New Perspectives on

MICROSOFT® ACCESS 2002

with Visual Basic® for Applications

Advanced

AF807628

THOMSON
COURSE TECHNOLOGY

Australia • Canada • Mexico • Singapore • Spain • United Kingdom • United States • Japan

New Perspectives on

MICROSOFT® ACCESS 2002

with Visual Basic® for Applications

Advanced

KRISTIE L. OXFORD
Santa Rosa Junior College

ANTHONY D. BRIGGS

THOMSON
COURSE TECHNOLOGY

Australia • Canada • Mexico • Singapore • Spain • United Kingdom • United States • Japan

THOMSON
COURSE TECHNOLOGY™

New Perspectives on Microsoft® Access 2002 with Visual Basic® for Applications—Advanced
is published by Course Technology.

Managing Editor:
Rachel Crapser

Senior Product Manager:
Kathy Finnegan

Technology Product Manager:
Amanda Young

Product Manager:
Karen Stevens

Associate Product Manager:
Brianna Germain

Marketing Manager:
Rachel Valente

Developmental Editor:
Jane Pedicini

Production Editor:
Catherine G. DiMassa

Composition:
GEX Publishing Services

Text Designer:
Meral Dabcovich

Cover Designer:
Efrat Reis

Printed in the United States of America

1 2 3 4 5 6 7 8 9 QWD 04 03 02

For more information, contact Course Technology, 25 Thomson Place, Boston, Massachusetts, 02210.

Or find us on the World Wide Web at: www.course.com

ISBN 0-619-04466-7

New Perspectives

Prefa

Course Technology is the world leader in information technology educ
Series is an integral part of Course Technology's success. Visit our Web s
perspective on teaching and learning solutions.

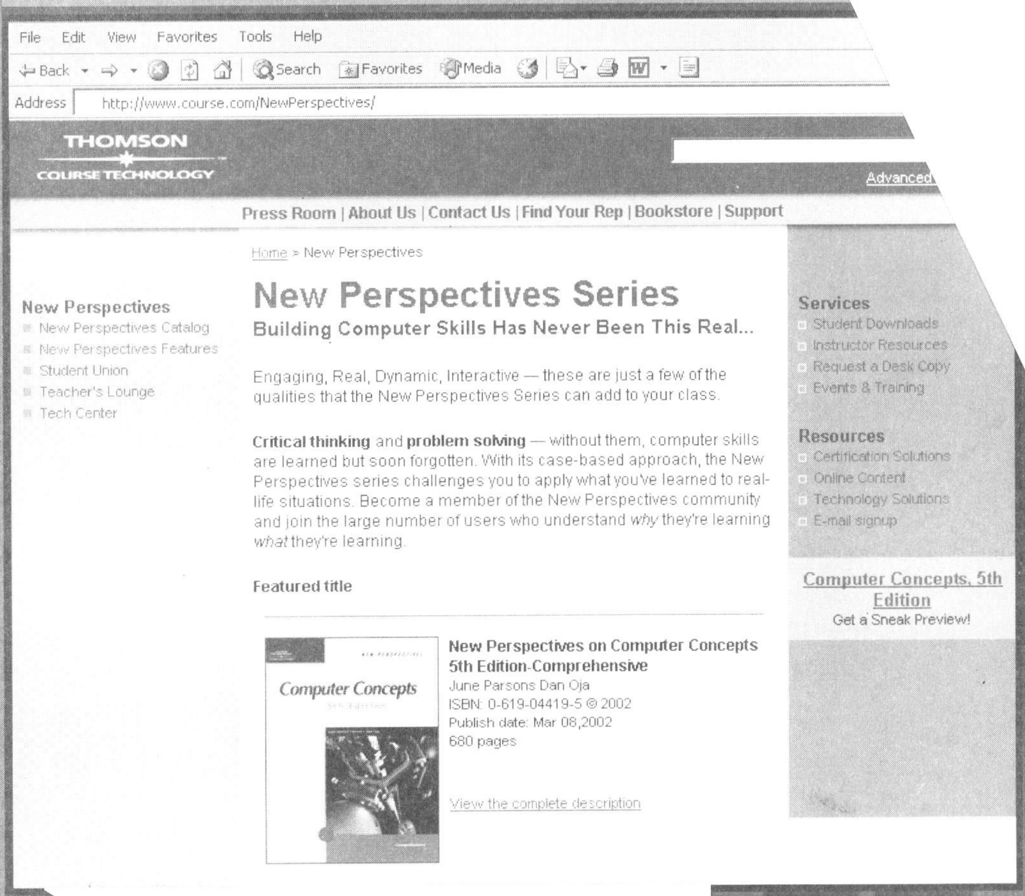

New Perspecti Bui Has Never Been This Real

Why New Perspecti… for you.

Critical thinking and **problem solving**—without them, computer skills are learned but soon forgotten. With its **case-based** approach, the New Perspectives Series challenges students to apply what they've learned to real-life situations. Become a member of the New Perspectives community and watch your students not only **master** computer skills, but also **retain** and carry this **knowledge** into the world.

New Perspectives catalog
Our online catalog is never out of date! Go to the Catalog link on our Web site to check out our available titles, request a desk copy, download a book preview, or locate online files.

Brief
Introductory
Comprehensive
Advanced

Complete system of offerings
Whether you're looking for a Brief book, an Advanced book, or something in between, we've got you covered. Go to the Catalog link on our Web site to find the level of coverage that's right for you.

Instructor materials
We have all the tools you need—data files, solution files, figure files, a sample syllabus, and ExamView, our powerful testing software package.

SAM xp and TOM

How well do your students know Microsoft Office?
Experience the power, ease, and flexibility of SAM XP and TOM. These innovative software tools provide the first truly integrated technology-based training and assessment solution for your applications course. Click the Tech Center link to learn more.

CIW™ — Microsoft Office User Specialist — APPROVED COURSEWARE

Get certified
If you want to get certified, we have the titles for you. Find out more by clicking the Teacher's Lounge link.

Bb Blackboard www.blackboard.com — WebCT courses · campus · community

Interested in online learning?
Enhance your course with rich online content for use through MyCourse 2.0, WebCT, and Blackboard. Go to the Teacher's Lounge to find the platform that's right for you.

Your link to the future is at www.course.com/NewPerspectives

Wha

"My compliments to the authors. This is a very well-written textbook. It contains an excellent collection of topics and skills. The order in which you have approached the topics is very good."
Rebekah L. Tidwell, Carson Newman College and Lee University

"I really like the addition of the industry standard explanations throughout—good job!"
Patricia Clerico, Davidson County Community College

"This text will be a guide to bridge the gap between the point that most beginning Access courses leave off and actually developing applications with Access."
Richard Heiges, High Point University

- Student Online Companion takes students to the Web for additional work.
- ExamView testing software gives you the option of generating a printed test, LAN-based test, or test over the Internet.
- Our clear and concise coverage of different types of queries—including pass-through queries, action queries, and union queries—also contains thorough explanations of query properties.
- Students will appreciate the in-depth coverage of building and programming forms, including templates, masters, data entry forms, subforms, and switchboards.
- This text provides an excellent introduction to SQL and ANSI standards.
- Students will tackle VBA and other related design issues in a simplified and efficient manner, which will help them to master these more complex topics.
- Advanced topics such as object models, database security, and data access pages are presented at just the right level for students using this text.

CASE

Tutorial Case
Each tutorial begins with a problem presented in a case that is meaningful to students. The case sets the scene to help students understand what they will do in the tutorial.

TROUBLE?

TROUBLE? Paragraphs
These paragraphs anticipate the mistakes or problems that students may have and help them continue with the tutorial.

SESSION 1.1

Sessions
Each tutorial is divided into sessions designed to be completed in about 45 minutes each. Students should take as much time as they need and take a break between sessions.

QUICK CHECK

Quick Check Questions
Each session concludes with conceptual Quick Check questions that test students' understanding of what they learned in the session.

RW

Reference Windows
Reference Windows are succinct summaries of the most important tasks covered in a tutorial. They preview actions students will perform in the steps to follow.

www.course.com/NewPerspectives

Microsoft Access 2002 with VBA

TABLE OF CONTENTS

Acknowledgments

I would like to thank the following reviewers for all their terrific, insightful feedback: Patricia Clerico, Davidson County Community College; Lisa Friedrichsen, Johnson County Community College; Richard Heiges, High Point University; and Rebekah Tidwell, Carson Newman College and Lee University. My thanks to many people on the Course Technology staff for helping to put this book together on such a tight timeline. Kathy Finnegan, Cathie DiMassa, and Jane Pedicini have put an incredible number of hours into this effort. We made it! Many thanks to Rachel Crapser for asking me to do this work and for her faith and support along the way. A special thank you to John Freitas for a top notch QA and Validation job. Many thanks to my extended family and close friends for putting up with all the missed gatherings, birthdays, anniversaries, and weddings. Finally, thank you to my wonderful wife, Robi, for her love and support while I have been sequestered in my office typing away these many months, night after night after night. Thanks to you all.

Anthony D. Briggs

I would like to thank the following reviewers of the previous edition for their helpful feedback: Roy Ageloff, University of Rhode Island; Sue Krimm, Los Angeles Pierce College; and Carrie Budd. My thanks to all of the Course Technology staff for all of their help and support. Special thanks to Joe Adamski for his incredible attention to detail, editorial expertise, guidance, support, and friendship. Finally, I want to thank Tim, Jon, and Justin for their love and support, hard work, and tolerance of all the lost weekends, evenings, and holidays. You guys are the best.

Kristie L. Oxford

New Perspectives on

MICROSOFT ACCESS 2002 WITH VBA

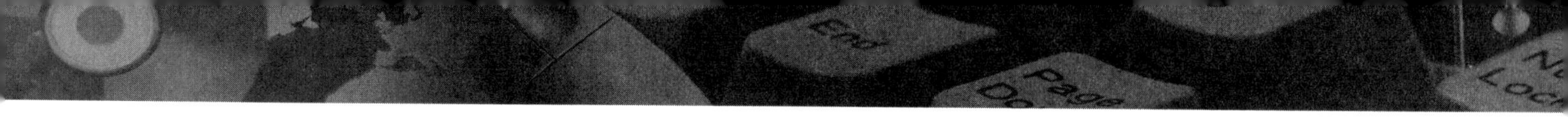

Read This Before You Begin

To the Student

Data Files

To complete the tutorials, Review Assignments, and Case Problems in this book, you will need access to a folder on your computer's local hard drive or a personal network drive. If you must complete work using floppy disks, you may not be able to complete some of the steps due to space limitations. Your instructor will either provide you with the necessary Data Files or ask you to obtain them.

You will need to copy a set of files and/or folders from a file server, standalone computer, or the Web, to your folder. Your instructor will tell you which computer, drive letter, and folders contain the files you need. You can also download the Data Files by going to www.course.com and following the instructions on the screen.

The information below shows you the structure of the Data File folders you use throughout the tutorials. To see the names of the files contained in each folder, refer to the File Finder chart at the back of this book.

Data File Folders

Tutorial.01
Tutorial.02
Tutorial.03
Tutorial.04
Tutorial.05
Tutorial.06
Tutorial.07
Tutorial.08
Tutorial.09
Tutorial.10

Note: Each of these main tutorial folders contains the following subfolders to further organize the Data Files:
\Tutorial
\Review
\Cases

When you begin each tutorial, be sure you are using the correct Data Files. Refer to the File Finder chart at the back of this text for more detailed information on which files are used in which tutorials. See the inside front or inside back cover of this book for more information on Data Files, or ask your instructor or technical support person for assistance.

Using Your Own Computer

If you are going to work through this book using your own computer, you need:

- **Computer System** Microsoft Windows 98, NT, 2000 Professional, XP Professional, or higher must be installed on your computer. This book assumes a typical installation of Microsoft Access.
- **Data Files** You will not be able to complete the tutorials or exercises in this book using your own computer until you have the Data Files. It is highly recommended that you work off your computer's hard drive or your personal network drive.

Visit Our World Wide Web Site

Additional materials designed especially for you are available on the World Wide Web:
Go to www.course.com/NewPerspectives.

To the Instructor

The Data Files are available on the Instructor's Resource Kit for this title. Follow the instructions in the Help file on the CD-ROM to install the programs to your network or standalone computer. For information on the Data Files, see the "To the Student" section above.

You are granted a license to copy the Data Files to any computer or computer network used by students who have purchased this book.

OBJECTIVES

In this tutorial you will:

- Review database terms, concepts, and standard database-naming conventions
- Review table design and field properties
- Create table and field validation rules to control data entry
- Review and use query features
- Work with advanced query features, such as building and sorting expressions
- Explore existing forms and their design
- Modify form design to improve overall appearance
- Explore an existing report and its design
- Modify report design to improve overall appearance
- Create a simple data access page
- Review use of macros and modules

REVIEWING DATABASE OBJECTS

Exploring the Database for MovieCam Technologies

CASE

MovieCam Technologies

MovieCam Technologies is a firm based in northern California that specializes in the development and manufacture of state-of-the-art imaging systems for the entertainment industry. In the 10 years of its existence, MovieCam has grown rapidly from a small consulting firm to a sophisticated engineering and manufacturing firm. MovieCam produces cameras that mount to virtually any type of moving platform, including helicopters, boats, and camera cars. Computer systems have been used in all aspects of business operations since the company's inception, but many of the methods and procedures are now outdated and ineffective.

One of the problems that MovieCam is experiencing is how to track and manage a growing number of orders for standard and custom-engineered camera systems. Currently, a product manager is responsible for coordinating the engineering and production of these camera systems from the time that a bid is requested through the final date of completion. Product managers traditionally have used spreadsheets to track the jobs for which they are responsible; however, this approach has led to long hours at the computer entering and compiling time card information. Some managers who are not proficient with spreadsheets have even opted to track products the old-fashioned way—making mental notes and acting on their gut feelings!

SESSION 1.1

In this session, you will review key database terms and concepts, learn to use a naming convention for Access objects, and review table design. You create table-level validation rules and field-level validation rules. You also create an expression in a query and sort a query based on that expression.

Introduction to Database Management Systems

Microsoft Access 2002, also referred to simply as Access, is a **database management system (DBMS)** that is used to manage, store, retrieve, and order large amounts of information. Unlike many desktop database management systems, Access stores all the data required to make the database operational in a single file. Access also is a **relational database management system (RDBMS)**. In an RDBMS, you can link tables through a common field and thereby combine data in new objects in order to minimize the duplication of data. An RDBMS can store a large amount of information; an Access database can be up to two gigabytes (GB) in size (minus the space needed for system objects) and can contain up to 32,768 objects.

From a general, broad-based programming perspective, an **object** can be thought of as a code-based abstraction of some real entity. From this same perspective, objects are composed of data and behavior, where data is in the form of some state information and behavior consists of a set of routines. It may be helpful to think of an object as a thing, much like a noun in the English language. An **Access object** is an item that can be created, manipulated, controlled, or programmed. From the Database window, you can see seven primary Access objects: tables, queries, forms, data access pages, reports, macros, and modules. It is important to remember that in Access, not only is a table an object, but each field in that table is also an object. A form is another type of Access object, and each of the sections and controls in a form are Access objects as well. Additional types of objects are introduced as they apply to topics presented in these tutorials.

A **property** is a characteristic, or attribute, of an object. Every object in Access has a set of specific properties that characterizes it. For example, a text box on a form or report has a Font Name property, a Font Size property, a Name property, and so on. Remember that an object's properties are not the same as its data.

MovieCam management decided that an employee, labor, and product tracking system should be designed and written using Microsoft Access 2002. Jason Thompson, an Access developer, began a prototype system, but he left the company before completing the project. Amanda Tyson, director of Information Systems, has asked you to help complete the system.

MovieCam Technologies needs an RDBMS to manage labor and product information. This type of database would allow managers to design tables to contain data that's specific to a certain subject, such as employees, time cards, products, and projects or jobs.

A sample of a spreadsheet that a MovieCam manager might use to track data on employees and time cards is shown in Figure 1-1.

Figure 1-1 **EMPLOYEE AND TIME CARD DATA IN THE TIMECARDDATA.XLS SPREADSHEET**

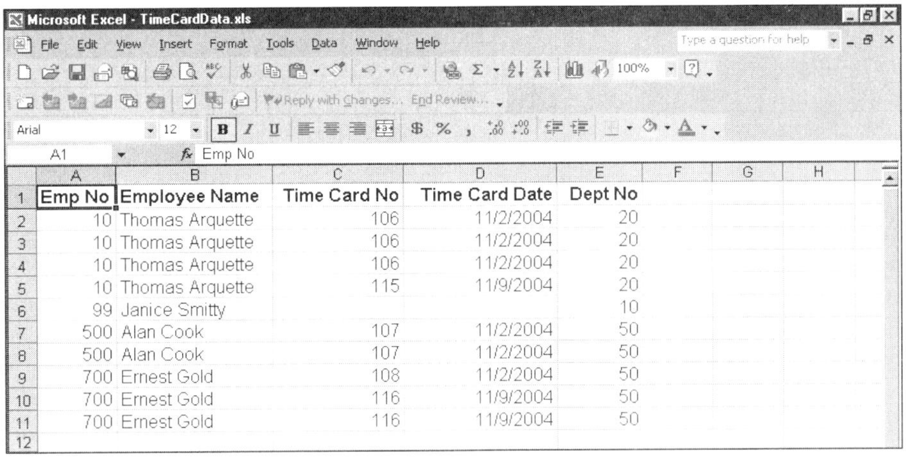

Emp No	Employee Name	Time Card No	Time Card Date	Dept No
10	Thomas Arquette	106	11/2/2004	20
10	Thomas Arquette	106	11/2/2004	20
10	Thomas Arquette	106	11/2/2004	20
10	Thomas Arquette	115	11/9/2004	20
99	Janice Smitty			10
500	Alan Cook	107	11/2/2004	50
500	Alan Cook	107	11/2/2004	50
700	Ernest Gold	108	11/2/2004	50
700	Ernest Gold	116	11/9/2004	50
700	Ernest Gold	116	11/9/2004	50

Though there is very little data entered in this sample, were this spreadsheet to represent multiple time card entries for many employees for a whole year, there would be a lot of repetition and it would be difficult to very easily extract specific information from it. For example, if you wanted to know how many hours Thomas Arquette worked on a specific job for a specific time period, or perhaps the same type information for *every* employee, you would have to filter and sort the data in the spreadsheet. You could probably add formulas to help calculate totals, but you would need to change the formulas each time someone wanted to know a slightly different piece of information.

Note that in the spreadsheet, entire employee names are listed multiple times, along with dates and other redundant data. Moving this data into a relational database can cut down on redundancy by splitting data into separate tables and linking these tables through key fields rather than unnecessarily repeating whole names, dates, and so on.

Figure 1-2 shows how the same data can be organized in a database. One table contains data on employees and another table stores data on time cards. As shown in Figure 1-2, the tables have a common field—EmpNo—by which they can be joined so that other database objects can be generated using data from both tables. Note the employee first name and last name are combined together into one column (the EmployeeName column); this violates industry best practices and you will go through an exercise to correct this in Tutorial 2. It is important to remember to always compartmentalize data into discrete fields, such as first name, last name, city, state, or zip code. By following these rules, searching, indexing, and sorting can be accomplished much faster. It is quicker to match an entire string of characters to a search criterion than to search for a subset of characters within a string. For example, it is much easier to sort or index by last name when that is a distinct field than when it is combined with a first name. It is also very easy to combine, or concatenate, two or more fields together for such things as forms, reports, and address labels.

Figure 1-2 **EMPLOYEE AND TIME CARD DATA IN TWO DATABASE TABLES**

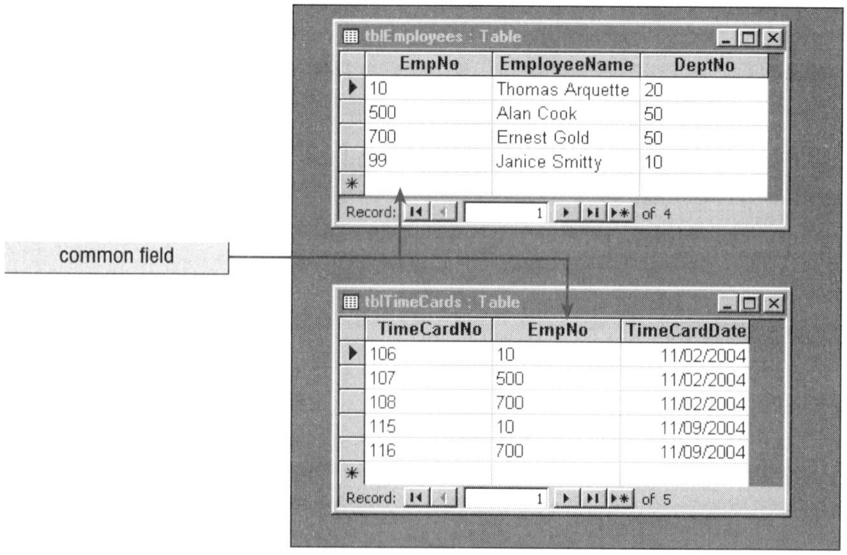

Opening **the MovieCam Technologies Database**

Earlier this week you met with Amanda and the product managers to discuss the objectives for the database. The list of objectives that the group compiled includes:

- The database should store employee-related information, time card data, hours worked, and product data.
- The database should be written so that the data entry process is intuitive and data entry errors are minimized.
- Product managers, company officers, and other personnel should be able to access reports on employees, products, and total hours spent on particular projects.
- All users should be able to access forms and reports via a user interface that is easy to understand.
- Employees should be able to update some portions of the system via the company intranet.
- A security system should be implemented that prevents unauthorized users from accessing the database window and modifying forms and reports in Design view.

Amanda has asked you to take a look at the database Jason started. She wants you to evaluate the objects that he has created so that you can determine the work that needs to be done to complete the system.

To open the MovieCam Technologies database:

1. Make sure that the data files have been copied to the local or network drive on which you are working.

   TROUBLE? If the data files have not been copied to your local or network drive, you must perform this task before you can proceed. Read the "Read This Before You Begin" page at the beginning of this book, or ask your instructor or technical support person for help.

2. Start **Access** and open the **Movie1** database located in the Tutorial.01\Tutorial folder on your local hard drive or network drive.

The Movie1 database is displayed in the Access window. The Tables option on the Objects bar of the Database window is selected, so you see the four tables that Jason created. Notice that he named each table with "tbl" preceding a descriptive name. This naming convention is discussed next.

Naming **Conventions**

Even the simplest Access database can have hundreds of objects. To keep track of all those objects, you might find it helpful to use a naming convention or standard that clearly defines the type and purpose of each object. A name also can help make the relationship between objects clear, as in the case of a linking table in a many-to-many relationship, which is discussed in Tutorial 2, or as in the case of a subform, which is discussed in Tutorial 4. A consistent naming convention brings order to your database, aids in documentation, and makes it easier for you and others to understand the database.

Before you can develop a naming convention, you need to understand the Access requirements for naming objects:

- Object names can be up to 64 characters long.
- Object names can include any combination of letters, numbers, spaces, and special characters, except a period (.), an exclamation point (!), a grave accent (`), or brackets [ ].
- Object names cannot begin with a space.
- Object names cannot include control characters (ASCII values 0 through 31).
- Table, view, or stored procedure names cannot include a quotation mark (").
- Table and query names must be unique in the database. However, other objects can have the same name. For example, you can name both a table and a form "Customer," but you cannot name both a table and a query "Customer." Although it is allowed, naming different objects with the same name can lead to confusion and is therefore *not* recommended.

The following are the suggested naming standards that many developers use. Examples of objects named using these conventions are shown in Figure 1-3.

- Include a tag in lowercase letters at the beginning of the object name to identify the type of object. For example, you might precede each table name with "tbl." A tag is typically three characters long (not counting an optional prefix). Some developers include a tag in field names to specify in which table the field is located, whereas others prefer to use tags to denote data type.
- Add a prefix to the tag to further identify an object. For example, if you use "frm" as a form tag, you could add the prefix "s" to the "frm" to identify a subform. The prefix "z" is often used to specify temporary objects in the database that you will delete, or "zap" later.
- Include a descriptive name that contains no spaces or special characters. Capitalize the first letter of each word to make the name easier to read.
- Keep object names short to avoid misspellings and excessive typing in expressions and Visual Basic for Applications (VBA) code.
- Use plural names for tables. For example, use the name "tblEmployees" rather than "tblEmployee."

Figure 1-3 SAMPLE OBJECT NAMES

OBJECT TYPE	TAG	DESCRIPTIVE NAME	NAME
Table	tbl	Employees	tblEmployees
*Field	emp	FirstName	empFirstName
Query	qry	EmployeesCurrent	qryEmployeesCurrent
Form	frm	Employees	frmEmployees
Report	rpt	EmployeesByDept	rptEmployeesByDept
Pages	dap	MovieEmployees	dapMovieEmployees
Macros	mcr	Global	mcrGlobal
**Macro group (prefix added)	mfrm	MainSwitchboard	mfrmMainSwitchboard
***Modules	mdl or bas	DateFunctions	mdlDateFunctions

* For a field, the tag here represents the table in which the field is located rather than the object type. Another option is to denote data type.

** The tag "mfrm" followed by a form name identifies in which form the macro is used. In this example, the "m" designates macro and "frmMainSwitchboard" is the form that uses that macro.

*** The tag "bas" is most often used in Visual Basic (VB) and denotes a "basic" code module. Many developers prefer to use the "bas" tag only in VB and the "mdl" tag in Access. Because there are some differences between code modules in VB versus VBA, using distinct tags for each helps to prevent possible confusion.

There are certainly exceptions and variations to the preceding guidelines. Some developers include tags in the names of all objects in the database except tables. Others forego using tags in field names or use singular names for their tables. Some developers prefer to abbreviate a table name into a tag and place that before every field name in a table, whereas others prefer to use tags to denote data type. Some developers find adding tags to field names to be cumbersome and not really helpful in practice. Fields are rarely referenced without their table name in both Structured Query Language (SQL) and Visual Basic for Applications (VBA); therefore, using a table name as a three-letter tag and placing it before every field name is considered cumbersome and rarely done. You learn more about queries and SQL in Tutorial 3 and about VBA in the latter half of this book.

Using data types as tags in front of field names can be helpful, but can also be as cumbersome as using tags derived from table names. Use of descriptive field names helps to preclude the necessity of data type tags. For example, fields named "HireDate" and "BirthDate" indicate not only the data that they contain, but also that they are a Date/Time data type. Data types are covered in more detail in *New Perspectives Comprehensive Microsoft Access 2002*. For a brief review of data types, search for the keyword "DataType" in Microsoft Access Help, and then select the "DataType Property" topic.

There is one consistent rule that developers follow: no spaces in any object names. Spaces in object names create more work when you write expressions and can produce naming conflicts in VBA and in expressions.

You should also make sure that object names don't duplicate the name of properties or keywords reserved for special purposes in Access. For example, the Name property is used in Access to assign a name to a property so that you can refer to it in macros, expressions, and VBA, as well as for documentation purposes. You should never use "Name" as a name for a field in one of your tables because unexpected behavior in some circumstances can result. Keywords reserved by Access for use in SQL and VBA are introduced as they apply to topics presented in these tutorials.

The naming convention used in these tutorials follows the guidelines listed above, with the exception of using tags in field names. Tags and prefixes precede all other object names.

The Database Window

An Access database contains the seven main object types mentioned earlier: tables, queries, forms, reports, pages, macros, and modules. The **Database window** shown in Figure 1-4 is what you see when you open an Access database. This window is the command center for working with Access objects.

Figure 1-4 DATABASE WINDOW

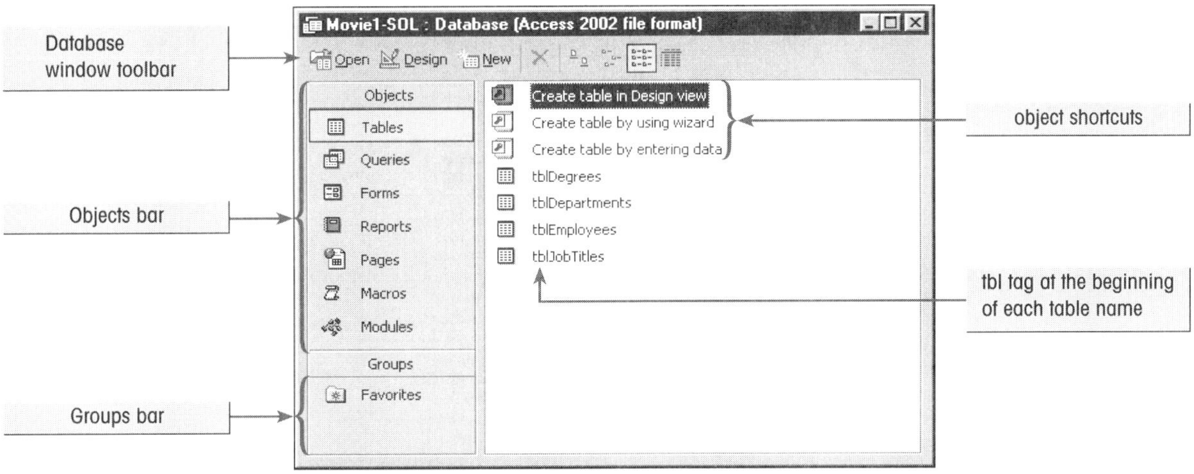

The **Database window toolbar** contains buttons for opening, creating, and deleting objects, and for changing views. Note that whatever object was selected, or highlighted, in the Database window when your copy of the Movie1 database was last closed (even if you have personally never opened or closed it before) will be the same object highlighted when you open the Movie1 database the next time. Therefore, the object highlighted in the Database window in the figure above may not be the same object highlighted in your Database window.

The **Objects bar** along the left side of the window contains buttons for viewing each of the seven main database object types.

Object shortcuts provide a quick method for creating an object. If you want to remove these shortcuts from the Database window, select Options on the Tools menu, select the View tab, and then deselect the New object shortcuts option. However, do not remove them at this time because they can be helpful to you and are referenced from time to time throughout the remaining tutorials.

The **Groups bar** is handy for organizing database objects according to subject. For example, you might create a group to contain all the queries and reports relating to employees. The Favorites group that you see on the Groups bar is a standard Access group.

Amanda now asks you to consider each of the seven main Access object types, both in general and as they specifically apply to the employee, labor, and product tracking system you are completing. You start with tables, which are the foundation of a database.

Tables

A table is composed of columns and rows, which in Access are also referred to as fields and records. The **field properties** you define in the table determine what data is to be stored in that column position of each row, or record. Each field provides a single piece of data about each record that helps describe that record. Tables store and retrieve data in the form of records and are used as the basis for all the other objects in the database. The properties associated with tables and with their fields allow you to control the data-entry process and validate data as it is entered.

The Movie1 database contains four tables. The tblEmployees table stores human resource, accounting, and labor-related information. The tblDepartments, tblDegrees, and tblJobTitles tables contain data on the company's departments, employees' academic degrees, and job titles, respectively. The currently defined relationships for those four tables are shown in Figure 1-5. You learn more about setting relationships in Tutorial 2.

Figure 1-5 **MOVIE1 TABLE RELATIONSHIPS**

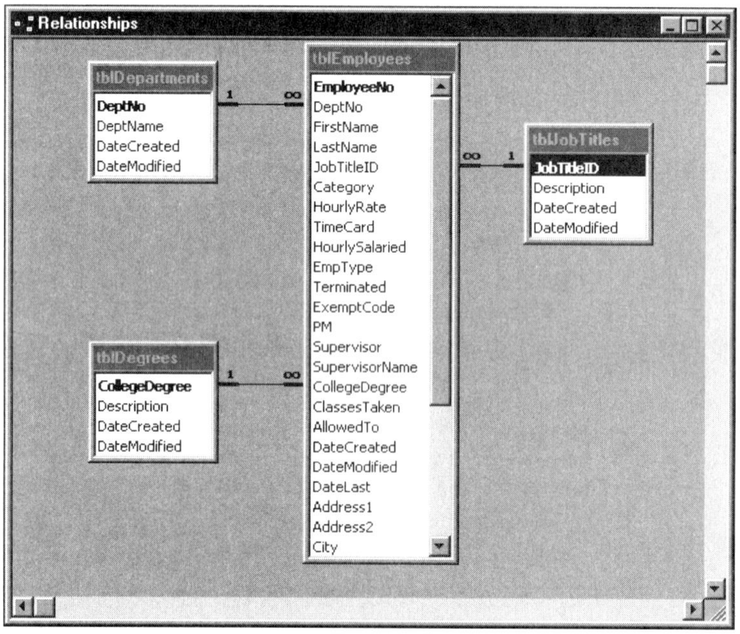

Table and Field Properties

You already know that tables, forms, and reports are considered objects in Access. Likewise, fields, controls, relationships, and indexes are considered objects as well. All objects in Access have public properties that describe them and that you can use to manipulate the objects.

To view the properties of a table, you must open it in Design view. The properties for the tblEmployees table are shown in Figure 1-6. As you can see, there are properties for validating data, filtering, and working with subdatasheets. (Subdatasheets are discussed in Tutorial 2.)

Figure 1-6 **tblEmployees PROPERTIES**

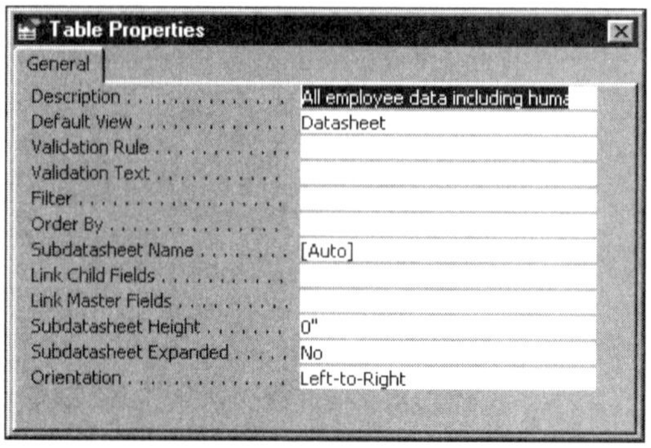

A **validation rule** is an optional expression (formula) that can be created at the table or field level. A **table validation rule** allows you to test the validity of one field compared to another. A **field validation rule** allows you to validate a field compared to a constant. **Validation text** appears in the warning message box that opens if the validation rule is violated. Figure 1-7 shows some sample validation rules and validation text for both tables and fields.

Figure 1-7 SAMPLE VALIDATION RULES FOR TABLES AND FIELDS

TYPE	FIELD(S) USED	VALIDATION RULE	VALIDATION TEXT
Field	EmpType	"R" or "P" or "T" or "C"	You must enter an R, P, T, or C code for this field
Field	HourlyRate	Between 7 and 150	You may enter a value as low as $7.00 or up to and including $150.00
Field	DateModified	>=#1/1/1900# Or Is Null	This date must be January 1, 1900, or later, or left blank
Table	DateCreated and HireDate	[DateCreated]>=[HireDate]	The DateCreated must be the same or later than the HireDate

Amanda suggests that you begin by evaluating the design of the tblEmployees table, including its fields and their properties.

To examine field properties of the tblEmployees table:

1. Make sure the **Tables** object is selected on the Objects bar in the Database window, click **tblEmployees** in the Database window, and then click the **Design** button on the toolbar in the Database window. The tblEmployees table opens in Design view. Note that to quickly open a table in Design view, you can right-click the table and click Design view on the shortcut menu that appears.
2. Scroll down the field list in the Table Design grid, located in the upper pane, until you see the HireDate field, and then click the **HireDate** field. Jason set the Required property (seen in the Field Properties pane, located in the lower portion) for the HireDate field to "Yes." The Caption property is set to "Hire Date;" if a caption had not been specified, the field name (HireDate) would be used to label the field in Datasheet view. The Format property is set to *mm/dd/yyyy*, a custom format designed to display a four-digit year.
3. Click the **BirthDate** field. This field also has the Required property set to "Yes," its Caption property is set to "Birth Date," and its Format property is set to *mm/dd/yyyy*.

Amanda asks you to create a validation rule to verify that the date of hire is later than the date of birth. It is not possible to test these dates against each other in a field validation rule, so you must create the validation rule at the table level.

REFERENCE WINDOW RW

Creating a Table Validation Rule

- Open the table in Design view.
- Click the Properties button on the Table Design toolbar to open the property sheet.
- Click the Validation Rule text box, and then type the validation expression.
- Click the Validation Text text box, and then type the text that appears when the rule is violated.
- Close the property sheet.

You now create a validation rule to test the dates against each other in order to avoid data-entry errors in these fields.

To create a table validation rule:

1. Click the **Properties** button on the Table Design toolbar to display the Table Properties dialog box.
2. Type **[HireDate]>[BirthDate]** in the Validation Rule text box, and then press the **Enter** key. Note that in this particular case, if you forget to use square brackets around the field names, Access automatically inserts quotation marks (" ") around the field names, which would prevent the validation rule from working properly.
3. Type **The hire date must be later than the birth date of the employee** in the Validation Text text box.
4. Click the **Close** button in the Table Properties dialog box to close the property sheet, and then click the **View** button for Datasheet view on the Table Design toolbar to switch to Datasheet view. You are asked to save the table.
5. Click the **Yes** button. The warning message shown in Figure 1-8 is displayed. This message states that data integrity rules have changed and asks if you would like to test the existing data against the new rules.

Figure 1-8 DATA INTEGRITY WARNING MESSAGE

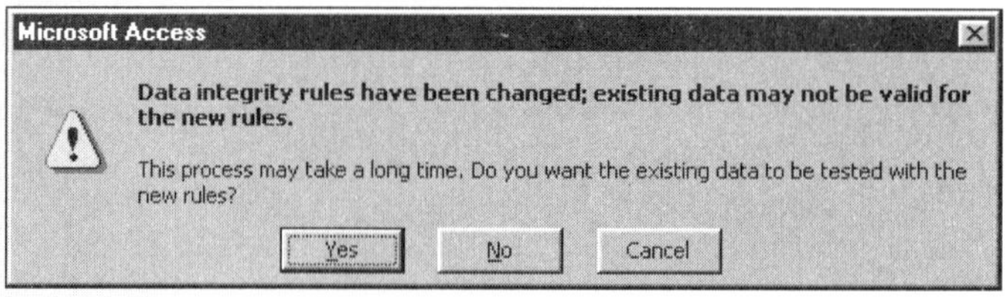

6. Click the **Yes** button to continue. Access tests the existing records against the new validation rule. If any of the records violate the rule, an error message is displayed, and you are prompted to continue testing or abandon the new rule.

Now that you have created the validation rule, you test it by temporarily changing a Birth Date to an invalid value. When referring to a field name in an expression, you need to use brackets [ ] to encapsulate the field name. Do not use parentheses ( ) or curly braces { }.

To test the table validation rule:

1. Scroll to the right to display the BirthDate field, select the first record in that field, and then enter *today's date*.
2. Press the ↓ key to move out of the record. The error message you entered in the Validation Text text box appears.

   TROUBLE? If a warning message does not appear, you might have made an error when typing the validation rule. If you did not type the brackets around each field name, Access places quotation marks around the field names, and your validation rule cannot work. Return to Design view and make sure that square brackets rather than quotation marks enclose the field names. Verify the validation rule has been typed correctly, and then repeat Steps 1 and 2 to verify that the rule is working properly.

3. Click the **OK** button, and then click the **Undo** button on the Table Datasheet toolbar to cancel the change you made and restore the original birth date value.

Because MovieCam has been in business since February 1, 1994, it is impossible for any employee to have been hired prior to that date. Amanda asks you to create a field validation rule to be sure that no hire date is earlier than that 1994 date. Because you are checking a field against a constant value, you can use a field validation rule.

REFERENCE WINDOW RW

Creating a Field Validation Rule

- Open the table in Design view.
- Click the field to be validated in the Table Design grid.
- Click in the Validation Rule text box in the Field Properties pane.
- Type the expression and then press the Enter key.
- Type the text that is displayed if the rule is violated.
- Click the Save button on the Table Design toolbar.

You now create a validation rule to test the date entered in the HireDate field against the date that the company started.

To create and test a field validation rule:

1. Click the **View** button for Design view on the Table Datasheet toolbar to return to Design view.
2. Click the **HireDate** field name in the Table Design grid.
3. Press the **F6** key to move the insertion point to the Field Properties pane of the window, and then press the **Enter** key until the insertion point is in the Validation Rule text box.

4. Type **>2/1/94** and then press the **Enter** key. The insertion point is now in the Validation Text text box, and the Validation Rule value automatically changes to >#2/1/94#.

   Depending upon your system settings, the date displayed in the Validation Rule text box after you press the Enter key might be formatted differently. In most Windows environments, you can specify the format for both date and time using the Date tab found in the Regional Settings of your Control Panel. Access picks up this system formatting. It is important to remember that in Access, and most windows applications, dates are all stored with the same precision, meaning they contain the same level of information and take up the same amount of data storage no matter how they are displayed on the screen. The date 2/1/94 is stored with the four-digit year of 1994 and also includes a time stamp, for example. The Operating System or Application settings determine how the date is displayed by default, which is something you can control.

5. Type **The hire date must be later than February 1, 1994** and then press the **Enter** key. See Figure 1-9.

Figure 1-9 FIELD VALIDATION

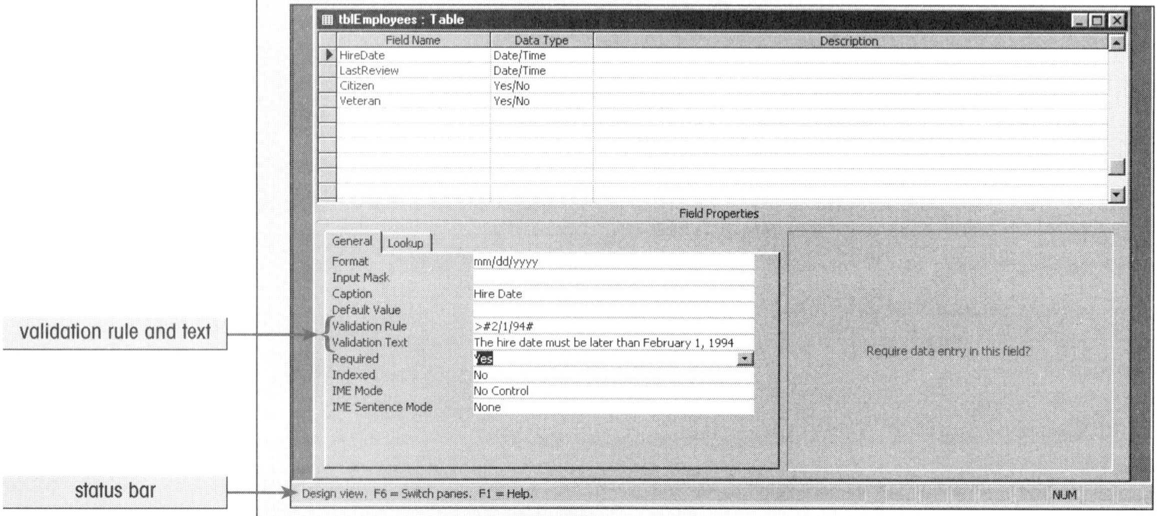

TROUBLE? The status bar is displayed at the bottom of the screens shown in the figures in this book. If you want your screen to match the figures, you can display the status bar: click Tools on the menu bar, click Options, click the View tab if necessary, click the Status bar check box, and then click the OK button.

6. Click the **View** button for Datasheet view on the Table Design toolbar to switch to Datasheet view, and then click the **Yes** button when prompted to save the table.

7. Click the **Yes** button to test the existing data with the new rules (you see the same message you saw after changing the table validation rule, as depicted in Figure 1-8). Next, you will enter an invalid Hire Date value to test the validation rule.

8. Scroll to the right and select the first record in the Hire Date field, type **2/1/93**, and then press the **Enter** key. The validation error message is displayed, so you know the validation rule correctly detects dates before 2/1/1994. Now you restore the original value.
9. Click the **OK** button to acknowledge and close the message box, and then press the **Esc** key to replace the original entry.
10. Click the **Close** button [X] on the Table window title bar to close the table and return to the Database window.

Note that while testing the table validation rule in regard to the Birth Date entry, you used the Undo button and then you used the Esc key. When you are editing a record and want to reverse changes you have made, pressing the Esc key once clears all the changes to that record, as long as it has not been saved. Clicking the Undo button or pressing the Undo button's shortcut keys (Ctrl + Z) reverses your changes whether or not the record has been saved. If you were to immediately edit a second record and then click the Undo button, then only the most recently edited record would be affected by the undo action.

If a record is still being edited, then the undo action might be "Undo Typing" or "Undo Current Field/Record," which has the same effect as the pressing the Esc key. Once the record is saved, the undo action would be "Undo Saved Record" and all changes just made to that record are lost and the record reverts to its unedited state, or values. Just remember that the Esc key only works when the changes to the record have not yet been saved. Recall that to save a record, you press and hold down the Shift key and press the Enter key, close the table, or simply tab to or click on any other record. All of these actions save the current record being edited.

Field Properties

Validation rules and text are only two of many field properties. Each data type has a set of field properties that apply to it. A few properties apply to all data types, whereas other properties apply to only specific data types. Many of the field properties are self-explanatory. Defined below are some fairly common, but not all, field properties that apply to more than one data type; these are field properties that many developers typically review and either accept the default settings or provide their own settings.

Field Size

This property defines the maximum size for data stored in a Text, Number, or AutoNumber field. Most developers consider it an industry best practice to determine the data types and field sizes for fields during table design. You most likely need to change these properties from the default settings to comply with your table design. Remember that the maximum possible setting for a Text field is 255 characters. Access does not reserve space for unused portions of a Text field. The Number data type can require 1, 2, 4, 8, 12, or 16 bytes of storage, depending upon the Field Size chosen. See the "FieldSize Property" Help topic for more information. An AutoNumber can be either a Long Integer (4 bytes) or a Replication ID (16 bytes). The Replication ID field size should only be needed if you plan on having two copies of a database in separate places and plan on synchronizing the changes between them regularly. For more information on the use of the Replication ID field size, see the Help topic entitled "About AutoNumber field size and replicated databases."

Format

You can use the Format property to specify a standard, predefined display format for AutoNumber, Number, Date/Time, Currency, and Yes/No fields. You can also use the Format property to create your own custom format for those five field types as well as for Text and Memo fields. For example, a commonly used custom format specification for a Text field is the greater than sign (>), which changes all characters to uppercase. The Format property does not affect the way data must be entered or how it is stored, only how it is displayed after it is entered. To reiterate, data is not converted back and forth by the Format property; it is simply a means of displaying the data differently than it is stored and has no impact on how it is stored in the database.

Input Mask

The input mask controls how data is actually entered into a field, as opposed to how it is displayed after it is entered (which is controlled by the Format property). An input mask is composed of a string of characters that act as placeholders for the characters that will be entered into the field. To start the Input Mask Wizard, you must be in Design view.

To view the available input mask options for a text field:

1. For the sake of simplicity, open the **tblEmployees** table in Design view and make sure the **EmployeeNo** field name is selected. Note that you could select any one of your Text, Number, Date/Time, or Currency fields to complete these steps.
2. In the Field Properties pane, move the insertion point to the Input Mask property text box.
3. Click the **Build** button ... for the Input Mask property. The Input Mask Wizard Dialog box opens, as shown in Figure 1-10.

   TROUBLE? If a message box opens and tells you this feature is not installed, insert the Office XP installation CD, and then click the Yes button to install the feature now. If you do not have an Office XP installation CD, ask your instructor or technical support person for help. The Input Mask Wizard feature is not one of the Wizards installed by default.

Figure 1-10 INPUT MASK WIZARD DIALOG BOX

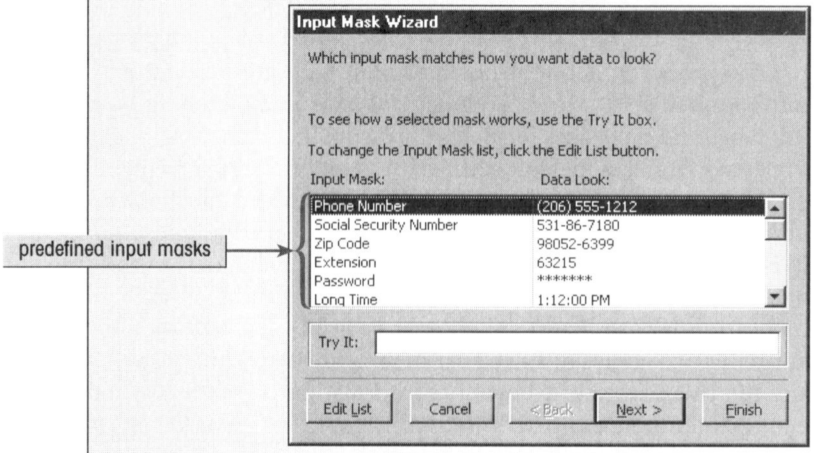

As shown in Figure 1-10, the Input Mask Wizard dialog box offers a number of predefined input masks, including masks for zip codes and Social Security numbers.

4. Scroll down the list of options to see predefined formats.
5. Click the **Cancel** button to close the Input Mask Wizard, and then close the table without saving any changes.

Caption

This property displays the specified caption text rather than the field name as the column heading in Datasheet view for a table or query. When you create a form or report based on a table, captions for table fields are used as the labels for the corresponding controls, as long as you have set the Caption properties before creating the form. If you change the Caption property of a field after the form has been created, the labels in the form are not automatically updated. This is one of the reasons many developers set this property during table design. There are no restrictions on the characters and symbols used in captions.

Default Value

When you specify a value in a field's Default Value property, Access automatically enters that value for that field in each new record. For Number or Currency fields, Access sets the Default Value property to 0 when you first specify Number or Currency as the data type. If you delete the setting for this property (in other words, the property setting is blank, nothing is entered), then there is no default value placed in that field for a new record; it would just be Null. In Access, there are two kinds of blank values: Null and zero-length strings. This is not always the case in other applications or programming languages.

Access defines the term **Null** as a value you can enter in a field or use in expressions and queries to indicate missing or unknown data. In Visual Basic, the Null keyword indicates a Null value. Some fields, such as primary key fields, can't contain Null values. Access defines a **zero-length string** as a string that contains no characters. You can use a zero-length string to indicate that you know there's no value for a field. You enter a zero-length string by typing two double quotation marks with no space between them (""). Null propagates through expressions (formulas), so if a value in an expression is Null, the result of the expression is Null. If you add two fields and one is Null, the result is Null. This is called propagation of Null values.

Required

If you set this property to Yes, you must enter text or a value into the field, or Access does not allow the record to be saved.

Allow Zero Length

This property applies only to Text, Memo, and Hyperlink fields. If you set it to Yes, you can enter a zero-length string. To enter a zero-length string, you simply type two consecutive quotation marks (""). Although zero-length string and Null both appear as an empty or blank field, they have different meanings. A zero-length string indicates that the data does not exist, whereas Null indicates that the data exists but is unknown. For fields with a Number data type, Null and zero-length strings do not seem to behave any differently when queried for Null values. This is most likely because by definition, numeric values do not accept string input, even a zero-length string, and simply accepts it as a Null value. In other words, if the value in a numeric field is Null in one record, and if you were to specifically enter a zero-length string as described above for the same field in another record, and then queried the same table with a condition of retrieving only Null values in that field (using the criteria Is Null), records with both Null values as well as those in which you entered zero-length strings are in fact returned in the query results. This is just something to bear in mind when working with these types of situations.

Here is another example If you know that a customer does not have an e-mail address, you should choose to actually enter a zero-length string in the field to indicate that no e-mail address exists. You should leave the field blank or Null for another customer who has an e-mail address, but you don't know what that address is. The reason this matters is that in the case of a Text field, the query results do in fact differ. If you were to query asking for Null values in a Text field (using Is Null as a criteria value for that field), but there were records that had zero-length strings entered in that Text field, those records are not returned by the query results (queries are reviewed in more detail in Tutorial 3). In contrast, only the records with zero-length string values in that same field would be returned if the field criteria in the query were changed to the equation = "" (that is, the equal sign followed by a set of quotation marks). This is a very important distinction and can be a useful concept when considering the design of your database. In the e-mail example here, this differentiation allows you to use a query to find out which customers do not have e-mail addresses compared to the customers for whom you do not know the e-mail address (or if one even exists). If Amanda asks you to be sure you have an e-mail address in your database for every customer who in fact has an e-mail address, you can do so without bothering those customers you know have no e-mail address, and you can focus just on the ones you were unsure about by querying for Null e-mail addresses.

Indexed

You can use the Indexed property to create an index on a field. Indexes speed up the process of searching and sorting on a particular field, but they can slow updates (data entry). There is no exact formula for figuring out how many indexes you can have before data entry performance suffers. As a general rule, you probably want to index the fields which you plan to frequently sort or search. (Indexes, in conjunction with primary keys, foreign keys, and table relationships, are discussed in more detail in Tutorial 2.)

Some field properties do not seem to have any Help topic associated with them, nor is it self-evident what the property represents. In many cases, they apply to only one data type or to a specific Field Size of a data type. Here are some, but not all, examples below:

- **New Values:** This property applies only to a field with an AutoNumber data type and specifies how a number is automatically generated for that field when a new record is added to a table. You can specify either Increment or Random for this property. The Increment setting automatically generates a new number in the AutoNumber field by adding one to the highest existing value. If you specify Random, Access instead generates a random integer.
- **Precision:** This property can be applied only to fields of Number data type with their Field Size property set to Decimal. The Precision property defines the total number of digits that can be stored both to the left and right of the decimal point. Precision indicates degree of detail. For example, the number 5.23 is less precise than the number 5.2347652, or even 52.347652. To reiterate, precision is not related to where the decimal point lies, but rather defines the total (maximum) number of digits allowed to the left and right of the decimal point. If anyone attempts to enter a number with more total digits than the Precision property setting, an error message results and the entry is not accepted. For example, if the Precision property were set to 6, both the numbers 52.3337 and 5.23337 are allowed. However, the numbers 523.3337 and 5.233336 are not allowed because the total number of digits in both values exceeds the precision setting of 6.

- **Scale:** This property can be applied only to Number fields with a Field Size property that has been specified as Decimal. The Scale property determines the maximum number of digits that can be stored to the right of the decimal point. Violating the Scale property setting does not result in an error message; Access simply truncates extraneous numbers to the right of the decimal point beyond the maximum allowed by the setting in the Scale property. For example, if the Precision property were set to 6 and the Scale property were set to 4, then 52.3337 would be an allowable entry. However, Access would truncate the 7 on the right of the 5.23337 and only accept 5.2333 as the entry, because 7 is the fifth digit to the right of the decimal point, which violates the Scale property that is set to only four digits to the right of the decimal point in our example here.
- **Decimal Places:** This property, which applies only to Number and Currency fields, determines the number of decimal places displayed to the right of the decimal point. If you specify Auto, the number of decimal places to the right of the decimal point depends on the choice made in the Format property. You may also specify a number of decimal places from the drop-down list or type in a value. Although this property does apply to the Decimal Field Size as well, in several tests it does not appear to have any bearing on what is shown to the right of the decimal. This property is also listed for Integer and Long Integer Field Sizes, but of course any setting has no impact because by definition integers do not contain decimals.
- **Unicode Compression:** Access 2002 uses the Unicode character-encoding scheme to represent data in a Text, Memo, or Hyperlink field. Unicode uses a fixed-width, 16-bit character-encoding scheme to represent all text characters from all languages except Chinese. Unicode allows mixing and sharing data between multiple languages. In Unicode, each character is represented by two bytes instead of by a single byte. When the Unicode Compression property of a field is Yes, any character with a first byte that is 0 is compressed from two bytes to one byte when it is stored, and uncompressed back to two bytes when it is retrieved. Because Unicode stores data in larger pages, some databases with a lot of textual data may increase in size. The default for Unicode Compression is Yes.
- **IME Mode:** Input Method Editor (IME) is a program that enters East Asian text into programs by converting keystrokes into complex East Asian characters. This property specifics a specific type of IME for that purpose.

Next, Amanda wants you to examine query database objects to learn why they are considered a powerful tool in database management systems.

Queries

Queries are often used to find records that meet a condition or criterion. Queries also are used to filter data from a single table, group data with totals, combine fields from more than one table, update or delete data, append data from one table to another, or create an entirely new table. The results (or the records found) of a query are referred to as the **recordset**.

Queries can be classified as select, parameter, crosstab, action, or SQL. You consider each of these in turn, beginning with select queries and expressions. There are two current ANSI standards for SQL, known as ANSI-89 SQL and ANSI-92 SQL. ANSI-89 SQL is also called Microsoft Jet SQL and ANSI SQL and is the traditional Jet SQL syntax. ANSI-92 SQL has new and different reserved words, syntax rules, and wildcard characters. ANSI-89 and ANSI-92 are not compatible. When you create a Microsoft Access database, you need to decide which query mode you are going to use, because mixing queries created in both query modes could produce run-time errors or unexpected results. The range of data types, reserved words, and wildcard characters are different in each query mode. You may want to use ANSI-92 SQL if you are connecting to a Microsoft SQL Server database. Changing this setting could cause existing queries not to run at all or to return unexpected results. For the purposes of this book, you do not select the ANSI-92 standard. This is an Access application setting that can be found on the Tables/Queries tab in the Options dialog box, as shown in Figure 1-11.

Figure 1-11 TABLES/QUERIES TAB OF THE OPTIONS DIALOG BOX

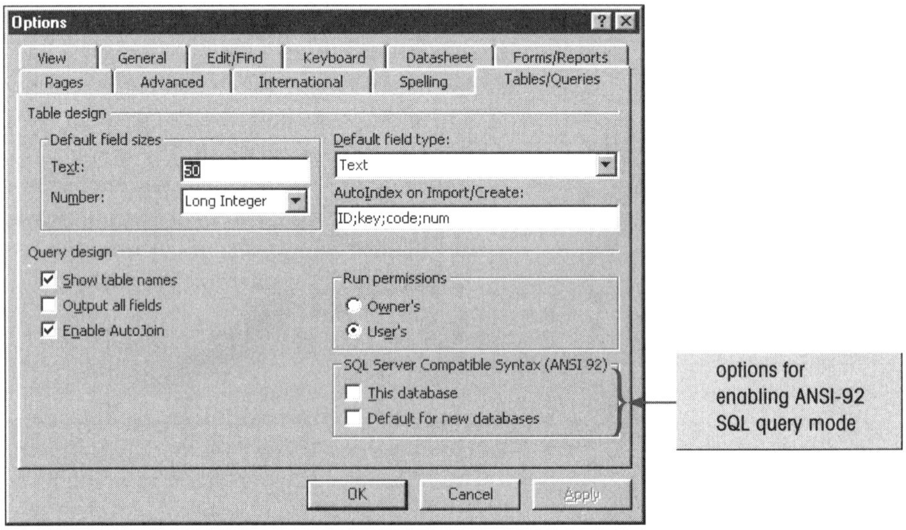

Access adds many of its own features to its brand of SQL, which extend its capabilities and make it a powerful tool within the application. You can even embed SQL in your VBA code, which you explore more in the latter half of this book. Access SQL is the language that underlies all of your queries.

Select Queries and Expressions

Select queries are commonly used to combine fields from more than one table into a single object. Up to 32 different tables can be used in the construction of one select query in Access 2002.

The Movie1 database contains a select query (qryEmployeesCurrent) that is used as the basis for a report that lists employees by department (rptEmployeesByDept). Both forms and reports have a property called Record Source, which identifies the sources of the data. The Record Source property is discussed in more detail throughout the book, but for now the Record Source property can be the name of a table, a query, or even a syntactically correct SQL statement.

The qryEmployeesCurrent query, which is based on the tblEmployees table, finds records for current employees. The query contains one field expression. An **expression** is a combination of symbols and values that produces a result. A few examples of how expressions can be used in Access follow:

- To set a property that establishes a validation rule or sets a default field property
- To enter a criteria expression in a query
- To create a calculated field in a query

- To set a condition for carrying out action(s) in a macro
- To construct functions or procedures in VBA
- To edit an SQL query

You should use the following guidelines when writing expressions in queries:

- Separate the name of the expression from the actual expression (formula) by a colon.
- Do not include spaces or special characters in the name of the expression. Although spaces and some special characters are allowed, this practice is discouraged. Capitalize each word in the name of the expression so that it is easy to read and recognize.
- You do not need to type brackets around field names referenced in expressions if you do not use spaces and special characters in the name of the field (thus reinforcing the recommendation earlier in this Tutorial not to use spaces in field names).

The qryEmployeesCurrent query contains an expression that concatenates, or joins, the FirstName and LastName text fields using the ampersand (&) operator and the Space(x) function, where *x* is the number of spaces you want between the first and last name. The expression looks like the following:

Name:[FirstName]&Space(1)&[LastName]

Amanda asks you to take a look at the query that Jason created.

To review qryEmployeesCurrent:

1. Click **Queries** on the Objects bar of the Database window.
2. Click **qryEmployeesCurrent** in the Database window, and then click the **Open** button on the toolbar in the Database window. The qryEmployeesCurrent query opens in the Select Query window, as shown in Figure 1-12. No sort was specified for this query, so Access automatically sorted the recordset in ascending order by the primary key, EmployeeNo. Because EmployeeNo is a text field, the employee numbers appear in text (alphanumeric) order rather than numeric order. Thus, as shown in Figure 1-12, record 99 appears at the end of the list.

Figure 1-12 qryEmployeesCurrent QUERY

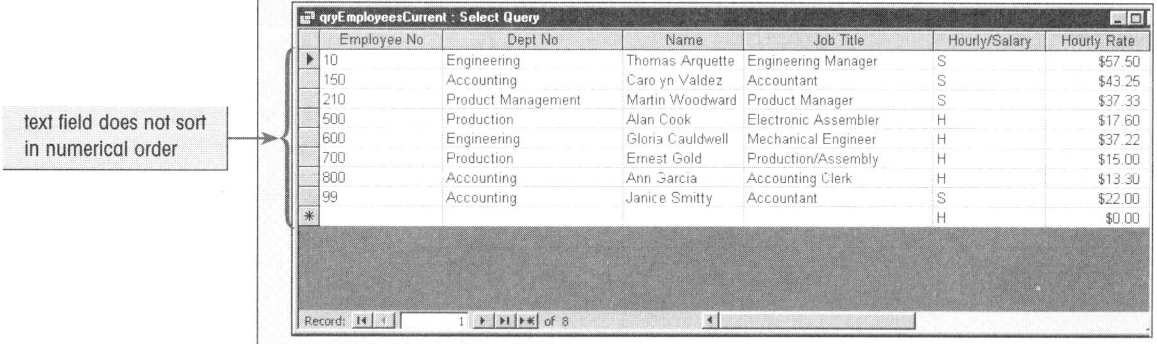

Employee No	Dept No	Name	Job Title	Hourly/Salary	Hourly Rate
10	Engineering	Thomas Arquette	Engineering Manager	S	$57.50
150	Accounting	Caro yn Valdez	Accountant	S	$43.25
210	Product Management	Martin Woodward	Product Manager	S	$37.33
500	Production	Alan Cook	Electronic Assembler	H	$17.60
600	Engineering	Gloria Cauldwell	Mechanical Engineer	H	$37.22
700	Production	Ernest Gold	Production/Assembly	H	$15.00
800	Accounting	Ann Garcia	Accounting Clerk	H	$13.30
99	Accounting	Janice Smitty	Accountant	S	$22.00
				H	$0.00

Amanda thinks the report based on this query would be more useful if the employee numbers were sorted in numerical order. She asks you to create an expression in the query that converts the EmployeeNo field from text to a number type and to sort the query results on that expression.

The CInt function is used to convert a text or date field to an integer. The syntax of the CInt function is: CInt([fieldname])

To create a field expression in a query and specify a sort:

1. Switch to Design view.
2. Click the **DeptNo** text box in the design grid, located in the lower portion of the Select Query window.
3. Click **Insert** on the menu bar, and then click **Columns**. A blank column is now positioned to the left of the DeptNo column.
4. In the Field text box of the column you added, type **EmpNoInt:CInt(EmployeeNo)** and then press the ↓ key twice.

   If you want to see the whole expression as you type, you can press Shift + F2 to open the Zoom window. This window provides a dialog box in which the expression you are typing appears, making it easier to see all of what you are typing. When you are finished, click the OK button to close the Zoom window and return to the design grid. EmpNoInt is the name of the field expression. CInt(EmployeeNo) is the function that converts the EmployeeNo field to an integer. You can also widen a column in the design grid. You can either click and drag the right edge of the column or double-click the right edge for the best fit.

5. In the Sort row of the new expression column, type the letter **a** to specify an ascending sort, and then press the **Tab** key. Notice how Access selects the complete word "Ascending" after you typed the letter "a." See Figure 1-13.

Figure 1-13 FIELD EXPRESSION AND SORT SPECIFICATION ADDED TO qryEmployeesCurrent

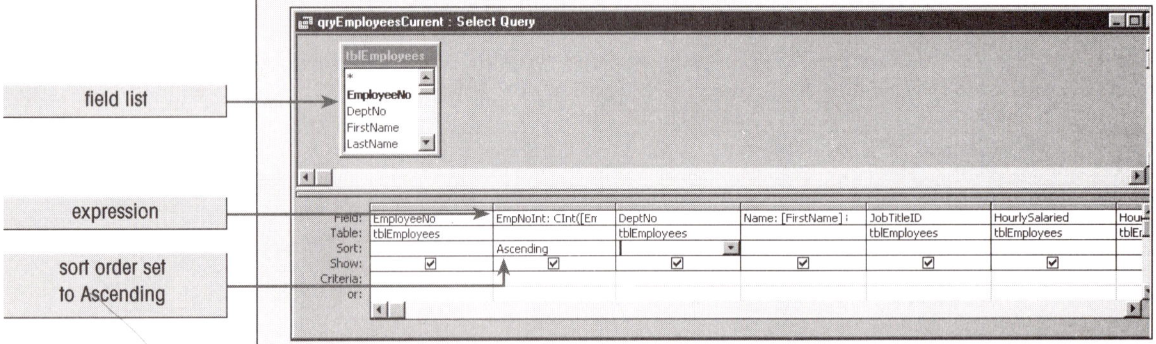

6. Click the **Run** button [!] on the Query Design toolbar. The employee numbers are now sorted from smallest to largest. See Figure 1-14.

Figure 1-14 RESULTS OF FIELD EXPRESSION AND SORT SPECIFICATION ADDED

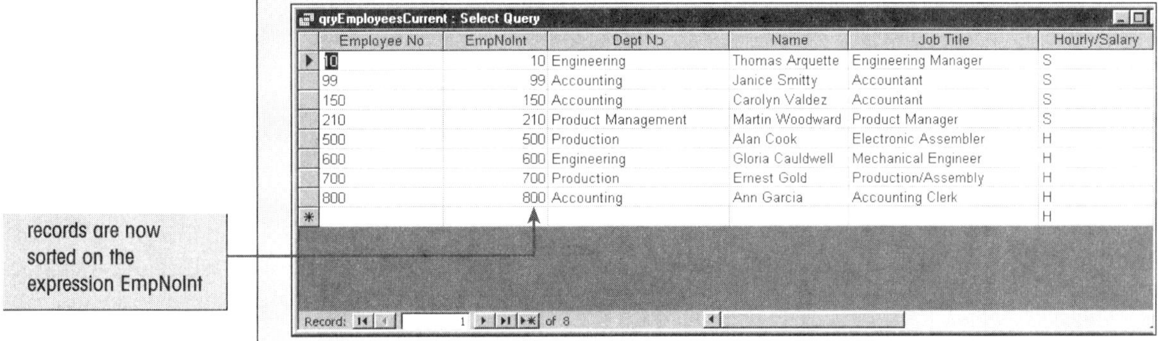

Employee No	EmpNoInt	Dept No	Name	Job Title	Hourly/Salary
10	10	Engineering	Thomas Arquette	Engineering Manager	S
99	99	Accounting	Janice Smitty	Accountant	S
150	150	Accounting	Carolyn Valdez	Accountant	S
210	210	Product Management	Martin Woodward	Product Manager	S
500	500	Production	Alan Cook	Electronic Assembler	H
600	600	Engineering	Gloria Cauldwell	Mechanical Engineer	H
700	700	Production	Ernest Gold	Production/Assembly	H
800	800	Accounting	Ann Garcia	Accounting Clerk	H
					H

7. Close the query and save your changes.

Note that when the query did not specify a sort order, it defaulted to the sort order imposed by its underlying table, tblEmployees, which sorts on the primary key. The primary key was the text field EmployeeNo. When numbers are entered into text fields, they are treated as ASCII characters and not numbers. ASCII characters are assigned a character value and they are sorted in that order, starting with the first character of the text. This is common alphanumeric sorting. For example, "700" precedes "99" in a text sort, because these digits are not treated as values, but rather a series of ASCII characters. An ASCII "7" comes before an ASCII "9" in the ASCII character set (a "7" has a lower character value than a "9"), just like the letter "a" comes before the letter "b." Once the "7" is found to be lower than the "9" in the first position of the EmployeeNo text field, the "700" is placed ahead of the "99" in the displayed recordset. This is why you entered an expression to convert the EmployeeNo to an integer and then sorted on that numeric column.

Parameter Queries

When a parameter query is run, a dialog box is displayed on the screen that prompts you for information such as a criterion for retrieving records or a value to be inserted in a field. A **parameter query** allows you to use a single query for different conditions. You can design a parameter query to prompt for more than one piece of information. For example, to retrieve all records that fall between two specified dates, you could use a parameter query that prompts for the two dates.

Parameter queries are especially handy when used as the basis for reports. For example, you can create a monthly time card report based on a parameter query. When you print the report, Access prompts you for the month and then prints the report for that month. The only disadvantage is that validation of the data entered is limited. If the parameter calls for a date and the user enters text instead of a date, the parameter query catches that and provides an appropriate message. But there is no simple validation for a month number to prevent someone from entering the number 13, for example. The results would just be that no data would be returned because there is no thirteenth month. This works out fine in many situations (users realize their error and rerun the report), but in the latter half of this book, you have the opportunity to learn more about programming user interfaces and controlling or validating parameter entry.

Crosstab Queries

A **crosstab query** displays summarized values from one or more tables in a spreadsheet format. Crosstab queries can calculate sums, averages, counts, or other types of totals for data that is grouped by two types of information—one down the left side of the datasheet and another across the top. Crosstab queries are very similar to PivotTables in Microsoft Excel.

Action Queries

Action queries include update, delete, append, and make-table queries. An action query is different from a select query in that it modifies the data in the underlying table when it is run. Action queries are frequently used to archive data. For example, assume that a Yes/No field identifies inactive records in a particular table. To archive those inactive records, you could use a one-time, make-table query to initially create an archive table, and then periodically run an append query to append the inactive records to that archive table. A delete query might then be run to delete the inactive records from the active table. These queries and the process of archiving are explored in greater detail in Tutorial 3.

SQL-Specific Queries

SQL-specific queries are written in SQL and cannot be created in Design view like other types of queries. Recall that for every type of query you create there is an underlying Access SQL statement. The query design grid, formerly known as the Query By Example, or QBE, grid (the use of this term was not unique to Access) is an interface tool within Access to make it simple to quickly put queries together without requiring any knowledge or direct use of Access SQL. However, recall that an Access SQL statement underlies every query. The main difference between all other types of queries and SQL-specific queries is that most SQL-specific queries *must* be written in SQL view. SQL view is accessed from the query's Design view by clicking View on the menu bar, and then clicking SQL view. You then create the query by entering SQL statements and clauses. There are four types of SQL-specific queries: union, pass-through, data-definition, and subqueries. There are ways to work a subquery into the design grid, which is explored in more detail in Tutorial 3. Pass-through and data-definition queries are not covered in detail in these tutorials.

Pass-through queries send commands directly to ODBC databases, such as SQL Server 2000, Microsoft FoxPro, or even other types of databases, using commands that are accepted by those database-specific query languages. For example, you can use a pass-through query to retrieve records or change data. With pass-through queries, you work directly with the tables on the database server instead of merely linking to them. Pass-through queries are also useful for running stored procedures on an ODBC server. You must know how to properly construct an SQL statement for the target database and set up the ODBC connection in order to make these types of queries function correctly. Other query languages are beyond the scope of this book, which is focused on Access 2002.

One of the great advantages of pass-through queries is that the query and data retrieval are actually run on the server side of the client server relationship, and only the results are returned across the network to Access. This tremendously helps performance of Access queries against large server side databases. In fact, it is the only acceptable way in many companies to query large databases from a client PC. Consider that a large company may have a data warehouse that contains many terabytes of data. Linking its table through ODBC to Access and running a normal Access query means that Access has to pull all the records in that linked table across the network and then use the Access query engine to sort through them all. This is very inefficient and time consuming.

For example, say you want to query a sales table, which has 50 million records in the form of two years of sales history and you are only looking for maybe one percent of those records (for instance, last week's sales results). The network gets bogged down with moving data to your PC that you do not actually need, and of course performance is so slow that you have unhappy users. By using a pass-through query, those 50 million records are sorted through on the server side, which most likely has multiple processors and far more memory than your PC. Now the one percent of the records that you are really interested in are placed in a result recordset, and only those records are passed across the network. This makes your users and the network administrators very happy. Can you imagine what would happen if 1000 people linked every day to a large data warehouse and ran multiple queries that required all the data in those tables to be pulled across the network instead of using pass-through queries and only pulling the data they really needed across the network? This does happen in companies, far too often, because sometimes people are not aware of the tools available to them, or how to use them effectively. The Movie1 database is not a large scale database and MovieCam technologies is not a large company, so you are not required nor have the opportunity to write pass-through queries while working on this project for Amanda. As a student of Advanced Access 2002, however, you should be aware of pass-through queries and the situations where you would use them.

Data-definition queries can create, delete, or alter tables, or even create indexes in a database table. This is a very powerful feature, but is a more advanced topic and is not within the scope of this book. Most developers using Access find that the action queries available to them are more than sufficient for these types of functions. Data-definition queries become more important when using SQL Server 2000 or other large database applications.

Union queries let you query for similar data from two or more unrelated tables. For example, you might want to compile a list of names and addresses of your vendors and customers for a mailing. The data for each is found in two separate, unrelated tables. A union query could be written to bring data together from these two tables. Union queries are discussed in greater detail in Tutorial 3.

Session 1.1 Quick Check

1. A(n) ____________ is used to manage, store, retrieve, and order large amounts of information.
2. Use a(n) ____________ validation rule when you want to test the validity of one field compared to another, but use a(n) ____________ validation rule when you want to validate a value in a field compared to a constant.
3. The ____________ operator is used to concatenate text fields in an expression.
4. The ____________ function can be used to convert data in a text field to an integer.
5. What is the purpose of a crosstab query?
6. List the four types of action queries.
7. List the four types of SQL-specific queries.

SESSION 1.2

In this session, you will review forms and their design. You change the Cycle property of a form, add rectangles for visually grouping controls, and add a text expression to a form. You review reports, add an expression to a report to count the number of records in each group, and add a page break to a grouping footer. Finally, you create a simple data access page so that employees can update their personal information via the company intranet.

Forms

Forms are used to display, edit, and enter data on screen. A form is basically a different way to display records; however, it can incorporate pictures, graphs, music, narration, and other controls that you do not see in a table or query. Forms are also used to create the user interface for a database. You learn more about the user interface in Tutorial 4.

The Movie1 database includes two forms. The frmEmployees(page_break) form is designed with a page break that splits the data from the tblEmployees table between two screens. As shown in Figure 1-15, you click a command button at the bottom of the first screen to display the second screen.

Figure 1-15 FIRST SCREEN OF THE frmEmployees(page_break) FORM

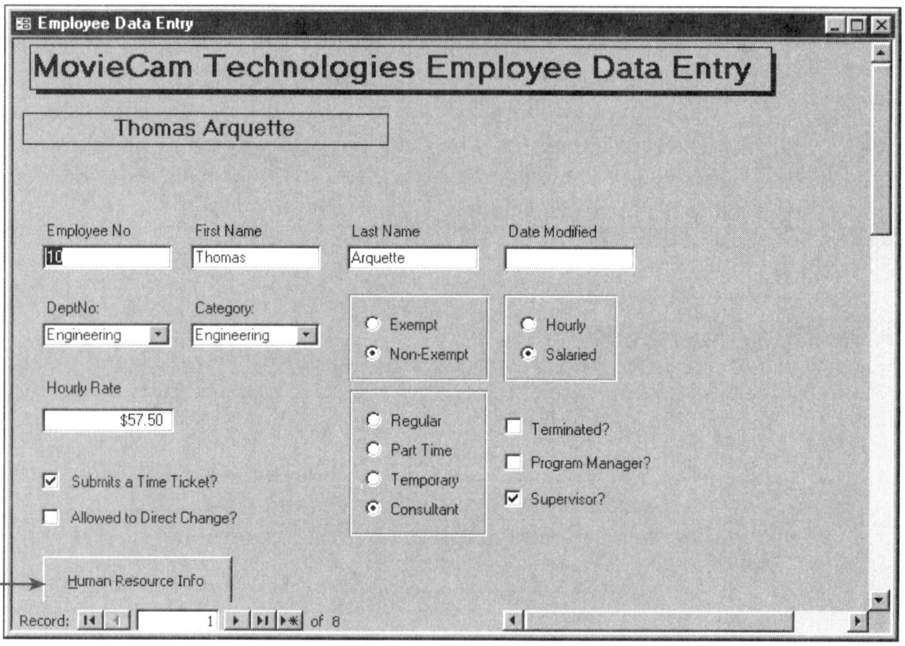

click to display the second screen

The very same information is displayed in the frmEmployees form shown in Figure 1-16. Instead of a page break, however, this form uses a tab control to present the two categories of data from the tblEmployees table. To display the second screen of information, you click the Human Resources Information tab.

Figure 1-16 **FIRST TAB OF THE frmEmployees FORM**

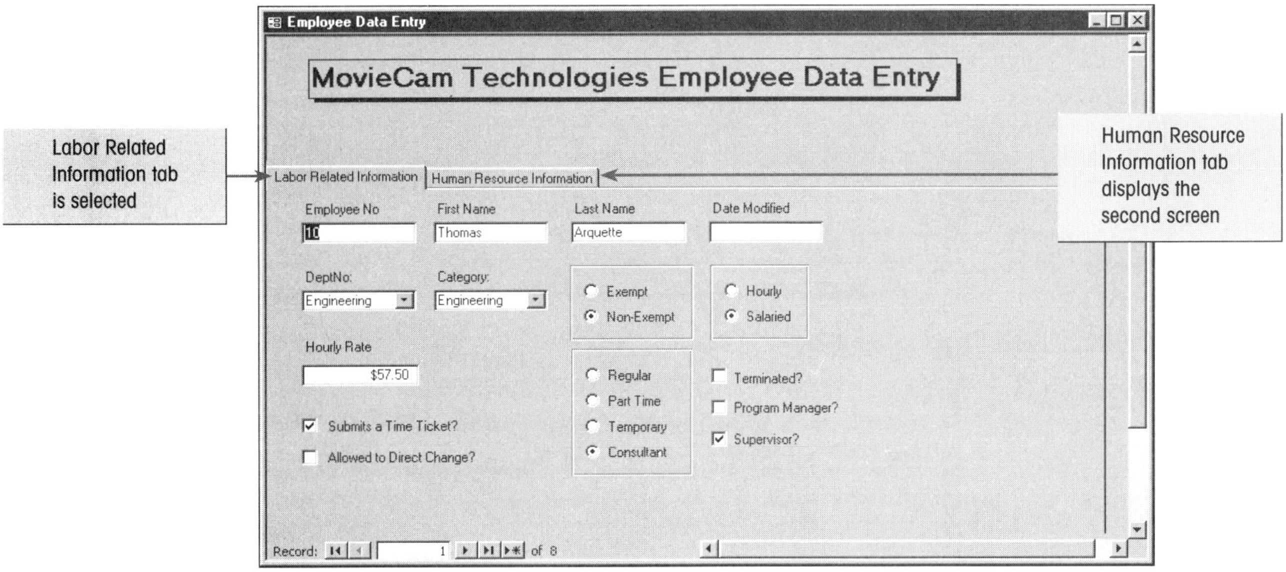

A form that uses the tab control is helpful when you want to segregate data or organize data when the underlying table has many fields. But the tab control can cause the form to load more slowly than a form that uses a page break. When you use a tab control, the tabs are created on the form, and then the text box, combo box, and check box controls are placed on top of the form. Overlapping controls in this manner causes a decrease in the form's performance.

Amanda explains that Jason created these two forms to show users of the database two options for entering and viewing employee records. Ultimately, the form that performs better will be retained and the other form discarded. She asks you to look at each form now. You decide to explore the page-break form first.

To explore the frmEmployees(page_break) form:

1. If you took a break after the previous session, make sure that Access is running and the Movie1 database is open.
2. Click **Forms** on the Objects bar of the Database window.
3. Click **frmEmployees(page_break)** and then click the **Open** button in the Database window. The form opens and displays the first page of information for the first record. See Figure 1-15.
4. Click the **Human Resource Info** button in the lower-left corner of the form. The second page of information for the first record is displayed. The command button on this page is the Labor Related Info button at the bottom of the page.
5. Scroll down the form, and then click the **Labor Related Info** button to redisplay the first page of the form.
6. Press the **Tab** key to tab through the controls on the form until the focus returns to the Human Resource Info command button. (When the command button has the focus, a dotted line outlines the text on the button.)
7. Press the **Tab** key one more time. The first page of the form *and* a portion of the second page are displayed simultaneously, and the text in the Address Line 1 text box of the second page is selected, as shown in Figure 1-17.

Figure 1-17 **VIEWING TWO PAGES OF A FORM SIMULTANEOUSLY**

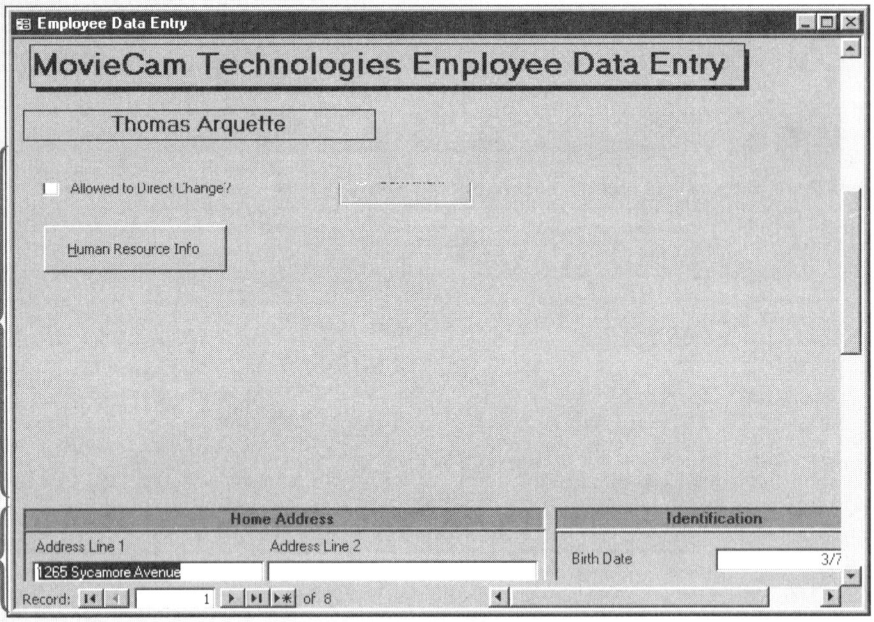

first page of the form

first part of the second page of the form

Amanda explains that the Cycle property is used to specify what happens when you press the Tab key and the focus is in the last control on a bound form. The default is All Records, which generically speaking, means that pressing the Tab key from the last control on a form moves the focus to the first control in the tab order in the next record in a form. But on a form with a page break, this setting causes a portion of two pages to be displayed on the screen simultaneously. Amanda suggests that in this form it would be preferable to cycle through the current page only, using only the command buttons to move between pages. This means that when you press the Tab key from the last control on the page the focus moves back to the first control in the tab order on the page. She asks you to make that change to the form.

REFERENCE WINDOW **RW**

Changing Form Properties

- Open the form in Design view.
- Click Edit on the menu bar, and then click Select Form.
- Click the Properties button on the Form Design toolbar.
- Change the appropriate property, and then close the property sheet.

Next you change the Cycle property of the frmEmployees(page_break) form.

To change the Cycle property of a form:

1. Switch to Design view. Note that the toolbox appears with the form.
2. Click **Edit** on the menu bar, and then click **Select Form**.

3. Click the **Properties** button on the Form Design toolbar, and then click the **Other** tab in the property sheet for the form.
4. Click the **Cycle** property text box, click its list arrow, and then click **Current Page** in the list. See Figure 1-18.

Figure 1-18 FORM PROPERTY SHEET

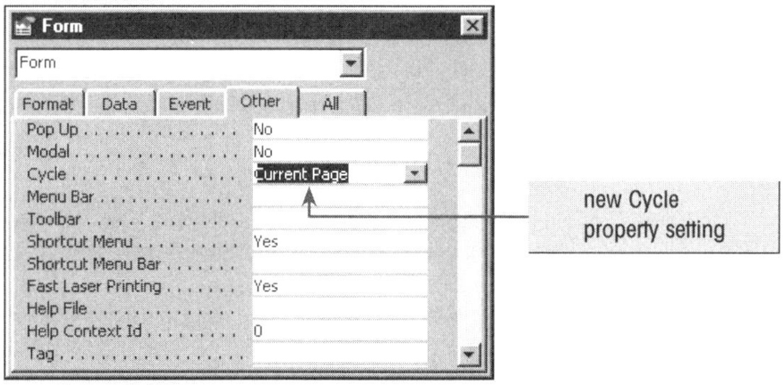

5. Close the property sheet.

   To test the change you made, you open the frmEmployees(page_break) form in Form view and tab through its controls.
6. Switch to Form view, and then press the **Tab** key to move through the controls on the first page until the focus returns to the Human Resource Info command button. At this point you could click the button or press the Enter key to move to the second page of the form and display that entire page.
7. Press the **Tab** key one more time. The focus returns to the first control on the page.
8. Close the form and save your changes.

Amanda is happy with the change you've made to the form. Now you want to take a look at the frmEmployees form to determine its ease of use.

To explore the frmEmployees form:

1. Open the **frmEmployees** form in Form view. It contains tab controls with the data divided into two categories. See Figure 1-16.

   TROUBLE? Depending on the size of your monitor, you might have to scroll to the top of the form to see the tabs.
2. Click the **Human Resource Information** tab at the top of the form to view the controls on the second tab. Notice that the Home Address and Identification sections on the form are accented with a rectangle that is formatted with a sunken special effect.

Amanda suggests that the form's design could be improved if the Job Related Information and Education & Training controls were boxed in the same manner as the Home Address and Identification sections.

REFERENCE WINDOW RW

Adding a Rectangle to a Form

- Open the form in Design view.
- Click View on the menu bar, and then click Toolbox (or click the Toolbox button on the toolbar) to display the toolbox.
- Click the Rectangle button on the toolbox, and then click and drag to draw the box on the form.

Next, you add rectangles to the form to create the boxed effect Amanda wants.

To add rectangles to the form:

1. Switch to Design view and then click the **Human Resource Information** tab.
2. If necessary, click the **Toolbox** button on the Form Design toolbar to display the toolbox, and then maximize the form.
3. Click the **Rectangle** button on the toolbox, and then move the pointer over the form.
4. Using Figure 1-19 as a guide, click and drag to create a rectangle around the Job Related Information controls.

Figure 1-19 ADDING A RECTANGLE TO frmEmployees FORM

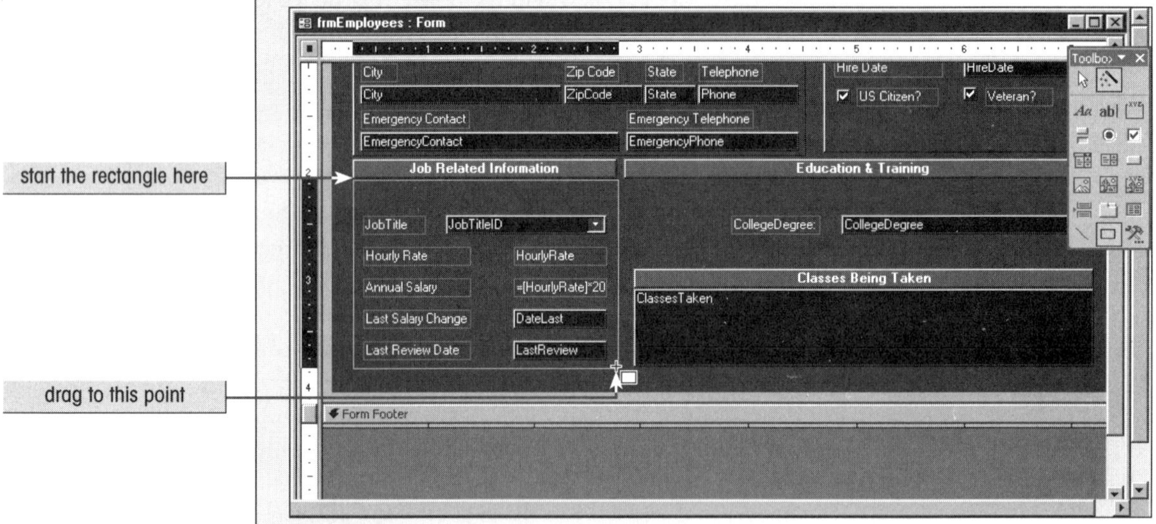

TROUBLE? If all of the Job Related Information controls are not visible, you can scroll down the form before performing Step 4 (although the form does scroll automatically as your drag the pointer over the form).

5. Click the list arrow on the **Special Effect** button on the Formatting toolbar, and then click **Special Effect: Sunken**.

TROUBLE? Your Special Effect button might have a different appearance, depending on which of its options were previously chosen.

6. Repeat Steps 2 and 3 to create a rectangle to enclose the Education & Training controls, and then apply the **Sunken** effect.

7. Switch to Form view, restore the window (so it is no longer maximized), and then click the **Human Resource Information** tab. The result should look similar to those in Figure 1-20.

Figure 1-20 COMPLETED frmEmployees FORM

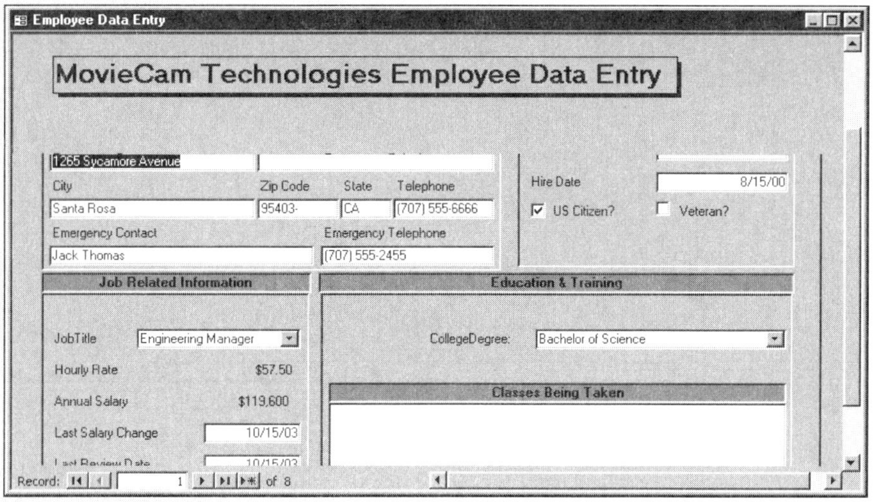

8. Click the **Save** button on the Form View toolbar to save your changes to the form.

The frmEmployees(page_break) form has a text box at the top of the form that displays the employee's first and last name. The text box value is a text expression that concatenates the values of the FirstName and LastName fields with a space between them. Amanda asks you to add this same expression to the frmEmployees form so that the employee's name shows regardless of which tab of the form is displayed.

To add a text expression to a form:

1. Switch to the Design view of the frmEmployees form.
2. Click the **Text Box** button ab| on the toolbox.
3. Click below the "MovieCam Technologies Employee Data Entry" label in the Form Header section. A label control and a text box control appear.
4. Click the label control to select it, and then press the **Delete** key.
5. Click the text box control to select it, click in the text box to position the insertion point, type **=FirstName&Space(1)&LastName** and then press the **Enter** key. Note that Access placed square brackets around the field names: (FirstName) and (LastName) for you, and put a space on each side of each ampersand (&).
6. Size the text box so that it is approximately 2 inches wide and ¼ inches tall, and then position it as shown in Figure 1-21.

TROUBLE? If you are having difficulty sizing the text box, open its property sheet and change the Width and Height values on the Format tab.

Figure 1-21 TEXT BOX WITH AN EXPRESSION ADDED TO frmEmployees FORM

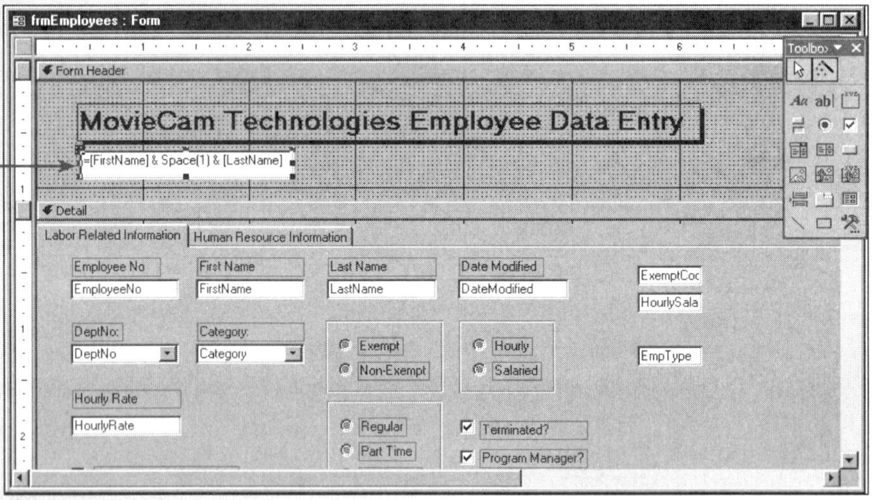

text box correctly positioned and resized

Now you format the text in the text box.

7. Click the **Font Size** list arrow, click **12** on the Formatting (Form/Report) toolbar, and then click the **Bold** button. The employee names should fit nicely within this text box at these settings.

Amanda asks you to change the background color of the text box to transparent and change the effect to flat.

8. Click the list arrow for the **Fill/Back Color** button on the Formatting (Form/Report) toolbar, and then click **Transparent**.

9. Click the list arrow for the **Special Effect** button on the Formatting (Form/Report) toolbar, and then click **Special Effect: Flat**.

10. Click the **Properties** button, and then change the Name property of the text box to **txtName**. When you create your own controls, they are generically named by Access with such names as "Text166" or "Command168." Although there is no specific harm in this, it can become very confusing when you set the tab order on a form. Text166 and Text168 have no particular or useful meaning, but EmployeeNo and FirstName do. In addition, when you want to refer to controls on a form in VBA code or in a macro, having a meaningful name for the controls also simplifies and speeds up your work. The forms are also easier to maintain by yourself and others in the future.

Now you test the form to verify that the expression is correct and that the text box is correctly formatted.

11. Switch to Form view, and then use the record navigation button at the bottom of the form to move through the records and click the tabs to switch from one page to the other. Notice that the employee name is always displayed, which is what Amanda wanted.

12. Close the property sheet and the form, and save your changes.

Amanda prefers the layout of the form with tabs to the page break form and is satisfied with its performance, but she doesn't yet know which layout the users prefer. While a system is still in development, you should keep any object that might come in handy later. So, rather than delete the frmEmployees(page_break) form, Amanda asks you to rename it with a prefix that indicates it is a temporary object. Then, if the users prefer that form, or if you ever need to refer to it again, it is available.

The prefix "z" is often used to specify a temporary object, such as a test object or an object saved for reference purposes. The letter "z" is used because all the objects that begin with "z" sort to the bottom of the list in the Database window, making it easier to locate and delete all temporary objects when the application is finished.

Next, you add this prefix to the name of the form.

To change the name of a form:

1. Right-click **frmEmployees(page_break)** in the Database window, and then click **Rename** on the shortcut menu.
2. Press the **Home** key to position the insertion point at the beginning of the name, and then type **z**. The form name should now read zfrmEmployees(page_break).
3. Press the **Enter** key to accept your changes.

You have completed your review of the forms in the database. Amanda asks you to continue exploring the existing database by examining the report that Jason created.

Reports

Reports are used primarily for printing records in an organized, attractive format. A report may be based on the contents of a table, the results of a saved query, or an SQL statement.

Jason created one report in the Movie1 database. Amanda explains that the report lists all employees grouped by the department in which they work, and contains information such as job title, salary, and labor category. The product managers use the report to project job costs based on employees' current earnings.

Amanda reminds you that you previously modified the query on which this report is based by creating a field expression that you used to properly sort employee numbers. The sort order in this report needs to reflect the changes you made in that query. This report is grouped on DeptNo so that all of the employees from a particular department print in one group. The report is then sorted by EmployeeNo so that the employees in each group or department are sorted in ascending order by employee number. To sort the employee numbers in true numerical order, Amanda asks you to change the Sorting and Grouping options so that the data is sorted by EmpNoInt instead.

To change the sort order in the rptEmployeesByDept report:

1. Click **Reports** on the Objects bar, and then open the **rptEmployeesByDept** report in Design view.

   TROUBLE? It is unlikely, but if a message box opens warning that the section width is greater than the page width, click the OK button to continue. You deal with this issue shortly.

2. Click the **Sorting and Grouping** button on the Report Design toolbar. The Sorting and Grouping dialog box opens.
3. Click **EmployeeNo** in the Field/Expression text box, click the list arrow that appears, and then click **EmpNoInt**. See Figure 1-22. You now have changed the second sort order of the report from EmployeeNo (a text field) to EmpNoInt (an integer).

Figure 1-22 SORTING AND GROUPING DIALOG BOX

second sort field changed to EmpNoInt

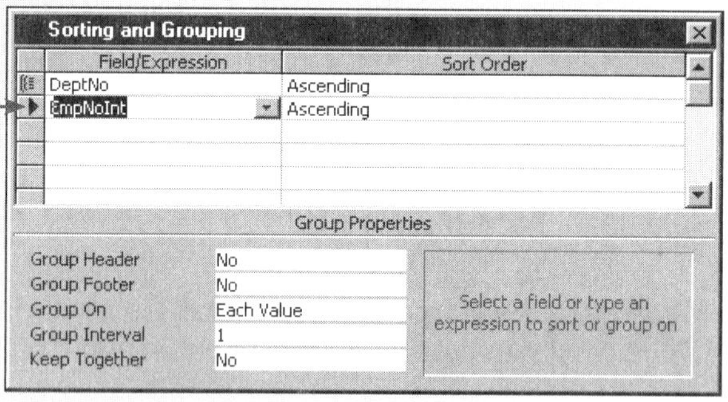

4. Close the Sorting and Grouping dialog box.
5. Preview the report and note that the employee numbers within each group appear in numerical order. Also notice that all the departments print on one page.

   TROUBLE? If a message box opens warning that the section width is greater than the page width, click the OK button to continue.

Amanda comments that the report would be easier to use if each new department began on a separate page. She tells you that this can be accomplished by applying the Force New Page property.

REFERENCE WINDOW RW

Applying the Force New Page Property

- Open the report in Design view.
- Display the property sheet of the section before or after which you want to break the page.
- Click the Force New Page text box, and then click its list arrow.
- Select the appropriate item from the list.
- Close the property sheet.

You now change the Force New Page property of the DeptNo footer to add a page break after each department.

To use the Force New Page property:

1. Switch to Design view.

2. Right-click the **DeptNo Footer** section band to display the shortcut menu, and then click **Properties** to open the property sheet.
3. Make sure the **All** tab is displayed, and then scroll to the top of the property list, if necessary.
4. Click the **Force New Page** text box, click its list arrow, and then click **After Section**. See Figure 1-23.

Figure 1-23 SECTION PROPERTIES

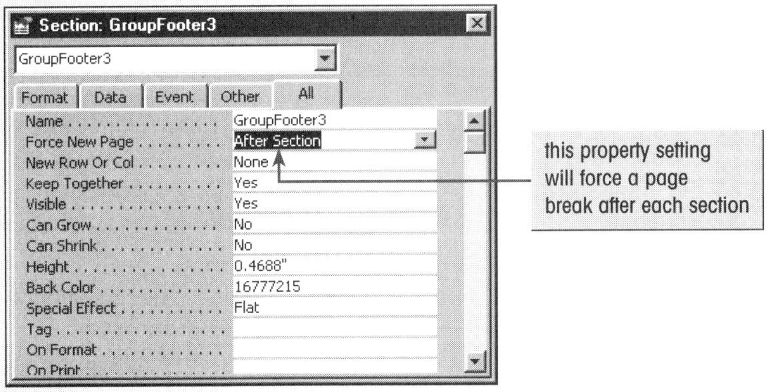

5. Close the property sheet.
6. Preview the report and then use the page selector buttons to page through the report.

   TROUBLE? If a message box opens warning that the section width is greater than the page width, click the OK button to continue.

   TROUBLE? You might see a blank page between every page of the report; if so, don't worry about that for now—it is related to the section-width message, if you are getting it. If portion of the section width exceeds the page width, it spills over onto a blank page. You correct this next.
7. Switch to Design view.

The horizontal ruler along the top of the report shows the width of the report, which is 6¾ inches. This report is designed to print on 8½ x 11-inch paper. The default left and right margins in Access reports are each 1 inch. Therefore, the report itself can be at most 6½ inches wide.

Amanda asks you to make the report narrower and to adjust the left and right margins to eliminate blank pages between each page of the report.

To size a report and change its margins:

1. Position the pointer on the right border of the report, as shown in Figure 1-24.

Figure 1-24 RESIZING THE rptEmployeesByDept REPORT

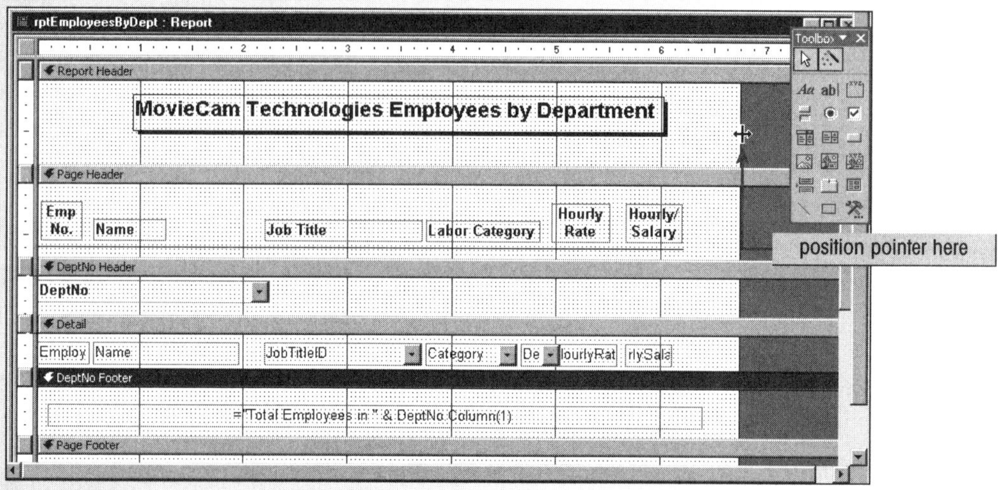

2. Using the ruler as a guide, click and drag the mouse to the left to size the report so that it is **6½** inches wide. For most printers, this page width change eliminates the blank pages. But Amanda wants you to also change the margin settings, just to be sure.
3. Click **File** on the menu bar, and then click **Page Setup**.
4. Type **.75** in the Left text box, type **.75** in the Right text box, and then click the **OK** button.
5. Preview the report to be sure that the blank pages are gone.

   TROUBLE? If the report still displays blank pages, it might be due to the printer you are using. Repeat Steps 3 and 4 and change both the left and right margins to .5.
6. Switch to Design view.

Jason included a text box control in the DeptNo Footer section for the total number of employees, but he did not include anything in its expression to calculate and display that total. Amanda wants you to edit the expression so that it totals the number of employees in each department and identifies the department's name. This also gives you a chance to center this data across the page by editing the existing text box.

To modify an expression in a text box:

1. Click the **txtDeptEmpCount** text box in the DeptNo footer.

   Now, you edit the expression to place the total the number of employees in that text box control to the right of the existing text.
2. Position the insertion point at the end of the expression, press the **spacebar**, type **& ": " & Count(EmployeeNo)** in the text box (making sure to insert a space after the colon and a space on both sides of each ampersand), and then press the **Enter** key. Note that Access automatically enclosed the EmployeeNo field name in brackets ( ) .

3. Click the **Bold** button **B**. See Figure 1-25.

Figure 1-25 EDITED EXPRESSION IN THE TEXT BOX IN rptEmployeesByDept

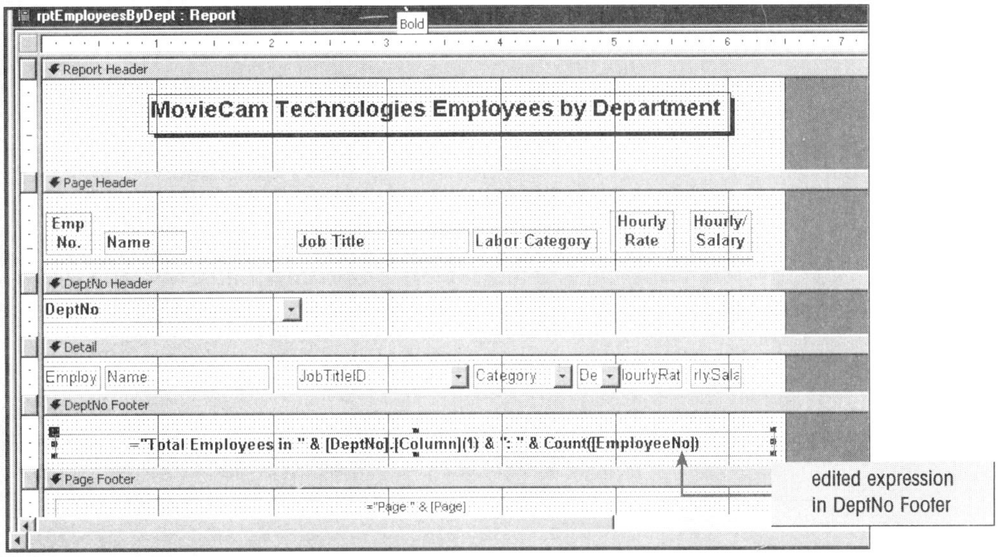

4. Save your changes, preview the report, and then close the report.

The next object that Amanda wants you to review is the data access page.

Pages

You can display a database object as a data access page that can be published to the Internet or an intranet. The **data access page**, which serves as a live link to that data, can be based on a table or on a query. Data access pages are written in HTML (Hypertext Markup Language) and are stored outside the database file. You create data access pages in much the same way that you create forms and reports.

Not all MovieCam employees have access to or use the Movie1 database; however, they still need access to some of the database information. This information can be made available via the company's intranet by placing it on a data access page that can then be viewed in a Web browser.

Creating a Data Access Page

One of the original objectives for the Movie1 database was to create a data access page to allow employees to update their personal information on the company intranet. Amanda asks you to create a data access page that is based on the tblEmployees table.

To create a data access page:

1. Click **Pages** on the Objects bar, and then double-click **Create data access page by using wizard**. The Page Wizard starts and opens the first Page Wizard dialog box, in which you specify the table or query to use and select the fields to be included.

2. Click the **Tables/Queries** list arrow, click **Table: tblEmployees**, and then move the following fields from the Available Fields list box to the Selected Fields list box, in the specified order: **EmployeeNo**, **FirstName**, **LastName**, **Address1**, **Address2**, **City**, **State**, **Phone**, **ZipCode**, **EmergencyContact**, and **EmergencyPhone**.
3. Click the **Next** button. The second Page Wizard dialog box asks if you want to add grouping levels, which you do not.
4. Click the **Next** button to move to the third Page Wizard dialog box.
5. Click the first list arrow, select **LastName** as the field to sort by in ascending order, and then click the **Next** button. The fourth Page Wizard dialog box prompts you for a title for the page.
6. Type **dapMovieEmployees** and then click the **Finish** button. After a few moments, the data access page is displayed in Design view.
7. Click the placeholder **Click here and type title text**, and then type **Employees Contact Information Page**.
8. Click the **Save** button on the Page Design toolbar, make sure that dapMovieEmployees appears as the filename, navigate to the Tutorial.01\Tutorial folder on your local or network drive (if necessary), and then click the **Save** button. If this is the very first time a data access page has been saved on your computer, a message should come up asking if you want to use this as the default path for data access pages. If so, you can accept this default; it doesn't matter at this stage. If you do not see this message, do not worry as this does not present a problem for the purpose of your exercises. You should now receive the warning message shown in Figure 1-26. The message states that the connection string of this page specifies an absolute path. The page might not be able to connect to data through the network and advises you to edit the connection string to specify a network (UNC) path if necessary.

Figure 1-26 ACCESS WARNING MESSAGE

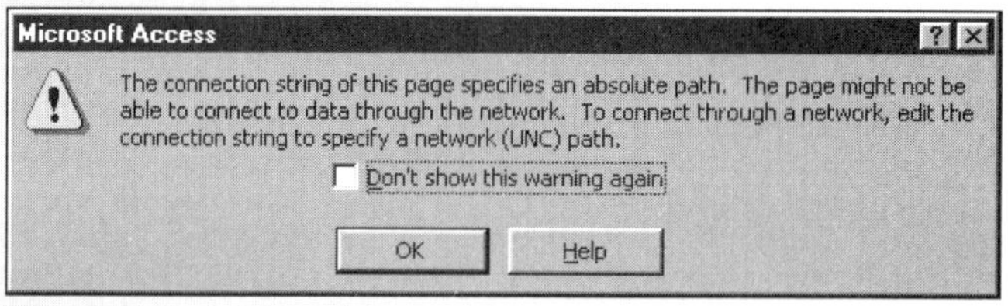

This means that if you design the data access page while the database is on a local drive, Access uses the local path when it associates the page to the file on which it is based. The data then won't be accessible to other users until it is moved to a network drive. When you move or copy a database to a network drive, you also need to specify the new location in the ConnectionString property of the data access page. When you do this, you should use the UNC network path. UNC stands for Universal Naming Convention and is a naming convention that uses the syntax:

\\server\share\path\filename

The ConnectionString property can be found by clicking Edit on menu bar, clicking Select Page, and then clicking the Data tab in the property sheet.

9. Click the **OK** button to continue and switch to Page view. The results of creating the data access page are shown in Figure 1-27.

Figure 1-27 COMPLETED dapMovieEmployees DATA ACCESS PAGE

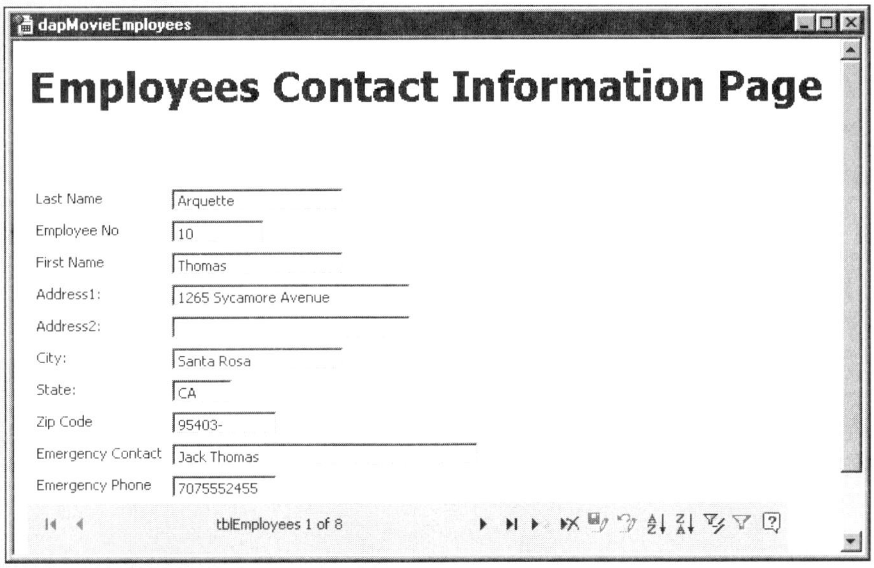

TROUBLE? If necessary, resize the data access page window so the navigation tools at the bottom of the window are visible. Close the toolbox if necessary.

10. Exit Access.

Macros

Macros can be used to automate common tasks. Although they are not the only method of automation, macros are the easiest to learn. To program with macros at the simplest level, you choose from a list of macro actions that parallel the manual actions you would take to perform a task. Macros are explored in depth later in these tutorials as an introduction to working with VBA. Generally speaking, most programmers do not make extensive use of macros. These are not the same kind of macros you may be used to working with from an end-user perspective in Excel. The vast majority of creation and control of a user interface for your database is best done in VBA. Macros, however, do provide a good means of automating various tasks until you become more comfortable working with VBA code. Another reasons macros exist are for those who want to automate Access without doing any actual coding. This, however, is not the case for this book.

Modules

A module is made up of subroutines and functions that are written in VBA and is a more flexible and powerful tool than a macro. Macros are not nearly as fast and cannot provide the same level of control or functionality that a module in VBA can. Although it takes some time to learn VBA, you will find that modules are the better choice for automating more complex or critical tasks, because all of the public properties and methods of each object are made available through VBA.

VBA also allows developers to trap errors; if a developer anticipates an error that could occur, the default response of Access can be trapped and replaced with custom messages and actions. It is not possible to trap errors using macro actions, although steps can be taken to try to avoid them. Proper error handling is an absolute necessity and is considered to be a programming industry best practice; yet this is not possible with macros. Trapping errors and providing the users with suggestions for avoiding errors is good programming practice because it makes the interface more user-friendly. In addition, trapping errors and forcing certain actions by way of VBA code can help to enforce business process rules, prevent user mistakes, and maintain good data integrity.

To truly control and lock down the user interface and properly manage how data in the database is entered, updated, and deleted, developers turn to VBA. It was created for this reason. VBA is covered in depth in the second half of this text.

Session 1.2 QUICK CHECK

1. What is the purpose of a form?
2. On which objects can a report be based?
3. The section property in a report used to create a page break is called ____________.
4. In what language are data access pages written?
5. What might be wrong if your data access page could not connect to data in the database through the network? What is one way to correct this problem?
6. What is a module?
7. ____________ ____________ is a feature available in modules, but not in macros, and this feature is considered a programming industry best practice.

REVIEW ASSIGNMENTS

In the Review Assignments, you work with the Hours database, which is similar to the Movie1 database you worked with in the tutorial. Complete the following:

1. Start Access and open the **Hours1** database, which is located in the Tutorial.01\Review folder on your local or network drive.
2. Open the **tblEmployees** table in Design view.
3. Add a validation rule to the HireDate field to test that it is later than April 1, 1993. Add validation text to explain what the user is doing wrong if the validation rule is violated.
4. Switch to Datasheet view, and then save the table when prompted to do so and acknowledge that changes been made to the data integrity rules.
5. Test the rule to be sure that it works by temporarily replacing an existing HireDate with a date that is prior to April 1, 1993.
6. Restore the original HireDate value, close the table, and save your changes.

7. Open the **frmEmployees** form in Design view, and then do the following:
   a. Add a text box to the Form Header below the label containing Employee Data Entry.
   b. Delete the label control that is created with the text box.
   c. Enter the text **=FirstName&Space(1)&LastName** inside the text box.
   d. Change the font size to 12-point.
   e. Change the special effect to Flat.
   f. Resize the text box so it is 1½ inches in width and ¼ inch in height.
   g. Switch to Form view to test the expression.
8. Click the Human Resource Information tab, switch to Design view, and then do the following:
   a. Add rectangles to enclose the Home Address, Identification, and Job Related Information sections.
   b. Change the effect of each rectangle you added to Sunken.
   c. Return to Form view to see your changes.
9. Print one page using landscape orientation of the form that has the Human Resource Information tab, and then close the form and save your changes.
10. Use the Page Wizard to create a data access page based on the tblEmployees table. Display the following fields: FirstName, LastName, Address1, City, State, Phone, ZipCode, EmergencyContact, and EmergencyPhone. Do not specify grouping levels, select LastName as the field to sort by, and change the title of the page to **dapHoursEmployees**.
11. Replace the placeholder text at the top of the page with **Employee Contact Info**.
12. Close the page and save it as **dapHoursEmployees** in the Tutorial.01\Review folder. If necessary, accept the default path for data access pages and acknowledge the warning about the Connection string property.
13. Close the database, and then exit Access.

CASE PROBLEMS

Case 1. Edwards and Company Edwards and Company is a CPA firm that provides tax planning and preparation services to individuals and businesses, plus real estate, finance, and investment consulting, estate and financial planning, and small business consulting. Managing partner Jack Edwards contacted you regarding the firm's database needs. His company needs a database to track employees, contractors, clients, and client services.

Complete the following:

1. Start Access and open the **Edward1** database located in the Tutorial.01\Cases folder on your local or network drive.
2. Open the **tblConsultants** table in Design view.
3. Add a table validation rule to test that the BirthDate field is prior to the HireDate field, add validation text to let the user know how to correct the error if the validation rule is violated, and then test your changes. Restore any original values that you change.
4. Change the Field Size property of the State field to 2.

5. Change the Format property of the State field so that all characters are forced into uppercase after being entered. The current data is all in uppercase, but you want to be sure that any new data entered for the State field is forced to uppercase.

Explore

6. Apply a validation rule to the ConsultantType field so that only the letter R or C may be entered. (R stands for regular employee and C stands for consultant.) Then add validation text to tell the user what the error is if the validation rule is violated.

7. Test the rule to be sure that it works by temporarily changing the ConsultantType field in one of the records to something other than the letter R or C.

8. Close the table and save your changes.

Explore

9. Use the Documenter to print the table properties. Open the Documenter from the Analyze submenu on the Tools menu. Select the tblConsultants table for printing. Open the Options dialog box to check the print options, making sure the Relationships and Permissions by User and Group check boxes are clear. Close the Print Table Definition dialog box, and then close the Documenter. After a moment, a report opens in Preview mode. You do not need to print the report, but you might want to print the first page or two to see how it comes out.

10. Close the report.

11. Close the database and then exit Access.

Case 2. San Diego County Information Systems You are the training coordinator and lead trainer for the San Diego County Information Systems Department. Your job includes planning, coordinating, and training all county employees on computer systems and applications. You develop classes, write course material, train other instructors, and publish a class schedule in the county newsletter each month. You also work closely with the PC team to schedule training for entire departments during major conversions or upgrades of software. To keep track of students and the classes they take, you have developed an Access database.

Complete the following:

1. Start Access and open the **ISD1** database located in the Tutorial.01\Cases folder on your local or network drive.

2. Open the **qryEmployeesByDept** query in Design view.

3. Add a column to the query after the DepartmentNo column, and then enter the following expression: **DeptNoInt:CInt([tblDepartments]![DepartmentNo])**. Note that the name of the table is required because there is a field in each table with the name DepartmentNo. (*Hint*: To see the whole expression, press Shift + F2.)

4. Run the query to test the expression. The results display the department number as an integer rather than as text.

5. Switch to Design view, and then delete the DepartmentNo column.

6. Specify an ascending sort on DeptNoInt, and then run the query to test your changes. Notice that department number 50 now displays at the top of the results, instead of after department 300.

7. Switch to Design view, add another column to the query after the DeptNoInt column, and then enter an expression named **StudentName** that concatenates FirstName with LastName and has a space between the two fields.

8. Run the query to test your expression.

9. Switch to Design view, and then delete the FirstName and LastName columns from the query.
10. Print the query results.
11. Close the query and save your changes.

Explore

12. Open the **frmClasses** form in Design view, and then change the Record Selectors and Dividing Lines properties to No.
13. Add an etched rectangle to the Detail section of the form to visually group all of the controls.
14. Print the form.
15. Close the form and save your changes.
16. Open the **rptStudentsPhone** report in Design view. Size the report so that a blank page is not printed after the first page of the report.
17. Add an unbound text box control to the Report Footer section, and type an expression in the text box that counts the total number of students on the report. (*Hint*: The expression should read *=Count(LastName)*.)
18. Preview the report and then print it.
19. Close the report and save your changes.
20. Use the Page Wizard to create a data access page based on the tblStudents table. Use all fields in the table, sort on LastName, and then change the title of the page to **dapISDStudents**.
21. Replace the placeholder text at the top of the page with **Student Information**.
22. Save the page as **dapISDStudents** in the Tutorial.01\Cases folder. If necessary, accept the default path for data access pages and acknowledge the warning about the Connection string property.
23. Close the page, close the database, and then exit Access

Case 3. Christenson Homes Christenson Homes is a builder and developer of custom homes. At any given time, two or three different subdivisions might be under construction. As office manager, it is your responsibility to keep track of the homes under construction based on lot number and subdivision location. In addition, each home comes with standard options such as doors, carpeting, and showers. Customers may choose from a variety of purchase options that upgrade the standard options and carry an added cost. To track all of the purchase options for each lot in each subdivision, you have begun an Access database.

Complete the following:

1. Start Access and open **Homes1** located in the Tutorial.01\Cases folder on your local or network drive.
2. Open the **frmLots** form in Design view.
3. Add a sunken rectangle to the detail section of the form to visually group all of the controls.
4. Change the Cycle property of the form to Current Record.
5. Switch to Form view, test your changes, and then print the form.

6. Close the form and save the changes.
7. Open the **rptLotsBySub** report in Design view.
8. Change the grouping properties of the SubdivisonID Footer section so that there is a page break after each subdivision.
9. Add an unbound text box control to the SubdivisionID Footer section that is aligned below the Elevation text box in the Detail section. Delete the label that is created when you created the text box.
10. Change the Name property of the text box to **txtCount**, and then enter an expression into the text box to count the total number of lots in each subdivision.
11. Add another text box control in the SubdivisionID Footer section, and align the text box below LotNo. Delete the label control that is created when you created the text box.
12. Change the Name property of the text box to **txtLabel**, and then enter the following expression as the Control Source property: **="Total Lots in " & [SubdivisionID].[column](1)**. This expression displays the subdivision name concatenated to the words *Total Lots in*. Be sure to include a space between the word *in* and the quotation mark.
13. Format both new text boxes to be Arial 8-point, bold (if necessary to change), and size each of the text boxes to display all of the text.
14. Save and preview the report.
15. Print the first page of the report. Close the report.
16. Use the Page Wizard to create a data access page based on the qryLotsBySubdivision query. Select all the fields in the query, group the data by SubdivisionName, and change the title of the page to **dapHomeLots**.
17. Replace the placeholder text at the top of the page with **Home Lots By Subdivision**.
18. Close the page and save it as **dapHomeLots** in the Tutorial.01\Cases folder. If necessary, accept the default path for data access pages and acknowledge the warning about the Connection string property.
19. Close the database and then exit Access.

Case 4. Sonoma Farms Sonoma Farms is a family-owned and -operated cheese factory located in Sonoma County, California. Known for their award-winning cheeses, Sonoma Farms attracts thousands of visitors each year. Visitors may observe the cheese being processed, sample from over 20 different kinds of cheese, or simply enjoy the picturesque setting. As marketing manager for Sonoma Farms, you work directly with the regional distributors and consumers of the Sonoma Farms products. You need to track the customers each distributor is responsible for servicing. You use customer information to value target product announcements and mailings, as well as promotional visits by customers to the factory.

Complete the following:

1. Start Access and open **Sonoma1** located in the Tutorial.01\Cases folder on your local or network drive.

Explore

2. Open the **qryVisitors** query in Design view, and then create an expression in the query that concatenates the FirstName field with the LastName field and has a space in between. Name the expression **VisitorName** and place it in the first column of the query grid.

3. Switch to Datasheet view and then resize the new column for best fit on the screen; be sure you can read all the text in that column for each record.
4. Save the changes, and then print the query results. Close the query.
5. Open the **rptDistributors** report in Design view.
6. There is a text box in the Detail section that contains a formula that concatenates the Address and City fields. The formula is missing the State and Zip Code fields. Add these two fields by typing **&", "&[State]&", "&[ZipCode]** after [City].
7. Add a text box control to the Report Footer section to count the total number of distributors, and then change the label of the text box to read **Total**.
8. Change the format of both the text box and label to Arial 12-point, bold. Preview the report. (*Hint*: If the Enter Parameter Value dialog box opens, click the OK button to close it without entering a value at this time.) Resize the text box for the best fit if necessary, and resize the report so that no blank pages are printed.
9. Save your changes and print the report. Close the report.
10. Open the **frmDistributors** form in Design view, and then add an etched rectangle that surrounds all the controls on the form.
11. Save your changes and print the form. Close the form.
12. Use the Page Wizard to create a data access page based on the tblDistributors table. Use all fields in the table. Do not specify grouping or sorting fields. Change the title of the page to **dapSonomaDistributors**.
13. Replace the placeholder text at the top of the page with **Distributors Web Page**.
14. Close the page and save it as **dapSonomaDistributors** in the Tutorial.01\Cases folder. If necessary, accept the default path for data access pages and acknowledge the warning about the Connection string property.
15. Close the database and then exit Access.

QUICK CHECK ANSWERS

Session 1.1

1. database management system (DBMS)
2. table; field
3. &
4. CInt
5. Crosstab queries display summarized values from one or more tables in a spreadsheet format.
6. make-table, delete, append, and update
7. union, pass-through, data definition, and subquery

Session 1.2

1. Forms are used to display, edit, and enter data on screen.
2. the contents of a table, the results of a saved query, or an SQL statement
3. Force New Page
4. HTML
5. Error trapping
6. A module is made up of subroutines and functions that are written in VBA.
7. The connection string of the page probably specifies an absolute path, such as to a local drive, which is not available to others on the network. To correct this, edit the connection string to specify a Universal Naming Convention (UNC) network path.

OBJECTIVES

In this tutorial you will:

- Learn about why and when to use Access as a database management solution
- Learn about data redundancy
- Create tables in Datasheet and Design view
- Study and create primary keys and indexes
- Identify one-to-one, one-to-many, and many-to-many relationships
- Learn about referential integrity and apply it when you establish relationships
- Add data using a subdatasheet
- Explore how Access handles dates, and set properties to manage date issues
- Document your database using the Database Documenter and printing relationships

DESIGNING AND DOCUMENTING A DATABASE

Completing the Tables and Establishing Relationships in the MovieCam Technologies Database

CASE

MovieCam Technologies

Amanda wants you to continue working on the MovieCam database project. She wants you to finalize the database's design by completing the tables and establishing relationships between them. She has requested that you use the Database Documenter tool to provide detailed information on the database's design and structure.

In your preliminary review of the Movie2 database, you found that the tblEmployees table is the central table in the database. The tblDepartments, tblDegrees, and tblJobTitles tables contain data on departments, academic degrees, and job titles, respectively, and are each related to the tblEmployees table.

Using what you've learned from reviewing the Movie2 database and understanding the objectives that Amanda and the other product managers have for it, you begin the task of completing the design of the database.

SESSION 2.1

In this session, you will learn about when to use Access as a solution and about avoiding data redundancy. You then add tables to the Movie2 database. You also set primary keys and indexes, and finally, you establish relationships between tables.

Database Design

As you learned in Tutorial 1, a database management system is designed to manage, store, retrieve, and organize large amounts of information. Some databases accomplish this with a single table, sometimes referred to as a flat file. Most real-world databases, however, contain numerous tables that store many records. This is where relational database management systems become essential.

Why Use Access?

You have used Access before and know that it is a versatile database management system, but you have never really used it to put together a real business application. So far you have been using Access without questioning its capabilities or why the company chose it. You know that there are other database management systems that are larger or more sophisticated; however, you also know that Access has all the basic elements and features that make it a good choice for managing data. But, you don't really know all the advanced capabilities of Access or why MovieCam Technologies chose it for their purposes here. You decide this is a good question for Amanda; after all, she is the Director of Information Systems and the person who oversees this project.

Amanda explains that MovieCam Technologies considered a number of factors, or criteria, which included, but were not necessarily limited to:

- Speed to market, or how soon the application could be built
- Ease of maintenance and enhancement
- Flexibility and power to control the user interface to the database
- Connectivity to existing spreadsheets used by product managers helps simplify and speed up data conversion
- Overall low cost of ownership
- Ability for up to 10 or 15 concurrent users (several employees could access the application at one time) while maintaining data integrity
- Security capabilities
- Initial estimated size indicates that the database will be far less than 100 MB (in the foreseeable future, but future needs may require an increase in size)
- Ease of upsizing or migrating the database to a larger platform in the future

Amanda explains these factors are not necessarily listed in order of priority, but they were all important considerations. She also explains that MovieCam chose Access because it can satisfy all of the above requirements.

Access is part of the Microsoft Office XP suite of applications, and as such integrates extremely well with other Office products. In particular, converting data from an Excel spreadsheet (called a worksheet in Excel), which is where many product managers keep their data, into an Access table is very easy. Access is very user-friendly and also utilizes Visual Basic for Applications (VBA), which has been standardized across the Office suite of applications. VBA is both a subset and a superset of Visual Basic (VB). VBA contains commands, key words, control structures, naming conventions, built-in functions, and types of procedures common to VB, though VBA does not have quite all the power and objects available through VB; this makes VBA a subset. VBA includes additional functionality specific to the application making use of it.

For example, there are naming and reference conventions available in the Excel form of VBA that are not available in either the Access or the Word form of VBA, and vice-versa.

Access not only manages tables and queries, but also offers forms, reports, data access pages, and the ability to control their use and automate a great degree of the functionality. Access also allows for user and group level security, which can be managed much in the same way as network security. Access can easily handle a 100 MB database that can grow as large as 2 GB, including system and hidden objects.

Access allows for up to 255 concurrent users, though Amanda mentions that she has noticed when more than 20 people use the database at one time it does not run very efficiently. Several factors such as number of processors, disk space and memory on the file server, individual PC processor speed and memory, and even network bandwidth and speed influence the efficiency and speed of various database operations. These factors, plus query efficiency and the types of activities performed by users concurrently all contribute to how well Access can perform in a multiuser environment. MovieCam's anticipated having only 10 to15 concurrent users, so Access is usually adequate under the current network, server, and local PC conditions.

Much of what has been mentioned to this point seems to indicate a relatively low cost of ownership, but what does that mean really? It is entirely relative to the size of the company, the annual Information Systems/Technology budget for expense and capital expenditures, as well as to the other options available at the time. Amanda states that one option considered was to jump right into an SQL Server 2000 database in a client/server environment and to write the front end of the application, such as the screens, reports and business logic, using other tools available as part of Visual Studio .NET. Much of the business logic could be handled by SQL Server, as well. In Amanda's experience, there has quite often been some middleware component to handle business rules or to provide application logic. Though this would have been a relatively low-cost solution compared to other large database platforms on the market, it was seen as overkill for a database that might grow to only 100 MB some day. You question whether it might become something much bigger as business needs and applications tend to quickly grow larger and more complex.

Amanda concedes the point, but assures you that for the reasons she mentioned, Access was still a good choice. One of the criteria is speed to market, as well as ease of upsizing or migrating to a larger database platform. Assuming Access could provide an adequate solution for the next three years or so, the money saved in using it would pay for itself, especially when compared to jumping into a three-tier client/server architecture. Three-tier architectures typically consist of a dedicated database server, an application server that enforces certain business rules and logic, and a front-end application (often referred to as a client-side application) user interface. Had the company wanted to seamlessly integrate the application to payroll, a purchase order system, or to create an online e-commerce site to handle millions of customer orders each year, then Access would have been ruled out as a viable solution.

Access provides advice in the Help files for using an upsizing wizard, when you should upsize, and what you should do in preparation for upsizing to SQL Server. Amanda explains that it is even possible to continue to use Access as a "front-end application," meaning that although tables and queries in Access could be converted to their appropriate counterparts in SQL Server, the forms, reports, data access pages, macros and modules you write now could still be used even after that migration. This is what makes Access even more of an ideal solution now, given the ease of upsizing or migration and the fact that much of the money spent today would not go to waste or be used to develop something you know for a fact would become obsolete in a year. For more information regarding upsizing, go to Access Help and look up the topic entitled, "About upsizing a Microsoft Access database."

Data Redundancy

One advantage of using a relational database is its capability to link tables, thus reducing the amount of data duplication. Duplication of data is referred to as **data redundancy**. Some duplication of data is always necessary, but the goal of good database design is to eliminate as much redundancy as possible.

The sample spreadsheet shown in Figure 2-1 is an example of a two-dimensional representation of the time card data. This file, you may recall from Tutorial 1, represents what MovieCam product managers use to track time spent on jobs. It is not possible to create and link tables in a spreadsheet program as it is in a relational database, as you shall explore next.

Figure 2-1 **SPREADSHEET TO TRACK TIME SPENT ON JOBS**

first and last names should be separated into two separate fields

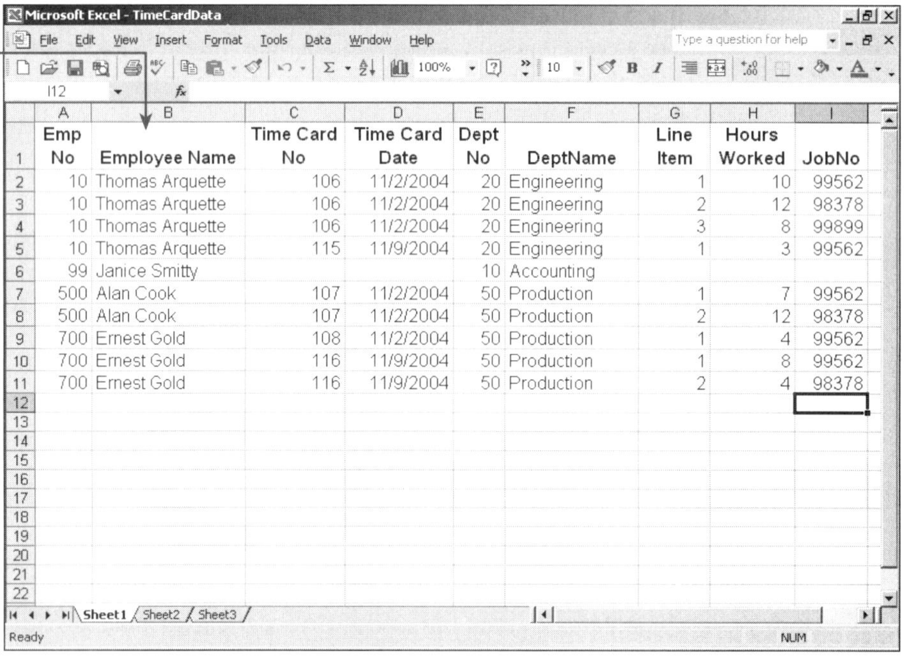

Emp No	Employee Name	Time Card No	Time Card Date	Dept No	DeptName	Line Item	Hours Worked	JobNo
10	Thomas Arquette	106	11/2/2004	20	Engineering	1	10	99562
10	Thomas Arquette	106	11/2/2004	20	Engineering	2	12	98378
10	Thomas Arquette	106	11/2/2004	20	Engineering	3	8	99899
10	Thomas Arquette	115	11/9/2004	20	Engineering	1	3	99562
99	Janice Smitty			10	Accounting			
500	Alan Cook	107	11/2/2004	50	Production	1	7	99562
500	Alan Cook	107	11/2/2004	50	Production	2	12	98378
700	Ernest Gold	108	11/2/2004	50	Production	1	4	99562
700	Ernest Gold	116	11/9/2004	50	Production	1	8	99562
700	Ernest Gold	116	11/9/2004	50	Production	2	4	98378

Notice the redundancy of information in practically every column of the spreadsheet file. This file contains only 10 records. Imagine the data redundancy problem you would have if you were dealing with thousands of records. In Figure 2-1, the term "Engineering" occurs four times. Assume that you're dealing with 100,000 records; the term "Engineering" would occur 50,000 times. The department name "Engineering" uses approximately 10 characters, so if Engineering is entered 49,999 times more than necessary, you would enter 499,990 characters. If each character requires two bytes of storage, the duplication of just one department name takes up 999,980 bytes!

In addition to wasting storage space, data redundancy can result in inefficiency and inaccurate data. For example, if Thomas Arquette and his address have been stored in a single table or spreadsheet 2,000 times, that information had to be typed each one of those times. What would happen if his address changed? All of the records containing his address would have to be changed. If one or two records were missed, it would be difficult to tell which address was correct.

With a relational database, you can reorganize data into separate tables to eliminate the redundant storage of data. You have come up with a plan for completing the table design for the Movie2 database. Ultimately, you want the database to include the following tables:

- *tblEmployees*: This table contains one record for each employee, and has data such as the employee's name, address, title, salary, and start date. This table has already been created by Jason and includes sample records.
- *tblDepartments*: This table contains one record for each department. It is related to the tblEmployees table via the DeptNo field. This means you can create another database object using fields from both tables. This table has already been created by Jason and includes sample records.
- *tblDegrees*: This table contains one record for the four types of academic degrees an employee might have. It also is related to the tblEmployees table via the CollegeDegree field. The table has been created by Jason and includes sample records.
- *tblJobTitles*: This table contains one record for each job title at MovieCam. It is related to the tblEmployees table via the JobTitleID field. This table has been created by Jason and includes sample records.
- *tblTimeCards*: This table has not yet been created. It will contain one record for each time card filled out for each pay period by each employee who uses a time card. It will contain fields for the time card number, the time card date, and the employee's identification number. Information will be entered in the table using the employee's actual time card, which is shown in Figure 2-2.

Figure 2-2 **EMPLOYEE TIME CARD**

MovieCam Technologies		Weekly Time Ticket For:	Thomas Arquette							Emp # 10
Time Card # 106		Week Ending (Saturday):	11-Nov-2004							Dept# 20
Line Item	Job#	Task Description	S	M	T	W	Th	F	S	Total
1										
2										
3										
4										
5										
6										
7										
8										
9										
10										
11										
12										
13										
14										
15										
16										
17										
18										
19	99998	Personal Time								
20	99999	Holidays								
		Total Time								
Signature:			Supervisor:							

This time ticket must be filled out daily in blue or black ink and signed by your supervisor at the end of the week. Report time in 15-minute increments. All time tickets are to be turned in to your supervisor by the end of work on Friday or Saturday. Supervisors must review and sign time tickets. Submit to Accounting no later than 9:30 a.m. Monday.

- *tblHours*: This table has not yet been created. It will contain a record for each line item on the time card (see Figure 2-2), including the time card number, the line item number, the hours worked, and the job number.
- *tblJobs*: This table has not yet been created. It will contain a record for each job or product made by MovieCam, and the product's model number.

When the database design phase is completed, the table structure for the database should look like that shown in Figure 2-3.

Figure 2-3 DESIGN FOR THE MOVIE2 DATABASE

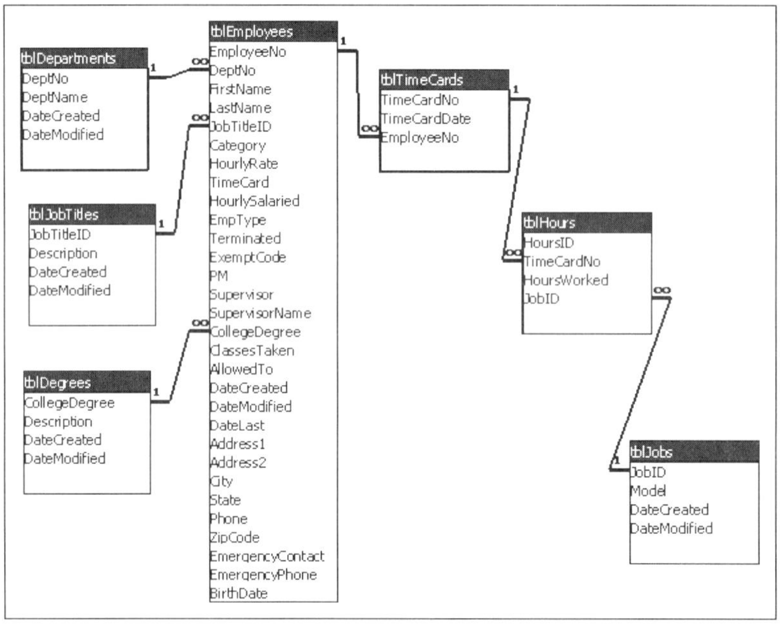

Creating **Tables**

You are ready to begin work on completing the design of the tables in the Movie2 database. You will start by creating the tblTimeCards table.

To create a table in Datasheet view:

1. Make sure that the data files have been copied to the local or network drive on which you are working.

   TROUBLE? If the data files have not been copied to your local or network drive, you must do so before proceeding. Read the "Read This Before You Begin" page at the beginning of this book, or ask your instructor or technical support person for help.

2. Start **Access** and open the **Movie2** database located in the Tutorial.02\Tutorial folder on your local or network drive.
3. If necessary, click **Tables** on the Objects bar in the Database window.

4. Double-click **Create table by entering data**. A new table opens in Datasheet view. The field name at the top of each column is generic. Rename the fields to indicate the type of data that will be stored in each field.
5. Right-click the **Field1** field name, and then click **Rename Column** on the shortcut menu.
6. Type **TimeCardNo** (without any spaces), and then press the **Enter** key.
7. Change the name of Field2 to **TimeCardDate**, and then change the name of Field3 to **EmployeeNo**.
8. Close the table and then click the **Yes** button when you are prompted to save the table.
9. Enter the name **tblTimeCards** in the Save As dialog box, and then click the **OK** button. A message box like that shown in Figure 2-4 warns you that there is no primary key for this table and asks if you would like to create one now.

Figure 2-4 PRIMARY KEY MESSAGE BOX

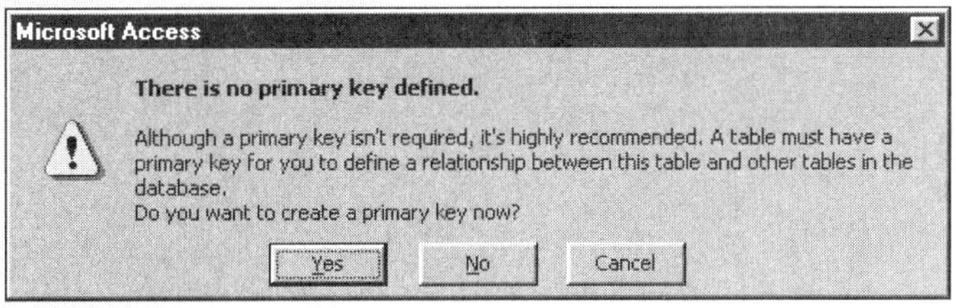

10. Click the **No** button to return to the Database window. You set the primary key and modify the table design in the next section.

You must open a table in Design view to set a primary key and modify its design. When you create a table using the shortcut, as you did in the previous set of steps, the fields are defined by default as Text, and the field size is automatically set to 50. You want to assign a primary key, change the data type for the TimeCardDate field from Text to Date/Time, and set the Caption property for each of the three fields in the table so the field names are easier to read.

To modify the table design:

1. Open the **tblTimeCards** table in Design view. Remember that you can open a table in the Design view by clicking the Design button on the toolbar or using the right-click method.
2. Click the **TimeCardNo** field if it is not already selected, and then click the **Primary Key** button on the toolbar.
3. Click the **TimeCardDate** field, and then change the data type to **Date/Time**.
4. Click the **TimeCardNo** field, press the **F6** key to move the insertion point quickly to the Field Properties pane, click in the **Caption** text box, and then type **Time Card No** to change the caption for the TimeCardNo field.

5. Repeat Step 4 to set the Caption property for the TimeCardDate field to **Time Card Date** and the EmployeeNo field to **Employee No**. Avoiding spaces in actual field names makes it easier to write expressions and use the field name in code; however, changing the caption properties to include spaces makes the field names easier to read in a normal view and is a generally accepted industry practice.
6. Close the table and save your changes.

Next, you need to create the tblJobs table to keep track of MovieCam's jobs.

To create the tblJobs table:

1. Double-click **Create table in Design view**.
2. Define the fields as shown in Figure 2-5 below:

Figure 2-5 tblJobs TABLE

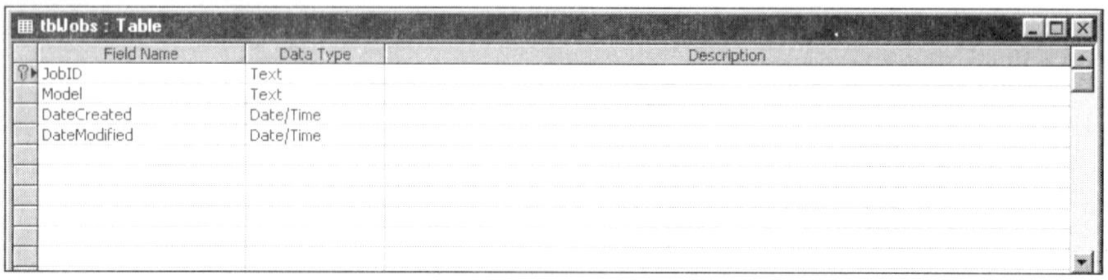

3. Change the Caption property of the JobID, DateCreated, and DateModified fields to **Job ID**, **Date Created**, and **Date Modified**, respectively.
4. Change the Data Type for both date fields to **Date/Time**, and change the Format property for these two fields to **Medium Date**.
5. Set the **JobID** field as the primary key.
6. Close the table and save it as **tblJobs**.

Before you can set relationships between the tables, you need to review primary keys and indexing.

Primary Keys, Foreign Keys, and Indexing

A **key** is a field in a table from which you can order (or sort) the rest of the values in the table. In Access, the field or set of fields that uniquely identifies each record stored in a table is called a **primary key**. Each table can have only one primary key, even if more than one field is unique. For example, if both a Social Security number and an employee number were stored in an employee table, each of these fields could contain unique data, but only one can be set as the primary key. A primary key that consists of two or more fields is called a **composite key**. Sometimes one field by itself is not unique, but when combined with another field, it is. The tblHours table in the Movie2 database has a composite key. As illustrated in Figure 2-6, the TimeCardNo field is not unique because the same number can be entered many times. However, when the data in this field is combined with the data in the LineItem field, the TimeCardNo field becomes a unique field. For example, there is only one record for TimeCardNo 106 and LineItem 1.

Figure 2-6 **COMPOSITE KEY IN THE tblHours TABLE**

these two fields combined are unique

TIMECARD NO	LINEITEM	JOBNO	HOURS WORKED
106	1	99562	2.5
106	2	98378	3.0
106	3	99899	1.5
115	1	99562	8.0
107	1	99562	3.0
107	2	98378	4.0
108	1	99562	8.0
108	2	99562	4.0
116	1	98378	4.0

Another type of key field is a **foreign key**, which is one or more table fields that refer to the primary key field or fields in another table. A foreign key indicates how the tables are related, so it exists only in terms of the relationship between two tables. There is no method for simply setting or appointing a foreign key in Access, other than by creating the relationship. The foreign key is also referred to as the **join field** in the secondary table in a relationship and refers to the primary key field in the primary, or base, table. Figure 2-7 identifies a primary key and foreign key in a relationship. The DeptNo field is used to create the relationship between the tblDepartments table and the tblEmployees table. The DeptNo field is the primary key in the tblDepartments table and the foreign key in the tblEmployees table.

Figure 2-7 **DeptNo AS PRIMARY KEY AND FOREIGN KEY**

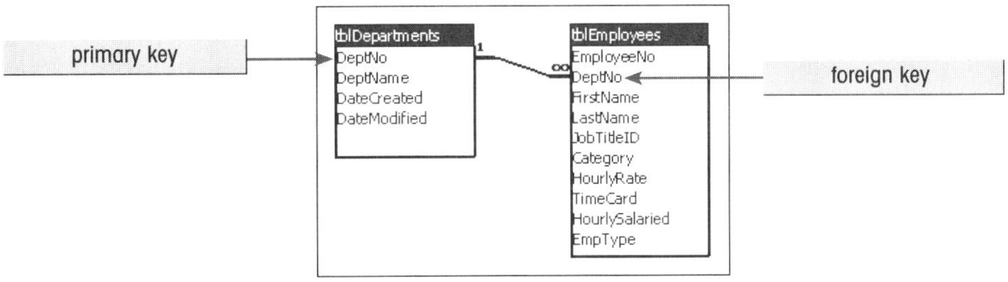

When you set a primary key, Access automatically creates an index that is based on the primary key field. An **index** is a separate hidden table that consists of pointers to records or groups of records. The purpose of an index is to make sorting and searching more efficient. Each table can have a maximum of 32 indexes, and each index can have up to a maximum of 10 fields. You cannot index Memo, Hyperlink, or OLE Object data type fields. You probably want to index fields that you search frequently and fields that you want to sort (order) by, but, at the minimum, index the fields that you will join to fields in other tables (creating relationships) or in queries. You also need to consider that indexes can slow down some action queries, such as append queries, whenever the indexes for many fields need to be updated while running these types of queries. Indexes also consume storage space and contribute to the overall size of the Access database file, which is limited to 2 GB for all objects (visible or hidden).

For other fields, you want to consider indexing a field if all of the following apply:

- The field's data type is Text, Number, Currency, or Date/Time
- You expect to search for values stored in the field
- You expect to sort values in the field
- You expect to store many different values in the field (*Note*: If many of the values in the field are the same, the index may not noticeably speed up queries)

Generally, you should index fields that you plan to sort, set criteria for, group, or on which you will establish relationships. Indexes can be set at any time in the development of the database. You might find that you need indexes when you generate a query or report.

For each record that you add, the indexes must be updated. For each record that is edited, Access must also update the indexed fields affected by the edit. For this reason, it is recommended that you limit the number of indexes in tables, especially for those tables that are considered transactional.

A **transactional** table is one in which the data entry process is ongoing. Orders entered in an order entry system, for example, would be transactional data. The tblTimeCards and tblHours tables in the Movie2 database are examples of transactional tables because new records will be entered into these tables on a frequently recurring basis. Creating a lot of indexes for transactional tables can hinder response time and overall performance because these indexes must be updated each time you enter a new record or change any value of an existing record for a field that is indexed. Transactional tables typically become very large and are frequently used, so slowing down response times with too many indexes in these types of tables can have an impact on the efficiency and productivity of employees using the database during the course of the day.

Tables that are not changed or updated frequently could easily support many indexes. An example of such a table is the tblEmployees table in the Movie2 database because data in this table is changed only when new employees are hired or when an employee's address or salary changes. Access must still update all indexes when you enter such changes, but this nontransactional table will likely be smaller than your transactional tables (consider how many time cards and hours are being entered each day or week for every employee). The time to update a larger number of indexes in this much smaller table may not even be noticeable to users as it would for a large, transactional table.

You anticipate that you will query the tblTimeCards table frequently. The product managers told you that they need reports based on cumulative hours for each pay period or time card date. For this reason, you decide to index the TimeCardDate field.

To create an index:

1. Open the **tblTimeCards** table in Design view.
2. Click the **TimeCardDate** field, and then press the **F6** key to move to the Field Properties pane.
3. Click in the **Indexed** property text box, click its list arrow, and click **Yes (Duplicates OK)**. You need to set the indexed property to Yes (Duplicates OK) because the same date is entered into this field for many records. The Yes (No Duplicates) property option is typically used for primary keys only, although it can be used to restrict duplicate entries in a field that is not the primary key field.
4. Close the table and save your changes.

Next, you will create the tblHours table and set the primary key, which will be a composite key.

REFERENCE WINDOW RW

Specifying a Composite Primary Key

- In the table's Design view, click the row selector of the first field you've chosen for the primary key, and drag over the row selector of the second field (or click the first field and press and hold the Ctrl key while you click the second field).
- Click the Primary Key button on the toolbar.

Now you will create the tblHours table and set the primary key, which is also a composite key. You will also assign captions for each of the field names.

To create the tblHours table and set a composite primary key:

1. Create a new table in Design view.
2. Define four new fields as shown below (after step 4) in Figure 2-8.
3. Change the Caption property of the LineItem, TimeCardNo, JobID, and HoursWorked fields to **Line Item**, **Time Card No**, **Job ID**, and **Hours Worked**, respectively.
4. Click in the **LineItem** field and then position the pointer on the row selector of the LineItem field until the pointer changes to a ➡ shape as shown in Figure 2-8.

Figure 2-8 SETTING A COMPOSITE PRIMARY KEY

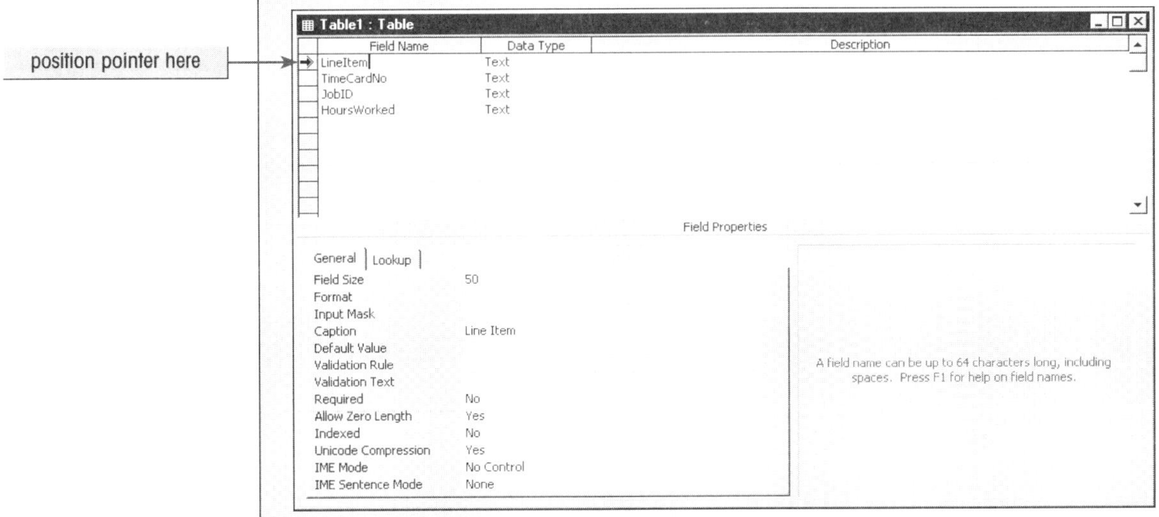

5. Click and drag down one row to select the **LineItem** and **TimeCardNo** fields.
6. Click the **Primary Key** button on the toolbar.
7. Close the table and save the table as **tblHours**.

Next, you will establish the relationships between the tables in the database.

Setting Relationships

Relationships are at the very heart of working with a relational database and storing data in multiple tables. Establishing relationships using primary and foreign keys enables you to reduce redundancy in your databases.

After relationships among tables have been established, you can build queries, forms, and reports that pull together information from the various tables. Relationships among tables are established in the Relationships window.

One-to-One Relationships

A **one-to-one relationship** between two tables exists when one entry in each table corresponds to only one entry in the other table. This is not a common relationship because in many instances the data in the two tables could be combined and stored more efficiently in one table. The few exceptions where separate tables are appropriate are the following:

- To avoid exceeding the 255 field number maximum per table
- To control access to fields in a table that are particularly sensitive or confidential
- To store data in a separate table when only a small group or subset of the records use those fields. (*Note:* This is a means of managing what is known as data sparsity. If you are unfamiliar with this term, do not be concerned; just understand that there are circumstances when certain fields are rarely used, and separating those into a different table with a one-to-one relationship to the primary, or base, table helps to cut down on wasted storage space in a relational database.)

One example of the appropriate use of a one-to-one relationship would be the tblEmployees table in the Movie2 database. You might split the table into two tables, one of which would contain confidential salary information that you want only certain users to be able to access. Both tables would have one record per employee and the primary key for each table would be the EmployeeNo field as shown in Figure 2-9.

Figure 2-9 ONE-TO-ONE RELATIONSHIP

EmployeeNo is the primary key in each table

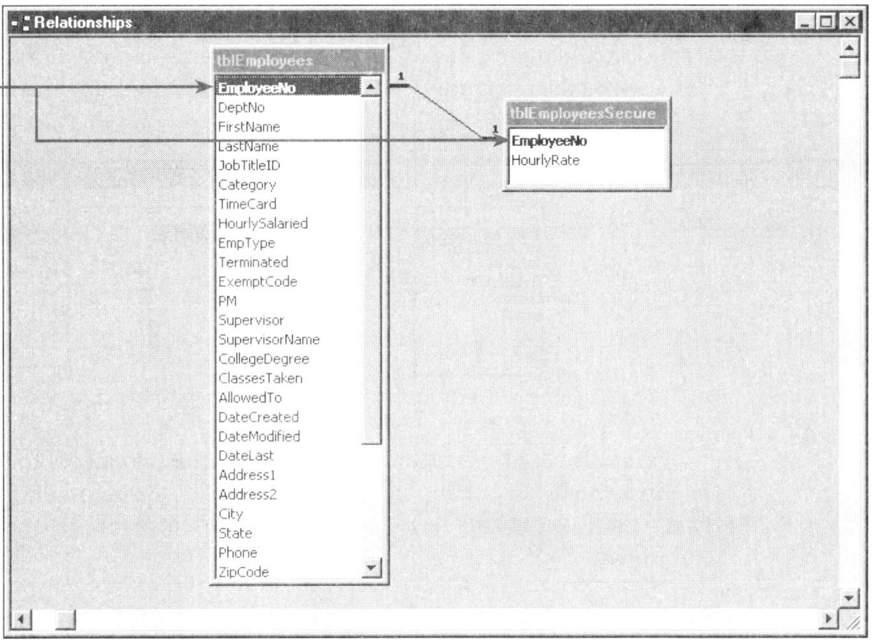

One-to-Many Relationships

A **one-to-many relationship** is a very common type of relationship between tables. It exists between two tables when a **related table** has many records that relate to a single record in the **primary table**. The term primary (or base) table describes the table that contains data about a person or an object when there is only one record that can be associated with that person or object. The tblEmployees table is one example of a primary table.

For example, one customer places many orders with a business, one employee submits many time cards, and one publisher publishes many books. When you implement a one-to-many relationship in Access, the join field in the table on the one side of the relationship must be unique. In almost all cases, the join field is the primary key.

In the Movie2 database, there are numerous examples of one-to-many relationships: tblDepartments has a one-to-many relationship with tblEmployees; tblDegrees has a one-to-many relationship with tblEmployees; tblEmployees has a one-to-many relationship with tblTimeCards; and tblTimeCards has a one-to-many relationship with tblHours.

Consider the employee and time card relationship as an example. An employee has a unique ID number, such as the number 10 for Thomas Arquette. The employee number is a primary key in the tblEmployees table, so the number 10 appears only once in this table. In the tblTimeCards table, Thomas has many time card records for each year, so his employee number (10) appears many times. The EmployeeNo field is the join field in the one-to-many relationship of tblEmployees to tblTimeCards; the values in this field appear only once in the primary, or base, table, but can appear many times in the secondary table.

Many-to-Many Relationships

A **many-to-many relationship** is defined between two tables and a third table, referred to as a **junction table**. A junction table contains common fields from two tables. It is on the many side of the one-to-many relationship with the other two tables. An example of a many-to-many relationship is that between students and classes. The relationship would consist of three tables: a students table containing fields such as names and addresses that describe the students; a classes table containing fields such as descriptions, dates, and times that describe the classes offered; and a students and classes table that contains links to the other two tables. Figure 2-10 illustrates a many-to-many relationship.

Figure 2-10 MANY-TO-MANY RELATIONSHIP

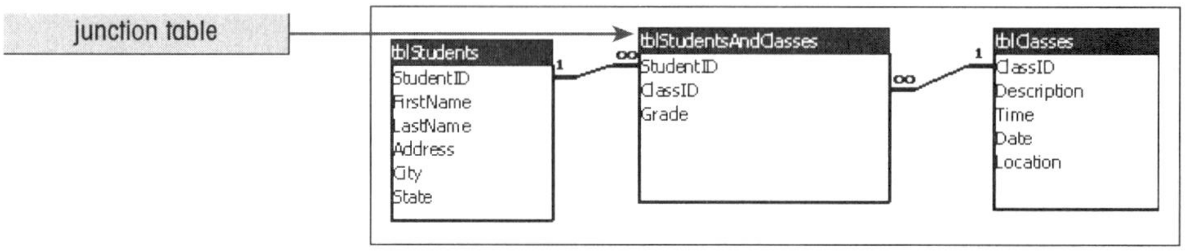

Junction tables are often named so that the two tables for which they provide the link is obvious. In the example in Figure 2-10, tblStudents has a one-to-many relationship with tblStudentsAndClasses and tblClasses also has a one-to-many relationship with tblStudentsAndClasses.

Referential Integrity

Referential integrity requires that a foreign key value in a related table match the value of the primary key for some row in the primary table. This requirement prevents the occurrence of orphaned records. An **orphan record** is a record in the related table that does not contain a record in the primary table. An example of an orphan record is a time card record in the tblTimeCards table that refers to an employee number that doesn't exist in the tblEmployees table. Enforcing referential integrity prevents orphan records from occurring; therefore, you do not have to develop separate procedures for preventing, finding, or fixing them.

Referential integrity also controls the order of operations in your database. For example, if a user tries to enter a time card for a new employee before the employee is entered into the database, referential integrity between the two tables does not allow the time card to be entered.

Access enforces a series of rules to make sure that relationships between records in related tables are valid and that you don't accidentally change or delete related data. When a relationship is created between two tables, the option to set referential integrity is displayed. The following conditions must be met in order to enforce referential integrity:

- The field on the one side of the relationship (in the primary table) must be a primary key.
- The fields on which the tables are joined must be the same data type with the following exceptions: an AutoNumber field can be related to a Number field that has its field size property set to Long Integer; an AutoNumber field that has a field size property set to Replication ID can be related to a Number field to which the same Replication ID field size property has been applied.
- Both of the tables that are related must be part of the same database format. Referential integrity cannot be enforced for linked tables from databases in other formats, although you can set referential integrity on Access-linked tables in the database file in which they exist.

The following rules apply to tables on which referential integrity has been set:

- You cannot enter a value in the foreign key field of a related table if the primary table doesn't contain that particular value. For example, you cannot enter an employee number in the tblTimeCards table for an employee who doesn't exist in the tblEmployees table. You can, however, enter null in the foreign key to indicate that the record is not related to any record in the primary table. A null value in the EmployeeNo field specifies that the time card is assigned to no one, rather than to an employee who doesn't exist (however, managing the data in this way is *not* recommended).
- You cannot delete a record from a primary table if there are matching records in the related table. For example, you cannot delete an employee from the tblEmployees table if time cards for that employee exist in the tblTimeCards table. See Figure 2-11.

Figure 2-11 **ENFORCING REFERENTIAL INTEGRITY WHEN DELETING A RECORD**

tblEmployees (primary table)

EMPLOYEENO	FIRSTNAME	LASTNAME	DEPTNO
10	Thomas	Arquette	20
99	Janice	Smitty	10
500	Alan	Cook	50
700	Ernest	Gold	50

cannot delete these records

tblTimeCards (related table)

TIMECARDNO	TIMECARDDATE	EMPLOYEENO
106	11/2/2004	10
115	11/2/2004	10
107	11/2/2004	500
108	11/2/2004	700
116	11/9/2004	700

related foreign key values

- By default, you cannot change the value in the primary key field if there is a related record(s) in the related table. EmployeeNo in the tblEmployees table cannot be changed if time cards exist for that employee number in the tblTimeCards table. See Figure 2-12.

Figure 2-12 **ENFORCING REFERENTIAL INTEGRITY WHEN CHANGING A PRIMARY KEY VALUE**

tblEmployees (primiary table)

EMPLOYEENO	FIRSTNAME	LASTNAME	DEPTNO
10	Thomas	Arquette	20
99	Janice	Smitty	10
500	Alan	Cook	50
700	Ernest	Gold	50

cannot change these primary key values

tbleTimeCards (related table)

TIMECARDNO	TIMECARDDATE	EMPLOYEENO
106	11/2/2004	10
115	11/2/2004	10
107	11/2/2004	500
108	11/2/2004	700
116	11/9/2004	700

related foreign key values

Some restrictions, such as deleting from a primary table those records that have matching records in a related table, and changing the value of the key in the primary table, can be overridden with the Cascade Update and Cascade Delete options. Though these features exist, they are not recommended or considered industry best practices. Next you explore the impact of using these features, and the reasons why you should not employ them.

Cascade Update and Cascade Delete

When enforcing referential integrity, you can apply the Cascade Update and Cascade Delete options. Because these features exist, you can learn something about them now, but mostly you should learn why you should not use them. The examples in your reading and the case problems are for illustrative purposes only and in no way should you consider these features as acceptable options when you create your own database solutions for real-world applications.

When you select the Cascade Update option, a change in the primary key of the primary table is automatically updated in the related table. For example, when you change an employee number in the tblEmployees table, that employee number is updated for each record in the tblTimeCards table and every other table where the EmployeeNo field is the foreign key. Consider, however, the power of this feature if someone accidentally keys through an employee number and changes it. The relationships may remain intact, but what if the employee number has some other significance or is used in other databases in the company that are not automatically linked to this one, such as payroll? If the Payroll Department depends upon time card data from this database, and someone mistakenly changes an employee number in this database, the hours shown for that employee would not match any employee number in the payroll system. Though there could be other safeguards against this, the example is mostly illustrative in terms of the type of problems that can arise as a result of using the Cascade Update feature. If the primary key in the primary table is an AutoNumber field, setting this option has no effect because you cannot change entries in AutoNumber fields.

When you select the Cascade Delete option, deleting a record in the primary table automatically deletes any related records in *all* related tables. For example, if you delete an employee record from the tblEmployees table, any related time card records are deleted from the tblTimeCards table. Although this may seem a quick and easy way to propagate a legitimate deletion of an employee throughout the database, this is *not* recommended and by industry standards is *not* acceptable. Allowing such deletions to take place without review through a standardized process represents an unacceptable risk to most businesses and is not considered best practices by software application architects. In short, Cascade Delete allows automatic deletions to occur in a domino effect throughout an entire database and these deletions cannot be reversed by a simple undo action. The consequences can be most grave.

For example, records in other tables related to an employee who is no longer with the company could have an impact on total hours and cost calculated on all jobs on which the employee worked. Consider that an accidental deletion of a record in a primary, or base, table could eradicate years of history in secondary tables; this loss of information would not be reversible without using a backup copy to restore the database or table. This type of selective restore can be very difficult and time consuming when other records (to many tables) have been added since the last backup copy was made. In later lessons, you learn ways to archive data and make appropriate changes to the database without the need for the crutch of a Cascade Delete or Cascade Update option. You must take steps in every database design to forbid and prevent any possible accidental (or purposeful) corruption or loss of data by enforcing processes and procedures. Use of Cascade Delete or Cascade Update is a systematic means of subverting procedures which prevent data corruption or loss.

REFERENCE WINDOW **RW**

Creating a Relationship Between Tables

- Click the Relationships button on the Database toolbar.
- Click the Show Table button on the Relationship toolbar.
- Add to the Relationships window the tables to be related, and then close the Show Table dialog box.
- Drag the common field in one of the tables to the common field in the other table.
- Click the Enforce Referential Integrity check box in the Edit Relationships dialog box.
- Click the Create button.

You are now prepared to establish relationships in the Movie2 database. You will start by creating a relationship between the tblEmployees and tblTimeCards tables.

To create a relationship between the tblEmployees and tblTimeCards tables:

1. Click the **Relationships** button on the Database toolbar. The Relationships window opens.
2. Click the **Show Table** button on the Relationship toolbar.
3. Double-click **tblTimeCards** and **tblHours** (in this order) to add them to the Relationships window.
4. Click the **Close** button to close the Show Table dialog box. See Figure 2-13.

Figure 2-13 RELATIONSHIPS WINDOW

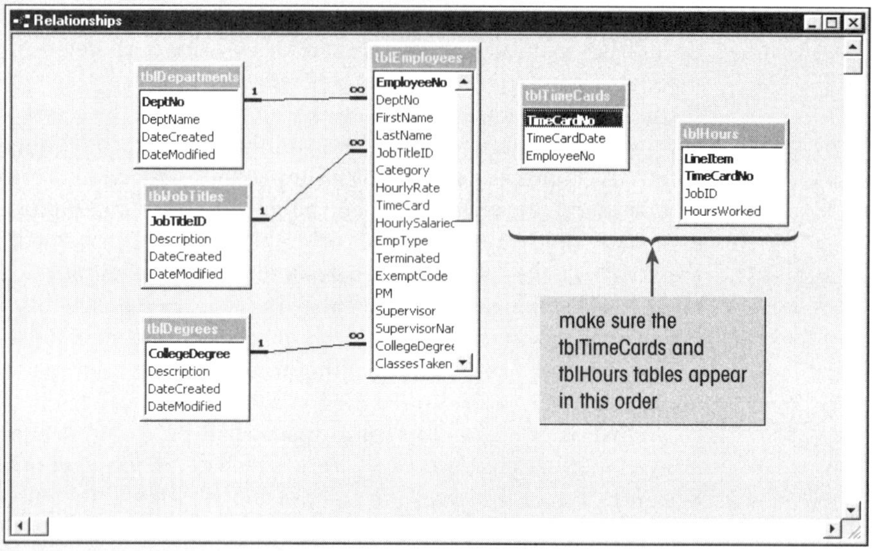

TROUBLE? If necessary, reposition the tblTimeCards and tblHours field lists in the Relationships window to match the positions shown in Figure 2-13.

5. Click the **EmployeeNo** field in the tblEmployees field list, and then drag the field to the EmployeeNo field in the tblTimeCards field list. The Edit Relationships dialog box appears. See Figure 2-14.

Figure 2-14 EDIT RELATIONSHIPS DIALOG BOX

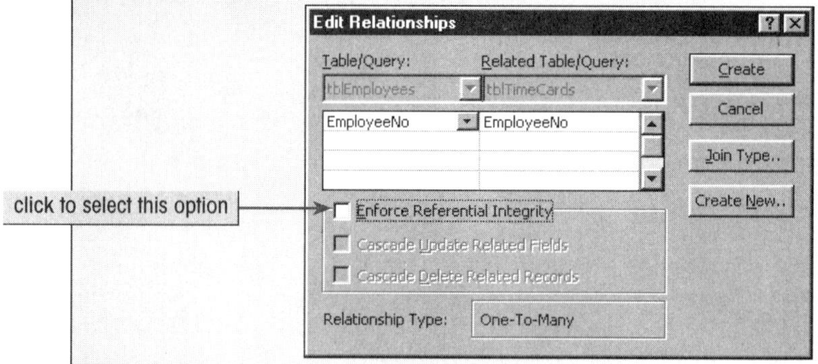

6. Click the **Enforce Referential Integrity** check box. Selecting this option prevents modifications to the EmployeeNo of an employee in the tblEmployees table that has a related time card(s) in the tblTimeCards table. Enforcing referential integrity also ensures that the record for that employee cannot be deleted.

7. Click the **Create** button. A one-to-many relationship is created.

Next, you will establish the relationship between the tblTimeCards and tblHours tables.

To create a relationship between the tblTimeCards and tblHours tables:

1. Click the **TimeCardNo** field in the tblTimeCards field list, and then drag the field to the **TimeCardNo** field in the tblHours field list.
2. Click the **Enforce Referential Integrity** check box in the Edit Relationships dialog box.
3. Click the **Create** button to create the one-to-many relationship.

Finally, you will create the relationship between the tblHours and tblJobs tables. The tblJobs table has a one-to-many relationship with the tblHours table, because one job may have hours applied to it from many days and/or from many employees. If a record is deleted from the tblJobs table, you don't want all of the records for the hours worked on that job deleted. This is an example of why you would not select the Cascade Delete option. This prevents a user from deleting a job that has related records.

To create the relationship between the tblJobs and tblHours tables:

1. Add the **tblJobs** table to the Relationships window.
2. Drag the **JobID** field in the tblJobs field list to the **JobID** field in the tblHours field list.
3. Click the **Enforce Referential Integrity** check box.
4. Click the **Create** button. The added relationships should now appear as they do in Figure 2-15 below.

Figure 2-15 COMPLETED RELATIONSHIPS

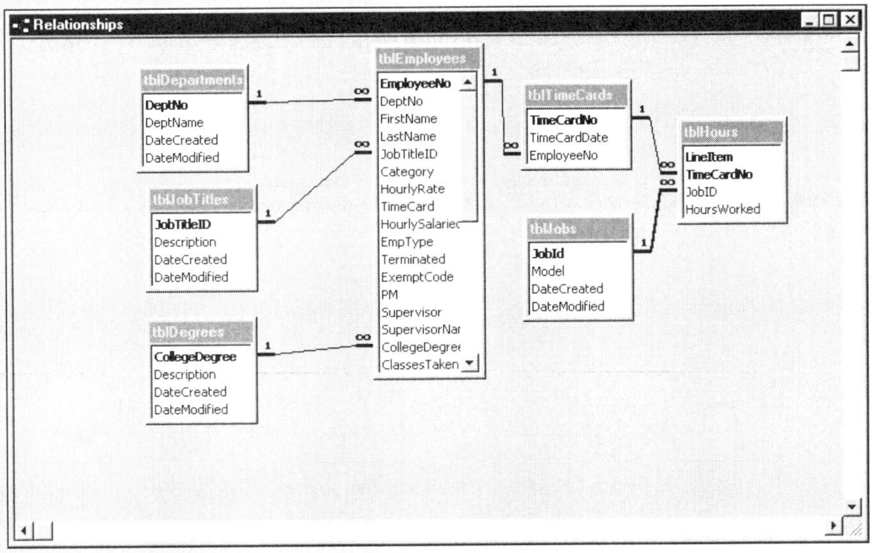

5. Close the Relationships window and save your changes.

Other than making some minor changes to field properties, you have finished the tables for the Movie2 database. Now that the structure is complete and the relationships are established, you can test the database, add any necessary finishing touches, and document the database to complete Amanda's request.

Session 2.1 Quick Check

1. Define the term "redundancy."
2. Access automatically creates a hidden index on ____________ key fields.
3. The maximum number of indexes in a table is ____________.
4. What is the benefit of adding indexes to a table?
5. A(n) ____________ relationship exists between two tables when only one entry in each table corresponds to only one entry in the other table.
6. What is a very common type of relationship between tables?
7. Which relationship requires a junction table?
8. What is an orphaned record?

SESSION 2.2

In this session, you will add data to the tables you created and refine the design of the tables by changing field properties. You then learn about subdatasheets and how to use them. You also document your work by printing relationships and using the Database Documenter.

Entering Records in Tables

You decide to add sample data to the tables that you created, so you can test the tables' relationship settings. Adding sample data also helps you determine field properties that might need to be set. Figure 2-16 shows the sample records you enter into the tblTimeCards table.

Figure 2-16 RECORDS TO ADD TO THE tblTimeCards TABLE

Time Card No	Time Card Date	Employee No
106	11/02/2004	10
107	11/02/2004	500
108	11/02/2004	700

To enter data in the tblTimeCards table:

1. If you took a break at the end of the previous session, make sure that Access is running, that the **Movie2** database located in the Tutorial.02\Tutorial folder on your local or network drive is open, and that **Tables** is selected on the Objects bar in the Database window.
2. Open the **tblTimeCards** table in Datasheet view.

3. Type the first record shown in Figure 2-16, and then press the **Enter** key to move to the second record.
4. Type **107** in the Time Card No field for the second record, and then press the **Enter** key.
5. Press **Ctrl + apostrophe (')** in the Time Card Date field to copy the previous entry in this field, and then press the **Enter** key to move to the next column.
6. Type **501** in the Employee No field, and then press the **Enter** key. You see an error message like the one in Figure 2-17. Because there is no EmployeeNo 501 in the tblEmployees table, the rules of referential integrity prohibit you from entering the value in this field.

Figure 2-17 REFERENTIAL INTEGRITY ERROR MESSAGE

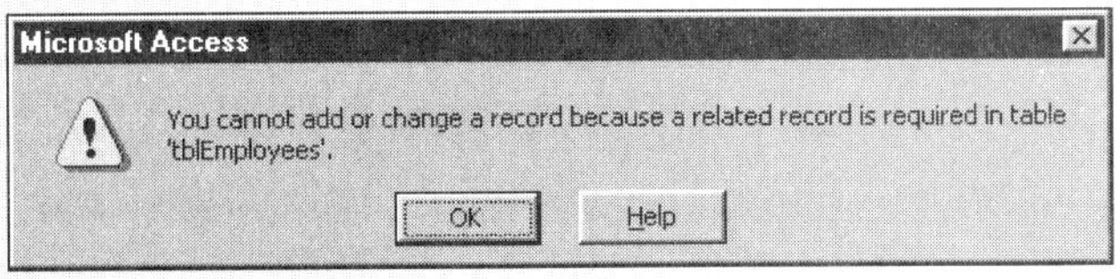

7. Click the **OK** button and then change the entry to **500**.
8. Enter the third record as shown in Figure 2-16.
9. Close the table.

Because the relationships that were set earlier control the order of data entry, you must enter records into the tblJobs table before you can enter them into the tblHours table. Otherwise you receive an error similar to the one you got when you tried to enter a nonexistent employee into the tblTimeCards table.

Next, you will enter the sample records into the tblJobs table.

To add data to the tblJobs table:

1. Open the **tblJobs** table in Datasheet view.
2. As shown in Figure 2-18, type the data for the **Job ID** and **Model** fields for the first record, and then press the **Enter** key to position the insertion point in the Date Created field.

Figure 2-18 RECORDS TO ADD TO THE tblJobs TABLE

Job ID	Model	Date Created	Date Modified
98378	XCAM1080SB	11/02/2004	
99562	ZTSM 1022	11/02/2004	

3. Press **Ctrl + semicolon (;)** to automatically insert the current date into the Date Created field. This is a good place to include a field property to default to the current date. You'll switch to Design view and make that change before you complete the data entry.
4. Re-enter **11/02/2004** as the date in the Date Created field, and then switch to Design view.

5. Click the **DateCreated** field and then click the **Default Value** property text box in the Field Properties pane. You enter the Date function so the current date is entered in this field when a record is entered.
6. Type **=Date()** and then press the **Enter** key.
7. Switch to Datasheet view and save your changes. Note that the current date has been automatically entered in the next row in anticipation of your entering another record.
8. Complete the data entry for the second record as shown in Figure 2-18.
9. Close the table.

Finally, you will add the sample records to the tblHours table.

To add data to tblHours:

1. Open the **tblHours** table in Datasheet view.
2. Add the two records listed in Figure 2-19.

Figure 2-19 RECORDS TO ADD TO THE tblHours TABLE

Line Item	Time Card No	Job ID	Hours Worked
1	106	99562	2.5
1	107	99562	3.0

3. Close the table.

Subdatasheets

A **subdatasheet** is a datasheet that is nested within another datasheet and contains data related or joined to the first datasheet. A subdatasheet allows you to view or edit related or joined data in a table, query, form datasheet, or subform. Access automatically creates a subdatasheet in a table that is in a one-to-one or a one-to-many relationship, as long as the Subdatasheet property of the table is set to Auto, which is the default. The tblTimeCards table is the primary table in a one-to-many relationship with the tblHours table. Because the Subdatasheet table property has not been changed, a subdatasheet for the tblHours table was created. You now can click the expand indicator to the left of TimeCardNo as shown in Figure 2-20 to see any records from the tblHours table that relate to the selected record in the tblTimeCards table.

Figure 2-20 SUBDATASHEET

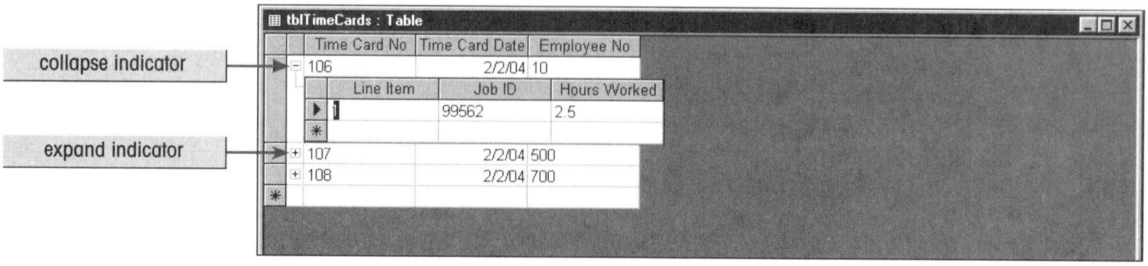

You now change the sample data in the tblHours table while working in the tblTimeCards table.

To add data using a subdatasheet:

1. Open the **tblTimeCards** table in Datasheet view, and then click the **expand indicator** [+] for the Time Card No 106 record. The subdatasheet for TimeCardNo 106 opens.
2. Click in the **Line Item** field for the second row, type **2**, and then press the **Enter** key.
3. Type **98378** in the Job ID field, and then press the **Enter** key.
4. Type **3.0** in the Hours Worked field, and then press the **Enter** key.
5. Click the **collapse indicator** [–] for Time Card No 106, and then close the table.
6. Open the **tblHours** table in Datasheet view. You see the new record you entered.
7. Close the table.

Dates in Access

The way Access handles dates can influence the way you set the properties for Date/Time fields. Most users type dates in the short format—MM/DD/YY. When a user types 1/1/29, Access interprets this as January 1, 2029. When a user types 1/1/30, Access interprets this as January 1, 1930. A two-digit year can include only a 100-year time span, and for several years that default time span has been defined as January 1, 1930, through December 31, 2029.

However, a Windows file (named OLEAUT32.DLL) controls this time span. If that file is damaged, Access could erroneously interpret two-digit years as falling into the range of January 1, 1900, through December 31, 1999.

There are three levels of precautions that you can take to prevent users from entering an incorrect date. First, you can set Access to always display a four-digit year. Second, you can force users to enter a four-digit year. Third, you can add validation rules to test dates that are entered, and to display an error message if a date is entered incorrectly.

The least restrictive approach to handling dates is to format all date fields so that a four-digit year is displayed. However, this method relies on the user to spot entries in which Access assumed the wrong century.

A more restrictive approach is to apply an input mask for all date fields. The input mask would require users to enter all four digits of the year. This isn't the most desirable option because input masks are effective only on new data, not on data that's already entered. Also, a validation rule limits the entries to a particular range of years based on the system date.

Amanda prefers that you take a conservative approach on matters such as these. She believes that taking higher precautions is the best course of action, considering the end users of this system. You decide to force all date formats to display four digits. You will also include input masks that require four-digit year data entry, and you will write validation rules for dates wherever possible.

REFERENCE WINDOW RW

Forcing a Four-Digit Year

- Click Tools on the menu bar, and then click Options.
- Click the General tab in the Options dialog box.
- To display a four-digit year in the current database, click the This database check box.
- To display a four-digit year in all databases, click the All databases check box.
- Click the OK button.

You will change this database's default date display option to a four-digit year.

To display four-digit dates in the Movie2 database:

1. Click **Tools** on the menu bar, and then click **Options**.
2. Click the **General** tab in the Options dialog box to display date formatting options as shown in Figure 2-21. Note that one of the Use four-digit year formatting options allows you to apply the formatting to the database in which you are currently working. If you want to apply the formatting to all databases, Access adds a Registry entry to your computer to force four-digit year formatting on any Access 2002 database.

Figure 2-21 DATE FORMATTING OPTIONS

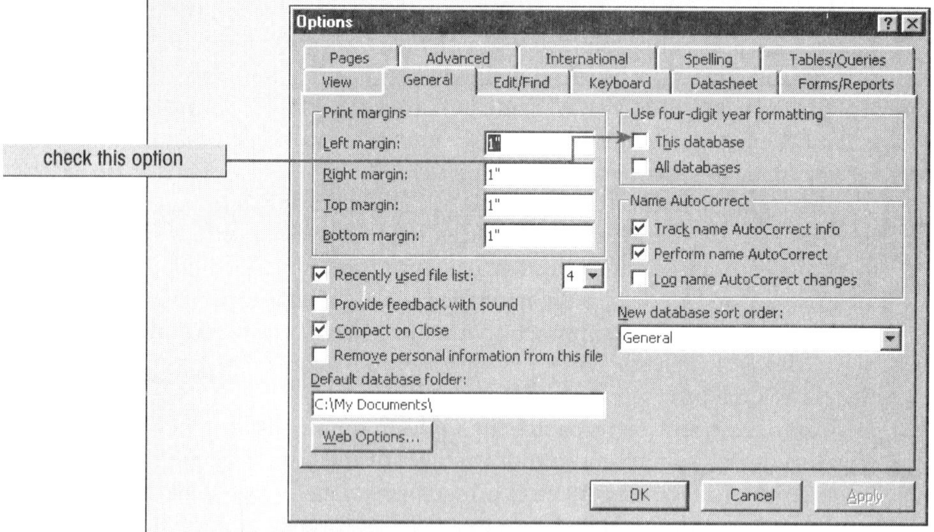

3. Click the **This database** check box.
4. Click the **OK** button to return to the Database window.

Next, you will change the format for the TimeCardDate field to Medium Date, which displays and prints dates in a format similar to 19-Apr-2004.

To change date field properties in the tblTimeCards table:

1. Open the **tblTimeCards** table in Design view.
2. Click the **TimeCardDate** field, and then change its Format property to **Medium Date**.
3. Switch to Datasheet view and save the changes to the table.
4. To test the way that Access handles dates, delete the current date in the TimeCardDate field for the first record, type **1/1/29**, and then press the **Enter** key. Notice that Access interprets the entry as the year 2029.
5. Delete the current date for the TimeCardDate for the second record, type **1/1/30**, and then press the **Enter** key. This time Access interprets the year as 1930.
6. Change both dates to **11/2/04**.
7. Switch back to Design view.

You will now create an input mask for the TimeCardDate field in the tblTimeCards table that requires the user to enter a four-digit year.

To create an input mask in the TimeCardDate field:

1. Make sure the **TimeCardDate** field is selected in the design grid.
2. Click in the **Input Mask** property text box, and then type **99/99/0000;0;_** as the input mask. Make sure you include the underscore character after the final semicolon.

An input mask is composed of three parts separated by semicolons. The first part represents the placeholders for the data to be entered. In the above step, the placeholders are 99/99/0000.

The 9s stand for optional numbers from 0 to 9, and the 0s stand for required numbers from 0 to 9. The slashes are character separators that are used for date input masks.

The second part of the input mask can be 0 or 1. In this case, it is 0. This means that Access stores any literals that are included in the input mask. A **literal** is a character in the mask that you don't have to type, such as dashes in a Social Security number 555-55-5555.

The date input mask does not have any literals, only separators for the month, day, and year. The 0 is a default value. It is a good idea to store literals when you create an input mask, because when you query the data, you probably type the literal character. If you haven't stored it, the query won't find the value you are looking for. A 1 in this position would indicate that only the typed data would be stored. In the case of the Social Security number example, Access would store 555555555.

The last part of the input mask is the placeholder character that you want to use. The placeholder character is the character that appears in the field and represents the number of characters the user should type. In this case, the placeholder is the underscore.

To test the TimeCardDate field's input mask:

1. Switch to Datasheet view and save your changes.
2. Test the input mask by typing **1/1/29** in the TimeCardDate field for the first record and then pressing the **Tab** key. You should see the error message shown in Figure 2-22.

Figure 2-22 **INPUT MASK ERROR MESSAGE**

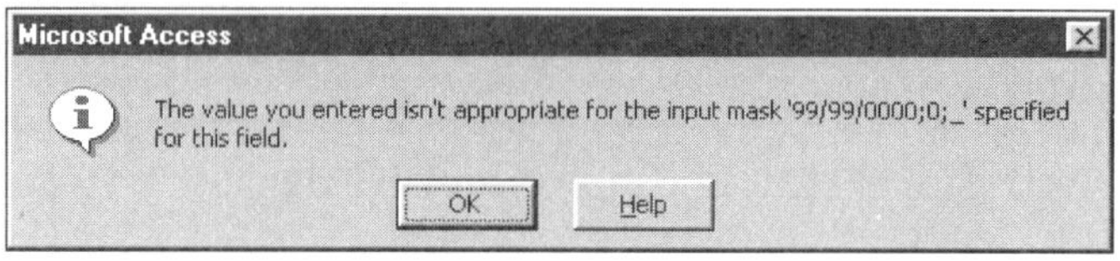

3. Click the **OK** button and then press the **Esc** key to cancel your changes.
4. Close the table.

Documenting **Your Database**

Amanda asks you to begin documenting the database that you are developing for MovieCam Technologies. Amanda wants you to gather documents which include: the objectives for the database; the information that you have compiled from your interviews with the product managers; notes you have taken at meetings; and the original system printouts, including the sample spreadsheet and the time card used by employees. She also wants you to print a report of the relationships between the tables you have developed and a data dictionary of the fields and their properties.

A **data dictionary** is a list and definition of the individual fields included in each of the tables in your database. It may also include table and field properties, such as primary keys, foreign keys, indexes, field data types, and validation rules.

The **Database Documenter** allows you to create a data dictionary quickly and easily. It generates a document that clearly identifies the objects in the database and their related properties.

The data dictionary for the tblEmployees table in the MovieCam Technologies database is over 10 pages long and doesn't even include all the information on the table. In fact, if you were to print documentation for all the properties applied to all the objects in a database such as MovieCam's, you could end up with a document that's hundreds of pages long! In most cases, it's necessary to print only the documentation for the tables in the database.

REFERENCE WINDOW **RW**

Using the Database Documenter

- Click Tools on the menu bar, point to Analyze, and then click Documenter.
- Select the tab of the object type that you want to document, and select the specific object(s) from the list.
- Click the Options button and select the options that represent the level of detail you want to print.
- Click the OK button to return to the Documenter dialog box.
- Click the OK button to preview the report.

Earlier in the week, you added field descriptions to the tblEmployees table as shown in Figure 2-23. Field descriptions print as a part of the documentation, as do table descriptions and properties. For this reason, it is a good idea to add them whenever possible. You also printed the data dictionary for all of the tables except tblEmployees, tblTimeCards, tblHours, and tblJobs.

Figure 2-23 **tblEmployees TABLE WITH FIELD DESCRIPTIONS**

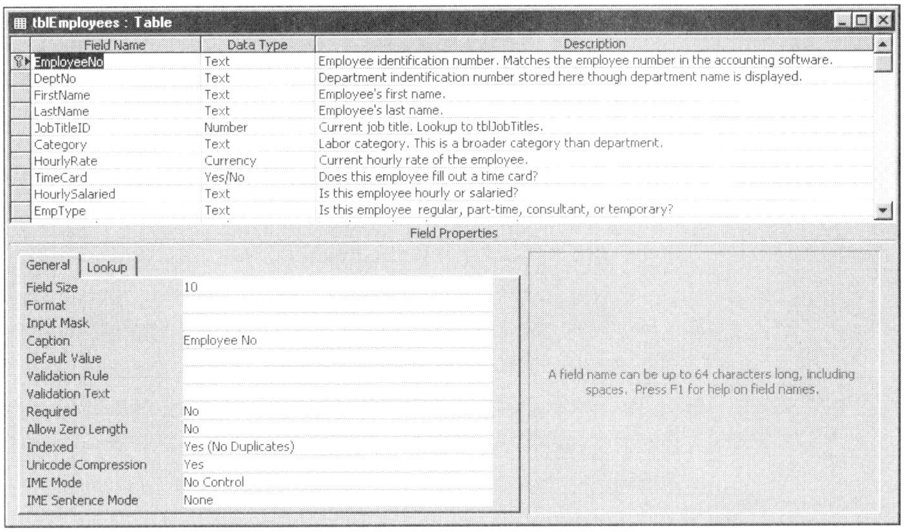

You will complete the data dictionary for these tables next.

To use the Database Documenter:

1. In the Database window, click **Tools** on the menu bar, point to **Analyze**, and then click **Documenter**. The Documenter dialog box opens with the Tables tab selected, as shown in Figure 2-24.

Figure 2-24 **DATABASE DOCUMENTER**

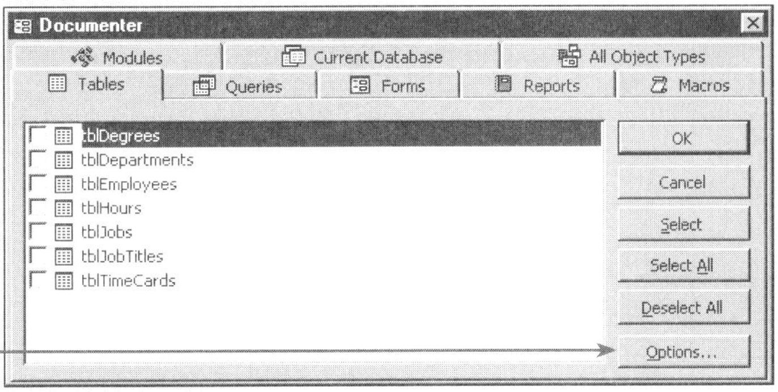

click to open the Print Table Definition dialog box

2. Click the **tblEmployees** check box to select this table, and then click the **Options** button to open the Print Table Definition dialog box, as shown in Figure 2-25. Access defaults to print all of the possible options for tables. If you have used the Database Documenter before, the options that you selected then are still displayed. Otherwise, all of the options are checked by default.

Figure 2-25 PRINT TABLE DEFINITION DIALOG BOX

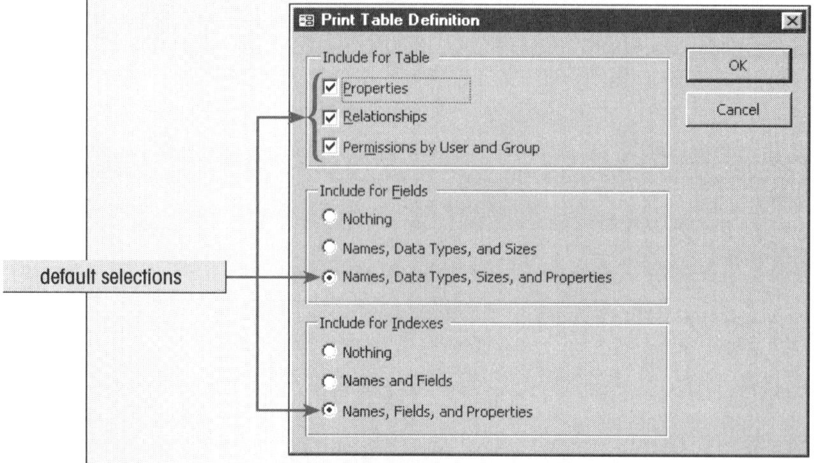

3. Clear the check boxes for **Relationships** and **Permissions by User and Group** in the Include for Table, if necessary.
4. If necessary, select the **Names, Data Types, Sizes, and Properties** option button in the Include for Fields section.
5. Select the **Names and Fields** option button in the Include for Indexes section, and then click the **OK** button.
6. Click the **OK** button in the Documenter dialog box. After a few moments, an Object Definition report opens in Print Preview.
7. Click to enlarge the preview of the report, and then scroll, as needed, to display the report as shown in Figure 2-26.

Figure 2-26 OBJECT DEFINITION REPORT

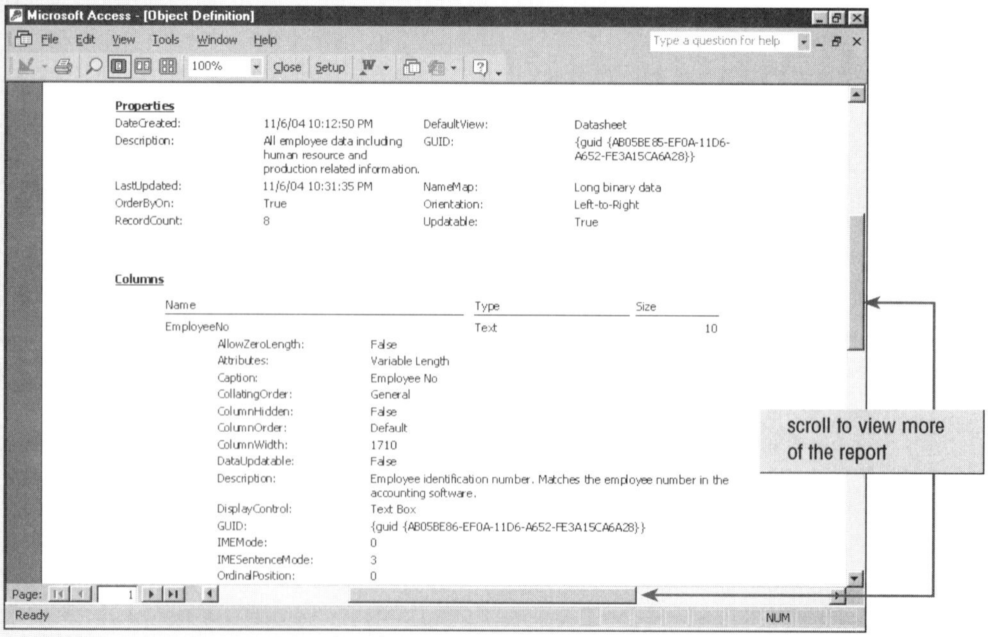

Rather than printing the report right now, you export it to Word and save the report with your other files.

To export the Object Definition report to Word:

1. Click the list arrow for the **OfficeLinks** button, and then click **Publish It with Microsoft Word**. A small window appears, indicating the progress of the transfer to Word. Word then opens and displays a document named doc_rptObjects.
2. Click **File** on the menu bar, and then click **Save As** to open the Save As dialog box.
3. Navigate to the drive that contains the Tutorial.02\Tutorial folder, which is where the Movie2 database is also stored.
4. Click the **Save as type** list arrow, and then select **Word Document**.
5. Click the **Save** button.
6. Close Word and then close the Object Definition window.

Next, you will add descriptions to the tblTimeCards, tblHours, and tblJobs tables and then print the data dictionary for these three tables.

To add field descriptions:

1. Open the **tblTimeCards** table in Design view.
2. Add the following field descriptions by typing the values in each field's description column:

TimeCardNo	**Time card number**
TimeCardDate	**Week ending date**
EmployeeNo	**Employee number, foreign key for relationship to tblEmployees**

3. Close the table and save your changes.
4. Open the **tblHours** table in Design view.
5. Add the following field descriptions:

LineItem	**Line item number from time card**
TimeCardNo	**Time card number**
JobID	**Job number, foreign key for relationship to tblJobs**
HoursWorked	**Total hours worked column from time card**

6. Close the table and save your changes.
7. Open the **tblJobs** table in Design view.
8. Add the following field descriptions:

JobID	**Job number**
Model	**Camera model number**
DateCreated	**Date record created**
DateModifed	**Date of last change**

9. Close the table and save your changes.

Now you print the Database Documenter report for these three tables.

To print the Database Documenter report:

1. In the Database window, click **Tools** on the menu bar, point to **Analyze**, and then click **Documenter**. The Documenter dialog box opens with the Tables tab selected.
2. Click the check boxes for **tblTimeCards**, **tblHours**, and **tblJobs** in this order, and then click the **Options** button to display the Print Table Definition dialog box.
3. Be sure that the check boxes for **Relationships** and **Permissions by User and Group** are cleared.
4. Be sure that the **Names, Data Types, Sizes, and Properties** option in the Include for Fields section is selected.
5. Be sure that the **Names and Fields** option in the Include for Indexes section is selected, and then click the **OK** button.
6. Click the **OK** button in the Documenter dialog box. After a few moments, an Object Definition report opens in Print Preview.
7. Click the **Print** button on the Print Preview toolbar.
8. Close the Object Definition window.

The last thing you need to do for documentation is print the Relationships window, which graphically illustrates the relationships among all the tables. One relationship was automatically created by the Lookup Wizard. It is the relationship between the tblHours and tblJobs tables.

To print the relationships report:

1. In the Database window, click **Tools** on the menu bar, and then click **Relationships** to display the Relationships window.
2. Click **File** on the menu bar, and then click **Print Relationships**. A preview of the Relationships for Movie2 window opens.
3. Click the **Print** button on the Print Preview toolbar to print the report.
4. Close the report without saving it, and then close the Relationships window.
5. Close the Movie2 database and then exit Access.

You have now compiled a data dictionary for all the tables in the Movie2 database. You have printed a report of the relationships between each set of tables in the database. You have a copy of the original time card, a copy of the original sample spreadsheet, handwritten notes of your interviews with product managers, and notes taken at meetings. You completed Amanda's request by compiling this documentation into a binder. You will add more to it as you continue to develop the database in later tutorials.

Session 2.2 Quick Check

1. The ____________ Column property of a combo box determines which column's data is stored in the field.
2. What is a subdatasheet?
3. What is the range of years that Access uses when a user types a two-digit year?
4. A(n) ____________ is a character you don't have to type that is included in an input mask.
5. What is a data dictionary?
6. The ____________ lets you create a data dictionary quickly and easily.

REVIEW ASSIGNMENTS

You have been asked to complete the tables for the Hours database and to set the relationships between the tables. The design is similar to the Movie2 database you worked on in this tutorial. Complete the following:

1. Start Access and open the **Hours2** database located in the Tutorial.02\Review folder on your local or network drive.
2. Create the tblTimeCards and tblHours tables in the Hours2 database:

Table	**tblTimeCards**
Field Name:	**TimeCardNo** (primary key)
Field Name:	**TimeCardDate**
Field Name:	**EmployeeNo** (this is the foreign key in a relationship with the tblEmployees table)

Table	**tblHours**
Field Name:	**LineItemNo** (forms composite key with TimeCardNo; together are the primary key)
Field Name:	**TimeCardNo** (forms composite key with LineItem; together are the primary key)
Field Name:	**HoursWorked**
Field Name:	**ProductNo**

3. Open the **tblTimeCards** table in Design view.
4. Set the data type for the TimeCardDate field to Date/Time. The data type for the EmployeeNo and TimeCardNo fields remain as Text.
5. Enter a caption for each field using the field name with a space between each word. For example, "Time Card No" is the caption for the TimeCardNo field.

6. Add the following field descriptions to the fields in the tblTimeCards table:

TimeCardNo	**Time card number from the original time card document**
TimeCardDate	**Period ending date**
EmployeeNo	**Employee number**

7. Save the changes you have made to the table.
8. Format the TimeCardDate field as Medium Date, and then create an input mask so that a four-digit year must be entered in the TimeCardDate field.

Explore

9. Create a validation rule so that only dates between March 1, 1995, and the current day's date can be entered. (*Hint*: Click the Validation Rule text box in the Field Properties pane, and then press the F1 key to access Help.)

Explore

10. Enter validation text to notify users about what they need to do if they enter an incorrect date.
11. Close the tblTimeCards table and save your changes.
12. Enable the option for this database to display four-digit years in the date/time fields.
13. Open the **tblHours** table in Design view.
14. Set the data type for the HoursWorked field to Number, and set its Field Size property to Double. The remaining fields in the tblHours table are set to Text.

Explore

15. Format the HoursWorked field to display positive numbers in #,###.00 format in black, negative numbers in red with the same format but enclosed in parentheses, and zero values as the word "Zero." (*Hint*: Click the Format property text box, press the F1 key, and then click the Number and Currency Data Types link to access Help.)
16. Enter a caption for each field using the field name with a space between each word in the field name. For example, "Line Item No" is the caption for the LineItemNo field.
17. Add the following field descriptions to the fields in the tblHours table:

LineItemNo	**Line item from time card**
TimeCardNo	**Time card number from the original time card**
HoursWorked	**Total hours worked per project**
ProductNo	**Product number**

18. Close the tblHours table and save your changes.
19. Open the Relationships window, add the tblTimeCards and tblHours tables, create a relationship between the tblTimeCards and tblHours tables based on the TimeCardNo field, and then create a relationship between the tblEmployees and tblTimeCards tables based on the EmployeeNo field. Set referential integrity for each relationship and apply the Cascade Update Related Fields option to each.
20. Print the Relationships window report, and then save it as **rptRelationships**.
21. Close the Relationships window, close the Hours2 database, and then exit Access.

CASE PROBLEMS

Case 1. Edwards and Company You completed the tblConsultants table for the Edwards and Company database, and now you need to complete the tblClients table. One consultant in the database can have many clients, so these tables have a one-to-many relationship between them.

Complete the following:

1. Start Access and open the **Edward2** database located in the Tutorial.02\Cases folder on your local or network drive.
2. Open the **tblClients** table in Datasheet view and note the values in the Address2 field.
3. **Explore** Switch to Design view and format the Address2 field to display text that is entered and to display the word "None" when the field is empty (null). (*Hint*: Press the F1 key for the Format property, and then click the Text and Memo Data Types link to access Help.) Save your changes and switch to Datasheet view to see the results of the change to the Format property.
4. **Explore** Switch to Design view and create a custom input mask for the ZipCode field that requires the entry of five digits with a placeholder of @. (*Hint*: Press the F1 key for the Input Mask property to access Help.)
5. Switch to Datasheet view and then widen the Company Name column to display the text more clearly. Save and close the tblClients table.
6. Open the Database Documenter and then select the tblClients table. Set the options to include only Properties for the table; the Names, Data Types, Sizes, and Properties for the fields; and only Names and Fields for the indexes. Print your results. Close the Object Definition window.
7. Close the Edward2 database and then exit Access.

Case 2. San Diego County Information Systems You have developed the tables and the test data for your database, which tracks students and classes. The tables need a few more changes, the documentation needs to be completed, and relationships between tables need to be established. Enforce Referential Integrity for all relationships and do not select Cascade Delete or Cascade Update options.

Complete the following:

1. Start Access and open the **ISD2** database located in the Tutorial.02\Cases folder on your local or network drive.
2. Open the **tblClasses** table in Design view.
3. Format the Date field as a Medium Date.
4. **Explore** Create a custom format for the StartTime and EndTime fields. The times should be displayed with hours and minutes and am or pm should be in lowercase. (*Hint*: Press the F1 key for the Format property, and then click the Date/Time Data Type link to access Help.) Switch to the Datasheet view to see how the values in the Start Time and End Time fields appear.
5. Use the Input Mask Wizard for the Date field to create an input mask that requires a four-digit year to be entered.
6. Set the Indexed property of the Date field so duplicates can be entered.

7. Close the tblClasses table and save your changes.
8. Open the Database Documenter and then select the tblClasses table. Set the options to include only Properties for the table; the Names, Data Types, Sizes, and Properties for the fields; and only Names and Fields for the indexes. Print your results. Close the Object Definition window.
9. Open the Relationships window and set the appropriate relationships for all tables in the database, enforcing referential integrity.
10. Print the relationships report, and then save it as **rptRelationships**. Close the Relationships window.
11. Close the ISD2 database and then exit Access.

Case 3. Christenson Homes You decide that it would be easier to enter the subdivision ID information in the tblLots table if the SubdivisionID field were a lookup to the tblSubdivisions table. You set the relationships between the tables.

Complete the following:

1. Start Access and open the **Homes2** database located in the Tutorial.02\Cases folder on your local or network drive.
2. Open the **Relationships** window and create a one-to-many relationship between the tblSubdivisions table and the tblLots table using the SubdivisionID field. (*Hint*: The tblLots table should be on the *many* side of the relationship.) Set referential integrity for the relationship.
3. Print the relationships report and save it as **rptRelationships**.
4. Use the Database Documenter to create a Word document for both the tblLots and tblSubdivisions tables. Set the options to include only Properties for the table; the Names, Data Types, Sizes and Properties for the fields; and only Names and Fields for the indexes. Save the document as **Homes2_docRpt.doc** in the Tutorial.02\Cases folder. Do not print the report unless instructed.
5. Close the Homes2 database and then exit Access.

Case 4. Sonoma Farms The Sonoma Farms database is only partially completed. You have completed the tblCustomers and tblDistributors tables, but you need to finish the design of the database and the remaining tables. You also want to store information about customer visits to the winery. You've listed the following attributes to include in the remaining tables: VisitDate, CustomerID, VisitorFirstName, VisitorLastName, Accommodations, Meals, and Gifts.

Complete the following:

1. Start Access and open the **Sonoma2** database located in the Tutorial.02\Cases folder on your local or network drive.
2. Create a table using the following structure:

Field Name:	**VisitID** (primary key)
Field Name:	**VisitDate**
Field Name:	**CustomerID** (this serves as a foreign key to the CustomerID field of the tblCustomers table)
Field Name:	**Accommodations**
Field Name:	**Meals**
Field Name:	**Gifts**

3. Define VisitID as an AutoNumber data type and the primary key. Define VisitDate as a Date/Time field. Define CustomerID as a Number field with the Long Integer format. The remaining fields are Text data types.

Explore

4. Create a custom format for the VisitDate field in the Format property text box. The date should be formatted to the full name of the month, the day (using digits), followed by a comma and a four-digit year. (*Hint*: Press the F1 key in the Format property text box, and then click the Date/Time Data Types link to access Help.)

5. Create an input mask for the VisitDate field requiring a four-digit year. Close the table and save it as **tblVisits**.

6. Create a table using the following structure:

   Field Name: **VisitorID** (primary key)

   Field Name: **VisitID**

   Field Name: **VisitorFirst**

   Field Name: **VisitorLast**

7. Define VisitorID as an AutoNumber data type and the primary key. Define VisitID as a Number data type with the Long Integer format, and the remaining fields as Text data types.

8. Close the table and save it as **tblVisitors**.

9. Set a relationship between the tblCustomers and tblVisits tables and the tblVisits and tblVisitors tables. Use the common field between each pair of tables. Set referential integrity, but do not select the Cascade Update or Cascade Delete options for either relationship.

10. Print the relationships report, and then save it as **rptRelationships**.

11. Open the Database Documenter, select the tblVisits and tblVisitors tables, and set the Properties option for the table and the Names, Data Types, Sizes, and Properties for the fields. Do not include anything for the Indexes. Print your results.

12. Close the Sonoma2 database and then exit Access.

QUICK CHECK ANSWERS

Session 2.1

1. Redundancy is the term for duplication of data.
2. foreign
3. 32
4. The benefit of adding indexes to a table is that they speed sorting and searching.
5. one-to-one
6. The most common type of relationship between tables is a one-to-many relationship.
7. Many-to-many relationships require a junction table.
8. An orphaned record is a record in a related table that does not contain a record in the primary table.

Session 2.2

1. bound
2. A subdatasheet is a datasheet that is nested within another datasheet and contains data related or joined to the first datasheet.
3. The range of years that Access uses when a user types a two-digit year is 1/1/1930 through 12/31/2029.
4. literal
5. A data dictionary is a list and definition of the individual fields that comprise each of the tables in your database.
6. Database Documenter

OBJECTIVES

In this tutorial you will:

- Use the Import Text Wizard to import a tab-delimited text file
- Create expressions using text manipulation functions in a query
- Create append, update, and delete queries
- Import a standard module from another Access database
- Import data from an Excel worksheet
- Create a query for unique values
- Create a subquery to assist in archiving data
- Learn about SQL-specific queries
- Write queries using the commands and clauses of SQL
- Write a union query in SQL
- Export query results to an Excel worksheet

USING IMPORT WIZARDS, ADVANCED QUERIES, AND SQL

Importing and Archiving Data for the MovieCam Technologies Database with Queries and SQL

CASE

MovieCam Technologies

MovieCam Technologies has accumulated a significant amount of employee data, production data, and other historical data that needs to be incorporated in its new database. Amanda asks you to determine the best method to import this existing data into the MovieCam database. As you have learned, the managers maintain much of the data, including time cards and employee information, in spreadsheets stored in Excel workbooks. Other data, such as personnel and payroll information, has been entered in MovieCam's accounting software program, ACC90.

The company's accounting software is an older version of ACC90 and does not export to a format recognized by Access. Randy Harper, an ACC90 consultant, has already exported some of the data to a tab-delimited text file. Amanda asks you to work out the importing process using both the sample accounting file Randy has provided and the sample Excel data provided by the product managers.

Amanda also wants you to develop queries for archiving data that is more than a year old. The time card and hours data go back three years. She wants you to optimize database performance by storing the outdated transactional data in separate tables. She would like you to look into the potential usefulness of subqueries as well as other commands and clauses available to you in Structured Query Language (SQL), which is the query language Access uses.

Finally, Amanda wants you to develop the queries to integrate the archived records with the active records for those situations when the product managers need to compile statistics from all the data. She then wants you to demonstrate to a product manager how to export this data back to Excel for statistical analysis.

SESSION 3.1

In this session, you will use the Import Text Wizard to import a tab-delimited text file. You then will write text manipulation expressions to extract first and last names to separate fields. Finally, you will append the imported data to an existing table.

Getting Data from Other Resources

You decide to import sample records to help develop the rest of the database. To develop the remaining objects and write VBA code to control the user interface, you need sample data with which to work. The Excel worksheet data and the ACC90 accounting software data will continue to be updated while you complete the database design, so it is neither necessary nor efficient to import all the present-day data at this point. Because you will need to import the current data into the database once it is complete, you need a plan for working with the data. Figure 3-1 illustrates your plan for importing and appending employee text data from ACC90.

Figure 3-1 IMPORTING AND APPENDING EMPLOYEE DATA

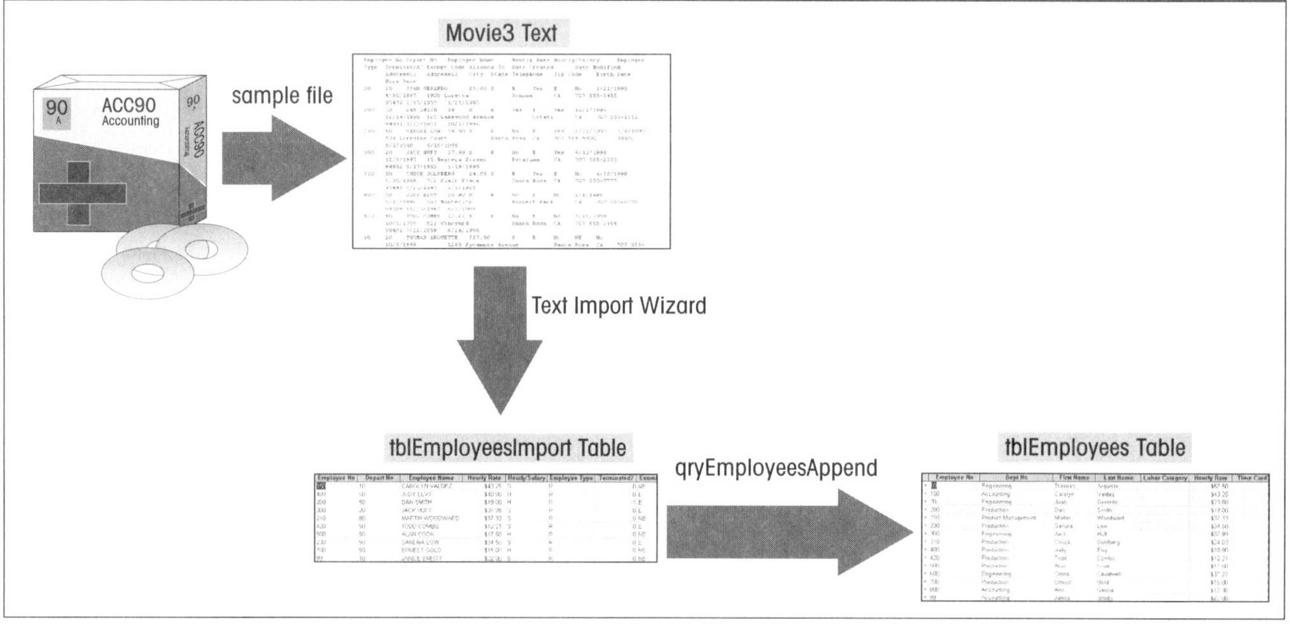

Figure 3-2 shows how you plan to import, append, and archive time card and hours data from Excel.

Figure 3-2 IMPORTING, APPENDING, AND ARCHIVING HOURS AND TIME CARD DATA

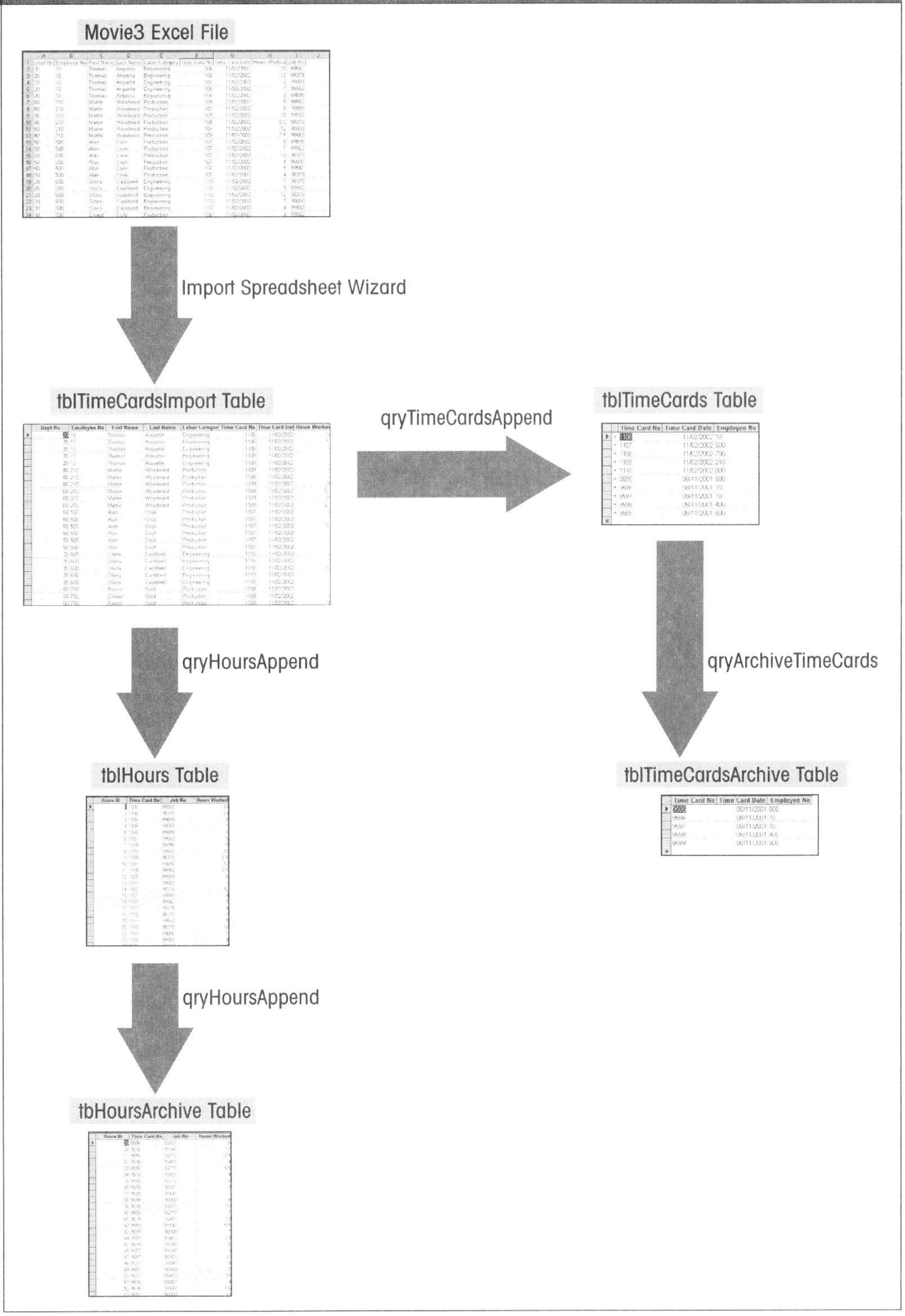

After the database is completed, tested, and documented, you will delete the sample records and then import the current records. You will also run queries to populate the tables, and you'll run queries to archive inactive records. Once the database is current, you can distribute it for use by the MovieCam employees.

Some of the objects in the Movie3 database have been fine-tuned since you worked with them in the Movie2 database. The tblHours table no longer contains a composite key field. The name of the LineItem field is now HoursID, and the HoursID field type is an AutoNumber so that each record added to the table is automatically assigned a unique number. Changing the HoursID field to an AutoNumber field saves time during data entry, and the field can also be set as the primary key. In general, the structure of the database is consistent with the one developed in Tutorial 2.

Importing and Linking Data

You can pull data into an Access database from an external source by using one of two methods: importing or linking. Importing brings the data into Access, usually into a new table. Linking leaves data in its current format and location, but does provide access to that data.

Linking is a good alternate method if the data is going to be used both in its original format and in Access. When you use Access to link to another RDBMS (relational database management system), Access acts as a database front end. The **front end** is a single file that contains the queries, forms, reports, macros, and modules. Tables are stored in another file referred to as the **back end**. Access can link to dBASE, Paradox, FoxPro, SQL Server, and many other RDBMS database files. Access also can link to Excel, Outlook, and text files.

Importing is a better method than linking if you know that you will be using the data only in Access and will not need to refer back to it in its original format. For example, perhaps the data was retrieved one time from a legacy system that is being retired, or is an initial feed of employees from another system, such as payroll or accounting. You can import data into an Access database from the same programs and file types from which you can link Access.

Using the Import Text Wizard

One means of importing data into an Access database is from a text file. The term **flat file** is a common industry term denoting a text file containing data that can be recognized or interpreted as records and fields for a database. The text is separated into records by placing a carriage return and linefeed character combination at the end of each row. The flat file differentiates fields typically by the use of a common **delimiter**. The term "delimiter" refers to the character that identifies the end of one field and the beginning of another field in a text file. The term **tab-delimited** refers to text files in which the fields are separated by tabs, and each record begins on a new line. Access also supports comma-delimited, space-delimited, and fixed-width files. In comma-delimited and space-delimited text files, fields are separated by commas and spaces, respectively. In a fixed-width text file, the fields are fixed in size so that a delimiter is not necessary because fields begin and end at fixed columnar positions, where each character represents a column.

You will begin working with records by importing the sample tab-delimited text file that Randy created. To import the tab-delimited text file to the Movie3 database, you will use the Import Text Wizard.

REFERENCE WINDOW RW

Using the Import Text Wizard

- Start Access and open the database to which you want to import the text file.
- Click File on the menu bar, point to Get External Data, and then click Import.
- Click the Files of type list arrow, click Text Files, navigate to the drive and folder that contains the file you want to import, select the file, and then click the Import button.
- Complete the Import Text Wizard dialog boxes selecting delimited or fixed-width fields, specifying a delimiter if necessary, marking the first row as field names or not, and selecting the table to which you want to import the data. Change the field options as necessary, choose whether you want to add a primary key or not, and name the table if you're importing to a new table.
- When you have completed all the wizard dialog boxes, click the Finish button.
- Click the OK button.

Next, you will open the Movie3 database and start the Import Text Wizard.

To import a tab-delimited text file:

1. Start Access and open the **Movie3** database located in the Tutorial.03\Tutorial folder on your local or network drive.
2. Click **File** on the menu bar, point to **Get External Data**, and then click **Import**.
3. Click the **Files of type** list arrow, and then click **Text Files**.
4. Be sure that the files from the Tutorial folder on your local or network drive are visible, click the **Movie3** text file, and then click the **Import** button. The Import Text Wizard dialog box opens. See Figure 3-3.

Figure 3-3 FIRST IMPORT TEXT WIZARD DIALOG BOX

make sure this option is selected

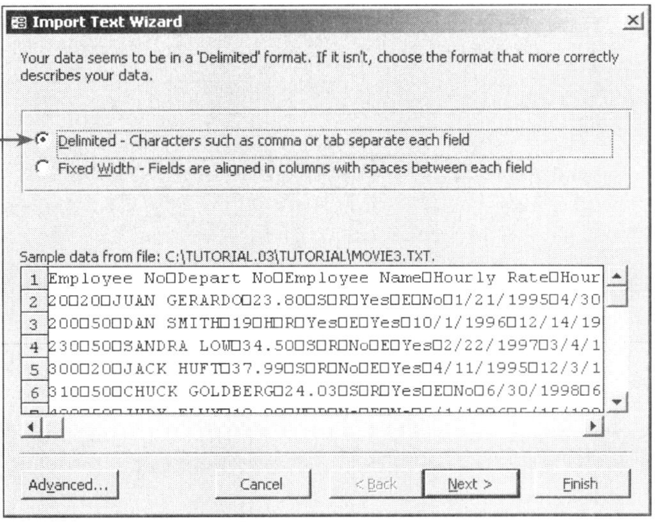

5. Be sure that the **Delimited** option button is selected, and then click the **Next** button.

6. Be sure that the **Tab** option button is selected, and then click the **First Row Contains Field Names** check box to select it, as shown in Figure 3-4. You choose the character that distinguishes text data from numeric data in the Text Qualifier list box. Some programs use quotation marks to enclose all data in a comma-delimited format; others that export to a comma-delimited format enclose only text data in quotation marks. Qualifiers are not used in tab-delimited files so you do not have to select a qualifier.

Figure 3-4 **CHOOSING A DELIMITER**

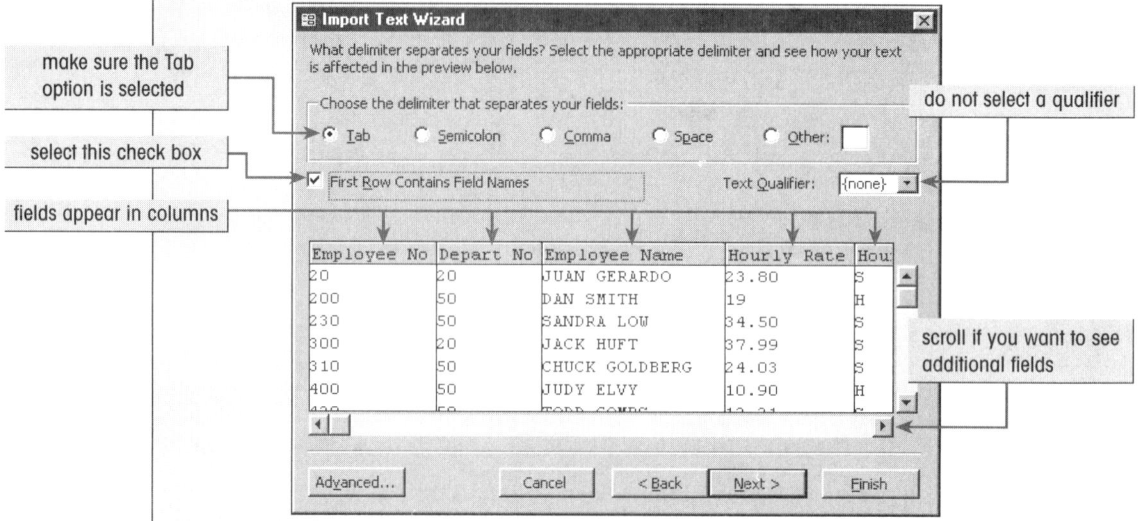

7. Make sure that **{none}** is selected in the Text Qualifier list box, and then click the **Next** button. The next wizard dialog box appears. You can choose to import the data into a new table or an existing table. In this case, you will import the data into a new table because you are working with sample data.

8. Be sure the **In a New Table** option button is selected, and then click the **Next** button.

In the next dialog box, you can change field names, add indexes to fields, change field data types, and skip fields that you don't want to import. Because you are importing the data into a new table and then appending the table to existing tables, you won't change the field names. The table to which you are importing this data will be temporary, so the name of each field is not critical. Changing the data types is a good idea, however, to reduce the risk of losing data during the import process. For example, the currency data in the Hourly Rate field or the dates in the date fields might not import properly if these fields are not changed from text fields. You need to change the data types of several of the fields next.

To change field data types:

1. With the Employee No column selected, click the **Data Type** list arrow, and then click **Text** to change the Employee No data type.

2. Click the **Depart No** column in the list box to select that field, click the **Data Type** list arrow, and then click **Text**. A text field can always be converted to a number field temporarily for sorting or comparison purposes if need be at some point.

3. Repeat Step 2 to change the data types for the following: Hourly Rate to **Currency** (if it is not already set to Currency), Terminated? to **Yes/No**, Allowed To to **Yes/No**, and Zip Code to **Text**. The Hourly Rate field is set to Currency because the field contains dollar values. The Terminated? and Allowed To fields are set as Yes/No fields because the data stored in them is always either Yes or No. The Zip Code field is changed to Text because this field is not be used for calculations and an input mask can also be applied to it. Also note that by using a Text field, any leading zeros, which might appear at the beginning of a zip code, are preserved.
4. Click the **Next** button and then click the **No primary key** option button. Because you'll use this table's records to populate other tables in the database and then delete the table, a primary key is not necessary.
5. Click the **Next** button, type **tblEmployeesImport** as the name of the new table, and then click the **Finish** button.
6. Click the **OK** button in the message box that tells you that Access has finished importing the file.

Next you'll build the query to append the sample data to the tblEmployees table.

Creating an Append Query

You have successfully imported the sample employee data into Access. The data imported smoothly, but the employee name information is not yet in the format you want. The first name and last name are in one field, as shown in Figure 3-5. You want the names to appear in two separate fields.

Figure 3-5 EMPLOYEE FIRST AND LAST NAMES APPEAR IN ONE FIELD

first name and last name need to be extracted from the Employee Name field

tblEmployeesImport : Table

Employee No	Depart No	Employee Name	Hourly Rate	Hourly/Salary	Employe
150	10	CAROLYN VALDEZ	$43.25	S	R
400	50	JUDY ELVY	$10.90	H	R
200	50	DAN SMITH	$19.00	H	R
300	20	JACK HUFT	$37.99	S	R
210	80	MARTIN WOODWARD	$37.33	S	R
420	50	TODD COMBS	$12.21	S	R
500	50	ALAN COOK	$17.60	H	R
230	50	SANDRA LOW	$34.50	S	R
700	50	ERNEST GOLD	$15.00	H	R
99	10	JANICE SMITTY	$22.00	S	R
10	20	THOMAS ARQUETTE	$57.50	S	R
310	50	CHUCK GOLDBERG	$24.03	S	R
600	20	GLORIA CAULDWELL	$37.22	H	R
20	20	JUAN GERARDO	$23.80	S	R
800	10	ANN GARCIA	$13.30	H	H

Record: 1 of 15

You need to write field expressions to extract the first name and last name from the Employee Name field in the same query that you create to append this data to the tblEmployees table. Before you do this, however, you want to be certain that the sample records Jason created in the tblEmployees table have all been deleted.

To check for records in the tblEmployees table:

1. Make sure **Tables** is selected in the Objects bar of the Database window.
2. Double-click the **tblEmployees** table to open it in Datasheet view. Note that there are no records entered in the table at this time.
3. Close the table.

Using Text Manipulation Functions

Before you can write the field expressions to extract first and last name from the Employee Name field in the imported data, you need to know more about working with functions in Access and about string functions in particular.

Functions return a value and are used to build validation rule expressions in tables, field expressions in queries, and text box expressions in forms and reports. Functions also are used to construct macros in VBA programming; this process will be discussed throughout these tutorials. Approximately 150 functions in Access and VBA are grouped into categories based on their purpose. The following is a list of functions commonly used in queries:

- *Date and time*: Used for manipulating dates and times, for example, adding values to dates, subtracting one date from another, extracting the month or year from a date, and extracting hours or minutes from the time.
- *Text manipulation*: Used for manipulating strings of text, such as trimming leading and trailing spaces from a string of text, extracting part of a string of text, and counting the number of characters in a string of text. Commonly used text manipulation functions are listed in Figure 3-6.

Figure 3-6 COMMONLY USED TEXT MANIPULATION FUNCTIONS

FUNCTION	DESCRIPTION	EXAMPLE	RETURNS
InStr	Returns the position of the first occurrence of one string within another (Note that if no starting position is specified, then the search begins at the first character in the string. In the second example, the search begins on the fourth character (k), so the first "o" found is in position 7.)	InStr("Bookstore", "o") InStr(4,"Bookstore", "o")	2 7
LCase	Returns the lowercase version of a string	LCase("JONES")	jones
UCase	Returns the uppercase version of a string	UCase("jones")	JONES
Len	Returns the number of characters in a string	Len("Jones")	5
Left	Returns the far left character(s) of a string	Left("jones",2)	jo
Right	Returns the far right character(s) of a string	Right("jones",2)	es
Mid	Returns a portion of a string	Mid("jones",2,2)	on
LTrim	Removes leading spaces from a string	LTrim(" jones")	jones

Figure 3-6 COMMONLY USED TEXT MANIPULATION FUNCTIONS (CONTINUED)

FUNCTION	DESCRIPTION	EXAMPLE	RETURNS
RTrim	Removes trailing spaces from a string	RTrim("jones ")	jones
Trim	Removes leading and trailing spaces from a string	Trim (" jones ")	jones
Space	Returns a string that consists of the specified number of spaces	Space(3)	Returns three spaces

- *Data type conversion*: Used to force a particular data type; for example, CInt (which you used in Tutorial 1 to force a text data type to an integer) is a data type conversion function.

To extract first name and last name from the Employee Name field, you need to find a common character in each entry that indicates where the first name ends and the last name begins. The apparent choice in this instance is the space. In other instances in which you extract one string of text from another, the common character might be a comma, a dash character, or a slash character. You will use the InStr function to find the position of the space in each entry.

You will use the Expression Builder, shown in Figure 3-7, to create the expression to extract first and last names from the Employee Name field. The Expression Builder is a useful tool for creating field expressions because it provides a list of built-in Access functions and therefore helps you avoid syntax errors. It does not always provide you with the exact syntax that you use in these functions, however. For example, quotation marks are required around arguments for some functions, and the Expression Builder does not include them when it displays the syntax of these functions. You should use Access Help for the correct syntax of functions, even if you use the Expression Builder.

Figure 3-7 EXPRESSION BUILDER

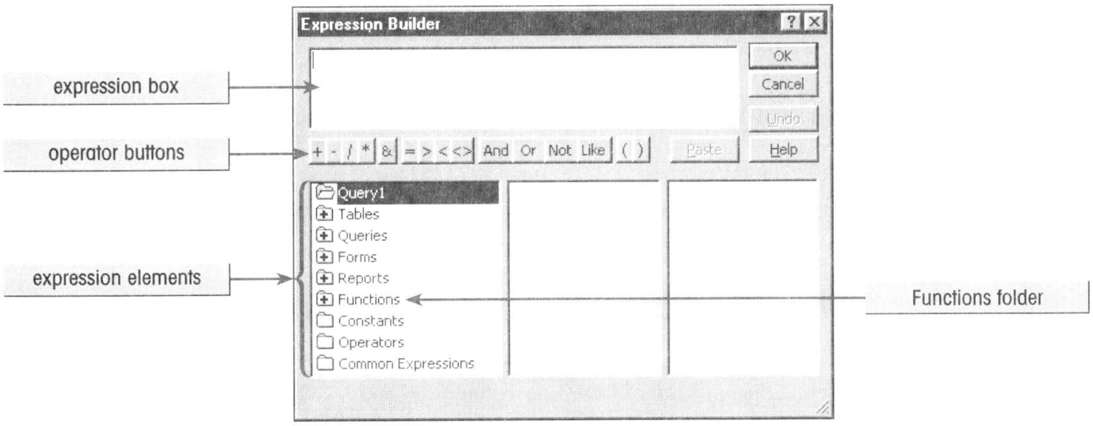

REFERENCE WINDOW RW

Using the Expression Builder

- Display the query in Design view.
- Position the insertion point in the Field text box of the field in which you want to create the expression.
- Click the Build button on the Query Design toolbar.
- Use the expression elements and operators to build the expression, or type the expression in the expression box.
- Click the OK button.

You will create a new query and use the Expression Builder to build an InStr function that determines the position of the space in the Employee Name field. Later you will use the results of this formula to extract the first name and last name from the Employee Name field.

To use the Expression Builder:

1. Click **Queries** in the Objects bar of the Database window, and then double-click **Create query in Design view.** The Select Query window and the Show Table dialog box open.
2. Add the **tblEmployeesImport** table to the Select Query window, and then close the Show Table dialog box.
3. Be sure that the insertion point is in the first Field text box, and then click the **Build** button on the Query Design toolbar. The Expression Builder dialog box opens (see Figure 3-7).
4. Double-click the **Functions** folder in the list of expression elements. The Built-In Functions and Movie3 folders appear below the Functions folder.
5. Click the **Built-In Functions** folder. A list of function categories appear in the center list box and a list of functions appear in the right list box.
6. Scroll down the center list box, click **Text** to display the text-related functions, click the **InStr** function in the right list box, and then click the **Paste** button to paste the function into the expression box. See Figure 3-8. Notice that the first argument <<start>> is the starting position of the search; this is also an optional argument. Because you want to start at the beginning of the string and that is the default for this argument, you omit this first argument. To delete or replace any argument in the expression box, click the argument to select it first.

Figure 3-8 BUILDING THE InStr EXPRESSION

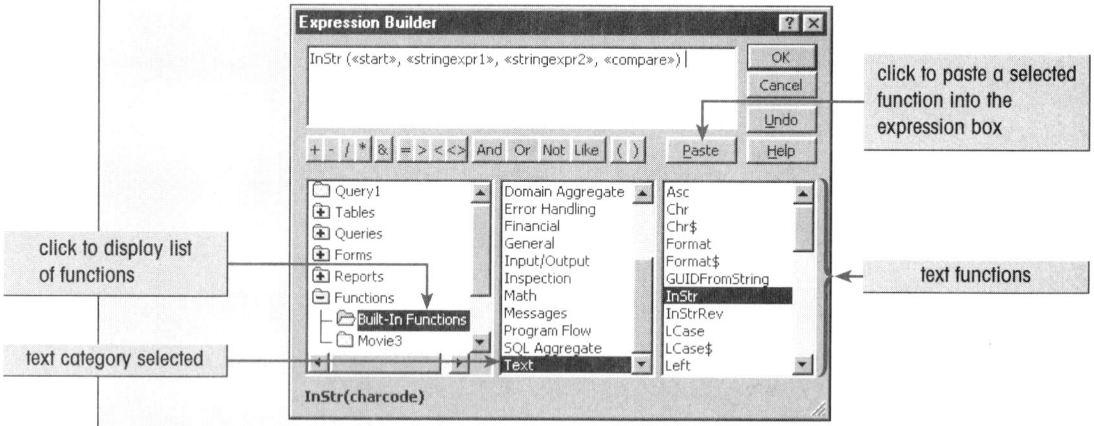

7. Click **<<start>>** in the expression box, press the **Delete** key to delete the argument, and then press the **Delete** key twice to delete the remaining comma and space.

   The second argument in the function <<stringexp1>> is required. This argument represents the string in which you are searching. You will replace the argument placeholder with a table.

8. Click **<<stringexpr1>>** to select it, and then double-click the **Tables** folder in the left list box to display the list of available tables.
9. Click **tblEmployeesImport** in the left list box, click **Employee Name** in the center list box, and then click the **Paste** button.

   The third argument in the function <<stringexp2>> is also required. This argument represents the string for which you are searching. This time you will replace the argument placeholder with a search string.

10. Click **<<stringexpr2>>** to select it and then type **" "** (quotation mark, space, quotation mark) to indicate that you are searching for a space.
11. Delete the remaining comma, delete **<<compare>>**, which is the last argument, but do not delete the closing parenthesis. (The <<compare>> argument is for conducting a binary or textual non-case-sensitive comparison, neither of which applies here. When this argument is omitted, this value defaults to the Option Compare setting for the database, which will be discussed in more detail when you read the tutorials on VBA).
12. Click the **OK** button in the Expression Builder dialog box, and then click the **Run** button ! on the Query Design toolbar to run the query. The result of the InStr function is a number that represents the position of the space character between the first and last names in the Employee Name string.

Next you will create another string function that uses the position of the space character as one of its arguments. Before you do that, however, you need to give a more meaningful name to the expression you just created.

To name the expression:

1. Switch to Design view.
2. In the Field text box, delete the word **Expr1** from the beginning of the expression, and then type **NameSpace** in its place. Do not delete the colon or the formula won't work. (Do not use the word "space" by itself as an object name because "space" is also the name of an Access function.)
3. Run the query again to be sure that it still works. "NameSpace" now appears as the name of the field expression.
4. Switch to Design view to prepare to build the next expression.

Now that you've located the space in each employee name, you'll use the Left function to extract the first name from the Employee Name string. For its first argument, the Left function requires the string from which you want to extract the far left characters; the second argument represents the number of characters to return.

To use the Left function to extract the first name:

1. Click the **Field** text box in the column to the right of the NameSpace expression.
2. Right-click the **Field** text box, and then click **Zoom** on the shortcut menu to open the Zoom window. You can also press and hold the Shift key and press F2 to open the Zoom window.

3. Type **FirstName:Left([Employee Name],NameSpace-1)** as shown in Figure 3-9. You must include square brackets around Employee Name because the field contains a space. However, you do not have to type the square brackets around NameSpace because it does not contain a space and Access automatically adds the brackets for you. You must subtract one (1) space from the second argument because NameSpace counts the position up to and including the space, and you don't want the space included at the end of the first name.

Figure 3-9 FirstName EXPRESSION

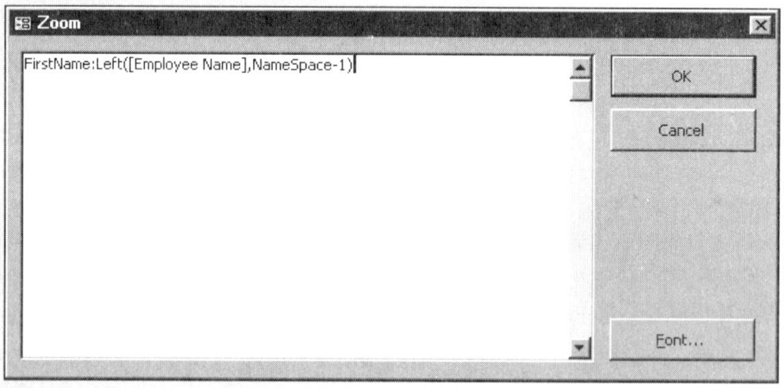

4. Click the **OK** button to close the Zoom window, and then run the query to test the expression. The first names should appear in the second column.

   TROUBLE? If an Enter Parameter Value dialog box opens, click its Cancel button. Reopen the FirstName expression in the Zoom window and make sure the expression matches the one shown in Figure 3-9. If not, make any necessary changes, and then repeat Step 4.

5. Return to Design view to write the expression to extract the last name.

The last name requires using two additional functions. To extract the far right characters from the Employee Name value, you need to know the number of characters in the value, starting with the space and counting to the end of the string. To determine this value, calculate the total number of characters in Employee Name using the Len function, and then subtract the value of NameSpace from the total. See Figure 3-10. You then use the Right function to extract the far right characters from the Employee Name field.

Figure 3-10 CALCULATING TOTAL STRING LENGTH LESS NameSpace

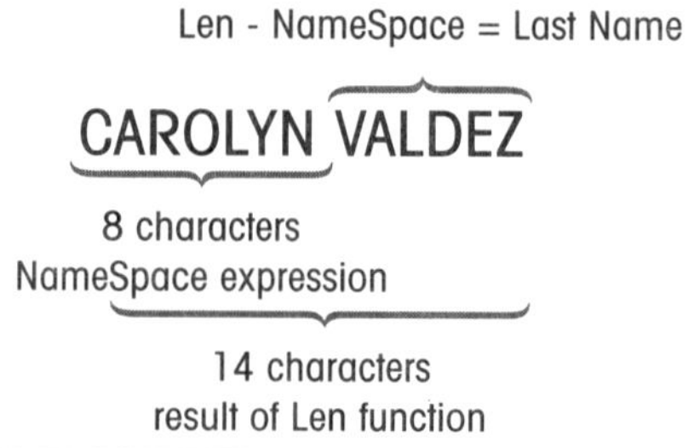

To use the Len function and the Right function to extract the last name:

1. Click the **Field** text box one column to the right of the FirstName expression.
2. Open the Zoom window, type **NameLen:Len([Employee Name])**, and then click the **OK** button to close the Zoom window. Be sure to include the brackets around EmployeeName.
3. Run the query to test the expression. The total number of characters in each employee name is displayed in the NameLen column.
4. Return to Design view and then click the **Field** text box one column to the right of the NameLen expression.
5. Open the Zoom window, type **LastName:Right([Employee Name], NameLen-NameSpace)**, and then click the **OK** button.
6. Run the query to test the expression. Your results should look like those shown in Figure 3-11.

Figure 3-11 **RESULTS OF LastName EXPRESSION**

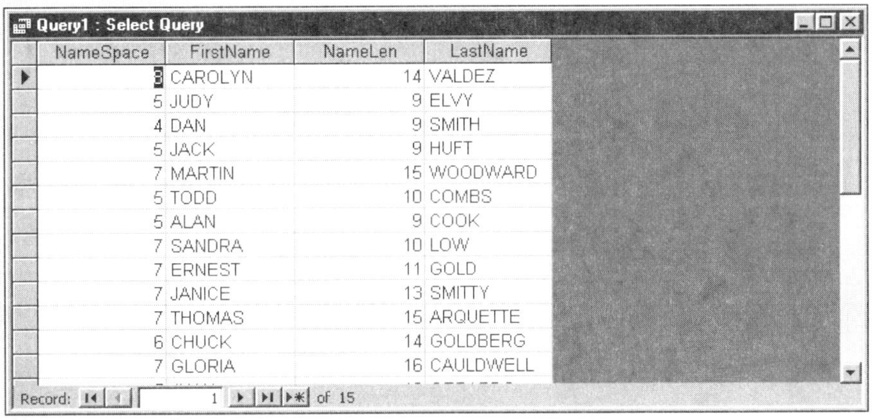

Query1 : Select Query

NameSpace	FirstName	NameLen	LastName
8	CAROLYN	14	VALDEZ
5	JUDY	9	ELVY
4	DAN	9	SMITH
5	JACK	9	HUFT
7	MARTIN	15	WOODWARD
5	TODD	10	COMBS
5	ALAN	9	COOK
7	SANDRA	10	LOW
7	ERNEST	11	GOLD
7	JANICE	13	SMITTY
7	THOMAS	15	ARQUETTE
6	CHUCK	14	GOLDBERG
7	GLORIA	16	CAULDWELL

Record: 1 of 15

To simplify the query, you want to combine the four expressions you just created into two expressions that you can then use to update the tblEmployees table. You will copy and paste the expressions for the NameSpace and NameLen fields in place of their names in the FirstName and LastName field expressions.

To complete the FirstName and LastName expressions:

1. Switch to Design view, click the **NameSpace** expression, open the Zoom window, and then click and drag from the **I** in InStr to the end of the expression to select it, as shown in Figure 3-12.

Figure 3-12 **SELECTING THE InStr FUNCTION**

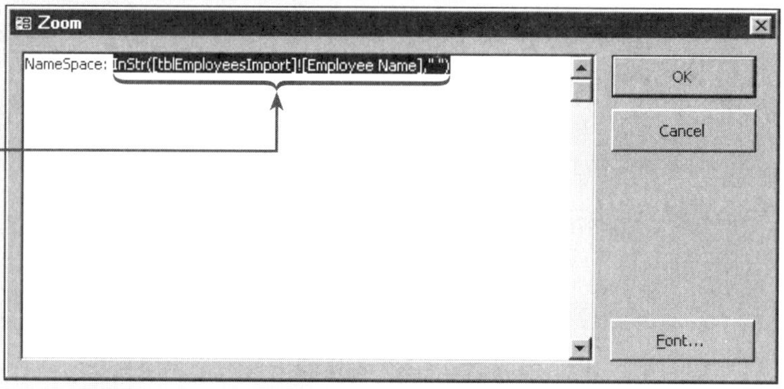

select from the letter "I" in InStr to the end of the function

TROUBLE? If you have trouble selecting the characters with the mouse, click at the beginning of the "I," press and hold down the Shift key, and then press the → right arrow key to select one character at a time until you reach the end of the expression.

2. Press and hold the **Ctrl** key and press **c** to copy the formula into the Clipboard, and then click the **Cancel** button to close the Zoom window.
3. Click the **FirstName** expression, open the Zoom window, and then select **(NameSpace)** (be sure to include the left and right brackets that Access has inserted around NameSpace for you).
4. Press and hold the **Ctrl** key and press **v** to past the formula in place of (NameSpace), making sure the operation to subtract 1 (one) remains at the end of the expression. See Figure 3-13.

Figure 3-13 **PASTING NameSpace IN THE FirstName EXPRESSION**

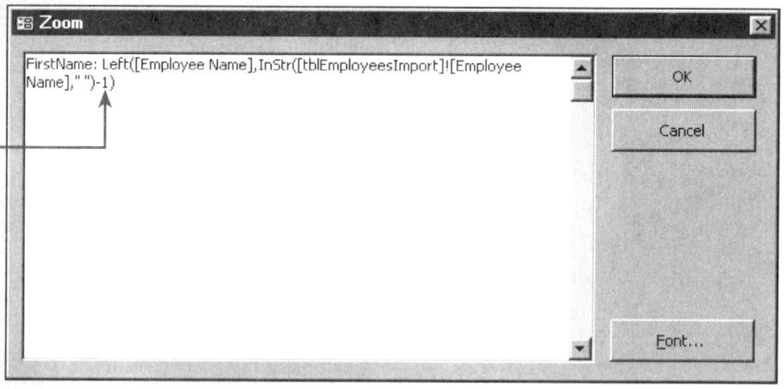

make sure that the 1 is subtracted at the end of the expression

5. Click the **OK** button to close the Zoom window.
6. Click the **LastName** expression, open the Zoom window, select **(NameSpace)**, and then press **Ctrl + v** to paste the formula again. Click the **OK** button to close the Zoom window.
7. Click the **NameLen** expression, open the Zoom window, select **Len([Employee Name])**, press **Ctrl + c** to copy the formula to the Clipboard, and then click the **Cancel** button to close the Zoom window.

8. Click the **LastName** expression, open the Zoom window, select **(NameLen)**, and then press **Ctrl + v** to paste the formula in place of (NameLen). The expression should look like that shown in Figure 3-14.

Figure 3-14 PASTING NameSpace IN THE LastName EXPRESSION

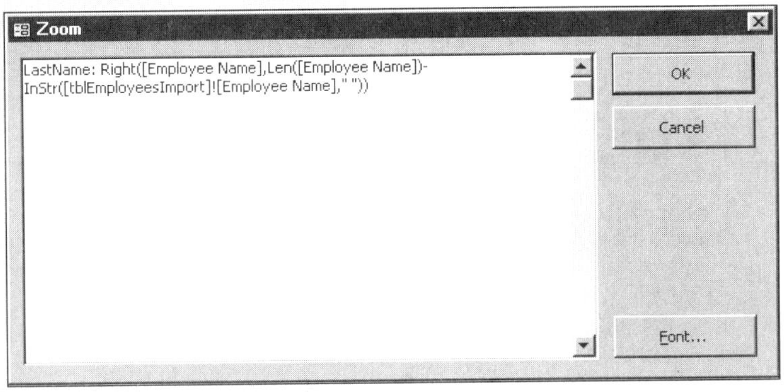

9. Click the **OK** button to close the Zoom window, run the query to be sure that both expressions still work, and then return to Design view.

   You no longer need the NameSpace and NameLen expressions so you can delete them from the query.

10. Position the pointer in the gray bar above the NameSpace expression so the pointer changes to ⬇, click to select the column, and then press the **Delete** key.
11. Repeat Step 10 to delete the NameLen expression.
12. Save the query as **qryEmployeesAppend**.

Review what you've completed so far. You imported the sample text file into Access as the tblEmployeesImport table. You created a query that extracts the first name and last name from the Employee Name column of this table. Now you need to complete the query by adding the other fields that you'll append to the tblEmployees table. You'll then convert the query to an append query.

REFERENCE WINDOW RW

Creating an Append Query

- Create a select query that includes the fields you want to append and the selection criteria.
- Click the Run button on the Query Design toolbar to be sure that you append the correct fields and records.
- Click Query on the menu bar, and then click Append Query to change the query type and open the Append dialog box.
- Click the Table Name list arrow, and then click the table to be appended. Be sure that the Current Database option button is selected so records are appended to the current database, or click the Another Database option button and enter the name of the database in the File Name text box. Click the OK button.
- Click the list arrow in the Append To row for each column, and click the field that corresponds to the field name in the top row of the column.
- Click the Run button on the Query Design toolbar.
- Click the Yes button to confirm appending the records to the table.

The query is almost complete. Next you will append the data to the tblEmployees table.

To create the Append query:

1. Add all the fields in the tblEmployeesImport table, *except* for the Employee Name field, to the design grid.
2. Run the query to make sure you are appending the correct data, and then switch to Design view.
3. Click **Query** on the menu bar, and then click **Append Query** to change the query type and to open the Append dialog box.
4. Click the **Table Name** list arrow to display the list of table names, click **tblEmployees**, and then click the **OK** button to close the Append dialog box.
5. Click the list arrow in the **Append To** row (fourth row in the design grid) for each column, and then select the field that corresponds to the field name in the top row. See Figure 3-15.

Figure 3-15 COMPLETING THE qryEmployeeAppend QUERY

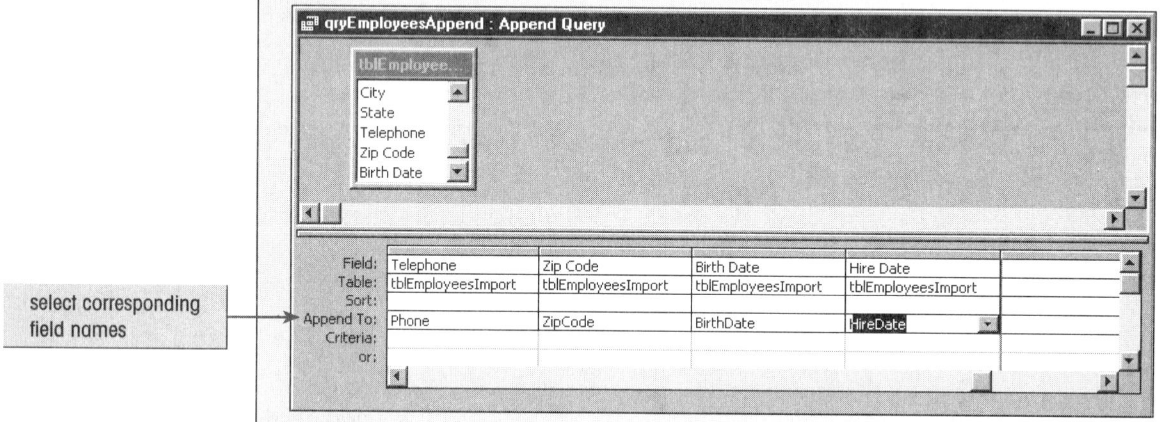

6. Run the query to append the rows to the tblEmployees table, and when the message box appears indicating the number of rows appended (15) and warns you that you cannot undo the append, click the **Yes** button.
7. Close the query and save your changes.
8. Click **Tables** in the Objects bar of the Database window, and then open the **tblEmployees** table. There are 15 records in the table. Earlier in the tutorial, you checked to be sure the tblEmployees table was empty, so at this point, the table has been appended and there are 15 more records than there were originally.
9. Close the table to return to the Database window.

You have completed the first part of Amanda's request; you successfully imported the data from the accounting software program and appended it to the tblEmployees table. Now you'll focus on reformatting the data you've imported and on importing the Excel data.

Session 3.1 Quick Check

1. If data from an external source is going to be used in its original format and in Access, which is a better method: linking or importing?
2. ______________ is the term that refers to characters that identify the end of one field and the beginning of another field in a text file.
3. ______________ ______________ functions allow you to force a particular data type, and are commonly used in queries.
4. Which function returns the position of a particular character in a string?
5. The ______________ function returns the number of characters in a string of text.

SESSION 3.2

In this session, you will import a standard module from another database and write an expression in an update query using a custom function in the module. You also will use the Import Spreadsheet Wizard to import data from Excel. You will write action queries to append and archive the data, and finally, you will employ a subquery to assist with archiving data.

Importing an Access Object

Now that you've appended the employee data to the tblEmployees table, you decide to write an update query to correct one other problem. When you imported the data from the accounting software to Access, the data in the FirstName and LastName fields was in all capital letters. You want to convert names to uppercase and lowercase. Another programmer in the company created a custom function, called ProperCase that can convert all caps to a combination of uppercase and lowercase. However, the function is stored in a module called mdlUtilityFunctions, which resides in another database, so you want to import the module to the Movie3 database. A **module** is simply an object in an Access database that is used to store VBA functions and procedures.

REFERENCE WINDOW RW

Importing Access Objects

- Start Access and open the database to which you want to import the Access object(s).
- Click File on the menu bar, point to Get External Data, and then click Import.
- Click the Files of type list arrow, and then click Microsoft Access.
- Navigate to the drive and folder that contains the file that you want to import, select the file to be imported, and then click the Import button.
- Click each object you want to import. To navigate to different object types, click the tabs at the top of the dialog box.
- Click the OK button.

Now, you will import the mdlUtilityFunctions module from the Samples database.

To import a standard module from another Access database:

1. If you took a break after the previous session, make sure that Access is running and that the **Movie3** database from the Tutorial.03\Tutorial folder on your local or network drive is open.
2. Click **File** on the menu bar, point to **Get External Data**, and then click **Import** to open the Import dialog box.
3. If necessary, click the **Files of type** list arrow, and then click **Microsoft Access**.
4. If necessary, navigate to the Tutorial.03 folder on your local or network drive, click **Samples**, and then click the **Import** button.
5. Click the **Modules** tab in the Import Objects dialog box. See Figure 3-16. The "mdl" tag preceding the module name stands for "module." Many developers name modules using "mdl" while working in Access, because "bas" is the tag typically reserved for Visual Basic modules. This way, one tag (bas) is used specifically for Visual Basic and the other (mdl) for VBA. Either is definitely fine as long as you are consistent.

Figure 3-16 IMPORTING THE mdlUtilityFunctions MODULE

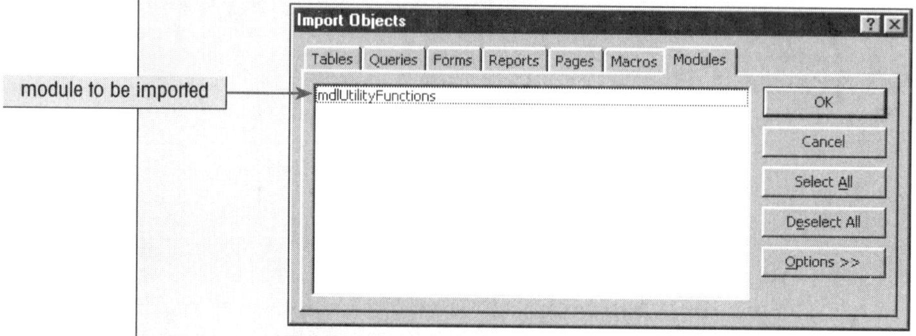

6. Click **mdlUtilityFunctions** and then click the **OK** button. The mdlUtilityFunctions module appears in the Movie3 Database window.

The mdlUtilityFunctions module contains a custom function, which you can use in the same way that you use the built-in functions of Access. Next, you'll write an update query using this function.

Creating an Update Query

It is generally a good idea to make a copy of any table you plan to update, delete, or append to before you run the action query to do so, because if you make an error, you cannot undo the results. Restoring a backup from the previous day or two is time consuming and can result in losing any data that has been entered since the last backup was made. In this instance, it is not necessary to make a copy of the tblEmployees table because you have just imported the data; you've saved the append query, and you can always reimport the data and run the append query again if something goes wrong during the update. If you were working with "live production" data, you would want to be sure you had an up-to-date backup of the entire database before running these types of operations or making any design changes.

REFERENCE WINDOW RW

Creating an Update Query

- Make a copy of the table you plan to update, or be sure that you have a current backup of the database file.
- Create a select query that includes the fields you want to update and the selection criteria.
- Click the Run button on the Query Design toolbar to be sure that you update the correct fields and records.
- Click Query on the menu bar, and then click Update Query to change the query type.
- Enter the expression for the new value(s) in the Update To rows for the field(s) you want to update.
- Click the Run button on the Query Design toolbar, and click the Yes button to confirm updating the records.

Because you do not need to make a copy of the table for this particular exercise, you are ready to write the update query to convert the FirstName and LastName fields to uppercase and lowercase.

To create an update query using the custom function you just imported from mdlUtilityFunctions:

1. Create a new query in Design view, add the **tblEmployees** table to the Select Query window, and close the Show Table dialog box.
2. Drag the **FirstName** and **LastName** fields into the first two columns of the design grid.
3. Click **Query** on the menu bar, and then click **Update Query** to change the query type.
4. Click in the **Update To** text box in the FirstName column, type **ProperCase ([FirstName])**, and then press the **Tab** key to move to the next column. Remember to type the square brackets around FirstName. Note that it is sometimes not necessary to type the square brackets around a field name that has no spaces in it, because Access often inserts the brackets for you when it recognizes a field name. However, in this instance, you are working with a custom function that accepts either a field or a string of text as its argument. If you do not include the square brackets around FirstName, Access assumes that the data you are modifying is a string and places quotation marks around it. When you run the update query, the ProperCase function would then convert "FirstName" to "Firstname," and every first name in your table would contain the string Firstname. The brackets ensure that Access knows you are referring to a field and not a string of text.
5. Type **ProperCase([LastName])**. Again, be sure to type the square brackets around LastName. See Figure 3-17.

Figure 3-17 USING A CUSTOM FUNCTION IN AN UPDATE QUERY

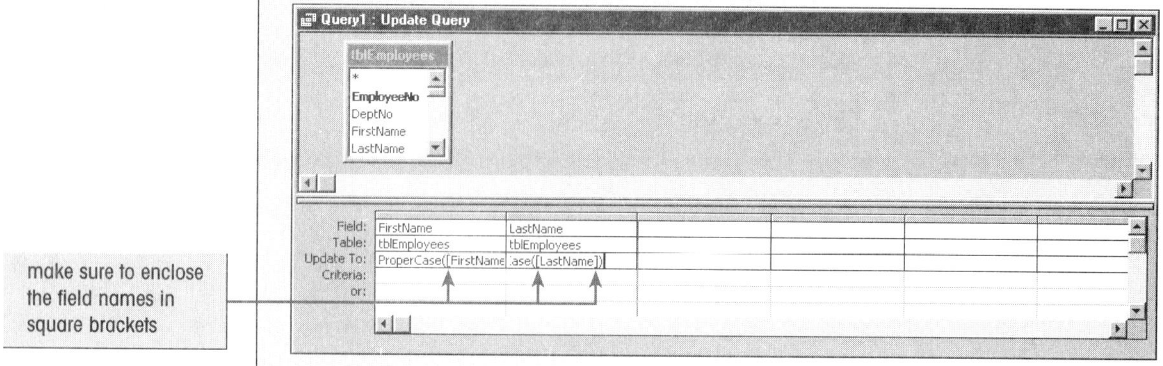

6. Run the query, click the **Yes** button to confirm that you want to perform the update, save the query as **qryUpdateNames**, and then close the query.
7. Open the **tblEmployees** table in Datasheet view to check the results. The names should be in uppercase and lowercase now.
8. Close the table to return to the Database window.

You've imported an Access object and a text file to the Movie3 database. Now you'll import the Excel data.

Using the Import Spreadsheet Wizard

Martin Woodward, one of MovieCam's product managers, has provided you with an Excel workbook file that contains sample data used to track time cards and hours. See Figure 3-18.

Figure 3-18 SAMPLE SPREADSHEET DATA

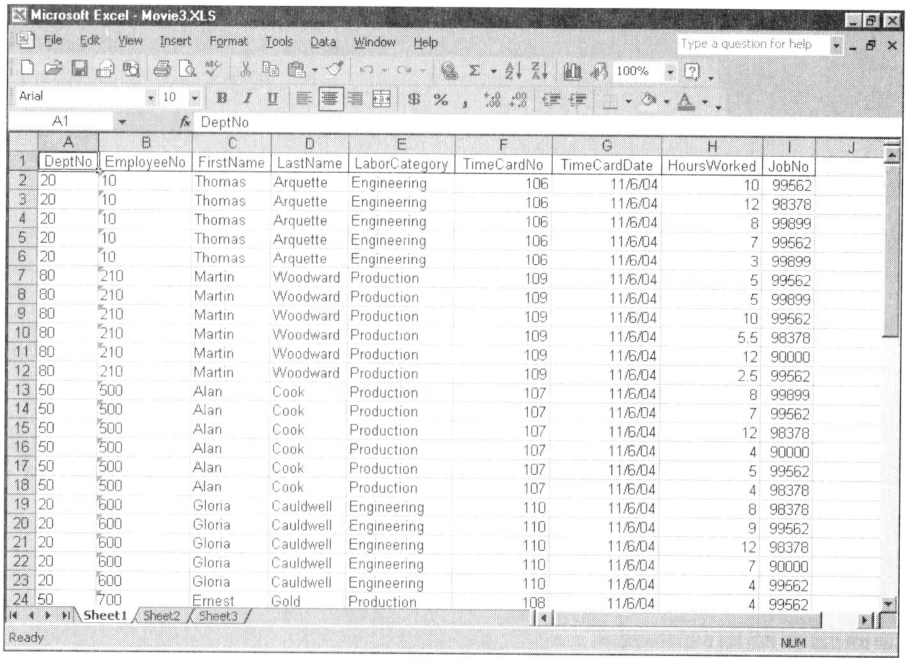

	DeptNo	EmployeeNo	FirstName	LastName	LaborCategory	TimeCardNo	TimeCardDate	HoursWorked	JobNo
2	20	10	Thomas	Arquette	Engineering	106	11/6/04	10	99562
3	20	10	Thomas	Arquette	Engineering	106	11/6/04	12	98378
4	20	10	Thomas	Arquette	Engineering	106	11/6/04	8	99899
5	20	10	Thomas	Arquette	Engineering	106	11/6/04	7	99562
6	20	10	Thomas	Arquette	Engineering	106	11/6/04	3	99899
7	80	210	Martin	Woodward	Production	109	11/6/04	5	99562
8	80	210	Martin	Woodward	Production	109	11/6/04	5	99899
9	80	210	Martin	Woodward	Production	109	11/6/04	10	99562
10	80	210	Martin	Woodward	Production	109	11/6/04	5.5	98378
11	80	210	Martin	Woodward	Production	109	11/6/04	12	90000
12	80	210	Martin	Woodward	Production	109	11/6/04	2.5	99562
13	50	500	Alan	Cook	Production	107	11/6/04	8	99899
14	50	500	Alan	Cook	Production	107	11/6/04	7	99562
15	50	500	Alan	Cook	Production	107	11/6/04	12	98378
16	50	500	Alan	Cook	Production	107	11/6/04	4	90000
17	50	500	Alan	Cook	Production	107	11/6/04	5	99562
18	50	500	Alan	Cook	Production	107	11/6/04	4	98378
19	20	600	Gloria	Cauldwell	Engineering	110	11/6/04	8	98378
20	20	600	Gloria	Cauldwell	Engineering	110	11/6/04	9	99562
21	20	600	Gloria	Cauldwell	Engineering	110	11/6/04	12	98378
22	20	600	Gloria	Cauldwell	Engineering	110	11/6/04	7	90000
23	20	600	Gloria	Cauldwell	Engineering	110	11/6/04	4	99562
24	50	700	Ernest	Gold	Production	108	11/6/04	4	99562

You plan to import this table and then use it to write the queries needed to populate the tblTimeCards and tblHours tables in the MovieCam database. Before you begin the import process, you examine the spreadsheet data in the Excel worksheet for the following:

- The data should be arranged in rows, and only one type of data should be entered in each column. For example, dates and text data should not be entered in the same column.
- Column headings should appear in the top row of the worksheet, with no blank rows above them. You might also want to remove spaces between words in multiword column names, although this can be done in Access. For example, you would use EmployeeName rather than Employee Name as the field name to represent that column heading of the worksheet. Recall that although it is permissible for field names to have spaces in them, this is not a best industry practice and it also makes it more difficult to use the field name in expressions.
- None of the cells to be imported should contain formulas. If they do, you need to replace the formula with its calculated value.

Use the Import Spreadsheet Wizard to import Martin's spreadsheet file.

REFERENCE WINDOW RW

Using the Import Spreadsheet Wizard

- Start Access and open the database to which you want to import the text file.
- Click File on the menu bar, point to Get External Data, and then click Import.
- Click the Files of type list arrow, and then click Microsoft Excel.
- Navigate to the drive and folder that contains the file you want to import, click the file to be imported, and then click the Import button.
- Complete the Wizard dialog boxes by selecting the worksheet and named range, marking the first row as field names or not, and choosing a new table or the table name of an existing table. Change the field options as necessary, indicate whether you want to add a primary key, and name the table if you're importing to a new table.

The data in Martin's spreadsheet looks good with the exception of spaces in the field names. You decide to leave those the way they are for now. If the names in the worksheet are the same as the field names in the table you plan to append to, creating the append query is simpler. Access automatically determines to which fields to append the data and you don't have to match up the fields. However, changing the field names in the spreadsheet is just as time-consuming as assigning the correct field names in the append query when you create it.

The data that Martin gave you is a sampling of time cards from this year and last. You wanted both so that you can work out the archive queries that you'll need after all the data has been imported.

To import an Excel spreadsheet into Access:

1. Click **File** on the menu bar, point to **Get External Data**, and then click **Import**. The Import dialog box opens.
2. Click the **Files of type** list arrow, and then click **Microsoft Excel**.

3. If necessary, navigate to the Tutorial.03\Tutorial folder on your local or network drive, click **Movie3** in the Import dialog box, and then click the **Import** button. The Import Spreadsheet Wizard starts, as shown in Figure 3-19.

Figure 3-19 IMPORT SPREADSHEET WIZARD

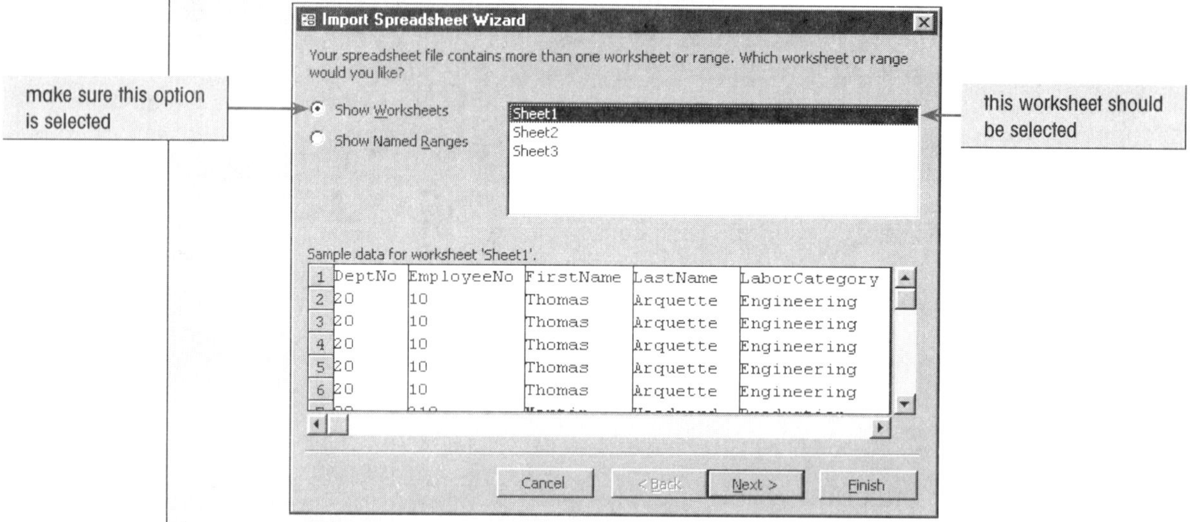

If you have a large spreadsheet that includes cells you do not want to import to Access, you should name the range in the Excel file that you plan to import. Any ranges you name in the Excel file will appear in the first Import Spreadsheet Wizard dialog box after you select the Show Named Ranges option. In this instance, you want to import all the data on the worksheet (Sheet1).

4. Be sure that the **Show Worksheets** option button is selected and that **Sheet1** is selected (see Figure 3-19), and then click the **Next** button. In the next dialog box, you are asked if there is a single row of column headings in the Excel worksheet. If more than one row contains column headings, Access assumes the second row of data represents the first record.

5. Be sure that the **First Row Contains Column Headings** option is checked, and then click the **Next** button.

6. Be sure that the **In a New Table** option button is selected, and then click the **Next** button.

   Next, you can change field names and add indexes. However, it is not necessary to make changes here because the table you are creating is temporary.

7. Click the **Next** button. Again, because this is a temporary table that you will delete when you are finished with it, no primary key is necessary.

8. Click the **No primary key** option button, and then click the **Next** button.

9. Type **tblTimeCardsImport** as the table name, and then click the **Finish** button.

10. Click the **OK** button in the message box that informs you that Access has finished importing the data.

Now that the transactional data is successfully imported to the database, you want to transfer it to the tables that you created. You will start by appending data to the tblTimeCards table.

As you already determined, storing data in the Excel file led to a lot of data duplication. Now that same redundant data appears in the table to which you imported it. To minimize duplicate data in a table, you apply the Unique Values property in a query.

Query Properties

The Unique Values and Record Locks query properties are particularly useful when you write action queries. There are some other query properties that are helpful to understand when you work with external data files. An explanation of these properties follows:

- *Output All Fields*: Use this property to show all the fields in the query's underlying data source. When this property is set to Yes, the only fields you need to include in the design grid are the fields on which you want to sort by or specify criteria.
- *Unique Values*: Use this property to include only unique results when the query is run. If the query results contain more than one field, then the query displays only the records that are unique given the combination of all the included, or specifically selected, fields.
- *Unique Records*: Use this property to return from the underlying data source only the unique records that are based on all the fields in the data source, not just the ones displayed in the query results. This property is ignored when the query uses only one table.
- *Source Database* and *Source Connect Str*: Use these properties to access external data that either is not or cannot be directly linked to your database. The Source Database property specifies the external source database where the data resides. The Source Connect Str specifies the name of the program used to create the external file. For an Access database, the Source Database property is the path and database name, such as C:\Clients\MovieCam. Access adds the .mdb file extension automatically. The Source Connect Str is not necessary for an Access database. For a database created by another program, such as dBASE, the Source Database property is also the path and the Source Connect Str is what specifies the database type, such as *dBASE III;* or *dBASE IV;* (the semicolon should be included).
- *Destination Table, Destination DB, Dest Connect Str*: Use these properties for append and make-table queries. The Destination Table property represents the name of the table to which you are appending. The Destination DB property is the name and path of the database to which you are appending, if it is outside the current database. The Dest Connect Str property specifies the destination database, such as dBASE IV. If you are appending to the current database, Destination DB is the current database, and Dest Connect Str is not used.
- *Record Locks*: Use this property to specify whether the records in a multiuser environment are locked so that other users cannot access them while the query is being run. This property is typically set for action queries, so it is of particular importance when you create queries to import and archive records. There are three choices for locking records. The No Locks option, the default for select queries, means that the records aren't locked while the query is being run. The All Records option allows users to read records but prevents editing, adding to, or deleting from the underlying record source until the query has finished running. The Edited Record option, the default for action queries, locks a page of records as soon as the query is run. A page is a portion of the database file in which record data is stored. A page is 4 KB in size in

Access 2002. Depending on the size of the record, a page may contain more than one record, or just a portion of a record. You can change this property, but be aware that it affects record locking in forms and reports as well.

Now you will create a query to append to the tblTimeCards table only those records with unique values.

REFERENCE WINDOW RW

Querying for Unique Values

- Create a query in Design view with the necessary fields and selection criteria.
- Right-click in the Query Design window to display the shortcut menu, and then click Properties to display the query properties.
- Click the Unique Values property text box, click its list arrow, and then click Yes.
- Run the query to check your results.

Next, you'll create the append query to append the imported records to the tblTimeCards table.

To append unique data to the tblTimeCards table:

1. Create a new query in Design view, add the **tblTimeCardsImport** table to the Select Query window, and close the Show Table dialog box.
2. Add the **TimeCardNo**, **TimeCardDate**, and **EmployeeNo** fields (in this order) to the design grid in the lower pane of the Select Query window.
3. Run the query to test the results. There should be 56 records in the results.
4. Switch to Design view and then right-click a blank area of the upper pane of the Select Query window to display the shortcut menu shown in Figure 3-20.

Figure 3-20 DESIGNING THE APPEND QUERY

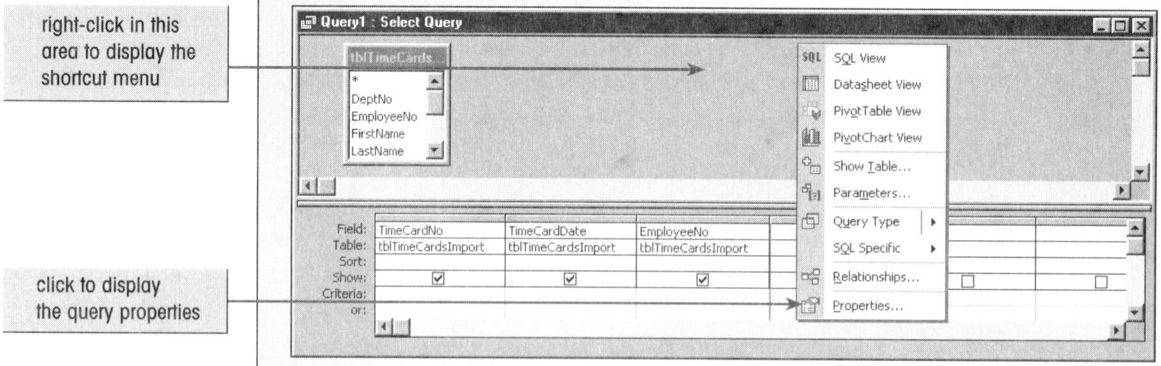

5. Click **Properties** on the shortcut menu, and then change the Unique Values property to **Yes**. The Unique Values property applies to select queries and make-table and append action queries. After this property is changed, the query results, or recordset, can no longer be updated. This means that you

cannot change the data in the recordset in Datasheet view. Most, but not all, queries can be used to change the data in the underlying table or tables (recordset) in Datasheet view. Use Access Help for detailed information regarding which type of query can and cannot be changed.

6. Close the property sheet, and then run the query again. Now the recordset should display 10 unique records.
7. Return to Design view, click **Query** on the menu bar, and then click **Append Query** to change the query type and to open the Append dialog box.

   Next you will select the tblTimeCards table to which the data will be appended. You will also need to select fields in that table that correspond as closely as possible with the fields in the tblTimeCardsImport table.

8. Select **tblTimeCards** from the Table Name list, and then click the **OK** button.
9. In the design grid, click the list arrow in the **Append To** row for each of the three columns, and then select the corresponding fields from the tblTimeCards table. See Figure 3-21. Note that the Time Card No field will be appended to TimeCardID.

Figure 3-21 CHANGING QUERY PROPERTIES

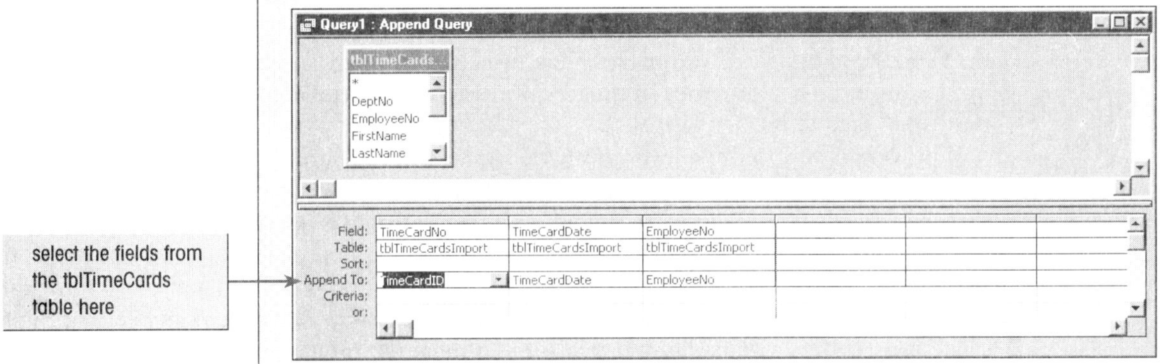

10. Run the query, click the **Yes** button in the message box that appears, save the query as **qryTimeCardsAppend**, and then close the query.
11. Open the **tblTimeCards** table to check your results. You should have 10 records.
12. Close the table to return to the Database window.

Now you will append the hours data to the tblHours table.

To append sample data to the tblHours table:

1. Create a new query in Design view, add the **tblTimeCardsImport** table to the Select Query window, and then close the Show Table dialog box.
2. Add the **TimeCardNo**, **HoursWorked**, and **JobNo** fields to the design grid. You do not need to include the HoursID field. It is an AutoNumber field that has been set as the primary key and will populate automatically.

3. Click **Query** on the menu bar, and then click **Append Query** to change the query type and to open the Append Query dialog box.
4. Select **tblHours** from the Table Name list, and then click the **OK** button.
5. In the design grid, click the list arrow in the **Append To** row for each of the three columns, and then select a corresponding field. The TimeCardNo field is appended to TimeCardID and the JobNo field to JobID.
6. Run the query, click the **Yes** button in the message box, save the query as **qryHoursAppend**, and then close the query.
7. Open the **tblHours** table to check the results. There should be 56 records in the table.
8. Close the table to return to the Database window.

Next you will work out the archiving queries that Amanda requested.

Archiving Data

The tblTimeCards and tblHours tables in the MovieCam Technologies database will contain the most records—many times more than the other tables. Because employees enter time cards and hours for various jobs each week of the year, these tables grow quite rapidly. To optimize the performance of queries, forms, and reports, you should store only the current year's data in the active tables.

This brings you to the question of whether to store the archive tables in this database or another. If you store them in another database, you have to run only the append queries so that the records are appended to the other database file. However, in this case it will be simpler if all the tables are stored in the same database file. Then when you create comprehensive reports and queries you can include the data in the archive tables without linking tables from a separate database back to the current one. This suits the company's needs at the present time. However, consider that if at some time in the future the current database grew to a much larger size, then you could move the archive tables into a separate database and link them back to the current one using the same table names. This way, you can save storage space in your primary database, and by linking those archive tables back to the primary database, you can still union the two tables together using union queries which can further serve as the basis for your reports or other comprehensive queries.

The Movie3 database already contains an archive table, named tblTimeCardsArchive. This table was created simply by copying and pasting the structure of the tblTimeCards table to a new table and saving it with a new name. You need to create the archive table for the tblHours table. You will use the same method of copying and pasting, and then you will change the HoursID field in the archive table from an AutoNumber type to a Number field, because you cannot add data to an AutoNumber field (it increments automatically). The HoursID field in the archive table must contain the same number it had in the tblHours table; therefore, you have to change the HoursID field to a Number data type. That way, the data from the tblHours table can be appended to the archive table without error.

The first time you archive data, you can create make-table queries to create the tables and write the records all in one step. In this instance, however, you will run the queries over and over to archive data as time goes by. If you use a make-table query rather than an append query, the existing data is overwritten each time you run the query. The purpose of creating the queries is for future use, so you will create the tables first, and then write and save the append and delete queries.

REFERENCE WINDOW RW

Copying and Pasting a Table Structure

- In the Database window, select the table to be copied.
- Click Edit on the menu bar, and then select Copy.
- Click Edit on the menu bar, and then select Paste.
- Select the Structure Only option button.
- Type the table name.
- Click the OK button.

You will create the tblHoursArchive table and its structure by copying and pasting the tblHours table structure.

To copy and paste the tblHours table structure:

1. In the Database window, click the **tblHours** table to select it.
2. Click the **Copy** button on the Database toolbar. The copy is placed on the Clipboard.
3. Click the **Paste** button on the Database toolbar. The Paste Table As dialog box opens.
4. Type **tblHoursArchive** in the Table Name text box, click the **Structure Only** option button, and then click the **OK** button.
5. Open the **tblHoursArchive** table in Design view, and then change the data type of the HoursID field to **Number**.
6. Close and save the table.

Now that you have created the archive table, you'll write the append queries. The append queries will contain a prompt that requests the user to enter the date. All records prior to that date will then be archived. This allows the query to be used over and over.

To create the append query from the tblTimeCards table:

1. Create a new query in Design view, add the **tblTimeCards** table to the Select Query window, and close the Show Table dialog box.
2. Double-click the title bar of the tblTimeCards field list to select all the fields, as shown in Figure 3-22.

Figure 3-22 **SELECTING ALL FIELDS**

double-click the title bar

drag the selected fields to the design grid

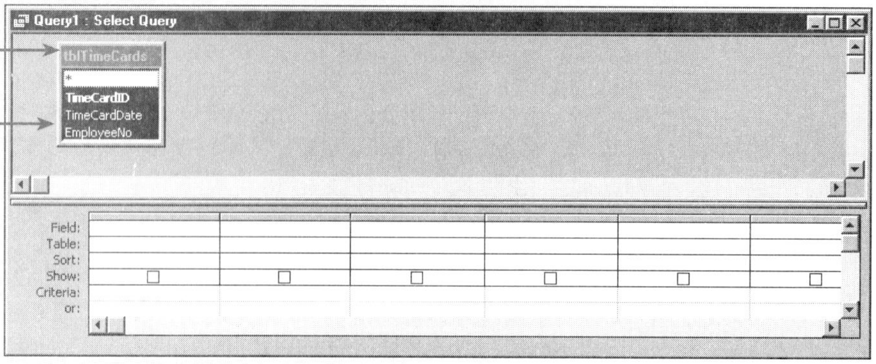

3. Drag the selected fields to the first column of the design grid. All the fields appear in the design grid.
4. Click the **Criteria** text box for the TimeCardDate column, type **<(Enter the first date of the current year)**. Creating this query as a parameter query enables the users to archive records over and over using one query. The less than (<) symbol indicates that all records entered before the date the user types will be found. Run the query to be sure you are archiving the correct records.
5. In the Enter Parameter Value dialog box, type **1/1/2004** as the first date of the current year, and then click the **OK** button. The records from the previous year, 2003, are displayed in Datasheet view.
6. Switch to Design view, click **Query** on the menu bar, and then click **Append Query**.
7. Select **tblTimeCardsArchive** from the Table Name list box, and then click the **OK** button. The Append To row fills in automatically because all the fields in both tables have the same name.
8. Run the query, type **1/1/2004** when prompted for the date, click the **OK** button, and then click the **Yes** button to append the five rows.
9. Save the query as **qryArchiveTimeCards**, and then close it.

Now that the records from the previous year are archived to the tblTimeCardsArchive table, you need to write a query to delete the records that were archived from the active table. However, you must consider the relationship between the tblTimeCards and tblHours tables. In the previous tutorial, you applied the Cascade Update option and not the Cascade Delete option, which prevents you from deleting the records from the tblTimeCards table before you archive the records from the tblHours table. If you had chosen the Cascade Delete option and archived the records from the tblTimeCards table first, then the related records in the tblHours table would be deleted also. This is one reason why you should never check the Cascade Delete option. As you will see, you can still delete the older data after archiving it, but you must do it in the right order. Following this rule helps to ensure data integrity and prevent accidental deletions from which you may not be able to recover unless you had a backup file of the database. However, having a backup file on disk or tape is no excuse for not following prudent industry practices. In addition, restoring a complete backup can be time-consuming and result in some data loss for any data added since the last backup was made.

With this in mind, you write the append query for the tblHours table before you delete records from the tblTimeCards table.

To create the append query from the tblHours table:

1. Create a new query in Design view, add the **tblTimeCards** and **tblHours** tables (in this order) to the Select Query window, and then close the Show Table dialog box.
2. Add the **TimeCardDate** field from the tblTimeCards table, and then add all the fields from the **tblHours** table to the design grid.
3. Type **<(Enter the first date of the current year)** in the Criteria text box for the TimeCardDate field, and press the **Tab** key. Your query should look like that shown in Figure 3-23.

Figure 3-23 APPENDING TO THE tblHoursArchive TABLE

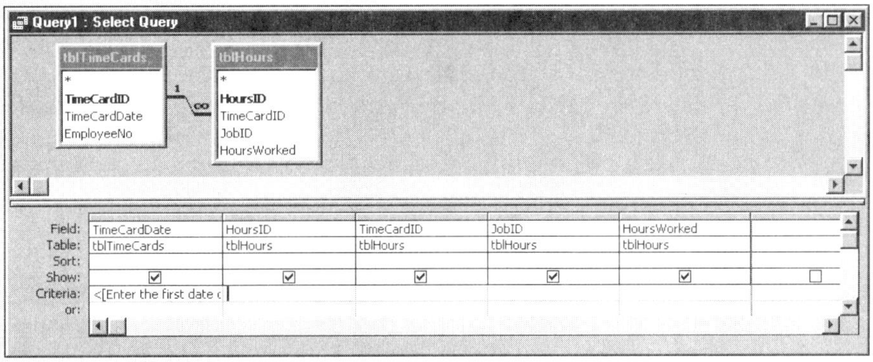

4. Run the query, type **1/1/2004** when prompted to enter the date, and then click the **OK** button. The recordset should display 28 records.
5. Switch to Design view, change the query to an **Append** query, select **tblHoursArchive** from the Table Name list box, and then click the **OK** button.
6. Right-click a blank area of the Append Query window, and then click **Properties** on the shortcut menu.
7. Change the Record Locks property to **All Records** so the records cannot be accessed until the query has finished running, and then close the property sheet. This is a good idea for all append queries, but especially for those run on transactional tables that might contain many records.
8. Run the query, type **1/1/2004** when prompted for the date, click the **OK** button, and then click the **Yes** button to confirm that you want to append the records.
9. Save the query as **qryArchiveHours**, and then close it.

REFERENCE WINDOW RW

Creating a Delete Query

- Make a copy of the table you plan to update, or be sure that you have a current backup of the database file.
- Create a select query that includes the fields you want to update and the selection criteria.
- Click the Run button on the Query Design toolbar to be sure you are deleting the correct fields and records.
- Click Query on the menu bar, and then select Delete Query to change the query type.
- Click the Run button on the Query Design toolbar, and then click the Yes button to confirm updating the records.

The last step in the archiving process is to create a query to delete the records from the tblTimeCards table that were archived to the tblTimeCardsArchive table. You must first delete the related records in the tblHours table, and then delete the primary records in the tblTimeCards table. This procedure may seem tedious, but it prevents accidental deletions in tables by avoiding the Cascade Delete option for the relationship between these two tables. See Figure 3-24.

Figure 3-24 RELATIONSHIP BETWEEN THE tblTimeCards AND tblHours TABLES

leaving this option deselected prevents irretrievable deletions of related records in the tblHours table when attempting to delete records from the primary tblTimeCards table

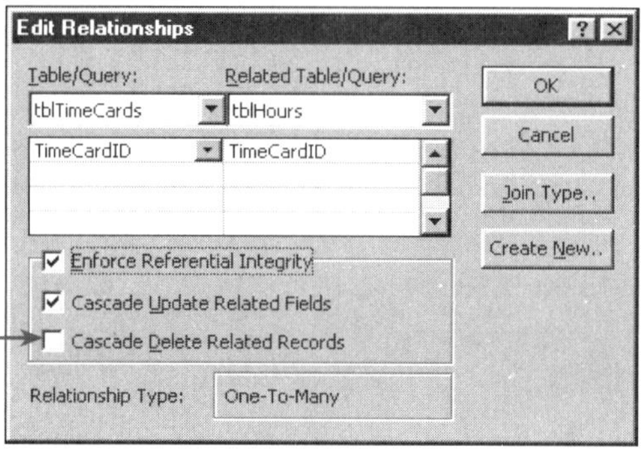

Employing a Subquery

To delete the archive records from the tblHours table, you use a **subquery**, which was discussed briefly in Tutorial 1. A subquery is a query within a query. A subquery can either be entered as field expressions or set up as criteria. You need to use a subquery here because the tblHours table does not have any date information in it. Therefore, the only way to know if you are removing the correct related records is to first select only those records which meet the date criteria as they relate to the records in the tblTimeCards table.

First you will delete the related records in the tblHours table.

To delete the archived records from the tblHours table:

1. Create a new query in Design view, add the **tblHours** table to the Select Query window, and then close the Show Table dialog box.
2. Double-click * (the asterisk) at the top of the tblHours table to add tblHours.* to the first field cell in the design grid.

3. Add the **HoursID** field to the design grid, clear its **Show** check box, click in the **Criteria** cell below HoursID, and then open the Zoom window.

   Next, you will enter the SQL statement in the Zoom window. For better readability, you will enter the statement on four separate lines. To start a new line within the Zoom window, you need to press the Ctrl key and press then Enter key at the end of each line. Note that you can allow the fourth line to wrap to the next line without forcing it.

4. Enter the following SQL statement into the Zoom window, as shown in Figure 3-25, pressing **Ctrl + Enter** at the end of the first three rows:

   In (SELECT tblHours.HoursID
   FROM tblTimeCards INNER JOIN tblHours ON tblTimeCards.TimeCardID = tblHours.TimeCardID
   WHERE (((tblTimeCards.TimeCardDate)<(Enter the first date of the current year)));)

   The keyword "In" at the beginning of the subquery tells Access to look for records in the tblHours table with HoursID values that are related to records in the tblTimeCards table with TimeCardDate values prior to the first date of the current year. The recordset returned by the query should display only the records in the tblHours table that match records in the tblTimeCards table. Then you can delete those records from the tblHours table. Note that the SQL statement itself must have parentheses around it when it is used as a subquery. The "In" keyword must be in front of the subquery and outside the opening parenthesis.

Figure 3-25 QUERY TO DELETE ARCHIVED RECORDS IN THE tblHours TABLEUSING A SUBQUERY

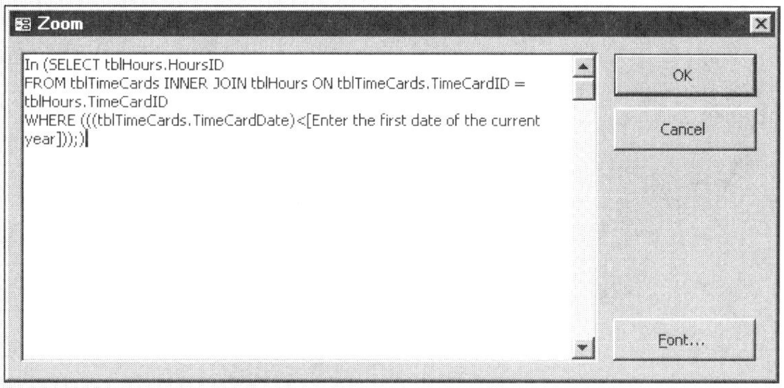

5. Close the Zoom window, run the query, type **1/1/2004** when prompted for the date, and then click the **OK** button. The recordset should have 28 records in it, and all the time card numbers shown should be four-digit numbers starting with the number 9. If you open the tblTimeCards table, you see that all the time cards numbers for 2004 have three-digit numbers beginning with the number "1," and all the time card numbers prior to 2004 have four-digit numbers beginning with the number "9."

6. Switch to Design view, click **Query** on the menu bar, and then click **Delete Query**.

7. Right-click in the upper pane of the Delete Query window, and then click **Properties** on the shortcut menu.

8. Change the Record Locks property to **All Records** so that the records cannot be accessed until the query has finished running, and then close the property sheet.
9. Run the query, type **1/1/2004** when prompted for the date, click the **OK** button, and then click the **Yes** button to confirm the deletion of 28 rows from the specified table.
10. Save the query as **qryDeleteHours**, and then close it.

Now you will delete the primary records in the tblTimeCards table.

To delete the primary records from the tblTimeCards table:

1. Create a new query in Design view, add the **tblTimeCards** table to the Select Query window, and then close the Show Table dialog box.
2. Double-click ***** (the asterisk) at the top of the tblTimeCards table to add tblTimeCards.* to the first field cell in the design grid.
3. Add the **TimeCardDate** field to the design grid, clear the **Show** check box, click in the **Criteria** cell below TimeCardDate, and enter **<(Enter the first date of the current year)**.
4. Run the query, type **1/1/2004** when prompted for the date, and then click the **OK** button. The recordset should have five records in it all with TimeCardDate values before January1, 2004.
5. Switch to Design view, click **Query** on the menu bar, and then click **Delete Query**.
6. Right-click in the upper pane of the Delete Query window, and then click **Properties** on the shortcut menu.
7. Change the Record Locks property to **All Records** so that the records cannot be accessed until the query has finished running, and then close the property sheet.
8. Run the query, type **1/1/2004** when prompted for the date, click the **OK** button, and then click the **Yes** button to confirm the deletion of five rows from the specified table.
9. Save the query as **qryDeleteTimeCards**, and then close it.
10. Open the **tblTimeCards** table, press the **F11** key to redisplay the Database window, and then open the **tblHours** table to check the records. The tblTimeCards table should contain five records, all dated in the year 2004. The tblHours table should contain 28 records with values in the TimeCardNo field matching one of the five values in the TimeCardNo field of the tblTimeCards table.
11. Close the tables.

When you work with action queries, take the following safeguards. Copy a table you plan to delete from or update to before you run the query. Run action queries that contain criteria as select queries first, as you did with the queries that archived and deleted the time cards and hours. A final precaution is to hide action queries in the Database window. Now, you will document and hide the queries.

To hide an object in the Database window:

1. Right-click the **qryHoursAppend** query, and then click **Properties** on the shortcut menu.
2. Type **Appends records to tblHours from imported data stored in tblTimeCardsImport** in the Description text box, and then click the **Hidden Attributes** check box. See Figure 3-26.

Figure 3-26 HIDING AN OBJECT IN THE DATABASE WINDOW

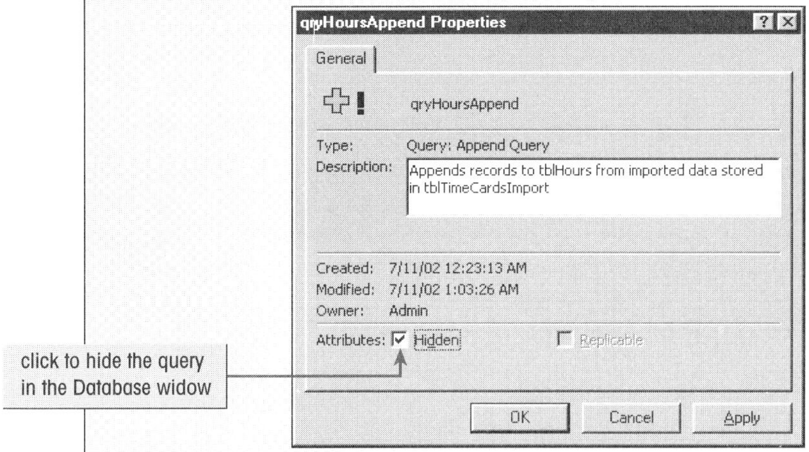

3. Click the **OK** button. The query disappears from the Database window.

   TROUBLE? If the query is still visible, but dimmed in the Database window, the option to display hidden objects in the Options dialog box (opened from the Tools menu) may have already been selected.

   After you've hidden an object, you still need to be able to display it to run or to modify it. Next, you'll redisplay the hidden query.

4. Click **Tools** on the menu bar, and then click **Options**.
5. On the View tab, click the **Hidden objects** check box to select it, and then click the **OK** button. In the Database window, you see that the qryHoursAppend query is visible, but dimmed.

You have completed the procedure for importing data, cleaning up imported data, and archiving, but you have a few more queries to write. The product managers are concerned that they won't know the new system well enough to generate the statistics they are using now in Excel. You can use a special query in Access to recombine the active and archive tables dynamically and then export the results of that query to Excel so the managers can continue to do their normal statistical analysis until they become accustomed to working with the new Access database system you are creating.

You can combine the data from the tblTimeCards table with the tblTimeCardsArchive table, and the tblHours table with the tblHoursArchive table by using a union query. You will create that query, and others, in the next session.

Session 3.2 Quick Check

1. It is a good idea to ____________ a table before you run an update query that changes the table's data.
2. The ____________ ____________ query property is used when you want to include only unique results when the query is run.
3. How do you keep users from accessing records while an action query is being run?
4. Which type of query should you use to archive only the most current data?
5. How do you hide an object, such as a table or query, in the Database window?

SESSION 3.3

In this session, you will learn about SQL-specific queries and utilize basic statements and clauses of Access SQL. You will also write a union query and export its results to Excel.

SQL-Specific Queries

Access uses a form of query language known as **Structured Query Language**, or **SQL**, which is often pronounced like the word "sequel," or by saying the three letters phonetically, as in "es-kew-el." SQL is the most common database query language used today. However, it is more than just a query language; it is a complete database management system language that gives you the capability to create components of a database, as well as to manipulate them. It is probably not necessary to use all the available commands and clauses of SQL to accomplish your assignments, but you need to explore them in order to determine which ones to use. SQL has three components:

- A data definition language to allow the creation of database components, such as tables and indexes
- A data manipulation language to allow manipulation of database components, using queries
- A data control language to provide internal security for a database

ANSI-92 SQL is the current version of SQL. Access 2002 databases use **ANSI-89 SQL**, which is the traditional SQL syntax. You can choose to set your Access 2002 databases to be ANSI-92 SQL compliant. However, Access 2002 does not implement the complete ANSI-92 standard and therefore is not considered to be fully compliant. For more information about the differences in ANSI standards, you can use the Access Help Answer Wizard to search for the associated Help topics entitled "About ANSI SQL query mode" and "Set ANSI SQL query mode."

Access adds some features of its own to the query language. For example, Access makes use of its built-in functions within SQL statements itself, as you did in the previous section with the ProperCase function. When you add expressions to create specific fields or to specify criteria for one or more fields in a query, Access embeds these expressions into the SQL statement.

Whether you use a query wizard or the grid in Design view to create your queries, it all comes down to SQL. However, SQL-specific queries cannot be generated by the query design grid; they must be written in SQL.

A subquery is an SQL statement that you may insert into the query design grid as a field expression or as criteria for an existing field. You may, of course, also incorporate a subquery into a query using the SQL View. A subquery is technically considered an SQL-specific query because you must actually type the SQL, as you did in Session 3.2 to archive data for the tblHours table.

Data-Definition Queries

Data-definition queries use the data-definition language component of SQL to create objects such as tables and indexes. The data-definition commands in Access SQL include Create Table, Alter Table, Drop Table, and Create Index. You will not create tables and indexes in SQL in the Movie3 database; however, here is an example of a data-definition query that could be used to create a table to store spouse information for your employees:

```
CREATE TABLE tblSpouses
([EmployeeID] integer,
[SpouseName] text (20),
[BirthDate] date,
[WorkPhone] text (20),
[Notes] memo,
CONSTRAINT [PrimaryKey] PRIMARY KEY ([EmployeeID]));
```

Pass-Through Queries

A pass-through query passes an SQL statement through to an external database server without trying to interpret the statement. This query is intended for the target database (such as SQL Server) to interpret and then to return only the results to Access. In other words, Access sends a pass-through query directly to the back-end database server without understanding it. Access acts as a front end in this case, yet the back-end database server may use a completely different dialect of SQL than Access. This type of query is also useful if the action you want to take is supported by your back-end database server, but not supported by Access SQL.

Another significant benefit of pass-through queries is that you can retrieve only the fields and records you want, rather than having to import an entire table from an external database server, which could alone be a great deal larger than the 2 GB limit imposed by Access on the entire database size. Keep in mind that Query recordsets are limited in size to 1 GB.

Larger companies, such as those in retail or manufacturing, may have data marts or data warehouses containing tables that are many gigabytes in size, with years of data. Trying to link directly to tables of this size and query them using Access SQL can take hours to transfer data, or even cause your ODBC connection to time out before returning any results.

Union Queries

A union query is a query that creates a union of two or more tables. In other words, this query allows you to combine data (records) from two tables with similar or the same structure.

Consider the tblHours and tblHoursArchive tables. Shortly, you will create a union query to merge the records in these two tables into one table for reporting purposes. Another example of a union query might be a mailing list composed of all the vendors stored in one table in your database and all the customers stored in another table. A union query allows you to produce a recordset that contains all the names and addresses from both tables in one listing.

Union queries cannot be created in the Query Design view, as this view is designed for applying a set of criteria to one table or for joining two or more tables in some fashion. When more than one table is added to the Query Design view, but without any join lines established, the result set is known as a "Cartesian join" where all possible combinations of rows for the tables are represented. This leads to a multiplicative result for the number of rows. In a union query, you seek an arithmetic result. For example, if both the tblHours and tblHoursArchive tables contain 28 records each, the result of a union query would be 56 records, which is the arithmetic result of adding 28 records together from each of the two tables.

If you were to add the same two tables to the Query Design view with a join line on the HoursID field, the result set would contain no records, because by definition, data in the archive table should not match any data in the active table. However, if you were to remove that join line and run the query, the result set would contain 784 records, which is the multiplicative result of multiplying 28 * 28.

In summary, when you want to combine the records from two similarly structured tables, you cannot do this in the Query Design view, but rather you must write a Union query.

Access SQL Statements, Commands, and Clauses

SQL has very few verbs. Knowledge of the basic constructs of SQL allows you to create queries that cannot be created using wizards or the grid in Design view, and can help you understand how all your queries work.

The SELECT Command

The **SELECT** command is used in an SQL statement to specify the fields you want to retrieve from a table and place in a resulting recordset. A SELECT command determines which columns, or fields, are actually displayed by the query. The simplest SQL statement, to retrieve and display all fields and all records from a table is:

SELECT *

If you use the command in a query that contains more than one table, include the table name and a period before the asterisk:

SELECT tblHours.*

This SELECT command returns all fields, but if you want to retrieve particular fields, such as TimeCardID and JobID, the SQL statement is:

SELECT TimeCardID, JobID

If the query contains more than one table, it would be:

SELECT tblHours.TimeCardID, tblHours.JobID

You also can include expressions in your SELECT command, just as you have done in the Design view grid. The following SQL statement retrieves the EmployeeNo field, combines FirstName and LastName into an EmployeeName field, and retrieves the DeptNo field:

SELECT EmployeeNo, FirstName & " " & LastName AS EmployeeName, DeptNo

Note that action queries use commands such as DELETE, INSERT INTO, and UPDATE rather than the SELECT command.

DISTINCTROW and DISTINCT Keywords

When you use the **DISTINCT** keyword, Access eliminates duplicate rows, based on the fields that you include in the query results. This also happens when you set the Unique Values property to Yes in the query Properties dialog box.

When you use the **DISTINCTROW** keyword, Access eliminates any duplicate rows based on all fields of all tables you include in the query (whether they appear in the query results or not). This also happens when you set the Unique Records property to Yes in the Properties dialog box.

For example, earlier in this tutorial you built a query to append unique values from the tblTimeCardsImport table to the tblTimeCards table. You changed the Unique Values property to Yes in that query. To write the same query in SQL, you use the DISTINCT keyword because you want all the fields displayed to be unique. Note the use of brackets around both the table name and the field name of those fields containing spaces.

SELECT DISTINCT [tblTimeCardsImport].[Time Card No],[tblTimeCardsImport].[Time Card Date], [tblTimeCardsImport].[Employee No]FROM tblTimeCardsImport;

Note there is a semicolon at the end of the SQL statement. Access does not require you to add the semicolon at the end of each SQL statement, but this is the proper syntax and you should use it to form good programming habits. Other forms of SQL and DBMS query languages that you may use in the future are not as forgiving as Access regarding this syntax. Note that when you create a query in Design View and then switch to SQL View, Access does indeed add the semicolon.

The FROM Clause

You use the **FROM** clause to specify the table or query from which the SELECT command takes its records. For example, the following SQL statement retrieves all fields from the tblHours table using the SELECT command and the FROM clause:

SELECT * FROM tblHours;

Again, in the case of more than one table in the query, you include the table name as follows:

SELECT tblHours.* FROM tblHours;

REFERENCE WINDOW RW

Creating a Query Using SQL

- Create a new query in Design view, but do not select any tables.
- Click View on the menu bar, and then click SQL View.
- Type the SQL statements and clauses.
- Save the query and close it.

Next, you'll begin writing the union query to combine records from the tblTimeCards and tblTimeCardsArchive tables.

To write a query in SQL:

1. If you took a break after the previous session, make sure that Access is running, that the **Movie3** database from the Tutorial.03\Tutorial folder on your local or network drive is open, and that **Queries** is selected in the Objects bar of the Database window.
2. Create a new query in Design view, and then close the Show Table dialog box without selecting a table.

3. Click the list arrow for the **View** button on the toolbar, and then click **SQL View**. The Query window opens in SQL view. Access automatically inserts and selects SELECT; into the otherwise empty SQL View window; if it does not, this is not a problem.
4. Type **SELECT tblHours.* FROM tblHours;** and then run the query to check the results. The recordset contains 28 records and four fields from the tblHours table.
5. Switch to SQL view.

Now you will add a WHERE clause to the query.

The WHERE Clause

You use the **WHERE** clause to limit the records that are retrieved by the SELECT command. A WHERE clause determines which rows, or records, are retrieved by a normal select query by applying criteria to any of the fields available in the underlying table(s). A WHERE clause can include up to 40 fields combined by the keywords AND and OR. A simple WHERE clause that limits the TimeCardID field in the results to 106 is:

WHERE TimeCardID = "106"

To specify which table the TimeCardID field comes from, the same clause would be written:

WHERE tblHours.TimeCardID = "106"

To combine a SELECT command, FROM clause, and WHERE clause into an SQL statement you would write:

SELECT tblHours.* FROM tblHours WHERE tblHours.TimeCardID = "106";

If only one table were included in the query, the following statement would have the same result:

SELECT * FROM tblHours WHERE TimeCardID = "106";

To add a WHERE clause in SQL:

1. Position the insertion point at the end of the SQL statement SELECT tblHours.* FROM tblHours, and then press the **Enter** key, making sure the semicolon (;) moves to the new line.
2. Type **WHERE tblHours.TimeCardID = "106";** as shown in Figure 3-27. Quotation marks are required around the number because the TimeCardID field is a text field. The line of code should end with the semicolon.

Figure 3-27 SELECT COMMAND, FROM CLAUSE, WHERE CLAUSE

3. Run the query to check your results. All four fields from the tblHours table with five records where the TimeCardID is 106 are displayed. Note that the values in the Hours ID field go from lowest to highest, and the values in the Job ID field are mixed.
4. Switch to back to SQL view.

Next, you want to sort the results by the JobID field and then by the TimeCardID field. In SQL, you use the ORDER BY clause to sort the data.

The ORDER BY Clause

The ORDER BY clause determines the order in which the returned records are sorted. It is an optional clause; an example of the ORDER BY clause is:

ORDER BY TimeCardID

The ORDER BY clause can include more than one field. When more than one field is used, just as in Design View, the far left field is the first sorted. For example, the following ORDER BY clause first sorts by the JobID field, and then by the TimeCardID field:

ORDER BY tblHours.JobID, tblHours.TimeCardID

If you combine the ORDER BY clause with the earlier query, you get the following SQL statement:

SELECT tblHours.* FROM tblHours WHERE tblHours.TimeCardID = "106" ORDER BY tblHours.JobID, tblHours.TimeCardID;

Next, you will change the query to add the ORDER BY clause.

To use the ORDER BY clause in SQL:

1. Click to position the insertion point before the semicolon at the end of the WHERE clause, and then press the **Enter** key.
2. Type **ORDER BY tblHours.JobID, tblHours.TimeCardID** (the semicolon should now be at the end of the ORDER BY clause) as shown in Figure 3-28.

Figure 3-28 **ORDER BY CLAUSE**

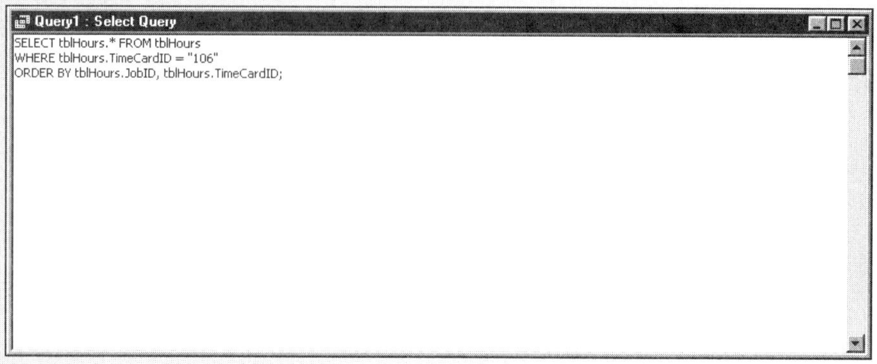

3. **Run the query and check the results.**
4. **Switch to SQL view.**

Next, you need to join the records from the tblTimeCards table to the tblHours table. Then you need to join the records from the tblTimeCardsArchive table to the tblHoursArchive table. First, you will look at the JOIN clause, and review the different types of joins possible.

The JOIN Clause

You often need to build SELECT commands that retrieve data from more than one table. When you build a SELECT command on more than one table, you must join the tables using a JOIN clause. The **JOIN** clause varies depending on whether you're using an inner join, left outer join, or right outer join.

The inner join property, the default when creating a query in the design grid, includes all the records or rows where the joined fields from both tables are equal. See Figure 3-29.

Figure 3-29 **JOIN PROPERTIES DIALOG BOX**

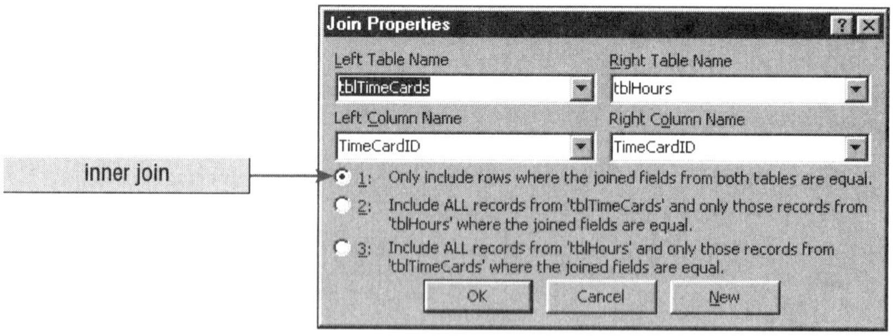

To create an inner join in SQL, you use the INNER JOIN clause. For example, to join the tblTimeCards table to the tblHours table using an inner join, you would type the following:

tblTimeCards INNER JOIN tblHours ON tblTimeCards.TimeCardID = tblHours. TimeCardID

The outer joins, left and right, are created in Design view by viewing the join properties, and choosing the appropriate join. A **left outer join** includes all records from the primary table and only the records from the related table where the joined fields from both tables are equal, as shown in Figure 3-30.

Figure 3-30 LEFT OUTER JOIN

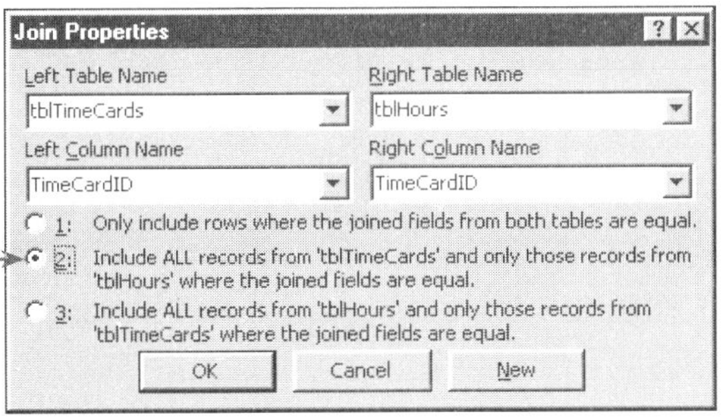

A **right outer join** includes all records from the related table and only the records from the primary table where the joined fields from both tables are equal, as shown in Figure 3-31. The SQL clauses for these are LEFT JOIN and RIGHT JOIN, respectively.

Figure 3-31 RIGHT OUTER JOIN

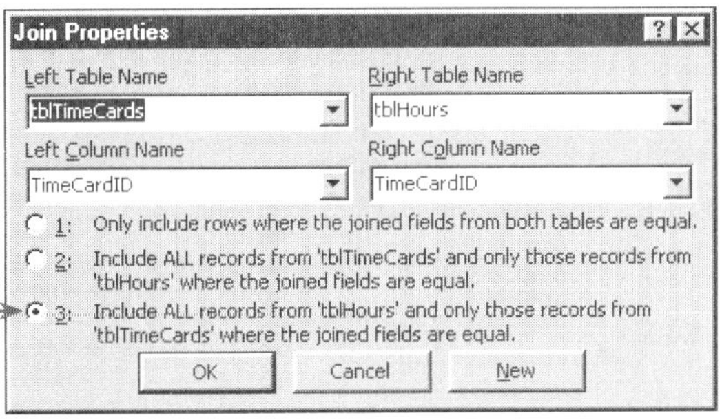

You will create the inner join between the tblTimeCards and tblHours tables next.

To use the JOIN clause in SQL:

1. Position the insertion point at the end of SELECT tblHours.*, and type **,tblTimeCards.*** (making sure to include the comma before tblTimeCards and the period and asterisk after it), and then press the **Enter** key. Delete the extra space in front of the word FROM on the second line, so it aligns to the left side of the SQL view window. See Figure 3-32.

Figure 3-32 COMPLETING THE SELECT COMMAND PORTION OF THE QUERY

2. Position the insertion point at the end of the second line, press the **spacebar**, and then type **INNER JOIN tblTimeCards ON tblHours.TimeCardID= tblTimeCards.TimeCardID** as shown in Figure 3-33.

Figure 3-33 COMPLETING THE INNER JOIN CLAUSE PORTION OF THE QUERY

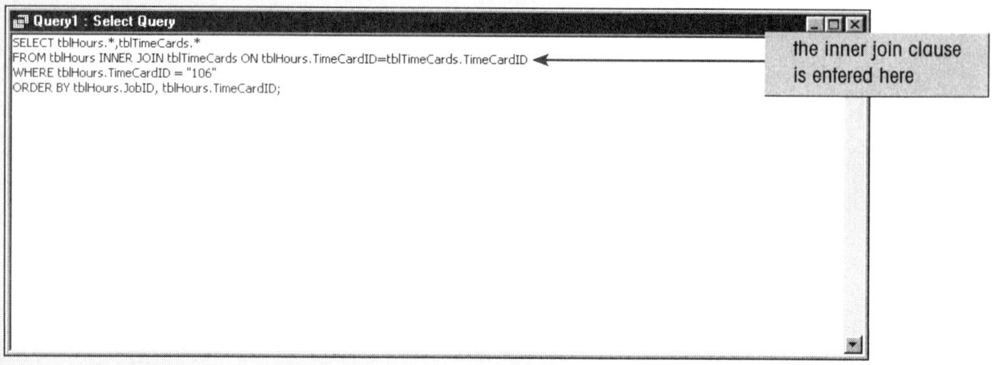

3. Run the query to check your results. All the fields from the tblHours and the tblTimeCards tables are displayed, along with five records.

4. Switch to SQL view, and then minimize this query window. You will use this query later to complete a union query.

The GROUP BY Clause and Aggregate Functions

When you want to keep rows of a query result set grouped together by some criteria, you use the **GROUP BY** clause. Another way to think about this is that a GROUP BY clause modifies the results of a SELECT command by organizing the query's recordset according to the fields named in the GROUP BY clause. For example, if your query was intended to tell you how many employees were from a particular city, you would GROUP them BY city. Once you GROUP BY city, you have to choose which aggregate function(s) to use for any field(s) which was (were) not specified as part of the GROUP BY clause.

Recall from Tutorial 3 of the New Perspectives Comprehensive Access 2002 book that Access provides a number of aggregate functions you can use to make calculations within a query, such as Sum, Avg, Min, Max, Count, StDev, Var, First, and Last. The Sum, Avg, StDev, and Var aggregate functions do not work on text. In the example here, you want to use the Count aggregate function for the employee name field. Because the employee names are correctly broken out into two fields, one called FirstName and one called LastName, you could use either of those fields, or even the EmployeeNo field for your purposes here.

To use the GROUP BY clause in SQL:

1. Create a new query in Design view, close the Show Table dialog box without selecting any tables, and then switch to SQL view. Access automatically inserts and selects SELECT;.

2. Type the following SQL statement:

   SELECT Count(tblEmployees.EmployeeNo) AS EmployeeCount, tblEmployees.City

   FROM tblEmployees

   GROUP BY tblEmployees.City;

3. Switch to the Design view to see how the query looks in the grid, as depicted in Figure 3-34. Note that the name that appears in the title bar of the query window is "Query2," unless you had other practice queries open as well. The number in the query name depends on how many queries you have created in a session and does not affect the query itself. You will save this query to a different name later.

Figure 3-34 DESIGN VIEW OF A QUERY USING A GROUP BY CLAUSE

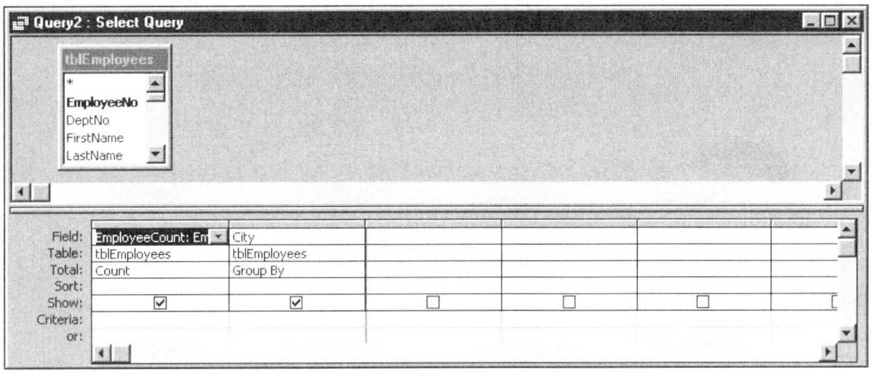

4. Run the query to test the SQL statement. The results should show the records grouped by city.

5. Switch to SQL view.

For more information about calculations in queries, aggregate functions, and the GROUP BY statement, use the Access Help Answer Wizard and search for the associated Help Topic entitled "About calculations in a query," and then select that topic for display.

The HAVING Clause

The **HAVING** clause is used in conjunction with a GROUP BY clause whenever you want to add a search condition or limiting criteria to the field(s) specified by the GROUP BY clause. Another way to think about this is that the HAVING clause essentially modifies the GROUP BY clause. The HAVING clause has its own set of criteria that you utilize to restrict the query results further. The next example returns employee counts only for cities beginning with the letter "S."

To use the HAVING clause in SQL:

1. Modify the SQL statement from Figure 3-34 in SQL view, adding the HAVING clause:

   SELECT Count(tblEmployees.EmployeeNo) AS EmployeeCount, tblEmployees.City

   FROM tblEmployees

   GROUP BY tblEmployees.City

   HAVING (((tblEmployees.City) Like "S*"));

2. Switch to the Design view to see how the query looks in the design grid, and note that the criteria *Like "S*"* has been added to the Criteria text box for the **City** field.

3. Switch to the Datasheet view and the resulting recordset should look like Figure 3-35:

Figure 3-35 RESULTS OF A QUERY USING A HAVING CLAUSE

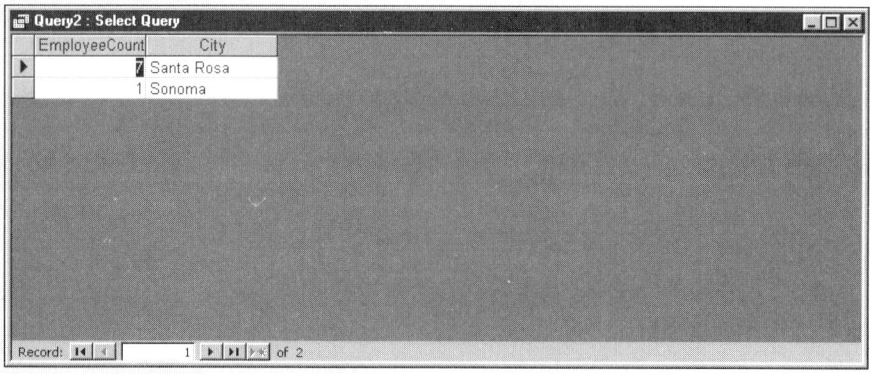

TROUBLE? Make sure you type the SQL statement exactly as indicated above, with the same number of left and right parenthesis, periods, commas and quotation marks shown.

4. Switch to SQL View.

The HAVING clause is similar to a WHERE clause, because they both apply criteria to fields in the query that further restrict or refine the query's resulting recordset. To better understand when to use the HAVING and WHERE clauses, it is helpful to understand the differences between the two clauses.

The most important distinction is that a HAVING clause can only be used in conjunction with a GROUP BY clause, yet a WHERE clause can always be used in a query. Recall that the WHERE clause limits or modifies the rows returned by the query by applying criteria to any of the fields available from the underlying table(s), whether those fields are part of the SELECT command or not. The HAVING clause can only apply criteria to the field(s) listed in the GROUP BY clause. You can use both a HAVING and a WHERE clause in the same SQL statement.

In the example shown in Figure 3-35, you limited the groupings in the query results to cities starting with the letter "S." If a manager only wanted to include employees in the aggregate count with an EmployeeNo less than 500, you could achieve this by using a criteria in a WHERE clause. Doing so would affect which employees were actually selected to be counted as part of the aggregated results, prior to the GROUP BY and HAVING clauses taking effect.

Because EmployeeNo is a text field, you need to make use of a function called the **Val** function that converts the text data type of the employee number into a numeric data type for the purposes of this query only. The syntax for using this function is Val(*stringexpr*), where *stringexpr* is any string, or ASCII text.

To use both the HAVING and WHERE clauses in SQL:

1. Modify the previous SQL statement in SQL view, adding the WHERE clause as follows:

   SELECT Count(tblEmployees.EmployeeNo) AS EmployeeCount, tblEmployees.City

   FROM tblEmployees

   WHERE Val(tblEmployees.EmployeeNo) < 500

   GROUP BY tblEmployees.City

   HAVING (((tblEmployees.City) Like "S*"));

2. Switch to the Design view to see how the query looks in the design grid.
3. Switch to the Datasheet view and resulting recordset should look like Figure 3-36.

Figure 3-36 **RESULTS OF A QUERY USING HAVING AND WHERE CLAUSES**

   TROUBLE? Make sure you type the SQL statement exactly as indicated above, with the same number of left and right parenthesis, periods, commas and quotation marks as shown.

4. Close and save the query as **zqryHavingWhere**, so you may reference it later if need be.
5. Hide this query in the Database window.

The order of query operations above is as follows: first, the fields are selected, then the records from the table are limited by the WHERE clause to only employees with an EmployeeNo less than 500, which is the first limitation placed on your resulting recordset. Next, this set of records is grouped by city so the employees can be aggregated into a count by city, further reducing the number of records in the final recordset. Finally, the HAVING clause reduces the query results to only two records, representing the employee counts for only the two cities that begin with the letter "S."

Note the differences in the resulting counts of employees from each city between the results shown in Figure 3-35 versus Figure 3-36. In both figures, the count for employees from Sonoma is 1, so that figure was not affected, but by limiting the selection of employees to only those employees with an EmployeeNo less than 500, your Santa Rosa city count of employees was reduced from 7 (see Figure 3-35) to 5 (see Figure 3-36).

Completing the UNION Query

You use the UNION operator in a query to create the union of two or more tables. The UNION ALL operator forces Access to include all records, which would then include duplicate rows. If you do not want any potential duplicate rows returned by the query results, then you must omit the word ALL and use only the UNION operator. The use of the UNION ALL operator does improve performance because the query runs faster. For example, to union the tblHours table to the tblHoursArchive table, you would use:

```
SELECT *
FROM tblHours
UNION ALL SELECT *
FROM tblHoursArchive;
```

This statement is in its simplest form and does not include references to tables, except in the FROM clauses. In the query you are creating, you need to use the UNION ALL operator to include all records from both tables. You will then construct the last half of the query that selects all the fields from both of the archive tables and joins them together on the common field, TimeCardID. If duplicate records did exist in your query results, this would actually alert you to a problem, because the same record should not appear in both your active and your archive table. You would then want to delete one of the duplicates from the appropriate table and double check your archiving process. You will complete the query next.

To complete the union query:

1. Go back to the query last shown in Figure 3-33, position the insertion point before the semicolon at the end of the line that contains the ORDER BY clause, and press the **Enter** key.

   TROUBLE? If this query is no longer open, create a new query in SQL view, enter the SQL statement as shown in Figure 3-33, and then repeat Step 1.

2. Type **UNION ALL** and then press the **Enter** key.
3. Type **SELECT tblHoursArchive.*,tblTimeCardsArchive.*** as shown in Figure 3-37.

Figure 3-37 COMPLETING THE UNION ALL AND SECOND SELECT COMMAND

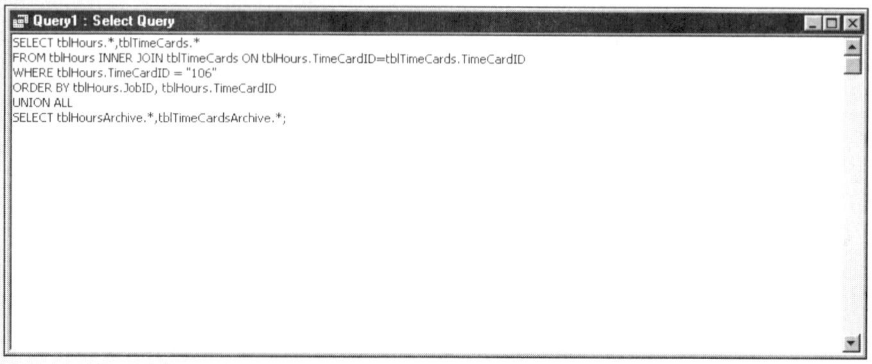

4. With the insertion point positioned before the semicolon at the end of the SELECT command that you just typed, press the **Enter** key, and then type the following as it appears here:

   FROM tblHoursArchive INNER JOIN tblTimeCardsArchive
   ON tblHoursArchive.TimeCardID=tblTimeCardsArchive.TimeCardID

5. Delete the WHERE and ORDER BY clauses and any blank rows that result. The final SQL statement should look like that shown in Figure 3-38.

Figure 3-38 UNION QUERY COMPLETED

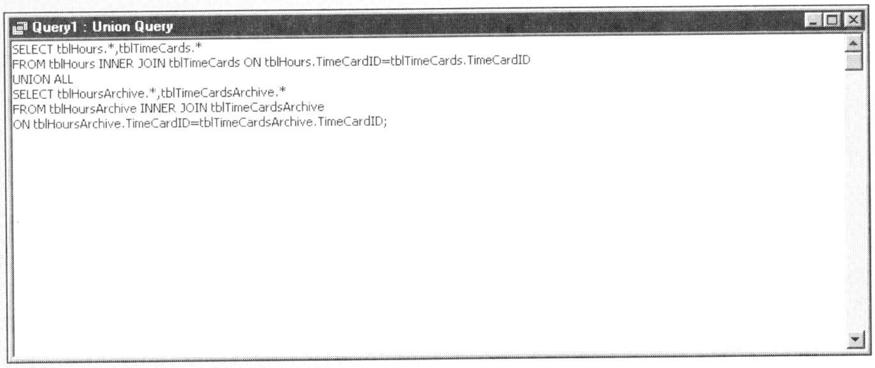

6. Run the query and check the results. All the fields from the tblTimeCards and tblTimeCardsArchive tables and from the tblHours and tblHoursArchive tables are shown. There are 56 records in the recordset.

7. Save the query as **qryUnionAllTCHours**, and then close it.

You will now export the results of the union query to Excel so that Martin can use the data with this program. You ask Martin to join you so that he can observe the process.

To analyze query results with Excel:

1. Open the **qryUnionAllTCHours** query in Datasheet view so that the resulting recordset is displayed.

2. Click **Tools** on the menu bar, point to **Office Links**, and then click **Analyze It with MS Excel**. The data now appears in an Excel worksheet (the name of a workbook file appears in the title bar).

Martin explains to you that he wants to be able to sort the data in various ways and to calculate subtotals. For example, he frequently sorts by the JobID field and then by the TimeCardDate field to get a subtotal of all the hours to date worked on the jobs.

To sort and subtotal the data in Excel:

1. Click **Data** on the Excel menu bar, and then click **Sort**.

2. Click the **Sort by** list arrow, and then click **JobID** in the list.

3. Click the **Then by** list arrow, click **TimeCardDate** in the list, and then click the **OK** button. A Sort Warning message box appears, regarding the data in the JobID field. You need to let Access know how to handle this situation.

4. Click the **Sort anything that looks like a number, as a number** option button, as shown in Figure 3-39.

Figure 3-39 EXCEL SORT WARNING

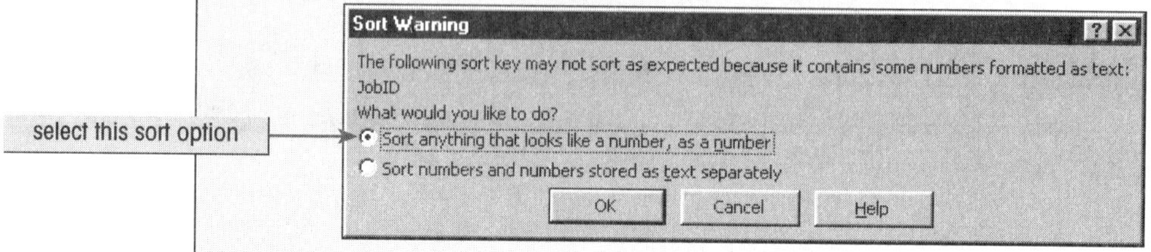

5. Click the **OK** button to close the message box.

6. Click **Data** on the menu bar, and then click **Subtotals**. The Subtotals dialog box opens.

7. Select the **JobID** field from the At each change in list box. The JobID field is the field in which Excel knows that a subtotal needs to be inserted.

8. Select the **Sum** function from the Use function list box.

9. In the Add subtotal to list box, make sure the **EmployeeNo** check box is clear, click the **HoursWorked** check box to select it, make sure no other boxes are checked, and then click the **OK** button. The subtotals display as shown in Figure 3-40.

Figure 3-40 CREATING SUBTOTALS IN AN EXCEL WORKSHEET

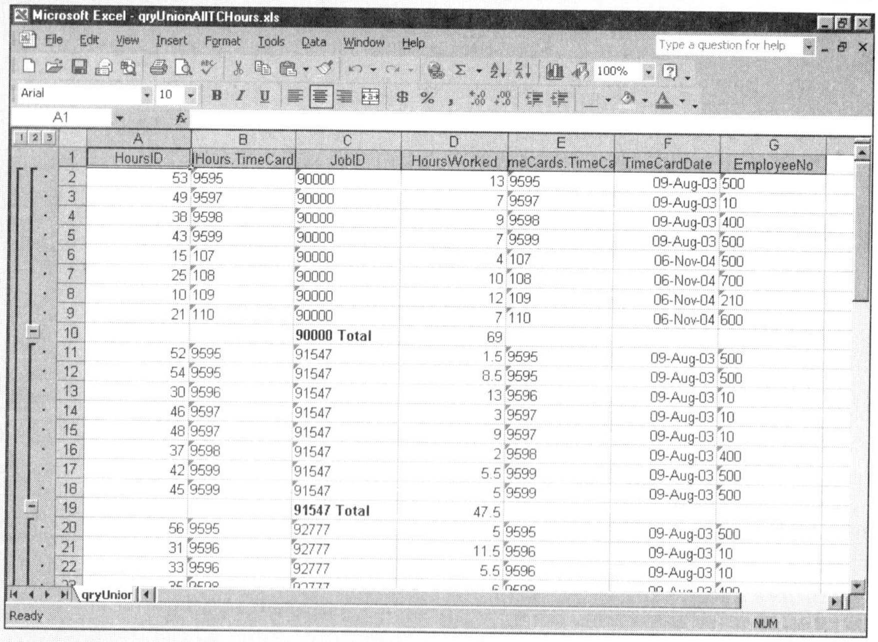

10. Close Excel to return to Access, saving your changes.

11. Close the query, close the Movie3 database, and then exit Access.

Now that you've completed the queries to append, archive, and compile the data, the actual importing and conversion of the historical data should run smoothly.

Session 3.3 QUICK CHECK

1. The current version of SQL is ____________.
2. Name the four SQL-specific queries covered in this tutorial.
3. The SELECT command in SQL is used to specify the ____________.
4. Using the DISTINCT keyword is the same as setting the ____________ property in a query.
5. The WHERE clause is used to limit the records retrieved by the ____________ command.
6. What is an inner join?
7. What is a right outer join?
8. The ____________ operator in SQL is used to create the union of two or more tables.

REVIEW ASSIGNMENTS

The Hours3 database has been modified slightly from Tutorial 2. It was determined that the tblTimeCards table was not necessary because the week-ending date isn't used for reporting purposes and the time card numbers are not tracked. The hours that an employee works is entered directly into the tblHours table. This table is related on the many side of a one-to-many relationship with the tblEmployees table. In this assignment, you import data from an Excel worksheet and write the append queries to append the data to the tblEmployees and tblHours tables. Complete the following:

1. Start Access and open the **Hours3** database located in the Tutorial.03\Review folder on your local or network drive.
2. Use the Import Spreadsheet Wizard to import the Hours3 Excel file from the Tutorial.03\Review folder on your local or network drive. (*Hint*: Be sure to set the Files of type option to Microsoft Excel). Make sure that the option for specifying that the first row contains field names is selected. Import the data into a new table. Do not set a primary key. Name the table **tblEmloyeesImport**.
3. Create a new query in Design view, and add the tblEmloyeesImport table to the Select Query window.
4. Create the following expressions in the query:

   FirstName:Left([EmployeeName],InStr([EmployeeName]," ")-1)

   LastName:Right([EmployeeName],Len([EmployeeName])-InStr ([EmployeeName]," "))
5. Add all fields to the query, *except* the EmployeeName, DateWorked, HoursWorked, and ProductNo fields.
6. Run the query to test the results.
7. Return to Design view, change the Unique Values property to Yes, and then run the query to test the results.
8. Change the query to an append query, and select tblEmployees as the table to append. All fields match up automatically because the names in the Excel file match the names in the table.
9. Run the query to append the records, save the query as **qryEmployeesAppend**, and then close the query.
10. Create another new query in Design view, and add the EmployeeNo, DateWorked, HoursWorked, and ProductNo fields from the tblEmployeesImport table to the design grid.
11. Change the query to an append query, and select tblHours as the table to append.
12. Run the query, save it as **qryHoursAppend**, and then close the query.
13. Copy and paste the structure of the tblHours table to the tblHoursArchive table.
14. Open the **tblHoursArchive** table in Design view, and change the HoursID field to a Number data type. Close the table and save your changes.

15. Create a new query to append the old data to the archive table. Add all the fields from the tblHours table to the design grid. Enter **<#1/1/04#** in the appropriate row inthe DateWorked column, change the query to an append query, select tblHoursArchive as the table to append, make sure that the fields match, and then run the query. Save the query as **qryHoursArchive**, and then close the query.

16. Create a new query to delete the data that you archived. Follow the instructions provided in Step 15 *except* change the query to a delete query. The criteria is the same. Run the query, save it as **qryDeleteArchivedHours**, and then close the query.

17. Create a union query in SQL view to union the records in the tblHours table with the records in the tblHoursArchive table. The query should be written as follows:

    SELECT * FROM tblHours
    UNION ALL
    SELECT * FROM tblHoursArchive;

18. Run the query to test the results, save the query as **qryUnionHours**, and then close it.

Explore 19. Create another union query that is identical to qryUnionHours *except* sort this query in descending order by the EmployeeNo field. Save the query as **qryUnionHoursSort**.

Explore 20. To begin tracking employee demographics, Human Resources wants to have a quick way to see employee counts by city and state as the company grows. Create a select query using the tblEmployees table. Add the EmployeeNo, City, and State fields. Change the query to an aggregation query. (*Hint*: Click the Totals button on the toolbar.) Group by the City and State fields, and count by the EmployeeNo field. Run the query. You should see three records, one for each city, with employee number counts. Save the query as **qryEmployeeCountByCityState**.

21. Close the Hours3 database and then exit Access.

CASE PROBLEMS

Case 1. Edwards and Company Jack Edwards has a list of clients that he exported from another software program into a text file. He wants you to import this data so that you can create a mailing list and run labels for all the clients and consultants in the database. He plans to do several different mailings to these people, so he needs the list sorted in ascending order by zip codes. He wants the CompanyName field in the tblClients table, the FirstName field and the LastName field from the tblConsultants table concatenated in to one field, and the Address, City, State, and ZipCode data in the remaining fields. You need to build a union query to accomplish this task.

Complete the following:

1. Start Access and open the **Edward3** database located in the Tutorial.03\Cases folder on your local or network drive.
2. Use the Import Text Wizard to import the Edward3 tab-delimited text file from the Tutorial.03\Cases folder on your local or network drive.

3. Specify that the first row contains field names, indicate that the data will be imported into a new table, change the data type of the ConsultantID and ZipCode fields to Text, do not set a primary key, and then enter **tblClientsImport** as the name of the table.
4. Open the **tblClientsImport** table in Datasheet view to verify Access imported four records, and then close the table.
5. Create a new query in Design view, and then add all the fields from the tblClientsImport table to the design grid *except* ClientID.
6. Change the query to an append query, select tblClients as the table to append, and then run the query. Save the query as **qryClientsAppend**, and then close it.
7. Create a new query in SQL view, and enter the following SQL statement:

   SELECT CompanyName, Address1, City, State, ZipCode FROM tblClients

   UNION ALL

   SELECT FirstName&" "&LastName, Address, City, State, ZipCode FROM tblConsultants

   ORDER BY ZipCode;
8. Run the query to check the results.
9. Save the query as **qryUnionClientsConsultants**, and then close the query.

Explore

10. Create another union query in SQL view that *selects* CompanyName, Address1, City & " " & State & " " & ZipCode AS Address2 from the tblClients table and *unions* it to FirstName & " " & LastName, Address, City & " " & State & " " & ZipCode AS Address2 *from* the tblConsultants table. Do not sort the results. The resulting query will display three columns: CompanyName, Address1, Address2. Run the query, save it as **qryUnionClientsConsultants2**, and then close it.
11. Close the Edward3 database and then exit Access.

Case 2. San Diego County Information Systems Richard Johnson from the Human Resources Department recently e-mailed an Excel spreadsheet to you that contains employee data. The file has some of the same data that you track for students who are employees of the county. He wants to share information after you complete your database and will send you a complete list of employees if this one is helpful to you.

You will import the data and write the queries necessary to update and append the appropriate tables. Complete the following:

1. Start Access and open the **ISD3** database located in the Tutorial.03\Cases folder on your local or network drive.
2. Use the Import Spreadsheet Wizard to import the ISD3 Excel file from the Tutorial.03\Cases folder on your local or network drive.
3. Make sure that the option for specifying that the first row contains column names is selected. Import the data into a new table. Do not set a primary key. Name the table **tblStudentsImport**.

4. Open the **tblStudentsImport** table in Datasheet view to see the 19 records, then close it.
5. Create a new query in Design view, and add the tblStudentsImport table to the Select Query window.
6. Create the following expressions in the query:

   FirstName: Left([EmployeeName],InStr([EmployeeName]," ")-1)

   LastName: Right([EmployeeName],Len([EmployeeName])-InStr([EmployeeName]," "))
7. Add the EMPLOYEEID, DEPARMENT, and TELEPHONE fields to the design grid.
8. Change the query to an append query, select tblStudents as the table to append, and make sure that the fields match up to the fields in the table (EMPLOYEEID should be appended to StudentNo and DEPARTMENT to DeptNo).
9. Run the query, save it as **qryStudentsAppend**, and then close the query.
10. Import the Microsoft Access Samples database from the Tutorial.03 folder on your local or network drive, and then import the mdlUtilityFunctions module object.
11. Copy the structure and data of the tblStudents table in the Database window and save the copy with the name **tblStudentsCopy**. This copy is a backup in case you make a mistake in the update query you will write next.
12. Create a new query in Design view. Add the FirstName and LastName fields from the tblStudents table to the design grid. Change the query to an update query, and enter the following expressions in the Update To row of the design grid:

    ProperCase([FirstName])

    ProperCase([LastName])
13. Run the query, save it as **qryUpdateNames**, and then close the query.
14. Open the **tblStudents** table in Datasheet view, print the records, and then close the table.

Explore

15. Research the Strconv function and then use it rather than the ProperCase function to convert text to proper case.
    a. Double-click the mdlUtilityFunctions module to open it in the Visual Basic Editor window. Use Microsoft Visual Basic Help to find information on the Strconv function. What is the correct syntax for the function? How many arguments does this function have and how many are required? What syntax would be required to convert the data in the EMPLOYEENAME field to proper case? Close Help, close the Visual Basic window, and then close the mdlUtilityFunctions module.
    b. Create a new query in Design view, and add the tblStudentsImport table to the Select Query window. Create an expression named **NameProper** that uses the Strconv function to convert the EMPLOYEENAME field to proper case. Run the query to check the results, and save it as **qryEmployeeNames**.
16. Close the query, close the ISD3 database, and then exit Access.

Case 3. Christenson Homes After you met with Roberta Christenson to discuss the design you created for her database, you made a few changes to the earlier structure. You added a table for customer data because there is often more than one buyer of a home. The relationship between the tblLots and tblCustomers tables is a one-to-many relationship to allow for additional buyers.

Roberta exported some of the data from her accounting system to a tab-delimited text file and has asked you to import it into Access. You will then write queries to format the imported data the way she asked to see it in the database. Complete the following:

1. Start Access and open the **Homes3** database located in the Tutorial.03\Cases folder on your local or network drive.
2. Use the Import Text Wizard to import the Homes3 tab-delimited text file from the Tutorial.03\Cases folder on your local or network drive to a new table. Specify that the first row contains field names. Change the ZipCode field to a Text data type. Do not set a primary key. Import the data to a new table named **tblCustomersImport**.
3. Create a new query in Design view, and add the tblCustomersImport table to the Select Query window.
4. Using the string functions from this tutorial as a guide, create expressions in the query to extract first and last names from the CUSTOMERNAME field. Then add the remaining fields to the query.
5. Change the query to an append query and select tblCustomers as the table to append.
6. Save the query as **qryCustomersAppend**, run it, and then close the query.
7. Import the module mdlUtilityFunctions from the Samples database located in the Tutorial.03 folder on your local or network drive.
8. Make a copy of the tblCustomers table in the current database, include structure and data, and name it **tblCustomersCopy**.
9. Write an update query. Use the ProperCase function in expressions to update all the text fields that are in uppercase (leave the State field in uppercase).
10. Run the query, save it as **qryUpdateNames**, and then close the query.

Explore

11. Create a new query based on the tblCustomers table. Name the query **qryCustomer CountZipCode**. Make it an aggregation query using the CustomerID and ZipCode fields. Group on the zip code and count on the customer IDs. Apply criteria to the zip code that limits the records returned to only those zip codes beginning with 954. (*Hint*: In SQL, you need to use a SELECT query with GROUP BY and HAVING clauses.) Run the query. The results should show five records, representing five different zip codes. Four of the zip codes will show a count of only one customer, and zip code 95402 will reflect a count of two customers. As the company grows, this query could be expanded to help provide customer demographic information to the sales force.
12. Close the Homes3 database and exit Access.

Case 4. Sonoma Farms The Sonoma Farms database has been redesigned to eliminate the tblVisits table. After you work with sample data, you decide that the tblVisits table information is not necessary, but a new field in the tblVisitors table that includes the CustomerID does meet your needs.

Now you want to import some historical data from one of your spreadsheets. Then you will construct a query to combine data from the tblDistributors and tblCustomers tables. You want to use the data for a promotional mailing. Complete the following:

1. Start Access and open the **Sonoma3** database located in the Tutorial.03\Cases folder on your local or network drive.
2. Use the Spreadsheet Import Wizard to import the Sonoma3 Excel file in the Tutorial.03\Cases folder on your local or network drive. Do not set a primary key. Save the file as **tblVisitorsImport**.
3. Open the **tblVisitorsImport** table in Datasheet view, print the imported records, and then close the table.
4. Write a query to extract the first name and last name from the VISITORNAME field, and then append these two fields (FirstName and LastName) plus the remaining fields to the tblVisitors table.
5. Save the query as **qryVisitorsAppend**, and then close the query.
6. Import the module mdlUtilityFunctions from the Samples database located in the Tutorial.03 folder on your local or network drive.
7. Write an update query using the ProperCase function to convert the FirstName and LastName in the tblVisitors table to the proper case.
8. Save the query as **qryUpdateNames**, and then close the query.
9. Convert the data in the Gifts field to lowercase. (*Hint*: Use the Format property of the field in the table.)
10. Write a union query in SQL to create a list from the tblCustomers and tblDistributors tables. The list should include the Name, Address1, City, State, and ZipCode fields from each table.
11. Sort the query by ZipCode, run it to check the results, and then print the results.
12. Save the query as **qryUnionCustomersDistributors**, and then close the query.
13. Close the Sonoma3 database and exit Access.

QUICK CHECK ANSWERS

Session 3.1

1. Linking is a better method if the data is going to be used in its original format and in Access.
2. delimiter
3. data conversion
4. The InStr function returns the position of a particular character from a string of text.
5. Len

Session 3.2

1. copy (or backup)
2. Unique Values
3. You use the Record Locks property, which specifies whether the records in a multiuser environment are locked so that users cannot access them while a query is being run.
4. Check the object's hidden attribute property so it won't display (or will be dimmed) in the Database window.

Session 3.3

1. ANSI-92
2. Data-definition queries, union queries, pass-through queries, and subqueries
3. columns (or *fields*) you want to retrieve
4. Unique Values
5. SELECT
6. An inner join includes all the records from the two tables where the joined fields are equal.
7. A right outer join includes all records from the related table and only the records from the primary table where the joined fields from both tables are equal.
8. UNION

OBJECTIVES

In this tutorial you will:

- Review form design guidelines
- Create a form template
- Create form masters
- Use templates and masters to create data entry forms
- Apply expressions to refer to a subform
- Use the column property of a combo box
- Create a switchboard containing an option group
- Understand macros and macro group-naming conventions
- Write a macro containing a conditional expression

DESIGNING COMPLEX FORMS

Building the User Interface for the MovieCam Technologies Database

CASE

MovieCam Technologies

Amanda is pleased with the progress that you have made on the MovieCam Technologies database. She approved the design and is satisfied that the importing and archiving processes will run smoothly.

Amanda asks that you now begin work on the forms for the user interface of the database. She wants you to identify and create the forms necessary for data entry, keeping in mind that the users of the system are not familiar with Access and do not have a lot of time to learn more about it. She also wants you to design switchboards that will prevent users from seeing the Database window, thereby eliminating the possibility of them unintentionally modifying or deleting a database object (for example, a table, query, or form).

Your goal, therefore, is to develop standardized forms that do not require a significant amount of training to use and to design switchboards that contain all the controls end users need to work within the database.

SESSION 4.1

In this session, you will study form design guidelines. You will create a form template and then set it as the database default form template. You will also create a form master to use as the basis for data entry forms. You will create data entry forms based on the template and master forms, add a subform to a main form, and make form changes based on the design guidelines. Finally, you will work with expressions designed to further enhance the user-friendliness of forms.

Introduction to Forms

Access forms are classified as either bound or unbound. **Bound forms** are tied to a table or a query. They are used for editing, entering, and reviewing data in those underlying tables and queries. **Unbound forms** are not tied to a table or query and are used to create an interface that provides the users controlled access to the application. An unbound form that is used to navigate to other forms and reports in the database is referred to as a **switchboard**. In most cases, you design a switchboard to display upon opening the database application and hide the Database window. The switchboard contains controls for only those objects to which you want the user to have access. Figure 4-1 shows the design and format of a typical switchboard. It includes a command button to open the data entry forms switchboard, a command button to open the Reports switchboard, and a command button to exit Access. Access includes a Switchboard Manager tool, which creates a different type of switchboard than you will be creating here.

Figure 4-1 SAMPLE SWITCHBOARD

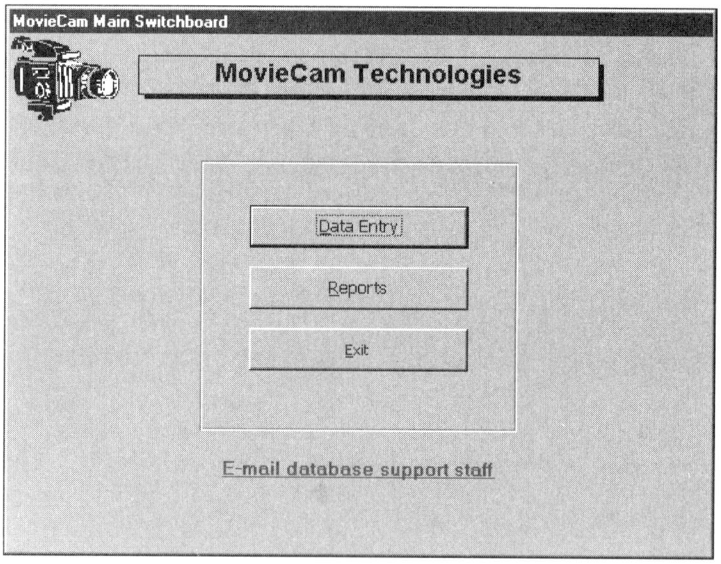

A splash screen is another type of unbound form. A **splash screen** form opens automatically when a database is opened, and its purpose is to give the user something to view while the application is loading. A sample splash screen is shown in Figure 4-2.

Figure 4-2 SAMPLE SPLASH SCREEN

Before leaving the company, Jason had created some of the data entry forms for the MovieCam Technologies database. However, changing the same properties over and over and adding the same controls to the forms is tedious. You suggest that it would be prudent to develop a form template you can use to design the rest of the forms. You can apply all the common properties that are characteristic of the forms to the form template, and then build individual forms using the template's basic structure and design. You also suggest creating a form master, which can contain items such as a company logo, company name, and other standard controls that you want to be part of any newly created form or switchboard.

Form Design

The user interface is one of the most important features you need to consider as you design forms. The **user interface** is the mechanism by which the user communicates and interacts with the application. From the user's perspective, the user interface is the application. In most instances, you design the user interface assuming the end user does not want to spend a lot of time learning how to use the application. Some design guidelines for meeting this goal are:

- If the application runs on the Windows platform, design your interface to look and feel like Windows. Because Access runs on Windows, Access database forms should look similar to the dialog boxes you see in the Access application, as well as other Office applications. For example, use option groups when you want the user to select only one option from a group of task-related options, and use check boxes when the user can select several options from a group of task-related options. Text boxes in which the user enters or edits data should have a white background and the sunken special effect. For controls the users cannot change, use flat text boxes with the same background color as the form. Figure 4-3 illustrates these examples.

Figure 4-3 EXAMPLE OF CONTROLS IN A DIALOG BOX

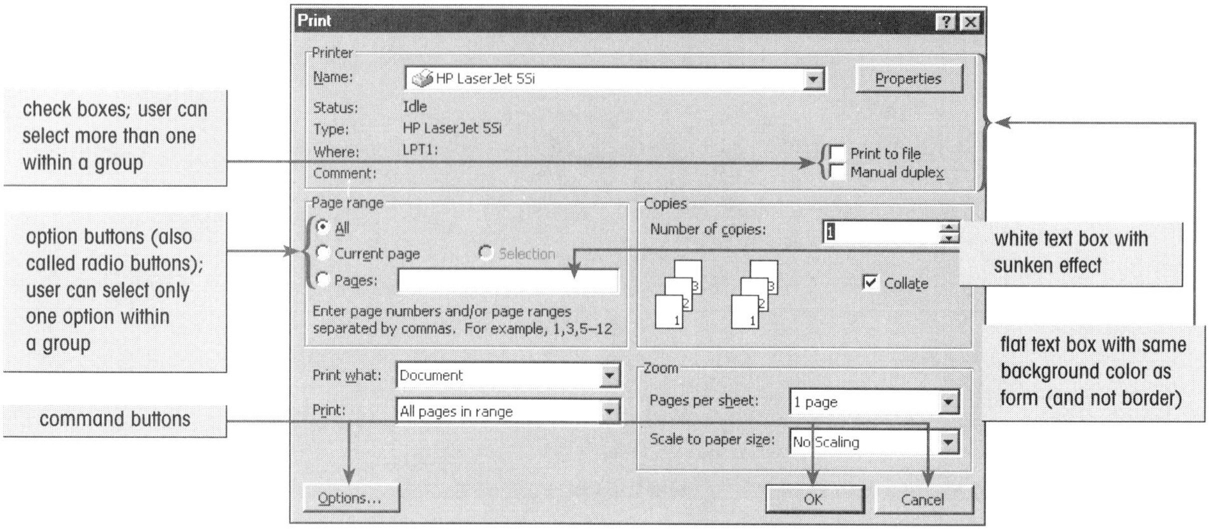

- Simple is better. Avoid the use of too many colors or fonts. It is visually confusing. Align controls and use rectangles to group information. The standard Windows look includes gray forms, as illustrated in the Print dialog box shown in Figure 4-3.
- Be direct. Provide linear, intuitive ways to accomplish tasks. Apply tab order (the order in which the focus moves from one control to the next) on forms to reinforce the visual order of the controls. Organize controls logically, based on how the user enters the data. Add keystroke shortcuts to command buttons and menu commands.
- Provide users with feedback. Create ScreenTip messages, such as shown in Figure 4-4. A **ScreenTip** is a message that appears when the pointer is positioned on a control on a form or on a button on a toolbar. Messages should be short and informative.

Figure 4-4 SCREENTIP MESSAGE ON A FORM

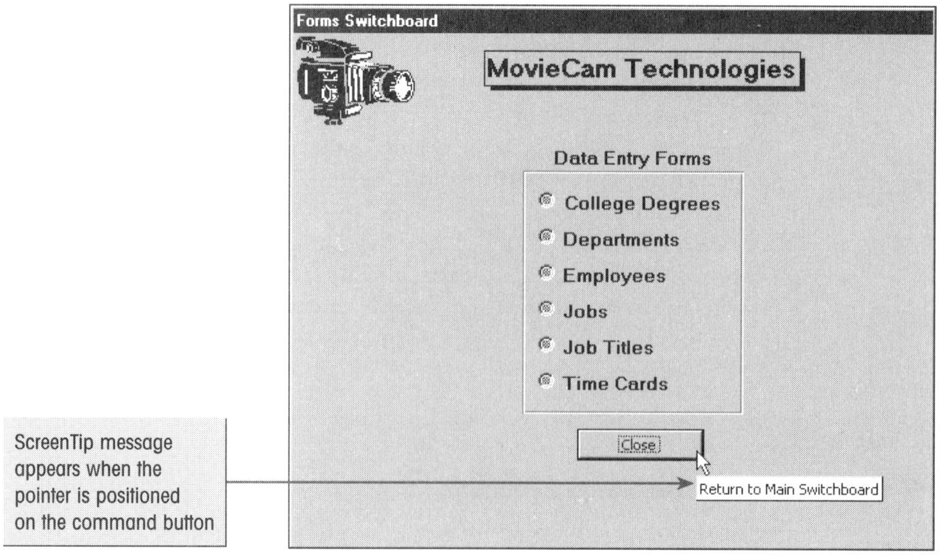

Visual consistency is another important consideration in form design. All forms in a database application should have the same color scheme and font properties, and the same consistent visual cues for controls. Form templates and masters help you achieve this consistency.

Creating a Form Template

A **form template** is a form on which you base other forms you create in the database. The template determines which sections a form will have and defines the dimensions of each section. A form template also contains the default property settings for the form, its sections, and controls.

When you create a form without using a wizard, Access uses the default template named *Normal* to determine the characteristics mentioned above. Creating a custom form template with new property settings and identifying it as your database's default template allows you to standardize properties for all forms in your database. You can reset the default template on the Forms/Reports tab in the Options dialog box.

REFERENCE WINDOW RW

Creating a Form Template

- Click Forms on the Objects bar in the Database window.
- Double-click the Create form in Design view option.
- Click the Properties button on the toolbar, change default control, section, and form properties as needed, and then close the property sheet.
- Save the form with a name that indicates that it is a template form, and then close the form window.
- Click Tools on the menu bar, and then click Options.
- Click the Forms/Reports tab, type the template form name in the Form template text box, and then click the OK button.

You now will create the form template for MovieCam Technologies. The template will contain a Form Header/Footer section. You will set a size for it, and you will set properties to eliminate record selectors and dividing lines. Because only one record is displayed in the form at a time, there is no need for a record selector.

To create a form template:

1. Start Access and then open the **Movie4** database located in the Tutorial.04\Tutorial folder on your local or network drive.
2. Click **Forms** on the Objects bar in the Database window, and then double-click **Create form in Design view**.
3. Click **View** on the menu bar, and then click **Form Header/Footer**. Be sure to select the form-related option and not the page-related option.
4. Maximize the form window to make it easier to size the form.
5. Position the pointer at the bottom edge of the Form Header section until it changes to a ✛ shape, and then drag the edge down to the ¾" mark on the vertical ruler.
6. Position the pointer on the right edge of the form until it changes to a ✛ shape, and then drag to the 6½" mark on the horizontal ruler.

7. Position the pointer at the bottom edge of the Detail section until it changes to a ✛ shape, and then drag down to the 3" mark on the vertical ruler.

8. Position the pointer on the bottom edge of the Form Footer section until it changes to a ✛ shape, and then drag down to the ½" mark on the vertical ruler.

9. Scroll to the top of the form, select the form by clicking the **form selector**, which is the box in the upper-left corner of the form where the two ruler bars meet. Note that when a form is selected a small black square appears in the middle of the form selector. The form selector is not a toggle button; clicking it again does not deselect the form.

10. Click the **Properties** button on the Form Design toolbar, and then click the **All** tab on the property sheet if necessary. See Figure 4-5.

Figure 4-5 FORM'S PROPERTY SHEET

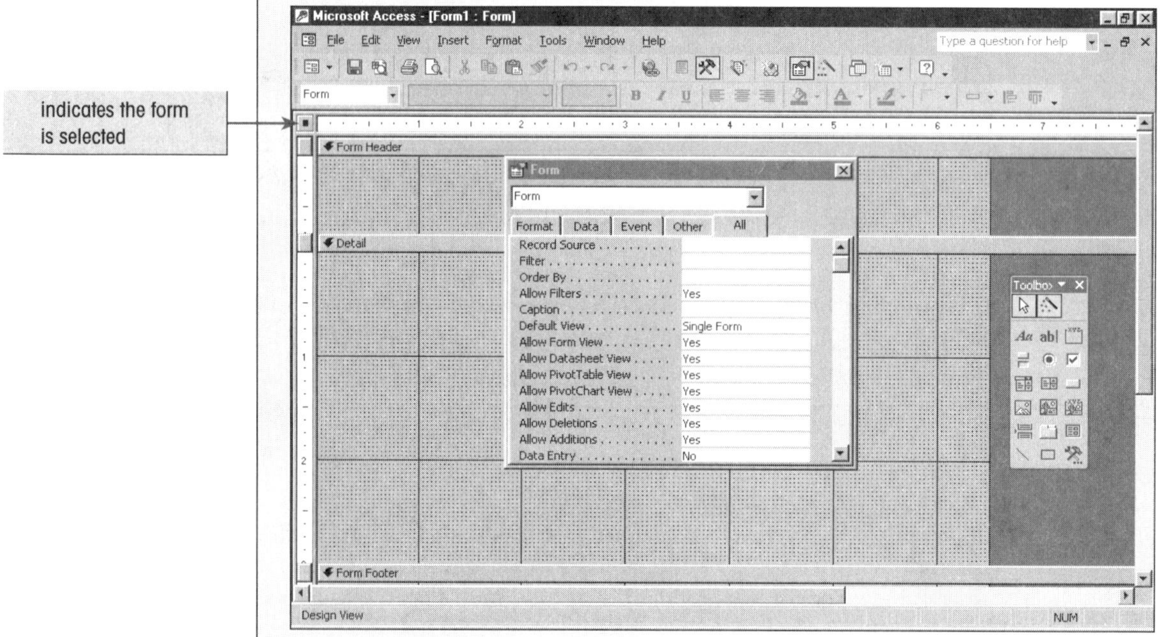

11. Scroll down the list of properties, and then change the Record Selectors property to **No** and the Dividing Lines property to **No**. This action removes the objects identified in Figure 4-6. Record selectors are not necessary on most of your MovieCam database forms. Dividing lines show the end of one form section and the beginning of another.

Figure 4-6 **ELIMINATING RECORD SELECTORS AND DIVIDING LINES**

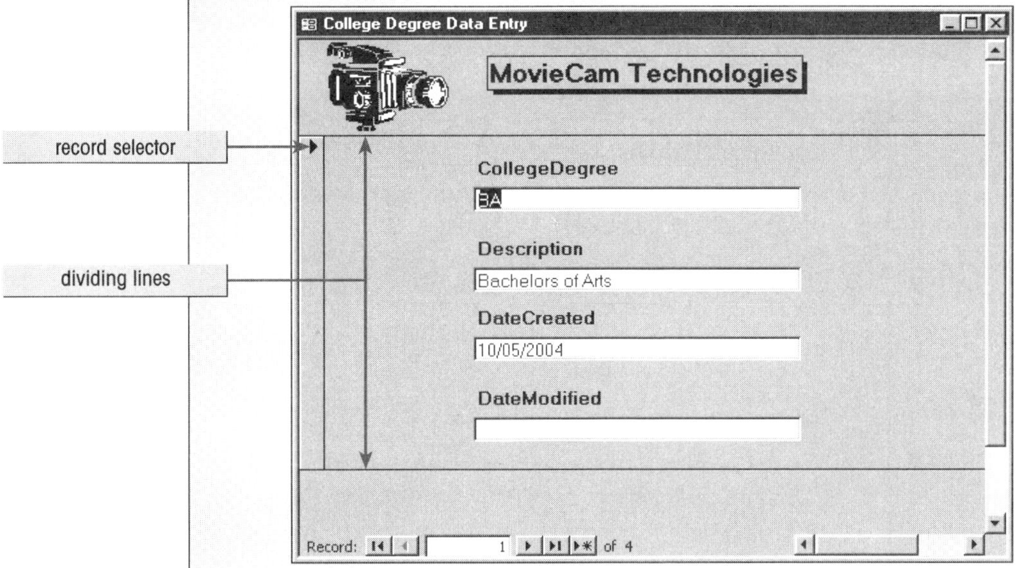

12. Click **File** on the menu bar, click **Save As**, and then type **dmfrmTemplate** in the Save Form 'Form1' To text box. The tag prefix "dm" can be used to identify objects that are part of the development and maintenance of your database application. Users normally do not work with these objects, so before moving your database application to production, you should hide them as shown in the previous tutorial. The "d" denotes development and the "m" denotes maintenance.
13. Click the **OK** button to close the Save As dialog box, and leave the form open.

Now you will focus on customizing the template's properties.

Changing Default Properties of Toolbox Controls

The properties of a toolbox control can be changed by selecting the toolbox control and then opening its property sheet. Modifying the properties of a control in the form template affects the use of that control in new forms based on the template.

Next you'll change some of the default controls on the template you created. The default Font Size of labels and text boxes is 8 point, which you think is too small. The default Font Weight is normal, but you want the labels to be semi-bold. When you insert a text box, the default position of its label is to the left of the text box, but for the most part, you want the label positioned above the text box.

To change the default properties of controls:

1. With the form's property sheet still open and the toolbox is visible, click the **Label** button Aa on the toolbox. The Default Label properties are now listed in the property sheet, as shown in Figure 4-7.

Figure 4-7 PROPERTIES OF THE TOOLBOX'S DEFAULT LABEL BUTTON

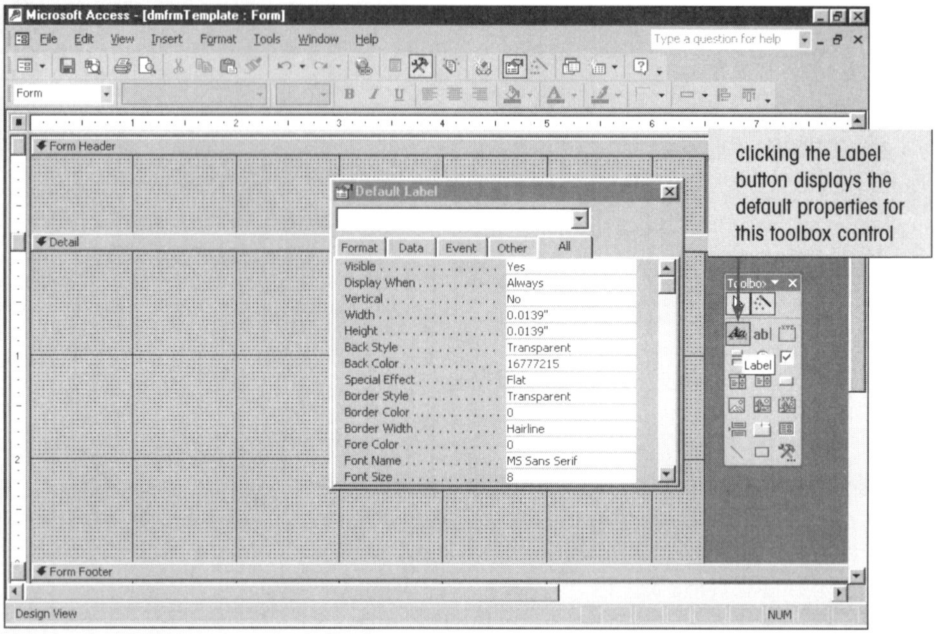

2. Make sure the Visible property is set to **Yes**, scroll down the list, and then change the Font Size property to **10** and the Font Weight property to **Semi-bold**.

   Now you will change the default settings for the Text Box control.

3. Click the **Text Box** button ab| on the toolbox so it displays the default Text Box properties in the property sheet.
4. Change the Font Size property to **10**.
5. Change the Label X property to **0** and the Label Y property to **-0.25**. Next when you add a Text Box control to a form, its accompanying label control will be positioned above the text box, instead of to its left. This is not always desirable, but it serves to illustrate this capability.
6. Change the Text Align and Label Align properties to **Left**.
7. Change the Add Colon property to **No** to eliminate the colon in the label.
8. Close the property sheet, and then restore the form window so it is no longer maximized.
9. Click the **Save** button on the Form Design toolbar to save the changes you have made, and then close the form.

After you complete the design of the form template, you will set it as the default for any new forms you create.

To set the dmfrmTemplate as the default:

1. Click **Tools** on the menu bar, and then click **Options**. The Options dialog box opens.

2. Click the **Forms/Reports** tab.
3. Double-click the text in the Form template text box, and then press the **Delete** key.
4. Type **dmfrmTemplate** and then click the **OK** button. The Options dialog box closes, and the dmfrmTemplate form has now been set as the default.

Creating Form Masters

A custom form template represents the basic structure for all forms in the database and determines the dimensions, properties, and form sections of new forms. It cannot contain any controls, however. To add the same controls to forms in a database, such as a label control for the company name or an image control for a company logo, you can create a form master. A **form master** is a form that contains the controls that are common to all forms in the database. Unlike a template, new forms created in the database do not inherit the characteristics of the form master. However, the form master can be copied and pasted to create new forms. You decide that all data entry forms should contain the company logo and the company name.

To create a data entry form master:

1. Create a new form in Design view. The form is automatically based on dmfrmTemplate.
2. Click the **Label** button on the toolbox, position the pointer in the Form Header section at the 1½" mark on the horizontal ruler and the ¼" mark on the vertical ruler, and then drag to create a label approximately 2½" wide and a little more than ¼" tall.
3. Type **MovieCam Technologies** inside the label control, and then press the **Enter** key. The text is entered in the control, and the control is automatically selected.
4. Click the **Font Size** list arrow on the Formatting (Form/Report) toolbar, and then click **14**. The text should already be bold, based on the Font Weight property you set for the default label control.
5. Click the list arrow on the **Special Effect** button on the Formatting toolbar, and then click **Special Effect: Shadowed**.
6. Resize and reposition the label as shown in Figure 4-8. Note that the size and position of the label does not have to be exact, but as close as possible to that shown in the figure.

   TROUBLE? If you are having trouble positioning the label control, open its property sheet, set the Left property to 1.5" and the Top property to 0.125", and set the Width property to 2.5" and the Height property to 0.3". Close the property sheet.

Figure 4-8 FORMATTED LABEL ON THE FORM MASTER

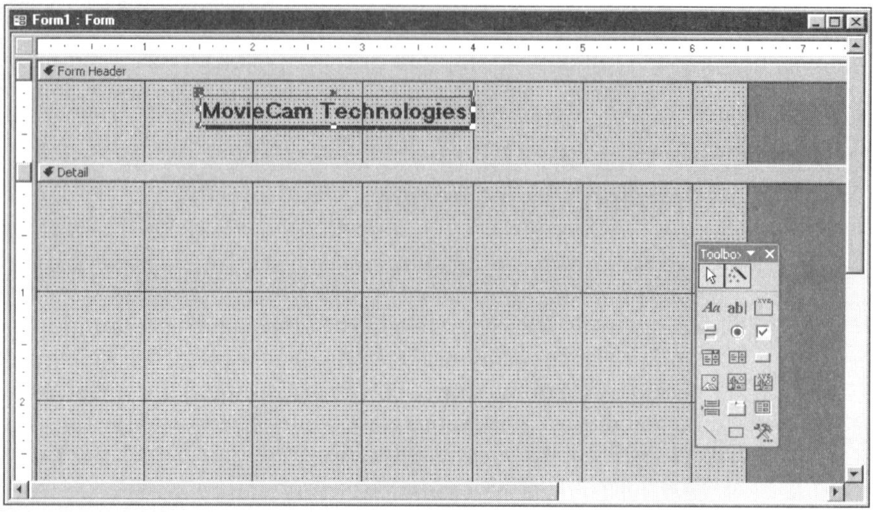

7. Save the form as **dmfrmMaster**.

Next you will use the Image button on the toolbox to create a control in which you will embed the company logo in the form master.

REFERENCE WINDOW RW

Adding a Picture to a Form

- Display the form in Design view.
- Click the Image button on the toolbox.
- Position the pointer on the form where you want the upper-left corner of the picture to be inserted.
- Click to place an image control in the form.
- Navigate to the drive and folder in which the picture file you want to insert is stored.
- Click the name of the picture file, and then click the OK button.

In addition to the company name, you decide to insert the company logo in the Form Header of the master.

To add a picture to a form:

1. Click the **Image** button on the toolbox, position the pointer in the upper-left corner of the Form Header section, and then drag to create an image control that is 1" wide by 3/4" tall. Note that you can just click to create an image control that uses default settings, or as instructed here you can drag the image pointer to create the image control in the size you want. The Insert Picture dialog box opens.

2. Click the **Look in** list arrow, navigate to the Tutorial.04\Tutorial folder on your local or network drive, and then make sure the **Logo** file is selected, as shown in Figure 4-9.

Figure 4-9 **INSERT PICTURE DIALOG BOX**

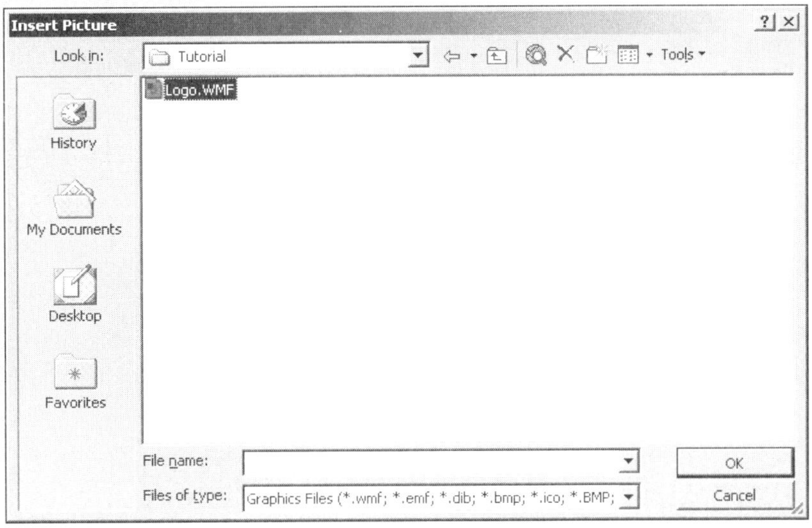

3. Click the **OK** button. The image is inserted on the form; however, the image is distorted and needs to be resized to fit better on the form.
4. Right-click the image control, and then click **Properties** on the shortcut menu.
5. On the All tab, click the **Size Mode** text box, and then click its **list arrow** to display the available property settings. The default Size Mode setting is Clip; this setting inserts the image inside the image control box that is created. The Stretch setting adjusts the entire logo to fit exactly within the boundaries of the image box, but does so by changing the image slightly from its original proportions. The Zoom setting makes the image fit within the image control, but the image retains its original width and height proportions.
6. Click **Stretch** in the list, and then close the property sheet. The image should now appear correctly in the image control.
7. Resize and reposition the image control as shown in Figure 4-10.

TROUBLE? If you are having difficulty positioning the image control on the form, open its property sheet, and then set the Left and Top properties to 0", the Width property to 1", and the Height property to 0.75". Close the property sheet when you are finished.

Figure 4-10 **SIZING AND POSITIONING THE IMAGE CONTROL**

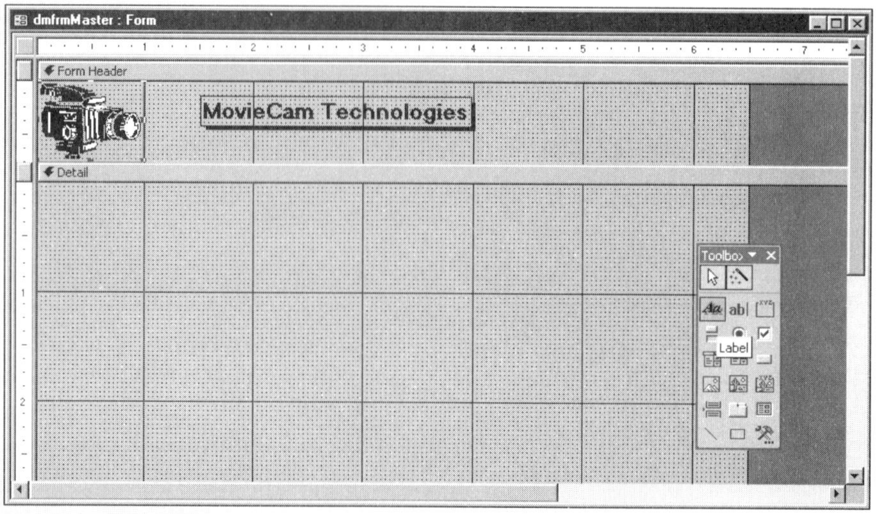

8. Save your changes and then close the form.

You have put together a list of data entry forms that you want the MovieCam database to contain. The form template and form master are completed, so you'll now create the remaining data entry forms.

Creating **Data Entry Forms**

The data entry forms that you plan for the database include the following:

- The *frmDegrees* form for data on college degrees. You have already created this form.
- The *frmDepartments* form for data on company departments. It has not yet been created.
- The *frmEmployees* form for data on employees. Jason created this form before he left, and you modified it so that its style matches the template and master.
- The *frmJobs* form for data on MovieCam's jobs. It will be used by management to review hours spent to date on existing jobs. You have already created the form. It contains a read-only subform that lists the hours spent on each job. The "hours spent" information comes from the tblHours table. Because this data is entered with the time card data on the frmTimeCards form, the data is read-only so the managers cannot change it.
- The *frmJobTitles* form for data on job titles. You have already created this form.
- The *frmTimeCards* form for data on labor and projects. The frmTimeCards form is the central form in the database. It will be used to enter data into both the tblTimeCards and tblHours tables. The tblTimeCards table is the record source for the main form that you already have begun. You also completed the *sfrmHours* subform, which is based on the tblHours table.

REFERENCE WINDOW RW

Creating a Form from a Form Master

- Right-click the form master in the Database window, and click Copy on the shortcut menu.
- Right-click an empty area of the Database window, and click Paste on the shortcut menu.
- Open the form in Design view, and click the Properties button on the Form Design toolbar.
- Click the Record Source list arrow, and then click the table or query that is the underlying record source for the form.
- Drag the appropriate fields from the field list to the form, and position the fields as needed.
- Size and align the controls.
- Save and close the form.

The frmDepartments form needs to be created, and the frmTimeCards form needs to be completed. You will create the frmDepartments form first.

To create a form using the master:

1. Right-click the **dmfrmMaster** form in the Database window, and then click **Copy** on the shortcut menu.
2. Right-click in an empty area of the Database window, and then click **Paste** on the shortcut menu. The Paste As dialog box opens.
3. Type **frmDepartments** in the Form Name text box, and then click the **OK** button.
4. Open the **frmDepartments** form in Design view, and then click the **Properties** button on the Form Design toolbar to open the form's property sheet.
5. Click the **list arrow** for the Record Source property, and then click **tblDepartments** to specify this table as the underlying table. Note that the tblDepartments table field list now appears on the screen.
6. Change the Caption property to **Department Data Entry**, and then close the property sheet.
7. Drag each field from the field list onto the form in the order shown in Figure 4-11. Try to keep the spacing between each control about equal (approximately ¼"). Next, you will align the controls so the left side of each is directly under one another.

Figure 4-11 **ADDING FIELDS TO THE FORM**

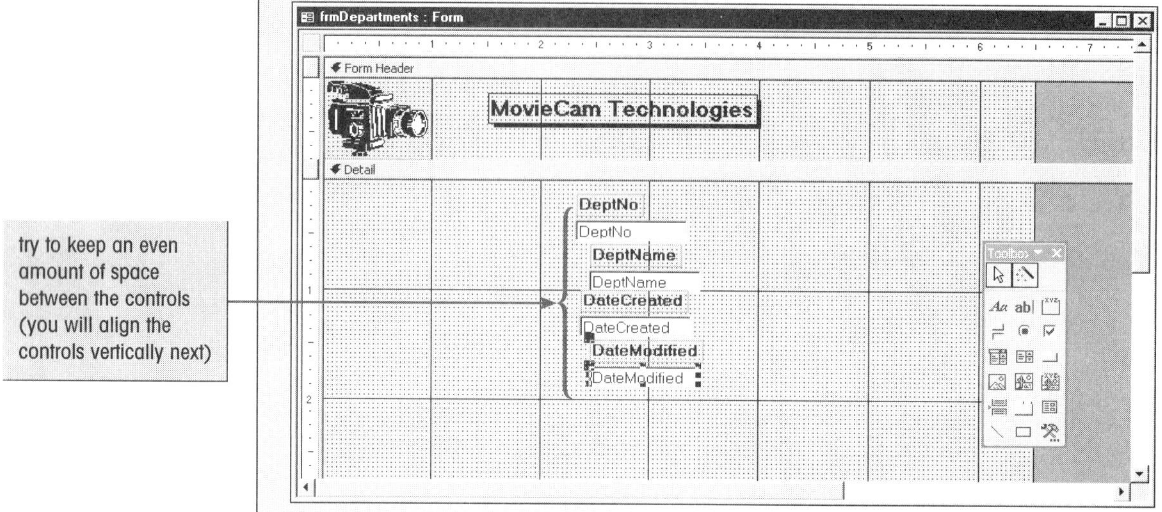

8. Select all the controls by dragging a rectangle around all them.
9. Position the pointer over the selected controls so that the pointer changes to a hand shape, right-click the selection, point to **Align**, and then click **Left** on the shortcut menu.
10. With the controls still selected, move the selection to the left to the 1¼" mark on the horizontal ruler.
11. Resize the DeptName text box control so it is 1½" wide.
12. Click the **DeptNo** label, change its text to **Dept No**, and then resize the label control to accommodate the width of the text.
13. Using Figure 4-12 as a guide, change the DeptName label to **Dept Name**, change the DateCreated label to **Date Created**, change the DateModified label to **Date Modified**, and rezsize each label control to adequately accommodate the new label.

Figure 4-12 **FORM WITH CONTROLS RESIZED, REPOSITIONED, AND RELABELED**

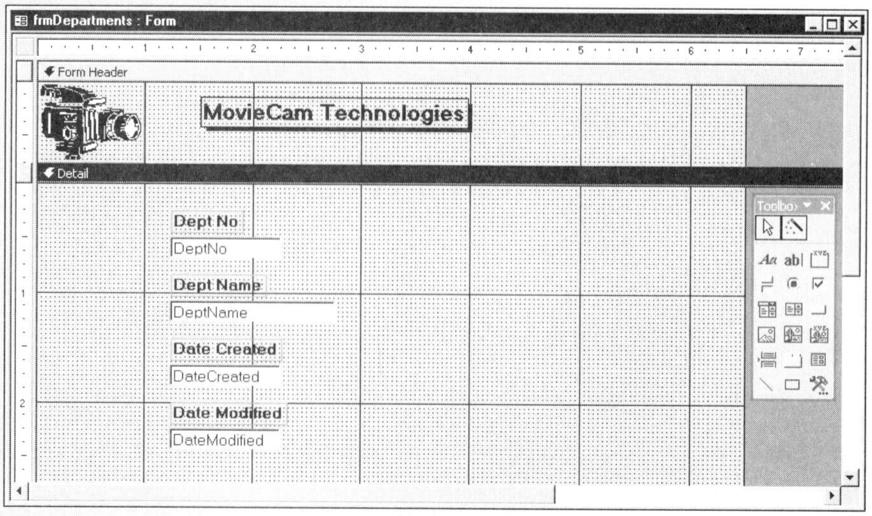

14. Save your changes and then close the form.

You will now complete the frmTimeCards form. The form consists of a main form that will be used to enter data into the tblTimeCards table and a subform that will be used to enter data in the tblHours table. The main form contains a formula that adds all the hours worked as noted on the subform for each time card. Figure 4-13 shows the completed frmTimeCards form.

Figure 4-13 PRELIMINARY DESIGN OF THE frmTimeCards FORM

(MovieCam Technologies Image) (Title)

Time Card No	Time Card Date	Employee No	Employee Name
XXX	XX/XX/XXXX	XXX	XXXXX XXXXXXX

Time Card No	Job No	Hours Worked
XXX	XXXXX	XXX
XXX	XXXXX	XXX
XXX	XXXXX	XXX
XXX	XXXXX	XXX
XXX	XXXXX	XXX
XXX	XXXXX	XXX
XXX	XXXXX	XXX

Total Hours XXXX

You have completed the subform and named it sfrmHours. You have also begun work on the main form and have named the form frmTimeCards. You will complete this form next.

To complete the frmTimeCards form:

1. Open the **frmTimeCards** form in Design view. You created the form by copying the form master, as you did for the frmDepartments form. You then added a text box control for the TimeCardNo and TimeCardDate fields, and a combo box control for the EmployeeNo field. Note that the tblTimeCards field list is also visible.
2. Click the **EmployeeNo** combo box to select it, and then click the **Properties** button on the Form Design toolbar to open the property sheet for the combo box control.
3. Click the **Row Source** text box, and then click its **Build** button ... . EmployeeNo is the first column of the combo box. The expression Name, which contains the FirstName and LastName fields, is the second column. LastName is the third column and is included for sorting purposes.
4. Close the Query Builder window to return to the form.
5. Change the Name property for the combo box to **cboEmployeeNo**. You will use this name in expressions or when you set the tab order of the form.
6. Close the property sheet and then save your changes to the form.

7. Switch to Form view, click the **Employee No** list arrow to see the options (a list of employee numbers with corresponding employee names), and then press the **Esc** key to cancel.

8. Switch to Design view.

Identifier Operators

Identifier operators are used in expressions, macros, and VBA code to identify objects and their properties.

The ! (exclamation point) is referred to as the **bang operator** and is used to separate one object from another or from the object collection. A **collection** is an object that contains a set of related objects (collections will be discussed in greater detail in Tutorial 6). For example, the Forms collection is the group of all currently open forms in the database, and the Reports collection is all the currently open reports.

The . (period) is referred to as the **dot operator** and is used to separate an object from its property or method (methods will be discussed in greater detail in Tutorial 7). Some examples of how identifier operators are used include the following:

- Combine the names of object collections and object names to select a specific object. For example, *Forms!frmTimeCards* identifies the frmTimeCards form in the MovieCam database. This identification is necessary because developers who do not use a naming convention might give a report the same name as a form.
- Combine object names with properties to set a specific property. For example, *txtTotalHours.Visible = False* specifies that the Visible property of the text box, txtTotalHours, is false.
- Identify specific fields in tables or controls on forms and reports. For example, *Forms!frmTimeCards!cboEmployeeName* identifies the combo box on the frmTimeCards form and *tblEmployees!FirstName* identifies the FirstName field in the tblEmployees table.

You will use a dot operator in an expression to display a particular column from the cboEmployeeNo combo box in the frmTimeCards form. The Column property of a combo box returns the value contained in a particular column of the combo box. It is **zero-based**, meaning it begins counting with the number 0. The first column is 0, the second column is 1, and so forth.

REFERENCE WINDOW RW

Creating an Expression in a Form

- Open the form in Design view.
- Click the Text Box button on the toolbox, position the pointer in the form where you want the upper-left corner of the text box, and then click to create an unbound text box.
- Open the property sheet for the text box control, click the All tab, and then click the Control Source property text box.
- Type the expression in the text box, or click the Build button for the Control Source property to open the Expression Builder, enter the expression, and then click the OK button.
- Save the form.

You might have noticed that when you tested the cboEmployeeNo combo box in Form view only the employee number was visible, even though the number and the name of the employee were on the drop-down list. Amanda wants you to add a control to show the employee name as well. This control will be based on an expression that refers to the combo box.

To add an expression to the form:

1. Click the **Text Box** button abl on the toolbox, and then click in the form to the right of the cboEmployeeNo combo box. An unbound text box control is inserted on the form. This control is considered unbound because it is not bound to a field in the underlying record source (table or query).
2. Click in the unbound text box, type **=cboEmployeeNo.Column(1)** and then press the **Enter** key. The expression specifies that the value appearing in the text box will be column 1 of the cboEmployeeNo combo box. Remember that column 1 is actually the second column because the property is zero-based, and this column contains the employee's name.
3. Click the label that was automatically added above the text box, replace the current text with **Employee Name**, and then press the **Enter** key.

   TROUBLE? You can also open the property sheet for the label control and enter "Employee Name" as the Caption property. If no label appeared above your text box automatically (although it should by default), you can just add a label to the form using the Label button Aa on the toolbox. Recall earlier in this tutorial that you set default properties for some controls. To ensure a label automatically appears above a text box in the future, open the property sheet for the Text Box button, and then set the Auto Label property to Yes.
4. Switch to Form view to verify that the text box contains an employee name as the results of the expression.
5. Switch to Design view, click the text box containing the expression, open its property sheet, set the Name property to **txtEmployee**, and then close the property sheet.
6. Select the new **Employee Name** label and the **Employee No** label.
7. Right-click the selection, point to **Size**, and then click **To Tallest** on the shortcut menu.
8. Right-click the selection again, point to **Align**, and then click **Top** on the shortcut menu.
9. Select the **cboEmployeeNo** combo box and the **txtEmployee** text box, right-click the selected controls, point to **Size**, click **To Tallest**, and then align the top of the labels.
10. Select the **Employee Name** label and the **txtEmployee** text box, right-click the selection, point to **Size**, click **To Widest** so the label and text box have the same width, and then align both controls to the left. See Figure 4-14. The changes you just made make the form appear more neat and orderly, aesthetically pleasing, and easier for people to work with.

Figure 4-14 **CREATING AN EXPRESSION IN THE frmTimeCards FORM**

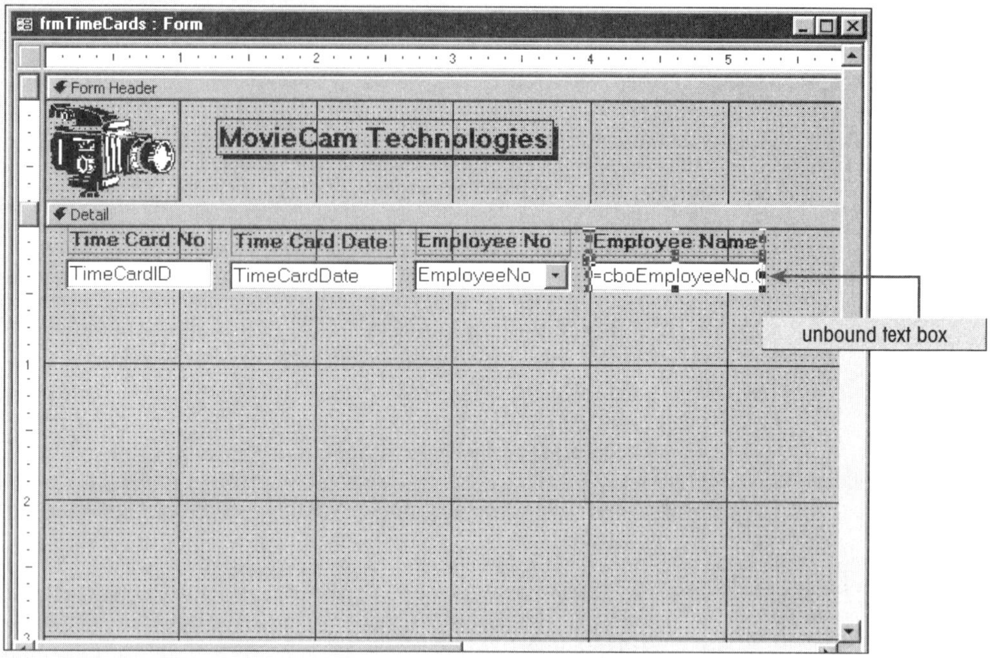

12. Save your form changes.

Because the txtEmployee text box contains an expression and is not a control in which data can be entered, you will change a few of the text box's properties to differentiate it from the other text box controls. You want the control to be flat and have the same background color as the form and you will remove it from the tab order so that the user is restricted from entering data in it. These changes are in keeping with industry standards for text boxes that are not intended for data entry or editing.

To change properties of the txtEmployee control:

1. Open the property sheet of the **txtEmployee** text box.
2. Click the **Format** tab on the property sheet, click the **Back Color** text box, and then click its **Build** button [...]. The Color dialog box opens.
3. Click the **gray** color box (bottom row, third color from the right) in the color palette, and then click the **OK** button. The text box's color will not change until you set the next property.
4. Click the **Special Effect** text box in the property sheet, click its list arrow, and then click **Flat**.
5. Click the **Other** tab on the property sheet, change the Tab Stop property to **No**, and then close the property sheet.
6. Save the changes and then switch to Form view. The form should look like that shown in Figure 4-15.

Figure 4-15 DISPLAYING THE EMPLOYEE NAME ON THE FORM

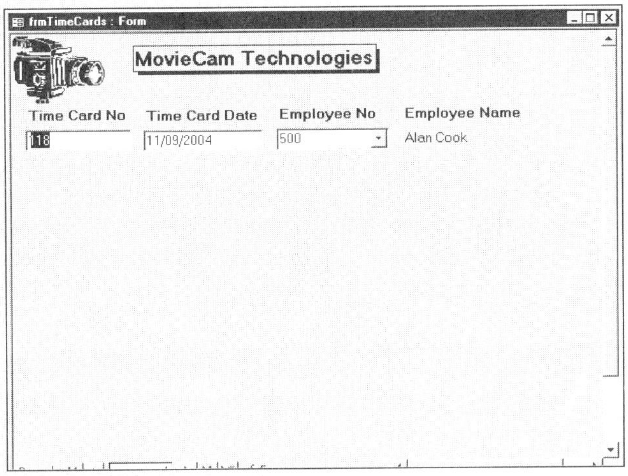

7. Press the **Tab** key to move through the controls. Notice that the Employee name field does not receive focus when you press the Tab key, but the name in the field changes as you move from record to record.
8. Switch to Design view.

Working with Subforms

Next you will insert the sfrmHours subform in the frmTimeCards form. You will do this simply by dragging the subform from the Database window to the frmTimeCards form in Design view.

To insert the sfrmHours subform in the frmTimeCards form:

1. Resize and position the frmTimeCards window as shown in Figure 4-16.

Figure 4-16 DISPLAYING THE FORM AND DATABASE WINDOWS SIDE-BY-SIDE

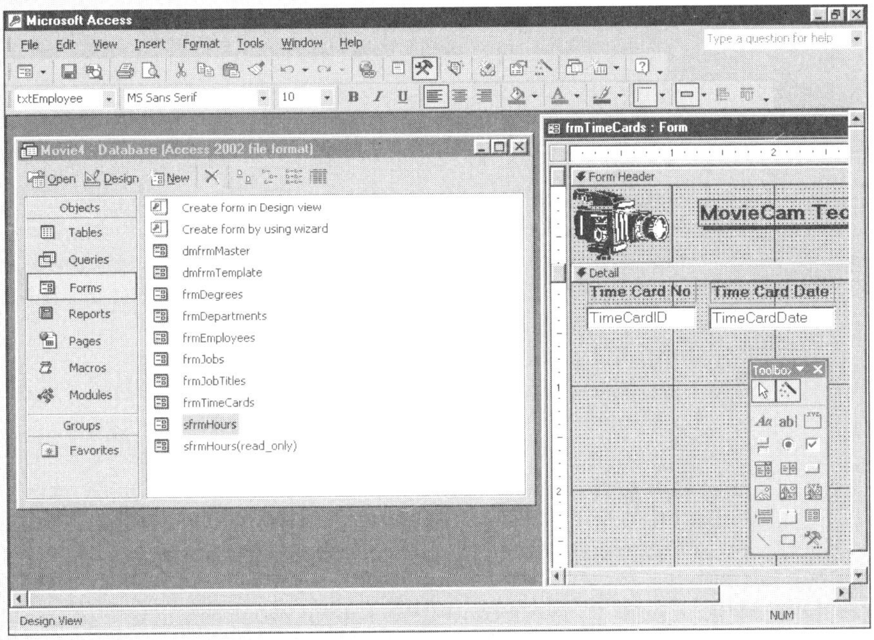

2. In the Database window, click the **sfrmHours** form, and then drag the form to a blank area about ¼" below the other controls in the Detail section of the frmTimeCards form. The sfrmHours becomes the subform in the frmTimeCards form.
3. Select the label control above the subform that contains the text tblHours, and press the **Delete** key.
4. Resize the Form window so the entire subform is visible, select the subform control, position the pointer on the lower-right corner handle so that it has a ↖↘ shape, and resize the selected control to approximately 3¾" wide and 2½" tall, as shown in Figure 4-17.

Figure 4-17 **SUBFORM RESIZED**

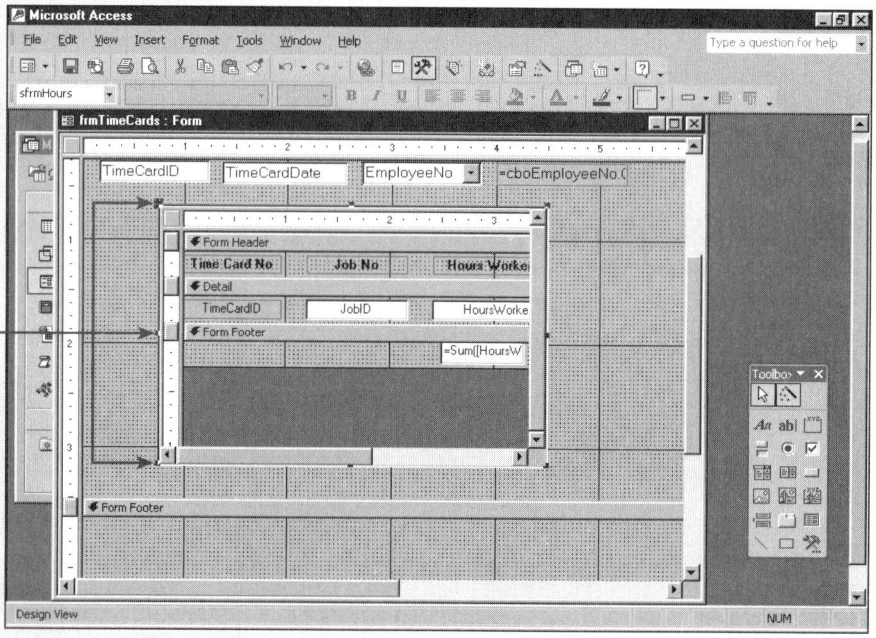

selection handles on the outside of the subform indicate it is selected

5. Open the property sheet for the subform, change the Name property to **sfrmHours**, and then close the property sheet.
6. Save the changes to the form.

Next you'll add to the frmTimeCards form an expression that will calculate total hours worked. This data is displayed on the subform. You included an expression named txtTotalHours in the footer of the subform that sums the HoursWorked field in the subform. The expression you'll add will be set equal to the txtTotalHours control. The txtTotalHours expression will look like this:

=sfrmHours.Form!txtTotalHours

In the expression above, the control in the frmTimeCards form that contains the subform is named "sfrmHours." The subform also has the name "sfrmHours," but in this syntax you are referring to the control rather than the subform itself. "Form" refers to the Form property of the control and specifies that you are now referring to the subform and not the control. The last part of the expression, "txtTotalHours," represents the name of the subform control that totals the HoursWorked field.

To refer to a subform in an expression:

1. Open the toolbox if necessary, click the **Text Box** button on the toolbox, and click below the subform in the Detail section to create another unbound text box. The label may be partially hidden by the subform.

2. Click the unbound text box, type **=sfrmHours.Form!txtTotalHours**, and then press the **Enter** key. See Figure 4-18.

Figure 4-18 EXPRESSION TO TOTAL RECORDS IN A SUBFORM

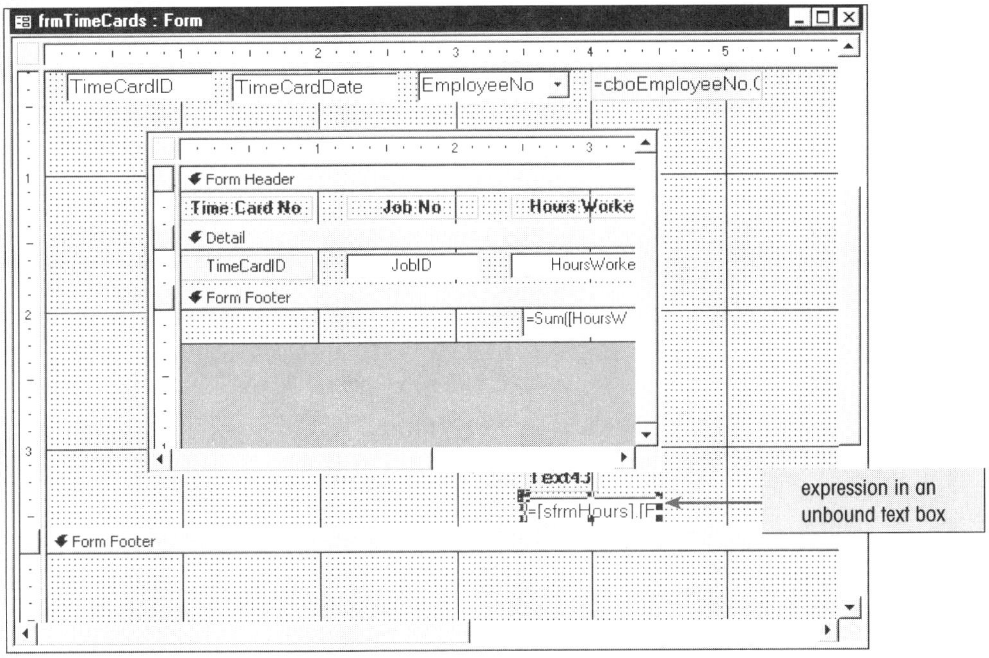

3. Position the label to the left side of the text box, change the label text to read **Total Hours**, and then resize the control so it is 1" wide.

4. Resize the label and text box controls so they are the same height.

5. Right-align the text box to the subform.

6. Select the new text box, open its property sheet, click the **Format** tab, click the **Back Color** text box, and then click its **Build** button. The Color dialog box opens.

7. Click the **gray** color box (bottom row, third color from the right) in the color palette, and then click the **OK** button. The color of the text box will not change until you set the next property.

8. Click the **Special Effect** text box, click its list arrow, and then click **Flat**.

9. Click the **All** tab, change the name of the new text box to **txtTotalHours**, close the property sheet, and then adjust the controls if needed so the form looks like that shown in Figure 4-19.

Figure 4-19 **MODIFIED DESIGN OF THE FORM WITH A SUBFORM**

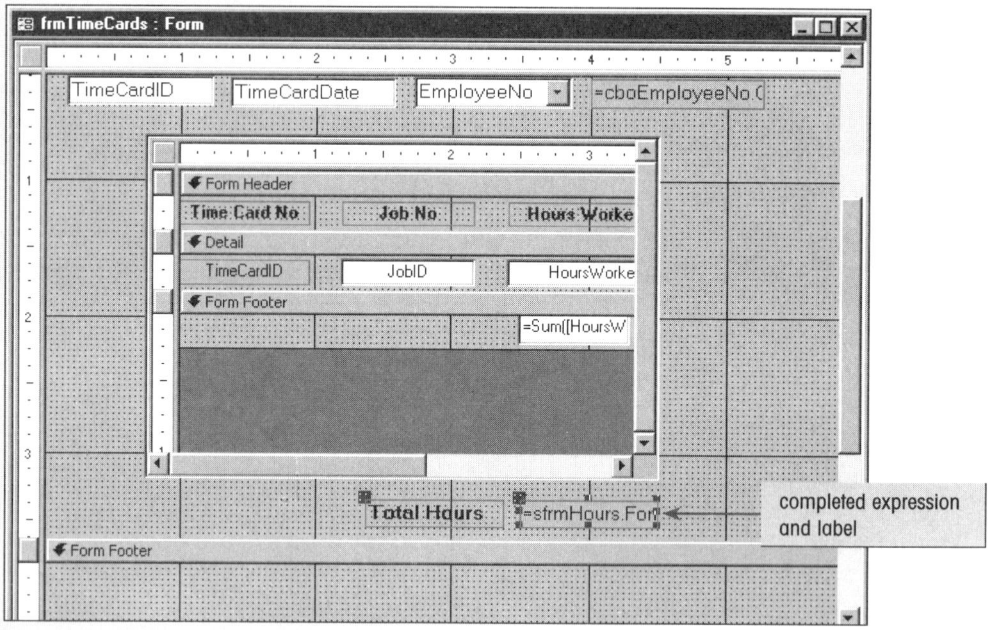

10. Set the Form Footer height to 0".

11. Save your changes and then close the form.

You have completed the template, the master, and the data entry forms for the database. Next you will plan the database's switchboard forms and macros.

Session 4.1 QUICK CHECK

1. What is the purpose of a splash screen?
2. The ______________ is the mechanism by which the user communicates and interacts with the computer program.
3. What is the drawback to using too many colors on a form?
4. How does a form template differ from a form master?
5. ______________ forms are not tied to a table or query and are used to create an interface that provides the users controlled access to the program.
6. What are the identifier operators?
7. What does the term "zero-based" mean?
8. All the open forms in the database belong to the Forms ______________.

SESSION 4.2

In this session, you will create a switchboard master and a switchboard. You will learn more about macros and macro groups and about macro naming conventions. You also will examine the Macro window. You will write a conditional macro and test it, and then you will be introduced to event properties and use them to run macros.

Creating **Switchboards**

You need to create a number of switchboard forms in the database. The design of the switchboards will be different from the design of the other forms in the database, so you'll need a different form master as well. The switchboard will contain the logo and company name just as the dmfrmMaster form does, but these items will be included in the body of the form instead of in the header. The switchboards will also have a different set of properties. You need to design a master for the switchboards that will be created in the database. To do this, you will copy and rename the dmfrmMaster form and then modify it for use with switchboards.

To create the switchboard master:

1. If you took a break after the previous session, be sure that Access is running, that the **Movie4** database from the Tutorial.04\Tutorial folder on your local or network drive is open, and that **Forms** is selected on the Objects bar of the Database window.
2. Right-click the **dmfrmMaster** form in the Database window, and then click **Copy** on the shortcut menu.
3. Right-click in an empty area in the Database window, and then click **Paste** on the shortcut menu. The Paste As dialog box opens.
4. Type **dmfrmMasterSwitchboard** as the name of the form, and then click the **OK** button. The new form master is displayed in the Database window.
5. Open the **dmfrmMasterSwitchboard** form in Design view.
6. Drag to select the image control containing the logo and the MovieCam Technologies label.
7. Click the **Cut** button on the Form Design toolbar, and then click anywhere in the **Detail** section of the form.
8. Click the **Paste** button on the Form Design toolbar to paste the two controls into the Detail section.
9. Click **View** on the menu bar, and then click **Form Header/Footer** to remove the header and footer sections from the form. You will not need header and footer sections in the switchboard forms.
10. Save your changes.

The form properties for switchboard forms differ somewhat from those for other forms in a database. You will now adjust the property settings in the switchboard master.

To change form properties of the dmfrmMasterSwitchboard:

1. Make sure the form is selected. The form is selected if the form selector in the upper-left corner of the form displays a small black square. Remember that this is not a toggle button; that is, clicking the button does not deselect the form.
2. Click the **Properties** button  on the Form Design toolbar to open the property sheet, and if necessary, click the **All** tab.
3. Change the Scroll Bars property to **Neither** because the switchboards will be designed so that all controls fit on the screen and scrolling will not be necessary.
4. Change the Navigation Buttons property to **No**. Switchboards have no underlying records through which to navigate.
5. Change the Auto Center property to **Yes** so that open switchboards will be centered on the screen.
6. Change the Border Style property to **Dialog** so that users cannot change the size of the form.
7. Change the Control Box property to **No** to remove the control box from the upper-left corner of the window.
8. Change the Min Max Buttons property to **None** so that the user cannot minimize or maximize the form.
9. Change the Close Button property to **No**. You want to design the switchboards so that users can navigate only where you want them to go. Eliminating the buttons for closing or minimizing the switchboards gives you more control of the database areas to which users have access.
10. Close the property sheet, and then switch to Form view. Your form should look like that shown in Figure 4-20.

Figure 4-20 COMPLETED dmfrmMasterSwitchboard FORM

11. Click **File** on the menu bar, click **Close** to close the form, and click the **Yes** button to save your changes. You must use the File menu because there is no Close button on the switchboard.

You are planning three switchboards for the MovieCam Technologies database. You will create a main switchboard that opens when a user opens the database, a switchboard for data entry forms, and another for reports.

You'll create the data entry forms switchboard first. This switchboard will contain the company logo and company name, and an option group with buttons to open each data entry form.

To create the data entry forms switchboard:

1. Right-click the **dmfrmMasterSwitchboard** form in the Database window, and then click **Copy** on the shortcut menu.
2. Right-click in an empty area of the Database window, and then click **Paste** on the shortcut menu. The Paste As dialog box opens.
3. Type **frmDataSwitchboard** in the Form Name text, and then click the **OK** button.
4. Open the **frmDataSwitchboard** form in Design view.

You can manually create an option group and the option buttons in it, but it is much simpler to use the Option Group Wizard, which is one of the Access Control Wizards. The Option Group Wizard automatically assigns numbers to each button in the group and then prompts you for the names of each item in the group. The Wizard also prompts you for a default button, the style of the option group, and the option group's caption.

REFERENCE WINDOW **RW**

Using the Option Group Wizard

- Open the form in Design view.
- Click the Control Wizards button on the toolbox to select it if it is not already selected.
- Click the Option Group button on the toolbox, and then click in the form to start the Option Group Wizard.
- Type the names of items in the group, pressing the Tab key between each item, and then click the Next button.
- Click a default option if necessary, and then click the Next button.
- Change the numbers assigned to each option if necessary, and then click the Next button.
- Choose the style for the option group and its buttons, and then click the Next button.
- Type a caption that will appear above the option group, and then click the Finish button.

You will add an option group to the switchboard. The buttons, or options, in the option group will represent the data entry forms in the database. You need to make sure the Control Wizards button is selected on the toolbox before you can start the Option Group Wizard. If there is a border around the Control Wizards button, then the button is selected.

To add an option group to the switchboard:

1. If necessary, click the **Control Wizards** button on the toolbox to select it, and then click the **Option Group** button on the toolbox. Note that when Control Wizards button is selected and you click the Option Group button, the Select Objects button is deselected.
2. Click anywhere in the Design section, drag to draw a form control that is approximately 2" tall and 2" wide. The Option Group Wizard dialog box opens, and you are instructed to enter the labels, or names, for each option in the option group.
3. Type the label names as shown in Figure 4-21, pressing the **Tab** key or the ↓ key to move to each text box. Each label represents the name of a data entry form in the database.

Figure 4-21 ADDING LABELS (FORM NAMES) FOR EACH OPTION

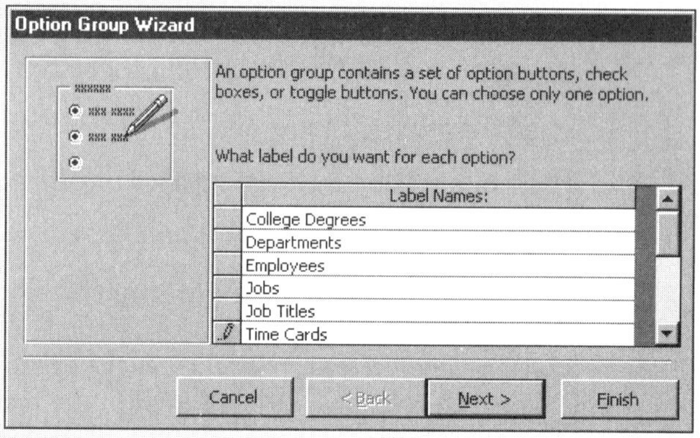

4. After you have entered all the label names, click the **Next** button. The next dialog box asks if you want the option group to show one choice as the default.
5. Click the **No, I don't want a default** option button, and then click the **Next** button. The next dialog box shows the numbers the wizard will assign to each choice in the option group. When the user clicks a button in the group, the value of the option group itself becomes the number that corresponds to the option button selected by the user. This allows you to test the value of the option group in a macro and then open the appropriate form.
6. Click the **Next** button to accept the numbers the wizard assigned to each option and continue. The next dialog box lists several style options. You accept the default etched option buttons selection, which is the standard Windows style for option groups.
7. Click the **Next** button to continue. In this last dialog box, you enter the caption, or heading, that you want to appear above the option group on the form.
8. Type **Data Entry Forms** as the caption that will appear over the option group, and then click the **Finish** button. The form control with the labels appears on the switchboard.

Next you will enhance the appearance of the option group.

To move controls on a form:

1. Drag the bottom border of the Detail section down so that it is approximately 4" in height.
2. Position the pointer on the lower-center handle of the option group frame, as shown in Figure 4-22, and then click and drag down approximately ½" to enlarge the frame slightly to better accommodate the options.

Figure 4-22 SIZING THE OPTION GROUP FRAME

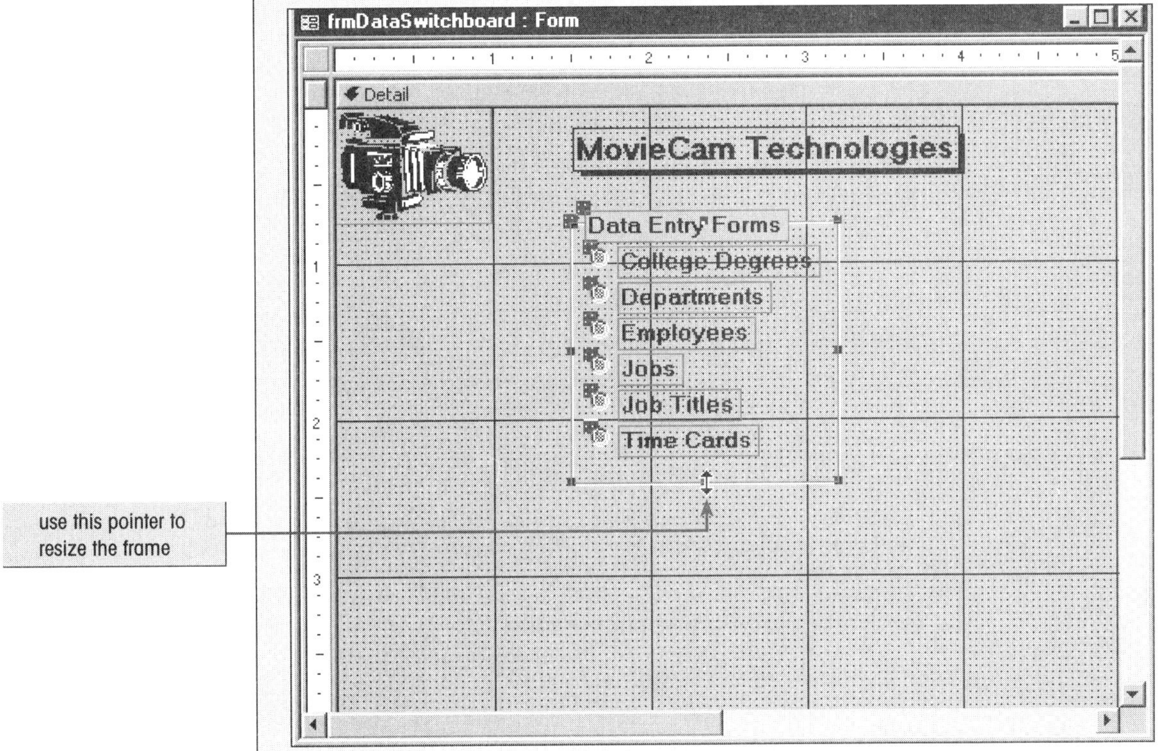

3. Drag around the option group, including its label and contents, to select them all, and then drag the selection down so that the top border of the label Data Entry Forms is approximately even with the 1" mark on the vertical ruler bar and directly under the MovieCam Technologies label.
4. Click a blank area of the form to deselect the option group, and then drag around all the options in the option group, *except* College Degrees, to select them. Be sure not to select the option group frame or the Data Entry Forms label at the top. See Figure 4-23.

Figure 4-23 SELECTING OPTION BUTTONS

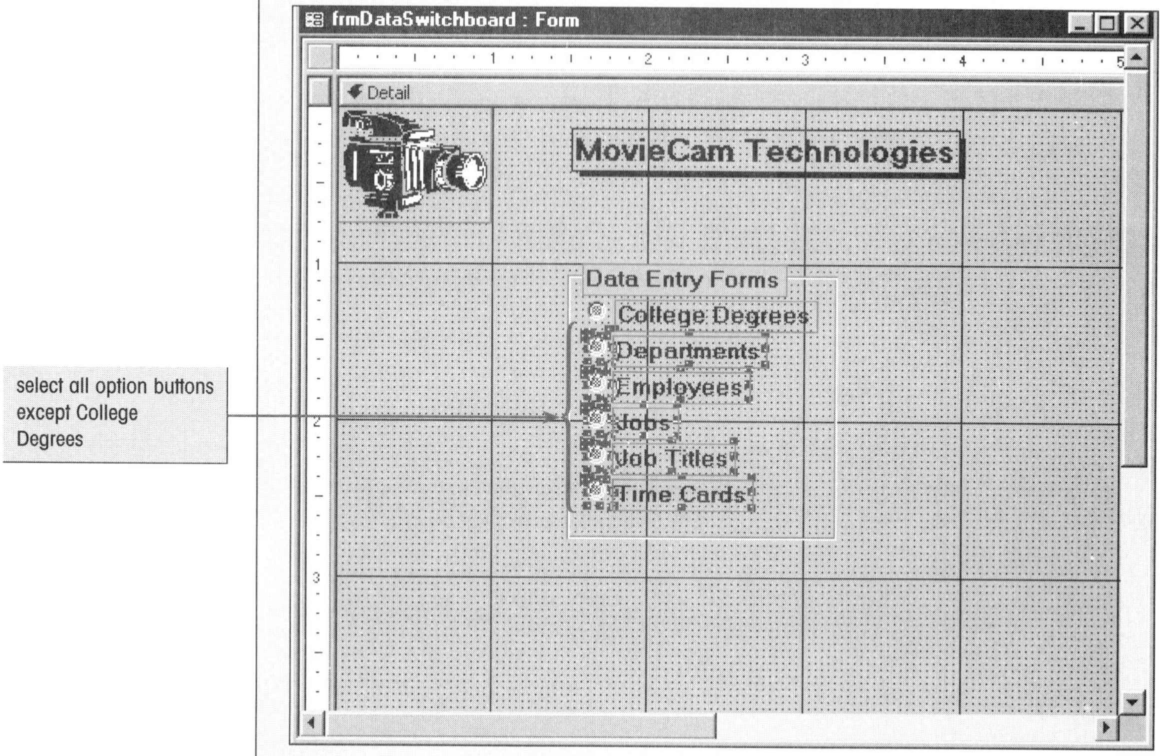

Next you want to space the controls evenly one above another.

5. Press and hold the **Ctrl** key and press the ↓ key five times. This moves down the selected options in slight increments.
6. Deselect the options, and then select all the options in the option group, *except* College Degrees *and* Departments.
7. Press and hold the **Ctrl** key and press the ↓ key five times, and then deselect the options.
8. Select the **Jobs**, **Job Titles**, and **Time Cards** options, and then press and hold the **Ctrl** key and press the ↓ key five times.
9. Repeat this process to insert the same amount of space between the remaining options in the option group. Adjust the bottom of the frame as neeeded to leave some space between the last option (Time Cards) and the bottom of the frame.
10. Click the **Data Entry Forms** label to select it, position the pointer on the upper-left corner handle until the pointer changes to a shape, and then drag to move the label above the option group. Size the label to the width of the option group frame, and click the **Center** button on the Formatting toolbar. Your screen should look similar to Figure 4-24.

Figure 4-24 MODIFYING THE OPTION GROUP

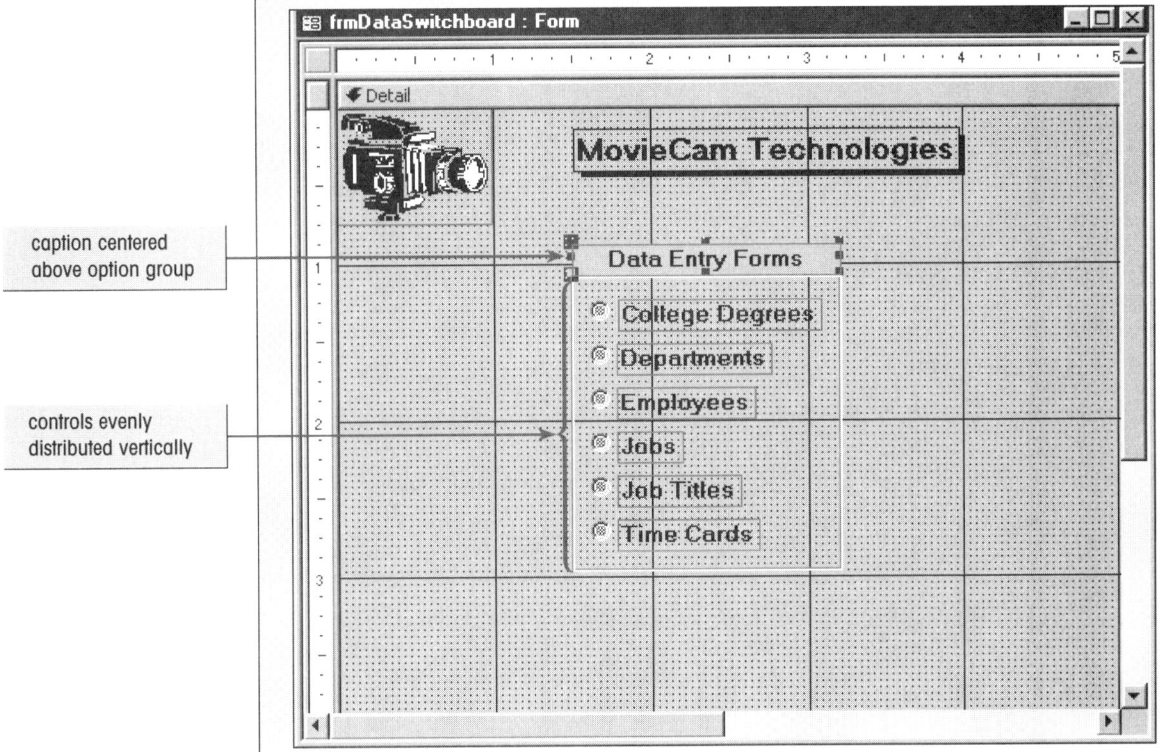

11. Select the option group frame, click the **Properties** button on the Form Design toolbar, change the Name property to **grpForms**, and then close the property sheet.
12. Save your changes and then close the form.

You now turn your attention to creating the macro that will open each form listed in the option group.

Working **with Macros**

A **macro** is a command or series of commands that you want Access to perform automatically for you. In Access, these commands are called **actions**. Some common actions you might want a macro to perform are opening a form, closing a form, exiting the database, finding a record, and so forth. The goal of macro programming is to duplicate those steps you take when you work interactively with the database, so that you don't have to repeatedly execute the steps.

You will explore the Macro Window and brush up on macro concepts.

To explore the Macro window:

1. Click **Macros** on the Objects bar of the Database window and then click the **New** button. The Macro window opens, as shown in Figure 4-25. In its default setting, the Macro window consists of the Action and Comment columns. For work you need to do, you also want to display the Macro Name and Condition columns.

Figure 4-25 OPENING THE MACRO WINDOW

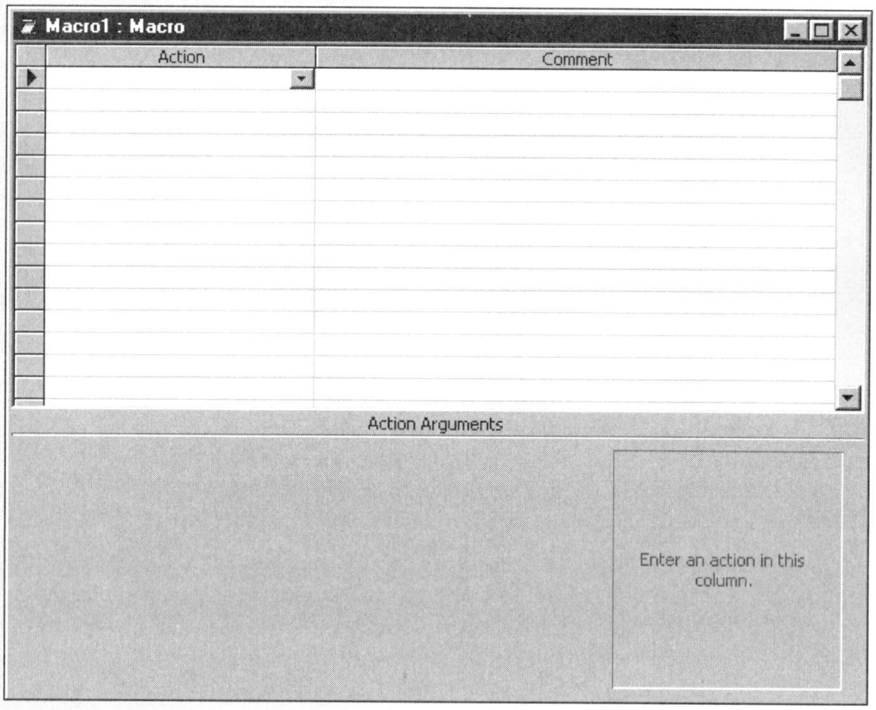

TROUBLE? The Macro Name and Condition columns might already be displayed; therefore, perform Step 2 or 3 only if the column is not visible.

2. Click the **Macro Names** button on the Macro Design toolbar to add the Macro Name column to the Macro window.

3. Click the **Conditions** button on the Macro Design toolbar to add the Condition column to the Macro window.

In the Condition column, you enter conditional expressions, which determine if an action will be carried out when the macro is run. If you want to create more than one macro in the Macro window, you enter the names of the individual macros in the Macro Name column. You can then organize the individual macros into a group. That group name is displayed in the Database window when Macros is selected on the Objects bar.

Naming Macros and Macro Groups

You will organize the macros you create for the frmDataSwitchboard form in a macro group. You have applied a naming convention to the objects with which you've worked so far in the database, and you also need to develop a standard naming convention for macros and macro groups.

You decide to name an individual macro according to the name of the object that initiates the macro, followed by the object's event property. Event properties are discussed in more detail below. For example, if the click event of a command button named cmdNext executes a macro, the name of the macro should be cmdNext_Click.

You decide to name a macro group with the same name as the form with which it is associated, preceded by the letter "m." The macro group that contains the macros for the frmDataSwitchboard form would be named mfrmDataSwitchboard. It is common to use the name "mcrGlobal" for a group of generic macros to be used on many different forms or reports.

Before you start designing macros, however, it's important that you understand event properties.

Events

An **event** is a specific action recognized by an object when it occurs on or with that object and for which you can define a response. Some events are the result of an action that the user takes; others are related to the retrieval or updating of data. Events include mouse clicks, clicking a button, opening or closing a form, keystrokes in text boxes, record updates, and more. Each event has an associated **event property** that specifies how an object responds when the event occurs. These event properties are listed in the property sheet for forms, reports, form and report sections, and form and report controls. Tables and queries do not have event properties. You can specify a macro name or the name of a VBA procedure, which is discussed later in this tutorial, in the event property of an object, and that macro or procedure runs when the event occurs. The use of event properties to run macros or to execute VBA code is called **event-driven programming**. (Event properties will be discussed in greater detail in Tutorial 6.)

Creating Macros

You are ready to begin writing the macro for the option group you created on the frmDataSwitchboard form. The macro will test the value of the option group grpForms to determine which option button was selected, and then, based on that value, open the form that corresponds to the button. You will use the OpenForm action in this macro and you will provide this action's required argument, which is Form Name. The arguments for the OpenForm action are summarized following:

- The *Form Name* argument is a required argument for the OpenForm action, and is the name of the form to open.
- The *View* argument lets you specify Form, Design, Print Preview, Datasheet, PivotTable, or PivotChart view when you open the form.
- The *Filter Name* argument lets you specify the name of a filter you save as a query to filter the records that open in the form.
- The *Where Condition* is a valid SQL WHERE clause (without the word WHERE) or an expression that Access can use to determine which records to select from the form's underlying table or query.
- The *Data Mode* argument lets you specify that the form accepts only new records (Add), that the form is Read Only, or the default is Edit, and allows you to enter, edit, and delete records. These settings correspond to the form properties Allow Edits, Allow Deletions, Allow Additions, and Data Entry. Add is the same as changing the Data Entry property to Yes. Read Only is the same as changing Allow Edits, Allow Deletions, and Allow Additions to No.
- The *Window Mode* lets you set the form so that it is Minimized(Icon), Hidden (it isn't visible even though it is open), or Dialog which sets the Modal and Pop Up properties to Yes. Modal means that you cannot use other open windows in Access, nor open any new windows until the current Modal form is closed. The Modal form is said to retain the focus, until it is closed. Pop Up means that the form stays on top of other open windows. The default is Normal, which means the form opens as it normally would from the Database window if the properties haven't been changed.

To create a macro:

1. Click in the **Macro Name** text box in the first row, type **grpForms_AfterUpdate** and then press the **Tab** key to move to the Condition column. The macro name indicates that you are using the AfterUpdate event property of the grpForms option group to execute the macro. The AfterUpdate event property sets the macro to execute *after* the user chooses an option from the group. As you recall, the grpForms option group contains a value based on the option selected by the user. Therefore, you are allowed to test what that value is and then open the appropriate form.

2. Type **grpForms=1** in the Condition text box, and then press the **Tab** key to move to the Action column. Access adds the square brackets around grpForms automatically so it is not necessary to type them. This expression tests to see if the value of the grpForms option group is equal to 1. If it is, you want to open the frmDegrees form. When you want to repeat the condition for the next action so that it is also executed conditionally, you don't have to retype the condition. Simply type … (an ellipses) to represent the same condition.

3. Click the **Action** list arrow, click **OpenForm** in the list, press the **Tab** key, and then type **Open frmDegrees form** to document the macro action. See Figure 4-26.

Figure 4-26 CREATING A MACRO

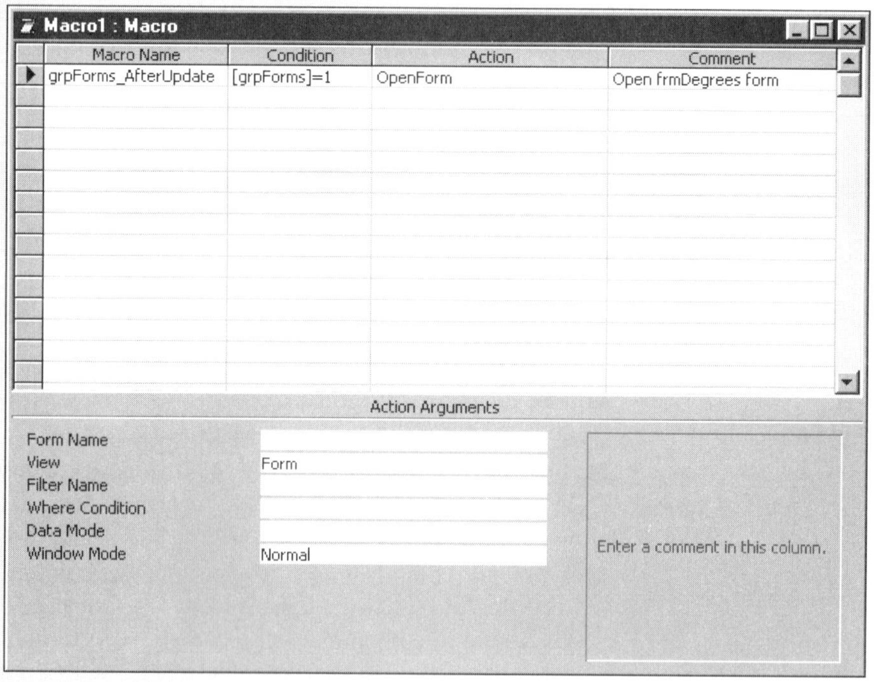

TROUBLE? If necessary, resize the Macro Name and Condition columns on your screen so your Macro window looks more like the one in Figure 4-26.

4. Press the **F6** key to move to the Action Arguments pane of the Macro window. The arguments are additional information that might or might not be needed to complete the macro action. A description of the selected argument appears in the right portion of the Action Arguments section.

5. Click the **Form Name** list arrow, and then click **frmDegrees**.
6. Click in the **Condition** text box in the second row, type **grpForms=2**, press the **Tab** key, click the **Action** list arrow, click **OpenForm**, press the **Tab** key, and then type **Open frmDepartments form**.
7. In the Action Arguments pane, click the **Form Name** the list arrow, and then click **frmDepartments**.
8. Click in the **Condition** text box in the third row, type **grpForms=3**, press the **Tab** key, click the **Action** list arrow, click **OpenForm**. press the **Tab** key, type **Open frmEmployees form**, press the **F6** key, click the **Form Name** list arrow, and then click **frmEmployees**.
9. Save the macro as **mfrmDataSwitchboard**.
10. Use Figure 4-27 as a guide for entering the conditions, actions, and comments for the three macro actions, and repeat Step 8 to create macro actions for opening the **frmJobs**, **frmJobTitles**, and **frmTimeCards** forms. Be sure to choose the correct Form Name in the Action Arguments for each row in the macro so that when a condition is met, the correct form opens.

Figure 4-27 CREATING MACROS FOR THE OPTION GROUP

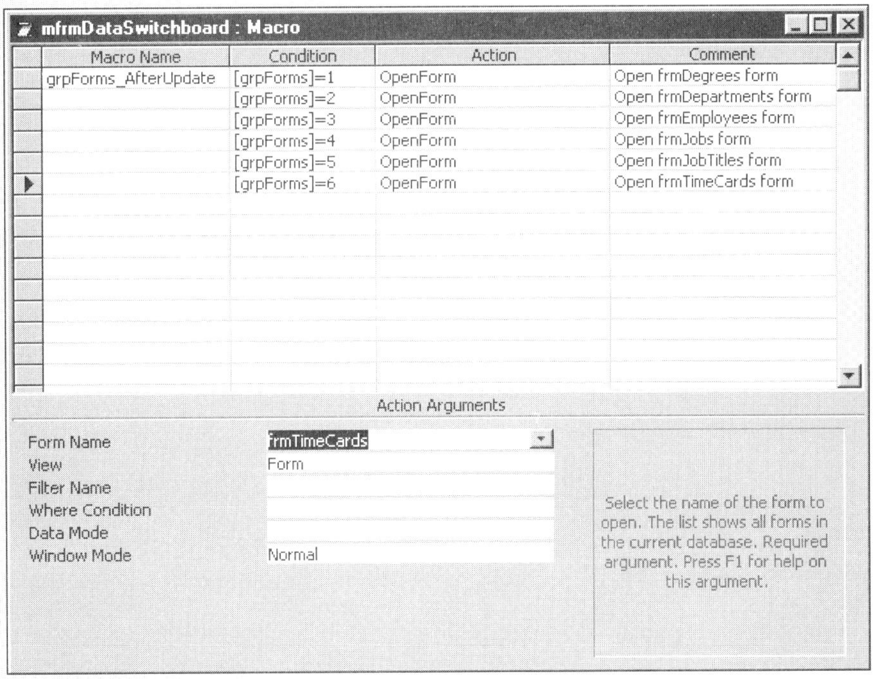

11. Click the **Action** text box in the seventh row, click its **list arrow**, and then click **SetValue**.
12. In the Action Arguments pane, click in the **Item** text box, type **grpForms**, press the **Tab** key, and then type **Null** in the Expression text box. The SetValue macro action and its arguments set the value of the option group back to null after the form is opened. Then when you return to the switchboard to select another form, the option group is ready.
13. Save your changes and then close the Macro window.

Next you will open the frmDataSwitchboard form and set the AfterEvent property of the grpForms option group to execute the macro you created.

To set the AfterUpdate property of the grpForms option group:

1. Open the **frmDataSwitchboard** form in Design view.
2. Click the **grpForms** option group frame, and click the **Properties** button on the Form Design toolbar.
3. Click the **Event** tab on the property sheet, click the **After Update** text box, click its list arrow, and then click **mfrmDataSwitchboard.grpForms_AfterUpdate**. This is the name of the macro group separated from the name of the macro by a period (.).
4. Click the **form selector** to display the form's properties, click the **All** tab, change the Caption property to **Forms Switchboard**, and then close the property sheet.
5. Resize the form so it is 5" wide, and then resize the form window so it is the approximately the same size as the form.
6. Move the MovieCam Technologies label and the option group as shown in Figure 4-28.

Figure 4-28 FINE-TUNING THE DESIGN OF THE frmDataSwitchboard FORM

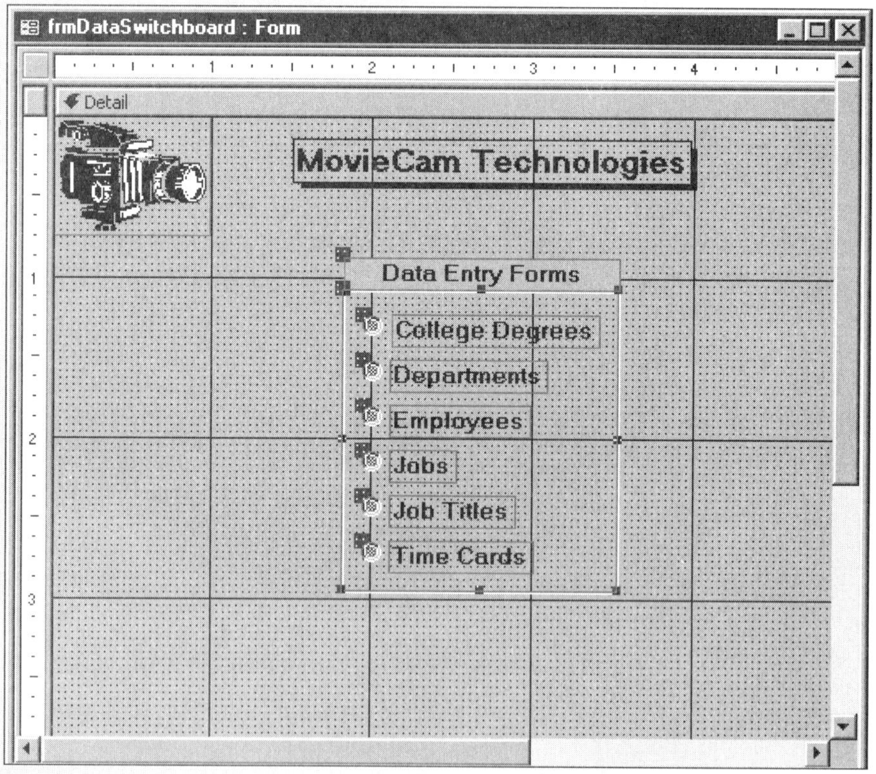

7. Save the changes and then close the form.
8. Open the form in Form view. It should look like the form shown in Figure 4-29.

Figure 4-29 **frmDataSwitchboard FORM**

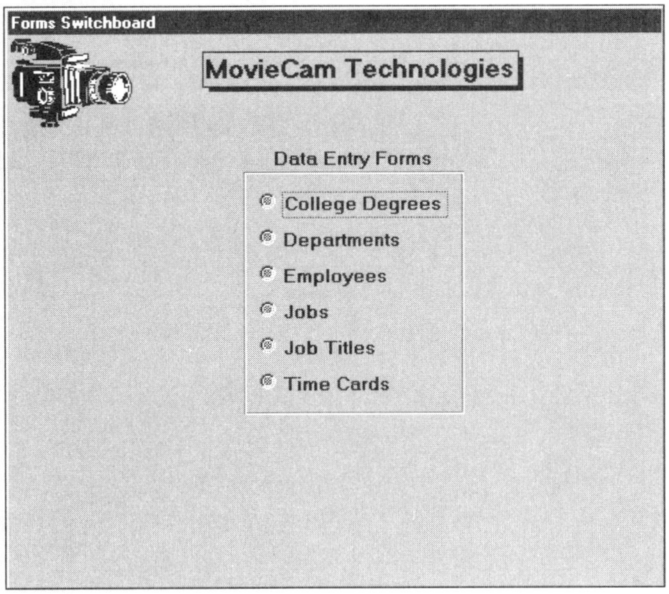

9. Click the **College Degrees** option button to test the macro. The College Degrees Data Entry form should open in Form view.
10. Close the form to return to the switchboard.
11. Open each form from the switchboard, and then close each form.
12. Close the frmDataSwitchboard form to return to the Database window.

You can change the default settings of the Macro window so that the Condition and Macro Name columns are included by default in each new macro you create. This is helpful if you plan to store your macros in groups, or when you want to test a condition before you execute it.

REFERENCE WINDOW RW

Changing Default Macro Window Settings
- Click Tools on the menu bar, and then click Options.
- Make sure that the View tab in the Options dialog box is selected.
- Click both the Names column and the Conditions column check boxes.
- Click the OK button.

Next you will change the default options for the Macro window.

To change macro design default options:

1. In the Database window, click **Tools** on the menu bar, and then click **Options**.
2. Make sure that the **View** tab in the Options dialog box is selected.

3. Click the **Names column** check box and the **Conditions column** check box, if necessary, as shown in Figure 4-30.

Figure 4-30 CHANGING MACRO DESIGN DEFAULT OPTIONS

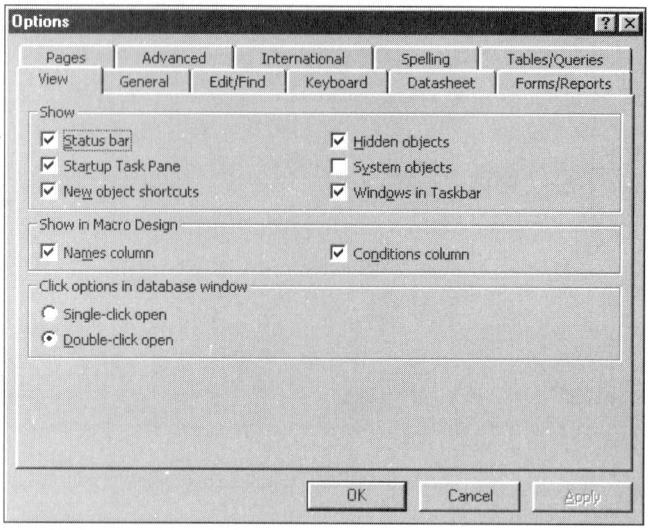

4. Click the **OK** button to return to the Database window.

Because these switchboards do not have a Close button in the upper-right corner, you want to add a command button that users can click to close the frmDataSwitchboard form. You now will create that macro as part of a new macro group, and then assign that macro to the On Click Event property of the new button.

This macro can be used on all the forms, so you will save it in a macro group named mcrGlobal. You will use the Macro Builder to create this macro.

To create a macro to close objects:

1. Open the **frmDataSwitchboard** form in Design view, and then scroll down to view the Detail section to make sure there is enough room under the option group to accommodate the new button you need to add to the switchboard. If not, increase the height of the Detail section.
2. Click the **Control Wizards** button on the toolbox to deselect it (that is, the button should appear without a border).
3. Click the **Command Button** button on the toolbox, click below the option group, and then drag to insert a command button control as shown in Figure 4-31.

Figure 4-31 CREATING THE COMMAND BUTTON

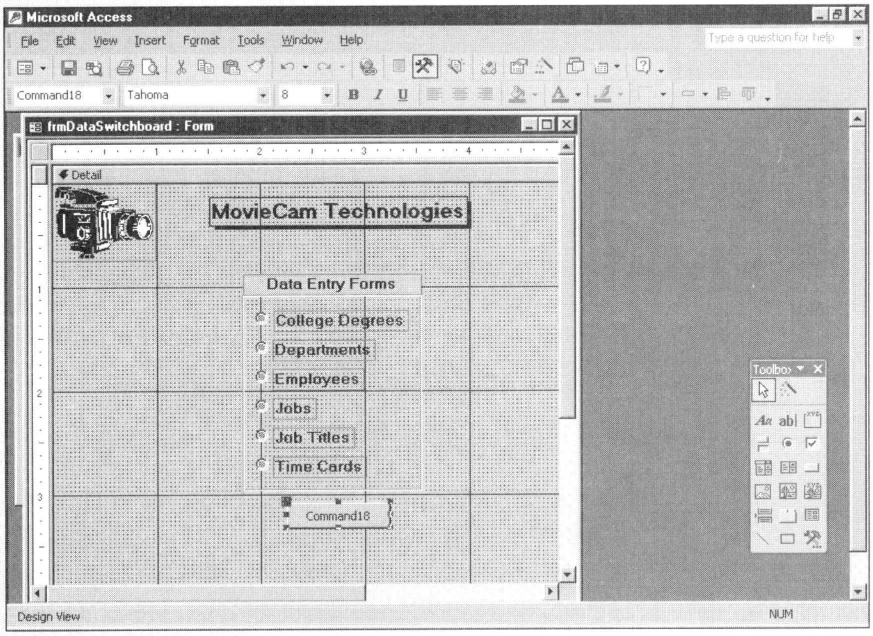

4. Click the **Properties** button on the Form Design toolbar, and then click the **Event** tab on the property sheet.
5. Click the **On Click** text box, and then click its **Build** button. The Choose Builder dialog box opens, as shown in Figure 4-32.

   TROUBLE? If the Visual Basic window opens automatically when you click the Build button, it is because the Always use event procedures option is checked in the Options dialog box. To disable this option, close the Visual Basic window, close the property sheet, click Tools on the menu bar, click Options, click the Forms/Reports tab, deselect the Always use event procedures option, click the Apply button, and then click the OK button. Open the property sheet, delete any text that might appear in the On Click text box , and then click its Build button.

Figure 4-32 OPENING THE MACRO BUILDER

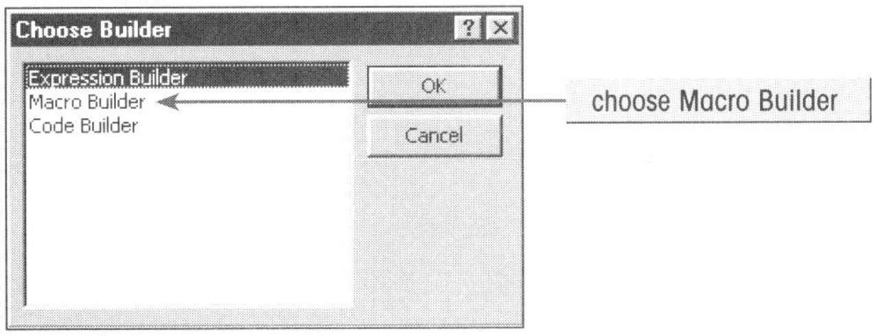

6. Click **Macro Builder** in the Choose Builder dialog box, and then click the **OK** button. The Save As dialog box opens, as well as a new Macro window.
7. Type **mcrGlobal** in the Macro Name text box, and then click the **OK** button.

8. Type **cmdClose_Click** in the Macro Name text box, press the **Tab** key twice, click the **Action** list arrow, click **Close**, press the **Tab** key, and then type **Close the active window**. The button used to execute this macro will be named cmdClose in any form in which it is used and the event property will always be On Click. The caption of the button, what the user sees, will be displayed as "Close."
9. Save your changes and then close the Macro window. The property sheet should still be open, although it may not be active.

Lastly, you'll add some finishing touches to the frmDataSwitchboard form. To make the form easier to work with, you will add a caption and a ScreenTip to the command button. The caption is what the user will see on the button in Form view and the ScreenTip will display when the user points to the button with the mouse.

To complete the frmDataSwitchboard form:

1. If necessary, click the **command button** control to select it, and then click the **All** tab in the property sheet.
2. Change the Name property to **cmdClose**, and then change the Caption property to **&Close**. The ampersand (&) indicates that the letter "C" will be underscored on the button, so the user can press the keyboard shortcut Alt + C to execute the action and does not have to click the button. If you want the ampersand character to be visible in a label or a command button, you must type two ampersands (&&). Otherwise, the only thing visible is the underscored character.
3. Click the **Other** tab, click the **ControlTip Text** text box, and then type **Return to Main Switchboard**. You will create the Main Switchboard in Tutorial 10, and it will be designed so you can open the frmDataSwitchboard form from it.
4. Click the **option group** frame to display its properties in the property sheet, click in the **ControlTip Text** text box, type **Select a data entry form**, as shown in Figure 4-33.

Figure 4-33 SETTING THE CONTROLTIP TEXT PROPERTY FOR THE OPTION GROUP

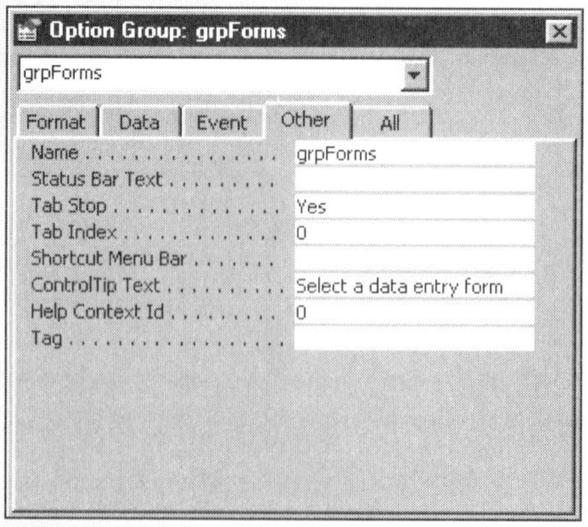

Now you'll test the form.

5. Close the property sheet, save your changes, and then switch to Form view.

6. Position the pointer on the center of the option group so that the ScreenTip text is visible.
7. Position the pointer on the **Close** command button to display its ScreenTip.
8. Press **Alt + C** to close the form.
9. Open the form in Form view again, and then click the **Close** command button to close the form and to return the Database window.
10. Close the Movie4 database, and then exit Access.

Amanda is pleased with the frmDataEntrySwitchboard form, the command button, and the macros that you have created. Your next challenge is to design reports and complete the remaining switchboards.

Session 4.2 Quick Check

1. A(n) ______________ is an instruction or sequence of instructions that is carried out as a unit.
2. ______________ are actions that are recognized by an object and for which you can define a response.
3. What is the purpose of the Condition column in the Macro window?
4. What is a macro group?
5. Which character precedes a letter on a command button to create a keyboard shortcut when that letter is used with the Alt key?
6. A(n) ______________ ______________ is a group of statements that execute when an event occurs.

REVIEW ASSIGNMENTS

Create a form template, a switchboard, and macros in the Hours4 database, which is similar to the MovieCam Technologies database you worked on in this tutorial. Complete the following:

1. Start Access and open the **Hours4** database located in the Tutorial.04\Review folder on your local or network drive.
2. Create a form in Design view, and add a header and footer to the form.
3. Size the form so it is 6½" wide, the Form Header section so that it is ½" tall, the Detail section so that it is 3" tall, and the Form Footer section so that it is ½" tall.
4. Open the form's property sheet, change the Record Selectors property to No, the Dividing Lines property to No, and the Auto Center property to Yes.
5. Display the properties of the default label control in the property sheet, and then change the Font Size property to 9 and the Font Weight property to Medium.

6. Display the default text box control properties in the property sheet, and then change the Font Size property to 9, the Text Align and Label Align properties to Right, the Label X property to -0.25, and the Add Colon property to No.
7. Save the form as **dmfrmTemplate**, and then close the form.
8. Set the **dmfrmTemplate** as the default form template.
9. Create an unbound form in Design view, and save the form as **frmMainSwitchboard**.
10. Open the form's property sheet, change the Caption property to **Main Switchboard**, the Navigation Buttons property to No, the Record Selectors property to No, the Border Style property to Dialog, the Min Max Buttons property to None, and then the Close Button property to No.
11. Use the Option Group Wizard to create an option group on the form. (*Hint*: Make sure the Control Wizards button is selected on the toolbox.) The option group frame should be about 2" by 2".
12. Enter the following as label names: **Department Data Entry**, **Employee Data Entry**, **Job Title Data Entry**, and **Close**. (*Hint*: Be sure to press the Tab key between each label name entry). Do not specify a default option button, accept the default numbering, and the default settings for the appearance of the option buttons, and then enter **Select from the following options:** as the caption for the option group.
13. Size the option group, and position the buttons and labels so that none overlap and they are easy to read.
14. Display the properties of the option group, change the Name property to **grpForms**.
15. Click the Event tab in the property sheet, click the Build button for the After Update property, click Macro Builder, click the OK button, and then save the macro as **mfrmMainSwitchboard**.
16. Specify the following macro action in the Macro window:

    Macro Name: **grpForms_AfterUpdate**

    Condition: **grpForms=1**

    Action: **OpenForm**

    Comment: **Open frmDepartments form**

    Form Name: **frmDepartments**
17. Using Step 16 as a guide, create the macro action to open the frmEmployees form and the frmJobTitles form.
18. In the fourth row, type **grpForms=4** as the condition, select Close as the macro action, and then enter **Close frmMainSwitchboard** as the comment.
19. In the fifth row, select SetValue as the macro action, enter **Set the option group to null** as the comment, set the Item action argument to **grpForms**, and set the Expression action argument to Null.
20. Save the changes, close the Macro window, switch to Form view, and then test the option group.

Explore

21. Use the Command Button Wizard to create a command button below the option group that closes the database and exits Access.
22. Open the Database Documenter from the Analyze submenu on the Tools, and then print only the actions and arguments of the mfrmMainSwitchboard macro.

23. Save the changes and close the form.
24. Close the Hours4 database, and then exit Access.

CASE PROBLEMS

Case 1. Edwards and Company Jack Edwards has asked you remove the Close, Minimize, and Maximize buttons from the frmClients form. He wants a command button to close the form and he wants a form for Consultants very similar to the frmClients form. You decide to use the frmClients form to create a form master so that when Jack wants additional forms in the future, you will not have to create them from scratch and can give the new forms the same look as the existing forms. Complete the following:

1. Start Access and open the **Edward4** database located in the Tutorial.04\Cases folder on your local or network drive.
2. Open the **frmClients** form in Design view, open the properties sheet, and then make the necessary changes to remove the Control Box, Minimize, Maximize, and Close buttons from the form.
3. Change the form width to 6 ½".
4. Add a Close button, centered in the Form Footer, as you did for the MovieCam database. Change the Name property to **cmdClose**, change the Caption property to **&Close**, and then set up the necessary macro to execute the close action. (*Hint*: Click the Build button for the On Click property on the Event tab to open the Macro Builder.)
5. Save your changes and then close the form.
6. Make a copy of the frmClients form, and name it **dmfrmMaster**.
7. Open the **dmfrmMaster** form in Design view. Delete all the controls from the Detail section and remove the words "Client Data Entry" from the label in the Form Header section.
8. Clear the Record Source and Caption properties of the form, because the form master does not need a caption and is not based on a table or query. Save your changes, and then close the form master.
9. Make a copy of the dmfrmMaster form, name the new form **frmConsultants**, and then open the new form in Design View.
10. Change the Record Source property to tblConsultants table, and change the Caption property to **Consultant Data Entry**. Add the same three words to the second line of the label in the Form Header section.
11. Drag all the fields from the field list to the form in an orderly manner, much the same way they were arranged on the frmClients form.

Explore

12. Add a Record Operations command button that deletes a record.
13. Open the form's property sheet, change the Auto Center property to Yes, the Modal and Pop Up properties to Yes, and the Border Style property to Dialog.
14. Switch to Form view and then test your changes.
15. Save your changes to the form, and then close the form.
16. Close the Edward4 database, and then exit Access.

Case 2. San Diego County Information Systems You have started the forms for the training database. So far you have completed a main form that contains data from the tblClasses table and a subform that is based on a query. The query contains all the fields from the tblStudents table. It also contains the ClassID field from the tblStudentsAndClasses table so that you can link the main form on the ClassID field. You have created the subform and named it sfrmStudents. The subform contains a footer text box named txtTotal. You want the text box to be visible on the main form. The txtTotal text box is the expression Count([StudentID]) and is designed to count the total number of students in each class. Complete the following:

1. Start Access and open the **ISD4** database located in the Tutorial.04\Cases folder on your local or network drive.
2. Open the **frmClasses** form in Design view. Position (and resize if necessary) the Form window so that the Database window is also visible. Move the sfrmStudents form below the other controls in the Detail section of the frmClasses.
3. Delete the label control containing the text "tblStudentsAndClasses" that appears above the subform. Resize the subform control so that it is approximately 5" wide and 3" tall, and then position the subform control so that it is centered on the form. (*Hint*: If necessary, increase the height of the Detail section in the frmClasses form so it is about 6" tall.)
4. Change the Name property of the subform control to **sfrmStudents**.
5. Change the Caption property of the frmClasses form to **ISD Classes**, the Record Selectors property to No, and then save the changes that you have made so far to the form.
6. Create an unbound text box in the Detail section below the subform.
7. Enter **Total Students** in the label control, and then enter the expression **=sfrmStudents.Form!txtTotal** in the unbound text box.
8. Resize the label and text box control so they are about 1" wide and 0.2" tall.
9. Open the property sheet for the unbound text box, and change the Name property to **txtTotalStudents**, change the Back Color property to the lightest gray color available, change the Special Effect property to Flat, and then change the Tab Stop property to No.
10. Save the changes, switch to Form view to view the changes, and then close the form.
11. Open the Database Documenter from the Analyze submenu on the Tools, and then print only the properties of the frmClasses form.
12. Close the ISD4 database, and then exit Access.

Case 3. Christenson Homes The forms for Christenson Homes are not yet completed. You have created one of the data entry forms, but now Roberta is considering adding tables to track the options for each new home that is sold. Being able to track those options will expand the use of the database program, but will require creating a number of new data entry forms. While Roberta works out the specifications for these new tables, you decide to create a form template and a master for the data entry forms. The template and master will contain the default property settings, the company name, and the company logo. Complete the following:

1. Start Access and open the **Homes4** database located in the Tutorial.04\Cases folder on your local or network drive.
2. Create a template for data entry forms. Add a header and footer to the form. Make the form 6" wide, the Form Header section ¾" tall, the Detail section 2" tall, and the Form Footer section ¼" tall.

3. Change the form properties as follows: Scroll Bars to Neither, Record Selectors to No, Dividing Lines to No, Auto Center to Yes, Border Style to Dialog, and Min Max Buttons to None.
4. Change the Label button properties as follows: Font Size to 10 and Font Weight to Semi-bold.
5. Change the Text Box button properties as follows: Font Size to 10, Label X to 0, Label Y to -0.25, Text Align and Label Align to Left, and Add Colon to No.
6. Save the form as **dmfrmTemplate**, and then close it.
7. Set the form as the default template in the database.
8. Create a new form in Design view. Create a label in the form header that contains the company name **Christenson Homes**, and change the font size to 16 points.
9. Add an image control to the left of the label in the form header, insert the **H4Logo** file located in the Tutorial.04\Cases folder on your local or network drive in the image control, and then change the Size Mode property of the image to Stretch.
10. Save the form as **dmfrmMaster**.
11. Open the **frmLots** form in Design view, and then open the **dmfrmMaster** form in Design view. Copy and paste the label containing the company name and the picture from dmfrmMaster to the Form Header section in frmLots. Align the controls so they do not overlap, and then save and close both forms.
12. Close the Homes4 database, and then exit Access.

Case 4. Sonoma Farms The Sonoma Farms database has three data entry forms. To make the application easier to work with, you will develop a switchboard that enables users to access each of the three forms or exit the database. Complete the following:

1. Start Access and open the **Sonoma4** database located in the Tutorial.04\Cases folder on your local or network drive.
2. Create a new form in Design view. Change the form properties as follows: Scroll Bars to Neither, Record Selectors to No, Navigation Buttons to No, Dividing Lines to No, Auto Center to Yes, Border Style to Dialog, Min Max Buttons to None, and Close Button to No.
3. Use the Option Group Wizard to create an option group control on the form with options for Customer Data Entry, Distributor Data Entry, and Visitor Data Entry. These will be the frmCustomers, frmDistributors, and frmVisitors forms in the macro.
4. Enter **Select a form to open:** as the caption for the option group. Change the Name property of the option group to **grpForms**.
5. Save the form as **frmMainSwitchboard**.
6. Write a macro named **grpForms_AfterUpdate** to open each of the forms, and set the value of the grpForms control to Null as the last macro step. Save the macro group as **mfrmMainSwitchboard**.
7. Type the macro name in the After Update property of the option group.
8. Add a Close button (as you did for the MovieCam database). Change the Name property to **cmdClose**, change the Caption property to **&Close**, and then set up the necessary macro to execute the close action. (*Hint*: Click the Build button for the On Click property on the Event tab to open the Macro Builder.)

9. Add a label with the text **Sonoma Farms** to the top of the switchboard form.
10. Test the switchboard to be sure that all the forms open.

Explore

11. Using the Command Button Wizard, create a button next to the Close button that closes the database and exits Access.
12. Save the form and then close it.
13. Open the Database Documenter from the Analyze submenu on the Tools, and then print only the actions and arguments of the mfrmMainSwitchboard macro.
14. Close the Sonoma4 database, and then exit Access.

Quick Check Answers

Session 4.1

1. A splash screen is designed to give the user something to view while the application loads.
2. user interface
3. The drawback to using too many colors on a form is that it is visually confusing.
4. A form template allows you to change form, section, and toolbox button properties. A template automatically affects all new forms if it is set as the default template. A form master contains controls common to many of the forms on your database.
5. Unbound
6. The identifier operators are the bang (!) and the dot (.).
7. "Zero-based" means that the first item in a group is numbered 0.
8. collection

Session 4.2

1. macro
2. Events
3. The Condition column in the Macro window is used to create a conditional expression to determine if an action will be carried out when a macro is run.
4. A macro group is a group of macros saved as a unit.
5. ampersand (&)
6. event procedure

OBJECTIVES

In this tutorial you will:

- Create a report master that uses the DLookup function
- Study report sections
- Create a self-join in a query
- Send a report as a snapshot file via e-mail
- Study event properties
- Use print events to run macros and code from reports
- Convert a macro to a VBA function
- Use the Running Sum property to add a line item to a report
- Use the Chart Wizard to embed a chart in a report
- Write VBA code to calculate an expression in a page footer
- Add blank rows to a report using report properties and VBA code

CREATING COMPLEX REPORTS

Reporting on Data in the MovieCam Technologies Database

CASE

MovieCam Technologies

You have completed most of the forms for the MovieCam Technologies database, and now need to turn your attention to reports. Just as you can create a form template, you also can design a template for the reports in a database. You have already created a report template for the MovieCam database. The next step is to use that template to develop the various reports that Amanda and other managers have requested.

Martin Woodward, for example, has requested a report on employees, categorized by supervisor. The report should contain data such as name, department, hourly rate, and whether the employee has to complete a time card. Each supervisor can then compare the report data to the time cards that employees turn in at the end of each week.

The product managers need a report that contains detailed information on the number of hours and the total dollars spent to date on each job. This report should include a summary of hours and dollars for each job. The summary needs to be broken down by each quarter of the year and illustrated in a chart.

Daniel Jenkins, Human Resources manager, has requested two reports. One report should list active employees, and the other should list terminated employees. Daniel will then compare these reports to the quarterly reports generated by the ACC90 payroll module. Both of the reports for Daniel should contain employee number, employee name, job title, labor category, whether employees are hourly or salaried, and hourly rate of pay.

You must consider one more requirement before you design the database's reports. In a staff meeting earlier in the week, it was announced that MovieCam Technologies is being purchased by TechCam Incorporated, a large corporation located in Southern California. It is uncertain whether the MovieCam Technologies name and logo will be retained once the buyout is complete. Amanda suggests that from this point on you design forms and reports that can be updated easily in the event the company name changes.

SESSION 5.1

In this session, you will create a new table that contains the company information (name and logo) that will be displayed on reports. You will create a report master that uses a domain aggregate function to look up the company name and logo in the new table. You also will work with report sections and learn to group records in a report based on a query containing a self-join. Finally, you will learn how to send a report in a snapshot file as an e-mail message.

Introduction to Reports

Reports are often the only component of a database that upper management or customers ever see. Most database administrators will tell you that reports generally require a great deal of maintenance and ongoing development. That's because management typically requests new reports or modifications to existing reports on a regular basis. For this reason, you should strive for efficient report design. Report templates and report masters can help you achieve that efficiency.

Creating a Report Master

You have already created a report template, named dmrptTemplate, following the same basic steps that you followed to create templates and masters for forms. You formatted the default controls to be in 10-point Arial and then set dmrptTemplate as the default report template.

You have also started work on a report master. You formatted the default controls and added the company logo to the report master. You need to complete the design of the report master; however, your first step is to create a new table that contains the company name and address information. If the MovieCam company name changes when TechCam takes over, you can easily modify the name in the table, and those modifications will be reflected in the reports.

To create the table to contain the company name and other data:

1. Start Access and open the **Movie5** database located in the Tutorial.05\Tutorial folder on your local or network drive.
2. Make sure that **Tables** is selected on the Objects bar of the Database window, and then double-click **Create table in Design view**.
3. Create the following fields: **CompanyName**, **Address**, **City**, **State**, **ZipCode**, **Telephone**, and **FAX**. Leave all the fields data types as Text.
4. Change the Caption property for the CompanyName field to **Company Name** and the Caption property for the ZipCode field to **Zip Code**, and then switch to Datasheet view. A message box opens, asking if you want to save the table. Earlier on you learned that the widely accepted naming convention specifies plural names for table. However, because this table will contain only one record, you will use a singular name.
5. Click the **Yes** button to close the message box and open the Save As dialog box, type **tblCorporate** as the table name, and then click the **OK** button. Another message box opens, asking if you want to define a primary key. You want Access to automatically add a primary key field.

6. Click the **Yes** button. The table appears in Datasheet view with a new primary key field. Access automatically added a new field named ID to the table, assigned the field the AutoNumber data type, and sets the field as the primary key.
7. Press the **Tab** key to move the insertion point to the Company Name field.
8. Add the record shown in Figure 5-1 to the table. As you begin to type in the company name, notice that Access assigns the value 1 to the primary key field named ID.

Figure 5-1 DATA FOR THE tblCorporate TABLE

COMPANY NAME	ADDRESS	CITY	STATE	ZIP CODE	TELEPHONE	FAX
MovieCam Technologies	1521 5th Street	Windsor	CA	94592	(707) 555-1111	(707) 555-2222

9. Close the table.

You will use the domain aggregate function, DLookup, to look up the report master objects in the new table.

Domain Aggregate Functions

Domain aggregate functions provide statistical information about a set of records, or **domain**. The domain can be a table or query. The domain aggregate functions, sometimes referred to as DFunctions, include:

- **DLookup( )**, which returns the value in the specified field
- **DMin( )**, **DMax( )**, which returns the minimum or maximum value in the specified field
- **DFirst( )**, **DLast( )**, which returns the value in the specified field from the first or last physical record
- **DAvg( )**, which returns the arithmetical average of the values in the specified field
- **DSum( )**, which returns the sum of the values in the specified field
- **DCount( )**, which returns the number of records with non-null values in the specified field

The syntax for all of the DFunctions is:

DFunction("*expression*","*domain*","*criteria*")

where the *expression* argument is the field you want returned. This argument is required. The *domain* argument is also required because it specifies the name of the table or query being searched. The *criteria* argument is optional and is a condition that you specify. If the criteria argument is not included, all the records are returned. Each argument must be enclosed in quotation marks.

You can also use the DLookup function to look up data in a table that is unrelated to the form or report in which you entered the function. The following is an example of the DLookup function:

DLookUp("CompanyName","tblCorporate","ID=1")

In this example, the DLookup function looks up and returns the CompanyName field value from the tblCorporate table when the ID field value is equal to 1. This is the expression that you will use in MovieCam reports. To change the company name or address on reports, all you have to do is change the data in the underlying table, and the changes are automatically reflected in the reports.

Before you complete the report master, you want to set the dmrptTemplate report as the default report template for Access.

To set the dmrptTemplate report as the default report template:

1. Click **Reports** on the Objects bar in the Database window to make sure the dmrptTemplate report is listed.
2. Click **Tools** on the menu bar, click **Options**, click the **Forms/Reports** tab, type **dmrptTemplate** in the Report template text box, and then click the **OK** button. All new reports you create in this database will be based on this template.

Now you will work on completing the report master.

To complete the report master with the DLookup function:

1. Open the **dmrptMaster** report in Design view. The report looks like that shown in Figure 5-2.

Figure 5-2 COMPLETING THE REPORT MASTER

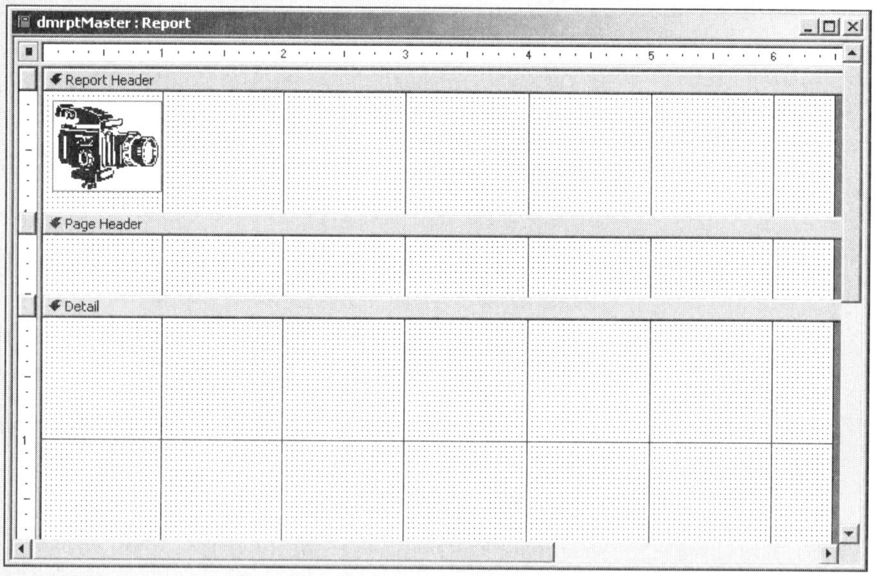

2. Display the toolbox if necessary, click the **Text Box** button abl on the toolbox, and then drag to create an unbound text box control approximately 4" wide and 3/10" tall in the Report Header section, located at the 1½" mark on the horizontal ruler and at the ¼" mark on the vertical ruler.

   TROUBLE? If you are having difficulty sizing or positioning the text box, open its property sheet and set the following property values: Left to 1.5", Top to 0.25", Width to 4", and Height to 0.3". Your settings do not have to be exact, but close enough so your screen is similar to the screen in the figures.

3. Type **=DLookup("CompanyName","tblCorporate","ID=1")** inside the text box, and then press the **Enter** key.
4. Change the font size to **14**, change the font style to **Bold**, and then change the text alignment to **Center**.
5. Change the Special Effect to **Shadowed**, and then close the toolbox. The report design should look like Figure 5-3.

Figure 5-3 COMPLETED REPORT MASTER

6. Save your changes and then close the report.

Now that the report master is complete, you can use it as the basis for new reports. To test the DLookup function you entered, you will change the company name in the underlying table and then view the report to see the result.

To test the DLookup function in the report master:

1. Open the **tblCorporate** table in Datasheet view.
2. Change the value in the Company Name field to **TechCam Incorporated**, and then close the table.
3. Open the **dmrptMaster** report in Print Preview. The report header portion is shown in Figure 5-4.

Figure 5-4 VIEWING CHANGES TO THE MASTER REPORT

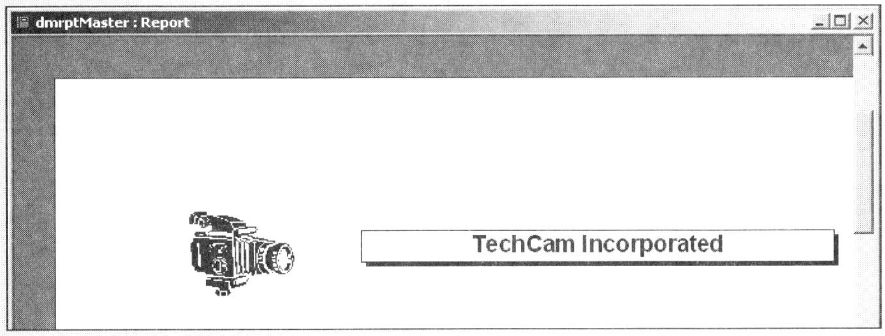

4. Close the report, open the **tblCorporate** table in Datasheet view, and then change the Company Name field entry back to **MovieCam Technologies**.
5. Close the table.

Because the report master is now complete, you are ready to create reports. You will review report sections next, and then you'll work on Martin's employees-by-supervisor report.

Report Sections

In Design view, a report's sections are represented as bands. An explanation of the various report sections follows:

- The **Report Header** section appears once at the beginning of a report. This section might contain information such as a company logo, report title, and company name and address. The report header can be either a single page or multiple pages.
- The **Page Header** section prints at the top of every page of the report. You might use the Page Header to print column headers or the report title on each page.
- The **Detail** section is the main body of the report. It prints one time for each record in the report's underlying record source (table or query).
- The **Page Footer** section appears at the bottom of every page of the report. Use the Page Footer section for items such as the date, time, and page numbers. Do not include numeric expressions, such as totals or averages, in the Page Footer section or an error will result. If you want to total a field in the report, that expression should be entered in the Group Footer section (discussed more in the next section) or the Report Footer section. If you absolutely must total a field at the bottom of each page, you have to write VBA code to do so.
- The **Report Footer** section appears once at the end of the report. You can use it to show the results of expressions such as totals or averages. The Report Footer section is the bottom section in the report's Design view, but it prints before the Page Footer on the last page of the report.

Grouping Records in a Report

By grouping records that share a common value, you can calculate subtotals and make reports easier to read. You can group on up to 10 expressions or values in a single report. When you choose to group on a field or expression, two other sections can appear on the report:

- A **Group Header** section appears at the beginning of a new group of records. You can use it to show information that applies to the group, such as a group name or a picture.
- A **Group Footer** section appears at the end of a group of records. You typically use it to show calculations, such as a total or average of the records in the group.

The first report that Martin requested for the product managers is a list of employees grouped by supervisor. He asked that the supervisor's name and department appear at the beginning of each group of employees that report to that supervisor. He also wants each group to print on a separate page. You have roughed out the report, as shown in Figure 5-5.

Figure 5-5 PLANNED DESIGN FOR THE rptEmployeesBySupervisor REPORT

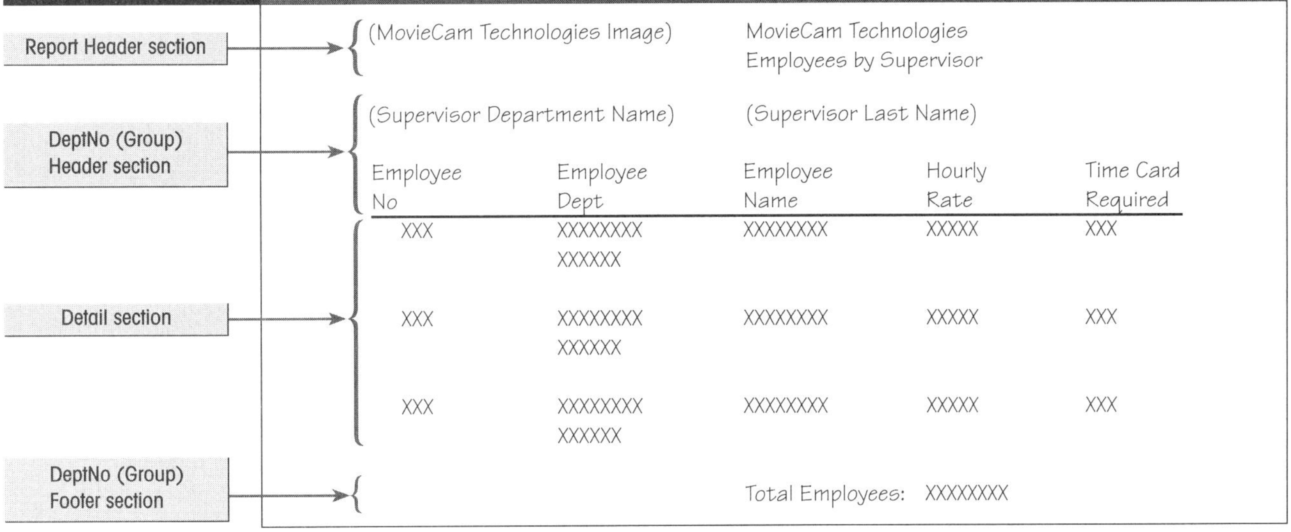

Creating a Query with a Self-Join

The rptEmployeesBySupervisor report will contain data from the tblEmployees table and the tblDepartments table. This report should contain a Group Header section based on the employee number of the supervisor and a Group Footer section. Using the Group Header section to meet Martin's requirements poses some interesting challenges. If you set the header to group on the DeptNo field, the report will group employees by their respective departments. In some cases, the supervisor's department name is different from the employee's. For example, Carolyn Valdez, supervisor in the Administrative and Accounting Department, supervises Ann Garcia, who is in the Accounting Department, as illustrated in Figure 5-6.

Figure 5-6 REVIEWING THE DIFFERENT MOVIECAM DEPARTMENTS

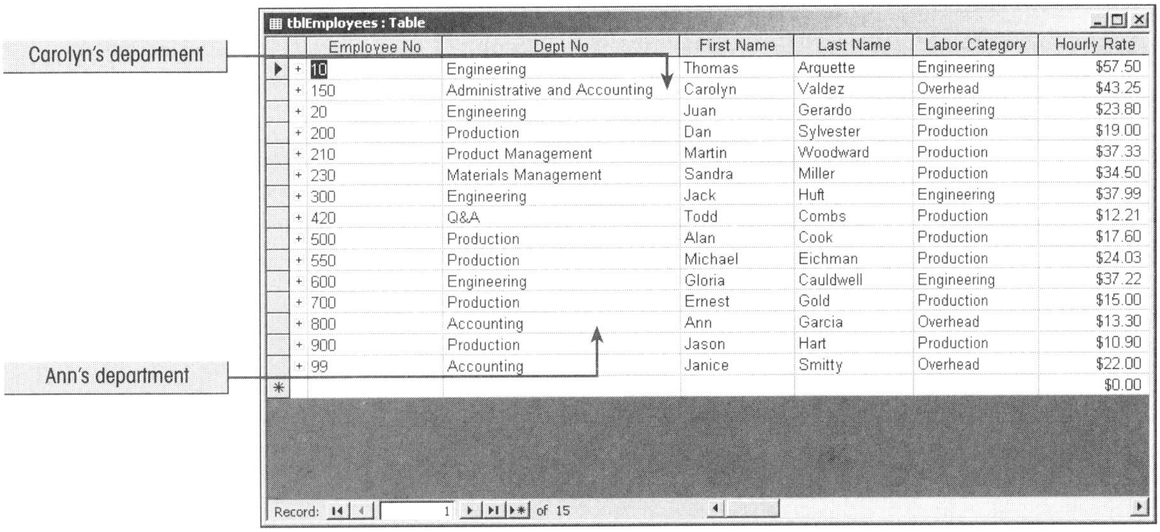

Employee No	Dept No	First Name	Last Name	Labor Category	Hourly Rate
10	Engineering	Thomas	Arquette	Engineering	$57.50
150	Administrative and Accounting	Carolyn	Valdez	Overhead	$43.25
20	Engineering	Juan	Gerardo	Engineering	$23.80
200	Production	Dan	Sylvester	Production	$19.00
210	Product Management	Martin	Woodward	Production	$37.33
230	Materials Management	Sandra	Miller	Production	$34.50
300	Engineering	Jack	Huft	Engineering	$37.99
420	Q&A	Todd	Combs	Production	$12.21
500	Production	Alan	Cook	Production	$17.60
550	Production	Michael	Eichman	Production	$24.03
600	Engineering	Gloria	Cauldwell	Engineering	$37.22
700	Production	Ernest	Gold	Production	$15.00
800	Accounting	Ann	Garcia	Overhead	$13.30
900	Production	Jason	Hart	Production	$10.90
99	Accounting	Janice	Smitty	Overhead	$22.00
					$0.00

The other issue you need to resolve is how to show the supervisor's name in the report's Group Header section. If you add the FirstName and LastName fields from the tblEmployees table to the Group Header and the Report Header, then each employee's name will appear in the header instead of only the supervisor.

If the records for supervisors were stored in a separate table, this would be a simple task. Because they are not, your solution is to create a query that actually joins the tblEmployees table to itself. Joining a table to itself in a query is referred to as a **self-join**.

A self-join can be either an inner or outer join. Remember from Tutorial 3 that an inner join is the default join type and is the one in which all the records with equal joined field values are displayed. Because each employee has a supervisor, this is the type of join you will use for this query.

REFERENCE WINDOW RW

Creating a Self-Join Query

- Create a query in Design view.
- Click the table for the self-join, click the Add button twice, and then click the Close button.
- Drag a field from one field list to the related field in the other field list.
- Right-click one of the tables, and then change the alias to another name to easily distinguish the two tables. (This step is optional.)
- Select the fields, define the selection criteria, and set the sort options for the query.
- Save the query.

You will include the tblEmployees table *twice* in the query and join the EmployeeNo field to the SupervisorNo field. You also will include the tblDepartments table twice, once for each of the tblEmployees tables. One table will be used to display the DeptName field for the employee, and the other will be used to display the DeptName field for the supervisor.

To create a query with a self-join:

1. Create a new query in Design view, click the **tblDepartments** table in the Show Table dialog box, and then click the **Add** button.
2. Click the **tblEmployees** table in the Show Table dialog box, and then click the **Add** button twice to add two copies of the tblEmployees table to the Query window.
3. Click the **tblDepartments** table again, click the **Add** button, and then close the Show Table dialog box. Now you have four tables in the Query window, as shown in Figure 5-7. The two tables on the left will be used to display data about the employees, and the two tables on the right will be used to display data about the supervisors.

Figure 5-7 ADDING THE TWO TABLES TWICE FOR A SELF-JOIN

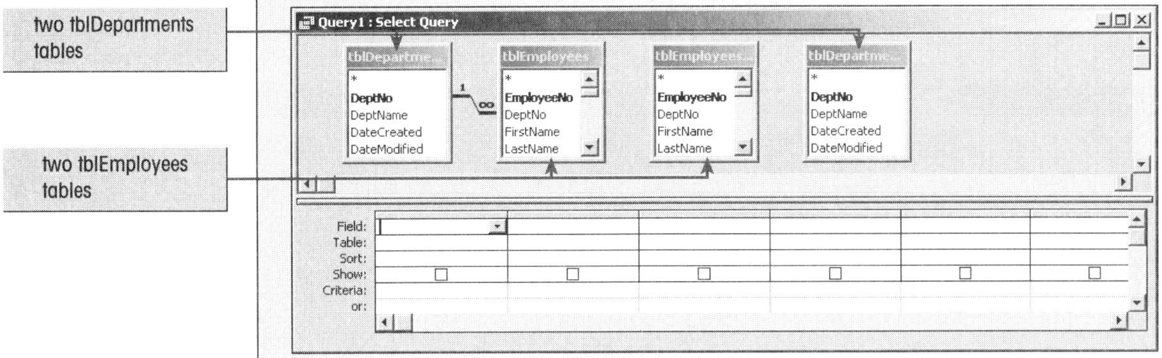

4. In the far left tblEmployees table, click the **SupervisorNo** field (scroll down the field list, if necessary), and then drag it to the **EmployeeNo** field in the other tblEmployees table (tblEmployees_1) to create the join, as shown in Figure 5-8.

Figure 5-8 CREATING THE SELF-JOIN

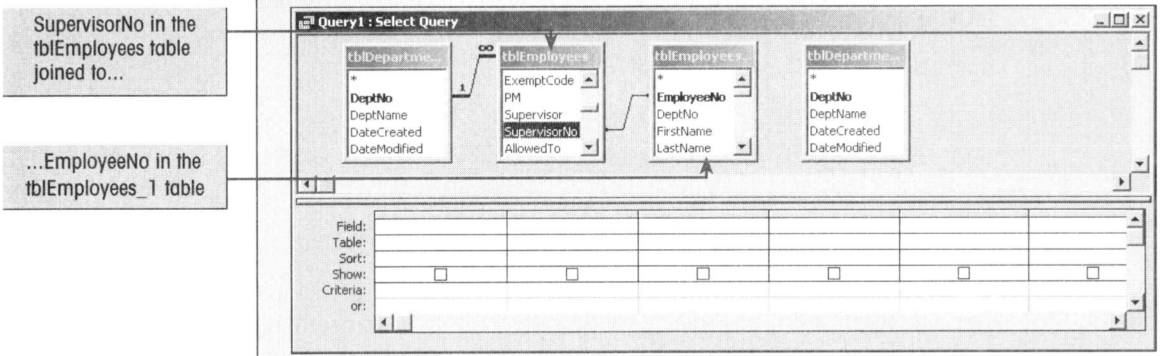

TROUBLE? If you are not sure which field list to use, widen the field lists so the table names are clearly visible.

5. Drag the **DeptNo** field in the tblEmployees_1 table to the **DeptNo** field in the tblDepartments_1 table (the far right tblDepartments table) to create a join.
6. Right-click the title bar of the field list for the **tblEmployees_1** table, click **Properties** on the shortcut menu, and then type **tblSupervisors** in the Alias text box. Changing the name of the field list makes it clear which fields contain the supervisor data and which fields contain the employee data when you build the report.
7. Click the title bar of the **tblDepartments_1** table to display its properties, type **tblSupervisorsDept** in the Alias property text box, and then close the property sheet.
8. Add the **EmployeeNo**, **LastName**, **HourlyRate**, and **TimeCard** fields (in this order) from the tblEmployees table to the design grid, and then add the **DeptName** field from the tblDepartments table to the design grid.
9. Add the **DeptNo** and **LastName** fields from the tblSupervisors table to the design grid, and then add the **DeptName** field from the tblSupervisorsDept table to the design grid. Scroll to the right so you can see the column containing the last

field you just added. The query should appear similar to Figure 5-9, depending upon where you stopped scrolling within the various field lists and if you resized any of the field lists or the Query window.

Figure 5-9 COMPLETING THE SELF-JOIN QUERY

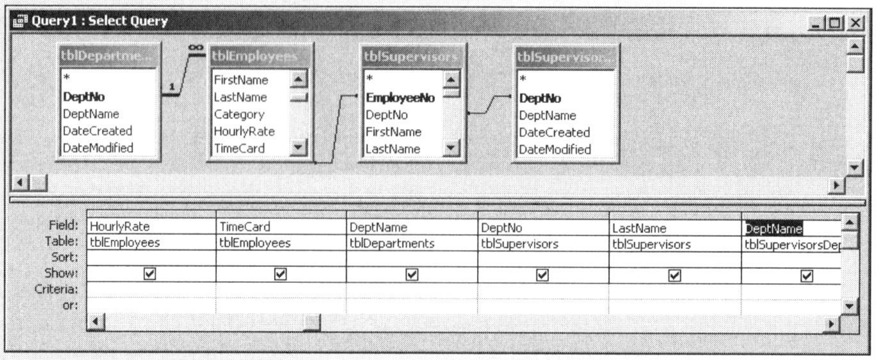

10. Run the query to test it. There should be 15 records in the query results.

11. Save it as **qryEmployeesBySupervisor**, and then close the query.

Now you're ready to create the report. You will copy the report master and rename it, and you will specify the qryEmployeesBySupervisor query as the record source.

To create the rptEmployeesBySupervisor report:

1. Click **Reports** on the Objects bar in the Database window, right-click the **dmrptMaster** report, click **Copy** on the shortcut menu, right-click an empty area of the Database window, and then click **Paste** on the shortcut menu. The Paste As dialog box opens.
2. Type **rptEmployeesBySupervisor** in the Report Name text box, and then press the **Enter** key. Recall that because the OK button is highlighted by default, pressing the Enter key is just like clicking the OK button.
3. Open the new report in Design view, and then open its property sheet.
4. Click the **All** tab if necessary, click the **Record Source** list arrow, and then click **qryEmployeesBySupervisor**. The field list for the query is automatically displayed and is resized, as shown in Figure 5-10, to make the field names easier to see. In the field list, any fields with the same name are preceded by the table name.

Figure 5-10 DESIGNING THE rptEmployeesBySupervisor REPORT

field list for the qryEmployeesBySupervisor query

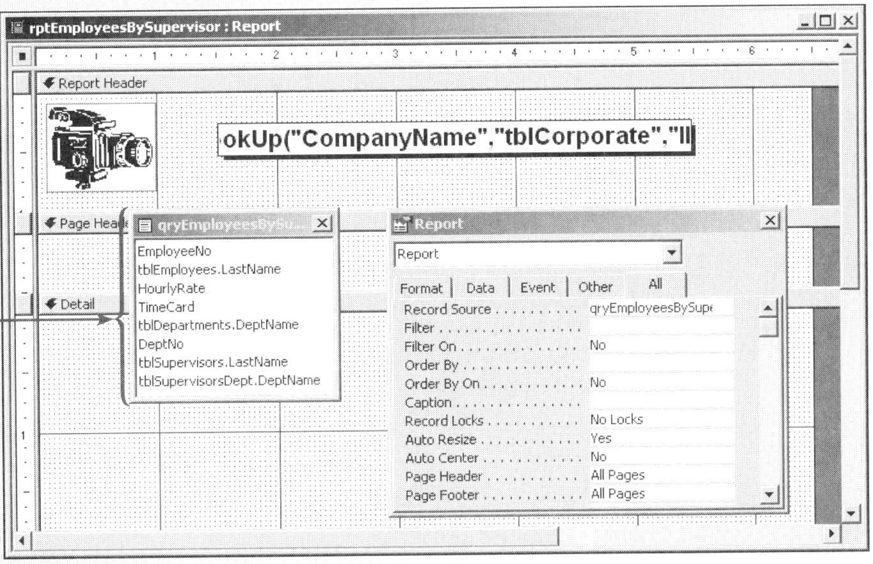

TROUBLE? If the field list does not display automatically, use the appropriate menu selections or toolbar button to open it.

5. Close the property sheet, click the **Sorting and Grouping** button on the Report Design toolbar. The Sorting and Grouping dialog box opens.
6. Click the **Field/Expression** list arrow for the first row, and then click **DeptNo**. This is the department number of the supervisor.
7. In the Group Properties section of the Sorting and Grouping dialog box, change both the Group Header and Group Footer properties for the DeptNo group to **Yes**. Do not change any other properties. Access adds a Group Header section, named DeptNo Header, and a Group Footer section, named DeptNo Footer, to the report. The Group On property lets you group on prefix characters, such as the first letter in a company name, rather than on the entire field. The Group Interval property is used to indicate the number of characters you want to group on if you select the Prefix Characters setting for the Group On property. The Keep Together property is used to keep a group together so it prints on one page. Don't change the Keep Together property because each group in this report begins on a new page.
8. Close the Sorting and Grouping dialog box.
9. Using Figure 5-11 as a guide, drag the **tblSupervisorsDepts.DeptName** field and the **tblSupervisors.LastName** field to the DeptNo Header section, and then drag the **EmployeeNo**, **tblDepartments.DeptName**, **tblEmployees.LastName**, **HourlyRate**, and **TimeCard** fields (in that order) to the Detail section.

Figure 5-11 ADDING CONTROLS TO THE REPORT

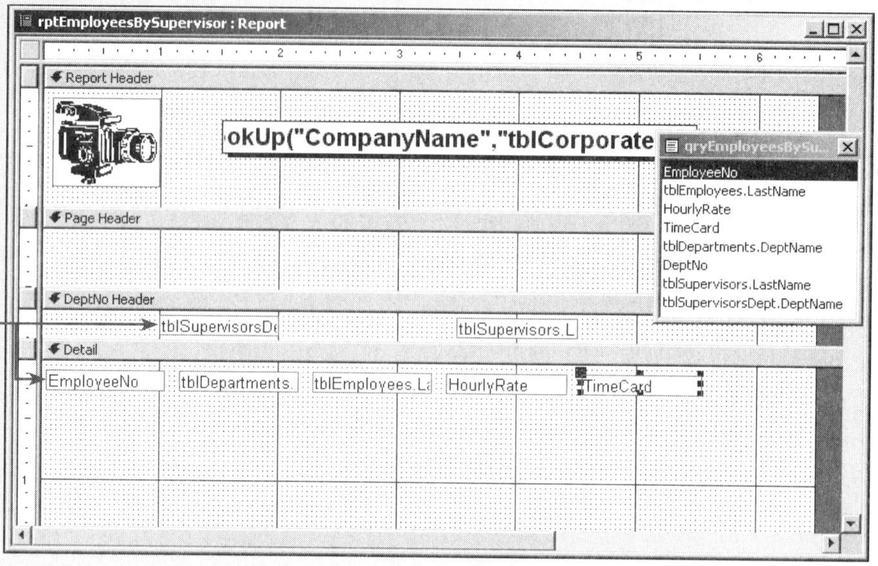

align the controls on your form as needed

10. Close the field list at this time, and then save your changes.

Next you will add labels to the report and align the labels with the fields in the Detail section. You also will change a property setting so that the full name of each employee's department is visible.

Can Grow and Can Shrink Properties

You can use the Can Grow and Can Shrink properties of sections or controls on printed or previewed forms and reports. Setting the **Can Grow** property to Yes enables the section or control to grow vertically so all of the data is visible. This is useful when the data in a few records is much longer than the data in the majority of records. Setting the **Can Shrink** property to Yes shrinks the section or control vertically to avoid printing blank lines.

When you set the Can Grow property to Yes for a control in a section, Access automatically sets that report section's Can Grow property to Yes. However, if you change the Can Grow property for the section back to No, this action does not in turn alter the Can Grow property of any controls residing within that section. If a control in a section is set to be able to grow (expand vertically), the entire section needs to be able to grow as well, because if it does not, then the control can grow to print more data than the section can display. If the controls and the section in which they reside are both set to grow or expand, then as controls grow vertically to display all of their data, the section grows to accommodate this. By default, Access automatically changes the section's Can Grow property to Yes if a control within that section is set to grow. That is the only scenario where Access automatically updates the Can Grow property of a section based on a setting changing for a control within that section. This automated property setting behavior does not apply for the Can Shrink property of a section.

The only time you would not want a section to grow when you allow the controls within it to grow is if the finished report absolutely must fit within a certain page count or perhaps has been designed to match some preexisting form, such as a medical or government form. In these such situations, you may not want to set controls to expand either, but rather size them to take up a fixed amount of space, just as the entry spaces for information on a preprinted form would.

REFERENCE WINDOW RW

Applying the Can Grow Property

- Open the report in Design view.
- Open the property sheet for the text box control for the field with data that uses more than one line.
- Click the list arrow for the Can Grow property, and then click Yes.
- Close the property sheet.

It is time to make some formatting changes to the report's design, and change the Can Grow property for the tblDepartments.DeptName field to Yes so that it wraps to two lines.

To format the rptEmployeesBySupervisor report:

1. Size the DeptNo Header section so that it is approximately 1" tall, click **View** on the menu bar, and then click **Page Header/Footer** to delete these sections from the report. Note that you might have to expand the menu to see all of its options if the Page Header/Footer item is not immediately visible.
2. Add a label below the MovieCam Technologies text box in the Report Header, type **Employees By Supervisor**, change the font size to **14**, and change the alignment to **Center**. Expand the label control to be approximately as wide as the as the text box above it, and resize the label control vertically, if necessary, to ensure all the text in the label is clearly visible.
3. Insert field labels in the DeptNo Header section as shown in Figure 5-12, pressing **Ctrl + Enter** to create a new line in a label. Make the labels the same width as the text boxes they represent, and line them up manually as close as you can, as shown in Figure 5-12. You are inserting the labels in the DeptNo Header section instead of in the Page Header section because each group begins on a new page.

Figure 5-12 ADDING LABEL CONTROLS TO THE REPORT

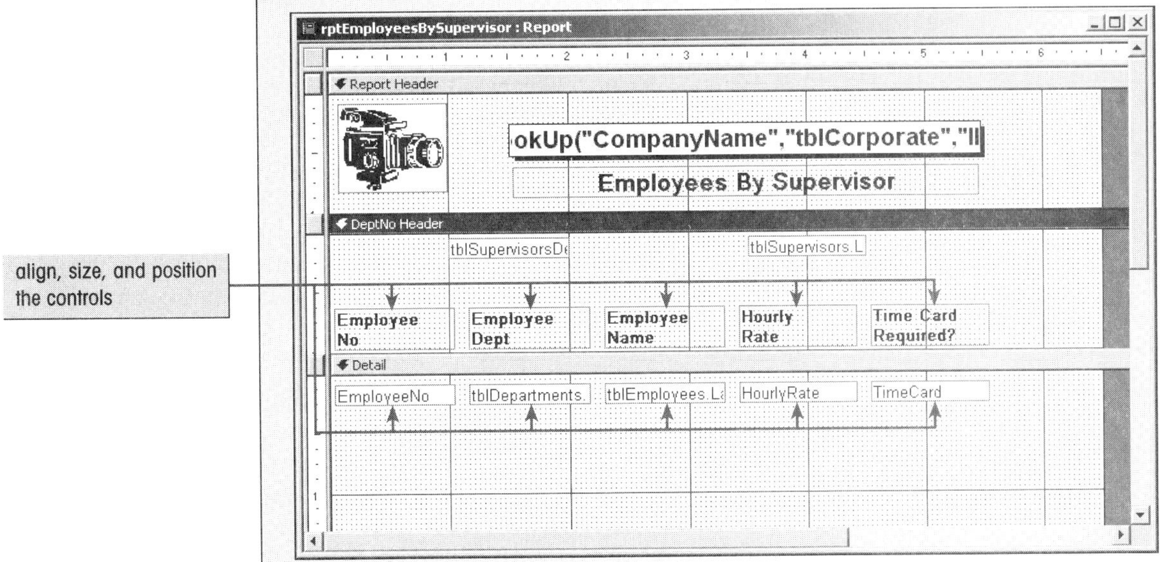

4. Click the **Line** button on the toolbox, press and hold the **Shift** key, and drag below the labels to create a straight horizontal line.
5. Align the line to the bottom of the label controls. The line should start at the left edge of the Employee No label and end at the right edge of the Time Card Required? label. This will present a more pleasing appearance and help to visually set the labels off from the data that will print on the report.
6. Scroll to the bottom of the report window so you can more easily work with the Detail section, drag the Detail section of the report up so that it is approximately 1/4" tall, and then adjust the vertical placement of the text box controls in the Detail section as shown in Figure 5-13.

Figure 5-13 **ALIGNING CONTROLS ON THE rptEmployeesBySupervisor REPORT**

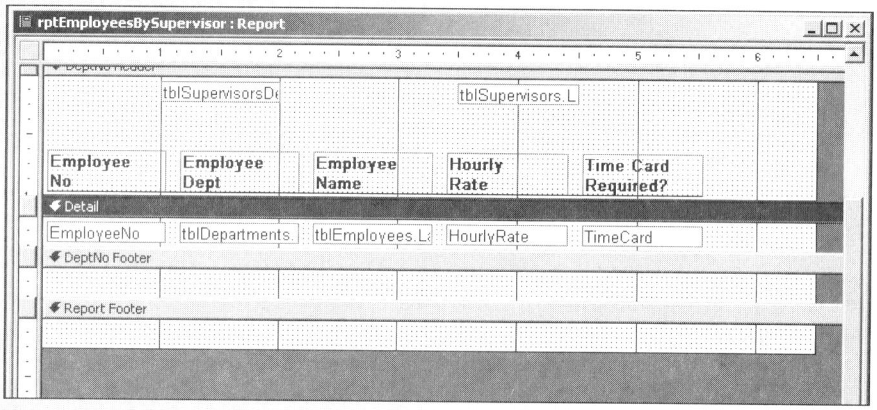

7. Left-align the labels in the DeptNo Header section with the text boxes in the Detail section, and adjust their width to be the same as each of their corresponding text boxes, if you have not already done so. Change the font size of the labels in the DeptNo Header section to **9**. The labels should already be bold because default labels in the template are bold.
8. Center the alignment of the **Employee No** and **Time Card Required?** labels and their corresponding text boxes. The rest of the labels and text boxes should be aligned left.
9. Click the **tblDepartments.DeptName** text box in the Detail section of the report, open the property sheet for the text box control, and then change its Can Grow property to **Yes**.
10. Size and align the **tblSupervisorsDept.DeptName** and **tblSupervisors.LastName** fields in the DeptNo Header section as shown in Figure 5-14, and then apply the **Bold** style to both fields. Leave the font size at 10. Note that you can use the property sheet to set the width for the tblSupervisorDept.DeptName control to 2.25" and the width of the tblSupervisors.LastName to 1.75".
11. Click the **DeptNo Footer** section, change the Force New Page property to **After Section**, and then close the property sheet.
12. Create a text box in the DeptNo Footer section, and then set its Control Source property to **=Count(EmployeeNo)**, or simply type the expression into the text box.

13. Create a label to the left of the text box, and then type **Total Employees** in the label control. This should ensure that all the text displays properly and is not cropped in any way when you preview or print the report. Size and align the new controls to be approximately as shown in Figure 5-14.

Figure 5-14 ADDING AN EXPRESSION TO THE DeptNo FOOTER SECTION

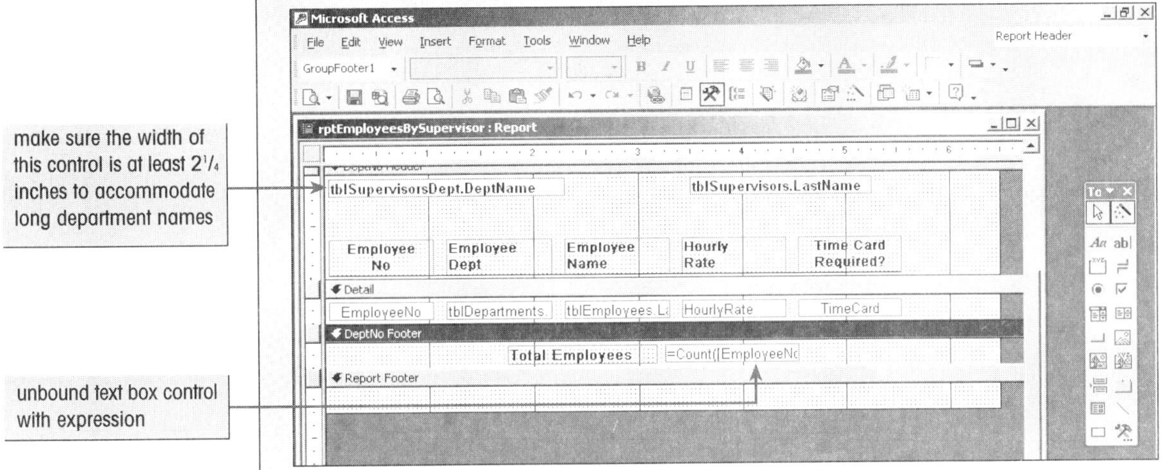

14. Preview the report. Use the navigation buttons at the bottom to move between pages. Note that the logo, company name, and title appear only on the first page. This is because these items are in the Report Header section of the report.

15. Save your changes, and then return to Design view.

You realized two things when you previewed the report. One is that because these pages will be distributed to various supervisors, the data in the Report Header section should be moved to the DeptNo Header section; then it will appear on each page of the report. As a result, you will no longer need the Report Header section. You also realized that you did not include criteria in the query so that only active employees are included in the report.

REFERENCE WINDOW RW

Modifying the Query from the Report Window

- Open the report in Design view.
- Open the property sheet for the report.
- Click the Record Source text box, and then click its Build button to open the query the report uses as its record source.
- Make the necessary changes to the query fields, criteria, and sort order.
- Save the changes and then close the query.
- Save the changes and then close the report.

All the test records in the tblEmployees table include active employees. However, the final data will include terminated employees. You need to add the field and criteria to the query to designate only active employees in this report.

To change the query of the report from Design view:

1. Click the **report selector** (the box in the left corner of the report at the intersection of the vertical and horizontal rulers) to select the report, and then open its property sheet.
2. Click the **Build** button ... for the Record Source property to open the qryEmployeesBySupervisor query in the Query Builder window.
3. Scroll to display the first empty column in the design grid, and then add the **Terminated** field from the tblEmployees table field list to the empty column.
4. Click the **Criteria** row in the Terminated column, type **No**, and then close the query.
5. Click the **Yes** button to save the change, returning focus to the Report design, and then close the property sheet.

Now you move the controls from the Report Header section to the DeptNo Group Header section, and remove the Report Header from the report. You need to resize the DeptNo Header section and move its existing controls down first.

To move the controls and eliminate the Report Header section:

1. Increase the height of the DeptNo Header section so that it is approximately 2" tall, and then select all the controls in the section, as shown in Figure 5-15. Be sure to select the horizontal line below the labels, as well.

Figure 5-15 SELECTING THE CONTROLS IN THE DeptNo HEADER SECTION

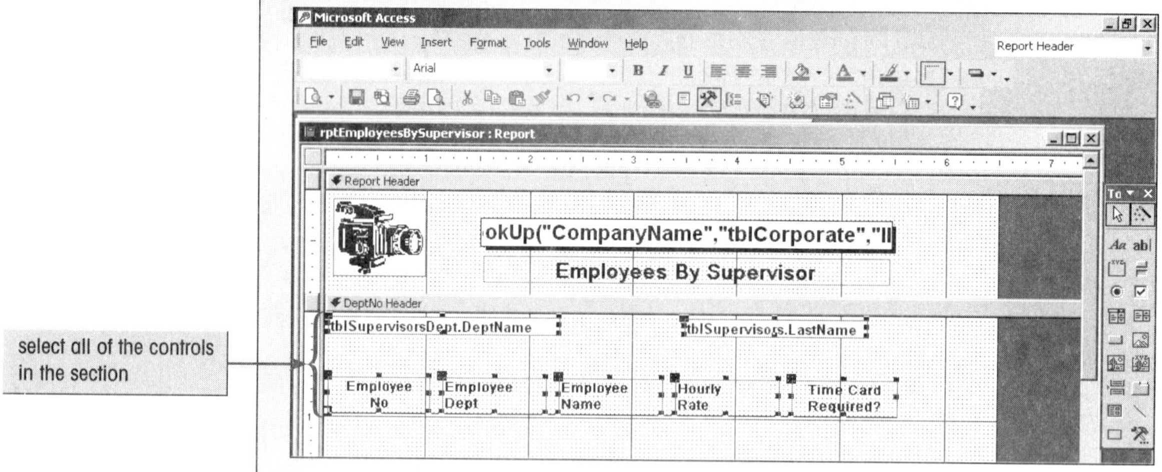

2. Drag all the controls towards the bottom of the section, select all the controls in the Report Header section, and then cut them either by using a menu item, shortcut keys, toolbar button, or shortcut menu.
3. Right-click in an empty area in the DeptNo Header section, and then click **Paste** on the shortcut menu.

4. Click **View** on the menu bar, and then click **Report Header/Footer** to deselect it. Your report should look like that shown in Figure 5-16.

Figure 5-16 MOVING CONTROLS AND DELETING THE REPORT HEADER/FOOTER SECTION

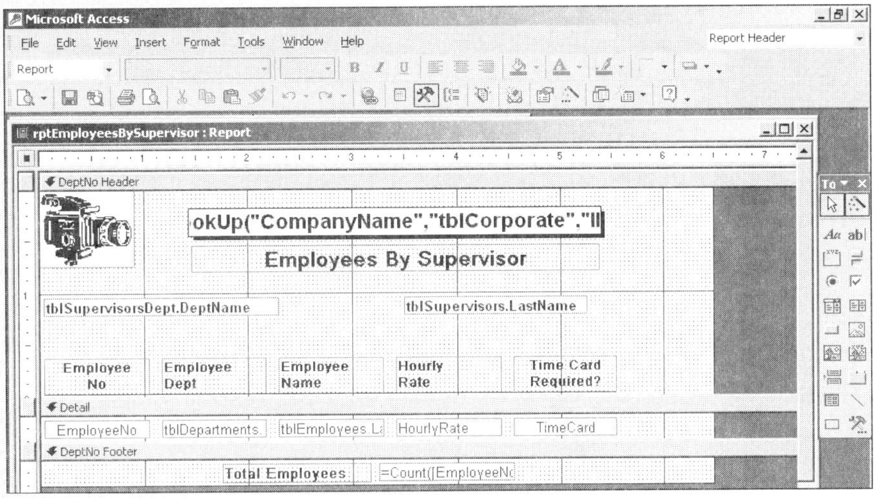

5. Click the **Logo control** in the DeptNo Header section, open the property sheet, and change the Size Mode property to **Stretch**, if necessary. It might have changed back to Clip when you cut and pasted the control.
6. Close the property sheet, save your changes, and then preview the report.
7. If any text from the department name and last name controls in the DeptNo Header section is not visible, increase the height of those two controls so nothing is cropped.

Now that you have completed the report for the product managers, you want Martin to take a look at it, so you decide to e-mail it to him in a snapshot format because you are not sure if he has Access installed on his computer. This way he can look at the report and then e-mail a response at his convenience. In this case, you are sending a snapshot as a file attachment.

REFERENCE WINDOW RW

Sending a Report in Snapshot Format

- Preview the report that you want to send.
- Click File on the menu bar, point to Send To, and then click Mail Recipient (as Attachment).
- In the Send dialog box, click Snapshot Format, and then click the OK button.
- Complete the e-mail message by entering the address of the recipient, the subject of the message, and an appropriate message.
- Click the Send button.

A report snapshot is a file (.snp extension) that contains a high-fidelity copy of each page of a report and that preserves the two-dimensional layout, graphics, and other embedded objects of the report. You can also embed a report snapshot as an icon or as a file in an e-mail message using such e-mail programs as Microsoft Outlook or Microsoft Exchange that support ActiveX controls.

Snapshot Viewer is a program used to view, print, and mail a snapshot, such as a report snapshot. Snapshot Viewer version 9.0 consists of a stand-alone executable program, a Snapshot Viewer control (snapview.ocx), a Help file, and other related files. The Report Snapshot feature is built into Access 2002. The advantage of sending a report snapshot is that the recipient doesn't need Access to view the report, but they do need the Snapshot Viewer. If the recipient does not have the Snapshot Viewer installed, it is available from the Microsoft Web site *www.microsoft.com/accessdev/prodinfo/snapshot.htm*. This Web site also provides additional information about working with snapshots.

Note: You must have a working e-mail account to export a report snapshot. For the purposes of this exercise, Microsoft Outlook 2002 is the e-mail program used, but you can use most any e-mail program. Your screen will differ somewhat from the figures shown if you are not using Outlook 2002. If you do not have an e-mail program installed on your computer, read the following set of steps without performing them.

To send the report in snapshot format:

1. Make sure that your e-mail program is open and operational.
2. With the report still displayed in Print Preview, click **File** on the menu bar, point to **Send To**, and then click **Mail Recipient (as Attachment)**.
3. In the Send dialog box, click **Snapshot Format**, and then click the **OK** button. Microsoft Outlook (or your default e-mail program) should already be open, but if you did not open it, you may be prompted to choose a profile. If so, choose your preferred e-mail program. In the illustration below, a new e-mail message is set up with the report attached in Outlook 2002, as illustrated in Figure 5-17.

Figure 5-17 ATTACHING A SNAPSHOT TO AN E-MAIL

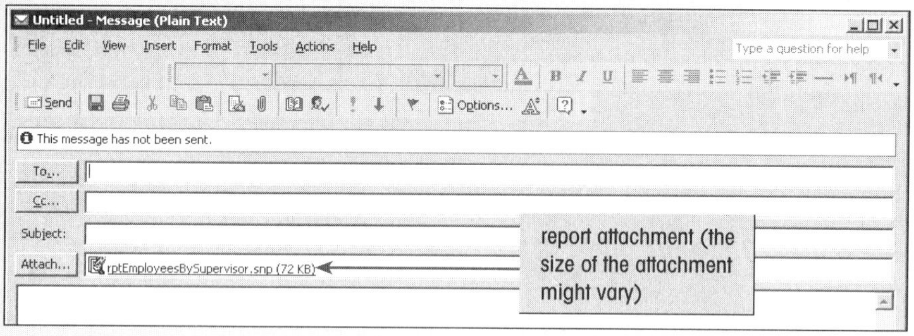

4. Address the e-mail to your instructor, and then type **MovieCam Technologies Report** in the subject line.
5. Complete the e-mail message text as shown in Figure 5-18, and then send the message.

Figure 5-18 **SENDING AN E-MAIL**

enter your instructor's actual e-mail address

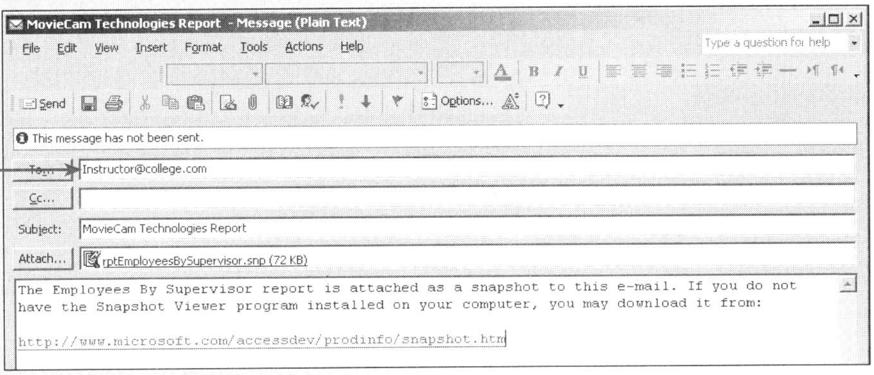

6. Close the report.

You have completed the report master and the first report for Martin. You will now direct your attention to a report for Daniel Jenkins. This report requires that you work with event properties. You will review event properties and design the remaining report in the next session.

Session 5.1 QUICK CHECK

1. What is the purpose of domain aggregate functions?
2. The ______________ argument in DLookup is optional. If it is not included, all records will be returned.
3. Which type of image control should be used for an object that will be updated automatically when the source file is changed?
4. The Report Header is printed before the ______________ on the first page of the report.
5. What is the Detail section of a report?
6. In which sections of a report can expressions be included without you having to write a macro or Visual Basic code?
7. What is a self-join?
8. What is the effect of setting the Can Grow property of a control to Yes?
9. Explain the advantage of sending a report as a snapshot.

SESSION 5.2

In this session, you will learn more about event properties and use the print event properties of reports to execute macros and VBA code. You will create a report that contains a summary subreport, add a chart to a report, and create an expression in a Page Footer section using VBA code. You also will create a macro to cancel printing a blank report and then convert the macro to a VBA function. Then you will add line items to a report using the Running Sum property, and learn a technique for adding blank rows to the Detail section of a report.

Event Properties

Events and event properties were discussed briefly in Tutorial 4. Remember that forms, reports, and controls and sections on forms and reports have event properties. Tables and queries do not. An explanation of the categories of events follows:

- **Data events**: These events occur when data is entered, deleted, or changed in a form or control. They also occur when the focus moves from one record to another. The AfterUpdate event you used to run a macro in Tutorial 4 falls into this category. Some other data events include Current, BeforeUpdate, Dirty, and Delete.
- **Error and timing events**: These events are used for error-handling and synchronizing data on forms or reports. They include the Error event found on forms and reports and the Timer event found on forms.
- **Filter events**: These events occur when you apply or create a filter on a form. The ApplyFilter and Filter events are included in this category.
- **Focus events**: These events occur when a form or control loses or gains the focus. They also occur when a form or report becomes the active or inactive window. Focus is the ability to receive mouse or user input through mouse or keyboard actions. In the Windows environment, only one item at a time can have the focus. If you try to type a string into a text box, but some other item on the form has the focus, the input is not accepted. You must click the text box so that it has the focus, and then type the string. Examples include the Activate, Deactivate, GotFocus, and LostFocus events.
- **Keyboard events**: These events occur when you type on a keyboard. They also occur when either keystrokes that use the Sendkeys macro action or keystrokes that use the Sendkeys statement in VBA are sent to a form or a control on a form. Some examples of keyboard events are KeyDown, KeyUp, and KeyPress.
- **Mouse events**: These events occur in a form or in a control on a form as a result of a mouse action, such as pressing down or clicking the mouse button. The Click event that you used in Tutorial 4 falls into this category. Other mouse events include DblClick, MouseDown, and MouseMove.
- **Print events**: These events are found on reports and report sections, and occur when a report is printed or formatted for printing. Examples are the NoData and Print events, which you will apply in this tutorial.
- **Window events**: These events occur when you open, resize, or close a form or report. Some examples of these events are Open, Close, and Load.

The Print Events

The Print events, which are triggered by reports and report sections, include the following:

- **Format**: This event occurs when Access determines what data goes in a report section, but happens before the section is formatted for previewing or for printing.
- **NoData**: This event occurs after Access formats a report for printing when the report has no data (the underlying recordset contains no records), but before the report is printed. This event is used to cancel printing a blank report.
- **Page**: This event occurs after Access formats a page for printing, but before the page is printed.
- **Print**: This event occurs after Access has formatted the data in a report section, but before the section is printed.
- **Retreat**: This event occurs when Access must back up past one or more report sections on a page in order to perform multiple formatting passes. Retreat occurs after the section's Format event, but before the Print event. The retreat event for each section occurs as Access backs up past the section. This allows you to undo any changes you have made during the Format event for the section.

Using the NoData Event

You created the report of terminated employees that Daniel Jenkins requested. It is named rptTermEmployees and uses the qryTermEmployees query for its record source. Although records for terminated employees will be stored in the final database, the sample records that you are working with do not include data on terminated employees; so this report contains no records. In the future, terminated employees might be archived out at year end, so at times there will be no records in this report.

REFERENCE WINDOW RW

Changing the NoData Event Property

- Open the report in Design view and open the property sheet.
- Click the Event tab in the property sheet, click the On No Data text box, and then click the Build button.
- Click Macro Builder, click the OK button, type a macro group name, and then click the OK button.
- If necessary, type a macro name in the first column, click the Action list arrow, click Msgbox, and then type a comment in the last column.
- In the Action Argument section, click the Message text box and type a message that tells the user the report has no data. If desired, change the Type argument to Information, and the information icon displays in the message box.
- Click the next row of the Action column, click the Action list arrow, and then click CancelEvent.
- Type a comment in the third column, and then save and close the macro.

You will create a macro that uses the NoData print event which, as you learned, stops the printing or previewing of a report that contains no data. This macro will be saved in the mcrGlobal macro and can be used by any of the reports in the database.

To change the NoData event:

1. If you took a break after the previous session, make sure that Access is running and that the **Movie5** database located in the Tutorial.05\Tutorial folder on your local or network drive is open.
2. Open the **rptTermEmployees** report in Print Preview, and then maximize the report window and zoom in on the report. There are no records in the report, and there is an error in the location where the expression in the Report Footer section that counts the total number of employees would appear.
3. Switch to Design view, resize the report window if necessary, and then open the property sheet for the report.
4. Click the **Event** tab, click in the **On No Data** text box, and then click its **Build** button [...].
5. Click **Macro Builder**, click the **OK** button, type **mcrGlobal** for the macro name, and then press the **Enter** key.
6. Type **Report_NoData** in the Macro Name column, click the **Action** list arrow, click **MsgBox**, press the **Tab** key, and then type **Displays a message box stating that there are no records in the report**.

   TROUBLE? If the Macro Name column is not displayed, click View on the menu bar and click Macro Names. To change the default settings so the Macro Name column is always displayed, click Tools on the menu bar, click the Options command, click the View tab, and then click the Names column option.

   The first argument of the Msgbox action is Message. You can enter up to 255 characters or an expression that you want shown in the message box. The second argument, Beep, can be Yes or No and specifies whether your computer beeps when the message is shown. The third argument, Type, specifies a type of icon that will be in the message box. The choices are None, Critical, Warning?, Warning!, or Information. The default is None. The fourth argument, Title, specifies the text you want in the title bar of the message dialog box. If it is left blank, "Microsoft Access" is used in the title bar.
7. In the Action Arguments section, click the **Message** text box, type **This report has no data**, click the **Type** list arrow, and then click **Information**, as shown in Figure 5-19.

Figure 5-19 SETTING THE ARGUMENTS FOR THE MSGBOX ACTION

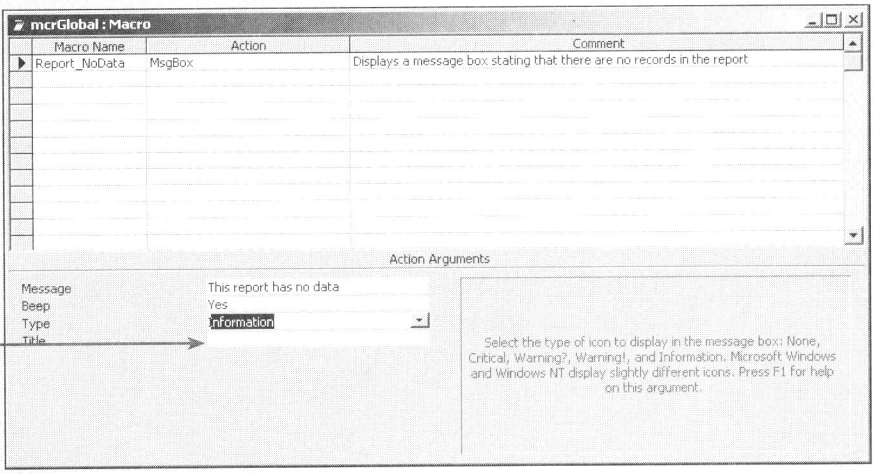

no title had been entered

8. Click the second row of the Action column, click the **Action** list arrow, click **CancelEvent**, press the **Tab** key, type **Cancels printing or previewing of the report**, and then save your changes and close the macro. The CancelEvent action has no arguments and cancels the event that caused this macro to run, which in this case is previewing the report.

9. In the property sheet, click the **On No Data** list arrow, and then click **mcrGlobal.Report_NoData** to select the specific macro that you want to run from within the mcrGlobal macro. See Figure 5-20. The property sheet has been widened for use in the figure below.

Figure 5-20 ASSIGNING THE MACRO TO TEST THE REPORT FOR NO DATA

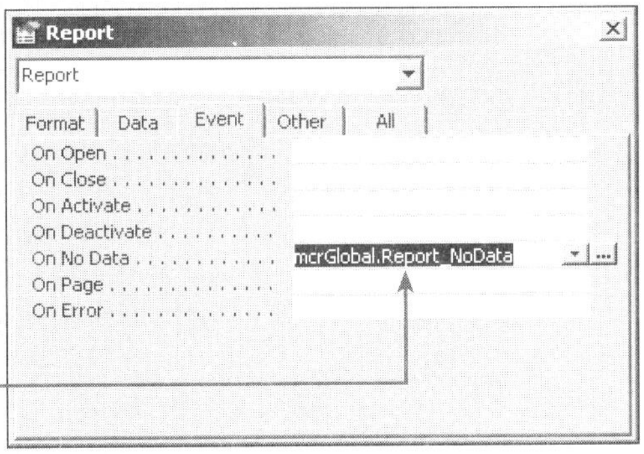

indicates the macro that will run for the On No Data event

10. Close the property sheet, save your changes, close the report, select the **rptTermEmployees** report, and then click **Preview** to test the macro. A message box opens and advises that there are no records.

11. Click the **OK** button to acknowledge the error message. The macro cancels the previewing event.

Converting Macros to VBA Code

You decide that you would rather use VBA code in place of macros whenever possible. Macros might be simpler to write, but VBA code executes faster, allows for error-handling and is a better way to automate the user interface.

Access can automatically convert macros to VBA event procedures or to modules that perform equivalent actions. You can convert macros on a form or report, or you can convert global macros that aren't attached to a specific form or report. You will convert the mcrGlobal macro you just wrote.

REFERENCE WINDOW RW

Converting a Macro to VBA

- Click Macros on the Objects bar of the Database window, and then click the macro you want to convert.
- Click Tools on the menu bar, point to Macro, and then click Convert Macros to Visual Basic.
- In the Convert Macro dialog box, be sure that the Add error handling to generated functions and the Include macro comments check boxes are selected, and then click the Convert button.
- Click the OK button.

Because the macro you are converting is a global macro, Access automatically converts it to a function in a standard module. A **function procedure**, often just called a function, returns a value, such as the result of a calculation. In addition to the Access built-in functions, you can create your own custom functions. A **sub procedure**, on the other hand, is a series of VBA statements that performs actions but does not return a value. Sub procedures and event procedures were introduced at the end of Tutorial 4.

Because functions return values, you can use them in expressions, property settings, or as criteria in queries and filters. Functions can also be used to do work and not return a value, which is referred to in some programming languages as a **Void** function, denoting that it returns nothing. Although the macro you will convert to a function procedure does not need to return a value, the procedure still needs to be a function rather than a sub. Recall from Tutorial 4 that event procedures are sub procedures and are stored in Access class modules associated with a specific form or report object. These event (sub) procedures have a consistent, mandatory naming convention in order to be associated with the intended event of the form or report object. Whenever you want to assign a procedure to an event that is not stored within that form or report's class module, the procedure must be a function procedure. Such a function procedure would be stored within a **standard module**.

Standard modules have general procedures that are not associated with any specific object in the database and are intended for frequently used procedures that can be run from anywhere within your database. As such, these typically apply to more than one object, but are coded once and stored in one place. This is considered to be a best programming practice in the industry and is the nature of what is called modular coding. Consider how much easier this code is to maintain or to change when it resides in one spot instead of copied and pasted into the class module of every form or report. Standard modules are listed as module objects in the Database window, but class modules for forms and reports are not shown in the Database window.

You need to convert the macro that you created to respond when no data was found for a report into VBA code as a function. This is a good example of when you would create a function and place it in a standard module. Just as you created one macro that could be called from any report if the **NoData** event was triggered, you will convert this macro to one VBA function that can be called by any report. This way, you do not place the same VBA code in every single Report class module. Rather, you write the code once and update or maintain it from a single location: a standard module.

To convert a macro to VBA:

1. Click **Macros** on the Objects bar of the Database window, and then make sure the **mcrGlobal** macro is selected.
2. Click **Tools** on the menu bar, point to **Macro**, and then click **Convert Macros to Visual Basic**.
3. In the Convert macro dialog box, be sure that the **Add error handling to generated functions** and **Include macro comments** check boxes are selected. See Figure 5-21. These options add some generic error handling to the function and add descriptions that are the same as those included in the macro.

Figure 5-21 CONVERT MACRO DIALOG BOX

4. Click the **Convert** button, and then click the **OK** button in the Convert macros to Visual Basic dialog box.
5. If necessary, resize the Visual Basic window so you can see all the code, but you do not need to maximize the window.
6. Click **Edit** on the menu bar, click **Replace**, type **mcrGlobal_Report_NoData** in the Find What text box, type **Report_NoData** in the Replace With text box, click the **Replace All** button, and then click the **OK** button in the message box that tells you six replacements were made. This search-and-replace procedure eliminates the mcrGlobal string, which can look confusing in the code.

   Trouble? If a message is displayed stating that the specified text was not found, make sure that there are no spaces at the beginning or end of the Find and Replace strings you entered in this step, that there are no extra code windows open, and that you are working within the new function that Access just converted from the macro. Try the step again.

7. Close the Replace dialog box. The procedure should now look like that shown in Figure 5-22.

Figure 5-22 **Report_NoData FUNCTION**

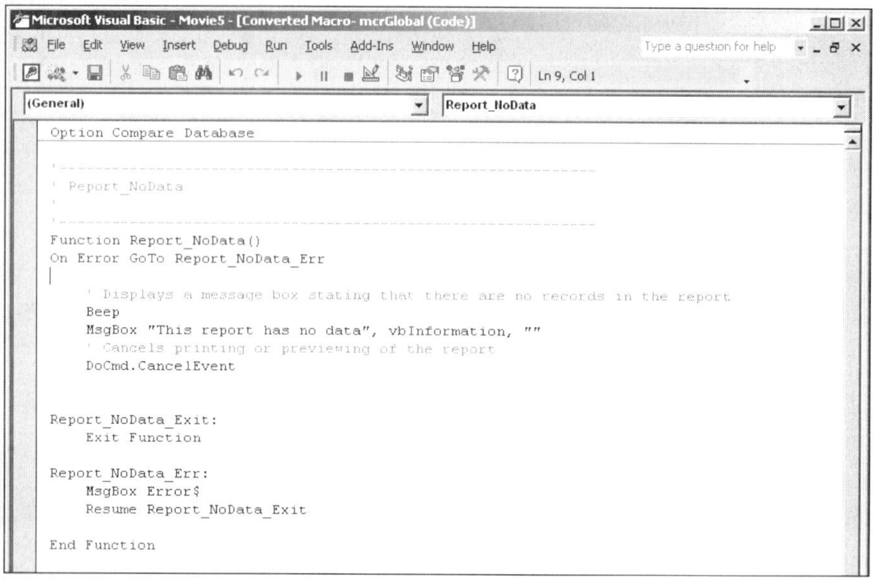

8. Click the **Debug** menu and then click **Compile MovieCam** to compile the code. Compiling checks for syntax errors. Save your changes and close the Visual Basic window.
9. Click **Modules** on the Objects bar of the Database window, right-click the **Converted Macro- mcrGlobal** module, click **Rename**, type **mdlReportFunctions**, and then press the **Enter** key. This name better describes the type of function contained in this module. Recall that the mdl tag is an abbreviation for module. The mdl tag is typically used by developers for modules in Access only (VBA), while the bas (for "basic") tag is typically used exclusively as a tag for basic modules in the complete Visual Basic programming integrated development environment.

Next you want to test the function. Before you delete the mcrGlobal macro, you will change the NoData event property of the rptTermEmployees report to the function name instead of the macro name, and then preview the report to test the function.

To assign a VBA function to an event property:

1. Open the **rptTermEmployee**s report in Design view, open the property sheet for the report, and then click the **Event** tab if necessary.
2. Delete **mcrGlobal.Report_NoData** from the On NoData event property text box, type **=Report_NoData()** as the new property value, and then close the property sheet.
3. Save your changes and then close the report.
4. Preview the report. A message box such as that shown in Figure 5-23 opens.

Figure 5-23 **ERROR MESSAGE DIALOG BOX**

5. Click the **OK** button. Note that there is no title in the message box. This is because you did not enter a title in the macro steps and so when you converted this to VBA, the title was left blank as well.

Daniel Jenkins also requested a report on all active employees. It is similar to the rptTermEmployees report. You designed the report, but you still need to add an expression to count the number of employees. This report has no grouping levels, so only the Report Footer section can contain the expression. However, the Report Footer prints on the last page of the report and Daniel wants to have the number of employees shown on each page of the report.

When you include a calculated expression in a Report Footer or a Group Footer, Access knows to which records the expression applies, and does the calculation for the expression before laying out the pages of the report in memory. If you try to calculate an expression in a Page Footer, an error results because Access does not know which records to include in the calculation of the expression until after the page has been laid out. To overcome this limitation you can create a macro or write VBA code to perform the calculation.

You can use the Print event to run the code that will perform calculations for a text box contained in a Page Footer. A report section recognizes the Print event after the section has been laid out, but before the section is printed or displayed in Print Preview.

To calculate a count of employees on each page, you can place an unbound text box in the Page Footer section. Use the unbound text box to tabulate the total number of employees on the page as Access lays out the records. A new page starts after Access recognizes the Print event as it lays out the Page Header. So you will use the Print event of the Page Header to initialize the unbound text box. You will set the value of the unbound text box to 0 before any records are added, and then increment the value of the text box by 1 for each record that is laid out.

The Print event of the Detail section is recognized each time a record is laid out in the Detail section, but before the record is printed. You will use this event to run a line of code that increments the value of the text box by 1 for each record in the Detail section. By the time all the records are laid out in a page of the report, the value in the text box will be equal to the total number of records on that page.

REFERENCE WINDOW RW

Using the Code Builder

- Open the form or report for which you are writing the VBA code in Design view.
- Click the control or section that will run the code.
- Open the property sheet, click the Event tab, and click the Build button in the text box of the property that will run the code.
- Click Code Builder and then click the OK button.
- Type the code and then close the Visual Basic window.

You will use the Code Builder to create two event procedures. Remember from Tutorial 4 that an event procedure is a group of statements that executes when an event occurs. You also will create these event procedures in a form class module. A **form class module** is saved as part of a form and contains one or many procedures that apply specifically to that form. Form class modules will be discussed in greater detail in Tutorial 7.

To create the report module for a page record count:

1. Open the **rptActiveEmployees** report in Design view, open the toolbox if necessary, click the **Text Box** button ab| on the toolbox, and then click in the **Page Footer** section at the 5" mark on the horizontal ruler to create an unbound text box control.
2. Open the property sheet for the new control, click the **All** tab, and then change the Name property to **txtCount**. Leave the property sheet open.
3. Insert a label control to the left of the text box, and then type **Total Employees**, as shown in Figure 5-24.

Figure 5-24 INSERTING A LABEL IN THE REPORT

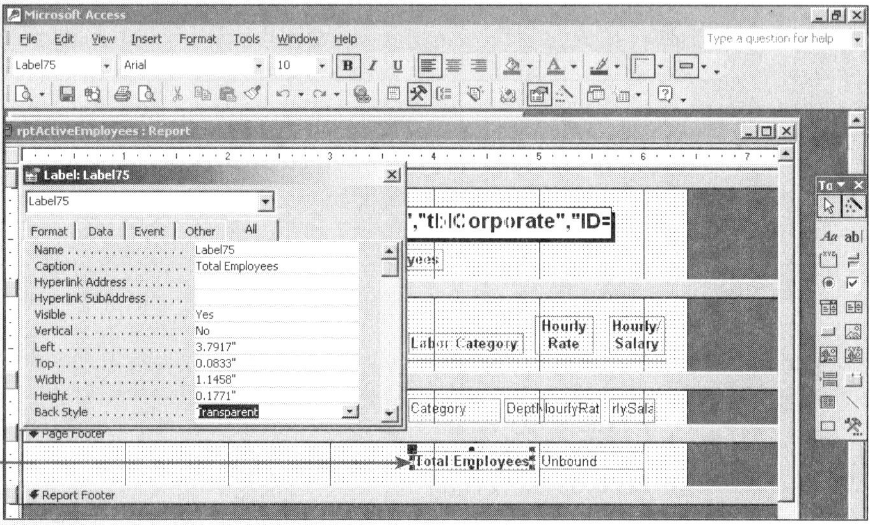

create label here

4. Change the Height property of the text box and label to **0.225"**.
5. Click the **PageHeader** section band, and then click the **Event** tab on the property sheet.
6. Click the **Build** button ... for the On Print property, click **Code Builder** in the Choose Builder dialog box, and then click the **OK** button. The Code window opens and the first and last line of the event procedure are created automatically, as shown in Figure 5-25.

Figure 5-25 **CODE WINDOW**

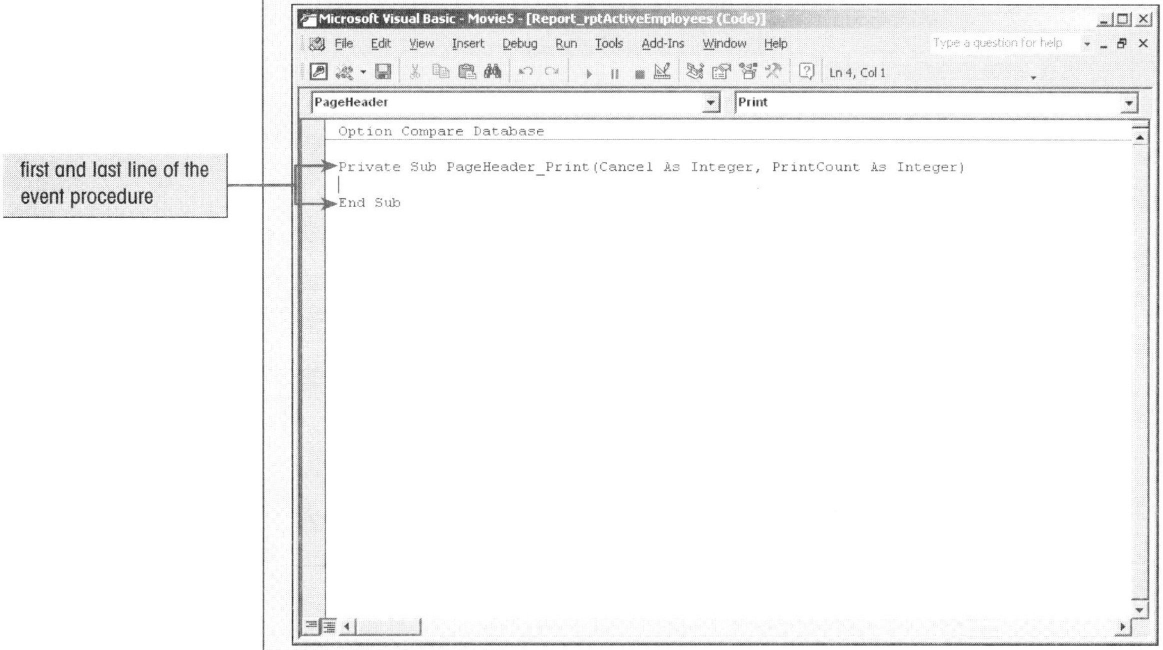

7. Press the **Tab** key to indent the line, and then type **txtCount = 0**. This statement sets the txtCount text box, which actually resides in the Page Footer section, equal to zero at the beginning of each new page before the detail section is laid out for that page.
8. Compile the code, save your changes, and then return to the Database window and the report design.
9. Click the **Detail** section band, click in the **On Print** text box in the property sheet, click its **Build** button [...], click **Code Builder**, and then click the **OK** button.
10. Press the **Tab** key to indent the line, and then type **txtCount = txtCount + 1**, as shown in Figure 5-26. This statement increments the value of the txtCount text box by 1 each time a record on the page is laid out.

Figure 5-26 **ENTERING CODE FOR THE EVENT PROCEDURES**

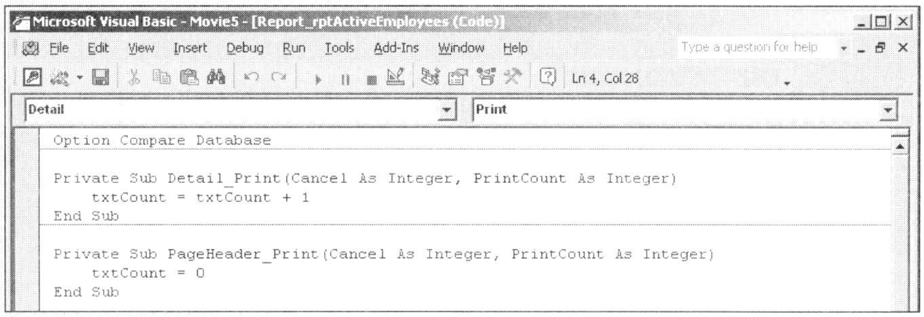

11. Compile the code, save your changes, and then close the Visual Basic window.
12. Close the property sheet, preview the report, scroll down to see the contents of the expression, and then close the report.

You need to create one last report for the product managers. It will show a detailed listing of hours by job, and a summary of hours by quarter of the year.

Creating **Numbered Lists**

You have begun the design of the report and named it rptHoursByJob. The report's record source is the qryHoursByJob query. This query contains a list of hours for each job by each employee. The report groups records on the JobID field. A page break has been inserted after the Group Footer section so each job number begins on a new page. The product managers want a line item number for each entry on the report to serve as a point of reference.

As you know, records are not numbered in the report, they simply appear in the order determined by the underlying query or table (the record source) if no sorting or grouping has been specified elsewhere in the report. Settings applied in the Sorting and Grouping dialog box override the sort order of the records in the record source. To create a reference number for each record, you can insert a text box and use the Running Sum property to increment the text box's value.

The Running Sum Property

You use the Running Sum property to calculate record-by-record totals or group-by-group totals in a report. You can specify that the text box display a running total, and you can set the range over which to accumulate the values.

For example, in the rptEmployeesByDept report, an expression in the DeptNo Footer section counts the number of employees in each department. If you set the Running Sum property on this control to Over All, it counts the number in the first group and continues counting all the records in each successive group, instead of starting over with each group. The value accumulates to the end of the report.

When you set the Running Sum property to Over Group, the running sum value accumulates until another group is encountered.

REFERENCE WINDOW RW

Using the Running Sum Property to Number Items in a Report

- Open the report in Design view.
- Create an unbound text box in the Detail section of the report, change the Name property, and change the Control Source property to 1.
- Change the Running Sum property to Over All if you want the numbering to continue to the end of the report or to Over Group to begin numbering at each new group.
- If necessary, insert a label for the text box.
- Save your changes and close the report.

As previously discussed, setting the Record Source property of a text box in the Detail section of a report to equal 1 while also changing the Running Sum property to Over Group or Over All will increment the value in the text box by 1 for each detail record.

To number each Detail section line in a report:

1. Open the **rptHoursByJob** report in Design view.

2. Make sure that the toolbox is open, and then click the **Text Box** button ab| on the toolbox.

3. Click to the left of the TimeCardDate control in the Detail section of the report to create a new unbound text box.

4. Make sure the property sheet is open, click the **All** tab, change the Name property to **txtLineItem**, set the Control Source property to **=1**, and then change the Running Sum property to **Over Group**.

5. Close the property sheet and then preview the report. Each group should have numbered line items and the numbers should start over for each group. Each group begins on a new page, but whenever a group extends to more than one page, the numbering will continue for that group until the next group is encountered or until the end of the report is reached.

6. Return to Design view, size the txtLineItem text box so that it is the same height (0.225") as the other controls in the Detail section of the report, and then reposition the text box so it is aligned with the other controls, as shown in Figure 5-27. You can use the sizing and aligning shortcut menu items or the property sheet to accomplish this step.

Figure 5-27 ADDING A RUNNING SUM OVER GROUP TO THE REPORT

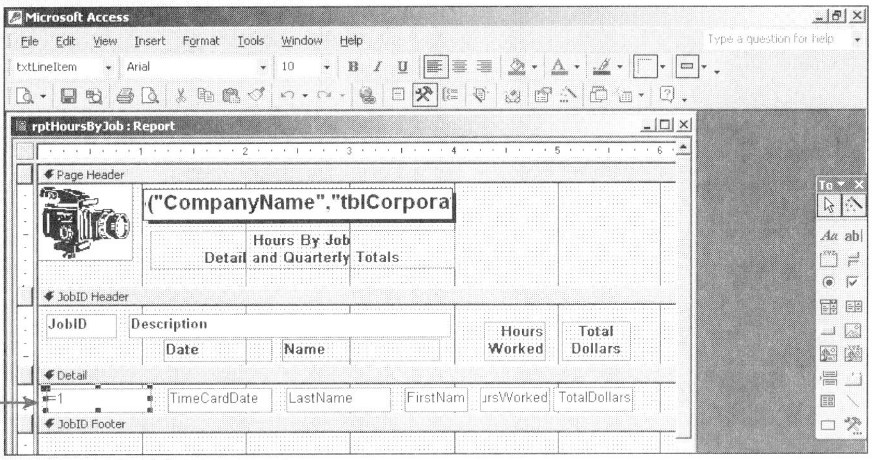

align text box with the other controls in the Detail section

7. Add a label to the JobID Header section, positioning it just below the Job ID label. Type **Line Item** in the label box. Align the label with the left edge of the txtLineItem control you just added in the Detail section. Size the height and align the bottom of the Line Item label to match the other labels in the header section.

8. Save your changes, maximize the report window, and then preview the report. Advance to page five. By scrolling a bit to the right and down slightly, page five of the final report should look like that shown in Figure 5-28.

Figure 5-28 **REPORT WITH LINE ITEM NUMBERS ADDED**

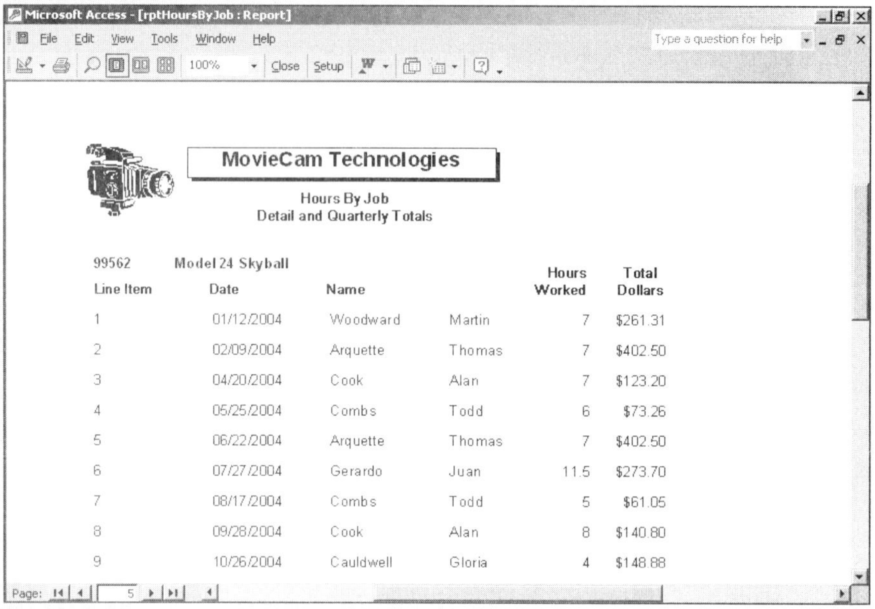

99562 Model 24 Skyball

Line Item	Date	Name		Hours Worked	Total Dollars
1	01/12/2004	Woodward	Martin	7	$261.31
2	02/09/2004	Arquette	Thomas	7	$402.50
3	04/20/2004	Cook	Alan	7	$123.20
4	05/25/2004	Combs	Todd	6	$73.26
5	06/22/2004	Arquette	Thomas	7	$402.50
6	07/27/2004	Gerardo	Juan	11.5	$273.70
7	08/17/2004	Combs	Todd	5	$61.05
8	09/28/2004	Cook	Alan	8	$140.80
9	10/26/2004	Cauldwell	Gloria	4	$148.88

9. Restore the report window and close the report.

The next step is to modify the report so that it sums the hours worked on a job during a specified quarter of the year. The quarterly totals can be calculated in a query, and then the query can be used to create a subreport on the main report.

Subreports

A **subreport** is a report that is inserted in another report. When you combine reports, one must be the main report. The main report can be bound to an underlying table, query, or SQL statement, or it can be unbound. An unbound main report can serve as a container for unrelated subreports that you want to combine. A bound report must contain a field in its record source that is also a field in its subreport(s).

A main report can contain several levels of subreports; there is no limit to the number of subreports a main report can contain, but there is a limit to what may be practical.

Subreports are often used to show summary data that is related to the detail data in the main report. In this way, subreports are similar to subforms and main forms. For example, when you view the page in the rptHoursByJob report for a specific job, you can include a subreport that has a summary of hours and dollars spent on that job during a calendar quarter.

The subreport will be based on a query you create that calculates total hours and dollars by quarter for each job. You will use the DatePart function in an aggregate query to perform these calculations.

To create a totals query for the subreport:

1. Create a new query in Design view.
2. Add the following tables to the Query window in this order: **tblEmployees**, **tblTimeCards**, **tblHours**, and **tblJobs**, and then close the Show Table dialog box.

3. Add the **JobID** field in the tblJobs field list to the design grid, click the **Field** text box of the second column in the design grid, and then type **Quarter: "Qtr" & Space(1) & DatePart("q",[TimeCardDate])**. This formula joins the abbreviation Qtr (for quarter) to the DatePart function that returns the quarter of the year in the TimeCardDate field. The quarter of the year value will be an integer value from 1 to 4.

4. Add the **HoursWorked** field in the tblHours field list to the third column of the design grid, right-click the third column, click **Properties** on the shortcut menu, and then change the Format property to **Fixed**. Leave the property sheet open.

5. Click the **Field** text box of the fourth column in the design grid, type **TotalDollars: Sum([HoursWorked]*[HourlyRate])**, and then change the Format property to **Currency**. This expression calculates the total dollars by quarter for each job. Close the property sheet. The query window should look like that shown in Figure 5-29.

Figure 5-29 DESIGNING A QUERY ON WHICH TO BASE THE SUBREPORT

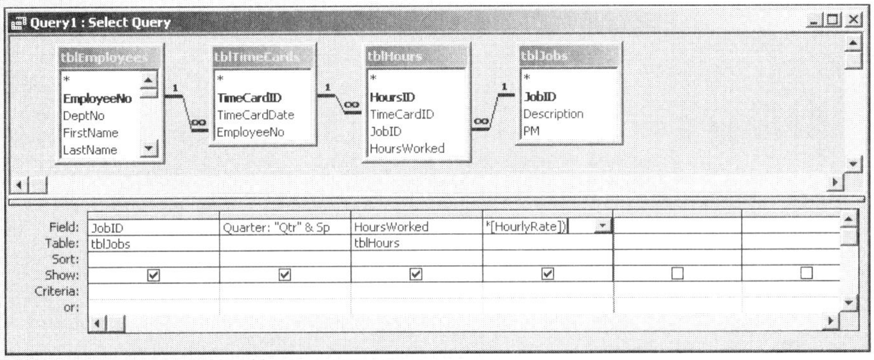

6. Click the **Totals** button Σ on the Report Design toolbar. The Total row in the design grid indicates that totals will be entered in the report.

7. Click the **list arrow** for the HoursWorked field in the Total row, click **Sum**, and then change the Total cell for TotalDollars to **Expression**. The design grid should look like that shown in Figure 5-30.

Figure 5-30 GROUPING IN THE QUERY DESIGN

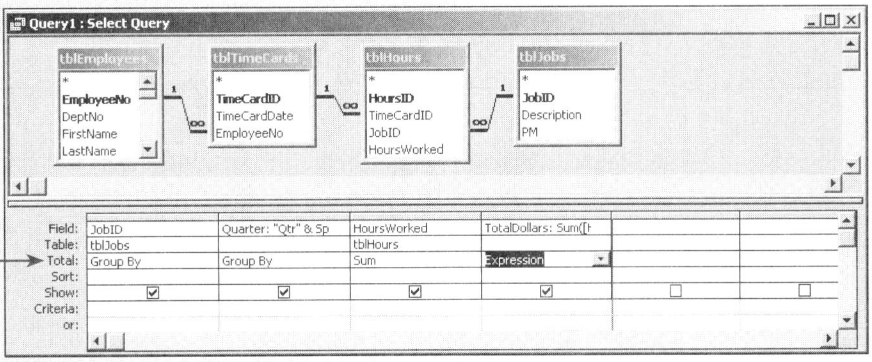

make sure the Total row is set as shown here

8. Run the query to check the results. The query results include 23 records and four columns.
9. Save the query as **qryQuarterlyTotalsByJob**, and then close the query.

Now you will create the subreport and add it to the main report. There is a button on the toolbox called Subform/Subreport, but an easy way to create one is to drag the query object from the Database window to the desired section of the report. Access will activate a wizard to insert a subreport and use the selected query as its underlying record source. After you've inserted the subreport, you can make formatting changes to it in Design view.

To create the subreport:

1. Resize the Database window horizontally to only take up the left half of your screen, if necessary. Open the **rptHoursByJob** report in Design view, close the toolbox, size the JobID Footer section to approximately 2½" tall, scroll up so you can see as much of the JobID Footer section as possible, and then size and position the report window so that you can see the Database window and the report window side by side, as shown in Figure 5-31.

Figure 5-31 POSITIONING WINDOWS TO DRAG AND DROP THE QUERY OBJECT

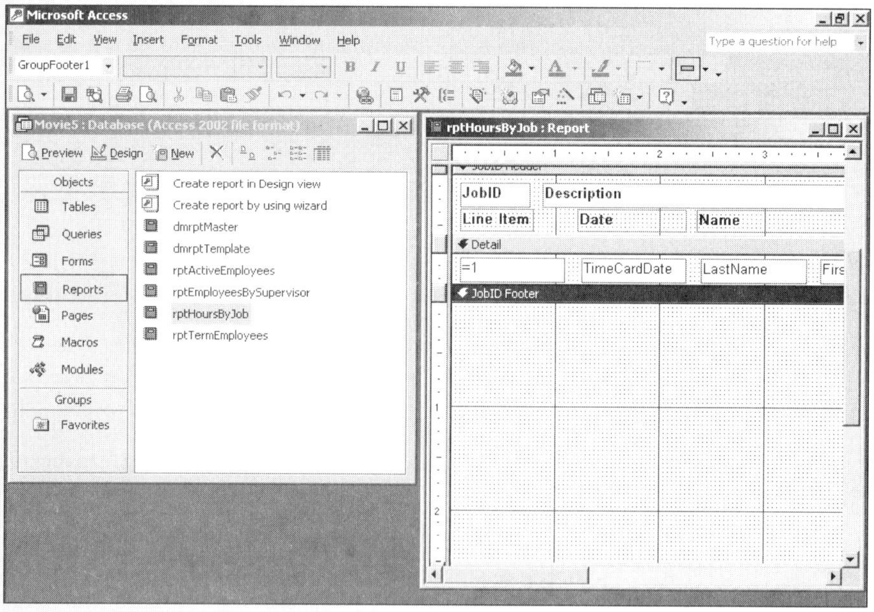

2. Click **Queries** on the Objects bar of the Database window, and then drag the **qryQuarterlyTotalsByJob** query to the upper-left portion of the JobID Footer section of the report. The SubReport Wizard opens, as shown in Figure 5-32.

Figure 5-32 SUBREPORT WIZARD DIALOG BOX

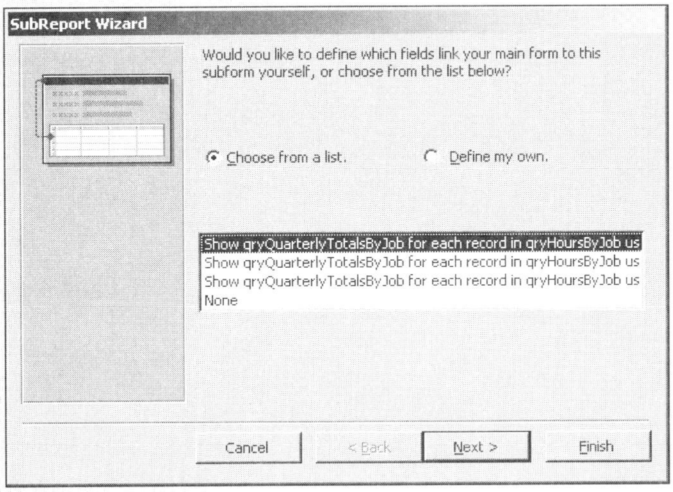

3. Click the **Define my own** option button so that you can identify the field(s) on which the main report and the subreport are linked.

4. Click the **Form/report fields** list arrow, click **JobID**, click the **Subform/subreport fields** list arrow, and then click **JobID** as shown in Figure 5-33.

Figure 5-33 LINKING THE MAIN REPORT AND SUBREPORT

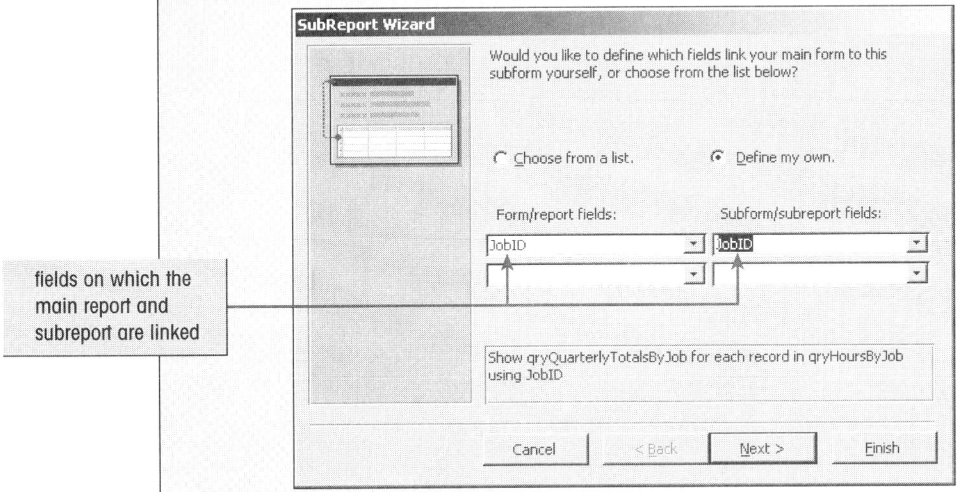

5. Click the **Next** button, type **srptQuarterlyTotalsByJob** as the name of the subreport, and then click the **Finish** button.

6. If necessary, resize the report window so it is easier to make changes to the report design, and then delete the **srptQuarterlyTotalsByJob** label above the subreport object in the JobID Footer section. If you placed the subreport in the upper-left corner of the section, you may have to reposition the subreport temporarily in order to select and delete the label. The label may only be partially showing above the subreport.

7. Reposition the subreport back to the upper-left hand corner of the JobID Footer section, leaving just a small amount of space from the edge. Notice that the Wizard also placed the subreport in such a way as to expand the report width, so you will resize both the report and subreport.
8. Reduce the subreport width to 2½", and then reduce the width of the main report back to 6½".
9. Save your changes and then close the report.

Next, you will format the subreport and add expressions to the Report Footer section that sum the hours worked and total dollars.

To complete the subreport:

1. Open the **srptQuarterlyTotalsByJob** report in Design view.
2. Delete the **JobID** label in the Report Header section, resize the JobID text box to approximately ¼" wide, and then set the Visible property of the JobID text box to **No**.

   The main report and subreport are linked by the JobID field, so this control must remain on the report; however, it does not need to be visible on the subreport when it's viewed or printed. The JobID field is located already in the JobID Header section of the main report.
3. Delete the **Quarter** label in the Report Header section because the abbreviation "Qtr" is included in the expression in the Detail section. The labels may already be bold because the subreport was created using the SubReport Wizard; therefore, the font style and color applied to the subreport is the same as the font style and color selected for the last report you created using the Report Wizard.
4. Move the Quarter text box control so it covers the JobID text box (you can use the align features to align the left edges of both controls). The JobID field is not visible now, so covering it with the Quarter text box has no negative affect on the report.
5. Using Figure 5-34 as a guide, rename, size, and reposition the labels in the Report Header section, and then size and reposition the text boxes in the Detail section.

Figure 5-34 FORMATTING CONTROLS IN THE SUBREPORT

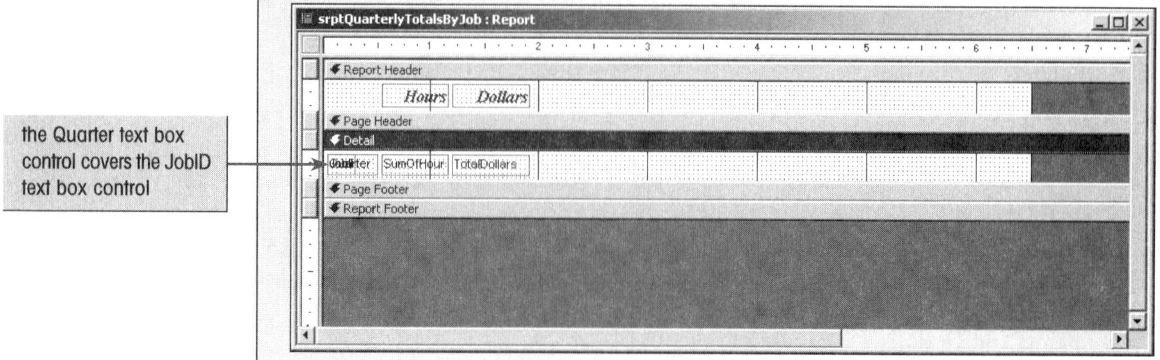

6. Size the Report Footer section of the subreport to approximately ¼" tall, and then add two text boxes to it: one beneath the SumOfHoursWorked control and the other beneath the TotalDollars control.
7. If necessary, delete any labels that Access may have added with the text boxes.
8. Click the text box control you inserted beneath the SumOfHoursWorked control, open the property sheet, change the Name property to **txtTotalHoursWorked**. Click the **txtTotalHoursWorked** text box, and then enter **=Sum([SumOfHoursWorked])** as the Control Source property. Change the Format property to **Fixed**.
9. Click the text box control you inserted beneath the TotalDollars control, and then change the Name property to **txtTotalDollars**, the Control Source property to **=Sum([TotalDollars])**, and the Format property to **Currency**.
10. Using Figure 5-35 as a guide, resize the controls and align them with those in the Detail section of the report. Select all labels and text boxes for all sections of the report, change the font to **Arial** and the font size to **8**, change the font color to **black** if necessary, and then size the report to be 2" wide. Deselect the controls, close the toolbox, close the property sheet, and your report should appear as shown in Figure 5-35.

Figure 5-35 COMPLETING THE SUBREPORT DESIGN

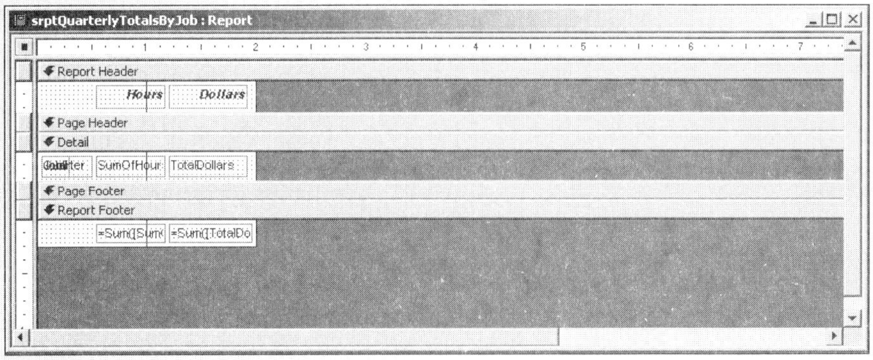

11. Save your changes, and close the report.

Next you'll size the subreport on the main report.

To size the subreport on the main report:

1. Open the **rptHoursByJob** report in Design view, and then maximize the Report window.
2. Scroll down enough so you can see the as much of the JobID Footer section as possible. Size the subreport control on the main report to approximately 2" tall and reposition it in the JobID Footer section as necessary to approximate its position as shown in Figure 5-36. The top of the subreport should be about 1/3" from the top of the section.

Figure 5-36 SIZING AND REPOSITIONING THE SUBREPORT

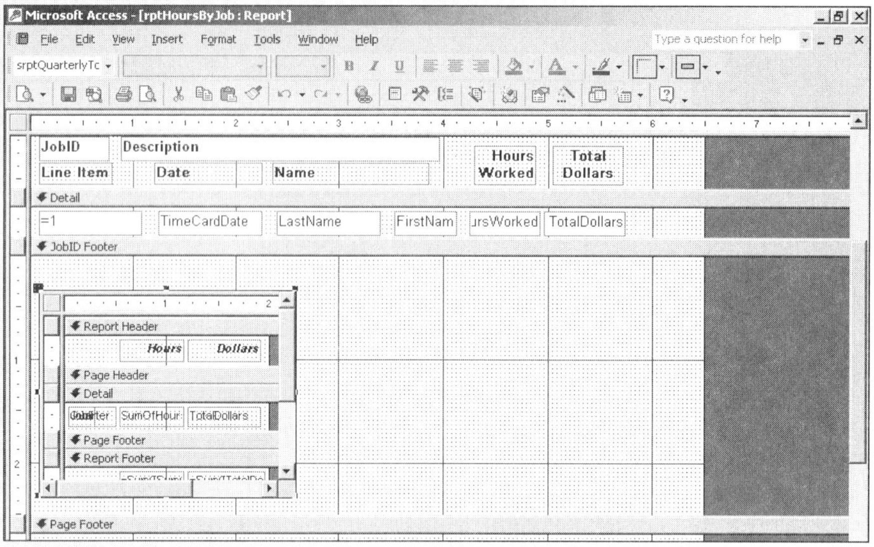

3. Open the toolbox if necessary, insert an unbound label control above the subreport control, type **Quarterly Hours and Dollars**, set the Label Height property to at least **0.25"**, widen the label to match that of the subreport (approximately 2.5"), and center the label text within the label control. Save the report.

4. Preview the report, move to the second page to see the subreport, and scroll down and to the right slightly to view the subreport as shown in Figure 5-37.

Figure 5-37 PREVIEWING THE SUBREPORT IN PRINT PREVIEW

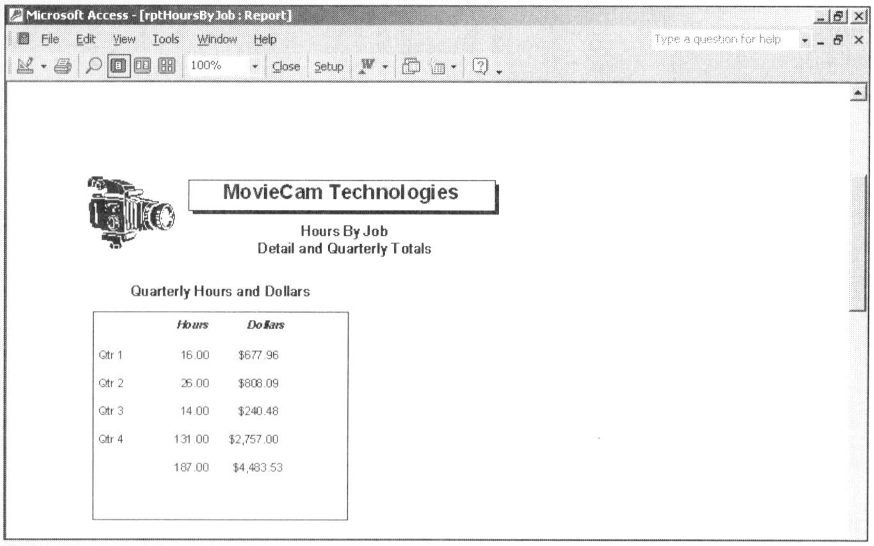

5. Restore the report window and close the report.

Next you will add a line chart to the report. The chart will graphically illustrate the summary data in the subreport.

Charting

You use the Chart Wizard to add graphs and charts to forms and reports. You must have Microsoft Graph 2002 installed to use the Chart Wizard. You can create two types of charts with the Chart Wizard: a global or unlinked chart that shows the data for each row in the record source; or a record-bound or linked chart that shows the data related to a specific record on the form or report in which it is embedded. Based on the data you specify, the Chart Wizard determines whether to use a global or record-bound chart. You can, however, change the results of a global chart so that it is linked to a specific record.

REFERENCE WINDOW RW

Inserting a Record-Bound Chart in a Report

- Open the report in Design view.
- Click Insert on the menu bar, and then click Chart.
- Click in the report where you want the chart to be positioned.
- Select the table or query on which the chart will be based, and designate the fields in the query that will be charted.
- Select the type of chart, move the fields to the correct location in the chart, establish the field(s) on which the chart and report are linked, change the summary data if necessary, and enter a chart title.

You will create a record-bound chart that shows summary data about each job. The chart will be based on the qryQuarterlyTotalsByJob query.

To insert a record-bound chart in a report:

1. Open the **rptHoursByJob** report in Design view. Maximize the report window if necessary, and scroll down far enough to view as much of the JobID Footer section as possible.
2. Click **Insert** on the menu bar, click **Chart**, and then drag to draw a rectangle to the right of the subreport in the JobID Footer section and approximately the same size as the subreport. The Chart Wizard dialog box opens, as shown in Figure 5-38.

Figure 5-38 CHART WIZARD DIALOG BOX

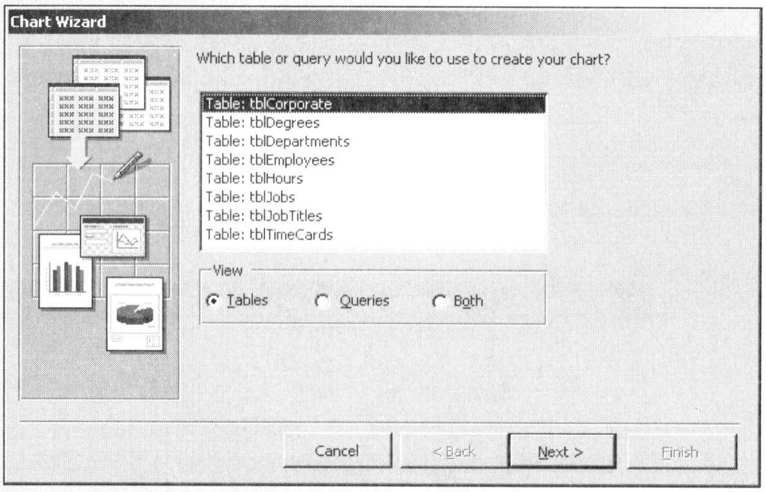

3. Click the **Queries** option button in the View pane, click **Query: qryQuarterlyTotalsByJob**, and then click the **Next** button.

   In the next dialog box, you need to specify the fields that contain the data you want to chart. Note that the chart is linked to the report via the JobID field, but it is not necessary to include the field in the data to be charted.

4. Add the **Quarter** and **TotalDollars** fields to the Fields for Chart list box by double-clicking each field, and then click the **Next** button.

   Now you need to specify the type of chart you want to create. A line chart is often used to show a trend over a specified time frame, and in this case, the line chart will illustrate a comparison of the hours worked and total dollars expended over time. The chart will show a line for each value with points plotted for each quarter of the year.

5. Click the **Line Chart** button in the chart palette (third row, third column), as shown in Figure 5-39.

Figure 5-39 SELECTING THE CHART TYPE

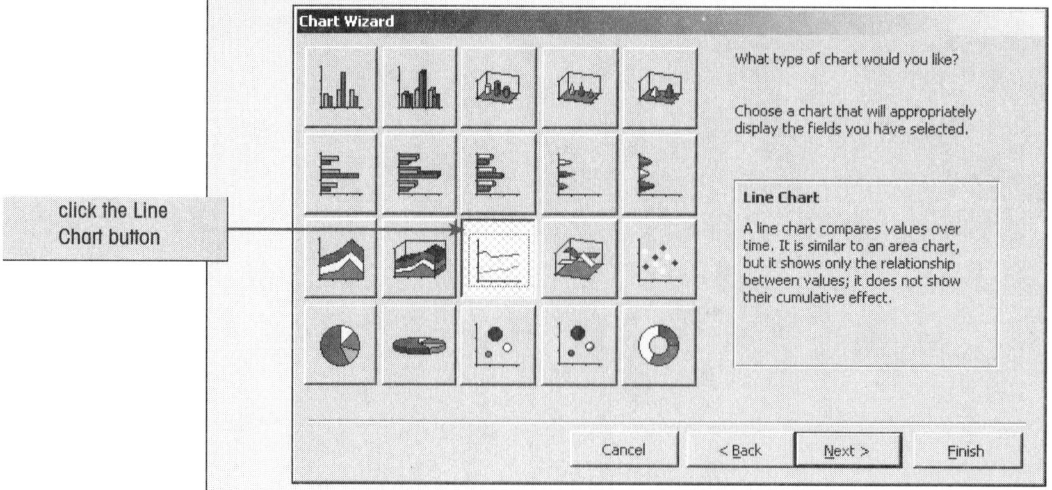

6. Click the **Next** button. The two fields or field expressions that you selected for this chart appear as buttons at the right of the next dialog box, as shown in Figure 5-40. You can drag and drop these buttons to determine where each will be placed in the chart. The x-axis is the horizontal line at the bottom of the chart and currently shows the Quarter. The sum of the TotalDollars field data is shown on the y-axis. The Chart Wizard automatically generates an SQL statement that totals the data for each field containing numeric values that you are charting, in this case for the TotalDollars field. You could double-click the button on the y-axis that contains the text SumOfTotalDollars to change the calculation from Sum to be Average, Min, Max, Count, or even no computation at all. You leave the calculation as is for the SumOfTotalDollars.

Figure 5-40 SUMMARIZING AND GROUPING DATA

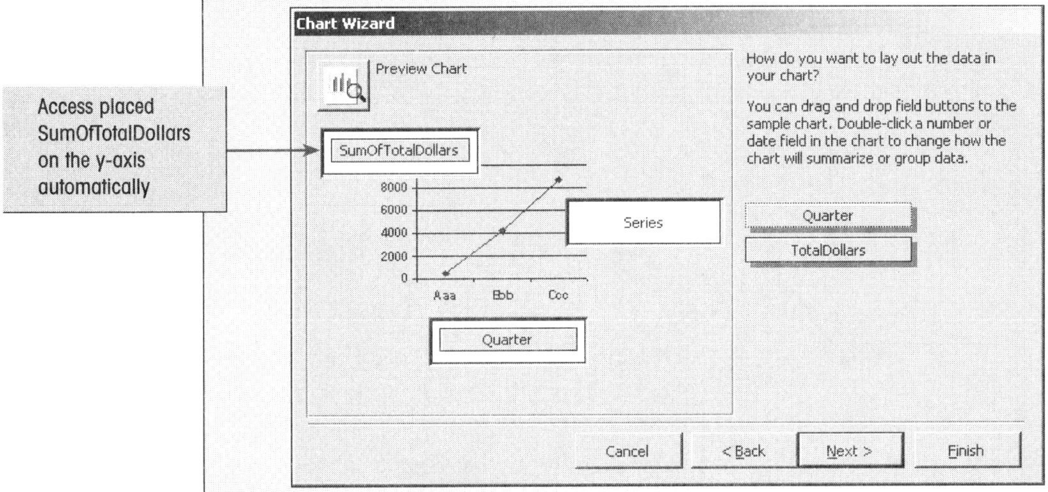

7. Click the **Next** button to move to the next Wizard dialog box, make sure that **JobID** is displayed in the Report Fields and the Chart Fields list boxes, as shown in Figure 5-41. This specifies JobID as the field on which the chart is linked to the report.

Figure 5-41 ESTABLISHING THE FIELD(S) ON WHICH THE CHART AND REPORT ARE LINKED

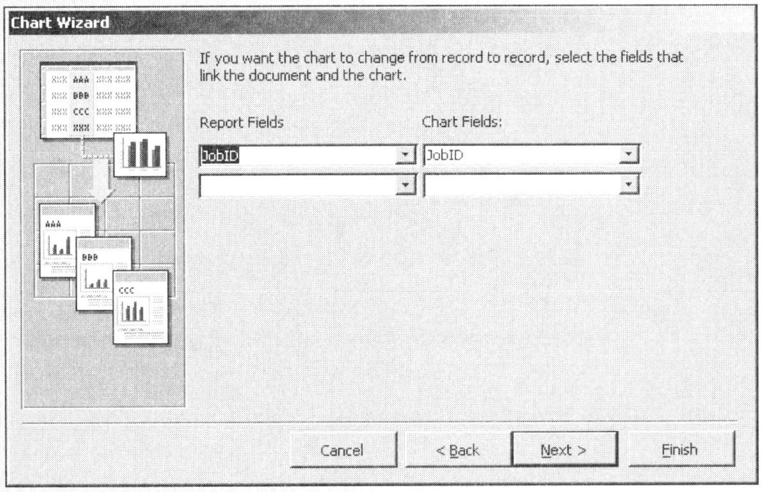

8. Click the **Next** button to move to the next Wizard dialog box, type **Quarterly Job Summary** as the title of the chart, make sure the **Yes, display a legend** option button is selected, and then click the **Finish** button.

9. Size the chart as shown in Figure 5-42. Microsoft Graph puts sample placeholders in the Design view that do not all apply to the graph you just created. When you preview the report, you will see what the graph really looks like based on the steps you followed to create it.

Figure 5-42 LINE CHART INSERTED IN THE REPORT'S DESIGN VIEW

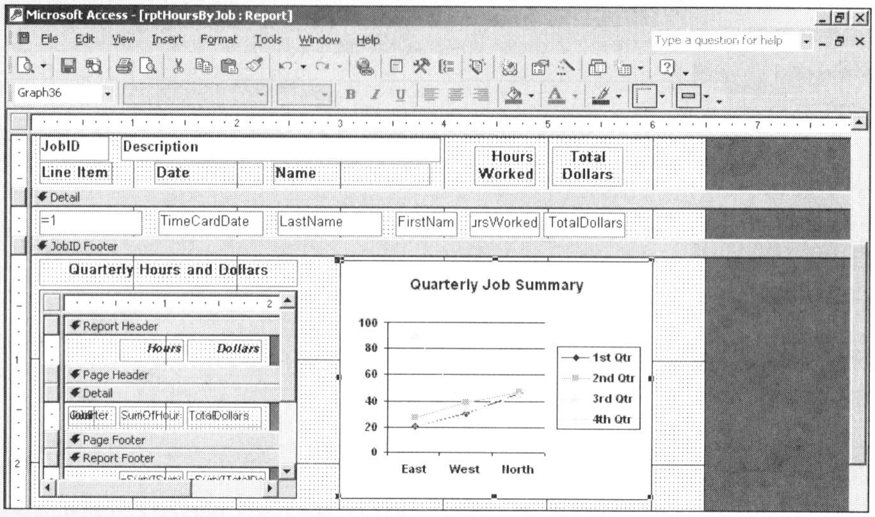

10. Preview the report and then move to page two to view the subreport and chart.

You would like to change the legend on the chart to be something that is easier to read and that fits better within the space reserved for the legend. To change the wording, you will modify the query on which the chart is based so that it is a saved query instead of an SQL statement. Then you will change the title of the dollars column in the query itself.

To create a saved query from the chart SQL statement:

1. Switch to Design view, click the chart to select it, and then open its property sheet.

2. Click the **All** tab if necessary, and then click the **Build** button ... for the Row Source property. The Query Builder window opens.

3. Right-click the **Table** cell in the **TotalDollars** column, click **Properties** on the shortcut menu, type **Dollars** in its Caption text box, and then close the property sheet.

4. Save the query as **qryProductsCharting**.

5. Close the query and then click the **Yes** button when asked if you want to save the changes and update the property. The name of the saved query is now the setting of the Row Source property on the property sheet.

6. Save your changes. Preview the report and navigate to the second page to see the chart. Scroll as needed to make your preview appear as shown in Figure 5-43.

Figure 5-43 MODIFIED LEGEND

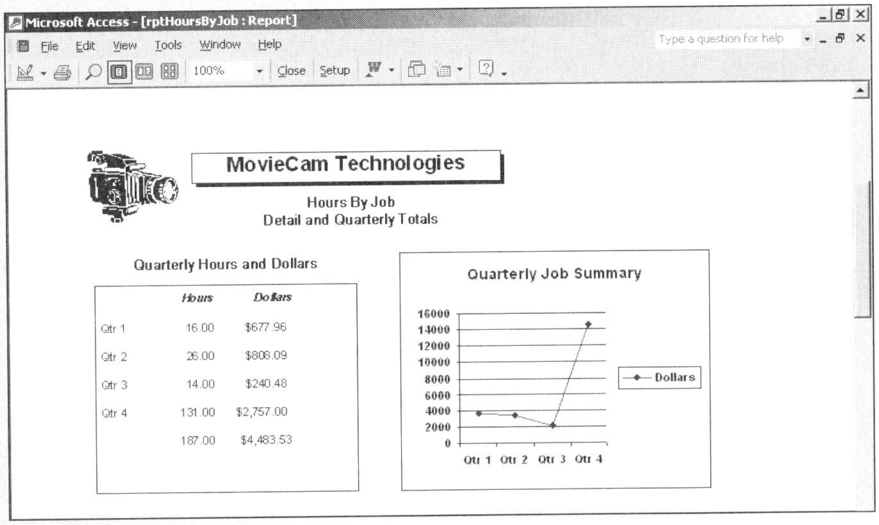

7. Return to Design view and then close the property sheet.

You want page numbers shown on the report, and you want each product group's page numbers to begin with the number 1. You will add an expression to show page numbers, and then you will write an event procedure to reset the page number to 1 at the beginning of each new product group.

Page Numbering

The Page and Pages properties can be used to print page numbers in forms or reports. The **Page property** specifies the current page number when a page is being printed. The **Pages property** specifies the total number of pages in the report. The Page and Pages properties can be used in an expression, in a macro, or VBA.

An example of an expression in a report that uses these properties is:

```
="Page " & Page & " of " & Pages
```

This expression will display *Page 1 of 15* on the first page of a 15-page report.

When a group of data in a report spans more than one page, you can reset the page numbering so that each group has its own page numbering sequence that starts with page number 1. The report's Page property is **read-write** at run time, which means that you can reset the Page property at any time by using a macro or code as the report prints. Resetting pagination in this manner is not typically recommended, but an example of where it would be useful is if you were starting a new page with each group and intended to separate and disseminate the grouped pages to multiple recipients rather than keeping the report bound together as one printout.

REFERENCE WINDOW RW

Adding Page Numbering to a Report

- Open the report in Design view.
- Create an unbound text box in the Page Footer section, and then click the text box.
- Type *="Page " & Page* to show the page number only, or *="Page " & Page & " of " & Pages* to show the page number and the total number of pages.
- Format the text box as desired.
- Save your changes and close the report.

You will use the On Format event property for the JobID Header to reset the Page property to the number 1. The Format event occurs when a header section is formatted, but before it is printed. This event procedure you create for the On Format event property will set the Page property to 1, the header will print, the records in the Detail section and the JobID Footer will print, and the page number will increment until the next JobID Header Format event is recognized.

To add page numbers to the rptHoursByJob report:

1. Return to the **rptHoursByJob** report in Design view, and maximize the report window if necessary. Display the toolbox if necessary, scroll down enough to view the entire Page Footer section, and then add a text box to the section.
2. Size the text box so that it is the same width as the report (see Figure 5-44), and set its Height property to **0.225"**. This allows you to center the page number in the text box, and as a result, center it on the report.
3. Position the insertion point in the text box, type **="Page " & Page**, press the **Enter** key, and then click the **Center** button on the Formatting toolbar to center the expression in the text box. The report should look as shown in Figure 5-44.

Figure 5-44 INSERTING A PAGE NUMBER EXPRESSION IN THE PAGE FOOTER

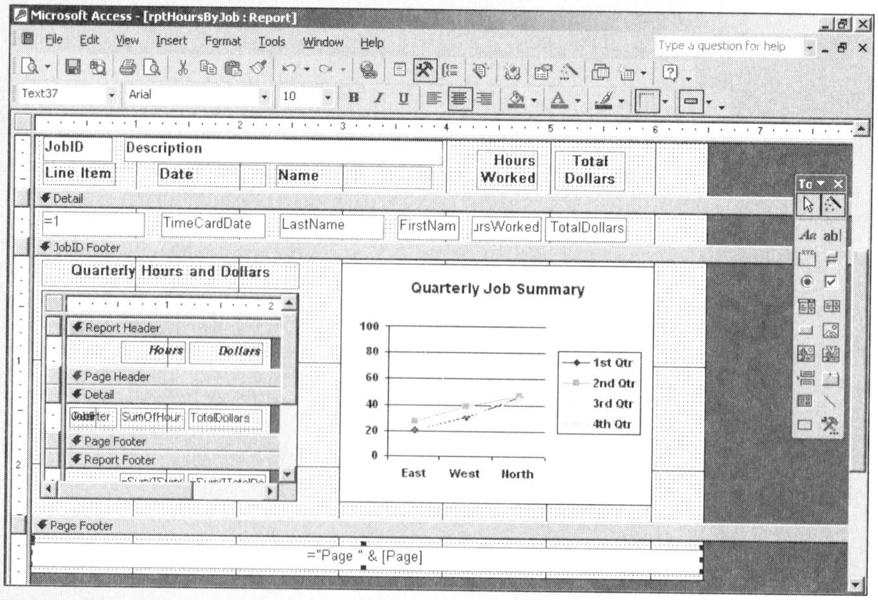

4. Click the **JobID Header** section band, open the property sheet, change the Name property to **hdrJobID** if necessary, and then click the **Event** tab on the property sheet.
5. Click in the **On Format** text box, click its **Build** button [...], click **Code Builder** in the Choose Builder dialog box, and then click the **OK** button. The Visual Basic window opens.
6. Press the **Tab** key to indent the line, type **Page = 1** as shown in Figure 5-45, compile and save the code, and then close the Visual Basic window.

Figure 5-45 CODE TO RESET PAGE NUMBER FOR EACH NEW GROUP

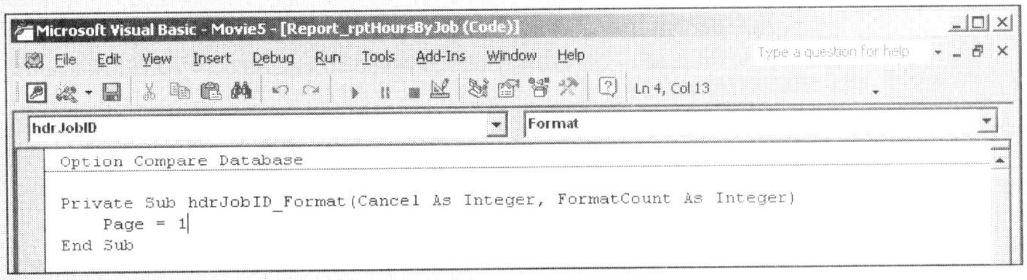

7. Preview the report again and move through the pages. As you move through the pages, note that the page numbers begin with 1 at the beginning of each new job grouping.
8. Return to Design view, close the property sheet, and then save your changes.

Next you will add the finishing touches to the report's design.

Adding Blank Rows to a Report

Some reports are easier to read if blank rows are inserted at certain intervals. Access does not provide a method to insert a blank row in the middle of a Detail section. However, you can use VBA code and the properties of controls and sections on a report to insert blank rows.

To add blank rows to a report, you insert a blank unbound text box in the Detail section of the report below the other text boxes, and name it "txtSpacer." Then set the Can Grow and Can Shrink properties of the txtSpacer text box and the Detail section to Yes. Remember that the Can Grow and Can Shrink properties allow controls and sections on a report to grow vertically and shrink vertically when necessary. Wherever you want the blank row to print, txtSpacer needs to contain " ", which is a space between quotation marks. This causes the text box to print, but nothing will be visible inside it. You can write VBA code to insert a blank row after a certain number of records. The VBA code tests which record is being laid out on the page. If you want a blank row after every fifth record, for example, the code tests to see if a record number is evenly divisible by 5. If it is, a blank row is inserted after it. You will use the txtLineItem text box in the rptHoursByJob report to determine which record is going to print.

To add blank rows to the rptHoursByJob report:

1. Drag the Detail section of the report down so that it is approximately ½" tall, and insert an unbound text box beneath the LastName text box, open the property sheet for the new control, and then set its Height property to **0.2"**.

2. Click the **All** tab if necessary, change the Name property of the new control to **txtSpacer**, and then change the Can Shrink property to **Yes**. It is not necessary to change the Can Grow property of the text box to Yes. That would only be necessary if you want to show more than one line vertically in the text box.
3. Click the Detail section band, and then change both the Can Grow and Can Shrink properties to **Yes**, if necessary. This allows the Detail section to grow larger when the txtSpacer field contains a space and to shrink when it does not.

Next you will learn how to incorporate a conditional VBA statement to complete the procedure.

Using an If...Then...Else Statement

An **If...Then...Else statement** conditionally executes a group of statements in VBA depending on the results of an expression. This type of conditional statement or control structure will be discussed in greater detail in Tutorial 6. **A control structure** is a series of VBA statements that work together as a unit. A VBA **statement** is a unit that expresses one kind of action, declaration, or definition in complete syntax. A VBA **expression** is a combination of keywords, operators, variables, and constants that yields a string, number, or object. Although you are not yet familiar with some of these terms, they will be introduced as they apply. **Operators** are used to perform arithmetic calculations, perform comparisons, combine strings, and perform logical operations. You have been using the ampersand (&) operator to create expressions in queries and reports that combine fields with other fields and strings of text. (Variables and constants will be introduced in Tutorial 6.) The If...Then...Else statement that you will write includes an expression that uses the Mod operator.

The **Mod operator** is an arithmetic operator used to perform modulo division, which divides two numbers and returns only the remainder. For example, 10 Mod 5 returns 0 because 10 divided by 5 equals 2 with a remainder of 0, and 10 Mod 3 returns 1 because 10 divided by 3 equals 3 with a remainder of 1.

You will use the Mod operator to determine the result of dividing the contents of the report's txtLineItem field by five. If the remainder (or the result) of the operation is zero, which will occur in multiples of five, you will add a blank space to the txtSpacer control and the blank line will print.

To complete the code for adding a blank line:

1. Return to the Design view of the rptHoursByJob report, click the Detail section band if necessary, click the **Event** tab in the property sheet, click in the **On Format** text box, click its **Build** button [...], click **Code Builder**, and then click the **OK** button.
2. Press the **Tab** key to indent, type **If (txtLineItem Mod 5) = 0 Then**, and then press the **Enter** key.
3. Press the **Tab** key to indent, type **txtSpacer = " "** (be sure to press the spacebar between the quotation marks), and then press the **Enter** key.
4. Press **Shift + Tab** to outdent, type **Else**, press the **Enter** key, press the **Tab** key to indent, type **txtSpacer = Null**, and then press the **Enter** key.
5. Press **Shift + Tab** to outdent, type **End If**. See Figure 5-46.

Figure 5-46 CODE FOR ADDING A BLANK LINE

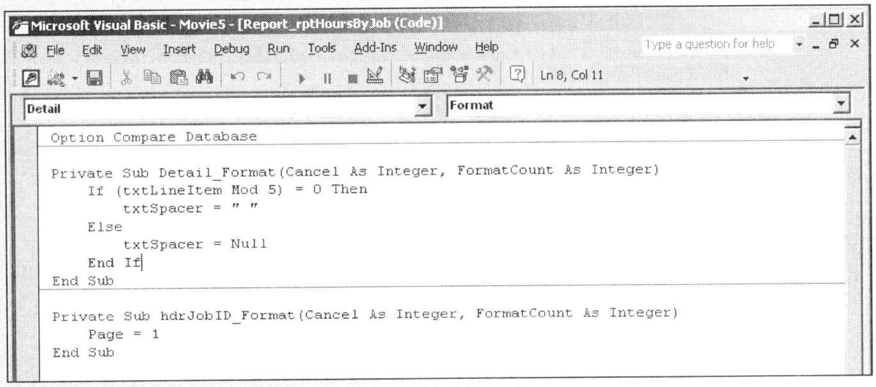

6. Compile the code, save your changes, and then close the Visual Basic window. Preview the report. A blank line should appear after every fifth record.
7. Return to Design view, restore the report window, close the property sheet, and then save your changes.
8. Close the report, close the Movie5 database, and then exit Access.

Martin is pleased with the report. The subreport provides the summary data he needs, and the chart provides a visual representation of that summary data. The detail data is included, and numbered and formatted so that it easy to read.

Session 5.2 Quick Check

1. Which events occur when data is entered, deleted, or changed in a form or control?
2. The ______________ event occurs after Access formats a report for printing that has no data, but before the report is printed.
3. A(n) ______________ procedure returns a value, such as the result of a calculation.
4. Where can VBA functions be used in Access?
5. The Code Builder allows you to create ______________ procedures in a class module.
6. The Running Sum property allows you to calculate ______________ totals or ______________ totals in a report.
7. What does the Page property specify?
8. A(n) ______________ in VBA is a unit that expresses one kind of action, declaration, or definition in complete syntax.
9. What is the Mod operator?

REVIEW ASSIGNMENTS

The Hours5 database is similar to the MovieCam Technologies database you worked with in the tutorial. It contains a report template named dmrptTemplate which is identical to the report template in MovieCam. Complete the following:

1. Start Access and open the **Hours5** database located in the Tutorial.05\Review folder on your local or network drive.

2. Create a table in Design view with the following fields, specify CompanyID as the primary key, add the new record shown below, and save the table as **tblCorporate**.

Field Name	Data Type	Description
CompanyID	Autonumber	**1**
CompanyName	Text	**Technologies Video**
Address	Text	**1010 West Street**
City	Text	**Santa Rosa**
State	Text	**CA**
ZipCode	Text	**95402**
Telephone	Text	**(707) 555-5555**
FAX	Text	**(707) 555-9999**

3. Create a new report in Design view. Create an unbound text box in the Report Header section that is approximately 4" wide and ½" tall. Type **=DLookup("CompanyName", "tblCorporate", "CompanyID=1")** inside the text box, and then press the Enter key.

4. Change the font size to 14, the style to Bold, and the alignment of the text to centered.

5. Save the report as **dmrptMaster**, and then close it.

6. Create a new query in Design view, click tblEmployees in the Show Table dialog box, and then click the Add button twice. Close the Show Table dialog box.

7. Click and drag the SupervisorNo field in the tblEmployees field list to the EmployeeNo field in the tblEmployees_1 field list to create a self-join.

8. Right-click the title bar of the tblEmployees_1 field list, click Properties on the shortcut menu, and then type **tblSupervisors** in the Alias property text box.

9. Close the property sheet, and then drag the EmployeeNo, DeptNo, LastName, HourlyRate, and TimeCard fields from the tblEmployees field list to the design grid.

10. Drag the DeptNo and LastName fields from the tblSupervisors field list to the design grid.

11. Save the query as **qryEmployeesBySupervisor**, and then close it.

12. Make sure that Reports is selected on the Objects bar in the Database window, right-click dmrptMaster, click Copy on the shortcut menu, right-click an empty area of the Database window, and click Paste on the shortcut menu.

13. Type **rptEmployeesBySupervisor** in the Report Name text box, and then click the OK button. Open the new report in Design view, and then open the property sheet.

14. Type **qryEmployeesBySupervisor** in the Record Source property text box, and then press the Enter key. Close the property sheet. Click View on the menu bar, click Sorting and Grouping, click in the first Field/Expression text box, click the list arrow, and then click tblSupervisors.DeptNo. Change Group Header to Yes and Group Footer to Yes, and then close the Sorting and Grouping dialog box. Increase the height of the tblSupervisors.DeptNo group header section to 0.5 inches.

15. Drag the EmployeeNo, tblEmployees.DeptNo, tblEmployees.LastName, HourlyRate, and TimeCard fields to the Detail section. Delete the labels that were created automatically with the text boxes, if necessary.

16. Insert appropriate field labels in the tblSupervisors.DeptNo Header section for its corresponding text box in the Detail section. Size and align them with the controls in the Detail section, and then apply the bold style to them.

17. Drag the tblSupervisors.DeptNo and tblSupervisors.LastName fields to the tblSupervisors.DeptNo Header section. Delete the labels that were created automatically with the text boxes, if necessary. Change the Font Weight of the tblSupervisors.DeptNo and tblSupervisors.LastName controls in the Header section to bold.

18. Resize the Detail section so that it is approximately ½" tall.

19. Preview the report, return to Design view, and size the text box controls so that the data is visible without being cut off.

Explore

20. Add an unbound text box to the tblSupervisors.DeptNo Footer section that averages the hourly rate paid to employees per supervisor department. Apply the currency format to the text box, and include a label to the right of it with the text **Average Hourly Rate**.

21. Preview the report, then close and save your changes.

CASE PROBLEMS

Case 1. Edwards and Company Jack Edwards has asked you to create a report that contains client names, their phone numbers, and contact names. You've created the report and now need to add some finishing touches to it. Jack wants a total at the bottom of the report of all of the clients on the page, and a count at the bottom of the report of all the clients in the report. The Edward5 database currently contains only sample records, so the report consists of only one page, but you anticipate that it will eventually be several pages long.

Complete the following:

1. Start Access and open the **Edward5** database located in the Tutorial.05\Cases folder on your local or network drive.

2. Open the **rptClientsPhone** report in Design view, and, if necessary, display the toolbox.

3. Click the text box button on the toolbox, and click in the Page Footer section below the ContactName control.

4. Open the property sheet and change the Name property to **txtCount**.

5. Click inside the label to the left of the text box, and type **Total Clients**.
6. Click the Page Header section, and then click the Event tab in the property sheet.
7. Use the Code Builder for the On Print property to initiate a code window and blank procedure for the Print event.
8. Press the Tab key to indent the line, set the txtCount to zero, and close the Visual Basic window.
9. Click the Detail section of the report, click the On Print event property text box, click the Build button, click Code Builder, and then click the OK button.
10. Press the Tab key to indent the line, increment the txtCount by 1, and then close the Visual Basic window.
11. Preview the report.
12. Move the text box and label to the right edge of the report, and then add a new unbound text box to the left side of the Page Footer section.
13. Delete the label that is drawn with the text box, click inside the text box, and type **="Page " & Page & " of " & Pages**.
14. Format the label and text boxes in the page footer to be Arial 10 point.

Explore

15. Add an unbound text box to the center of the Page Footer section that displays the current day's date. It should be formatted to display the day and the date.
16. Preview the report to test your changes.
17. Save your changes and close the report.
18. Close the Edward5 database, and then exit Access.

Case 2. San Diego County Information Systems You have created a new report for your database. The report is named rptEmployeesPhone, and contains a list of all employees sorted alphabetically by last name. You want to add a line item to the report to identify a specific employee, and a blank row after every fourth employee record to make the report easier to read.

Complete the following:

1. Start Access, open the **ISD5** database located in the Tutorial.05\Cases folder on your local or network drive, and open the **rptEmployeesPhone** report in Design view.
2. Make sure that the toolbox is visible, click the Text Box button on the toolbox, and click to the left of the FirstName text box control in the Detail section.
3. Open the property sheet, change the Name property to **txtLineItem**, type **=1** in the Control Source property text box, and then change the Running Sum property to Over All.
4. Close the property sheet, and then size and align the txtLineItem text box so that it is the same height as and aligned with the other controls in the report's Detail section.

5. Add a label in the Page Header section above the txtLineItem control, and type **Line Item**. Size and align the label to match the other labels in the Page Header section.

6. Drag the Detail section of the report down so that it is approximately ½" tall, insert an unbound text box beneath the LastName text box, open the property sheet, change the name of the text box to **txtSpacer**, and change the Can Shrink property to Yes.

7. Click the Detail section of the report and change the Can Grow and Can Shrink properties to Yes, click the Event tab in the property sheet, click in the On Format property text box, and click the Build button.

8. If necessary, click Code Builder in the Choose Builder dialog box, click the OK button, press the Tab key to indent, type **If (txtLineItem Mod 4) = 0 Then**, and then press the Enter key.

9. Press the Tab key to indent, type **txtSpacer = " "** (be sure to insert a space between the quotation marks), and then press the Enter key.

10. Press Shift + Tab to outdent, type **Else**, press the Enter key, press the Tab key to indent, type **txtSpacer = Null**, and then press the Enter key.

11. Press Shift + Tab to outdent, type **End If**, close the VB window, and then preview the report.

12. Save your changes.

13. Close the ISD5 database and exit Access.

Case 3. Christenson Homes The reports for Christenson Homes are not yet completed. Roberta told you that the company is considering incorporating and might change the company name and logo. You created the template for the database, and now need to create a report master that contains the company name and logo. You want these items stored in a table so that you can change them easily if necessary.

Complete the following:

1. Start Access and open the **Homes5** database located in the Tutorial.05\Cases folder on your local or network drive.

2. Create a new table in the Design view and define the following fields:

Field Name	Data Type
CompanyID	Autonumber
CompanyName	Text

3. Set CompanyID as the primary key.

4. Save the table as **tblCorporate**.

5. Switch to Datasheet view and then type **Christenson Homes** in the CompanyName field.

6. Close the table.

7. Create a new report in Design view, and insert a text box in the Report Header section that contains a DLookup function to look up the company name from the tblCorporate table. Delete the label that's automatically created when you add the text box, if necessary.

8. Format the text box to be Arial, 14 point, bold, and size it to fit the text.

Explore 9. Click the Image button on the toolbox, and click and drag to the left of the text box containing the company name. Select the H5Logo.wmf file from the Tutorial.05\Cases folder as the picture to insert.

Explore 10. Display the property sheet, click in the Control Source text box, type **=DlookUp ("Logo", "tblCorporate", "CompanyID=1")**.

11. Change the Size Mode property of the bound object frame to Stretch.

12. Save the report as **dmrptMaster**, and preview it to ensure it looks correct.

13. Close the Homes5 database, and then exit Access.

Case 4. Sonoma Farms The Sonoma Farms database contains a report named rptVisitorsByDistributor. The report contains information about each visitor to the farm, grouped by the distributor name. You want to add a subreport to the Report Footer that shows data that summarizes the number of visitors to the farm, by distributor.

Complete the following:

1. Start Access and open the **Sonoma5** database located in the Tutorial.05\Cases folder on your local or network drive.

2. Open the **rptVisitorsByDistribuor** report in Design view, and drag the qryVisitorsCount query from the Database window to the Report Footer section of the report.

3. Choose none when asked which fields link the main report to the subreport, and name the subreport **srptVisitorsCount**. Delete the label that's automatically created when you insert the subreport. Save your changes and then close the rptVisitorsByDistribuor report so that you may make changes to the design of the subreport.

4. Open the **srptVisitorsCount** report in Design view, and change the CountofVisitorID label to **Total Visitors**. Using Figure 5-47 as a guide, size and align the labels, then for all controls change the font to Arial, the font color to black (if necessary), and then save and close the report.

Figure 5-47

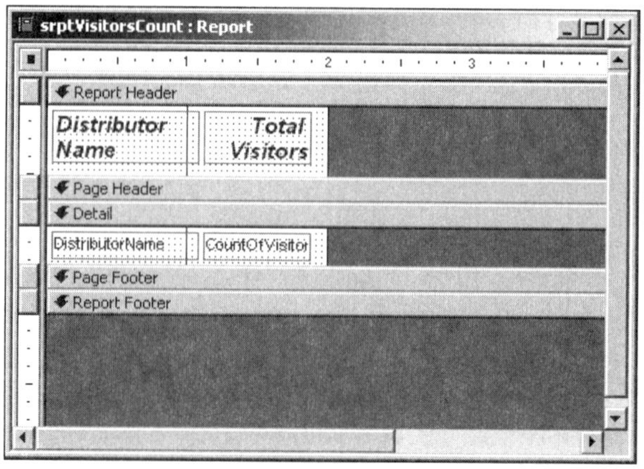

5. Open the **rptVisitorsByDistributor** report in Design view, maximize the report window if necessary, scroll down enough to view as much of the Report Footer on your screen as possible, and then size and reposition the subreport control as shown in Figure 5-48.

Figure 5-48

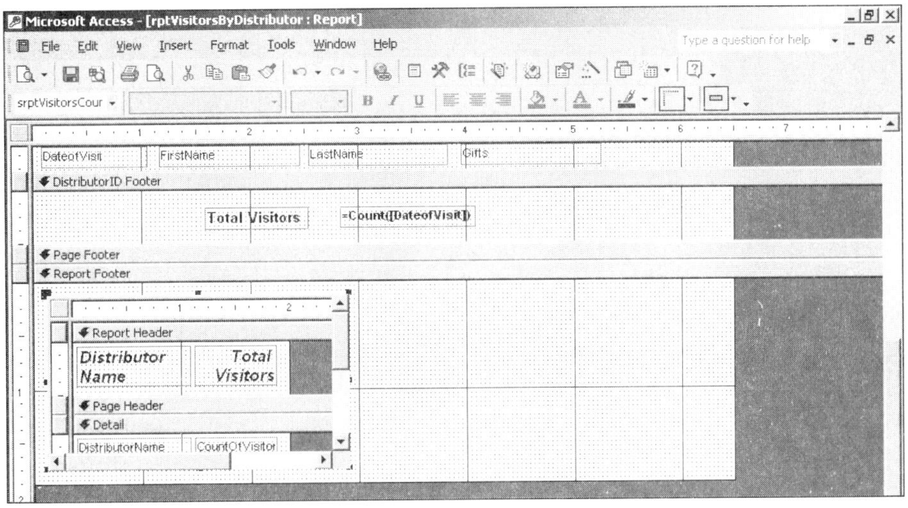

6. Save the report and preview it.

7. Restore the report window, close the report, close the Sonoma5 database, and then exit Access.

QUICK CHECK ANSWERS

Session 5.1

1. Domain aggregate functions provide statistical information about a set of records or domain.
2. criteria
3. An unbound object frame should be used to link to the source file.
4. Page Header
5. The Detail section is the main body of a report.
6. Expressions can be included in Group Headers/Footers and the Report Header/Footer.
7. Joining a table to itself is a self-join.
8. The effect of setting the Can Grow property to Yes is that it allows the control to grow vertically in order to display all the data.
9. The advantage to sending a report as a snapshot is that the recipient does not need to have Access installed on their computer in order to view the report.

Session 5.2

1. Data events occur when data is entered, deleted, or changed in a form or control.
2. NoData
3. function
4. VBA functions can be used in expressions, property settings, or as criteria in queries and filters.
5. event
6. record-by-record; group-by-group
7. The Page property specifies the current page number when a page is being printed.
8. statement
9. The Mod operator is an arithmetic operator used to perform modulo division, which divides two numbers and returns only the remainder.

OBJECTIVES

In this tutorial you will:

- Study properties, events, objects, methods, and collections
- Create an event procedure to validate data entered in a form
- Create an event procedure for the frmDataSwitchboard form
- Learn about If...Then...Else and Select Case conditional statements
- Use the DoCmd object, and learn the syntax of the OpenForm method
- Modify an Access toolbar, and create a custom menu bar and a custom shortcut menu
- Change the Startup properties for the MovieCam database
- Copy VBA code from the Access Help system and use it with an AutoKeys macro
- Split the MovieCam database into a front and back end

CUSTOMIZING THE USER INTERFACE

Redesigning the User Interface for the MovieCam Technologies Database

CASE

MovieCam Technologies

You now have confidence in your ability to write VBA code, so you want to revisit some of the objects that you created in the MovieCam database and apply your knowledge to enhance their design. Amanda has also asked that you complete the user interface. She wants you to customize the menus, toolbars, and Startup properties to make the database even more user-friendly for MovieCam employees.

Amanda has also suggested that you split the MovieCam database into a front-end file containing all the database objects except for the tables, and a back-end file containing only the tables. You will then move the back end to a shared network drive and distribute copies of the front end to key users for testing the database at its current level of completion. You will continue development of the database in a developmental copy of the front end that is located on a network drive to which the general user population does not have access.

There are a number of advantages to splitting a database in this manner. Recall that data is stored only in tables. One advantage of splitting off the tables from the other objects is that users who need to access the data can customize their own forms, reports, pages, and other objects while maintaining a single source of data on the network. Another advantage is speed. Particularly in a multiuser environment, allowing every user to have their own copy of the queries and forms on their own machine means that only data they are querying, viewing, or printing has to be pulled across the network. If all objects are in one file on the network in a multiuser environment, then many people are trying to access the same queries and forms at the same time, instead of just the data in the tables. By running the queries and working with forms and reports on a local desktop machine, the activity of all these other objects does not have to be carried across the network—just the data from the tables that is needed for a particular user operation.

With a small user base of five to ten simultaneous users, there may be very little noticeable difference in performance. There are many factors to be considered in terms of network bandwidth, server memory and CPU speed, desktop computer memory and CPU speed, the design of the database, and the amount of data being accessed. Amanda feels that enough users in the company may be using the database at the same time to warrant splitting the database into two parts. Maintenance is typically a little easier this way as well. By maintaining a developmental copy of the front-end database in a separate location, you can develop and test enhancements, then simply deploy the revised front-end database to the users, and never have to disturb the back-end data.

SESSION 6.1

In this session, you will learn more about objects and properties. You will be introduced to VBA methods, specifically, the DoCmd.OpenForm method. You'll study data events and use them to write an event procedure to validate data and to open forms from the frmDataSwitchboard form. You also will learn to work with the If...Then...Else and Select Case conditional statements, as well as work with the DoCmd object.

Methods, and Properties

You are familiar by now with the term "objects." It is used in reference to database tables, queries, forms, controls, fields, relationships, and other components. Objects have certain characteristics called "properties." Another way to think of a **property** is as a named attribute of an object that defines a certain characteristic, such as size, color, or a behavioral aspect, such as whether the object is visible or whether it is automatically centered. The objects that you have been working with are referred to as Microsoft Access objects. They are created and maintained by the Access programming environment and are related to the user interface and modules.

In addition to properties, objects have methods. A **method** is a procedure that acts on an object. For example, the Undo method for a control or a form lets you reset the control or the form when its value has been changed. You would use this method in VBA to clear a change to a record that contains an invalid entry. Methods will be introduced as they apply to writing VBA code. Methods are somewhat similar to macro actions.

Collections and Classes

Collections and classes were mentioned briefly in Tutorial 4 when the identifier operators were introduced. A **class** is the definition for an object and includes the object's name, its properties and methods, and any events associated with it. When you create an **instance** of a class, you create a new object with all of the characteristics defined by that class. The properties and methods associated with one form in the database are the same as the properties and methods of the Form object class. Objects in Access can contain other objects. For example, form objects contain control objects, and table objects contain field objects. In Access, it is common to group related objects together.

A **collection**, as you may recall, is an object that contains a set of related objects (objects of the same class). For example, a Forms collection contains all open forms in the database, and a Reports collection contains all open reports. A collection is not created by the user; rather, it is simply a means of referring to all the open forms or all the open reports. VBA, macros, and queries identify an object by specifying the collection to which it belongs. For example, Forms!frmDataSwitchboard!grpForms identifies the option group named grpForms in the frmDataSwtichboard form. The Forms collection is followed by the form name, frmDataSwitchboard, which is followed by the name of the control, grpForms. This is similar to specifying a filename in Windows by typing the name of the drive, the name of the folder, and then the filename itself, for example, C:\Tutorial.06\Tutorial\Movie6.

Figure 6-1 summarizes these terms.

Figure 6-1 NEW TERMS AND EXAMPLES

TERM	DEFINITION	EXAMPLES
Class	Definition for an object, including the object's name, its properties and methods, and any events associated with it	The Form object class is the definition for forms in the database.
Collection	An object that contains a set of related objects (objects of the same class)	The Forms collection is all the open forms at any given time.
Method	A procedure that acts on an object	The Requery method of a form updates the data in a form by requerying the underlying record source. The Undo method for a control lets you reset the control when its value has been changed.
Property	Named attribute of an object that defines a certain characteristic	The Visible property of a control determines whether you can see it displayed in Form view. The Back Color property of a control determines its background color.

Data Event Properties

You applied a number of Print events to reports in Tutorial 5. In this tutorial you will use Data events to trigger code. These events occur when data is entered, deleted, or changed in a form or control. The various data events are described below:

- *AfterDelConfirm*: This is a Form event that occurs after you confirm record deletions and the records are actually deleted, or after the deletions are canceled.
- *AfterInsert*: This is a Form event that occurs after a new record is added to the database.
- *AfterUpdate*: This is a Form and Control event that occurs after a control or record is updated with changed data. This event occurs when the control or record loses the focus, or you click Save Record on the Records menu or toolbar. This event occurs for new and existing records.
- *BeforeDelConfirm*: This is a Form event that occurs after one or more records are deleted, but before Access displays a dialog box asking you to confirm or cancel the deletion. This event occurs after the Delete event.
- *BeforeInsert*: This is a Form event that occurs when you type the first character in a new record, but before the record is added to the database.
- *BeforeUpdate*: This is a Form and Control event that occurs before a control or record is updated with changed data. This event occurs when the control or record loses the focus or when you click Save Records on the Records menu bar or toolbar. This event occurs for new and existing records.
- *Change*: This is a Control event that occurs when the content of a text box or the text box portion of a combo box changes. This event occurs when you type a character in the control or change the Text property of a control using a macro or VBA.
- *Current*: This is a Form event that occurs when the focus moves to a record, therefore making it the current record, or when you requery a form's source

of data. This event occurs when a form is first opened and whenever the focus leaves one record and moves to another.

- *Delete*: This is a Form event that occurs when a record is deleted, but before the deletion is confirmed and actually performed.
- *Dirty*: This is a Form event that occurs when the contents of a form or the text portion of a combo box change. It also occurs when you move from one page to another page in a tab control.
- *NotInList*: This is a Control event that occurs when a value entered in a combo box isn't in the combo box list.
- *Updated*: This is a Control event that occurs when an OLE object's data has been modified.

Validating **Data Using an Event Procedure**

In Tutorial 1, you learned how to apply table and field validation rules. By writing code in a form module, you can also validate data as the user enters it. At MovieCam Technologies, time cards are always dated the Saturday following the work week. The product managers want the database to prevent the data entry clerk from entering a date that does not fall on a Saturday. You will write an event procedure to perform this validation.

Before you write the event procedure, you will change a default setting so that the Code window opens automatically when you click the Build button for an event property in a form or report. This will bypass the Choose Builder dialog box (see Figure 6-2) that opens when you click the Build button.

Figure 6-2 CHOOSE BUILDER DIALOG BOX

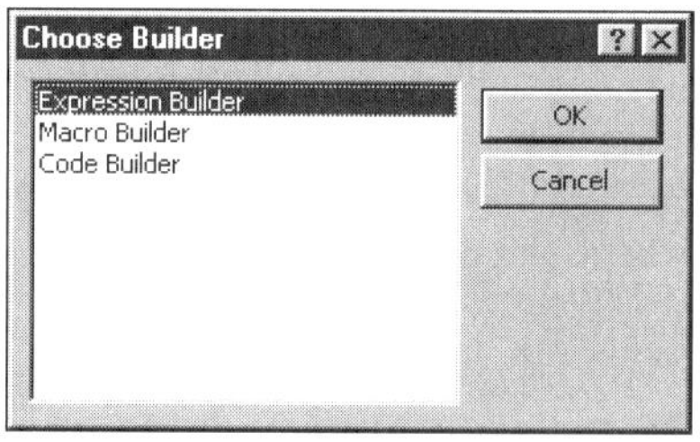

REFERENCE WINDOW RW

Bypassing the Choose Builder Dialog Box

- Click Tools on the menu bar, and then click Options.
- Click the Forms/Reports tab.
- Click the Always use event procedures check box.
- Click the OK button.

You will change the default setting next.

To change default settings so that the Code window opens automatically:

1. Start Access and open the **Movie6** database located in the Tutorial.06\Tutorial folder on your local or network drive.
2. Click **Tools** on the menu bar, and then click **Options**.
3. Click the **Forms/Reports** tab in the Options dialog box.
4. Click the **Always use event procedures** check box, as shown in Figure 6-3.

Figure 6-3 CHANGING DEFAULT SETTINGS IN THE OPTIONS DIALOG BOX

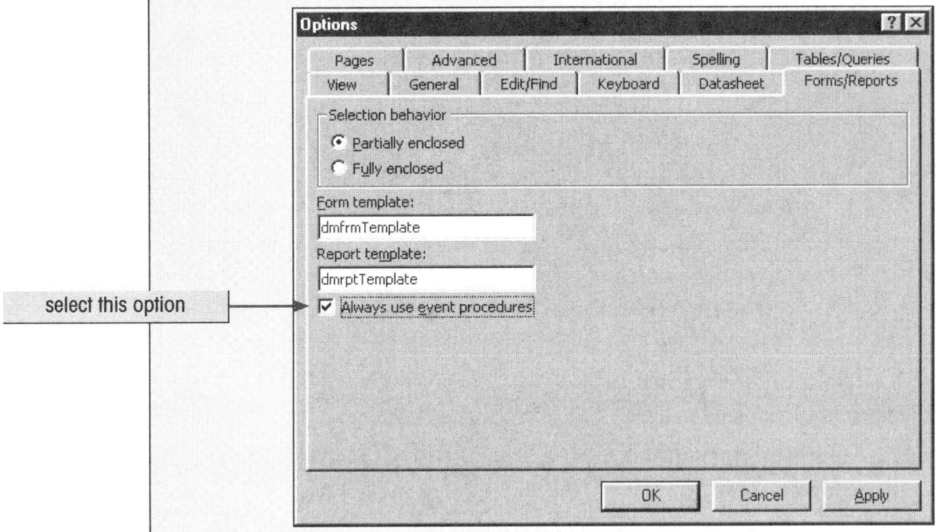

5. Click the **OK** button.

Canceling the Default Behavior Following an Event

After an object recognizes an event, Access carries out the default behavior. For some events, Access runs the event procedure or macro *before* the default behavior takes place. To cancel the user action for these events, you can include the Cancel event action in a macro (as you did in Tutorial 5) or include the Cancel = True statement in the VBA Sub procedure.

One of the events for which Access runs the event procedure before the default behavior takes place is the BeforeUpdate event. Others include the Apply Filter, Dbl Click, Delete, and No Data events.

You will use the BeforeUpdate event in the frmTimeCards form to test an entry in the TimeCardDate field. If the date entered does not fall on Saturday, the entry is canceled. You'll use the DatePart function to test the day of the week entered in the TimeCardDate field. The DatePart function returns an integer containing the specified part of the given date. For example, you can use it to extract the day of the week, the year, or the day of the month. As it is listed in Access Visual Basic Help, the syntax of the DatePart function is

```
DatePart(interval, date[,firstdayofweek[, firstweekofyear]])
```

The *interval* argument is a required string that represents the interval of time you want returned. The *date* argument is the date you are testing. The brackets indicate optional arguments and are part of a Microsoft syntax convention for built-in functions. The *firstdayofweek* argument is optional and is used to specify the first day of the week if you don't want Sunday used. The *firstweekofyear* argument is optional and is used to specify the first week of the year, if you do not want the week of January 1 used.

Because Access sets Sunday as day 1 of the week, Saturday is day 7. The procedure you write will test to see if the date entered is any day other than Saturday, and if it is, it will cancel the entry and display a message on the screen.

To validate the data entered in the TimeCardDate field in the frmTimeCards form:

1. Open the **frmTimeCards** form in Design view.
2. Click the **TimeCardDate** text box, and then click the **Properties** button on the toolbar.
3. If necessary, click the **Event** tab, and then click the **Build** button ... for the Before Update property. Your screen should look like that shown in Figure 6-4. The insertion point is positioned between the first statement of the event procedure and the last. The first and last statements of the event procedure are called the **stub**. The statements you will use in the code include an If...Then conditional statement to test the entry. You will also include a MsgBox statement to give the user an error message if the date entered does not fall on a Saturday.

Figure 6-4 CODE WINDOW IN THE VISUAL BASIC WINDOW

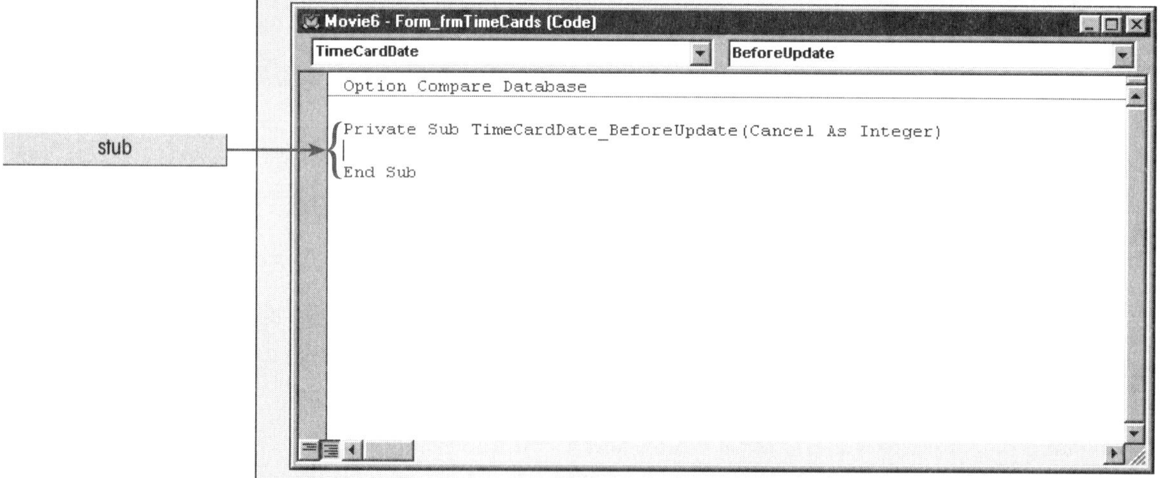

TROUBLE? If other windows, such as the Immediate window, are displayed in the Visual Basic window, close them.

4. Press the **Tab** key to indent the line, and type **If DatePart(**. A banner opens below the function and provides syntax information for the DatePart function. See Figure 6-5.

Figure 6-5 TYPING THE SUB PROCEDURE

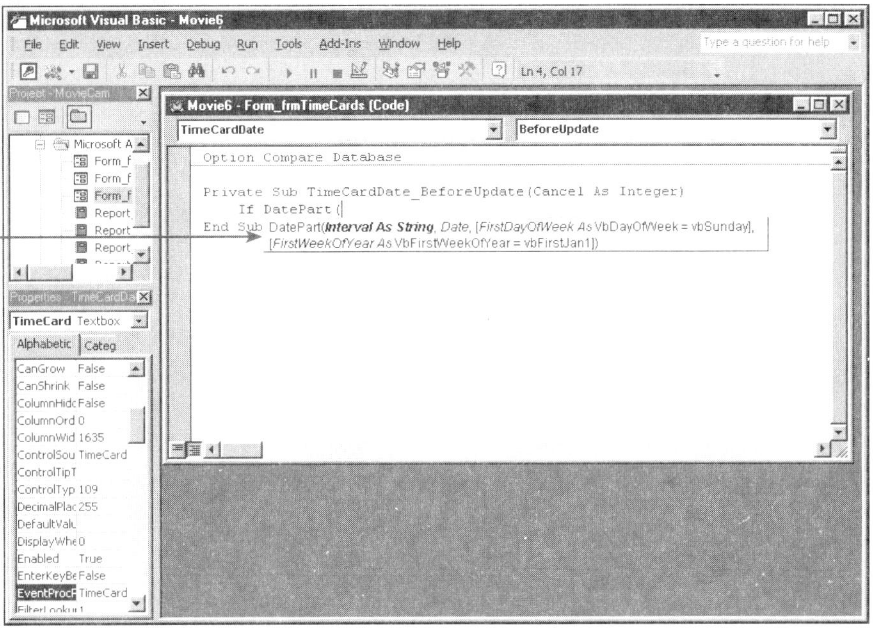

syntax information banner for the DatePart function

TROUBLE? If the banner does not open, click Tools on the menu bar, click Options, click the Editor tab, click the Auto Quick Info check box to select it, and click the OK button. Then press the Backspace key to delete the open parenthesis, and then retype it.

5. Type **"w", TimeCardDate) <> 7 Then** and then press the **Enter** key.
6. Press the **Tab** key, type **Cancel = True**, press the **Enter** key to move to the next line, and then type **MsgBox "You must enter a date that corresponds to a Saturday."**
7. Press the **Enter** key, press **Shift + Tab** to outdent the line, and then type **End If**.
8. Click **Debug** on the menu bar, and then click **Compile Movie6**. The process of translating modules from VBA to a translated form is called compilation. Access will compile all the modules in the MovieCam database and check them for syntax errors.
9. Close the Visual Basic window, close the property sheet, and switch to Form view to test the procedure.
10. Add a new record, type **200** in the Time Card No field, type **2/1/04** in the Time Card Date field, and then press the **Enter** key. You will see the error message shown in Figure 6-6.

Figure 6-6 DATA VALIDATION ERROR MESSAGE

11. Click the **OK** button, and then press the **Esc** key twice to cancel the entry.
12. Save your changes and close the form.

Now that you have completed the validation procedure for the frmTimeCards form, you will focus on converting the macros in the MovieCam database forms switchboard. To understand the VBA code needed to open the forms, you will learn about the DoCmd object and its OpenForm method. You also will learn about writing conditional statements in VBA, such as If…Then… Else and Select Case statements.

The DoCmd Object

The DoCmd object carries out macro actions in VBA procedures. Most macro actions have corresponding DoCmd methods, and the arguments correspond to the action arguments found in the macro window. For example, the DoCmd.OpenForm method in VBA is a code version of the OpenForm macro action. You will use the DoCmd object and its methods to create the code to open forms in the frmDataSwitchboard form.

The syntax for the DoCmd.OpenForm object is:

```
DoCmd.OpenForm (FormName, View, FilterName, WhereCondition,
DataMode, WindowMode, OpenArgs)
```

The *FormName* argument is the only required argument, and it must be included in quotation marks. The remaining arguments are optional. Microsoft syntax for a method does not make use of brackets for optional arguments, as you will see if you look up the OpenForm method of the DoCmd object in Microsoft Visual Basic Help. If you include an optional argument, you must include a comma for each argument that precedes the optional argument, even though the argument itself is not typed. You do not need to include commas after the optional argument. For example, if you were to include a *WhereCondition* argument, the Docmd.OpenForm statement would be written as follows:

```
DoCmd.OpenForm "FormName" , , , WhereCondition
```

The commas between *FormName* and *WhereCondition* represent the *View* and *FilterName* arguments. No commas are required after the *WhereCondition* argument. The OpenForm method arguments are as follows:

- *FormName*: A string expression that is the valid name of a form in the current database.
- *View*: One of the following intrinsic constants (an intrinsic constant is a word that has particular meaning in VBA; for example, in the list that follows, the intrinsic constant acDesign means Design view):
  - acDesign (Design view)
  - acFormDS (Form Datasheet view)
  - acFormPivotChart (Form Pivot Chart view)
  - acFormPivotTable (Form Pivot Table view)
  - acNormal (Form view, which is the default)
  - acPreview (Print Preview)
- *FilterName*: A string expression that is the valid name of a query in the current database.
- *WhereCondition*: A string expression that is a valid SQL where clause without the word "where."

- *DataMode*: One of the following intrinsic constants:
  - acFormAdd (the form accepts only new records)
  - acFormEdit (the form allows entering, editing, and deleting records)
  - acFormPropertySettings (the form opens based on the form's property settings; this is the default)
  - acFormReadOnly (the form is read-only)
- *WindowMode*: One of the following intrinsic constants:
  - acDialog (the Modal and Pop Up properties are set to Yes)
  - acHidden (form is open but hidden from view)
  - acIcon (form opens minimized as a small title bar at the bottom of the screen)
  - acWindowNormal or acNormal (form opens in the mode set by its properties; this is the default)
- *OpenArgs*: Use this to set the OpenArgs property of the form. The OpenArgs property lets you specify a particular record you want to move to, and then you use the OpenArgs property in another line of code to move to the specified record.

Control Structures for Decision Processing

VBA provides you with several different control structures for looping. A control structure is a series of VBA statements that work together as a unit. You often need to test for specific conditions in your procedures. VBA provides a number of ways to test for specific values using decision structures, such as If...Then, If...Then...Else, If...Then...ElseIf, and Select Case.

If...Then and If...Then...Else

The If...Then construct lets you specify a condition to be evaluated and then specify the action(s) to be taken if the condition is true. No action is taken if the condition is false. You used this construct when you executed the steps to validate data entered in the TimeCardDate field (these same steps included Figures 6-4 through 6-6).

The If...Then...Else construct lets you specify a condition to be evaluated, and then specify the action(s) to take if the condition is true, and the action(s) to take if the condition is false. In the following example, if the value of grpForms is equal to 1, the frmDegrees form is opened; otherwise, a screen message prompts the user to select a form. The Else portion of the construct is optional, so if no action is required when the condition is false, it can be omitted. The alignment of the If, Else, and End If key words is the industry best practice, as is indenting the code lines for actions to be taken when an if-part or else-part of the construct is true. Typing your code this way helps to make it more readable for yourself and others and is easier to debug and maintain.

```
If grpForms = 1 Then
   DoCmd.OpenForm "frmDegrees", acNormal, "", "", , acNormal
Else
   MsgBox "Select a form to open"
End If
```

ElseIf

You use the If...Then...ElseIf structure to test for multiple conditions. To understand the order in which Access evaluates the conditions, review the following example:

```
If grpForms = 1 Then
       DoCmd.OpenForm "frmDegrees"
ElseIf grpForms = 2 Then
       DoCmd.OpenForm "frmDepartments"
ElseIf grpForms = 3 Then
       DoCmd.OpenForm "frmEmployees"
End If
```

Access evaluates the first condition, grpForms = 1, and if it is true, the DoCmd.OpenForm "frmDegrees" line is executed. Its execution is directed to any code following the End If statement. If grpForms = 1 evaluates to false, Access proceeds to grpForms = 2, and so on.

Select Case

You might want to use the Select Case statement instead of multiple If...Then...Else statements. Access evaluates the expression that follows the Select Case statement to produce a result, and then compares the result of the expression to each Case statement. The advantage of using the Select Case construct is that is easier to read than multiple If...Then...Else constructs, and the code performs better because only one statement is evaluated. Following is an example:

```
Select Case grpForms
       Case 1
              DoCmd.OpenForm "frmDegrees"
       Case 2
              DoCmd.OpenForm "frmDepartments"
       Case 3
              DoCmd.OpenForm "frmEmployees"
```

Adding an Event Procedure to the frmDataSwitchboard Form

Access can automatically convert macros to VBA procedures that perform equivalent actions using Visual Basic code. You can convert macros on a form or report, or you can convert global macros that aren't attached to a specific form or report. You want to learn more about writing VBA in lieu of macros and to use the Macro Converter to help you.

You ran the Macro Converter to convert the mfrmDataSwitchboard macro to VBA code. The results are shown in Figure 6-7.

Figure 6-7 THE MACRO CONVERTED TO VBA CODE

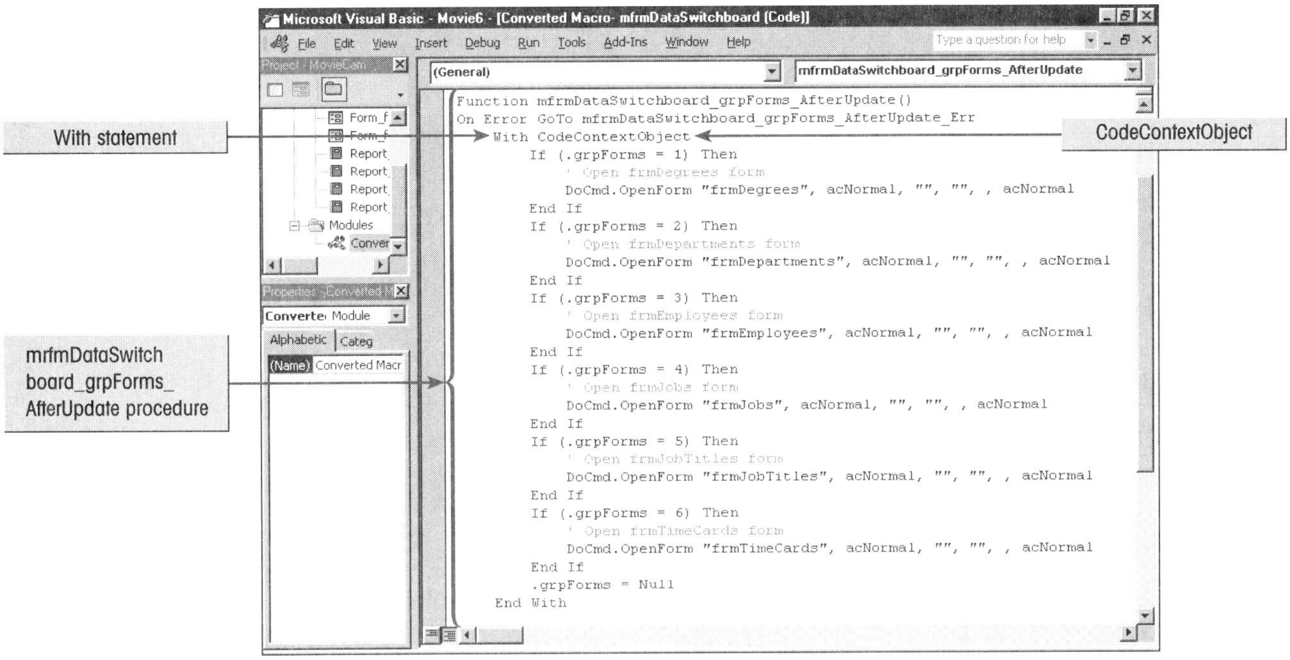

This mfrmDataSwitchboard macro does not exist in your data file for Movie6 database, and is shown in its converted form above as an illustration only, so you will not be able to run this macro conversion. However, the actual module shown in Figure 6-7, named Converted Macro- mfrmDataSwitchboard, does exist in the Movie6 database. You will review this code next, then explore some alternatives to it, and then enter one of those alternatives into a code module for the frmDataSwitchboard form.

Notice that a series of If...Then...Else statements were created in the conversion. No Else statement exists because no action is required if the condition evaluated is false. These statements test the value of the grpForms option group, which is set when the user clicks one of the option buttons in the group. The DoCmd.OpenForm method is used then to open the form specified by the option button. All the arguments in the DoCmd.OpenForm statement after the form name are the default choices, and are not required. When Access converts a macro to VBA, it includes the default arguments in the statements even if they are not required.

The Macro Converter also inserted some error handling into the procedure (note the second line in Figure 6-7 that begins with *On Error GoTo...*) that you will not explore at this time. You will learn more about error handling in Tutorial 8.

The With Statement

Also notice the With statement in Figure 6-7. The With statement lets you perform a series of statements on a specified object, such as a form or a control on a form, without restating the name of the object.

Recall from Tutorial 4 that the bang and dot identifier operators are used in VBA code to specifically identify objects and their properties. The bang is used to separate one object from another or from the object class, and the dot is used to separate an object from its property or method. In the following example, the dot is used to separate the lblFirstName object from its BackColor, Caption, and BorderStyle properties.

```
lblFirstName.BackColor = 12632256
lblFirstName.Caption = "First Name"
lblFirstName.BorderStyle = Solid
```

In the above example, the BackColor property is set to gray, the Caption property is set to First Name, and the BorderStyle property is set to Solid.

You can achieve the same effect by using a With statement and identifying the control one time, as shown below:

```
With lblFirstName
     .BackColor = 12632256
     .Caption = "First Name"
     .BorderStyle = Solid
End With
```

Notice the CodeContextObject property referenced in the With statement in Figure 6-7. This property's purpose is to determine the object in which a macro or VBA code is executing. In this instance, the CodeContextObject property represents the frmDataSwitchboard form.

In the converted macro, the CodeContextObject property is used because the mfrmDataSwitchboard_grpForms_AfterUpdate() procedure is a function. Remember that a function in a standard module can be called from properties, expressions, or even from other procedures. As a function in a standard module, the mfrmDataSwitchboard_grpForms_AfterUpdate() procedure can be run from any form in the database, and the CodeContextObject property will then represent the form that called the function. The grpForms=Null at the end of the procedure sets the option group back to null after the chosen form opens, which effectively clears the option you just selected. If grpForms were not set back to null, the last option chosen would still show as being selected the next time the switchboard is used. By setting the option group back to null, no form is preselected, and once again any form can be opened by clicking on the desired option.

If the procedure in Figure 6-7 were a form module in the frmDataSwitchboard form, then the With statement and CodeContextObject property would not be necessary, and the procedure would look like this (the indentation and comments identifying the form that will open have been removed to save space):

```
Private Sub grpForms_AfterUpdate()
If grpForms = 1 Then
   DoCmd.OpenForm "frmDegrees", acNormal, "", "", , acNormal
End If
If grpForms = 2 Then
   DoCmd.OpenForm "frmDepartments", acNormal, "", "", ,
   acNormal
End If
If grpForms = 3 Then
   DoCmd.OpenForm "frmEmployees", acNormal, "", "", , acNormal
End If
If grpForms = 4 Then
   DoCmd.OpenForm "frmJobs", acNormal, "", "", , acNormal
End If
If grpForms = 5 Then
   DoCmd.OpenForm "frmJobTitles", acNormal, "", "", , acNormal
End If
```

```
If grpForms = 6 Then
   DoCmd.OpenForm "frmTimeCards", acNormal, "", "", , acNormal
End If
grpForms = Null
End Sub
```

A more efficient way to write the same code would be to use the ElseIf form of the If...Then... Else statement, and to leave off the default arguments of the DoCmd.OpenForm as shown below:

```
Private Sub grpForms_AfterUpdate()
        If grpForms = 1 Then
               DoCmd.OpenForm "frmDegrees"
        ElseIf grpForms = 2 Then
               DoCmd.OpenForm "frmDepartments"
        ElseIf grpForms = 3 Then
               DoCmd.OpenForm "frmEmployees"
        ElseIf grpForms = 4 Then
               DoCmd.OpenForm "frmJobs"
        ElseIf grpForms = 5 Then
               DoCmd.OpenForm "frmJobTitles"
        ElseIf grpForms = 6 Then
               DoCmd.OpenForm "frmTimeCards"
        End If
grpForms = Null
End Sub
```

Next you will add the code to the frmDataSwitchboard form using the Select Case statement to open a particular form based on the user's choice from the switchboard.

To add code to the frmDataSwitchboard form:

1. Open the **frmDataSwitchboard** form in Design view.
2. Click the frame of the option group once to select it, click the **Properties** button on the toolbar, and then click the **Event** tab on the property sheet. See Figure 6-8.

Figure 6-8 DISPLAYING PROPERTIES FOR THE OPTION GROUP

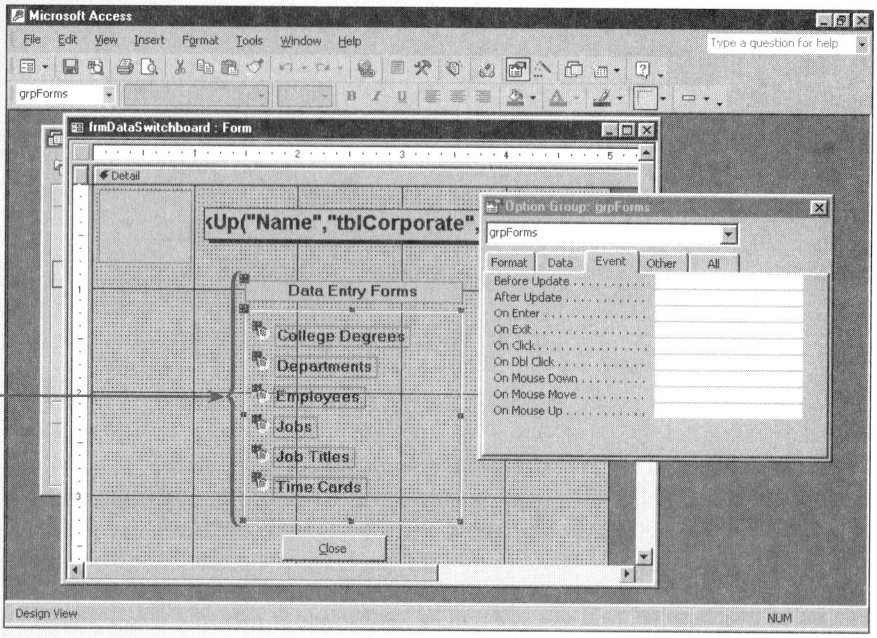

option group frame

3. Click the **After Update** property text box, and then click its **Build** button [...]. The Code window opens in the Visual Basic window. The new event procedure for the option group's AfterUpdate event property contains the Private Sub and End Sub statements. You can now enter the statements to open a form, based on the option the user selects in the option group.

   TROUBLE? If more than one code window opens, close those that you are not currently working with. Make sure that you type in the Form_frmDataSwitchboard (Code) window.

4. Type **Select Case grpForms**, press the **Enter** key, press the **Tab** key to indent, and then type **Case 1**.
5. Press the **Enter** key, press the **Tab** key, and then type **DoCmd.OpenForm "frmDegrees"**.
6. Press the **Enter** key, copy the **Case 1** and **DoCmd.OpenForm** statements and paste them in the blank line you just created before the End Sub statement, change Case 1 to **Case 2**, and then change frmDegrees to **frmDepartments**. If necessary, indent or outdent these statements so that they are aligned as shown in Figure 6-9.
7. Repeat Step 6, change the Case to **3** and the form to **frmEmployees**.
8. Repeat Step 6, change the Case to **4** and the form the **frmJobs**.
9. Complete the code (starting with the Case 5 statement) as shown in Figure 6-9.

Figure 6-9 **COMPLETED grpForms_AfterUpdate PROCEDURE**

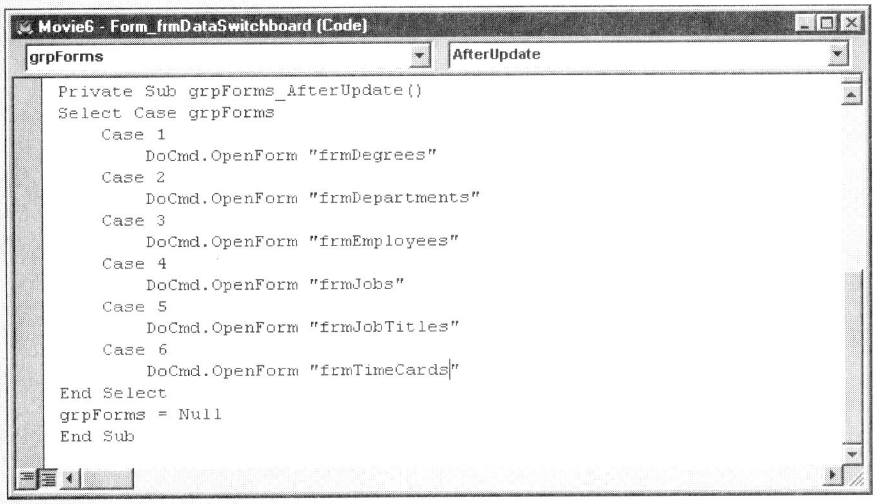

10. Compile your code, close the Visual Basic window, close the property sheet, and switch to Form view to test the procedure.
11. Click each of the forms in the option group to be sure that the correct form opens, and then close each form to return to the switchboard.

    TROUBLE? If you encounter any runtime errors, one option you have is to debug the code. Once Access takes you to the Code window, select Reset from the Run menu. Make sure your code looks like that shown in Figure 6-9. Compile it again and return to the switchboard to test the procedure again.

12. Save your work, and then close the switchboard to return to the Database window.

The product managers are pleased with the validation of data entered in the TimeCardDate field in the frmTimeCards form, and you have written some code using VBA. The frmDataSwitchboard form works well, and next you are ready to customize toolbars and menus, change Startup properties, and split the database.

Session 6.1 QUICK CHECK

1. A(n) ______________ is a named attribute of an object that defines a certain characteristic, such as size or color.
2. A(n) ______________ is a procedure that is similar to a statement or function that operates on an object.
3. When does the After Update event occur?
4. What does the DatePart function return?
5. What is the DoCmd object?
6. The ______________ argument in Docmd.OpenForm is a string expression that is a valid SQL WHERE clause without the word "where."

7. The ______________ is a good alternative to the ElseIf form of the If...Then... Else statement.
8. What is the purpose of the CodeContextObject property?
9. What is the purpose of using a With statement?

SESSION 6.2

In this session, you will learn how to modify an existing toolbar, create a custom menu bar, and create a custom shortcut menu. You will learn how to modify Startup properties to control user access to objects in the database. You also will learn to work with AutoKeys macros. The last task you will perform for this session is to split the database into two parts, a front end and a back end.

Introduction to Menus and Toolbars

Menus and toolbars are common in most Windows-based programs. Commands, such as opening, saving, and closing files, exiting a program, printing, and more are organized on toolbars and menus so that you can quickly and easily access them.

Access automatically "personalizes" menus and toolbars based on how often you use the commands they contain. When you first start Access, the most basic commands appear on the menus, and are represented by buttons on the toolbars. As you work, Access adjusts the menus and toolbars to display the commands and buttons you use most often. As you already know, clicking the double arrow at the bottom of a menu expands the menu to show all the commands it contains. You can also double-click the menu to expand it. For example, when you double-click Tools on the menu bar, the entire menu is visible. When you click a command on the expanded menu, it is automatically placed on the personalized menu the next time you open it. A command is dropped from your personalized menu if you use Access many times without using that command. You can change settings so that the full set of commands is always on the menus; however, if you are working in the Office 2002 suite, changing this setting in Access affects the other programs in the suite.

REFERENCE WINDOW RW

Displaying the Full Set of Menu Commands

- Click Tools on the menu bar, and then click Customize.
- Click the Options tab in the Customize dialog box.
- Clear the Menus show recently used commands first check box to deselect the option.
- Click the Close button.

You will now change the menu settings so that all menu commands are available when the menu is opened. You will also explore menu animation, the term used to describe how the menu opens. For example, a menu can slide down or it can unfold when you click it.

To display the full set of menu commands and explore menu animation:

1. If you took a break after the previous session, make sure Access is running and the **Movie6** database is open.
2. Click **Tools** on the menu bar, click **Customize**, and then click the **Options** tab in the Customize dialog box.
3. If necessary, click the **Always show full menus** check box to select the option, as shown in Figure 6-10.

Figure 6-10 **CHANGING MENU OPTIONS**

selecting this option displays a fully extended menu

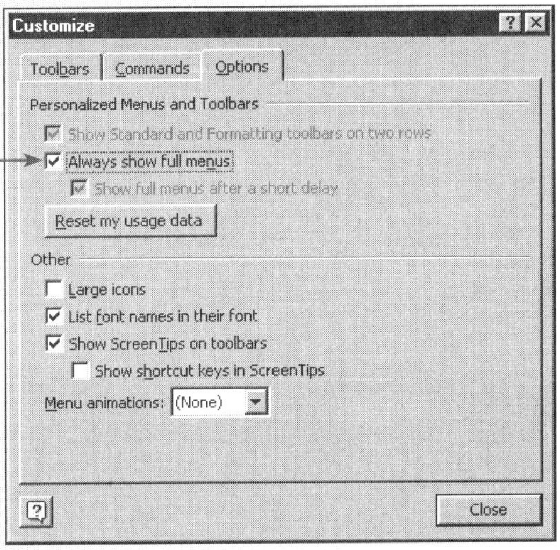

4. Click the **Close** button, and then click **Tools** on the menu bar. Note that all the commands are visible.
5. With the Tools menu still open, click **Customize** to reopen the Customize dialog box.
6. Click the **Menu animations** list arrow, click **Slide**, and then click the **Close** button.
7. Click **Tools** on the menu bar to test the change. The menu options display one at a time very rapidly, which you find distracting, so you will remove it.
8. Click **Tools** on the menu bar, click **Customize**, change the Menu animations setting back to **(System Default)**, and then click the **Close** button.

Access 2002 provides you with the flexibility to move and position toolbars. You can position them side by side by clicking the move handle along the left edge of the toolbar and then dragging the toolbar so that it is positioned to the right or left of another toolbar. See Figure 6-11.

Figure 6-11 POSITIONING TOOLBARS SIDE BY SIDE

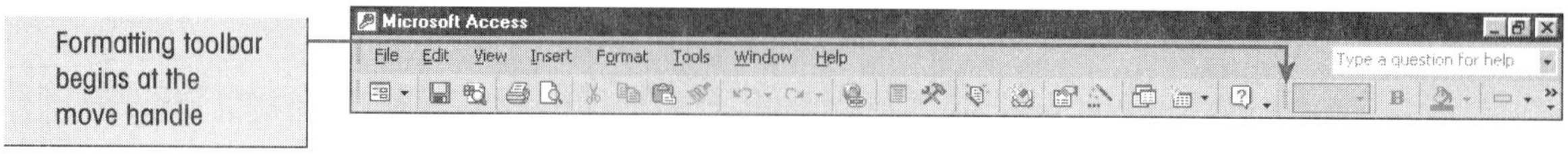

When you position toolbars side by side, however, there might not be enough room for all the buttons. In this case, only the buttons you have used most recently are visible. To resize a toolbar when it is positioned on the same row as another toolbar, click the move handle and then drag the edge of the toolbar. See Figure 6-12.

Figure 6-12 SIZING A TOOLBAR

To see a list of the buttons that are not visible on a built-in, docked toolbar, click the Toolbar Options button at the end of the toolbar. When you use a button that is not visible on the toolbar, that button is moved to the toolbar, and a button that has not been used recently is dropped to the Toolbar Options list, as shown in Figure 6-13.

Figure 6-13 BUTTONS THAT DO NOT FIT ON THE TOOLBAR

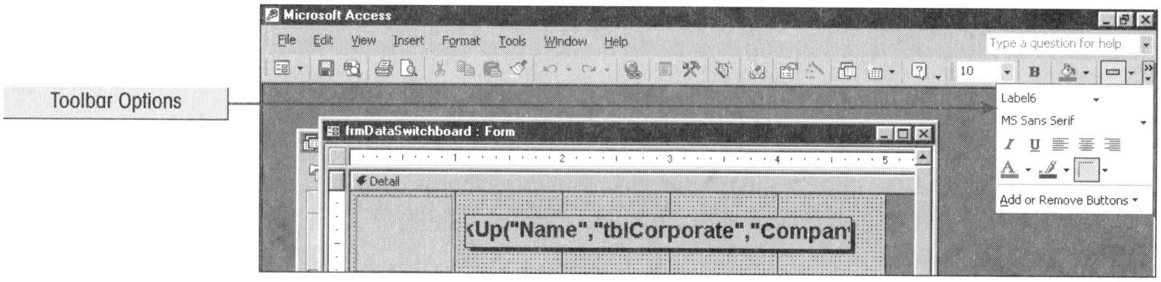

Because the menus and toolbars are personalized to show the commands that you use most often in Access, you might find at some point that you want to return them to their original state. To do this, open the Customize dialog box from the Tools menu, and click the Reset my usage data button, as shown in Figure 6-14.

Figure 6-14 RESETTING THE TOOLBAR

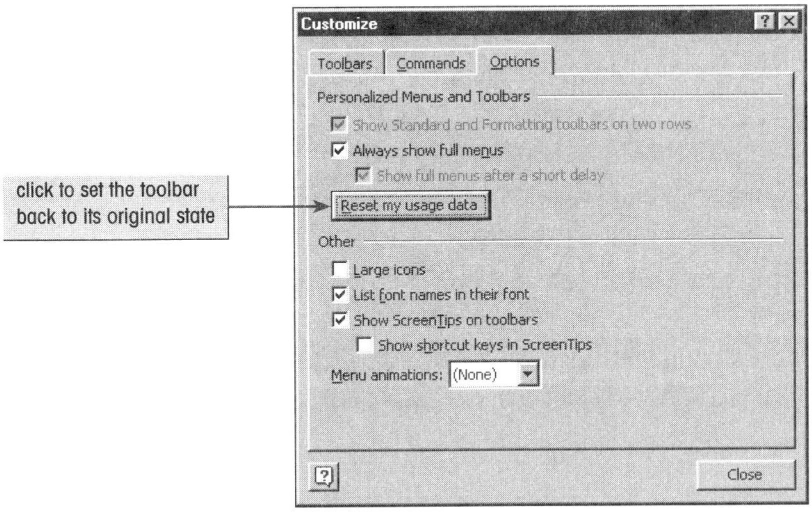

You can further customize the built-in menu bar by adding or removing menu items, or by moving a menu to a different location. You also can create your own custom toolbars, menu bars, and shortcut menus.

Creating and Customizing Menus and Toolbars

Creating custom menus and toolbars in a program is an important part of the database development process. In many instances, you will want to restrict access to certain features and objects so that users cannot inadvertently delete data, view sensitive data, modify the design of an object, modify macros or VBA code, and so forth. A simple way to do this is to customize existing menus and toolbars, or create new ones.

You determine that it is in the best interest of MovieCam Technologies to give database users access to only those menu commands and toolbar buttons that they need to enter and edit records. You need to restrict access to the default toolbars and create a custom shortcut menu so that the command to switch to an object's Design view is not available. You also need to create a custom toolbar that contains only those buttons users need to work in the database.

Customizing Toolbars

Access stores customized toolbars in a file named System.mdw. This file contains preference and security information and will be discussed in greater detail in Tutorial 9.

REFERENCE WINDOW RW

Customizing a Toolbar

- Make sure that the toolbar you want to customize is visible.
- Click View on the menu bar, point to Toolbars, and then click Customize.
- Click the Commands tab, and click a category from the Categories list box.
- Drag the command(s) you are adding from the Commands list box to the toolbar.
- Click the Close button.

Before you modify the menus and toolbars for users, you want to customize the menus and toolbars you're using to design and develop the database. Because you spend a lot of time aligning controls on forms, you will add Align Left and Align Top buttons to the Formatting (Form/Report) toolbar.

To customize a toolbar:

1. Make sure that **Forms** is selected on the Objects bar in the Database window, and then open the **frmJobs** form in Design view.
2. Be sure the Formatting (Form/Report) toolbar is visible, as shown in Figure 6-15.

Figure 6-15 CUSTOMIZING A TOOLBAR

Formatting (Form/Report) toolbar

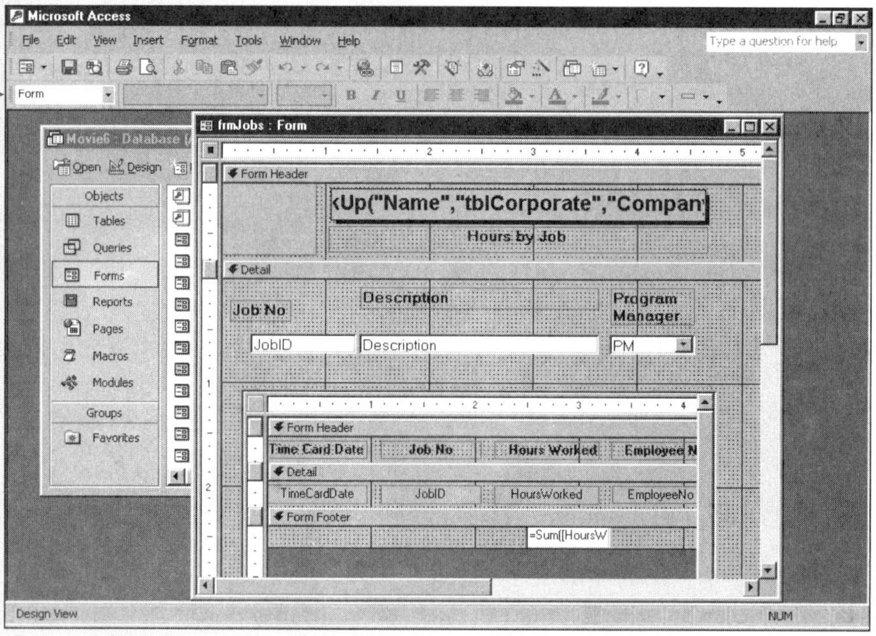

3. Click **View** on the menu bar, point to **Toolbars**, click **Customize** to open the Customize dialog box, and then click the **Toolbars** tab. See Figure 6-16. The first tab of the dialog lists the existing toolbars and menu bars in the program. Those that are currently visible are checked.

Figure 6-16 CUSTOMIZE DIALOG BOX

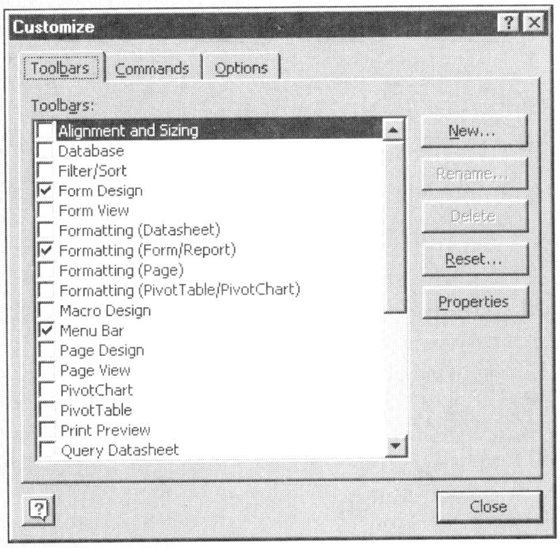

4. Click the **Commands** tab. The Categories list is comparable to the names of existing menus and toolbars; the Commands list box lists the commands that can be added to menus or toolbars.

5. Click **Form/Report Design** in the Categories list box, scroll down the Commands list box to the Align Left command, as shown in Figure 6-17.

Figure 6-17 TOOBAR COMMANDS

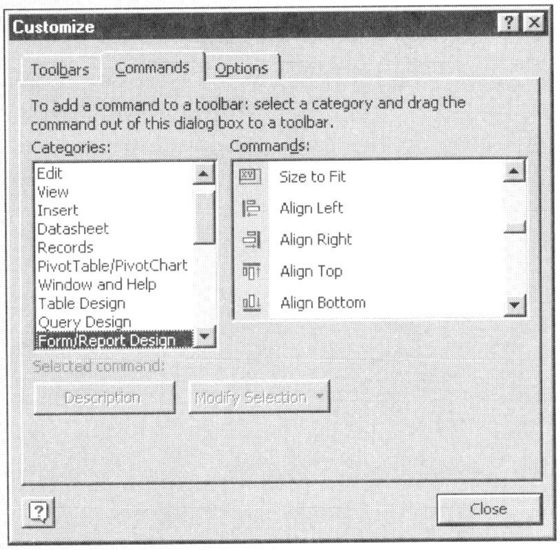

6. Drag the **Align Left** command from the Commands list box to the end of the Formatting toolbar, and then release the mouse button when the button is positioned on the toolbar.

7. Drag the **Align Top** command from the Commands list box to the right of the Align Left button on the toolbar, release the mouse button when the button is positioned on the toolbar, and then click the **Close** button to close the Customize dialog box. Your toolbar should look like that shown in Figure 6-18.

Figure 6-18 FORMATTING (FORM/REPORT) TOOLBAR

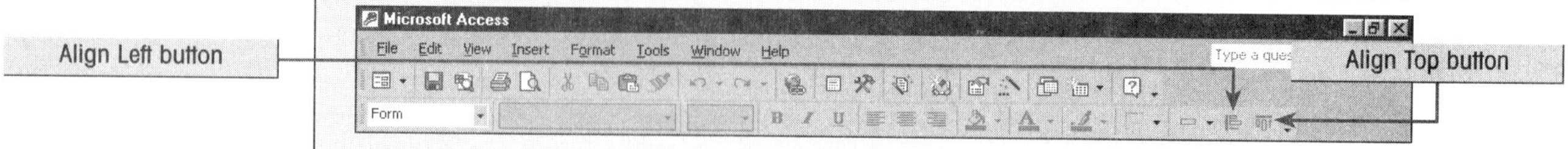

TROUBLE? If you have previously customized this toolbar, those changes will remain in effect until you select the toolbar in the Customize dialog box and click the Reset button.

8. Select the **Job No** label and **Description** label in the Detail section in the main form, click the **Align Top** button on the Formatting (Form/Report) toolbar, and then deselect these controls.
9. Select the **Job No** label and the **JobID** text box in the Detail section in the main form, and then click the **Align Left** button on the toolbar. The results are shown in Figure 6-19.

Figure 6-19 ALIGNING CONTROLS USING NEW TOOLBAR BUTTONS

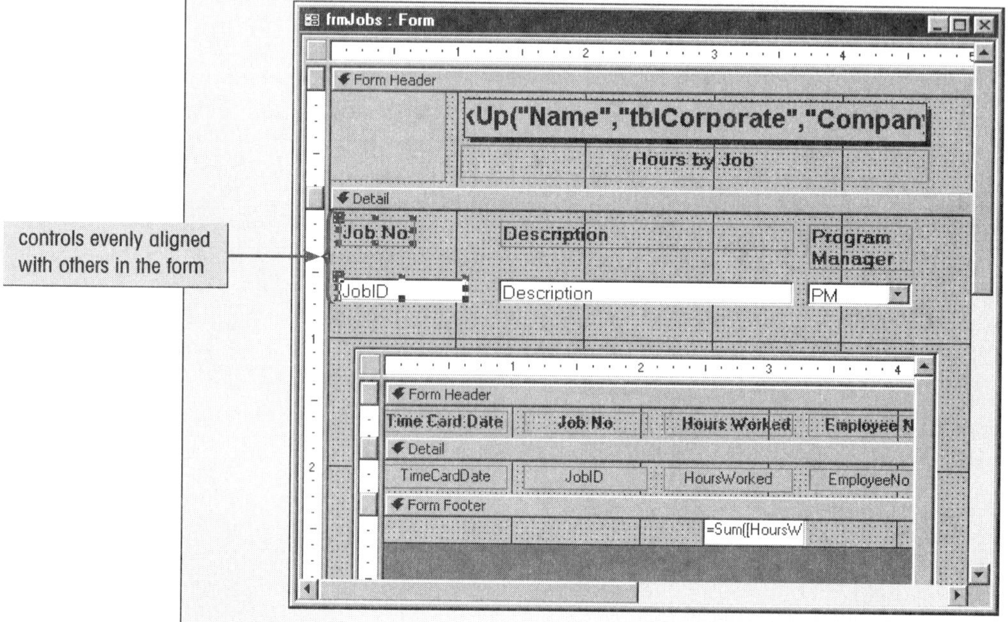

10. Save the form and then close it.

Next you will design a custom menu for the MovieCam database. You then will need to identify the new menu in the Startup properties.

Creating a Custom Menu Bar

When you create a new menu, it's a good idea to follow the standards used by most programs in the Windows environment. That is, for each of the menu items on the menu bar, use names that users are familiar with, such as File and Edit. You also should display the menu items in the order that users are accustomed to seeing them.

REFERENCE WINDOW RW

Creating a New Menu Bar and Menu Items

- Click View on the menu bar, point to Toolbars, and then click Customize to open the Customize dialog box.
- Click the Toolbars tab, click the New button, and type the toolbar name in the New Toolbar dialog box, and then click the OK button.
- Click the Properties button to open the Toolbar Properties dialog box, click the Type list arrow, click Menu Bar, and then click the Close button.
- Click the Commands tab, scroll to the bottom of the Categories list box, and then click New Menu.
- Click and drag the New Menu command in the Commands list box to the new menu bar.
- Right-click the new menu item on the menu bar, click Properties on the shortcut menu, and change the Caption property to specify the type of commands the menu item will contain.
- Click the Close button.

The new menu that you want to create will contain some of the same menu items that are currently available on the File, Edit, and Records menus. It will not contain any menu items that are on the View, Insert, Window, and Tools menus.

To create a new menu bar:

1. Click **View** on the menu bar, point to **Toolbars**, and then click **Customize** to open the Customize dialog box.
2. Click the **Toolbars** tab, click the **New** button, type **mnuMovieCam** in the Toolbar Name text box, and then click the **OK** button. The mnuMovieCam toolbar is visible, as shown in Figure 6-20.

Figure 6-20 **CREATING A NEW TOOLBAR**

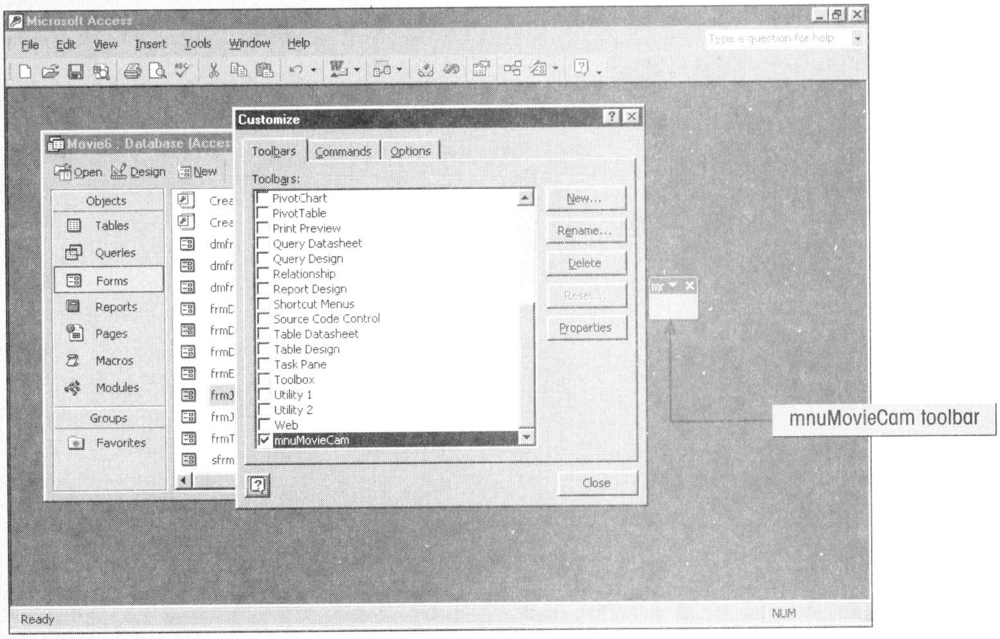

3. Click the **Properties** button to open the Toolbar Properties dialog box.
4. Click the **Type** list arrow, click **Menu Bar**, and then click the **Close** button. Now the toolbar will appear as a menu bar rather than as a standard toolbar. Next you will add a New Menu command to the menu bar.
5. Click the **Commands** tab in the Customize dialog box, scroll to the bottom of the Categories list box, and then click **New Menu**.
6. Click and drag the **New Menu** command in the Commands list box to the **mnuMovieCam** menu bar. Next you will name the new menu item on the toolbar.
7. Right-click the **New Menu** item on the mnuMovieCam menu bar, as shown in Figure 6-21.

Figure 6-21 RENAMING THE NEW MENU ITEM

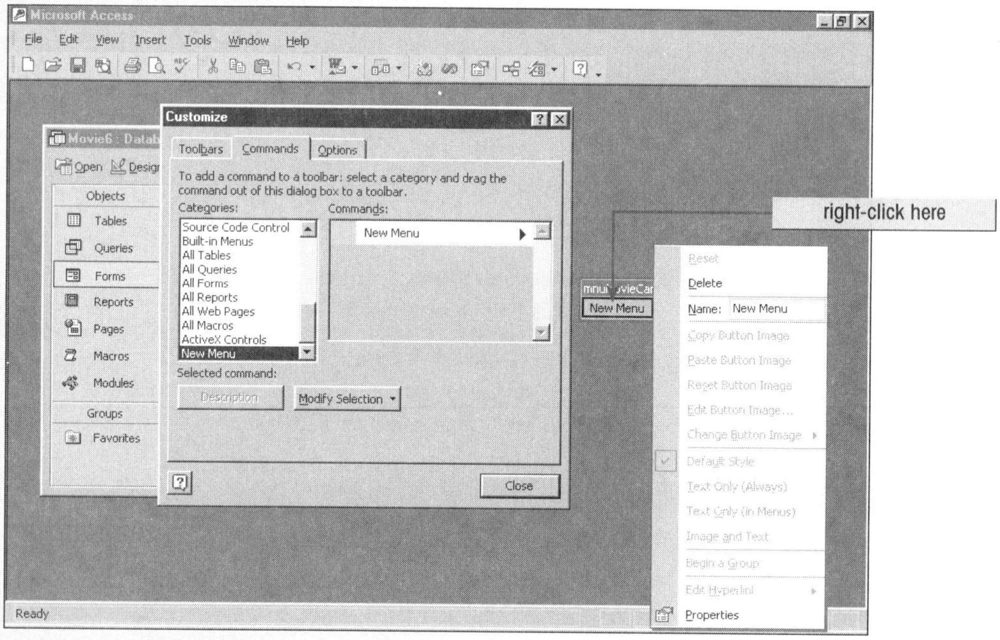

8. Click **Properties** on the shortcut menu.
9. Change the Caption property to **&File** and then click the **Close** button. The ampersand (&) preceding the F in File enables a keyboard shortcut to open the menu.

The next step in building the custom menu bar is to add commands to the new menu items. To do this you click and drag a command from the Commands list box in the Customize dialog box to the menu item on the menu bar.

REFERENCE WINDOW RW

Adding Commands to a Menu Item

- Display the menu to which you want to add an item, and then open the Customize dialog box.
- Click a category in the Categories list box, and then drag the desired command(s) from the Commands list box to the menu item, positioning the pointer on the menu item so that it drops down, and then release the mouse button to drop the command below the menu item.
- Click the Close button.

You decide to include the Close, Save Record, Page Setup, Print, Print Preview, and Exit commands on the new File menu.

To add commands to a new menu:

1. Click **File** in the Categories list box.
2. Drag the **Close** command in the Commands list box to the mnuMovieCam menu bar, position the pointer on the File menu so that the menu drops down, and then release the mouse button to drop the command below the File menu name.

   TROUBLE? If you drop the command on the menu bar itself, drag the command to a blank area of the screen to delete it, and then repeat Step 2.

3. Drag the **Save Record** command in the Commands list box to the menu bar, and then drop the command below the Close command.
4. Repeat this process to add the **Page Setup**, **Print Preview**, **Print**, and **Exit** commands, in that order, to the File menu. The menu should look like that shown in Figure 6-22.

Figure 6-22 ADDING COMMANDS TO THE FILE MENU ON THE mnuMovieCam MENU BAR

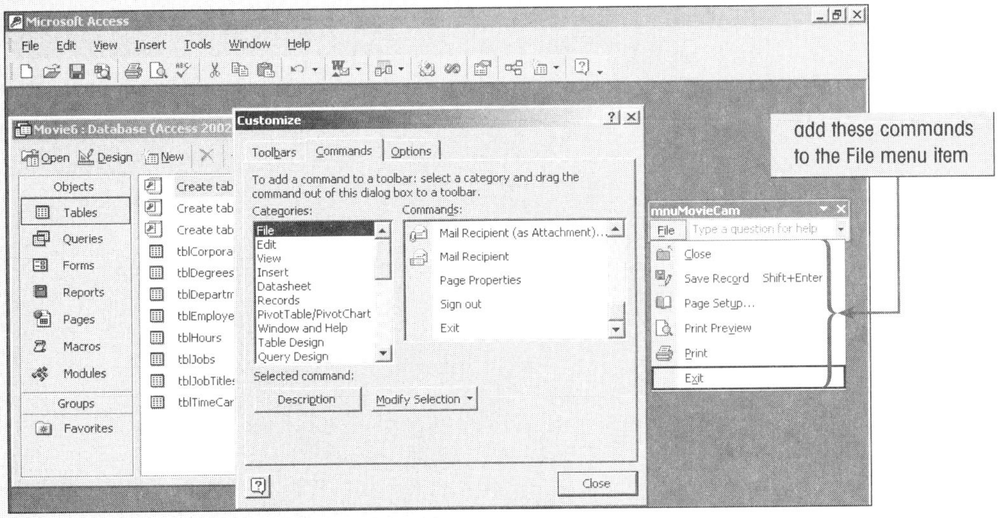

5. Click **New Menu** in the Categories list box, drag the **New Menu** command from the Commands list box and drop the command to the right of the File menu on the mnuMovieCam menu bar.

6. Right-click the **New Menu** item, click **Properties** on the shortcut menu, change the Caption property to **&Edit**, and then click the **Close** button.

7. Repeat Steps 5 and 6 to create a new menu item with a caption of **&Records**.

8. Click **Edit** in the Categories list box of the Customize dialog box, and drag the **Undo**, **Cut**, **Copy**, **Paste**, **Delete**, and **Find** commands, in that order, to the Edit menu on the mnuMovieCam menu bar. If you have multiple choices for Undo, use the first Undo command. If two Delete commands display, use the one with the red X next to it. The Undo button will appear on the menu as Can't Undo. It will change to Undo when the menu is used and an action has been taken that can be undone.

9. Click **Records** in the Categories list box, and drag the **Sort Ascending**, **Sort Descending**, **Filter By Selection**, **Filter By Form**, **Apply Filter/Sort**, **Remove Filter/Sort**, and **Spelling** commands, in that order, to the Records menu in the mnuMovieCam menu bar, as shown in Figure 6-23.

Figure 6-23 ADDING COMMANDS TO THE RECORDS MENU

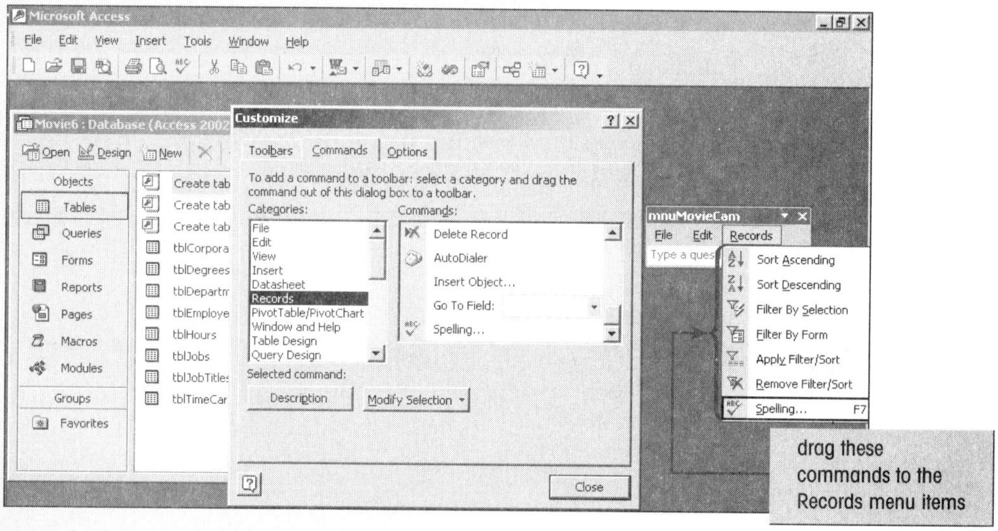

10. Click the **Toolbars** tab in the Customize dialog box, scroll down to the bottom of the toolbars list box, click **mnuMovieCam** to turn off the menu, and then click the **Close** button in the Customize dialog box.

Next you will create the shortcut menu that will replace the default shortcut menu in Access.

Creating a Custom Shortcut Menu

A shortcut menu opens when you click the right mouse button. Next you'll create a custom shortcut menu for your database.

REFERENCE WINDOW RW

Creating a Custom Shortcut Menu

- Click View on the menu bar, point to Toolbars, and then click Customize.
- Make sure that the Toolbars tab in the Customize dialog box is selected, and then click the New button.
- Type the name of the toolbar, and then click the OK button.
- Click the Properties button, click the Type list arrow, click Popup, and then click the OK button.
- Click the Close button on the Toolbar Properties window, scroll down in the Toolbars list box, and click the Shortcut Menus check box.
- Click Custom at the far right of the Shortcut menus toolbar, and then click the shortcut menu you created.
- Click the Commands tab in the Customize dialog box, click the category of command desired in the Categories list box, and then drag the command(s) from the Commands list box to the short-cut menu.
- Click the Close button to close the Customize dialog box.

The default shortcut menus in Access contain commands to open forms and reports in Design view, to open the Relationships window, and so on. You do not want users to have access to these commands.

To create a custom shortcut menu:

1. Click **View** on the menu bar, point to **Toolbars**, click **Customize**, and then click the **Toolbars** tab in the Customize dialog box.
2. Click the **New** button, type **MovieCam**, and then click the **OK** button.
3. Click the **Properties** button, click the **Type** list arrow, and then click **Popup**. The message box shown in Figure 6-24 opens.

Figure 6-24 POPUP MESSAGE BOX

4. Click the **OK** button, and then click the **Close** button in the Toolbar Properties window.

5. Scroll down in the Toolbars list box, and click the **Shortcut Menus** check box. The Shortcut Menus toolbar appears.

6. Click **Custom** on the Shortcut Menus toolbar (see Figure 6-25), and then click **MovieCam**.

Figure 6-25 CREATING THE SHORTCUT MENU

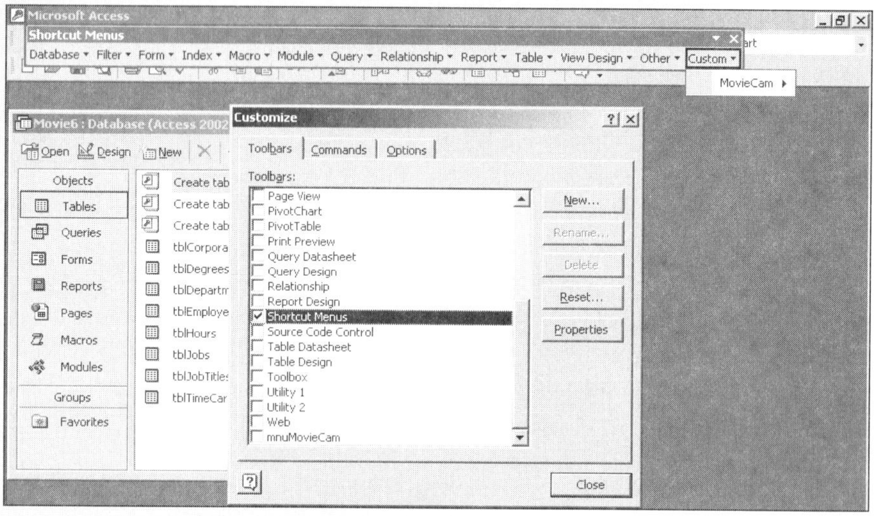

7. Click the **Commands** tab in the Customize dialog box, click **Edit** in the Categories list box, and drag the **Undo** command from the Commands list box to the MovieCam shortcut menu.

8. Add the **Copy**, **Paste**, and **Find** commands from the Commands list to the shortcut menu. You may need to reposition your Shortcut Menus toolbar so that you can better see the items you have added, as shown in Figure 6-26.

Figure 6-26 ADDING COMMANDS TO THE MovieCam SHORTCUT MENU

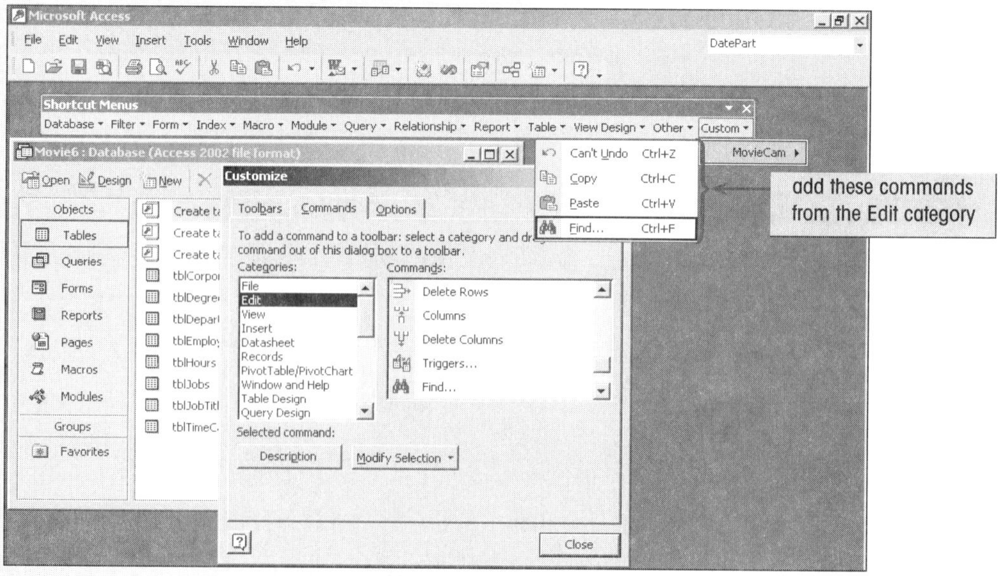

9. Click **Records** in the Categories list box, and then add the **Sort Ascending**, **Sort Descending**, and **Filter by Selection** commands to the shortcut menu.
10. Close the Customize dialog box.

You realize that the shortcut menu that you just created is not named properly. For consistency, you should add a tag to the menu name specifying that it is a shortcut menu as you did with the menu bar you created earlier. You decide to delete the shortcut menu and re-create it.

Deleting a toolbar or a menu bar is simple. In the Customize dialog box, you select the toolbar to be deleted, and then click the Delete button. Deleting a shortcut menu is more complicated; you must first convert it to a toolbar, and then delete it.

To delete a shortcut menu:

1. Click **View** on the menu bar, point to **Toolbars**, and then click **Customize**.
2. Click the **Toolbars** tab, and then click the **Properties** button.
3. Click the **Selected Toolbar** list arrow, and then point to **MovieCam** on the list, as shown in Figure 6-27.

Figure 6-27 CHANGING THE MovieCam SHORTCUT MENU TO A TOOLBAR

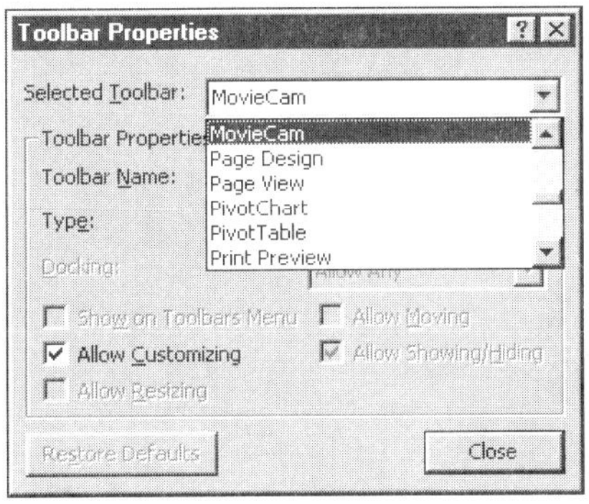

4. Click the **MovieCam** selection, click the **Type** list arrow, and then click **Toolbar** to change the MovieCam shortcut menu to a toolbar.
5. Click the **Close** button to return to the Customize dialog box, and then click **MovieCam** in the Toolbars list box to select it, as shown in Figure 6-28.

Figure 6-28 SELECTING THE MovieCam TOOLBAR FOR DELETION

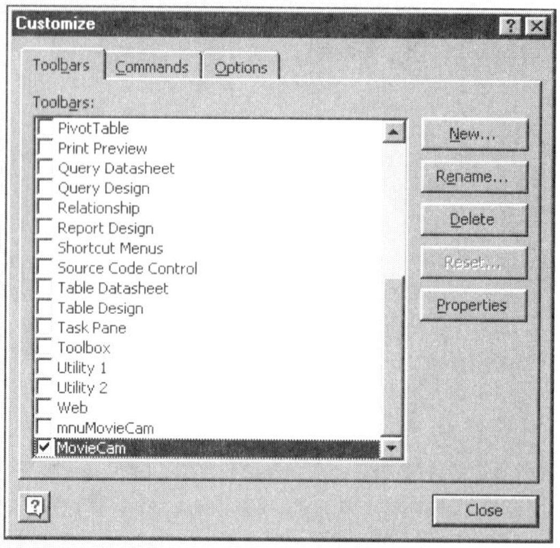

6. Click the **Delete** button, and then click the **OK** button to confirm the deletion.
7. Re-create the shortcut menu, naming it **smnuMovieCam**, following Steps 2 through 8 in the previous set of steps.
8. Close the Customize dialog box.

Now that you have completed the custom menus and toolbar, you will change the Startup properties in the MovieCam database so that the toolbar and menus appear by default. You also will set the frmDataSwitchboard form to open automatically when the database opens. Although it is not the Main Switchboard, frmDataSwitchboard will be used as the startup form to test the menus and some of the other startup features.

Startup Properties

The Startup properties control user access to areas of the database. These properties are set in the Startup dialog box, which you open by selecting Startup on the Tools menu. The changes you make to the Startup properties apply only to the database in which they are set; changing Startup properties in MovieCam will not affect any other databases. In addition, changing the Startup properties for the database does not override the property settings for a custom toolbar, menu bar, or shortcut menu that's been created for a specific form or report. When you specify a menu bar or shortcut menu in the Startup dialog box, it appears when the database opens.

The Startup properties include:

- *Application Title*: A program name that displays in the database title bar.
- *Application Icon*: A bitmap or icon file of an image that you use as the application icon in the Windows title bar, as shown in Figure 6-29. (You will be changing startup options shortly which will result in the Application icon and title appearing as they do in the figure below.)

Figure 6-29 APPLICATION ICON

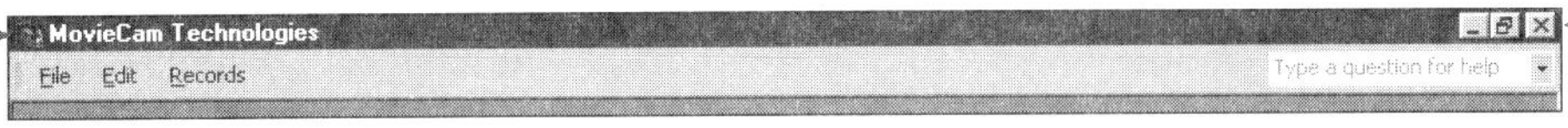

- *Menu Bar*: A menu bar that will appear as the default menu bar for the current database.
- *Allow Full Menus*: An option that allows the use of all Access menu commands. If this option is not selected, a predefined subset of the full built-in menus is shown. This subset of menus doesn't include menus and commands that enable users to change the design of the database objects. Clearing this option also disables the toolbar buttons that correspond to the disabled menu items.
- *Allow Default Shortcut Menus*: Use this property to specify whether or not the program allows the display of built-in shortcut menus. Clearing Allow Full Menus does not disable the shortcut menus, so if you want to keep users from changing the database design, this option also must be deselected.
- *Display Form/Page*: A form or data access page that you want shown when the database opens. Usually a switchboard or splash screen is specified here.
- *Display Database Window*: Deselecting this check box means the Database window will not be visible when you open the database. You can still see it, however, by pressing the F11 key.
- *Display Status Bar*: Deselect this option to hide the status bar.
- *Shortcut Menu Bar*: Use this property to specify a custom shortcut menu that you want to appear in your application. If you want to restrict users from Design view of the database objects, you should also clear Allow Default Shortcut Menus.
- *Allow Built-in Toolbars*: Deselect this option to disable the built-in toolbars.
- *Allow Toolbar/Menu Changes*: Deselect this check box to lock toolbars. This disables the feature that allows you to right-click the toolbar to open the Customize dialog box. It also disables the Toolbars command on the View menu, and the Close button on toolbars.
- *Use Special Access Keys*: Click the Advanced button in the Startup dialog box so this option is visible. Deselect this option to prevent users from pressing the F11 key to show the Database window, pressing Ctrl + F11 to toggle to the Database window, pressing Ctrl + Break to enter the break mode in a Visual Basic module, or pressing Ctrl + G to display the Immediate window. (The Immediate window is discussed in Tutorial 8.)

REFERENCE WINDOW RW

__Setting the Database Startup Properties__

- Click Tools on the menu bar, and then click Startup.
- Specify the options that you want.
- Click the OK button.
- Close the database and reopen it to enable the specified options.

You now will set the Startup properties to display the new menu you created. You will also change some of the other Startup properties.

To change Startup properties:

1. Click **Tools** on the menu bar, and then click **Startup**. The Startup dialog box opens, as shown in Figure 6-30.

Figure 6-30 STARTUP DIALOG BOX

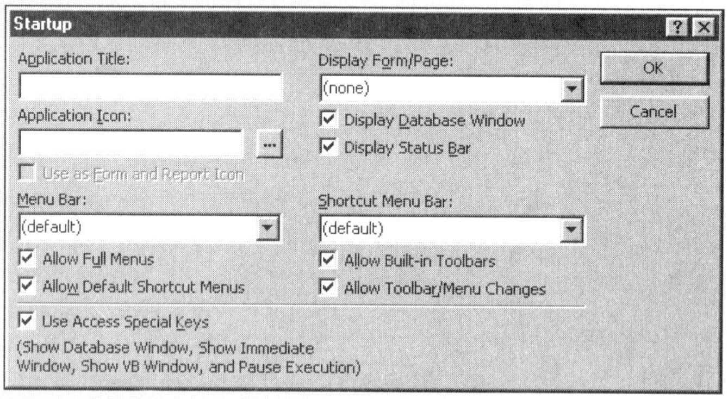

2. In the Application Title text box, type **MovieCam Technologies** and then click the **Build** button ... at the right of the Application Icon text box. The Icon Browser dialog box opens.
3. Navigate to the Tutorial.06\Tutorial folder on your local or network drive, click the **MovieCam** file, and then click the **OK** button. This is an icon of a camera that you will insert as the application icon in the Windows title bar and taskbar.
4. Click the **Menu Bar** list arrow, and then click **mnuMovieCam** to select your custom menu.
5. Click the **Display Form/Page** list arrow, click **frmDataSwitchboard**, clear the **Display Database Window** check box, click the **Shortcut Menu Bar** list arrow, and then click **smnuMovieCam**.
6. Clear the **Allow Built-in Toolbars** and the **Allow Toolbar/Menu Changes** check boxes to deselect these options, and then clear the **Use Access Special Keys** check box to deselect it. See Figure 6-31.

Figure 6-31 CHANGING STARTUP PROPERTIES

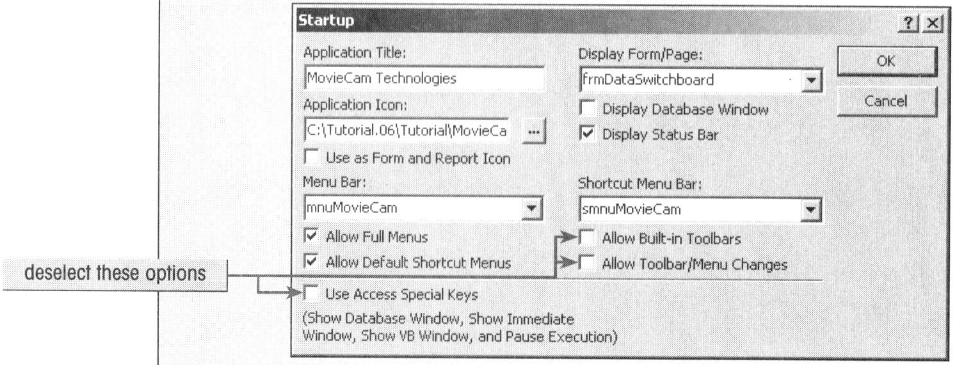

7. Click the **OK** button to close the Startup dialog box, and then exit the database. You must reopen the database to test your changes.
8. Open the database to see the effect of changing the Startup properties.
9. Right-click anywhere on the switchboard to open the custom shortcut menu.
10. Click **File** on the custom menu bar, and then click **Exit**.
11. Start Access, point to **Movie6** in the Task Pane, and then press and hold the **Shift** key and click to open the Movie6 database. The Startup properties are bypassed, and the database opens with the original Startup options in effect.

You do not want users to be able to bypass the Startup properties that you have set, so you will now disable the Startup properties bypass feature.

Disabling the Bypass Key

Access database programmers refer to the Shift key as the bypass key. Disabling the bypass key is a common method for securing a database; however, you must understand that most savvy database users are familiar with this security measure.

You also can disable the bypass key by writing VBA code, which is more difficult for users to undo. The trick here is that the VBA code must also include a method to enable the Shift key, so that you and other authorized users can get into the design and programming areas of the database.

One method to trigger the code that enables or disables the bypass key is to include transparent command buttons on the switchboard. As the developer, you know where they are located and can click them to perform the desired operation. Another method is to trigger the code with a series of keystrokes. An AutoKeys macro provides this functionality and is the method you decide to use. This type of macro, also referred to as global key assignment, is one example of when you would use a macro instead of VBA because you can only create the global key assignments with a macro. However, by setting startup options and employing VBA code modules, you can completely control the rest of the user interface in an efficient manner that is also easier to maintain.

Using Code Samples in Visual Basic Help

The code to disable or enable the bypass key is somewhat complex. However, Access Help contains many code samples that can be copied and pasted into your database application.

To copy code from Access Help:

1. Click **Modules** on the Objects bar in the Database window, then click the **New** button to create a standard module. Press and hold the **Alt** key and then press the **F11** key. When the Visual Basic window opens, click **Help** on the menu bar, and then click **Microsoft Visual Basic Help**.

TROUBLE? If a message box appears indicating that the Microsoft Visual Basic Help feature has not been installed and asking if you want to install it now, click the Yes button. You will be prompted to insert the Microsoft Office XP Professional CD. Insert the installation CD and then click the OK button. The files will be installed on your computer. Remember to remove the CD after the installation is complete, and then repeat Step 1. If you do not have the installation CD, ask your instructor or technical support person for assistance.

TROUBLE? If the Office Assistant appears, click the Options button, clear the Use the Office Assistant check box, and then click the OK button. Open the Microsoft Visual Basic Help from the Help menu.

2. Make sure the **Answer Wizard** tab is displayed in the Help window.
3. Type **Disable Shift Key** in the What would you like to do? text box, and click the **Search** button. The first topic, AllowBypassKey Property, is visible as shown in Figure 6-32.

Figure 6-32 LOOKING UP CODE IN HELP

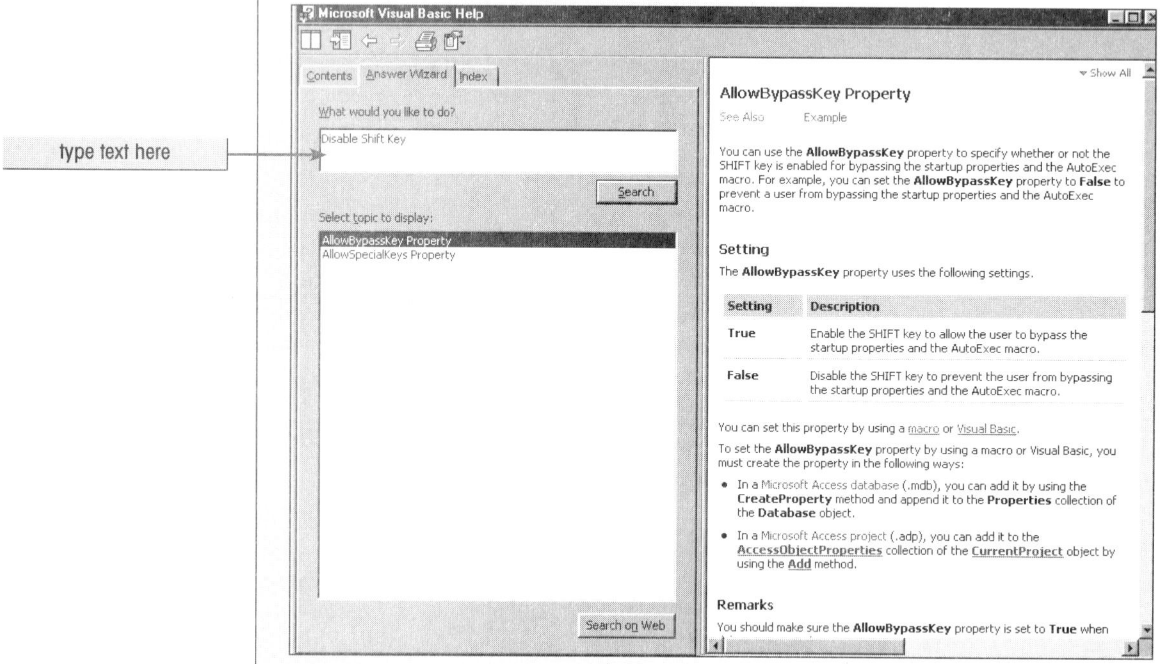

TROUBLE? If the Answer Wizard did not find the AllowBypassKey Property topic, or if it did, but the Example link is not available, then you may have gone into Microsoft Access Help from the Database menu. You must be in the Visual Basic window. Try Steps 1 through 3 again.

4. Click the **Example** link.
5. Select the entire code sample, as shown in Figure 6-33, from the Sub SetBypassProperty() line to the End Function line, and then press **Ctrl + C** to copy this code to the Clipboard.

Figure 6-33 SELECTING THE SetBypassProperty CODE

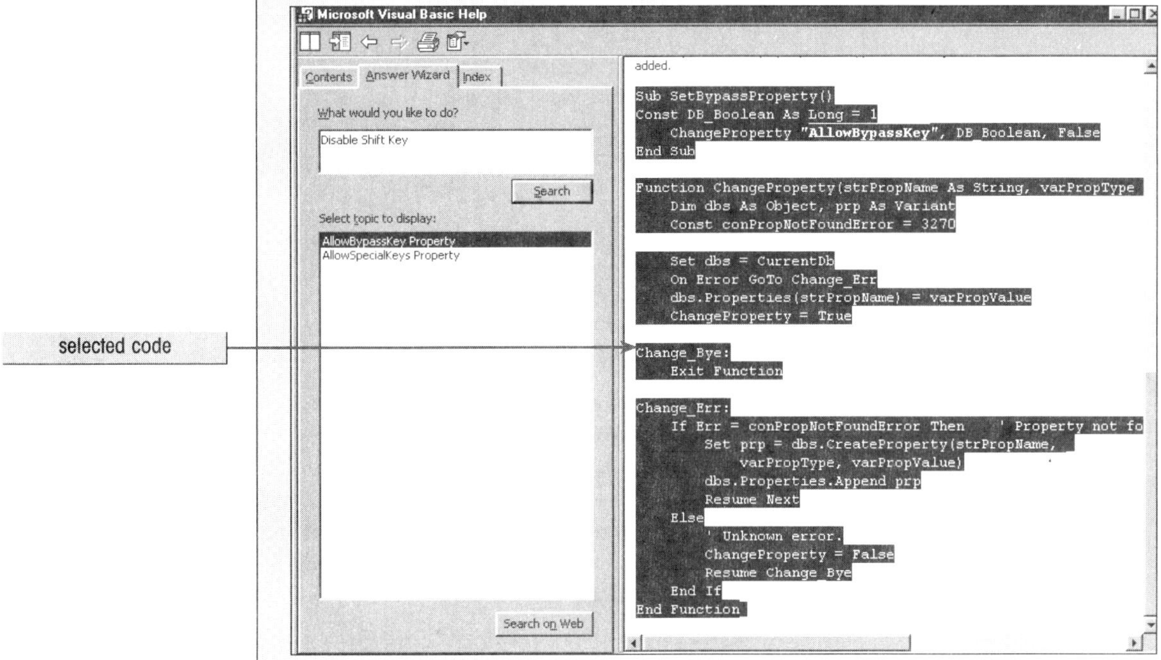

6. Close the Help window. Because you opened the Visual Basic window in Step 1 above, you may use the blank module that was started for you. If you have closed the Visual Basic window, simply click **Modules** on the Objects bar of the Database window, and then click the **New** button to create a new standard module.

7. Maximize the Code window, right-click to display the shortcut menu, and then click **Paste**.

8. Click the **Save** button on the toolbar, type **mdlFunctions** in the Module Name text box, and then click the **OK** button. As discussed in Tutorial 5, you can call a function from a macro, an event property, and an expression. The code that you copied into the mdlFunctions module contains two procedures. One is a Sub procedure and the other is a function. The Sub procedure calls the function. Again, this code is somewhat complex, which is why you copied it from Help instead of writing it yourself. Because you want to call the SetBypassProperty Sub procedure from a macro, you need to change the Sub procedure to a function.

9. Double-click the word **Sub** in the first line of the code to select it, type **Function**, and then press the ↓ key. Note that End Sub line of code changes automatically to "End Function."

   TROUBLE? If both procedures are not visible in the Visual Basic window, click Tools on the menu bar, and then click Options. If necessary, click the Editor tab in the Options dialog box, click the Default to Full Module View checkbox, and then click the OK button.

To use this function effectively, you need to be able to set the AllowBypassKey Property to false, and also to set it to true. One way to set the AllowBypassKey Property to true or to false using the code you copied from the Help system, would be to include two functions—one sets the AllowBypassKey Property to false, as shown below:

```
Function SetBypassPropertyFalse()
Const DB_Boolean As Long = 1
      ChangeProperty "AllowBypassKey", DB_Boolean, False
End Function
```

The other function sets the AllowBypassKey Property to true, and is shown below:

```
Function SetBypassPropertyTrue()
Const DB_Boolean As Long = 1
      ChangeProperty "AllowBypassKey", DB_Boolean, True
End Function
```

Another way to set the AllowBypassKey Property to True or False is to include in the function an argument to be supplied when the function is called. If you include an argument in the function that represents true or false, and then supply that true or false argument when the function is called by the macro, it is not necessary to write two separate functions.

The following code sample shows what this function would look like if you included the bValue argument for the reason stated previously:

```
Function SetBypassProperty(bValue As Boolean)
Const DB_Boolean As Long = 1
      ChangeProperty "AllowBypassKey", DB_Boolean, bValue
End Function
```

The argument name is bValue. The "b" prefix indicates that it is Boolean, which is the data type for True/False or Yes/No data, and Boolean is the argument data type required in the ChangeProperty function. You determine that passing true or false from the macro is the most efficient way to write the function procedure.

To add a variable to the SetBypassProperty function:

1. Position the insertion point between the parentheses in the first line of the SetBypassProperty function.
2. Type **bValue As** and then press the **spacebar**. Note the syntax information banner opens.
3. Type **B** and notice that the list shows the items that begin with the letter B.
4. Double-click **Boolean** to complete the statement.
5. Select the word **False** in the ChangeProperty statement, and then type **bValue**. The function should look like that shown in Figure 6-34.

Figure 6-34 **MODIFYING THE SetBypassProperty CODE**

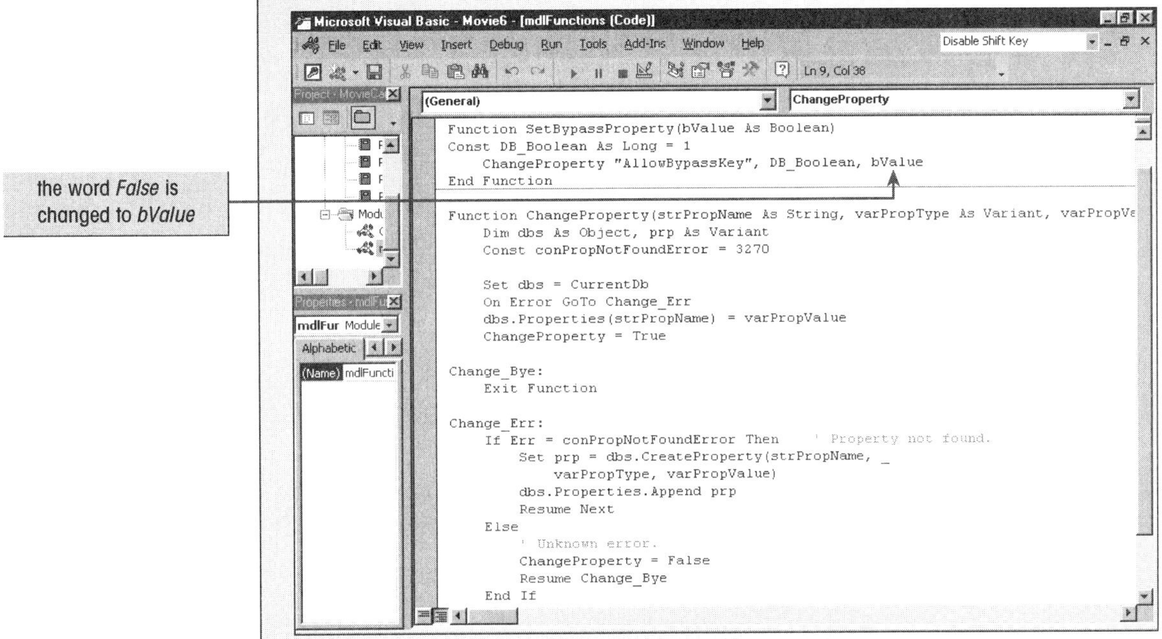

6. Save your changes, click the **Debug** menu, and click **Compile Movie6** (this is always a good idea after adding or changing a code procedure to verify there are no syntax errors), and then close the Visual Basic window.

Now that you have completed the code, you need to create a way to execute it. You decide that using a series of keystrokes to enable the Shift key, and a different series to disable the key is the best approach. You will be the only one who knows the appropriate key combinations, but you will also document this information for safekeeping and future database maintenance.

AutoKeys Macro Group

You can create a macro group to assign custom commands to key combinations. You use the special name AutoKeys to name the macro group. When you press a key combination, Access searches for an AutoKeys macro, and then runs the macro assigned to that combination. You can use an AutoKeys macro to make key assignments that replace the default key assignments (such as F11, which you can press to display the Database window), or you can create entirely new key combinations.

You also can specify in the macro Conditions column if you want the key to be effective under only certain circumstances. Not all key combinations are available for assignment in the AutoKeys macro. Figure 6-35 lists the key combinations that can be used.

Figure 6-35 KEY COMBINATIONS FOR AutoKeys MACRO

KEY COMBINATION	AUTOKEYS SYNTAX
Ctrl+Any letter or number key	^A or ^4
Any function key	{F1}
Ctrl+Any function key	^{F1}
Shift+Any function key	+{F1}
Ins	{INSERT}
Ctrl+Ins	^{INSERT}
Shift+Ins	+{INSERT}
Del	{DELETE} or {DEL}
Ctrl+Del	^{DELETE} or ^{DEL}
Shift+Del	+{DELETE} or +{DEL}

To create an AutoKeys macro:

1. Click **Macros** on the Objects bar of the Database window, and then click **New** to create a new macro.
2. Click the first row's **Macro Name** text box, type **^{F4}**, and then press the **Tab** key to move to the Action column.

   TROUBLE? If the Macro Name column is not visible, click View on the menu bar, and then click Macro Names.

3. Click the **Action** list arrow, click **RunCode**, press the **Tab** key, and then type **Set Bypass property to true**.
4. Press the **F6** key to move to the Function Name text box in the Action Arguments pane, and then click the **Build** button ... to open the Expression Builder.
5. Double-click the **Functions** folder in the first column. The Built-In Functions and Movie6 folders appear, as shown in Figure 6-36.

Figure 6-36 EXPRESSION BUILDER

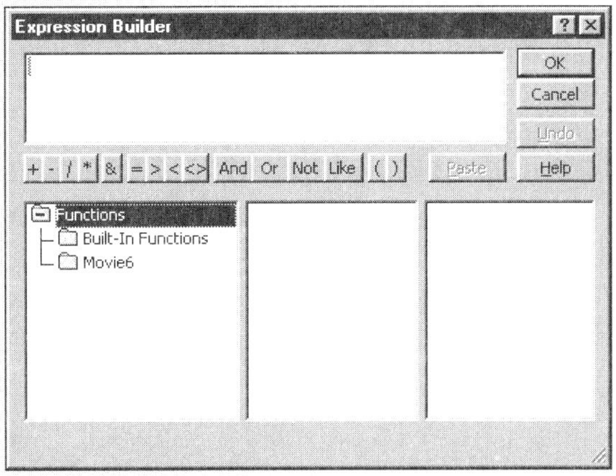

6. Click the **Movie6** Functions folder. A list of standard module names is shown in the center column, and the third column shows the functions within the selected module.
7. Click **mdlFunctions**, click **SetBypassProperty**, and then click the **Paste** button. Your screen should look like that shown in Figure 6-37.

Figure 6-37 SELECTING THE FUNCTION

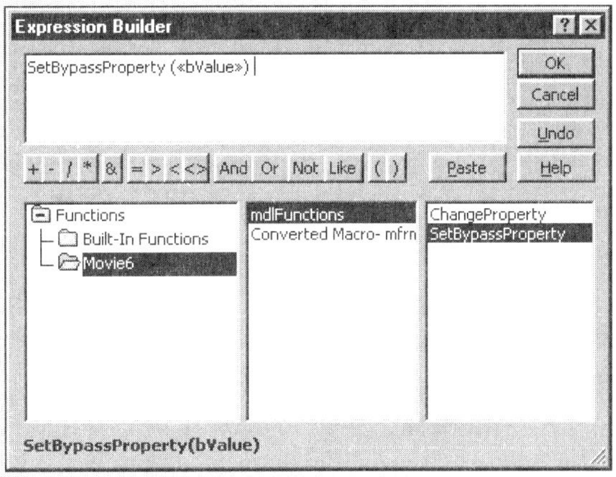

8. Click the **bValue** argument in the Expression Builder to select it, type **True**, and then click the **OK** button.
9. Save your changes, type **AutoKeys** in the Macro Name text box, and then click the **OK** button.

Next you will complete the macro group by adding the macro to run the SetBypassProperty function with the false argument to disable the bypass key.

To complete the AutoKeys macro:

1. Click in the third row **Macro Name** text box, type **^{F5}**, and then press the **Tab** key to move to the Action column.

2. Click the **Action** list arrow, scroll through the list, click **RunCode**, press the **Tab** key, and then type **Set Bypass property to false**.

3. Press the **F6** key to move to the Function Name Action Argument, and type **SetBypassProperty (False)**, as shown in Figure 6-38.

Figure 6-38 COMPLETING THE AutoKeys MACRO

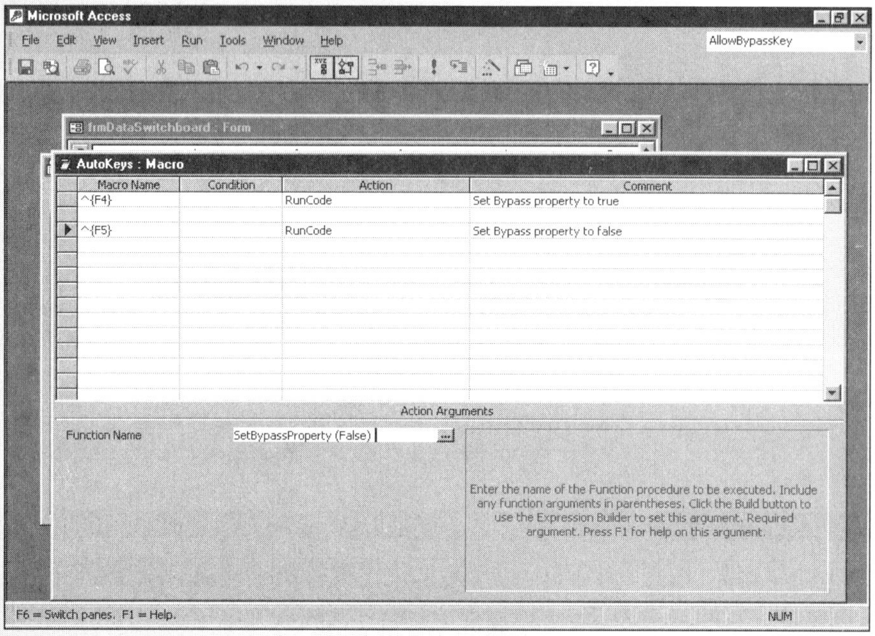

4. Save your changes and close the Macro window.

Next you'll test the code you wrote and the AutoKeys macro. First, be sure that you have a back-up copy of the entire database file. You might need to go to Windows Explorer and make a copy before you continue.

To test the AutoKeys macro and SetBypassProperty function:

1. Press **Ctrl + F5** to disable the Shift key, and then close the Movie6 database.
2. Hold down the **Shift** key as you reopen the **Movie6** database. The bypass key doesn't work.
3. Press **Ctrl + F4** to enable the Shift key, and then close the Movie6 database.
4. Open the **Movie6** database while you hold down the **Shift** key. The bypass key works this time, and the Startup property settings are bypassed.

The final step in the process is to split the MovieCam Technologies database. After this is completed, you can make copies of the front end for users, and continue development in the master front end.

Splitting the Database

Most Access developers agree that Access databases should be split into two files: one containing only Access tables, often called the back end, and another containing all other objects, often called the front end.

Splitting a database like this allows you to link tables from the shared back end to the front end, which is often placed on local drives. Keeping the front end on the user's computer minimizes network traffic and improves performance. The major benefit, however, is that ongoing development of the database objects can be accomplished without interfering with users working in the database. If one file is placed on a shared network drive, the forms and reports cannot be modified when users are working in them. If the database is split, however, changes can be made to a master copy of the front end and then copied to an individual user's machine.

Finally, splitting the database and providing users with a unique copy of the front end allows them to develop their own forms and reports without affecting the database of other users. If a user accesses Design view of a form or report and damages it, only that user's copy is affected.

REFERENCE WINDOW RW

Using the Database Splitter Wizard

- Make a back-up copy of the database that you want to split.
- Start Access and open the database you want to split.
- Click Tools on the menu bar, point to Database Utilities, and then click the Database Splitter.
- Click the Split Database button, select the drive and folder for the back-end database, type a name for the database in the File name text box, and then click the Split button.
- Click the OK button.

Now you'll use the Database Splitter Wizard to split the MovieCam database. Before you do, make a back-up copy of the database containing the work that you have done up to this point.

To split the Movie6 database:

1. Close the Movie6 database, but do not exit Access.
2. Right-click the **Start** button on the taskbar, and then click **Explore** on the shortcut menu to open Windows Explorer.
3. Navigate to the Tutorial.06\Tutorial folder, right-click the **Movie6** file, click **Copy** on the shortcut menu, right-click an empty area of the window, and then click **Paste** on the shortcut menu. A file named Copy of Movie6 is created in the Tutorial.06\Tutorial folder.
4. Close Windows Explorer to return to Access, and then open the **Movie6** database while holding down the **Shift** key to bypass the Startup properties options.
5. Click **Tools** on the menu bar, point to **Database Utilities**, and then click **Database Splitter**. The Database Splitter dialog box opens, as shown in Figure 6-39.

Figure 6-39 **DATABASE SPLITTER DIALOG BOX**

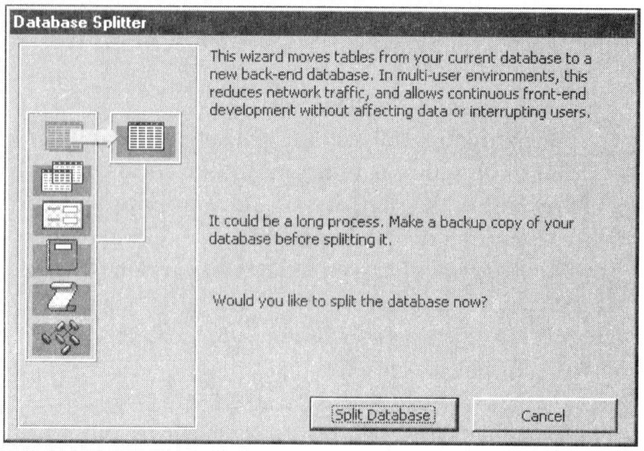

TROUBLE? If a dialog box opens and asks if you want to install the Database Splitter feature, insert your Office 2002 installation CD in the correct drive, and then click the Yes button. If you do not have the Office 2002 installation CD, see your instructor or technical support person for assistance.

6. Click the **Split Database** button. The Create Back-end Database dialog box opens. The back-end database will contain the tables from the MovieCam database. You will use the default filename for the back-end database.
7. Click the **Save in** list arrow, navigate to the Tutorial.06\Tutorial folder, and then click the **Split** button.
8. Click the **OK** button when the message box opens and tells you that the database has been successfully split.

Now that the database is split, you want to move the back-end database to the shared drive of the network. If you move the back-end database to a new folder or drive, the links to the front-end database will need to be refreshed.

REFERENCE WINDOW RW

Using the Linked Table Manager

- Start Access and open the database containing links to another Access database.
- Click Tools on the menu bar, point to Database Utilities, and then click Linked Table Manager.
- Select the tables link to be refreshed, click the Always prompt for new location check box, and then click the OK button.
- Navigate to the drive and folder for the file containing the tables, type a name for the database in the File name text box, and then click the Open button.
- Click the OK button.

The Linked Table Manager is a utility that allows you to refresh links to tables that are contained in a separate database. To see how this feature works, you will move the back-end database to the My Documents folder on your computer. Then you will open the Movie6 front-end database, test the linked tables, and then refresh the links to the back-end database.

To move Movie6_be to the My Documents folder and update the linked tables:

1. Close the Movie6 database and then exit Access.
2. Open Windows Explorer.
3. Navigate to the Tutorial.06\Tutorial folder, drag the **Movie6_be** database to the **My Documents** folder on the same drive as your Tutorial.06\Tutorial folder. Do not drag the file to a different drive or you will copy it and this exercise will not work.

   TROUBLE? If you do not have a My Documents folder on the same drive as the Tutorial.06\Tutorial folder or you don't have copy access to it, check with your instructor or technical support person to see which folder to use. The name of the folder is not important here, only that the file is moved to a new location.

4. Close Windows Explorer, start Access, and then open the **Movie6** database while holding down the **Shift** key.
5. Click the **Tables** button on the Objects bar of the Database window, and then double-click the **tblEmployees** table. An error message, explaining that the location of the tables is incorrect, is displayed.
6. Click the **OK** button to close the error message, click **Tools** on the menu bar, point to **Database Utilities**, and then click **Linked Table Manager**. The Linked Table Manager dialog box displays, as shown in Figure 6-40.

Figure 6-40 LINKED TABLE MANAGER DIALOG BOX

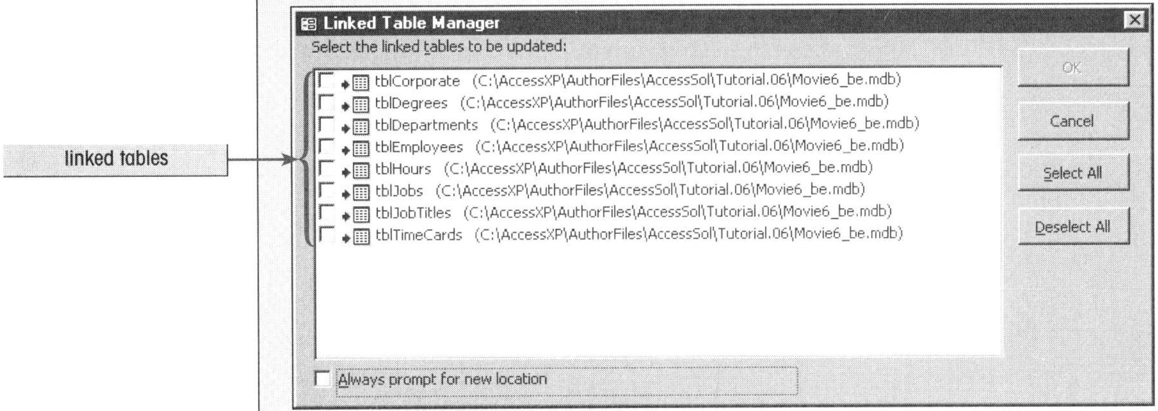

7. Click the **Select All** button to select all the tables in the database, and then click the **Always prompt for new location** check box so that the Linked Table Manager will prompt you for the location of the back-end file.

8. Click the **OK** button, navigate to the My Documents folder, click **Movie6_be** to select it, and then click the **Open** button.
9. Click the **OK** button when the message box opens and tells you that all selected linked tables were successfully refreshed, and then click the **Close** button in the Linked Table Manager.
10. Close the Movie6 database, and then exit Access.
11. If you are working in a lab and need to move the Movie6_be database back to the Tutorial.06\Tutorial folder, repeat Steps 2 through 9, dragging the file from the My Documents folder back to the Tutorial.06\Tutorial folder and running the Linked Table Manager again.

The database is split into a front and back end, and is ready to be copied for use on individual computers. The menus and switchboards are in place, and the Startup property settings cannot be bypassed by users.

Session 6.2 QUICK CHECK

1. In what way are built-in menus and toolbars personalized?
2. Access stores custom toolbars in a file called ______________.
3. To delete a shortcut menu, you must first convert it to a(n) ______________.
4. After you change the Startup property settings in Access, how do you test the results?
5. What is an AutoExec macro?
6. Which executes first, Startup property settings or the AutoExec macro?
7. What function does the bypass key perform?
8. What is the purpose of the AutoKeys macro?
9. After splitting the database, the file containing the tables is called the ______________.

REVIEW ASSIGNMENTS

The Hours6 database is similar to the MovieCam Technologies database you worked on in the tutorial. You'll modify the switchboard to include VBA code and create a custom menu bar.

1. Start Access and open the **Hours6** database located in the Tutorial.06\Review folder on your local or network drive.
2. Open the **frmMainSwitchboard** form in Design view.
3. Click the frame of the option group once to select it, open its property sheet, and then click the Event tab.
4. Click the Build button for the After Update event property to open the Visual Basic window with the beginning and ending line of the procedure.
5. Type the following code:

```
Select Case grpForms
        Case 1
               DoCmd.OpenForm "frmDepartments"
        Case 2
               DoCmd.OpenForm "frmEmployees"
        Case 3
               DoCmd.OpenForm "frmJobTitles"
End Select
grpForms = Null
```

6. Compile the code and then print the code.
7. Close the Visual Basic window, switch to Form view to test the procedure, and then save your changes and close the form.
8. Open the Customize dialog box from the View Toolbars menu.
9. Create a new toolbar with the name **mnuHours**, and then change the type to Menu Bar.
10. Add the New Menu command from the New Menu category to the mnuHours menu bar.
11. Change the Caption property to **&File**.
12. Add the Close command from the File category to the mnuHours menu bar below the File command.
13. Add the Page Setup, Print Preview, Print, and Exit commands from the File category (one under the other) to the mnuHours menu bar.
14. Add a new menu item named **Edit** that contains commands for Cut, Copy, and Paste from the Edit category.
15. Add a new menu item named **Records** that contains commands for Sort Ascending and Sort Descending from the Records category.

Explore

16. Create a new custom toolbar named **tlbHours** (the "tlb" tag stands for toolbar). Add the Save Record, Page Setup, Print Preview, and Print commands from the File category to the tlbHours toolbar. Add the Undo, Find, and Find Next commands from the Edit category. Add the Sort Ascending, Sort Descending, Filter by Selection, and Toggle Filter commands from the Records category.
17. Close the Hours6 database, and then exit Access.

CASE PROBLEMS

Case 1. Edwards and Company Jack asks you to create a custom shortcut menu to use in the frmClients data entry form. He wants the shortcut menu to contain the following commands: Undo, Copy, Paste, Delete, Find, Sort Ascending, Sort Descending, and Filter by Selection. Complete the following:

1. Start Access and open the **Edward6** database located in the Tutorial.06\Cases folder on your local or network drive.
2. Open the Customize dialog box from the View Toolbars menu, and then create a new toolbar with the name **smnuClients**.
3. Change the toolbar type to Popup, display the Shortcut Menus toolbar, and then select smnuClients from the Custom drop-down list.
4. Add the Undo command from the Edit category to the smnuClients shortcut menu.
5. Add the following commands from the Edit category: Copy, Paste, Delete, and Find.
6. Add the following commands from the Records category: Sort Ascending, Sort Descending, and Filter by Selection.
7. Close the Customize dialog box.
8. Open the **frmClients** form in Design view, and then click the Properties button on the toolbar.
9. If necessary, click the All tab in the properties dialog box, click in the Shortcut Menu Bar property text box, click the list arrow, and select smnuClients.
10. Switch to Form view, and right-click to test the shortcut menu.
11. ***Explore*** Switch to Design view. Create a new custom menu named **mnuClients** that contains File, Edit, and Records menu items. Add the Close, Save Record, and Exit commands (from the File category) to the File menu item. Add the Undo, Cut, Copy, Paste, and Find commands (from the Edit category) to the Edit menu item. Add the Sort Ascending, Sort Descending, and Spelling commands (from the Records category) to the Records menu item. Deselect the mnuClients menu on the Toolbar tab of the Customize dialog box so that this menu does not display automatically. Open the form's property sheet, and set the Menu Bar property to mnuClients.
12. Save your changes, and then switch to Form view to display the mnuClients menu.
13. Close the form.
14. Close the Edward6 database, and then exit Access.

Case 2. San Diego County Information Systems In the ISD6 database, classes are stored and entered into the system using the frmClasses form. Because classes are always held on Monday and Wednesday, you decide to add validation code to this form to test the data entered. Complete the following:

1. Start Access and open the **ISD6** database located in the Tutorial.06\Cases folder on your local or network drive.
2. Open the **frmClasses** form in Design view, select the Date text box, and then open its property sheet.
3. Click the Event tab, and then click the Build button for the Before Update property.
4. Type the following code, making use of the intrinsic constants available for the DatePart function (open Visual Basic Help and search for the DatePart function if you want to review available constants):

```
If DatePart("w", Date) <> vbMonday Then
       If DatePart("w", Date) <> vbWednesday Then
              Cancel = True
              MsgBox "Classes must be on Monday or Wednesday!"
       End If
End If
```

5. Compile and print the code, close the Visual Basic window, and switch to Form view to test the procedure.
6. Enter a new record with the date **10/17/04** (a Sunday) in the Date field, and then click the OK button to close the error message box.
7. Enter the new date **10/18/04** (a Monday) in the Date field, and then press the Enter key.
8. Delete the new record.
9. Save your changes and then close the form.
10. Close the ISD6 database, and then exit Access.

Case 3. Christenson Homes Roberta Christenson primarily uses the frmLots form in the Homes6 database. She asks you to set it as the default form for the database. She wants you to modify the database design so she doesn't see the Database window, and also wants you to create a custom menu that includes only the File, Edit, and Records commands. Complete the following:

1. Start Access and open the **Homes6** database located in the Tutorial.06\Cases folder on your local or network drive.
2. Create a custom menu named **mnuHomes** that contains the following menu items: File, Edit, and Records.
3. Add the following commands to the File menu: Close, Print Preview, and Exit.
4. Add the following commands to the Edit menu: Cut, Copy, Paste, and Find.
5. Add the following commands to the Records menu: Sort Ascending, Sort Descending, Filter By Selection, and Filter By Form.
6. On the mnuHomes custom menu, add a command to the File menu just above the Exit command that opens the frmLots form. (*Hint*: Click All Forms in the Categories list box in the Customize dialog box.)
7. Change the Startup options to meet the following conditions:
   a. The Application Title is **Christenson Homes**.
   b. The Menu Bar is **mnuHomes**.
   c. The frmLots form opens automatically.
   d. The Database window does not display.
   e. Displaying default toolbars and changing any toolbar is not allowed.
8. Close the Homes6 database.
9. Open the Homes6 database and then close the database using the Exit command on the mnuHomes menu.
10. Exit Access.

Case 4. Sonoma Farms The frmMainSwitchboard form in the Sonoma Farms database contains an option group named grpForms. You will add the VBA code to automate this form, and then set the Startup properties so that this form opens automatically when the database opens. You also will create code to turn off the bypass feature of the Shift key when the database opens. Complete the following:

1. Start Access and open the **Sonoma6** database located in the Tutorial.06\Cases folder on your local or network drive.
2. Open the **frmMainSwitchboard** form in Design view, select the grpForms control, display its property sheet, and click the After Update event.
3. Using the instruction in this tutorial as a guide, write the code using the Select Case statement to open each form in the option group, and then set the value of the option group back to null.
4. Test the form to be sure it works.
5. Set the Startup property options in the database so that the frmMainSwitchboard form opens automatically. Change the Application Title to **Sonoma Farms**. Clear the options to display the Database window, allow full menus, built-in toolbars, and toolbar/menu changes. Disable the function keys so that pressing the F11 key will not display the Database window.
6. Copy and paste the SetBypassProperty code from Visual Basic Help that you learned about in the tutorial exercise to a new module. Save the module with the name **mdlFunctions**. Modify the code so that it is written exactly as it was in the tutorial exercise, compile the code, and then print it.
7. Write an AutoKeys macro that sets the bypass key to true when the F11 key is pressed and that sets the bypass key to false when the key combination Ctrl + F11 is pressed.
8. Test the changes to the database.
9. Close the Sonoma6 database, and then exit Access.

QUICK CHECK ANSWERS

Session 6.1

1. property
2. method
3. The After Update event occurs after a control or record is updated with changed data.
4. The DatePart function returns an integer that contains the specified part of the given date.
5. DoCmd is a special object that you use to carry out macro actions in Visual Basic procedures.
6. WhereCondition
7. Select Case statement
8. The CodeContextObject property's purpose is to determine the object in which a macro or VBA is executing.
9. The With statement allows you to perform a series of statements on a specified object, such as a form or a control on a form, without restating the name of the object.

Session 6.2

1. Access automatically personalizes menus and toolbars based on how often you use the commands.
2. system.mdw
3. toolbar
4. by closing the database and reopening it
5. An AutoExec macro runs automatically when the database opens.
6. The Startup properties execute before the AutoExec macro.
7. The bypass key bypasses the Startup property setting changes, and the database opens normally.
8. The AutoKeys macro is a macro group used to assign custom commands to key combinations.
9. back end

OBJECTIVES

In this tutorial you will:

- Build the switchboard form for reports
- Examine the syntax of the DoCmd.OpenReport method
- Study variables, scope, and constants
- Apply common VBA syntax and construction standards in code
- Construct an OpenReport WhereCondition in VBA code
- Use variables in code
- Use the Immediate window
- Set breakpoints in code
- Step through code and check variable contents at different points
- Modify code to further refine the user interface

USING VISUAL BASIC FOR APPLICATIONS

Creating the Reports Switchboard for the MovieCam Technologies Database

CASE

MovieCam Technologies

Amanda asks you to talk with the managers who will be using the MovieCam application. She wants you to determine the variations of reports that they will need. Amanda does not want managers to have access to the Database window, so she wants you to design a switchboard form that will give managers access to the reports they need. She wants you to use VBA procedures to design the switchboard form.

Richard Jenkins in Personnel told you that he wants to be able to print a report that is based on whether an employee is terminated or not, another based on whether an employee is salaried or hourly, and a third according to department. He also wants to be able to generate these reports using filters. Martin Woodward in Production wants to be able to print job reports that are based on job number. He wants to be able to specify the first few digits in a job number, such as "92" or "99," so that he can print a report of the jobs that start with those numbers. He also needs to run reports that are based on time card date and on a range of dates, such as a month or a year.

In the past, you might have used the Access Switchboard Manager to generate generic switchboards for you. Although this is useful for creating a simple switchboard to open other forms or reports, you can develop a much more extensible user interface by creating your own switchboards and utilizing your programming skills. Switchboards are typically the initial point of entry for a user, and when designed properly, multiple switchboards can help control workflow and simplify a series of tasks.

In this tutorial, you create a switchboard form that looks like the one shown in Figure 7-1. It will contain two option groups: one for Employee Reports and one for Job Reports. You anticipate that you will add more reports to each option group. The switchboard will contain check box, combo box, and text box controls from which users can select the criteria for the report that they need to run. One set of controls will apply to Employee Reports, and another set of controls will apply to Job Reports. Because the reports in each category are based on the same tables or queries, the controls for selecting criteria will be nearly the same for each report in a category.

Figure 7-1 **SWITCHBOARD FORM FOR REPORTS**

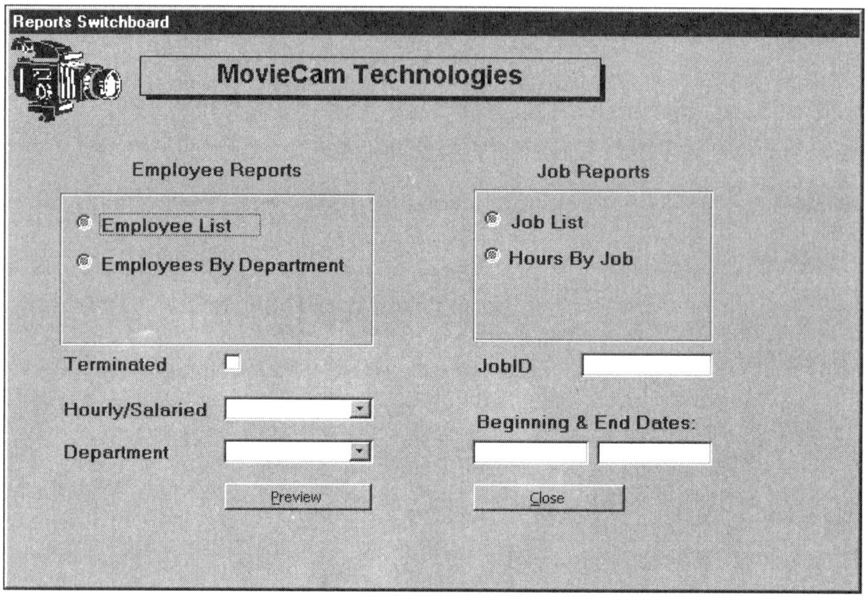

SESSION 7.1

In this session, you will learn the syntax of the DoCmd.OpenReport method and use this method to begin coding the frmReportsSwitchboard form. You also will learn to declare variables and constants, study their scope or lifetime, and use a variable in the procedure that you will write.

Introduction

In earlier tutorials you worked with simple Sub procedures using the Code Builder and by copying and pasting VBA code from a Help topic. In this tutorial, you will review terms and concepts that were introduced in previous tutorials and learn new terms and concepts that are fundamental to programming in VBA.

All Windows applications are event driven, which means that an event, such as a mouse click on a command button or the change of focus on a form, executes individual blocks of application programming code. The current version of VBA for Microsoft Access 2002 at the time of this writing is *Retail 6.3.8863*. VBA is a programming language that relies upon the Windows operating system and, as you have seen from writing macros and VBA code in previous tutorials, uses this event-driven model.

Modules

A **module** is an object that contains VBA code. Modules were discussed briefly in Tutorial 1, and you created modules in previous tutorials. Recall that you imported a standard module, mdlUtilityFunctions, into Access from another database; created a new standard module, mdlFunctions, by copying and pasting sample code from the Help system; and created form and report class modules using the Code Builder. These three types of modules are defined further in the following:

- *Standard*: You create a standard module the same way you create any other new object in a database. Click Module on the Objects bar of the Database window, and then click New. You use a standard module to store procedures that apply to more than one form or report in the database, or that you want to call from a query expression or a macro. For example, the mdlUtilityFunctions module you imported in Tutorial 3 was a standard module. You imported it so that you could use its ProperCase function in an update query to change first and last names to the proper case. See Figure 7-2.

Figure 7-2 STANDARD MODULE

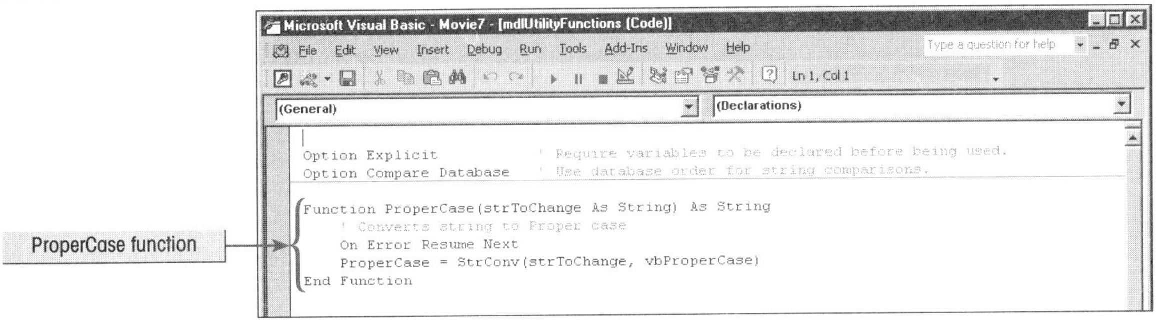

- *Form class*: You create a form class module when you add VBA code to a form. The code can be triggered by the event properties of the form, its sections or controls, or by other code contained within the module. Code in a form class module cannot be called or triggered by code or events in another form or report. The code is available only to the specific form in which it is contained. The event-handling procedures that you create when you write Sub procedures or functions in a form are the form's new methods; hence, the term "class module." You open a form class module by clicking the Code button on the Form Design toolbar or by selecting the Code command on the View menu. You created form class modules when you wrote the Sub procedures for the frmTimeCards and frmDataSwitchboard forms in previous tutorials.
- *Report class*: You create a report class module when you add code to a report. The code can be triggered by the event properties of the report, sections of the report, or other code contained within the module. Controls on reports do not have event properties and therefore do not trigger code or macros. Code in a report class module cannot be called or triggered by code or events in another form or report. The code is available only to the specific report in which it is contained. A report module is considered a class module for the same reasons as is a form module. You open a report class module the same way you open a form class module. You created report class modules in Tutorial 5 when you wrote code to add line numbers to a report and when you calculated a total in a page footer.

Sub Procedures and Functions

Modules are made up of procedures. **Procedures** in any programming language perform actions and tasks. Procedures are ideal for automating repetitive or complex tasks, so in some ways they are comparable to macros. In addition, they are commonly used in building a user interface, as you discovered in earlier tutorials.

Sub procedures and functions are the most commonly used types of procedures. These types of procedures are similar in that both contain VBA statements, accept arguments, perform operations or calculate values, and can be called from other Sub procedures or functions. They differ in that a function can return a value, can be called from a macro, and can be executed from event properties on forms and reports. In Tutorial 6, you changed a Sub procedure to a function for disabling and enabling the bypass key. You did that so the procedure could be called from the AutoKeys macro.

Indenting and Spacing Procedures

You've already had a little practice entering code in a readable format. In the procedures you've written so far, you indented some of the code lines, specifically those with decision structures like Select...Case and If...Then...Else. Procedures are easier to read and understand when you indent code. It is also helpful to add blank lines between groups of statements that perform a specific task. Indentations and blank lines do not affect the compilation or performance of your code; they simply make it easier to read.

Procedure Scope

You now know that all procedures are created and stored in modules. Although you could create and store all procedures in one module, your application will be better organized if you group the procedures logically according to their function. In addition, procedures should be stored in different modules so that you can determine their scope.

Scope describes the visibility and accessibility of one procedure from another procedure. For example, a procedure in a form class module is only visible and accessible to the specific form in which it is contained. The **Public** keyword indicates that the procedure can be called from outside the module in which it is contained. The **Private** keyword indicates that the procedure can be called only from within the module in which it is contained. You can declare procedures to be Public or Private by inserting the keyword *Public* or *Private* at the beginning of the first line of the procedure. All procedures are Public by default unless you specify otherwise. So why would you want to declare a procedure to be Private? Take a look at the procedures you copied and pasted from the Visual Basic Help topic in Tutorial 6. Two function procedures from the Movie6 database exist in the mdlFunctions standard module, as shown in Figure 7-3.

Figure 7-3 mdlFunctions STANDARD MODULE

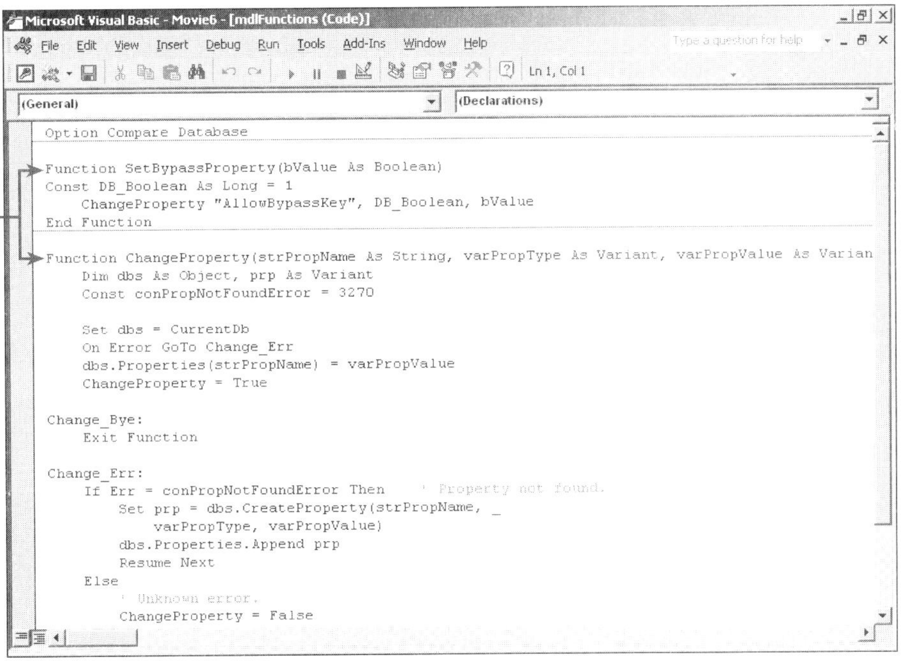

One function calls the other from within the same module. The first function, SetBypassProperty, needs to be called from a macro, so it should be Public. However, the SetBypassProperty function then calls the ChangeProperty function from within the module, so the ChangeProperty function could be declared Private. Declaring a procedure as Private is a more efficient use of memory because that memory storage is released more quickly. Public procedures and variables are retained in memory for a much longer period of time.

Creating the Reports Switchboard

Jason had previously worked on a reports switchboard. It currently looks as shown in Figure 7-4. It contains two option groups, grpEmployees and grpJobs, and each option group contains two option buttons. Each option button represents a report.

Figure 7-4 REPORTS SWITCHBOARD

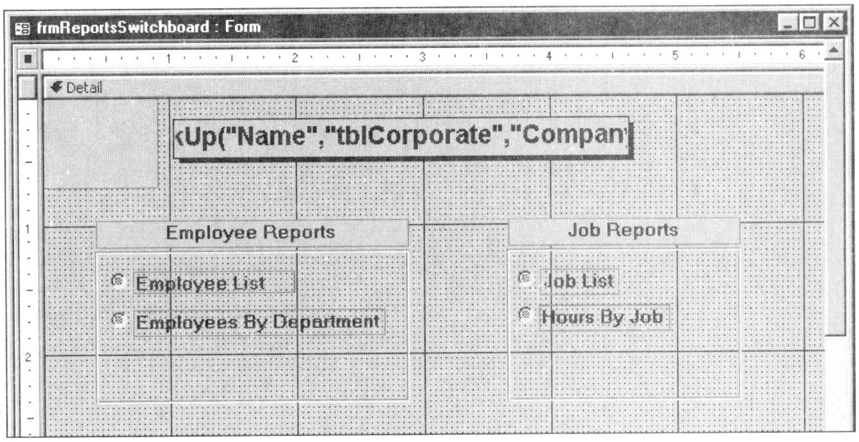

When the reports switchboard is completed, clicking the Employee List button in the Employee Reports group will open the rptEmployeesList report shown in Figure 7-5. This report is identical to the rptActiveEmployees report you worked on in Tutorial 5 except that it no longer filters out the terminated employees. You plan to design the switchboard so that the user can open a report that shows records for active employees or terminated employees. To do that you need to add a check box to the frmReportsSwitchboard form. You will test the value of this check box in the event procedure that you will write later in this tutorial and use its value to filter the records for the report when it opens. Recall that an event procedure is a procedure that is triggered by an event in a form or report and is stored in the form or report class module.

Figure 7-5 **rptEmployeesList REPORT**

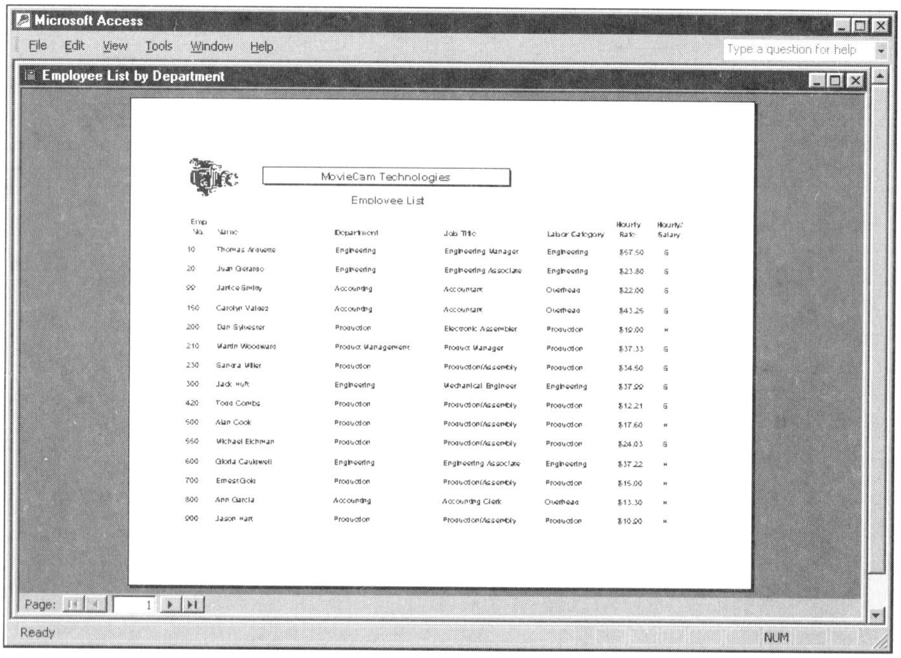

To add a check box to the frmReportsSwitchboard form:

1. Start Access and open the **Movie7** database located in the Tutorial.07\Tutorial folder on your local or network drive.
2. Open the **frmReportsSwitchboard** form in Design view, and then make sure the toolbox is open.
3. Click the **Check Box** button ☑ in the toolbox, and then click the form below the grpEmployees option group to insert the check box, as shown in Figure 7-6.

Figure 7-6 **INSERTING A CHECK BOX CONTROL**

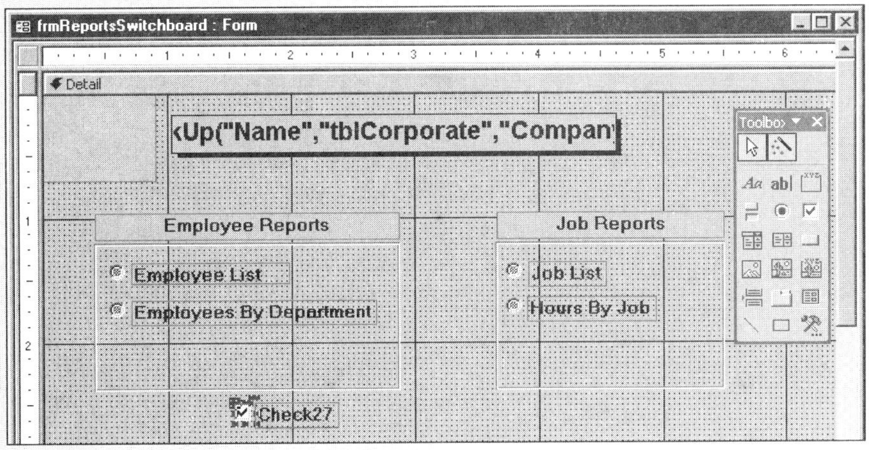

4. Click the **Properties** button on the toolbar, click the **All** tab if it is not already displayed, change the Name property of the check box to **chkTerm**, and then change the Default Value property to =**No**. This sets the check box so that it will default to No; therefore, the check box will not be checked. Later in this tutorial when you write code to test the value of the check box, you will want it to default to No if nothing has been checked on the form.
5. Click the **label control** for the check box to display its properties, change the check box label's Caption property to **Terminated**, move the label to the left of the check box, and then resize the label so that the entire label text is visible.
6. Close the property sheet, and then click in an empty area of the form to deselect the control. The Design view of the form should appear as shown in Figure 7-7.

Figure 7-7 **LABELING AND ALIGNING THE CHECK BOX CONTROL**

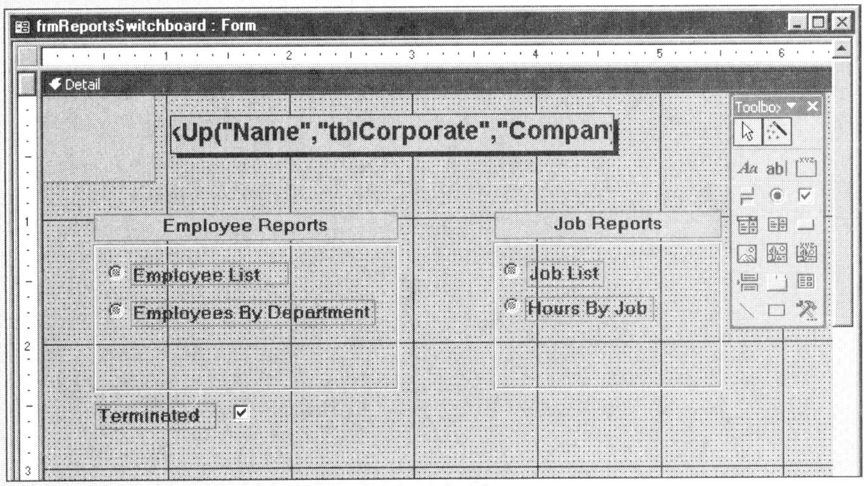

Before you write the event procedure for opening the reports, you will review the syntax of the OpenReport method of the DoCmd object.

OpenReport Method

You will use the OpenReport method of the DoCmd object to open reports from the reports switchboard. The OpenReport method contains a WhereCondition argument that will be used to filter the records of the report that is being opened. The syntax of this method is as follows:

```
DoCmd.OpenReport(ReportName, View, FilterName,
WhereCondition, WindowMode, OpenArgs)
```

The OpenReport method arguments are as follows:

- *ReportName*: A string expression that is the valid name of a report in the database.
- *View*: One of the following intrinsic constants. (Recall from Tutorial 5 that an intrinsic constant is a word that has particular meaning in VBA.) For example, in the list that follows, the intrinsic constant acDesign means Design view.
  - *acViewDesign*: Design view
  - *acViewNormal*: Prints the report immediately and is the default; so, if you leave this argument blank the report will print without allowing you to preview it first
  - ac*ViewPreview*: Print preview
- *FilterName*: A string expression that is the valid name of a query in the current database.
- *WhereCondition*: A string expression that is the valid name of an SQL WHERE clause without the word WHERE. The maximum length of this argument is 32,768 characters. (Remember from Tutorial 3 that the WHERE clause is used to specify the criteria or condition for which you are querying.) The WhereCondition argument must query fields contained in the underlying record source (table or query) of the report you are opening.
- *WindowMode*: acWindowMode is optional and can be one of these acWindowMode constants: acDialog, acHidden, acIcon, or acWindowNormal (the default). If you leave this argument blank, the default constant (acWindowNormal) is assumed.
- *OpenArgs*: This is an optional Variant that sets the OpenArgs property in a form or report. This property setting is read-only in all views and can only be set by using the OpenArgs parameter with the OpenForm method or the OpenReport method of the DoCmd object. This argument is available only in Visual Basic. The OpenArgs property cannot be set using a macro, but once the property has been set using VBA, a macro or an expression can reference it.

To illustrate a use for the OpenArgs property, consider the following example. Suppose that you open a form that is a continuous-form list of employees. If you want to go to a specific employee record when the form opens, you could specify the employee number, name, or such, with the OpenArgs argument. You could then use the FindRecord method to go to that employee's record right after the form opens.

Just as with the DoCmd.OpenForm method, you can leave an optional argument blank in the middle of the syntax, but you must include the argument's comma. For example, the following statement opens the rptEmployeeList report in Print Preview and displays the data for all employees who are terminated by placing "Terminated = Yes" in the designated placeholder for the WhereCondition argument. Notice that because the WindowMode and OpenArgs arguments are optional, you do not need to include commas at the end of the statement:

```
DoCmd.OpenReport "rptEmployeeList", acViewPreview, ,
"Terminated = Yes"
```

REFERENCE WINDOW RW

Adding an Event Procedure

- Open the form or report in Design view, select the control for the event property you want to set, and then open the property sheet for that control.
- Position the insertion point in the appropriate event property, and then click the Build button.
- Enter the Sub procedure statements in the Code window.
- Compile the procedure, fix any statement errors, and then save the event procedure.

You will use the OpenReport method in the code you write for the reports switchboard next.

To add an event procedure to the frmReportsSwitchboard form:

1. Click the **grpEmployees** option group, click the **Properties** button on the toolbar, click the **Event** tab, click in the **After Update** text box, and then click its **Build** button. The Visual Basic window opens, and the insertion point is positioned between the two lines of the stub.

   TROUBLE? If the Choose Builder dialog box opens, click Code Builder and then click the OK button.

2. Indent the first line, and then type the following code with additional indenting as indicated:

```
Select Case grpEmployees
   Case 1
      DoCmd.OpenReport "rptEmployeesList",
      acViewPreview, , "Terminated = " & chkTerm
   Case 2
      DoCmd.OpenReport "rptEmployeesByDept",
      acViewPreview, , "Terminated = " & chkTerm
End Select
grpEmployees = Null
```

   The code should look like that shown in Figure 7-8.

Figure 7-8 ADDING CODE FOR THE grpEmployees OPTION

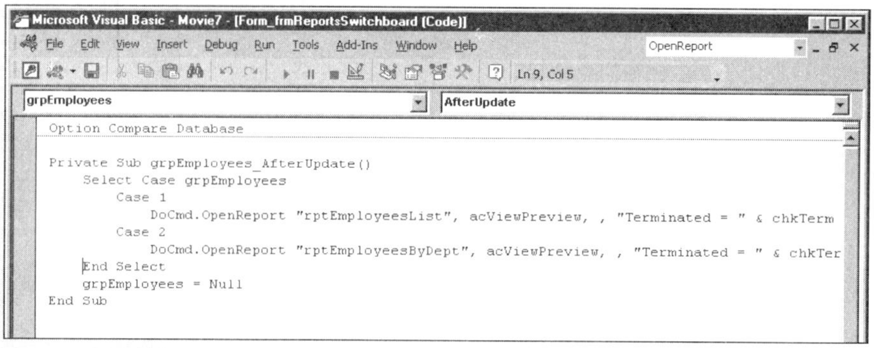

TROUBLE? If other windows are open in your Visual Basic window, click their Close Window buttons to close them.

The WHERE clause argument in each OpenReport method concatenates, or joins, the string "Terminated = " to the value of the chkTerm check box control. If the value of the check box is Yes, the report will show the records for all employees for whom the Terminated field in the tblEmployees table is Yes. If the value of the check box is No, the report will show the records for all employees for whom the Terminated field in the table is No. This is why it was important to specifically set a default value for the chkTerm check box.

A check box has three states: Yes, No, and Null. The Terminated field should be set specifically to either Yes or No. Because the tblEmployees table in the Movie7 database forces a default value of No for the Terminated field, none of the values for this field should ever be null. If you allowed the chkTerm check box on the reports switchboard to ever contain a null value, the WhereCondition would resolve to "Terminated = Null", and the report would contain no records, since none of the field values in any record would match the condition of the Terminated field being equal to Null.

Based upon this, note how the design considerations for both the employees table and the reports switchboard need to align or the results could be unpredictable and incorrect when the users run one of these reports. Business rules dictate that an employee either works for the company or does not. There is no Null state allowed in that business rule; therefore, your employee table design for the Terminated field must reflect that and the reports switchboard must enforce it or the reports will not contain complete information.

Figure 7-9 shows a query that searches the tblEmployees table for records where the Terminated field is equal to Yes.

Figure 7-9 DESIGNING A QUERY TO FIND RECORDS WITH YES IN THE TERMINATED FIELD

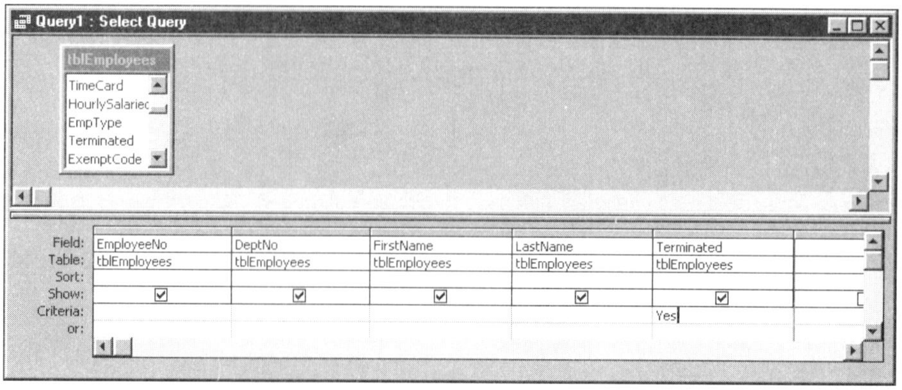

Figure 7-10 shows the SQL view of the same query. Note the syntax of the WHERE clause. If you have trouble constructing the WHERE clause, you can always write a query using the QBE grid and then switch to SQL view to copy and paste the WHERE clause (without the word WHERE) into your code.

Figure 7-10 **SQL VIEW OF QUERY TO FIND RECORDS CONTAINING YES IN THE TERMINATED FIELD**

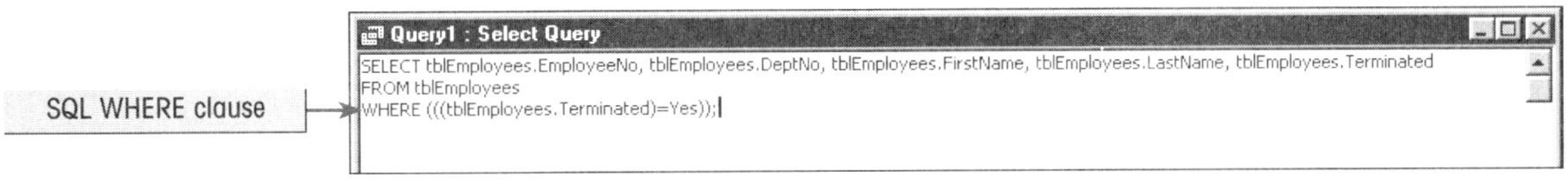

Compiling Code

Access checks each line of code as you enter it to make sure that it doesn't contain errors. Sometimes errors aren't obvious until each line of code is written and then compared to the entire procedure. Although Access doesn't check the entire procedure as you enter it, Access does check the entire procedure when you run it.

When the program is run, Access checks for overall consistency and translates the VBA statements into a language that the computer understands. This process is called **compilation**. If you want to check the code for errors before it is run, you can select the Compile command on the Debug menu.

Next you will compile the code you have just written.

To compile and test the code in the frmReportsSwitchboard form:

1. Click **Debug** on the menu bar, and then click **Compile MovieCam**.

   TROUBLE? If Access identifies any errors in your code, correct the errors and repeat Step 1.

2. Click the **Save** button on the toolbar, and then close the Visual Basic window.
3. Switch to Form view.
4. Test the code by clicking the **Terminated** check box, and then by clicking the **Employee List** button. The report opens with only three records.
5. Close the report, clear the **Terminated** check box, and then click the **Employee List** button again. The report opens with 12 records.
6. Close the report to return to the switchboard.

Adding Comments

A **comment** is text included in a procedure and briefly describes what the procedure does. Commenting your code is useful to help you remember why you did something a particular way or what a variable does. Comments can provide valuable information to future developers. A comment at the beginning of a procedure should simply explain what the procedure does, rather than how it actually works, because these details might change over time. Additional inline or local comments in your code can be used to describe the details of how the code actually works.

To designate a comment in a procedure, you start each comment line with the apostrophe character ('), as shown in the following example:

```
Sub cmdCustomer_OnClick
     'This Sub procedure opens the frmCustomers form and then
     maximizes it.
     DoCmd.OpenForm "frmCustomers"
     DoCmd.Maximize
End Sub
```

There are currently no comments in the code that you wrote for the frmReportsSwitchboard form. You will now add a descriptive comment to the beginning of the code. Although you will be making some other changes in the code, you won't add other comments until the Sub procedure is complete.

To add a comment to the code in the frmReportsSwitchboard form:

1. Switch to Design view and then click the **Code** button on the toolbar to open the Visual Basic window.
2. Position the insertion point at the end of the first line of the Sub procedure, and then press the **Enter** key twice.
3. Press the **Tab** key to indent the line, type **'Open rptEmployeesList or rptEmployeesByDept**, and then press the **Enter** key.
4. Type **' based on criteria entered into the form by the user.** (be sure to include two spaces at the beginning of the comment line to indicate that the text is a continuation of the comment started on the preceding line and a period at the end of the comment), and then press the **Enter** key. Your code should look like that shown in Figure 7-11. Notice that the comments are a different color than the code itself.

Figure 7-11 ADDING COMMENTS TO YOUR CODE

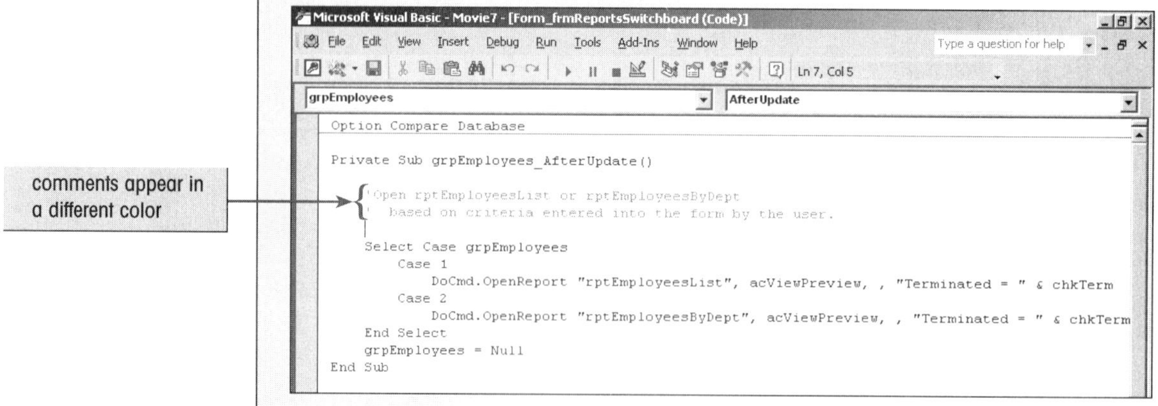

You are satisfied with your progress, but if you were to add variables to your coding, you could cut down on some of the repetitive statements. You will study how to declare variables first.

Variables

VBA lets you store values temporarily in memory. These values are called **variables**, which are named locations in memory that are used to store data of a particular type. For example, suppose you wanted to calculate the sales tax for an order and add the tax to the cost of the order. To do this without variables for a $150.00 order, you would type the following statements:

150 * .075 = 11.25
11.25 + 150.00 = 161.25

The disadvantage here is that you have to obtain the result of the first calculation before you can perform the second calculation. However, if you use variables you can simplify the process and make it more generic. Simply changing the value of Sale will compute the value of the TotalSale as shown below:

Sale = 150
SalesTax = Sale *.075
TotalSale = Sale + SalesTax

Another advantage to using variables is that they reduce the amount of coding necessary. For example, suppose you wanted to use a long and complex WhereCondition argument like the following in more than one DoCmd.OpenReport statement.

```
"Terminated = " & chkTerm & "AND HourlySalaried = " & "'" &
cboHS & "'"
```

The DoCmd.OpenReport statement would look like the following:

```
DoCmd.OpenReport "rptEmployeesList, acViewPreview, ,
"Terminated = " & chkTerm & "AND HourlySalaried = " & "'" &
cboHS & "'"
```

When you use the variable strSQL in place of the WhereCondition argument, the statements look like this:

```
strSQL = "Terminated = " & chkTerm & "AND HourlySalaried =
" & "'" & cboHS & "'"
DoCmd.OpenReport "rptEmployeesList, acViewPreview, , strSQL
```

You can implicitly or explicitly declare a variable. With **implicit declaration** you don't need to declare a variable before using it. You simply use it in a procedure. One problem with implicit declaration is that you might misspell a variable name the second or third time you use it and as a result create a new variable rather than refer to an existing one. Another problem with implicit declaration is that no data type is defined for the variable. When you do not assign a data type to a variable, Access assigns the Variant data type in the case of a constant, variable, or argument. This requires additional overhead for memory and forces Access to assign data type and commit memory storage while the code is executing, which is far less efficient than declaring variables before you use them. You will learn more about the Variant data type following Figure 7-14.

The following example demonstrates one simple type of problem that can arise if you allow implicit declaration. The following would result in four variables instead of three:

Sale = 150
SalesTax = Salee *.075
TotalSale = Sale + SalesTax

The misspelled Salee (vs. Sale) represents the fourth variable. This implicitly declared variable has not yet been assigned a value, so the resulting erroneous value of the

SalesTax variable in this situation would be zero, further resulting in an incorrect TotalSale value. Use of implicit variables makes it very hard to debug and maintain code. This example is not a syntax error, but rather causes a computational error that you or someone else would have to track down. The computational error may not even be caught right away, and invoices or accounting documents may be incorrect for some time before anyone noticed, which could create quite a problem. Though this is a very simple example, as you write larger procedures and create more and more applications, tracking down these types of errors is very difficult, can potentially cause serious computing or logical errors, and yet is easily avoidable if you simply require that all variables be declared before you use them.

Explicit declaration requires that you declare a variable before you use it, which is the best practices standard for writing code in any programming language. To force explicit declaration, you include the Option Explicit statement in the Declarations section of the module, as shown in Figure 7-12.

Figure 7-12 VBA MODULE

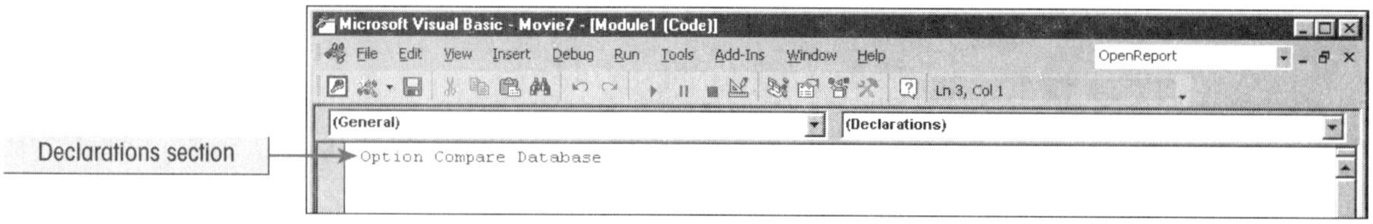

When Option Explicit is set for a module, all variables must be defined before they can be used in a procedure. If Option Explicit had been set in the preceding example, the three variables—Sale, SalesTax, and TotalSale—would have been declared at the beginning of the procedure, and if you attempt to use a variable named Salee, you would receive an error message.

Although variables are typically defined at the beginning of a Sub procedure or function, they can be declared at any point as long as they are declared before they are used. However, best practices standards dictate that you declare variables at the beginning of your procedures.

To be sure that Option Explicit is included every time you create a code module, you can set this option in the Visual Basic window. You will do that next. Setting this option will not force Option Explicit to be added to any existing modules, but it will be automatically inserted into any new modules you create.

To require variable declaration:

1. Click **Tools** on the menu bar, and then click **Options**.
2. Make sure the **Editor** tab is selected, and then make sure the **Require Variable Declaration** check box is selected, as shown in Figure 7-13.

Figure 7-13 **REQUIRING VARIABLE DECLARATION**

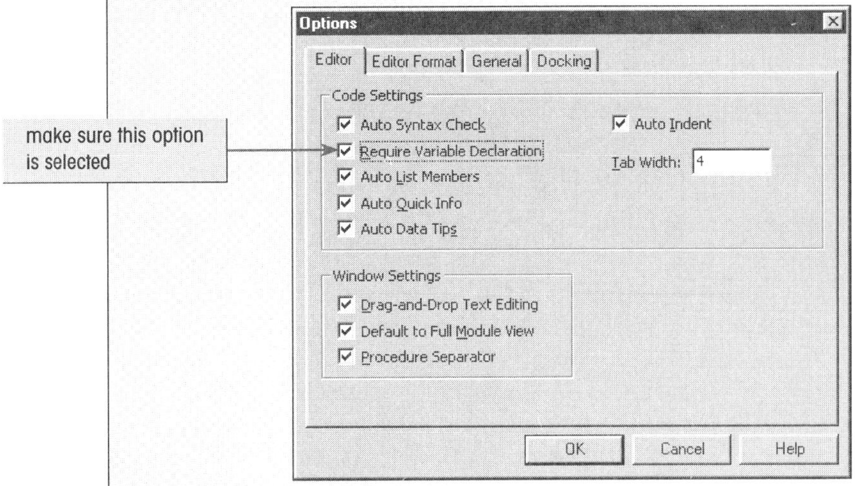

3. Click the **OK** button to return to the Visual Basic window.

Variable Scope

Variable scope is similar to the procedure scope discussed earlier in this tutorial. When you define a variable, you also define the scope of the variable. The time during which a variable retains its value is known as its **lifetime**. Although the value of a variable may change over its lifetime, it still retains some value. When a variable loses scope, it no longer has a value. Scope can be thought of as the variable's lifetime or life span. Once a variable goes out of scope, you cannot refer to its contents. Variable scope is determined by its declaration and its location in a module. You can use four different scopes of variables for declaration: Public, Private, Static, and Dim.

Declaring Variables

You normally use a Dim statement (Dimension statement) to declare variables. For example:

```
Dim strSQL As String
```

This declares the strSQL variable as a String data type variable. Data types will be discussed in the next section.

This declaration statement can be placed within a procedure to create a procedure-level variable, or it can be placed at the top of a module in the Declarations section to create a module-level variable. A **procedure-level variable** exists only when the procedure is running. When the procedure is finished executing, the variable is removed from memory. A **module-level variable** can be referenced by another function or Sub procedure within the same module.

The Static keyword can be used only in a function or Sub procedure, and can only be referred to by that same function or Sub procedure. The Static keyword differs from the Dim keyword in that the variable retains its value after the procedure has finished running, so that the next time the procedure is run you can refer to the previous value of the variable. Use the Static keyword as follows:

```
Static strSQL As String
```

The Private keyword can be used only in the General Declarations section of a module. It has the same effect as using the Dim keyword in the General Declarations section; that is, the variable is available to any function or Sub procedure in the module. For example:

```
Private strSQL As String
```

The Public keyword also can be used only in the General Declarations section of the module. The variable can then be referenced from any module anywhere within the database application. For example:

```
Public strSQL As String
```

Variable Data Types

All variables, whether explicitly or implicitly defined, are of a specific data type. When you declare a variable, you declare its scope as you have just learned. In addition, you declare its data type, which defines the kind of values that will be stored in the variable and how much memory space to allocate for the variable. Figure 7-14 summarizes the variable data types and the amount of memory required to hold each variable.

Figure 7-14 DATA TYPES

DATA TYPE	MEMORY	RANGE
Byte	1 byte	0 to 255
Boolean	2 bytes	True or False
Integer	2 bytes	-32,768 to 32,767
Long (long integer)	4 bytes	-2,147,483,648 to 2,147,483,647
Single (single-precision floating-point)	4 bytes	-3.402823E38 to -1.401298E-45 for negative values; 1.401298E-45 to 3.402823E38 for positive values
Double (double-precision floating-point)	8 bytes	-1.79769313486231E308 to -4.94065645841247E-324 for negative values; 4.94065645841247E-324 to 1.79769313486232E308 for positive values
Currency (scaled integer)	8 bytes	-922,337,203,685,477.5808 to 922,337,203,685,477.5807
Decimal	14 bytes	+/-79,228,162,514,264,337,593,543,950,335 with no decimal point; +/-7.9228162514264337593543950335 with 28 places to the right of the decimal; smallest non-zero number is +/-0.0000000000000000000000000001
Date	8 bytes	January 1, 100 to December 31, 9999
String (variable-length)	10 bytes + string length	0 to approximately 2 billion
String (fixed-length)	Length of string	1 to approximately 65,400
Variant (with numbers)	16 bytes	Any numeric value up to the range of a Double data type
Variant (with characters)	22 bytes + string length	Same range as for variable-length String data type

Normally, when a procedure begins running, all variables (except static variables) are initialized. A number variable is initialized to zero, a variable-length string is initialized to a zero-length string (""), and a fixed-length string is filled with the ASCII character code 0. Variant variables are initialized to Empty. An Empty variable is represented as 0 in a numeric context, or a zero-length string ("") in a string context.

Variant Data Type

If no data type is defined for a variable, the Variant data type is assigned by default, and VBA automatically performs any necessary conversions. Variables of Variant data type may contain date, time, numeric, string, or Boolean values. Although you might be tempted to code your procedures using the Variant data type, there is a drawback. It uses a greater amount of memory and can therefore make your application less efficient. See Figure 7-14 for specific information regarding memory storage requirements. Using a Variant data type is unnecessary overhead for memory storage in cases when you know precisely what data type is needed. For example, when you know the values to be assigned to a variable will be numeric, declare it as the appropriate numeric data type.

Recall that when you declare a variable implicitly, Access uses the Variant data type unless the Deftype statement is used. This statement allows you to specify that variables that begin with a particular letter are a particular data type. For example, DefStr L-Z would cause all variables that begin with letters "L" through "Z" to default to a String type variable. This statement can be overridden by explicit declaration with a Dim statement. For more information on Deftype statements, open the Help system in the Visual Basic window, click the Answer Wizard tab, and then search for the term "Deftype."

Variable Naming Conventions

A naming convention for variables is a good idea because it helps you to easily identify the data type or object type of a variable. (Object variables will be discussed in greater detail in Tutorial 9.) For the steps in this tutorial you will use a three-character prefix to identify the data type of the variable, followed by the base name. Some developers use a single-character prefix. However, for the sake of consistency, you will use three characters. Figure 7-15 defines the variable name prefixes that are used in this tutorial.

Figure 7-15 THREE-CHARACTER PREFIXES USED IN VARIABLE NAMES

PREFIX	DATA TYPE
ary	Array
bln	Boolean
cur	Currency
dbl	Double
dtm	Date and Time
lng	Long
int	Number/Counter/Integer
str	String
udt	User-defined
vnt	Variant

Declaring **Constants**

A **constant** is a meaningful name that takes the place of a number or string. It is like a variable except that you can't change its value after you declare it. You might want to use a constant for a string that occurs frequently in your code or for numbers that are difficult to remember and have no obvious meaning. You have already used some Access predefined constants, such as acViewPreview, in your code. The predefined constants in Access do in fact represent numbers, set in the base code of Access, and cannot be changed. Using these predefined constants is more user-friendly to you as a developer by not making it necessary for you to remember the underlying values of these constants. For example, the MsgBox constant to denote use of the OK button only on a message box is vbOKOnly, which is set to the value of "0" by Access. But you do not have to remember that a "0" is the OK button.

Constants that you create yourself work the same way, except that you name them and you assign the value to them. You declare constants with the Const statement. For example:

```
Const conAppName = "MovieCam Technologies"
```

Constants, like variables, have scope. Declaring a constant in the Declarations section allows you to use it throughout the module. Declaring a constant in a procedure makes it available to only that procedure. The Public and Private keywords are used to declare constants, just as they are used to declare variables.

Because you created the Sub procedure grpEmployees_AfterUpdate() before you selected the option to require variable declaration, the Option Explicit statement is not included in the Form_frmReportsSwitchboard class module. You will correct that next, and then substitute a variable for the WhereCondition argument in the OpenReport statement.

To modify the code in the frmReportsSwitchboard form:

1. Position the insertion point at the end of the Option Compare Database statement in the Declarations section, and then press the **Enter** key.
2. Type **Option Explicit** and then click at the beginning of the line immediately below the Private Sub grpEmployees_AfterUpdate() line.
3. Type **Dim strSQL As String** and then press the **Enter** key. Your Sub procedure should look like that shown in Figure 7-16.

Figure 7-16 DECLARING VARIABLES

type Option Explicit here

declare strSQL here

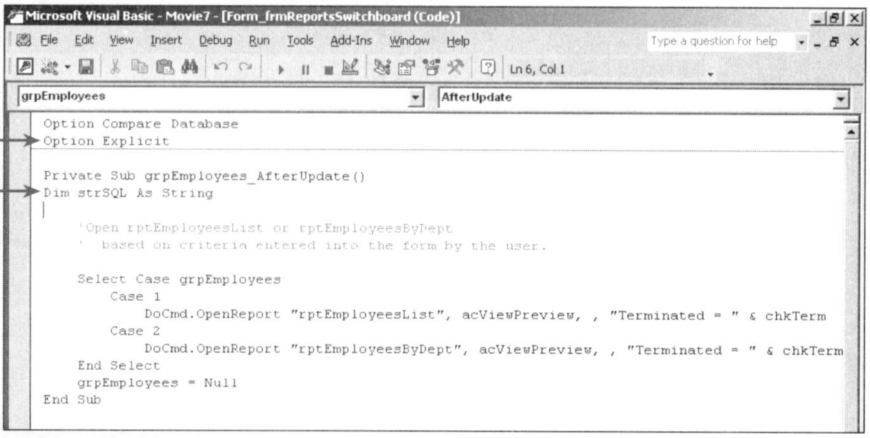

4. Position the insertion point at the end of the comment "based on criteria entered into the form by the user." (after the period), press the **Enter** key twice, type **strSQL = "Terminated =" & chkTerm** to set the value of the strSQL variable, and then press the **Enter** key.

5. Delete the string **"Terminated = " & chkTerm** in each of the DoCmd.OpenReport statements, and type **strSQL** in its place. Your code now should look like that shown in Figure 7-17.

Figure 7-17 USING A VARIABLE IN CODE

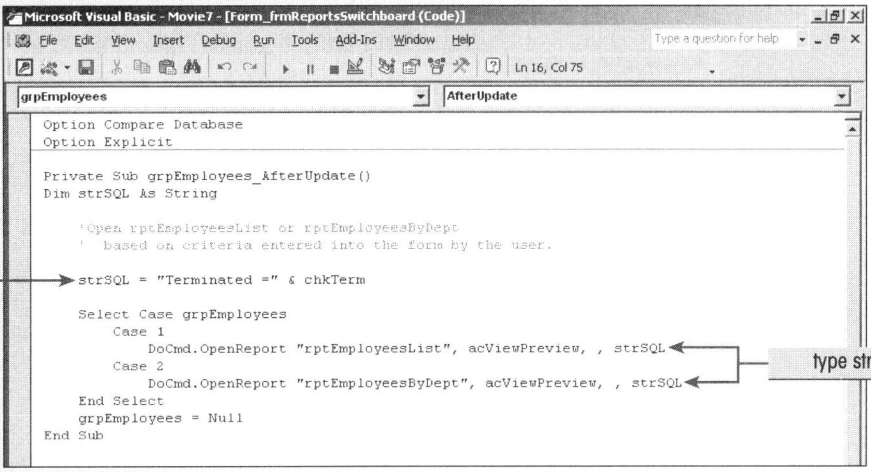

6. Click **Debug** on the menu bar, and then click **Compile MovieCam** to compile the code and check for errors.

7. Click the **Save** button on the toolbar to save your changes, and then close the Visual Basic window.

8. Switch to Form view and test the form by running the Employee List report for terminated employees, closing it, and then running it again for active (nonterminated) employees. The list of terminated employees should include three records, and the list of active employees should include 12.

   TROUBLE? If a report does not contain the correct number of records, return to Design view, open the code window and check the code carefully against that shown in Figure 7-17. Make any corrections necessary and then repeat Steps 6 through 8.

9. Switch to Design view.

Now you plan to add more flexibility to the switchboard. In the next session you will modify the code you've written so that users can use more than one condition or criteria to open the reports they need.

Session 7.1 Quick Check

1. VBA is a(n) ______________ programming language.
2. What is a form class module?
3. What term describes the visibility and accessibility of one procedure from another procedure?
4. What does the term "compiling" mean?
5. In ______________ declaration you don't need to declare a variable before using it.
6. The time during which a variable retains it value is known as its ______________.
7. How does the Static keyword differ from the Dim keyword when it is used to declare variables?
8. How does a constant differ from a variable?

SESSION 7.2

In this session, you will learn how to write the VBA code to create a multiple condition WhereCondition for the DoCmd.OpenReport method. You will use the Immediate window to test code, and you will learn to use breakpoints to run your procedure up to a particular point. You will also use the Locals window to see the contents of variables and step through code one line at a time so you can watch it execute. Finally, you will modify your code to further refine the user interface.

Creating the WhereCondition for Employee Reports

You are going to modify the code for the frmReportsSwitchboard form. Richard Jenkins in the Personnel Department told you that he needs to run the employee reports for various conditions. He wants to be able to print reports of all active employees or all terminated employees. At other times, he might need reports on all terminated employees who were salaried, or all active employees who are salaried. And occasionally he needs to see all the salaried, active employees for one department only.

The reports switchboard can be much more efficient for enabling this functionality when compared to writing predefined queries or even multiple reports. If you chose the predefined query approach, in order to provide for all the scenarios the Personnel Department needs, you would have to write several different queries and possibly several different reports. You could still use one report and change the Record Source property in code to point to the appropriate query, but that still requires several queries to be set up. Every query and report definition requires space in your database file and is part of the overall 2 GB file size limitation. You will learn how to provide for all these different scenarios without having to create multiple queries and reports, but rather by expanding the functionality of your user interface, specifically the reports switchboard. The approach you work with next often precludes the need for constant modifications or additional queries, because the reports switchboard can provide so many variations from one screen.

Creating Combo Boxes

Before modifying the code for the frmReportsSwitchboard form, you need to add some controls to the form. First you will add a combo box from which members of the Personnel Department can choose either Hourly or Salaried. You plan to use a combo box because the data is stored in this field as H for Hourly or S for Salaried, and that is what needs to be typed in on the form. You are concerned that Richard might input the word "Hourly" or the word "Salaried" if you simply use a text box. You will use a combo box with a value list to ensure the users can only choose an appropriate value that will match a value in the HourlySalaried field of the tblEmployees table. Your combo box with the value list will store the value selected in memory for later use, rather than storing it in an underlying table or query.

You also will add a combo box with the DeptName and DeptNo fields so that the appropriate department can be selected from the list, and the user does not misspell a department or type in a department that does not exist.

To create a combo box:

1. If you took a break after the previous session, make sure that Access is running, that the **Movie7** database from the Tutorial.07\Tutorial folder on the local or network hard drive is open, and that the **frmReportsSwitchboard** is open in Design view.
2. Make sure that the toolbox is open and that the **Control Wizards** button is selected in the toolbox, as shown in Figure 7-18.

Figure 7-18 CREATING THE COMBO BOX

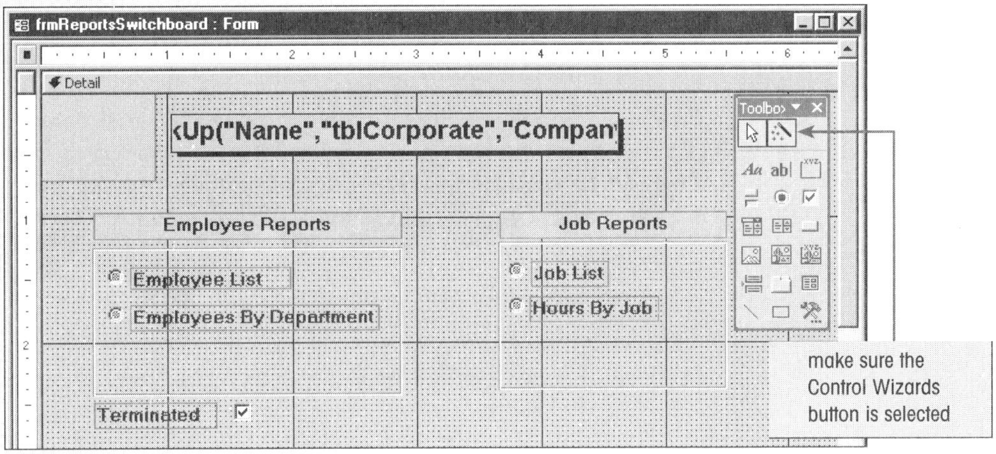

3. Click the **Combo Box** button in the toolbox, and then click beneath the Terminated check box to insert a combo box. The Combo Box Wizard opens.
4. Select the **I will type in the values that I want** option, and then click the **Next** button.
5. Type **2** in the Number of columns text box, position the insertion point in the first row of Col1, and then type **H**.
6. Press the **Tab** key to move to Col2, type **Hourly**, and then press the **Tab** key. This allows you to display the word "Hourly," but store the "H" for use in the WhereCondition.
7. Type **S**, press the **Tab** key, and then type **Salaried** as shown in Figure 7-19.

Figure 7-19 **SPECIFYING COLUMN VALUES IN THE COMBO BOX WIZARD**

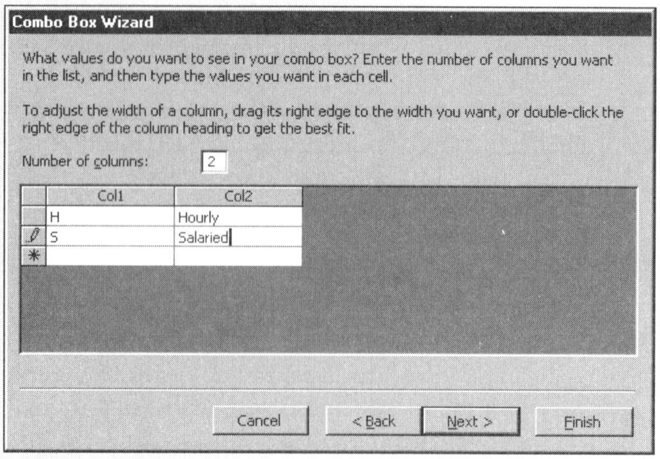

8. Click the **Next** button to move to the next Combo Box Wizard dialog box in which you specify the column that contains the value you want to store or use later.
9. Make sure that **Col1** is selected, and then click the **Next** button. This will save "H" or "S" to be used later. The last dialog box prompts you to enter a label for the combo box.
10. Type **Hourly/Salaried** and then click the **Finish** button.
11. Click the **Properties** button on the toolbar, click the **All** tab if necessary, change the Name property to **cboHS**, change the Column Widths property to **0";1"**, change the List Width property to **1"**, and then close the property sheet. These changes will hide the first column, which contains H and S, although the first column values will be retained for later use.
12. Resize the label to the left of the combo box so that all of the text is visible.
13. Switch to Form view and test the combo box by clicking the Hourly/Salaried list arrow. Hourly and Salaried should appear in the drop-down list.

Next you'll create the combo box to show the DeptNo and DeptName field values. You will set the combo box properties so that the values are looked up in the tblDepartments table.

To create the cboDept combo box:

1. Switch to Design view, click the **Combo Box** button on the toolbar, and then click below the cboHS combo box control to create the combo box.
2. Click the **Next** button to accept the default option of **I want the combo box to look up the values in a table or query**, click **tblDepartments** in the next dialog box, and then click the **Next** button.
3. Add the **DeptNo** and **DeptName** fields to the Selected Fields list box, click the **Next** button, and then widen the DeptName column by dragging the edge of the column to the right or by double-clicking the right edge of the column so the width accommodates the widest entry, making the entire department

name for each department visible. Note that the check box above the department names titled "Hide key column (recommended)" should already be checked; if it is not, check it.

4. Click the **Next** button, type **Department** as the label for the combo box, and then click the **Finish** button.
5. Click the **Properties** button on the toolbar, change the Name property to **cboDept**, and then close the property sheet.
6. Save the form, and then size and align the controls on the form so they look like those shown in Figure 7-20. Remember that you can use the Align and Size commands available on the shortcut menu for the controls and their labels.

Figure 7-20 ADDING CONTROLS TO THE frmReportsSwitchboard FORM

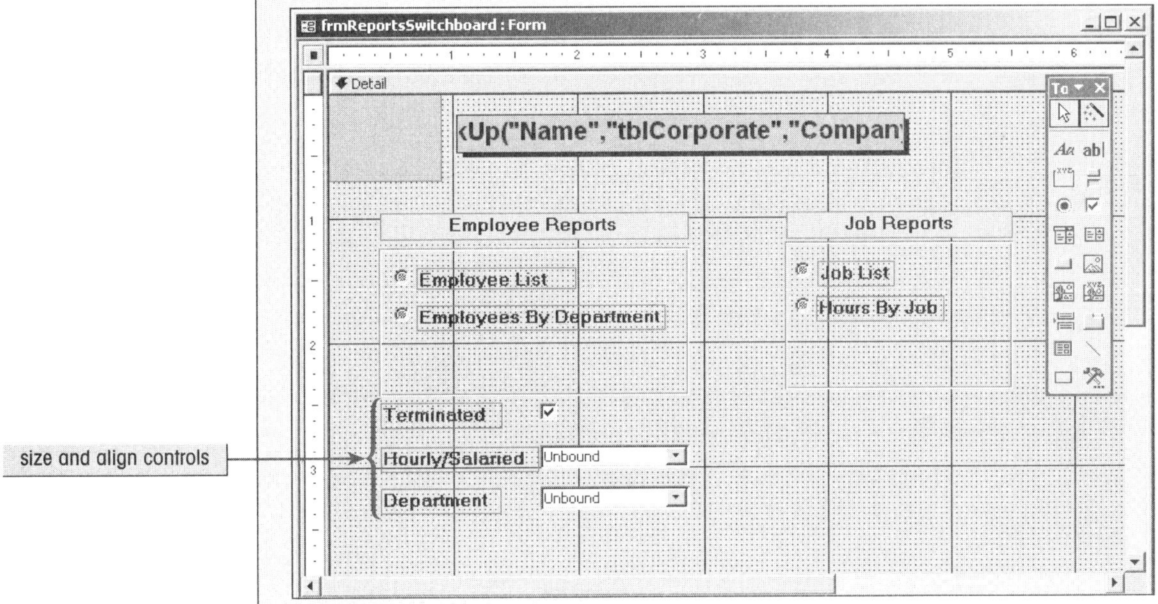

Now that you have completed the controls for the Employee Reports portion of the form, you are ready to plan the code that you will need.

Building the WhereCondition

Recall that the WhereCondition argument in the OpenReport method is a SQL WHERE clause without the word WHERE. There is an existing query that can help you to determine what this argument will look like when it is completed. The OpenReport method will open a report based on the tblEmployees table, and the WhereCondition argument will supply the condition for opening the report. Essentially, the WhereCondition argument will substitute for a query underlying the report.

The query contains the Terminated, HourlySalaried, and DeptNo fields from the tblEmployees table. The design for this select query, named qryWhere, is shown in Figure 7-21.

Figure 7-21 **qryWhere**

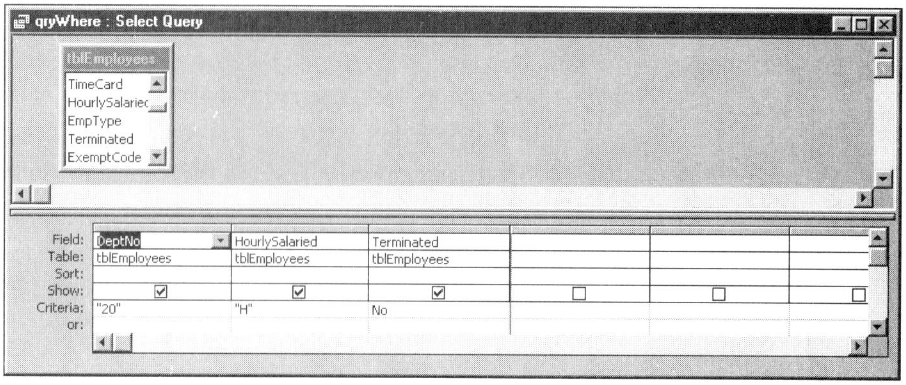

The results of the query after switching to SQL view are as follows:

```
SELECT tblEmployees.DeptNo, tblEmployees.HourlySalaried,
tblEmployees.Terminated
FROM tblEmployees
WHERE (((tblEmployees.DeptNo)="20") AND
((tblEmployees.HourlySalaried)="H")
AND ((tblEmployees.Terminated)=No));
```

Take a closer look at the WHERE clause. After you remove the SELECT and FROM clauses and the word WHERE from the WHERE clause, it looks like this:

```
(((tblEmployees.DeptNo)="20") AND
((tblEmployees.HourlySalaried)="H") AND
((tblEmployees.Terminated)=No));
```

Next you remove the parentheses, which are unnecessary syntax in this WhereCondition, and the expression looks like the following:

```
tblEmployees.DeptNo="20" AND tblEmployees.HourlySalaried="H"
AND tblEmployees.Terminated=No
```

When Access displays a query in SQL, it includes the complete syntax, just like the Expression Builder does when you create an expression in it. The table names are necessary only if there is more than one table in the query. Because this query has only one table, the field names are all you need in the WhereCondition argument of the DoCmd.OpenReport statement. After you remove the references to the table name, you have the following:

```
DeptNo="20" AND HourlySalaried="H" AND Terminated=No
```

Your switchboard form now contains the cboDept combo box, the cboHS combo box, and the chkTerm check box. If you substitute the names of these controls for the actual data in the previous expression, you get the following:

```
DeptNo="cboDept" AND HourlySalaried="cboHS" AND
Terminated=chkTerm
```

To construct the above statement so that it can be used as the WhereCondition argument in the OpenReport method, you must construct a string expression that joins together strings of text and special characters with the values contained in the cboDept, cboHS, and chkTerm controls in the frmReportsSwitchboard form.

To understand the syntax of this expression, you will examine it in various stages of completion. Each new string added to the end of the expression is in boldface to make it easier for you to identify.

The beginning of the WhereCondition follows. It must be enclosed in quotation marks because it is a string that you are going to concatenate to another string, and then to the contents of the cboDept combo box.

```
"DeptNo = "
```

In the following code, an apostrophe has been concatenated to the DeptNo = string because the contents of the cboDept combo box are text and must be surrounded by quotation marks. You place the apostrophe inside the set of quotation marks in order to properly concatenate it into the WhereCondition argument.

```
"DeptNo = " & "'"
```

In the following example, the contents of the cboDept combo box are now concatenated to the end of the expression:

```
"DeptNo = " & "'" & cboDept
```

In the next example, another quotation has been concatenated to the end of the expression. The quotation marks are necessary because DeptNo is a text field. Recall that this is the correct syntax for a text field value in an SQL statement.

```
"DeptNo = " & "'" & cboDept & "'"
```

The following example now concatenates the string AND HourlySalaried = to the end of the expression:

```
"DeptNo = " & "'" & cboDept & "'" & " AND HourlySalaried = "
```

The next example shows another quotation mark concatenated to the end of the expression. The contents of the cboHS combo box are text, and therefore must be surrounded by quotation marks. A single quotation mark is used inside the double quotation marks to make it easier to read.

```
"DeptNo = " & "'" & cboDept & "'" & " AND HourlySalaried = "
& "'"
```

The completed expression follows. Note that chkTerm is not surrounded by quotation marks in the original SQL statement, and therefore you do not have to concatenate the additional quotation marks to it here.

```
"DeptNo = " & "'" & cboDept & "'" & " AND HourlySalaried = "
& "'" & cboHS & "'" & " AND Terminated = " & chkTerm
```

This syntax might seem confusing at first. If you were to write down each string inside quotation marks and join it to the next string where an ampersand (&) exists, then substitute a value for cboDept, cboHS, and chkTerm, one possible completed string expression would look as shown in Figure 7-22.

Figure 7-22 **STRING EXPRESSION**

DeptNo = '10' AND HourlySalaried = 'H' AND Terminated = Yes

A disadvantage of using two apostrophes to offset, or delimit, the values used for comparison in a WhereCondition argument is that an error would occur if the text within the field being searched contained an apostrophe. For example, a company with the name Smith's ABC Widgets has an apostrophe in the actual company name. If you were to build a WhereCondition for company name using the apostrophe in code to delimit the name, Access would interpret the apostrophe in the word "Smith's" to be the ending delimiter.

This has the effect of forming 'Smith' as the search text for the company name, which is a problem because the intention was to search for the name Smith's ABC Widgets, not just the name Smith. The next problem that occurs in this example is the remaining text in the company name following the apostrophes—ABC Widgets—becomes superfluous text within the WhereCondition argument that the OpenReport method cannot interpret. The extraneous text does not fit within the proper syntax of the WhereCondition argument. As a result, Access would return an error message.

The apostrophe can work fine in many situations, such as the example shown in Figure 7-22, and is a fairly simple syntax to follow. To learn additional means of building strings in code to avoid any potential problems with using the apostrophe, go to Microsoft Visual Basic Help and search for the topic entitled "Quotation Marks in Strings." Recall that to go to Microsoft Visual Basic Help, you use the Help menu from the Microsoft Visual Basic window.

Writing the Code

Now that you have determined what the completed WhereCondition should look like, you will write the code so that the user can choose any combination of the three options on the form. To do this, you will first test to see if each of the controls is null. You will use the IsNull function.

The IsNull syntax is IsNull(expression). This function tests the expression to see whether it is null or not. In this case, you want to know if the expression (value of the control) is not null, that is, whether it contains a value, so you will include the Not operator before the function. Then you will set a variable called strWhere. At the beginning of the procedure you will declare that variable equal to whatever is already contained in strWhere, and equal to the part of the WhereCondition string that applies to the control you are testing.

You will then use a series of If...Then...Else statements to test each of the three controls on the form.

To write the code for building the WhereCondition:

1. Click the **Code** button on the toolbar to open the Visual Basic window, position the insertion point at the end of the Dim strSQL As String line, and then press the **Enter** key.
2. Type **Dim strWhere As String** to declare another string variable. It will be used to build the WhereCondition. The variable strSQL will be used to trim off leading characters after you build the WhereCondition.
3. Press the **Enter** key twice, press the **Tab** key, and type the following comment: **'Build the wherecondition to use in the OpenReport method.**
4. Press the **Enter** key twice, and then type the following:

```
If Not IsNull(cboDept) Then
    strWhere = strWhere & " AND DeptNo= " & "'" &
cboDept & "'"
End If
```

TROUBLE? In your text book, the second line of code above (the assignment of the strWhere variable) appears to wrap to a second line, but when you enter each line of code, be sure to type it on one line only without forcing any portion of it to wrap to the next line or this will result in an error. Later in this chapter, you will learn a technique for continuing a line of code to additional lines.

5. Select the **strSQL = "Terminated=" & chkTerm** line of code, press the **Delete** key, and then delete any extra blank lines until there is only one blank line separating the comment and the Select Case line of code.

6. Compare your code to that shown in Figure 7-23 to be sure that your code is correct.

Figure 7-23 **ADDING TO THE WHERECONDITION**

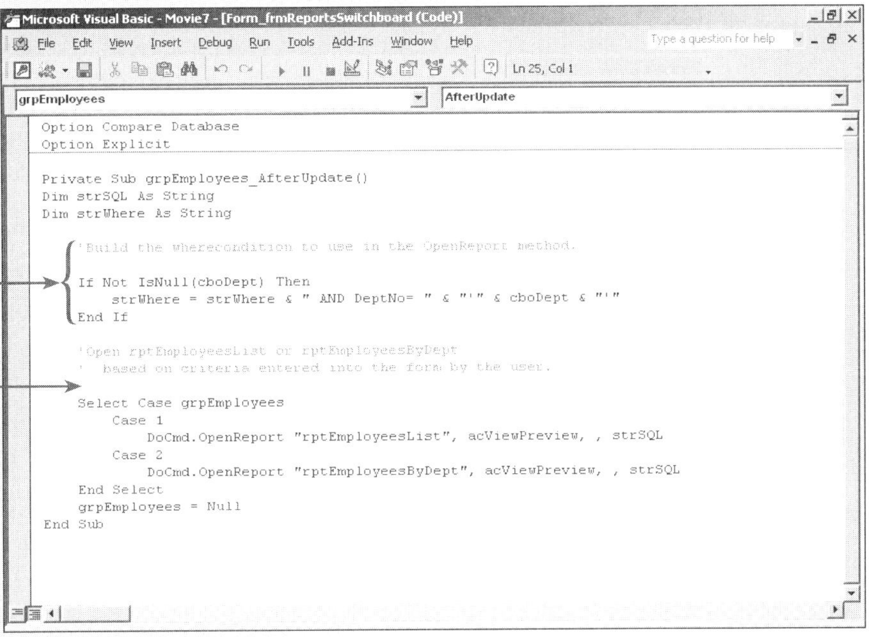

enter this comment and these lines of code

be sure to delete the code strSQL = "Terminated =" & chkTerm

You cannot be certain from which of the three controls (cboDept, cboHS, or chkTerm) the user will choose. To allow for this, you construct the WhereCondition so that it always concatenates whatever is already contained in the strWhere variable to the keyword AND and then to the remaining string expression for that particular control. This way, no matter which of the three controls is chosen, they are joined together with the keyword AND. Once you have finished building strWhere, you will use a function to trim off the leading AND keyword as well as any unneeded spacing before or after AND.

7. Position the insertion point at the end of the End If statement, press the **Enter** key twice, and then type the following (make sure you type the second line of code on one line):

```
If Not IsNull(cboHS) Then
    strWhere = strWhere & " AND HourlySalaried = " & "'"
& cboHS & "'"
End If
```

8. Press the **Enter** key twice, and then type the following:

```
If Not IsNull(chkTerm) Then
    strWhere = strWhere & " AND Terminated = " & chkTerm
End If
```

Technically, because you have previously forced a default value for chkTerm, this check box should never be null; however, it is always good coding practice to be sure that the value in a field or variable is not null before you use it in a calculation or as part of a WhereCondition.

9. Click the **Save** button on the toolbar. Your code should look like that shown in Figure 7-24. Delete any extra blank lines that may have been inserted as you entered the preceding code.

Figure 7-24 COMPLETING THE WHERECONDITION

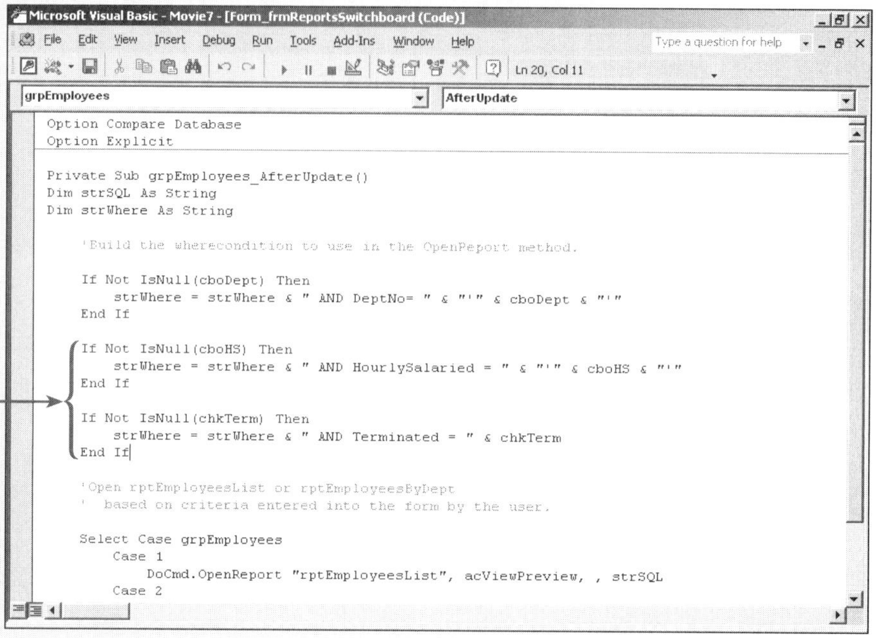

Next you test the contents of the strWhere variable to determine if it is not null. If it is not null, then it contains a string of text that has a leading AND keyword along with the spaces surrounding it. The way you built the value for the strWhere variable in code allows for the inclusion of as many of the three criteria available to which the user could assign a value. As long as the user chooses at least one value from the available selection, the strWhere string would not be null. All the preceding If...Then statements have to be identical, so that no matter how many of the three criteria the user chooses, you can easily trim the string to a WhereCondition with the proper syntax.

After building the strWhere string, you use the Mid string function to trim the leading AND keyword along with the spaces surrounding it. Some VBA functions have two versions: one that returns a Variant data type and another that returns a String data type. When the function name is followed by a dollar sign ($), it returns a string rather than a variant. Remember that the drawback to Variant data types is that they use more memory, which is not an efficient use of computer resources. You will use the Mid$ version of this function so that a string is returned.

The Mid$ function returns a variant or string with a specified number of characters from a string. The syntax of the Mid$ function is as follows (the length argument is optional, and if length is not used, you would not place a comma after the start argument.):

```
Mid$(string, start[, length])
```

The *string* argument is the variable or string from which you are taking the new string. The *start* argument is the character position in the string where the part to be taken begins.

The *length* argument is the total number of characters to return. The length argument is optional, so if it is left blank the remaining portion of the string is returned, beginning with the character designated by the start argument.

To add code to trim leading characters and spaces from the strWhere variable:

1. Press the **Enter** key twice to add a blank line after the third End If statement, and then type the following comment: **'Trim the leading " AND " off strWhere and store the new string in strSQL**.
2. Press the **Enter** key twice, and then type the following code:

```
If Not IsNull(strWhere) Then
    strSQL = Mid$(strWhere, 6)
End If
```

   The start argument in the Mid function is 6 because " AND " is a total of five characters, and you want the string to now begin at the sixth character. The strSQL variable now contains the contents of strWhere without unnecessary leading characters.

3. Change the comment before the DoCmd.OpenReport statement to the following, as shown in Figure 7-25:

```
'Open rptEmployeesList or rptEmployeesByDept based on
' the contents of strSQL
```

Figure 7-25 CHANGING A COMMENT IN THE CODE

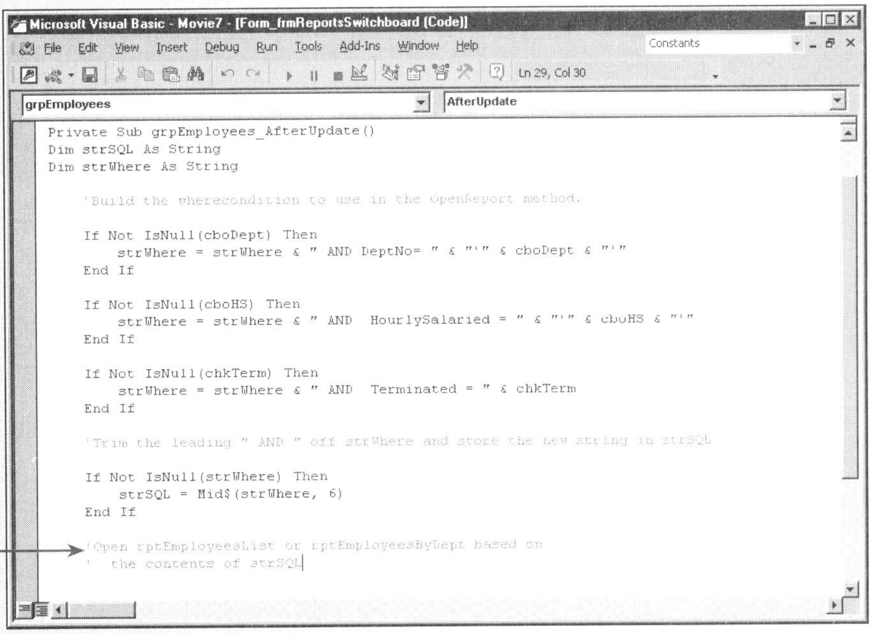

modified comment

4. Position the insertion point at the end of the End Select statement, and then press the **Enter** key twice.

5. Type the following comment: **'Set the option group and combo boxes back to Null, and clear the check box**, and then press the **Enter** key.
6. Position the insertion point at the end of the grpEmployees = Null statement, press the **Enter** key, and then type the following:

```
cboDept = Null
cboHS = Null
chkTerm = False
```

   These statements set the option group and combo boxes back to Null and clear the check box by setting its value to False after the report opens. This way the user can make a different choice without any residual value left in any of the controls. Setting the value of the chkTerm check box to False in VBA is the equivalent of setting its default value to No, which is an unchecked check box.
7. Press the **Enter** key to add a blank line between these statements and the End Sub statement, as shown in Figure 7-26.

Figure 7-26 ADDING BLANK LINES TO MAKE THE CODE EASIER TO READ

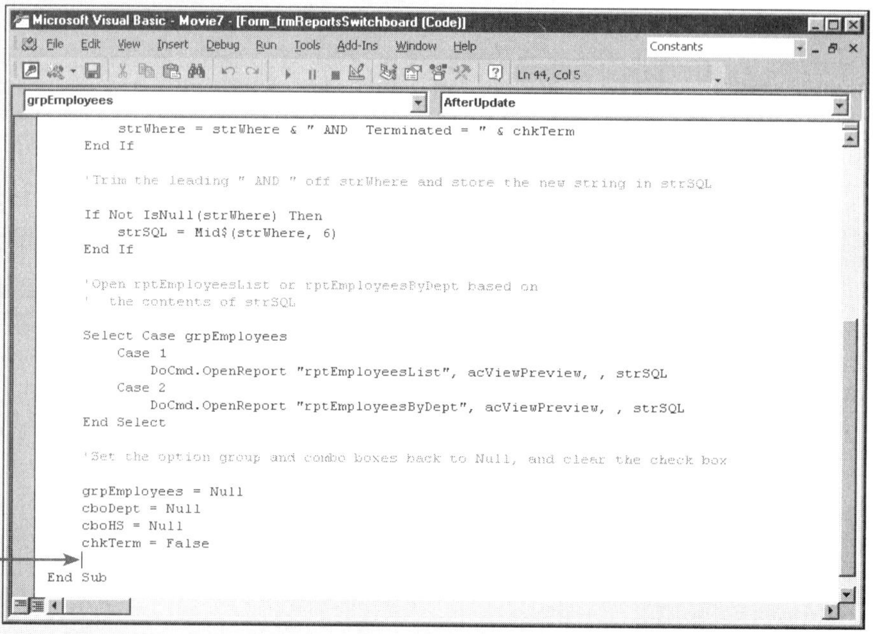

8. Click **Debug** on the menu bar, and then click **Compile MovieCam**. If any of your variables are misspelled, you should correct them now.
9. Click the **Save** button on the toolbar.
10. Close the Visual Basic window, switch to Form view, and test the reports.
11. Switch back to Design view, and click the **Code** button on the toolbar to open the Visual Basic window again.

The procedure that you have written should be working fine, but you may be curious to validate that the WhereCondition actually changes correctly for the different combinations the user can choose. Next you will use the Immediate window so that you can see the value of each of the variables when you run the procedure. You use the Immediate window to look for errors that are not caught during compilation. The types of errors you might encounter, including syntax and logic errors, are discussed in more detail in Tutorial 8. For now you will see the contents of the variables during testing.

Using the Immediate Window

The **Immediate window** shows information that results from debugging statements in your code or from commands typed directly into the window. To see the Immediate window in the Visual Basic window, you select Immediate Window on the View menu, or press Ctrl + G on the keyboard. You can use the Immediate window to check results of a line of code, and to check the value of a control, field, property, or variable. You might think of it as a scratch pad on which statements, methods, and Sub procedures can be evaluated immediately.

You can view the results of an expression or a variable in the Immediate window by entering the Print method of the Debug object, followed by the expression. For example, the following would display the results of the expression:

```
Debug.Print Mid$(strWhere, 6)
```

The Debug.Print method also can be represented by the question mark character (?), as shown below:

```
?Mid$(strWhere,6)
```

You also can use the Debug.Print method (or the question mark character) to run a function and display its results in the Immediate window. Recall the mdlUtilityFunctions module that you imported into the database in Tutorial 3. The module contained a function named ProperCase. To run this function in the Immediate window you would type:

```
?ProperCase("TEST")
```

The function would return "Test."

REFERENCE WINDOW **RW**

Testing a Function in the Immediate Window

- In the Code window, click View on the menu bar, and then click Immediate Window (or press Ctrl + G) to open the Immediate window.
- Type a question mark (?), the name of the function, and the function's arguments in parentheses.
- Press the Enter key.

First you'll test the Immediate window by typing in some simple formulas and running the ProperCase function.

To test the Immediate window:

1. Press **Ctrl + G** to open the Immediate window at the bottom of the Visual Basic window.
2. Type **Debug.Print 2+3** and then press the **Enter** key. The result is shown on the next line.

3. Type **?2+3** and then press the **Enter** key.

   The database contains the mdlUtilityFunctions module, so you'll now run the ProperCase function.

4. Type **?ProperCase("THIS IS A TEST")** and then press the **Enter** key. The results should look like those shown in Figure 7-27.

Figure 7-27 USING THE IMMEDIATE WINDOW

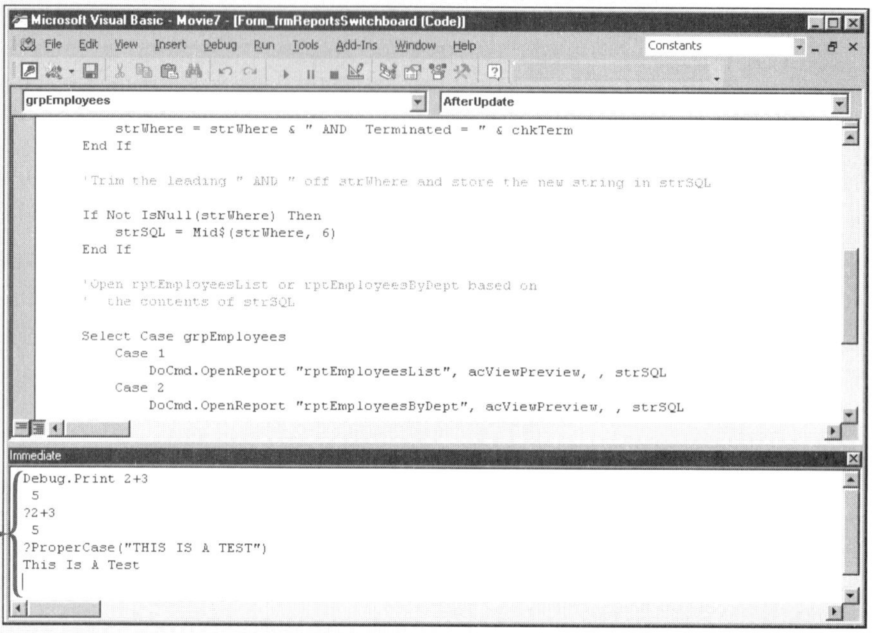

TROUBLE? If your Immediate window does not show all six lines as they are shown in Figure 7-27, then you just need to enlarge the window to increase its height.

Now that you've tested the Immediate window, you need a way to stop the code at a particular point so that you can test the value of expressions and variables before the procedure finishes running.

Setting Breakpoints in Code

A **breakpoint** is a selected line of your program at which execution automatically stops. There are various reasons you might want to set a breakpoint to suspend execution at a specific statement in a procedure. You might want to stop running the procedure at a statement where you suspect a problem exists. You might use a breakpoint to suspend execution so that you can use the Immediate window to test the value of variables or expressions at a particular point in the program. When you no longer need them to stop execution, you clear breakpoints. Breakpoints are not saved with your code.

REFERENCE WINDOW RW

Using Breakpoints to Step Through a Procedure

- In the Code window, click View on the menu bar, point to Toolbars, and then click Debug.
- Click the gray margin to the left of the statement for which you want to set a breakpoint, and start running the code.
- Execute the procedure, and then click the Step Into button on the Debug toolbar to run each line of code in the procedure.

Next you will use breakpoints in conjunction with the Immediate window to see the value of the variables in your code, and to test the Mid$ expression.

To test the code using the Immediate window:

1. Click the gray margin to the left of the Select Case grpEmployees line to set a breakpoint, as shown in Figure 7-28.

Figure 7-28 **SETTING A BREAKPOINT IN CODE**

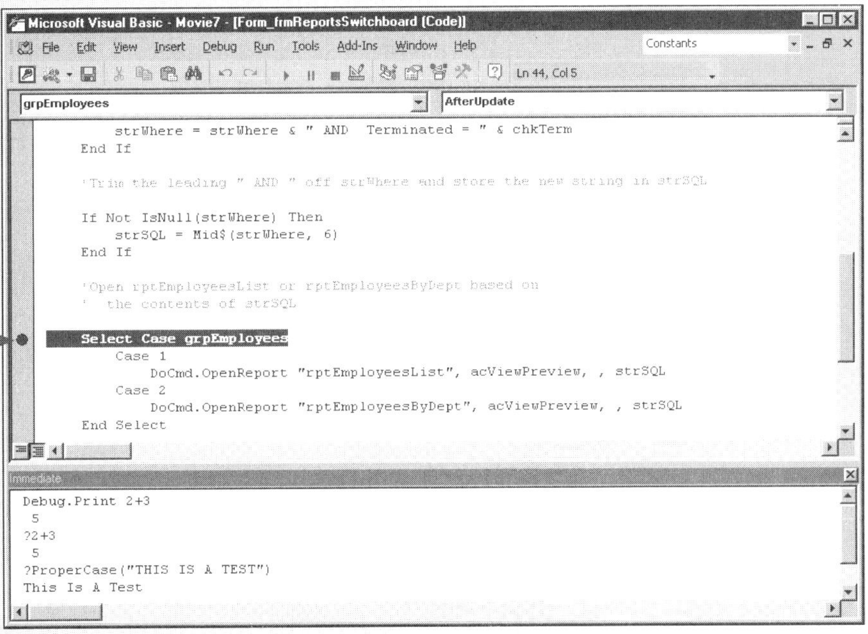

click the gray margin to the left of the Select Case

2. Minimize the Visual Basic window, and then switch to Form view to test the frmReportsSwitchboard form.
3. Select **Salaried** from the Hourly/Salaried combo box, and then select **Engineering** from the Department combo box.
4. Click the **Employee List** option in the Employee Reports option group. The Visual Basic window shows a highlighted line where you created the breakpoint.

5. Position the insertion point in the Immediate window, type **?Mid$(strWhere, 6)** to test the Mid function, and then press the **Enter** key. The results are visible as shown in Figure 7-29.

Figure 7-29 VIEWING RESULTS IN THE IMMEDIATE WINDOW

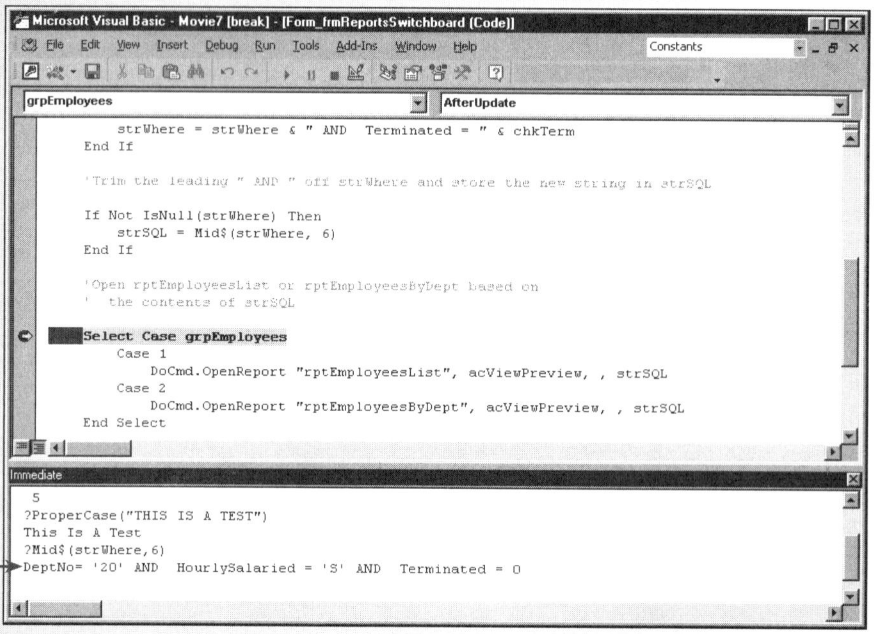

results of testing the Mid function

6. Type **?strSQL** in the Immediate window, and then press the **Enter** key. The contents of the strSQL variable are shown.

7. Click the **Continue** button on the toolbar to continue running the code. The Employee List report shows the records that meet the criteria entered on the form.

8. Close the report to return to the switchboard.

To further investigate how the procedure works, next you will step through the code one line at a time. This is useful for finding errors that don't show up during compilation, because you can check the value of your variables at various points in the execution of the code.

Reviewing **Code Line by Line**

Access provides tools that enable you to step through your code line by line. After you have seen the code run through the lines, you can step out of the code. This means that it finishes running. You will use breakpoints and commands on the Debug menu or on the Debug toolbar to step through the procedure. In addition, you will use the Locals window to see the contents of the strWhere and strSQL variables as each line of code executes.

The Locals Window

The Immediate window is useful for running functions, testing expressions, and displaying variables. You should use the Locals window if you need to see only the contents of the variables. In the **Locals window**, Access automatically displays the name, current value, and type of all the variables and objects in the current procedure. The values in the Locals window are updated each time you suspend code execution. If you step through the code, execution is suspended after each statement executes. With the Locals window open, you are able to see the variables change at each step.

To step through code one line at a time:

1. Restore the Visual Basic window by clicking its icon on the taskbar, and then close the Immediate window by clicking its **Close** button ×. It is simpler to step through the code if the Debug toolbar is visible.
2. Click **View** on the menu bar, point to **Toolbars**, and then click **Debug**. The toolbar, which contains a Step Into button that you can click each time you want to run another line of code, might be floating, as shown in Figure 7-30.

Figure 7-30 THE DEBUG TOOLBAR

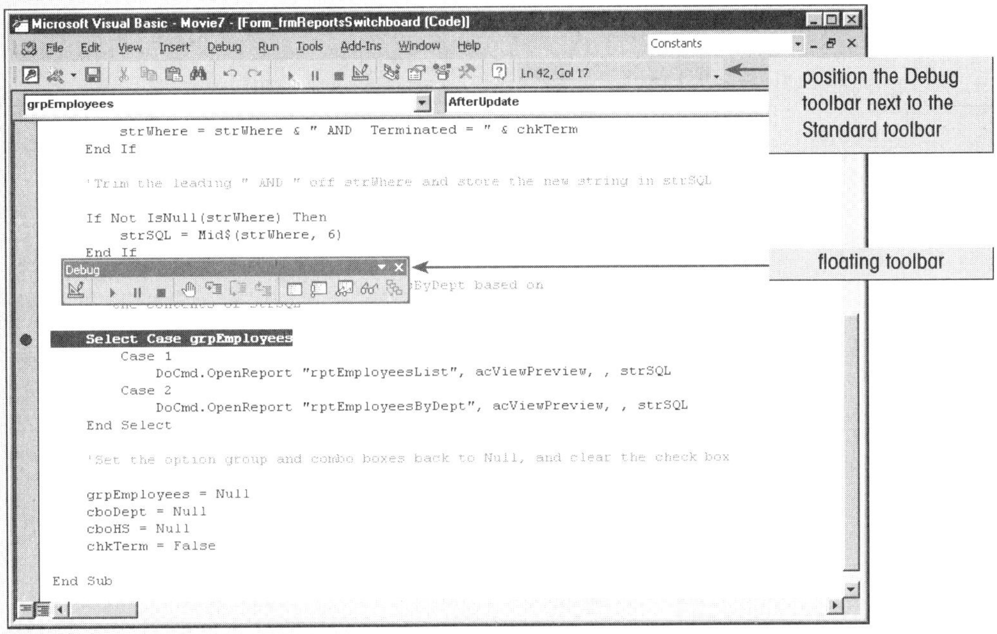

3. If necessary, drag the Debug toolbar by its title bar to the top of the screen, and dock it next to the Standard toolbar. The breakpoint that you set earlier should still exist. You will clear it and set another breakpoint now.
4. Clear the breakpoint by clicking the dot in the gray margin to the left of the Select Case grpEmployees line.
5. Scroll to the top of the code, and then set a breakpoint at the Private Sub grpEmployees_AfterUpdate() line, as shown in Figure 7-31. This will stop the code at the beginning of the procedure so that you can step through it one line at a time.

Figure 7-31 SETTING A BREAKPOINT AT THE BEGINNING OF THE PROCEDURE

set the new breakpoint here

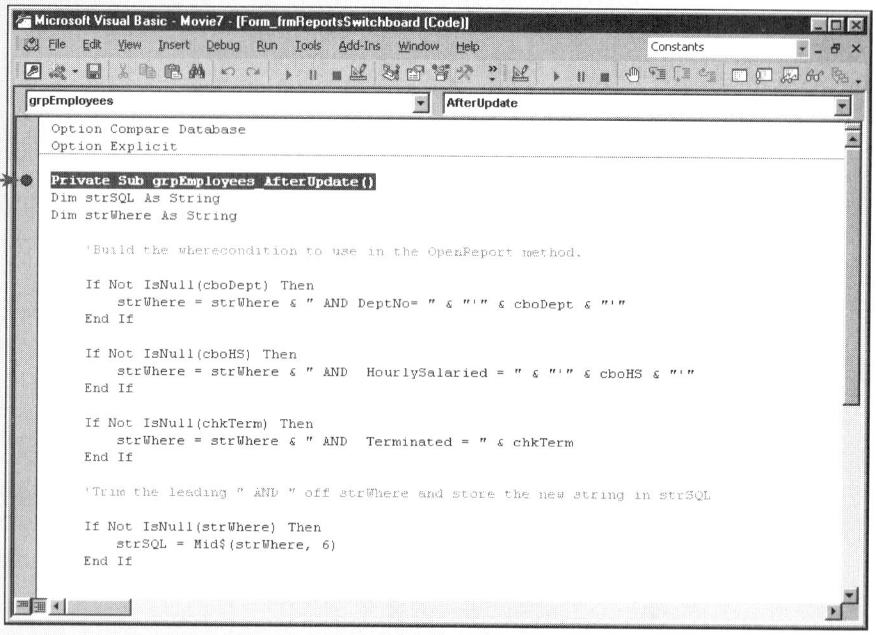

6. Click **View** on the menu bar, and then click **Locals Window**. The Locals window opens at the bottom of the Visual Basic window.
7. Minimize the Visual Basic window, select **Hourly** from the Hourly/Salaried combo box, select **Production** from the Department combo box, and then click the **Employee List** option. The Visual Basic window is redisplayed, and the code stopped running at the beginning of the procedure.
8. Click the **Step Into** button on the Debug toolbar. The first statement of code is highlighted as shown in Figure 7-32.

Figure 7-32 STEPPING INTO THE FIRST LINE OF CODE

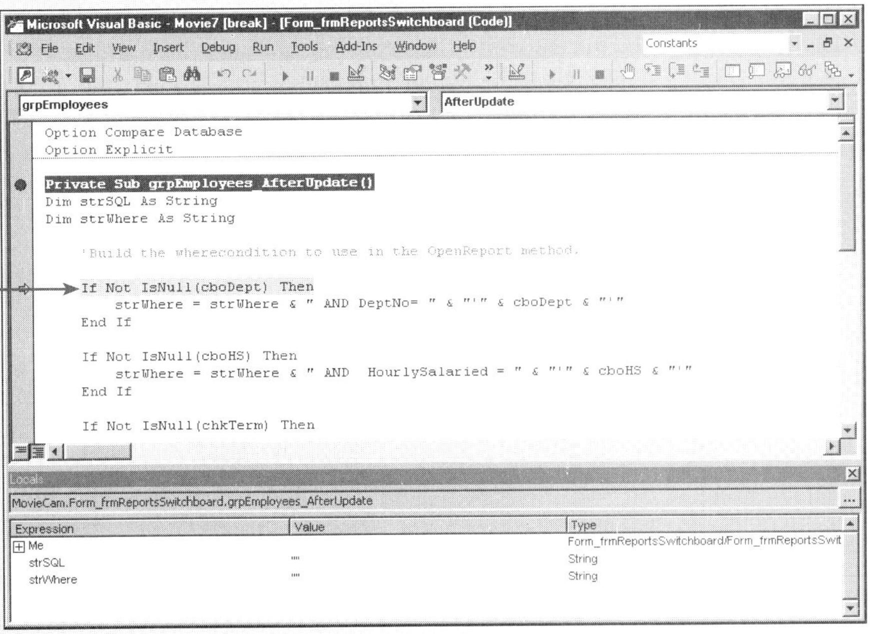

highlighted code

9. Click [Step Into] to step through each of the three lines of the first If...Then statement. Note the contents of the strWhere and strSQL variables, as shown in Figure 7-33, once you reach the first End If. The first portion of the WhereCondition is complete.

Figure 7-33 STEPPING THROUGH THE CODE

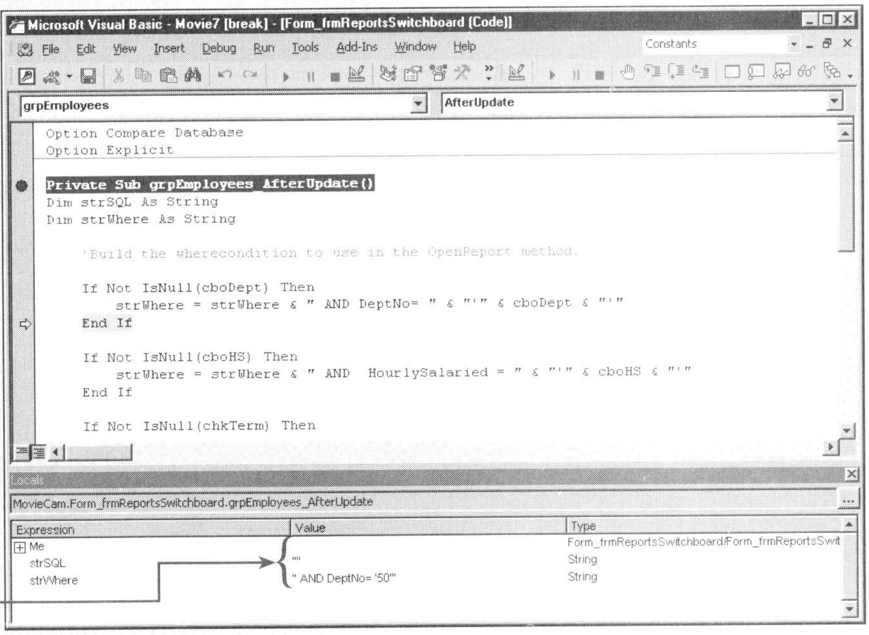

contents of the strSQL and strWhere variables

You also can see the code execute as you step through it. For example, to begin running the procedure, you chose a value from the Hourly/Salaried combo box and from the Department combo box, but you did not mark the Terminated check box on the frmReportsSwitchboard form. As you step through the If...Then statements, note that Access steps through each line of code when the condition is True. If you had not chosen a value for the Hourly/Salaried or Department combo boxes, their values would be null. Access would execute the first line of each If statement (the test condition) to check for a null value. Whenever the value was null, Access would skip past the second line and move to the *End If* line, without adding any conditions for that field value to the strWhere string being built.

To continue stepping through the code:

1. Click the **Step Into** button again to step into the first line of the next If...Then statement, and then click twice. The contents of the Locals window change to show the new contents of the strWhere variable. The strSQL variable is still a zero-length string.
2. Click to move to the first line of the next If...Then statement, and then click twice. The End If line is highlighted as shown in Figure 7-34. Note how Terminated = 0 in the strSQL and strWhere string variable assignments. For programming, 0 is False and -1 is True and are completely interchangeable for Boolean comparisons. Terminated is a Yes/No field, which is a Boolean-type field.

Figure 7-34 WATCHING THE EXECUTION OF THE PROGRAM

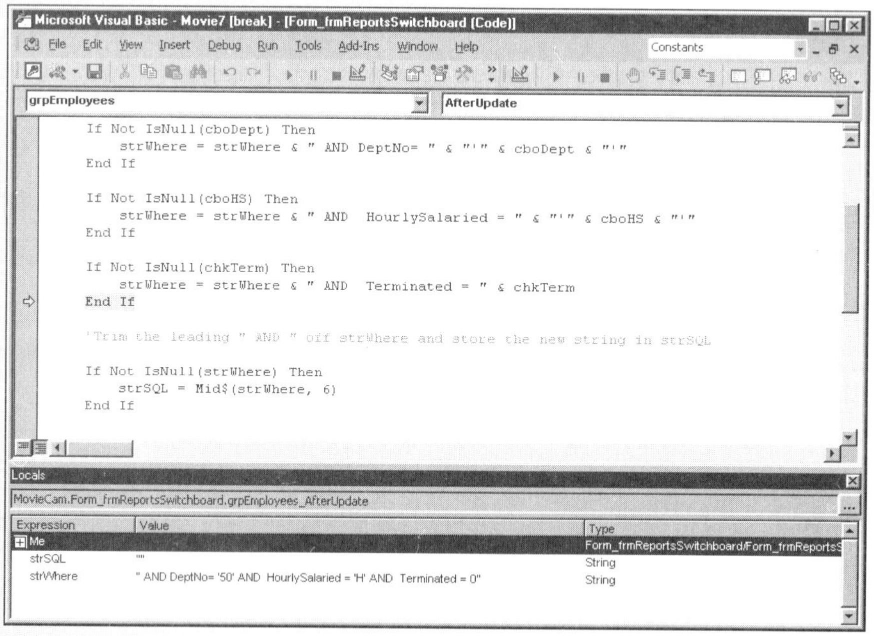

TROUBLE? If your screen does not look like Figure 7-34 in the Locals window, adjust the column widths of the Expression and Value columns so you can see the entire value of the strWhere variable.

3. Step through the next If...Then statement. The value of the strSQL variable has now changed, as shown in Figure 7-35.

Figure 7-35 STEPPING THROUGH THE CODE

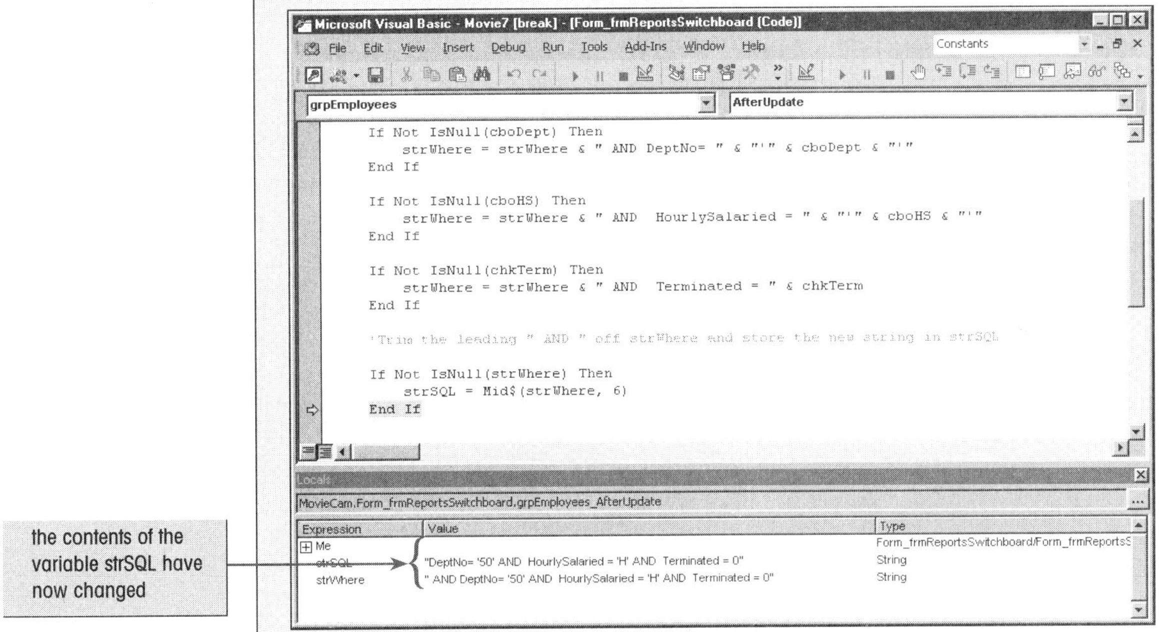

4. Click the **Step Out** button on the Debug toolbar to finish running the code. The report is shown.
5. Close the report and restore to the Visual Basic window.
6. Click **Debug** on the menu bar, and then click **Clear All Breakpoints**.
7. Close the Locals window by clicking its **Close** button.

You will make one more change to the design of the Employee Reports section of the frmReportsSwitchboard form. The users could click an option button to run a report before first choosing conditions from the three controls. You will add a command button to preview the report after the report is chosen from the option group and the conditions are selected from the other controls on the form. Next, you will make the code changes to accomplish this.

Modifying the Code for Employee Reports

If you add a command button to the form that triggers the DoCmd.OpenReport method, you will use that command only once. This is another case where a variable will come in handy. If you declare a variable, such as strReport, for the report name, you can then set the variable equal to the name of the report in the Select Case statement. Then the command button will trigger a DoCmd.OpenReport statement that uses the variable for the ReportName argument.

To add a command button to the frmReportsSwitchboard form:

1. Minimize the Visual Basic window, switch to Design view, and make sure the toolbox is open.
2. Make sure the **Control Wizards** button is deselected, click the **Command Button** button on the toolbox, and then click below the cboDept control.
3. Click the **Properties** button on the toolbar, change the Name property to **cmdPreview**, and then change the Caption property to **&Preview**.
4. Click the **Save** button on the toolbar, and then restore the Visual Basic window.
5. Click the **Object** list arrow, and then click **cmdPreview**. See Figure 7-36. The stub is created, and the insertion point is positioned between the two lines of code.

Figure 7-36 CREATING THE cmdPreview_Click STUB

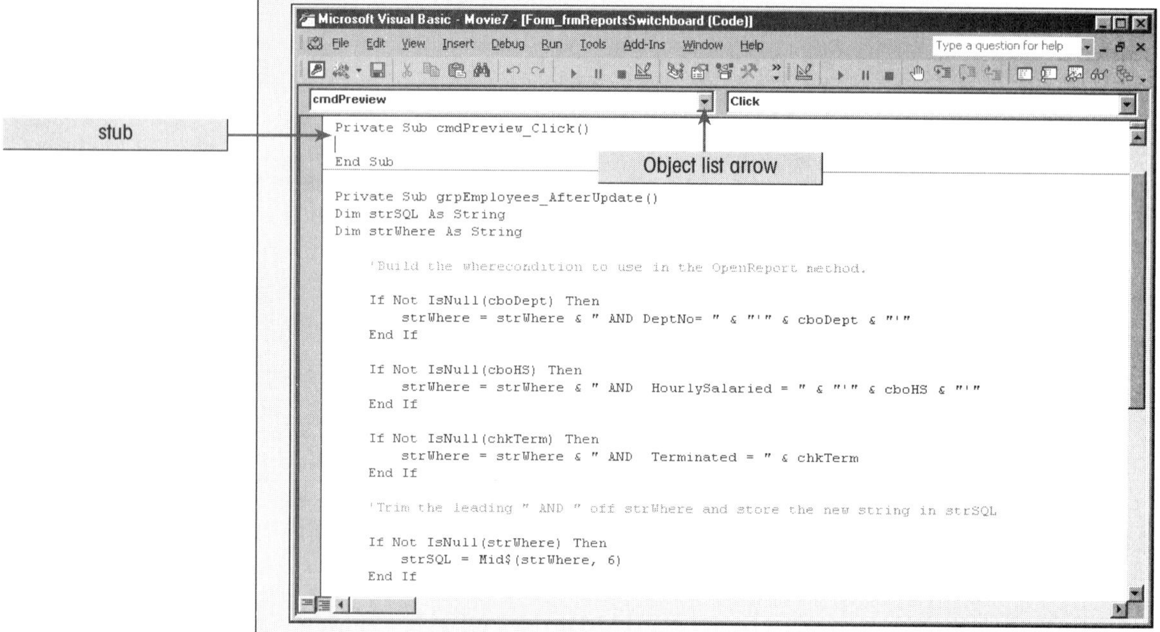

Before you continue, consider the rest of the code. Because the statement to preview the report will be a separate Sub procedure triggered by the cmdPreview button that you just created on the form, the code to populate the WhereCondition also needs to be included in this procedure. This is determined by the order of operations that the user will take:

1. The user will click a button in the grpEmployees option group to choose a report. The name of that report will be stored in a new variable named strReport.
2. The user will select Terminated, Hourly or Salaried, and/or a department. These values need to remain in the controls until the report is previewed.
3. The user will click the Preview button.

As you can determine from these steps, the code to build the WhereCondition must be run after the user selects Terminated, Hourly or Salaried, and/or the Department from the controls on the form. If this portion of the code remains in the AfterUpdate procedure, the WhereCondition will be built before these choices are made, because the AfterUpdate event fires as soon as an option is selected in the option group.

You will include the code for populating the strWhere and strSQL variables and the DoCmd.OpenReport statement in the new Sub cmdPreview_Click() procedure. You also will need to declare these variables at the beginning of this new procedure.

Recall from the discussion of variables that a variable must be declared in the Declarations section if you want it to be available to the entire module. This, as you learned, is because the lifetime of a variable declared in a procedure ends when the procedure stops running. The new strReport variable needs to be declared in the Declarations section of the module because it will be referred to in both procedures.

To complete the coding for the Employee Reports section of the switchboard form:

1. Position the insertion point at the end of the Option Explicit statement in the Declarations section, and then press the **Enter** key.
2. Type **Private strReport As String**.
3. Change Case 1 in the Select Case statement to:

```
strReport = "rptEmployeesList"
```

4. Change Case 2 in the Select Case statement to:

```
strReport = "rptEmployeesByDept"
```

5. Cut the following statements from the Private Sub grpEmployees_AfterUpdate() procedure, and paste them under the Private Sub cmdPreview_Click() statement:

```
Dim strSQL As String
Dim strWhere As String
```

6. Cut the following comments and statements from the Private Sub grpEmployees_AfterUpdate() procedure, and paste them below the two Dim statements in the Private Sub cmdPreview_Click() procedure, as shown in Figure 7-37:

```
'Build the wherecondition to use in the OpenReport
method.
If Not IsNull(cboDept) Then
    strWhere = strWhere & " AND  DeptNo= " & "'" &
cboDept & "'"
End If
If Not IsNull(cboHS) Then
    strWhere = strWhere & " AND  HourlySalaried = " & "'"
& cboHS & "'"
End If
If Not IsNull(chkTerm) Then
    strWhere = strWhere & " AND  Terminated = " & chkTerm
End If
'Trim the leading "AND " off strWhere and store the new
string in strSQL
If Not IsNull(strWhere) Then
    strSQL = Mid$(strWhere, 6)
End If
```

Adjust the spacing of your code to reflect that shown in Figure 7-37.

Figure 7-37 MODIFYING THE CODE IN THE frmReportsSwitchboard FORM

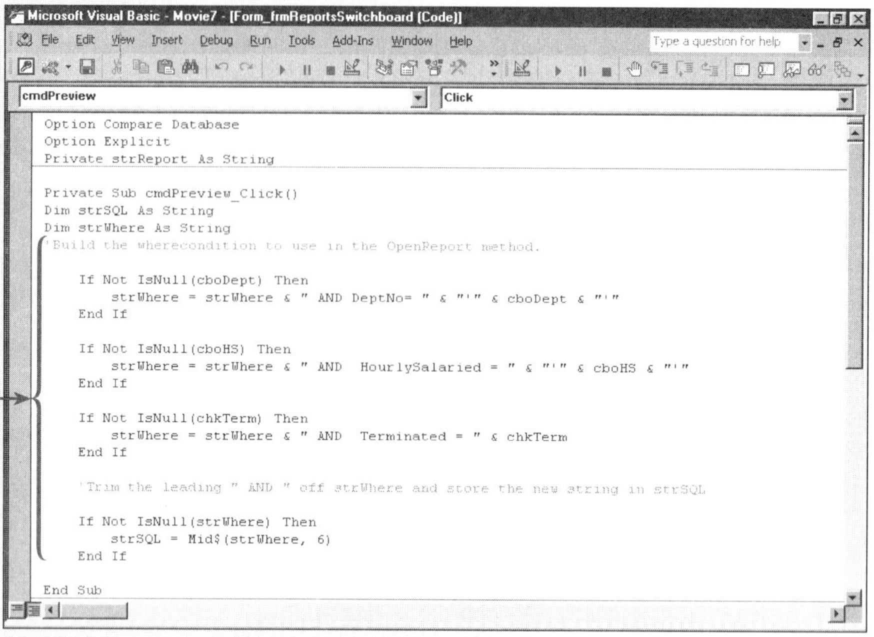

code cut and pasted

7. Press the **Enter** key twice after the last End If statement that you just entered, and then type the following comment and statement:

```
'Open report based on the contents of strSQL
DoCmd.OpenReport strReport, acViewPreview, , strSQL
```

8. Press the **Enter** key twice, cut the following comment and statements from the Private Sub grpEmployees_AfterUpdate() procedure, paste them at the end of the Private Sub cmdPreview_Click() procedure between the DoCmd.OpenReport strReport, acViewPreview, strSQL statement, and the End Sub statement, and then adjust any line spacing as shown in Figure 7-38.

```
'Set the option group and combo boxes back to Null, and
clear the check box
grpEmployees = Null
cboDept = Null
cboHS = Null
chkTerm = False
```

Figure 7-38 CUTTING AND PASTING MORE CODE IN THE frmReportsSwitchboard FORM

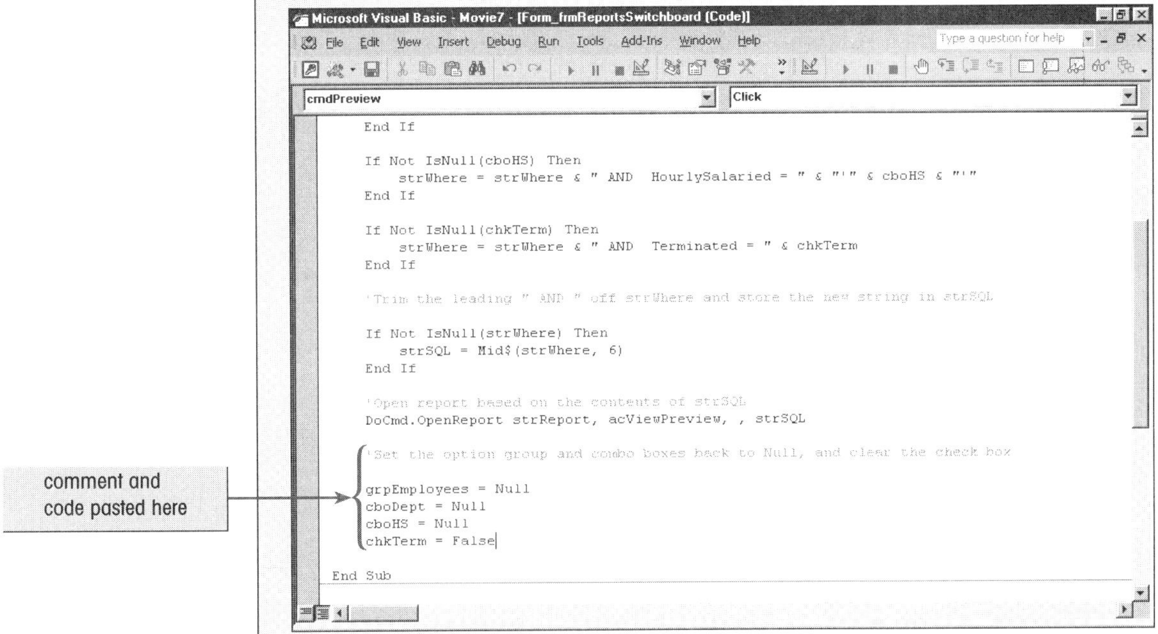

9. Click **Debug** on the menu bar, and then click **Compile MovieCam**.

Now that you've completed the coding for the grpEmployees option group, you need to test it again. You'll run through various conditions for each of the reports.

To test the frmReportsSwitchboard form:

1. Close the Visual Basic window, close the property sheet if necessary, and then switch to Form view.
2. Click the **Employee List** option, click the **Terminated** check box, and then click the **Preview** button. The report opens and shows the records for three employees.
3. Close the report to return to the switchboard, click the **Employee List** option, select **Salaried** from the Hourly/Salaried combo box, select **Engineering** from the Department combo box, and then click the **Preview** button. The report matching these criteria opens and there should be two records.
4. Close the report, click **Employees By Department**, select **Hourly** from the Hourly/Salaried combo box, select **Production** from the Department combo box, and then click the **Preview** button. The results match the condition you specified and there should be three records.
5. Close the report and then click the **Preview** button without selecting a report. Notice that the last report selected is shown with all records for nonterminated employees. This is because the chkTerm check box defaults to No and shows only active employees. This is fine for now, but in the future you will want to include a method that forces the user to choose a report in order to avoid confusion. (You will work on this in Tutorial 8.)
6. Close the open report.

Next you will address Martin Woodward's request that he be able to run job reports according to JobID and by a range of dates. To do this, you will add a text box for the JobID field, another one for a beginning date, and another for an ending date.

To add text boxes to the frmReportsSwitchboard form:

1. Switch to Design view and make sure that the toolbox is open.
2. Click the **Text Box** button in the toolbox, and then click below the Job Reports option group to create a text box.
3. Click the **Properties** button on the toolbar, change the Name property to **txtJobID**, type **Job ID** in the label control, move the label to the left of the text box, close the property sheet, and then resize and align the label and text box controls as shown in Figure 7-39

Figure 7-39 SIZING AND ALIGNING THE JobID CONTROLS

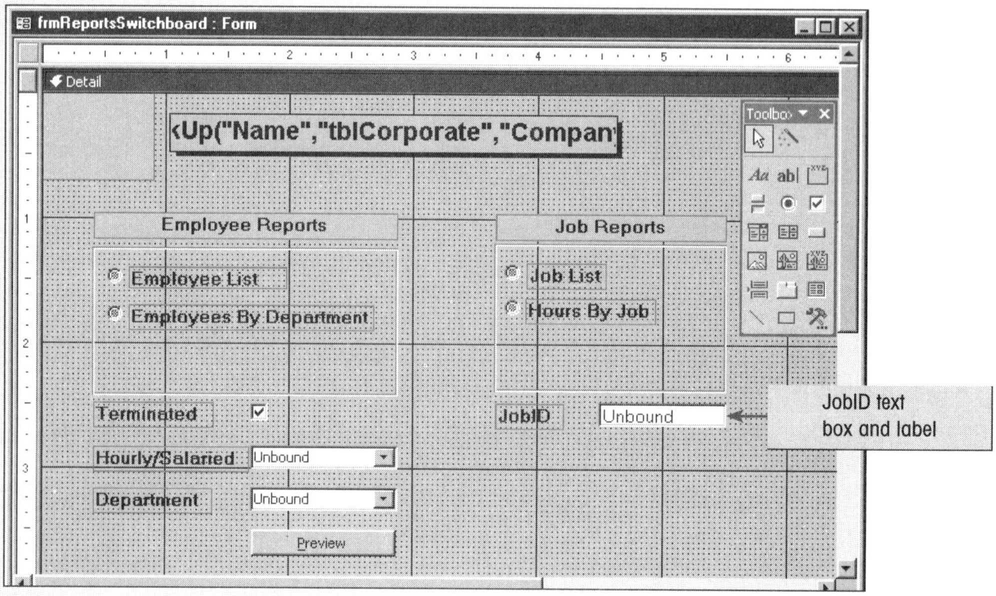

4. Create two more text boxes on the form, delete the label from one of them, and position them as shown in Figure 7-40. Open the property sheet for the text box on the left, change its Name property of the to **txtStartDate**, and then change the Name property of the other text box to **txtEndDate**.

Figure 7-40 **ADDING THE TEXT BOXES FOR DATES**

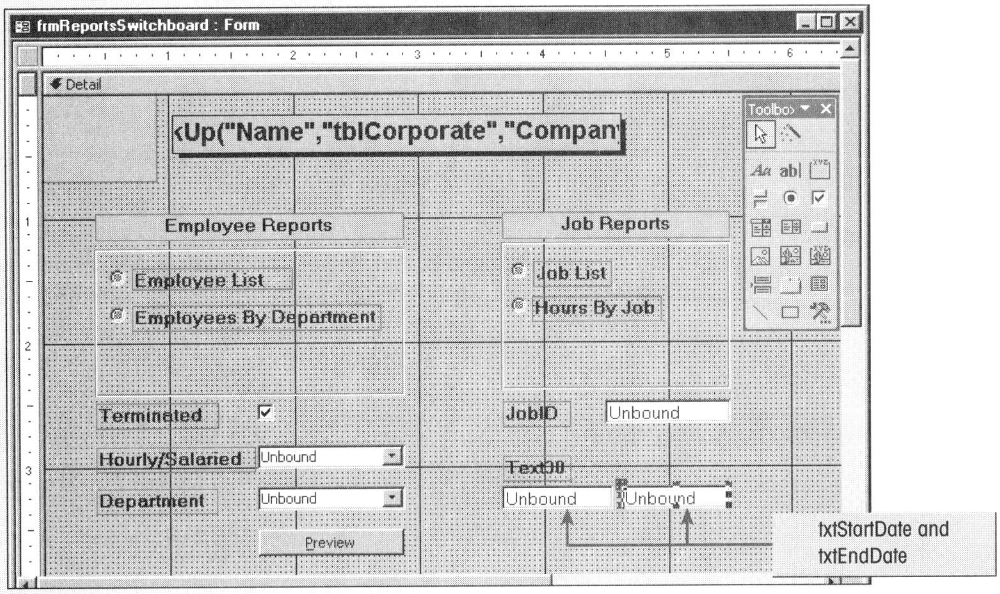

5. Change the Caption property of the label control to **Beginning && Ending Dates:** (including the colon). You must include two ampersands to display one in the label. Recall that one ampersand is a shortcut key combination and is used to indicate that the character following it is underscored, except when it is used with another ampersand. You must use two ampersands together in a label or caption to override the underscore feature and allow one ampersand to appear in the finished label or caption as shown below.

6. Close the property sheet, size and align the controls as shown in Figure 7-41, and then save the form.

Figure 7-41 **SIZING AND ALIGNING THE CONTROLS FOR BEGINNING AND ENDING DATES**

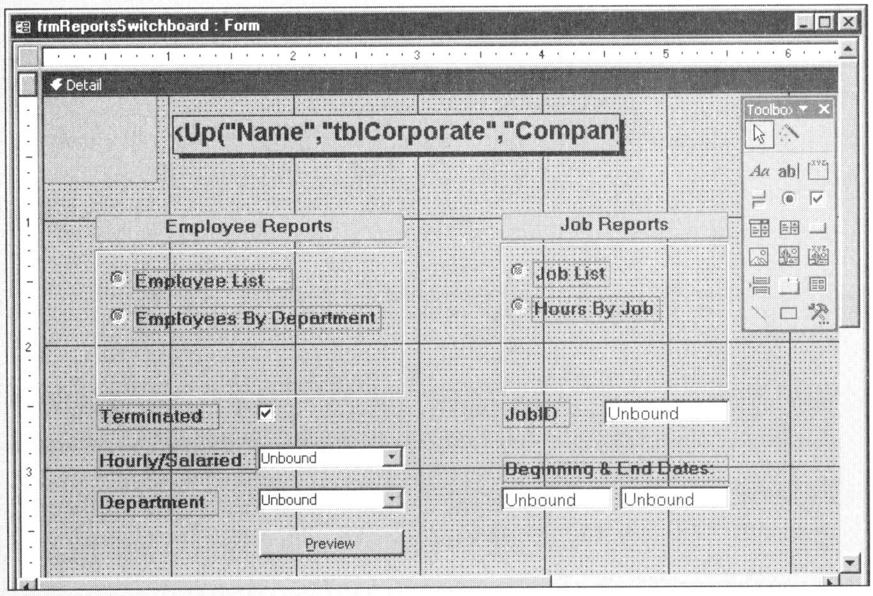

Next you need to add the code necessary to open reports from the Job Reports option group. First you will add a Sub procedure that is triggered by the AfterUpdate event property of the grpJobs option group.

To add a Sub procedure to open the job reports:

1. Click the **grpJobs** option group, click the **Properties** button on the toolbar, click the **Event** tab, click in the **After Update** property text box, and then click its **Build** button.
2. Complete the code as shown in Figure 7-42, including the change to the comment for the grpEmployees_AfterUpdate() Sub procedure. You are changing this comment to match the comment in the new Sub procedure for grpJobs so the two procedures are consistent.

Figure 7-42 COMPLETED grpJobs_AfterUpdate EVENT PROCEDURE

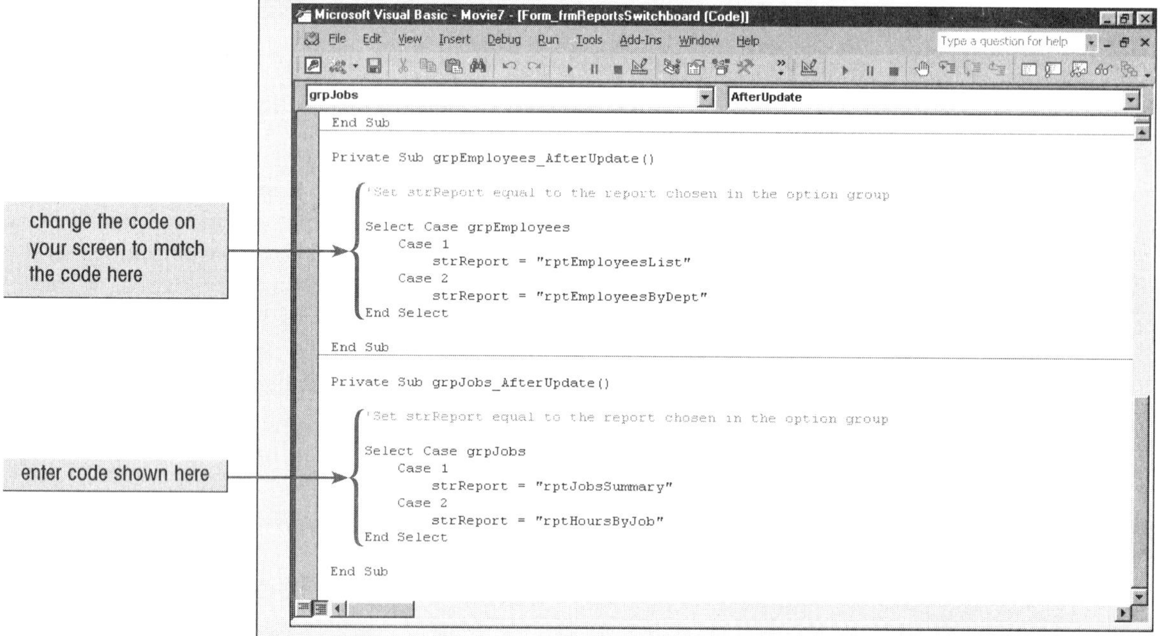

3. Click **Debug** on the menu bar, and then click **Compile MovieCam**.
4. Click the **Save** button on the toolbar.

Adding to the WhereCondition for Job Reports

Now that you have a feel for working with the WhereCondition, you will add more conditions to it. Recall that Martin said he wants to run reports for specific job numbers by typing in the first few numbers of the job. For example, if he types "92", he wants all the jobs that begin with those numbers to run. His other request is that he be able to run job reports by a single date or range of dates. The SQL WHERE clause that searches for records where the JobID field starts with "92" and includes any characters following it, looks like this:

```
WHERE JobID Like "92*"
```

You might remember from working with simple queries that the asterisk (*) wildcard stands for any group of characters and that the Like operation must be used in conjunction with a wildcard.

The SQL WHERE clause to query for records that include a single date for the TimeCardDate field looks like this:

```
WHERE TimeCardDate =  #11/9/2002#
```

Finally, the SQL WHERE clause to query for records that include a range of dates for the TimeCardDate field looks like this:

```
WHERE TimeCardDate Between #1/1/2002# And #12/31/2002#
```

You will start by adding the code for the JobID field.

To add code to query Job Reports:

1. Position the insertion point at the end of the third End If statement in the Sub cmdPreview_Click procedure as shown in Figure 7-43, and then press the **Enter** key twice.

Figure 7-43 ADDING TO THE WHERECONDITION CODE

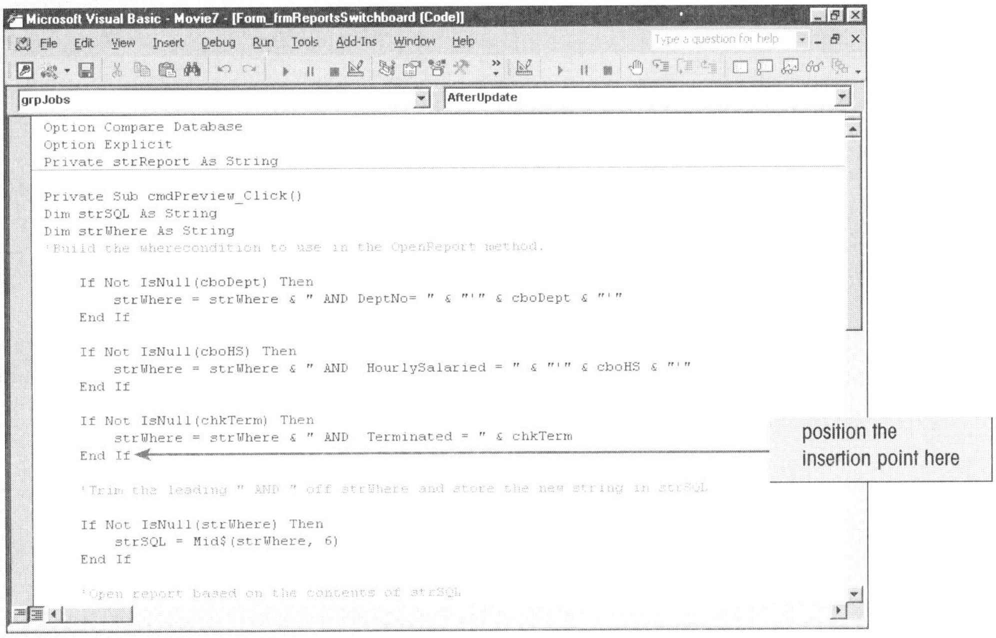

2. Type the following code (you can copy and paste one of the other If...Then statements, and then make the changes that are necessary):

```
If Not IsNull(txtJobID) Then
    strWhere = strWhere & " AND JobID Like " & "'" &
txtJobID & "*'"
End If
```

3. Position the insertion point at the end of the grpEmployees = Null statement, press the **Enter** key, and then type **grpJobs = Null**.

4. Position the insertion point at the end of the chkTerm = False statement, press the **Enter** key, and then type **txtJobID = Null**.
5. Compile the code and save your changes.
6. Check your code carefully against Figure 7-44, and make any changes necessary.

Figure 7-44 **ADDING TO THE WHERECONDITION CODE**

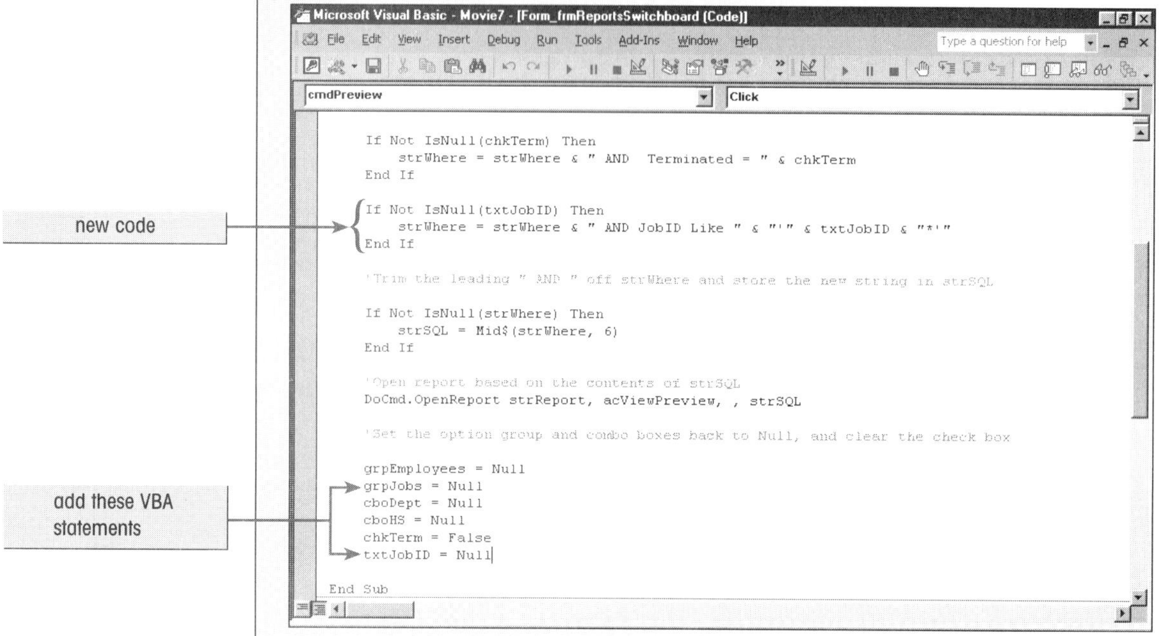

Next you need to plan the remaining statements to query for dates. If the user enters the beginning date in the txtStartDate text box and enters nothing in the txtEndDate text box, you want the report to show records for only one date. The following WHERE clause would accomplish this:

```
WHERE TimeCardDate =  #11/9/2002#
```

If both a start date and an end date are entered, you want to display that range of dates on the report, as this WHERE clause would do:

```
WHERE TimeCardDate Between #1/1/2002# And #12/31/2002#
```

If the start date is left blank and an end date is specified, you want to provide an error message that tells the user to enter both dates for a range, then clear the controls on the form, and exit the Sub procedure without previewing a report. To do this, you will use a nested If...Then...ElseIf statement inside an If...Then...Else statement. The first If statement tests to see if the txtStartDate field has an entry (If Not IsNull(txtStartDate)). If it does, the nested If statement tests to see if the txtEndDate field has an entry. If it does not, you add a string to the WhereCondition to query for only one date. If the txtEndDate field has an entry, you will add a different string to the WhereCondition that queries for the range of dates.

Using the Line Continuation Character

Up to this point, it has not been necessary to extend a statement over more than one line. However, the WhereCondition for a range of dates is quite long. In VBA, an underscore serves as a **line continuation character** that you can use when your code is too long to fit on a single line. An ampersand is required to concatenate strings, so if a string extends beyond one line, use an underscore (_) and an ampersand (&). The following example shows how you will use the underscore in the next series of steps:

```
strWhere = strWhere & " AND TimeCardDate Between " & "#" & _
& txtStartDate & "#" & " AND " "#" & txtEndDate & "#"
```

To complete the code to query Job Reports:

1. Position the insertion point at the end of the fourth End If statement in the Sub cmdPreview_Click procedure, as shown in Figure 7-45, and then press the **Enter** key twice.

Figure 7-45 COMPLETING THE WHERECONDITION CODE

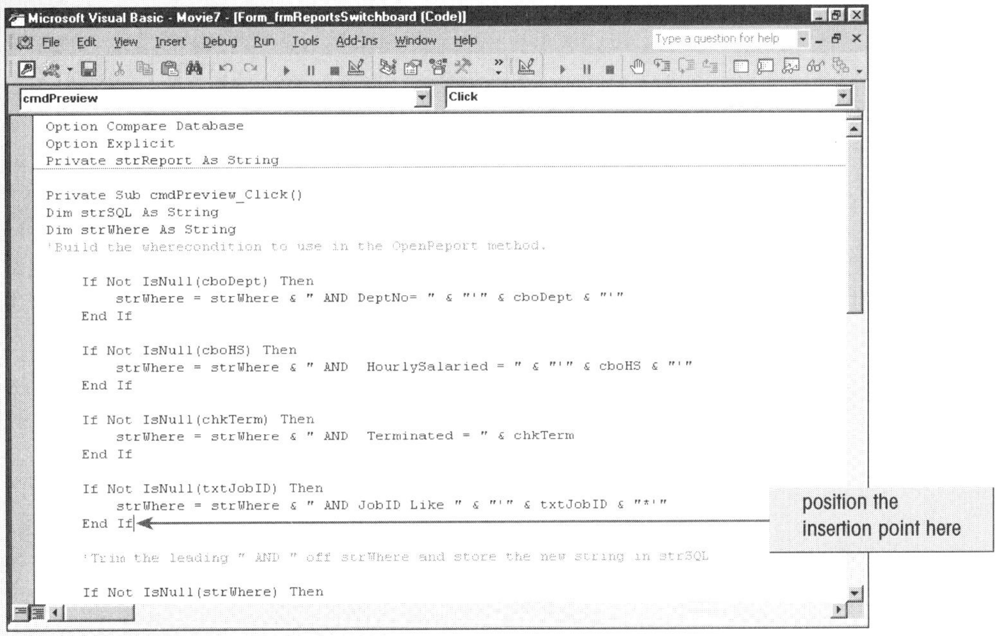

2. Type the following code:

```
If Not IsNull(txtStartDate) Then
    If IsNull(txtEndDate) Then
        strWhere = strWhere & " AND TimeCardDate = " & "#"
& _
          txtStartDate & "#"
    ElseIf Not IsNull(txtEndDate) Then
        strWhere = strWhere & " AND TimeCardDate Between "
& "#" & _
          txtStartDate & "#" & " AND " & "#" & txtEndDate
& "#"
    End If
End If
```

3. Check your code carefully against Figure 7-46, and make any changes necessary.

Figure 7-46 ADDING THE WHERECONDITION CODE FOR txtStartDate AND txtEndDate

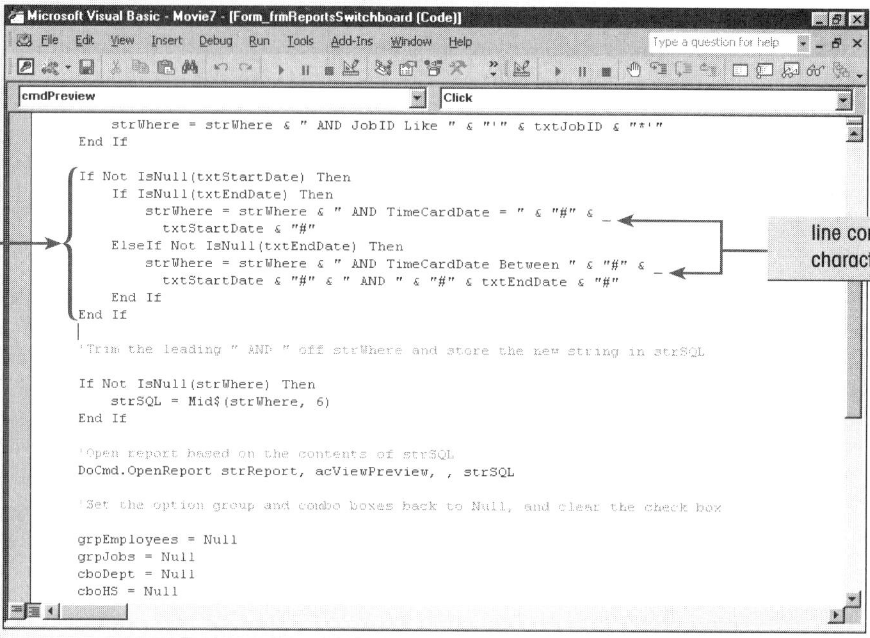

code should look like this

line continuation character

4. If necessary, position the insertion point at the end of the last End If statement you just typed, press the **Enter** key twice, and then indent and type the following code (the Clear_Controls code represents the name of a portion of the code that you will add in Step 5):

```
If IsNull(txtStartDate) And Not IsNull(txtEndDate) Then
    MsgBox "You must enter a starting date to run the
report for a range"
    GoTo Clear_Controls
End If
```

5. Position the insertion point at the beginning of the grpEmployees = Null line, and then press the **Enter** key.

6. Position the insertion point on the blank line above the grpEmployees = Null statement, and then type **Clear_Controls:** (including the colon), as shown in Figure 7-47. This names this series of statements so that after the message box is shown, you continue at this point in the program.

Figure 7-47 ADDING THE Clear_Controls: STATEMENT

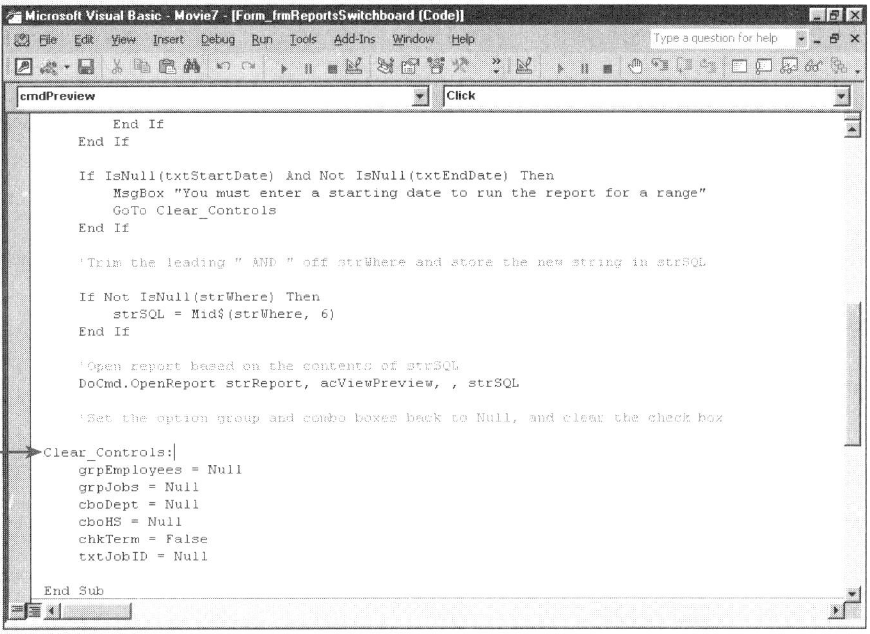

type this statement above grpEmployees = Null

7. Position the insertion point at the end of the txtJobID = Null statement, press the **Enter** key, and then type **txtStartDate = Null**.
8. Press the **Enter** key and then type **txtEndDate = Null**.
9. Check your code carefully against Figure 7-48, and make any necessary changes.

Figure 7-48 SETTING THE txtStartDate AND txtEndDate FIELDS TO NULL

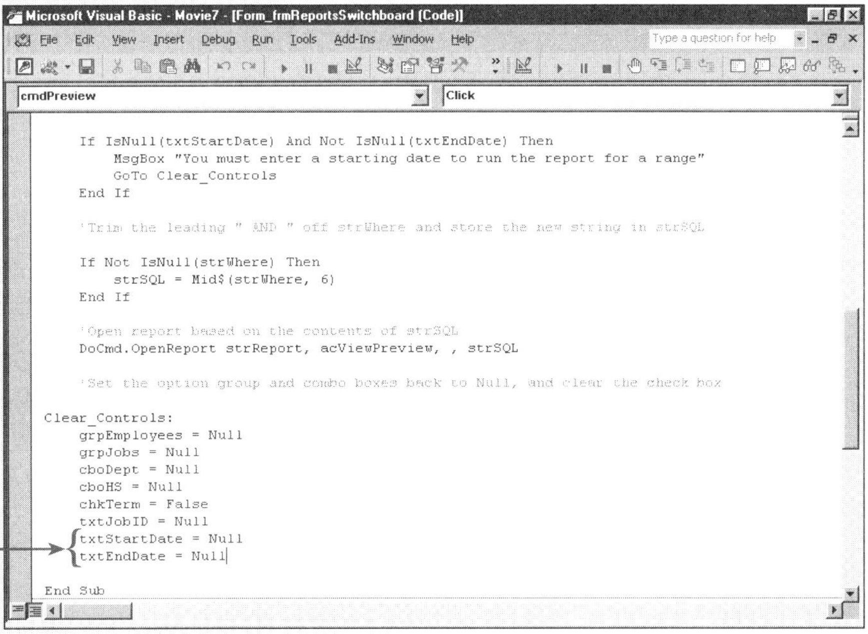

add these statements

Finally, because you have modified the code for the cmdPreview button to run any of the reports, you must alter one of your If...Then statements to ensure the chkTerm check box is ignored if you are running a Jobs report. You do not want Terminated criteria included for any of the Jobs reports, as the reports will not run properly. Recall that you set the default for chkTerm to No for use in the Employees reports. But whether it is checked or unchecked, when you run jobs reports, you want to see all hours related to the job(s), regardless if the employee who worked hours on any given job is still employed or has left the company. You do not want the Terminated criteria to be part of the WhereCondition for Jobs reports at all, so you selectively exclude it if one of the jobs options in the grpJobs option group is selected.

10. In the cmdPreview_Click Sub procedure, change the third If condition for chkTerm from *If Not IsNull(chkTerm) Then* to **If Not IsNull(chkTerm) And IsNull(grpJobs) Then** as shown in Figure 7-49.

Figure 7-49 MODIFYING THE IF... THEN STATEMENT TO EXCLUDE TERMINATED CRITERIA

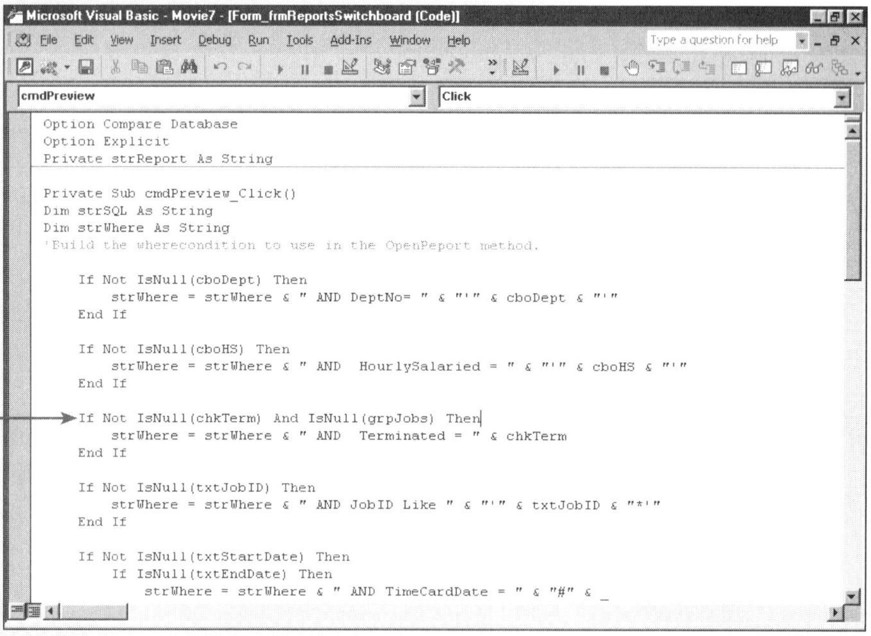

11. Compile the code and then save your changes.

12. Close the Visual Basic window, close the property sheet, and then switch to Form view.

13. Test the form by opening **Hours By Job** for a single date and then for a date range in the year 2004. Test the **Job List** by first using **92** and then using **99** as the Job ID number.

Technically, the reports switchboard form will allow users to select a department or an hourly versus salaried option and run a Jobs report, but this will be less likely of an issue, as these items are set to Null after you run each report. Because the Personnel Department wanted the employee reports to default to active employees, and they did not wish to run employee list or department reports that included both terminated and active employees, you had to default the chkTerm check box to No and reset it to something other than Null after each report was run.

You may also notice that currently users could mix and match criteria by choosing a department and then running a job report, or by entering a JobID and then running an Employee report. These scenarios would prompt users for missing parameters in reports because they would effectively be supplying a WhereCondition, like a department name, to a job report that does not include department name in the report. This is not how the application should behave, and this situation is not acceptable. When you create a user interface, it should not allow the users to select options which can cause erroneous reports to run, untrapped errors to occur, or basically anything that halts or crashes the application. This sounds fairly intuitive, but is rarely easy to implement.

In Tutorial 8, you will learn techniques for error trapping and a way to disable portions of the report switchboard when appropriate in order to prevent users from mismatching a set of criteria with the wrong set of reports.

There is one last feature you need to provide now for the reports switchboard. You need to provide the users with a way to exit or close it. They will not have access to the default menu that you are now using when the database is completed, and even then, it would still be more convenient for the user to have a button on the form. You will use the Command Button Wizard to complete this feature.

To add a Close button to the frmReportsSwitchboard form:

1. Switch to Design view, click the **cboDept** combo box on the form, hold down the **Shift** key, select the **Preview** command button, right-click the command button, point to **Align** on the shortcut menu, and then click **Right**.
2. Click the **Control Wizards** button in the toolbox to select it, click the **Command Button** button in the toolbox, and then click to the right of the Preview command button.
3. In the Command Button Wizard dialog box, click **Form Operations** in the Categories list box, click **Close Form** in the Actions list box, and then click the **Next** button.
4. Click the **Text** option button, type **&Close** in the text box, and then click the **Next** button.
5. Type **cmdClose** as the name of the button, and then click the **Finish** button.
6. Size and align the button with the Previous command button on the form. You can use Figure 7-1 at the beginning of the tutorial to see how this form should look on your screen.
7. Click the **Save** button on the toolbar to save the form, switch to Form view, and then click the **Close** button to test the button and close the form.

   TROUBLE? If an error message displays after you click the Close button, switch to Design view, display the properties for the Close button, and be sure that (Event Procedure) is displayed in the On Click text box. If it is not, click the text box list arrow, and select (Event Procedure).

8. Close the MovieCam7 database, and then exit Access.

Richard and Martin are pleased with the reports switchboard. They have requested a few additions, such as an option to print directly to the printer without opening the Print Preview window, and access to the Page Setup options so that they can change margins and other page elements. The Page Setup request can be addressed with a menu or a toolbar.

You have made notes on features that you want to add or change. Amanda is happy with your work because it is structured in a way that can be easily updated and modified.

Session 7.2 QUICK CHECK

1. The ______________ argument in the OpenReport method is a SQL WHERE clause without the word WHERE.
2. You can view the results of an expression or a variable in the Immediate window by entering the ______________ method of the Debug object, followed by the expression.
3. What is the shortcut method for viewing the results of an expression in the Immediate window?
4. A(n) ______________ is a selected line of your program at which execution automatically stops.
5. What is the Locals window?
6. What does "stepping through" your code refer to?
7. What does a dollar sign following the name of a function mean?
8. In VBA, a(n) ______________ serves as a line continuation character that you can use when your code is too long to fit on a single line

REVIEW ASSIGNMENTS

The Hours7 database is similar to the MovieCam Technologies database you worked on in this tutorial. A form named frmReportsSwitchboard has been created in the database. It contains a check box named chkTerm and a combo box named cboDept so that employee reports can be filtered by these criteria. You will write the code to set the strReports variable equal to the report name and then write the code to build the WhereCondition and print the report.

1. Start Access and open the **Hours7** database located in the Tutorial.07\Review folder on your local or network drive.
2. Open the **frmReportsSwitchboard** form in Design view, click the option group frame to select it, and then click the Properties button on the toolbar.
3. Click the Event tab, click in the After Update text box, and then click its Build button. (*Hint*: If the Choose Builder dialog box opens, click Code Builder, and then click the OK button.)
4. Indent lines of code and add blank lines as appropriate as you type the following comment and code:

```
'Set strReport equal to report chosen in the option group
Select Case grpEmployees
  Case 1
   strName = "rptEmployeesList"
  Case 2
   strName = "rptEmployeesByDept"
End Select
```

5. Insert two blank lines after the Option Explicit statement, and then type **Private strName As String**.
6. Select cmdPreview from the Object list to create the Sub.
7. Indent lines of code and add blank lines as appropriate as you type the following comments and code:

```
Dim strSQL As String
Dim strCondition As String
'Build the WhereCondition to use in the OpenReport method
If Not IsNull(chkTerm) Then
   strCondition = strCondition & " AND  Terminated = " &
chkTerm
End If
If Not IsNull(cboDept) Then
   strCondition = strCondition & " AND  DeptNo= " & "'" &
cboDept & "'"
End If
'Trim the leading "AND " off strCondition and store the new
string in strSQL
If Not IsNull(strCondition) Then
   strSQL = Mid$(strCondition, 6)
End If
'Open report based on the contents of strSQL.
DoCmd.OpenReport strName, acViewPreview, , strSQL
'Set the option group, combo boxes, and check box back to
null
grpEmployees = Null
cboDept = Null
chkTerm = Null
```

8. Compile the code, correct any errors, and then print the code. Close the Visual Basic window.
9. Switch to Form view to test the code. Open both reports using different combinations of conditions.
10. Save the changes and close the form.
11. Close the Hours7 database, and then exit Access.

CASE PROBLEMS

Case 1. Edwards and Company Jack Edwards asks you to create a method to make it simple for him to find specific clients in the Clients form. He wants to search based on Company Name and/or Contact Name, and does not want to input the entire name to conduct the search.

To do this, you have created a form named frmCriteria that is similar to the frmReportsSwitchboard form you worked with in this tutorial. It contains a text box named txtCompany and a text box named txtContact. It also contains a Search button that can be used to search for a particular record in the form. The DoCmd.OpenForm method contains a WhereCondition argument that works the same way as the WhereCondition argument in the DoCmd.OpenReport statement. You will write the code needed to populate the WhereCondition and open the frmClients form. Complete the following:

1. Start Access and open the **Edward7** database located in the Tutorial.07\Cases folder on your local or network drive.
2. Open the **frmCriteria** form in Design view, click the Search button, and click the Properties button on the toolbar.
3. Click the Event tab, click in the On Click text box, and then click its Build button. (*Hint*: If the Choose Builder dialog box opens, click Code Builder, and then click the OK button.)
4. Indent lines of code and add blank lines as necessary as you type the following Sub procedure:

```
Dim strSQL As String
Dim strWhere As String
'Build the WhereCondition to use in the OpenForm method
If Not IsNull(txtCompany) Then
   strWhere = strWhere & " AND CompanyName Like " & "'" &
txtCompany & "*'"
End If
If Not IsNull(txtContact) Then
   strWhere = strWhere & " AND ContactName Like " & "'" &
txtContact & "*'"
End If
'Trim the leading "AND " off strWhere and store the new
string in strSQL
If Not IsNull(strWhere) Then
   strSQL = Mid$(strWhere, 6)
End If
'Open form based on the contents of strSQL.
DoCmd.OpenForm "frmClients", , , strSQL
'Set the text boxes to null
txtCompany = Null
txtContact = Null
```

5. Compile the code, correct any errors, and then print the code.
6. Save the code, close the Visual Basic window, and switch to Form view.
7. To test the form, type **West** in the Company Name text box, and then click the Search button. The frmCriteria form is a modal form, which means it remains on top of other forms. You can move it by dragging it by the title bar.
8. Click in the Contact Name text box, type **T**, and then click the Search button.
9. Save your changes and close the forms.
10. Close the Edward7 database, and then exit Access.

Case 2. San Diego County Information Systems You have started to create a report switchboard in the ISD database, but are having trouble getting it to work properly. Each time you try to display the Student Phone List report for a particular department, you see all departments. You will troubleshoot the problem. Complete the following:

1. Start Access and open the **ISD7** database located in the Tutorial.07\Cases folder on your local or network drive.
2. Open the **frmReportsSwitchboard** form in Design view, and click the Code button on the toolbar.

3. Click in the gray margin to the left of the Private Sub cmdPreview_Click() procedure to set a breakpoint.
4. Minimize the Visual Basic window, and switch to Form view.
5. Click the Student Phone List option button, select Information Systems from the Department combo box, and then click the Preview button.
6. Make sure the Debug toolbar is displayed in the Visual Basic window.
7. Click the Step Into button twice, and note that the If…Then… statement is not executed. Looking more closely, you realize that this is because the Not operator is missing.
8. Click the Step Out button in the toolbar to complete running the code. When the Report Preview window opens, close it, and then return to the Visual Basic window.
9. Click Debug on the menu bar, and then click Clear All Breakpoints.
10. Change the statement If IsNull(cboDept) Then to **If Not IsNull(cboDept) Then** so that the Not operator is included.
11. Compile the code, correct any errors, and then close the Visual Basic window.
12. Save your changes and close the form. (*Hint*: Because there is no Close button on this form, you must use the File menu to close the form.) Reopen the form to reset the controls.
13. To test the form, click the Student Phone List option, select Sheriff from the Department combo box, and then click the Preview button.
14. Close the report and then close the form.
15. Close the ISD7 database, and then exit Access.

Case 3. Christenson Homes Roberta Christenson asks you to create a method to make it simple for her to find specific lots in the frmLots form. She wants to search based on any part of the address, and/or on any plan. Recall that the data for each lot in a subdivision is stored with a street address and a plan number to identify it.

To grant Roberta's request, you have created a criteria form named frmCriteria that contains a text box named txtAddress, and a text box named txtPlan. The form also contains a Search button. The DoCmd.OpenForm method contains a WhereCondition argument that works the same way as the WhereCondition argument in DoCmd.OpenReport. You will write the code needed to populate the WhereCondition and open the frmLots form. Complete the following:

1. Start Access and open the **Homes7** database located in the Tutorial.07\Cases folder on your local or network drive.
2. Open the **frmCriteria** form in Design view, click the Search button, and click the Properties button on the toolbar.
3. Click the Event tab, click in the On Click text box, and then click its Build button.
4. Indent lines of code and add blank lines as appropriate as you type the following comment and statements:

```
Dim strSQL As String
Dim strWhere As String
'Build the WhereCondition to use in the OpenForm method
If Not IsNull(txtAddress) Then
   strWhere = strWhere & " AND Address Like " & "'*" &
txtAddress & "*'"
End If
```

5. Write another If…Then…Else statement to concatenate the strWhere text for txtPlan.
6. To complete the code, type the following comments and statements, indenting lines of code and adding blank lines as appropriate:

```
'Trim the leading "AND " off strWhere and store the new string
in strSQL
If Not IsNull(strWhere) Then
   strSQL = Mid$(strWhere, 6)
End If
'Open form based on the contents of strSQL.
DoCmd.OpenForm "frmLots", , , strSQL
'Set the text boxes to null
txtAddress = Null
txtPlan = Null
```

7. Compile the code, correct any errors, save your changes, and then close the Visual Basic window.
8. Switch to Form view and test the form. Close the form.
9. Close the Homes7 database, and then exit Access.

Case 4. Sonoma Farms The Sonoma Farms database contains a report named rptVisitorsByDistributor. You have been asked to create a switchboard that can be used to open the report. The switchboard should be based on two types of criteria: the distributor name and the contact name. Complete the following:

1. Start Access and open the **Sonoma7** database located in the Tutorial.07\Cases folder on your local or network drive.
2. Create a switchboard form named **frmReportsSwitchboard** that contains an option group named grpReports. Add the label Reports to the option group.
3. Use the Option Group Wizard to create the option group. It should contain one option button that should be labeled **Visitor By Distributor**.
4. Add text boxes named **txtDistributor** and **txtContact** below the option group.
5. Add a command button named **cmdPreview** that triggers the code to open the report.
6. Complete the code for opening the **rptVisitorsByDistributor** report from the switchboard. Base the code on the contents of the txtDistributor and txtContact text boxes. The code for both Sub procedures is shown below. Be sure to add spacing and indenting as well as comments to complete the code.

```
Private strReport As String
Private Sub cmdPreview_Click()
Dim strSQL As String
Dim strWhere As String
If Not IsNull(txtDistributor) Then
   strWhere = strWhere & " AND DistributorName Like " & "'" &
txtDistributor & "*'"
End If
If Not IsNull(txtContact) Then
   strWhere = strWhere & " AND ContactName Like " & "'" &
txtContact & "*'"
End If
If Not IsNull(strWhere) Then
   strSQL = Mid$(strWhere, 6)
End If
```

```
DoCmd.OpenReport strReport, acViewPreview, , strSQL
'Set the option group, combo boxes, and check box back to
null
Clear_Controls:
  grpReports = Null
  txtDistributor = Null
  txtContact = Null
End Sub
Private Sub grpReports_AfterUpdate()
Select Case grpReports
  Case 1
   strReport = "rptVisitorsByDistributor"
End Select
End Sub
```

7. Compile the code, correct any errors, and then close the Visual Basic window.
8. Switch to Form view and test the code by typing **ABC Distribution** in the Distributor Name text box.
9. Save the form and then close it.
10. Close the Sonoma7 database, and then exit Access

QUICK CHECK ANSWERS

Session 7.1

1. event-driven
2. A form class module is created when you add code to a form.
3. Scope describes the visibility and accessibility of one procedure from another procedure.
4. Compiling is the process of checking for overall consistency and translating the VBA statements into a language that the computer can understand.
5. implicit
6. lifetime
7. The Static keyword differs from the Dim keyword in that the variable that is declared with it retains its value after the Sub procedure or function has finished running.
8. You cannot change the value of a constant after you declare it.

Session 7.2

1. WhereCondition
2. Print
3. Typing the question mark (?) instead of Debug.Print prior to the expression is the shortest method for viewing the results of an expression in the Immediate windows.
4. breakpoint
5. The Locals window is a window where Access automatically displays the name, current value, and type of all the variables and objects in the current procedure.
6. Stepping through code means that execution is suspended after each statement executes.
7. The dollar sign ($) means that the function returns a string data type.
8. underscore (_)

OBJECTIVES

In this tutorial you will:

- Review VBA decision structures
- Learn VBA looping structures
- Test a switchboard form for errors
- Learn about the *Me* keyword and use it in code
- Study error types, including syntax, run-time, and logic errors
- Study collections and the bang vs. dot notation
- Write code to handle a VBA error
- Write code to handle Access errors
- Create a combo box for selecting a record on a form
- Learn about ActiveX controls
- Create a form using the Calendar control

TRAPPING ERRORS AND AUTOMATING ACTIVEX CONTROLS WITH VBA

Trapping Errors and Refining Forms in the MovieCam Technologies Database

CASE

MovieCam Technologies

Amanda is pleased with the frmReportsSwitchbord form you created, but she is concerned that users might encounter error messages. She asks you to test the switchboard form for potential problems, and design the VBA code necessary to handle them. Amanda also wants you to test the other forms in the database for possible errors, and write error-trapping code for them.

In a recent meeting, Martin Woodward requested that you add some features to the frmTimeCards data entry form. Specifically, he wants to be able to easily search for the record of a particular time card. In addition, you will add a form feature that allows users to enter dates more easily.

SESSION 8.1

In this session, you will study decision structures and looping structures. You will test the frmReportsSwitchboard form for errors and add code to it so users cannot choose criteria that do not exist for a specific report. You will learn the difference between the Visible property and the Enabled property. You will review collections and compare bang versus dot notation and how they are used to specify objects in Access. You also will write code that uses a looping structure and the Controls collection on a form.

Control Structures for Decision Processing and Looping

VBA provides you with several different control structures for looping and decision processing. A **control structure** is a series of VBA statements that work together as a unit. You use decision structures to test for specific conditions in your procedures. You studied the three most common decision structures in Tutorial 6, If...Then...Else, If...Then...ElseIf, and Select Case. In this tutorial you will learn about commonly used structures for looping.

Frequently, you need to execute certain portions of program code multiple times. Rather than writing the line of code multiple times, you can write the code to be executed inside a loop. The most commonly used loop structures are Do...Loop, For...Next, and For Each...Next.

Do...Loop

You use the **Do...Loop** structure to repeat statements in your procedure either while a specified condition is true or until a specified condition is true.

The Do...Loop construct has several variations. You can use the following syntax:

```
Do [{While | Until} condition]
      [statements]
      [Exit Do]
      [statements]
Loop
```

Or, you can use this syntax:

```
Do
      [statements]
      [Exit Do]
      [statements]
Loop [{While | Until} condition]
```

You can also use the **Exit Do** statement to exit a loop, as shown above as part of the Microsoft VBA syntax. However, according to best practices programming standards, it is not advisable to do so. This is considered to be an unnatural exit from the loop. Rather, you should write your code so the test conditions ensure proper exiting from the loop. You might come across situations as a programmer where there seem to be compelling exceptions, but whenever possible, do not use an Exit Do statement.

In the first syntax example above, when Access encounters the Do statement in the procedure, it tests the specified condition. In the case of the Do While statement, Access enters the loop as long as the condition is true. As soon as the condition is false, Access continues the program's execution at the first statement after the Loop keyword. In the case of a Do Until statement, Access enters the loop until the condition is true. Use of While or Until is really more a preference of how you want to construct your test. Consider the following example.

```
Dim intCounter As Integer
intCounter = 1
Do While intCounter < 5
   MsgBox intCounter
   intCounter = intCounter + 1
Loop
```

The first line of the code declares a variable as an integer, and the next line sets the variable equal to 1. The looping construct performs the loop as long as the variable intCounter is less than 5. The looping construct also contains a statement that increments the variable each time the loop statements are executed.

Another way to achieve the same result using the Do Until statement would be:

```
Dim intCounter As Integer
intCounter = 1
Do Until intCounter > 4
   MsgBox intCounter
   intCounter = intCounter + 1
Loop
```

The use of While or Until is usually a matter of preference for programmers and as you can see from the examples above, you have to write the code for your test differently depending upon which one you use. The above examples do not ensure that the code executes at least once. If the intCounter variable had somehow been set to 5 or greater, the code would not execute at all. To be sure that the code executes unconditionally at least once, the code should look like the following:

```
Dim intCounter As Integer
intCounter = 5
Do
   MsgBox intCounter
   intCounter = intCounter + 1
Loop While intCounter < 5
```

If you wanted to use the Loop Until statement for your test, one possible solution for the code would look like this:

```
Dim intCounter As Integer
intCounter = 5
Do
   MsgBox intCounter
   intCounter = intCounter + 1
Loop Until intCounter > 4
```

The difference between the two sets of examples is that in the first example set, the Do While/Until...Loop evaluates before the code is executed. In the second example set, the Do...Loop While/Until is evaluated at the end of the loop so that it is guaranteed to execute at least once. This code would execute at least once even though the variable is set to 5. Logically, you would probably not write a code segment like this, but it serves to generically demonstrate the use of the test conditions at the beginning versus the end of the Do...Loop construct.

For...Next Loop

Unlike the Do...Loop, the **For...Next loop** executes statements of code a specified number of times. When you use the Do...Loop construct you do not know how many times it will be executed because it continues until some condition is met. You use the For...Next loop construct when you have an exact number of iterations you want to perform. Unlike with the Do...Loop, you specify the number of times through the loop at the beginning of the For...Next loop. The loop shown below will execute five times, once for each value specified in the "For intCounter = 1 to 4" statement.

```
Dim intCounter As Integer
For intCounter = 1 To 4
   MsgBox intCounter
Next intCounter
```

The start and stop values, which are 1 and 4 in the example above, also can be variables. Compare this code segment to the examples provided for the Do...Loop construct. This code segment achieves the same result in fewer lines of code. A For...Next construct can also be given a step value. A **step value** lets you increment the loop by a given amount. For example:

```
Dim intCounter As Integer
For intCounter = 1 To 5 Step 2
    MsgBox intCounter
Next intCounter
```

The preceding loop repeats three times: once when intCounter equals 1; once when intCounter equals 3; and once when intCounter equals 5.

For Each...Next Loop

The **For Each...Next** construct executes a group of statements on each member of an array or collection. (Recall from Tutorial 6 that a collection is an object that contains a set of related objects.) For example, the Controls collection contains all of the controls found on an open form. An **array** is a series of variables of the same data type, arranged contiguously in memory. Arrays can be useful for storing a series of values.

The For Each...Next construct works similarly to the For...Next construct. It iterates through a collection or array, and moves through each object until it reaches the end of the collection. For example, if you want to set the Enabled or Visible property to false for all of the controls on a form, you can use For Each...Next structure to loop though each control in the collection and make the change to its property. The following example sets the Fore Color property (the text color) of all of the controls on the form to red:

```
Dim ctl As Control
For Each ctl In Controls
   ctl.ForeColor = 255
Next ctl
```

The first statement declares ctl as a control object variable. The next statement specifies that for each control in the Controls collection the next statement(s) should execute. The ctl.Fore Color part of the statement sets the Fore Color property of each control to 255, which is red. Next you apply some of these concepts to make some enhancements to the Reports Switchboard, such as enabling and disabling controls as appropriate so that only the applicable options are available on the switchboard based on the report you choose to preview.

Testing and Refining the Reports Switchboard

When you use the frmReportsSwitchboard form, notice that when choosing combo box and text box options, you could actually choose options that do not apply to the report you are trying to run. You should disable the controls that don't apply to specific reports in the class module, and then enable those controls after the report is run. Also note that an error occurs if the user does not choose a report from one of the two option groups. To verify these issues, you will test the switchboard next.

To test the frmReportsSwitchboard form:

1. Start Access and open the **Movie8** database located in the Tutorial.08\Tutorial folder on your local or network drive.
2. Click **Forms** on the Objects bar in the Database window, and double-click the **frmReportsSwitchboard** form.
3. Click the **Employee List** option button, type **92** in the Job ID text box, and then click the **Preview** button. An Enter Parameter Value dialog opens, as shown in Figure 8-1, because Access cannot find the JobID field in the rptEmployeesList report.

Figure 8-1 ENTER PARAMETER VALUE DIALOG BOX

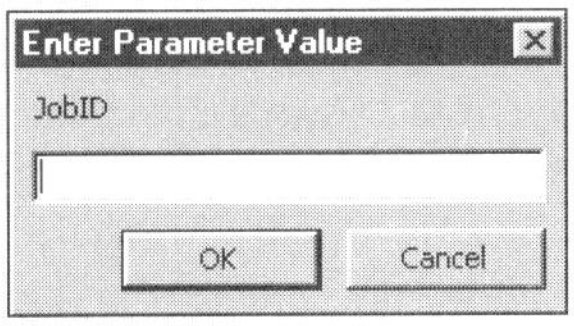

4. Click the **OK** button. The report opens, but no records are visible, as shown in Figure 8-2.

Figure 8-2 rptEmployeesList REPORT

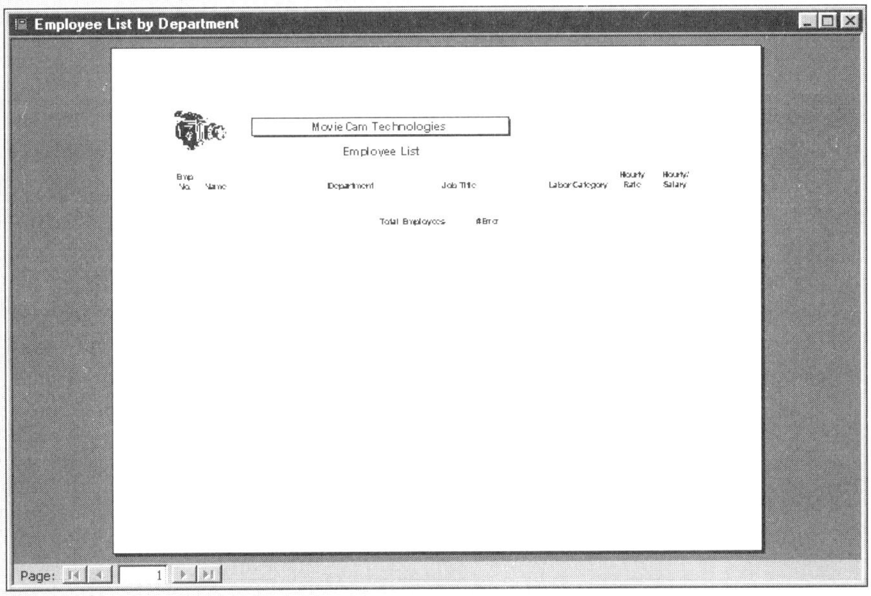

5. Close the report, click **File** on the menu bar, and then click **Close** to close the switchboard. Closing and reopening the frmReportsSwitchboard form resets it.
6. Open the **frmReportsSwitchboard** form in Form view, and click the **Preview** button. You should see an error message like that shown in Figure 8-3. You receive this error because no report has been selected yet.

Figure 8-3 RUN-TIME ERROR MESSAGE

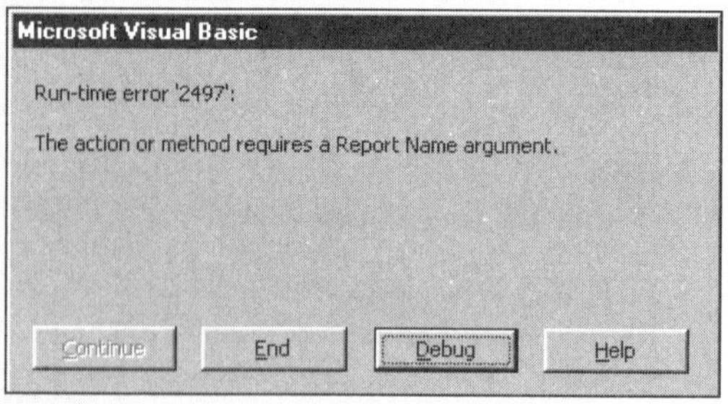

7. Click the **End** button to close the error message, and then switch to Design view.

You can use a couple of ways to rectify an error that's caused when a user specifies criteria that do not apply to a given report. One way is to set the Visible property to false for the controls on the switchboard that do not apply to the selected report, thereby making the controls "invisible." Another way is to leave the controls visible, but disable them by changing the Enabled property to false.

You also can use the Visible property to show or hide a form, report, data access page, or a section or control in a form or report. This property can be set in macros or in VBA code; you can also change it in the properties dialog box for some objects.

The Enabled property specifies whether a control can have the focus in Form view. Focus, as you have learned, means that a control can receive user input through the mouse or keyboard. In the Windows environment, only one item at a time can have the focus. When the Enabled property is set to false, the control on the form is dimmed.

Figure 8-4 shows the frmReportsSwitchboard form with the Visible property set to false for all the controls related to the Job Reports option group.

Figure 8-4 SWITCHBOARD FORM WITH CONTROLS' VISIBLE PROPERTY SET TO FALSE

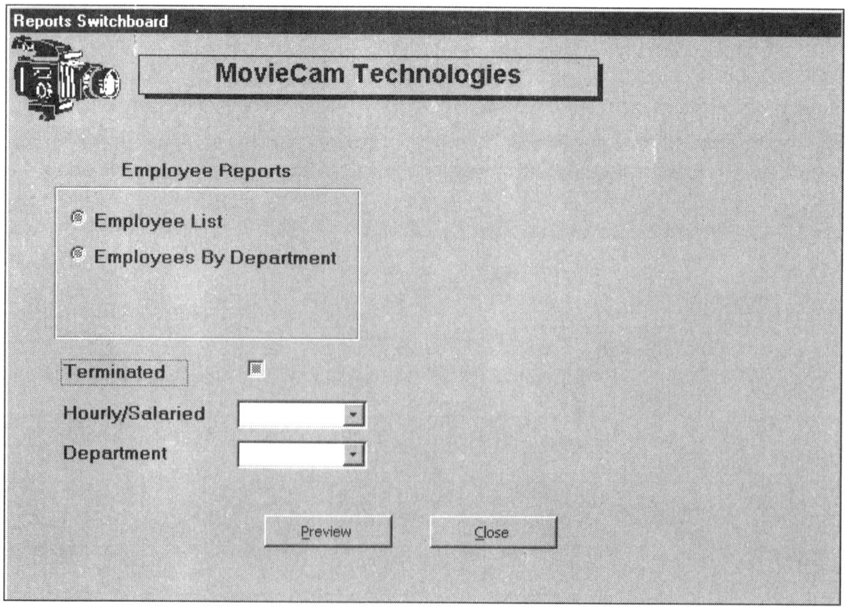

Figure 8-5 shows the Enabled property set to false for the controls related to the Employee Reports option group.

Figure 8-5 SWITCHBOARD FORM WITH CONTROLS' ENABLE PROPERTY SET TO FALSE

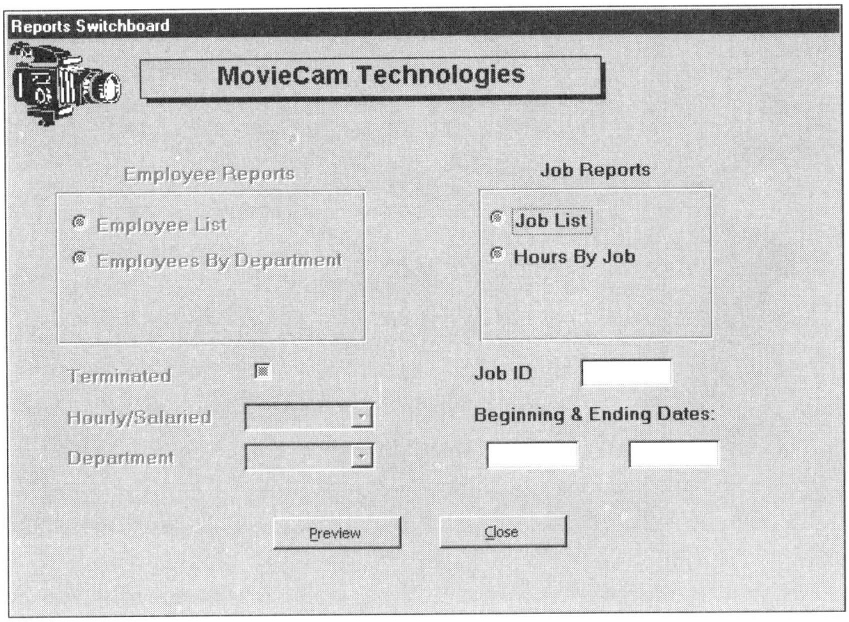

After reviewing the two options, you decide that you don't want to confuse or alarm users by having controls disappear completely from the form. Therefore, you will set the Enabled property to false for all controls that don't apply to particular reports in each option group.

Next you will write the code to set the Enabled property to false. The code will execute so that the Enabled property for the controls for the Employee Reports option group is set to false *after* the user selects a Job Report from the grpJobs option group.

To use code to set the Enabled property to false:

1. Click the **Code** button on the Form Design toolbar.
2. Click the **Object** list arrow, and click **grpJobs**, and then if necessary click the **Procedure** list arrow, and click **AfterUpdate**.
3. Position the insertion point at the end of the End Select statement, as shown in Figure 8-6.

Figure 8-6 VISUAL BASIC WINDOW

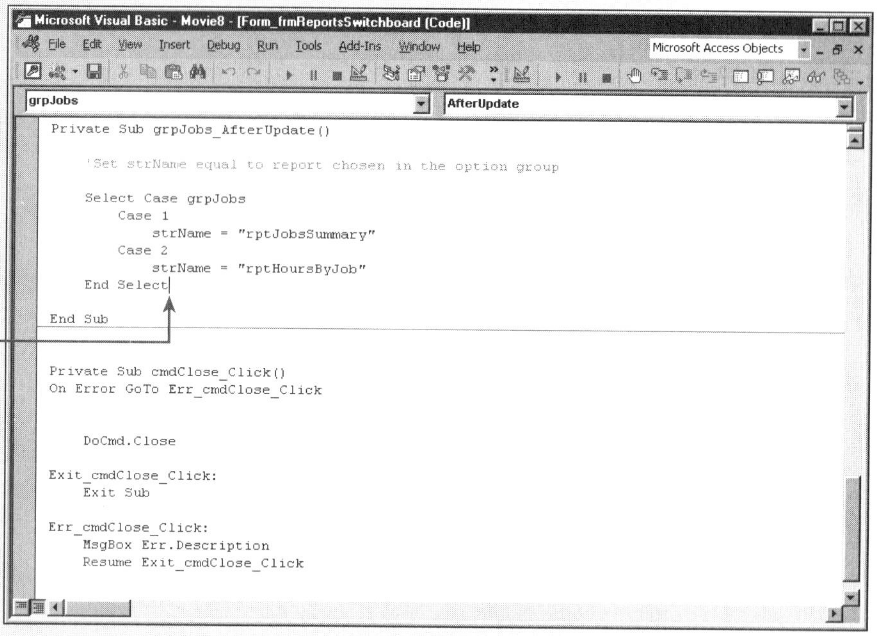

position the insertion point here

4. Press the **Enter** key twice, and then type the following comment and statements, indenting and spacing as shown in Figure 8-7.

```
'Disable controls for Employee Reports after a Job
' Report is selected
grpEmployees.Enabled = False
cboDepartment.Enabled = False
cboHourlySalaried.Enabled = False
chkTerminated.Enabled = False
```

Figure 8-7 MODIFYING THE grpJobs_AfterUpdate PROCEDURE

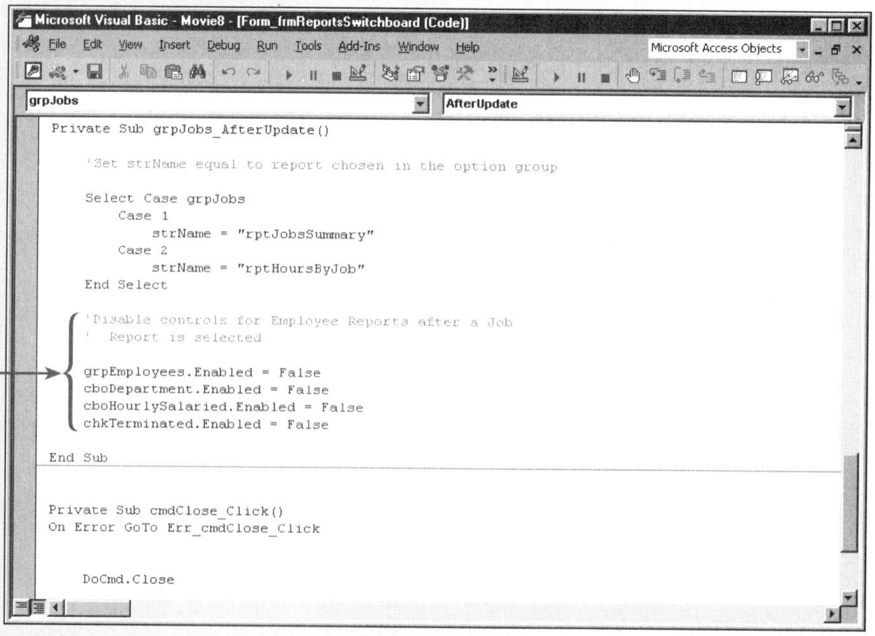

add this comment and these statements to the procedure

5. Compile the code, fix any errors, save your changes, close the Visual Basic window, switch to Form view, and click the **Job List** option button. Your switchboard should look like that shown in Figure 8-5.

6. Switch to Design view and then click the **Code** button on the toolbar.

Job List, the first report in the Job Reports option group, does not contain a TimeCardDate field. If the user attempts to type in dates and then run this report, the Enter Parameter Value dialog box will open. To prevent this, you will disable the txtStartDate and txtEndDate text boxes for this report and also disable the Job text boxes when an option from the Employee Reports group is selected.

To disable the date text boxes:

1. Position the insertion point at the end of the strName = "rptJobsSummary" line in the grpJobs_AfterUpdate() Sub procedure, and then press the **Enter** key.

2. Type the following code. Your code should look like that shown in Figure 8-8 when you are finished.

```
txtStartDate.Enabled = False
txtEndDate.Enabled = False
```

Figure 8-8 ADDING CODE TO DISABLE DATE TEXT BOXES

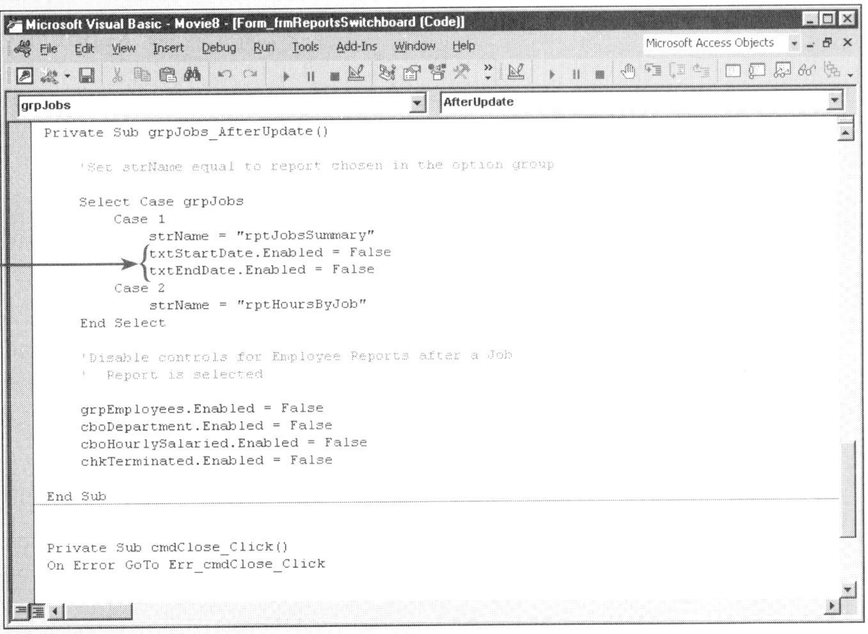

add these two statements to the procedure

3. Select **grpEmployees** from the Object list, and then make sure the **AfterUpdate** property is selected in the Procedure list.

4. Position the insertion point at the end of the End Select statement in the grpEmployees_AfterUpdate() Sub procedure.

5. Press the **Enter** key twice, and then type the following comment and code statements, indenting and spacing as shown in Figure 8-9.

```
'Disable controls for Job Reports after Employee Report
' is selected
grpJobs.Enabled = False
txtJobID.Enabled = False
txtStartDate.Enabled = False
txtEndDate.Enabled = False
```

Figure 8-9 ADDING CODE TO THE grpEmplyoees_AfterUpdate PROCEDURE

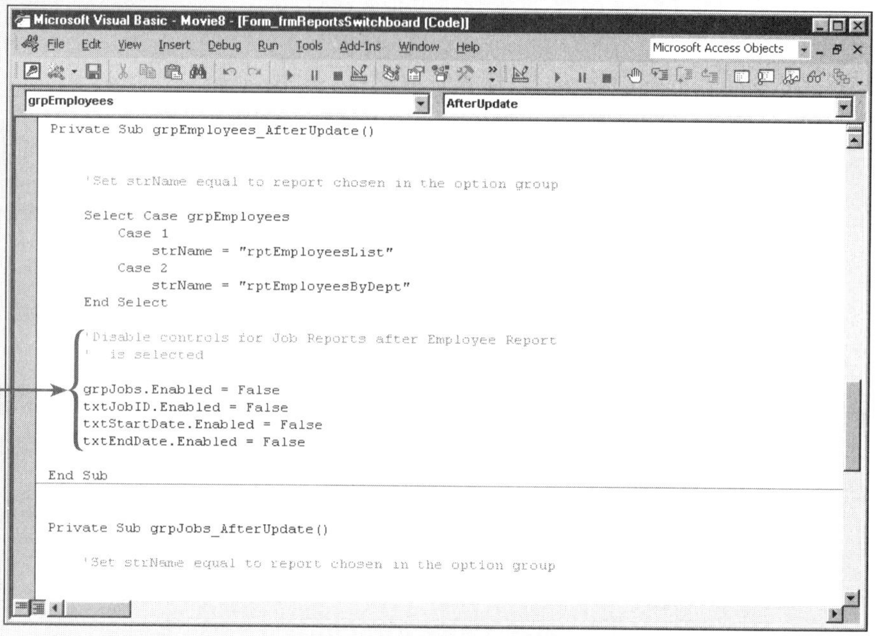

add this comment and these statements to the procedure

6. Click the **Save** button on the toolbar, and then close the Visual Basic window.
7. Switch to Form view and test the form by clicking the **Job List** option button. The Employee Reports options and the Beginning and Ending Date text boxes are dimmed.
8. Close the form.

   TROUBLE? If you receive the error message "You can't disable a control while it has the focus," be sure that the code to disable the grpJobs, txtJobID, txtStartDate, and txtEndDate controls is in the grpEmployees_AfterUpdate() Sub procedure and not in the grpJobs_AfterUpdate() Sub procedure.

9. Open the **frmReportsSwitchboard** form, and click the **Employee List** option button. All the Job Reports controls are now dimmed.
10. Switch to Design view.

The controls that you have disabled now need to be enabled before the frmReportsSwitchboard form is used again. To do this you will add code that sets the Enabled property for the controls back to true *after* the selected report is previewed.

Rather than typing a line of code for each control, you will use a loop construct to loop through each control except for the label controls in the Controls collection. Label controls do not have an Enabled property, and the code will not execute if a label control is included in the procedure.

Collections

You know that a collection is a group of objects of the same type or class. The Forms collection contains open forms, and the Reports collection contains open reports. Even though forms and reports are similar, they are not the same and you must refer to them in separate collections. Many different collections are available when you are programming in Access, a portion of which are shown in Figure 8-10. Remember that collections can also contain other collections.

Figure 8-10 ACCESS OBJECTS AND COLLECTIONS

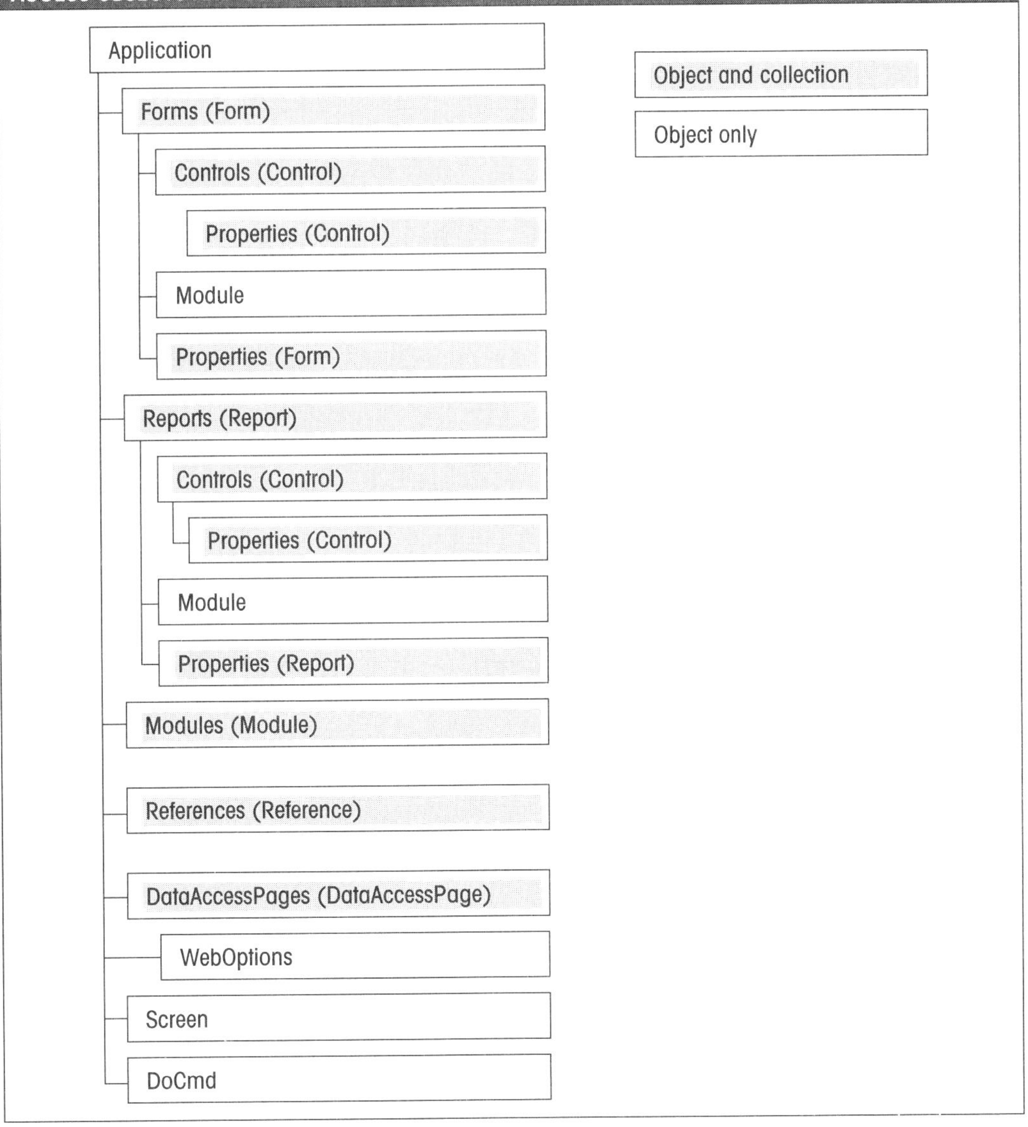

For example, each form object has a Controls collection that contains all of the controls on the form. The name of a collection is often the starting point in the path for a particular object. For example, Forms!frmReportsSwitchboard specifies the frmReportsSwitchboard form that is a part of the Forms collection. More than one correct notation can specify the path to an object or property. Understanding each type of notation makes it easier to understand the syntax that you see in sample code in the VBA Help system, and the code that you use in this tutorial.

To see a full list of Access objects and collections, open Microsoft Visual Basic Help from within the Visual Basic window, type "Microsoft Access Objects" in the Answer Wizard text box, and then click the Search button to display the Microsoft Access Objects topic in the Help window.

Dot vs. Bang Notation

Dot notation uses the dot (.) operator to indicate that what follows is an item defined by Access. For example, the properties of an object are items defined by Access. In the step exercise where you referred to the Enabled property by typing "grpEmployees.Enabled," you used dot notation to refer to properties.

Dot notation also is used to indicate the sequence of steps that you take to specify a particular object. Consider, for example, the steps required to change the Enabled property of the grpEmployees control on the frmReportsSwitchboard form to false. First you open the frmReportsSwitchboard form in Design view, and then you click the grpEmployees option group, display the properties dialog box for that control, find the Enabled property, and, finally, change the property to false. Dot notation enables you to simply provide a path to a particular property. Using dot notation, the preceding example looks like the following:

```
Forms("frmReportsSwitchboard").Controls("grpEmployees").
Enabled
```

As you can see, dot notation can result in long paths. The collection is specified, then the specific item in the collection, then the next collection, and then the specific item in it, and so on. Default collections and properties reduce the size of dot notation. For example, Controls is the default collection of a form, so the word Controls does not need to appear in the path. Therefore, the following statement has the same meaning as the previous one:

```
Forms("frmReportsSwitchboard")("grpEmployees").Enabled
```

You can use **bang notation**, which uses the bang operator (!), in place of dot notation when the collection referenced by an object is the default collection. Therefore, the following statement is the same as the previous two examples:

```
Forms![frmReportsSwitchboard]![grpEmployees].Enabled
```

Note that the brackets do not need to be typed as long as there are no spaces in the object names. You can see why developers are encouraged to use bang notation over dot notation. It is much shorter. In addition, you can use keywords and special objects to make the path shorter still.

Me Keyword

In a VBA class module, the Me keyword can be used to refer to the associated form or report in which the class module is located. "Me" always refers to the object that is running the code. For example, using the Me keyword in the frmReportsSwitchboard form refers to this form even if other forms are currently open or have the focus. Using the Me keyword, you could shorten the example used in the preceding section to the following:

```
Me!grpEmployees.Enabled
```

CodeContextObject Property

The CodeContextObject property determines the object in which a macro or VBA code is executing. When you converted a macro to VBA code in Tutorial 5, the CodeContextObject property was used in the resulting procedure. The CodeContextObject is mentioned again here because it has the same functionality as the Me keyword, except that it can be used in a class module or a standard module. Functions using the CodeContextObject can be called from an event property in either a form or report. In this instance, the name of the form or report calling the procedure containing CodeContextObject will be substituted for CodeContextObject. The Me keyword can only be used in a class module in which it substitutes for the name of the form or report that contains the class module. The CodeContextObject property can be used in standard modules, but the Me keyword cannot.

The Screen Object

The **Screen object** is the particular form, report, or control that currently has the focus. The Screen.ActiveForm and Screen.ActiveReport objects refer to the form or report that currently has the focus. The Screen.ActiveControl object refers to the control that currently has the focus. The Screen objects can be used only when a form or report is active or an error will result.

For example, the following statement refers to the switchboard form in the database that has the focus, and changes the form's Caption property to Current Switchboard:

```
Screen.ActiveForm.Caption = Current Switchboard
```

Controls Collection

You can refer to a control on a form either by implicitly or explicitly referring to the **Controls collection**. It is faster to refer to a control implicitly, as demonstrated in the following examples (these two examples also use the dot and bang notation discussed earlier):

```
Me!grpEmployees
Me("grpEmployees")
```

You also can refer to a control by its position in the collection index. The **collection index** is a range of numbers that begin with a zero, and in turn represent each object in the collection. Most indexes are zero based, meaning they begin counting with a zero. Recall that the Column property of combo boxes discussed in earlier tutorials was zero based. The following example refers to the control by its position in the collection index:

```
Me(0)
```

To refer to the same control explicitly, use any of the following three examples:

```
Me.Controls!grpEmployees
Me.Controls("grpEmployees")
Me.Controls(0)
```

You can only use the Me keyword in a form or report class module to refer to the current form (the form that has the current focus). In other words, when you are writing code within the form module of a form, you can use the Me keyword in place of the form's name when referring to one of the controls contained on that form. The same is true within a report module. If you refer to a form or report from a standard module, or from a different form's or report's module, you must use the full reference to the form or report.

You will use the Controls collection of the frmReportsSwitchboard form and set the Enabled property for all the controls (except for the label controls) in the collection to true.

You will use the For Each...Next loop construct to do this. To test the form controls to determine if they are not labels, you will use the If...Then decision construct and include the Type Of expression. You also will need to declare an object variable in your code to represent the controls in the Controls collection. Object variables are discussed next.

Object Variables

You use **object variables** when you want to declare variables in your procedures to use in place of object names. For example, to refer to the frmReportsSwitchboard form, you could declare a variable as follows:

```
Dim frmMyForm As Form_frmReportsSwitchboard
```

You must precede the name of the form or report with Form_ or Report_ when you define the object variable, because forms and reports share the same namespace. For example, the name "Customers" could be used for both a form and a report in a database that does not follow the naming conventions used in this tutorial.

Another way to declare an object variable and to assign a particular object to it is to declare the variable, and then use the Set statement to initialize it as illustrated in the following example:

```
Dim frmMyForm As Form
Set frmMyForm = frmReportsSwitchboard
```

You can then use the frmMyForm object variable to manipulate the frmReportsSwitchboard form properties and methods.

Object variables do, however, use memory and associated resources. Setting an object variable equal to Nothing discontinues the association and frees these resources. In addition, setting an object variable to Nothing when you finish using it prevents you from accidentally changing the object by changing the variable. To set the object variable referred to in the preceding example to Nothing, simply include the following:

```
Set frmMyForm = Nothing
```

Now you are ready to write the code to set the Enabled property to true for the controls on the form.

To set the Enabled property to true for controls on the form:

1. Click the **Code** button on the toolbar.
2. Position the insertion point at the end of the Dim strSQL As String in the cmdPreview_Click() Sub procedure, and then press the **Enter** key.
3. Type **Dim ctl As Control** to declare the variable ctl an object variable. See Figure 8-11.

Figure 8-11 **DECLARING THE OBJECT VARIABLE**

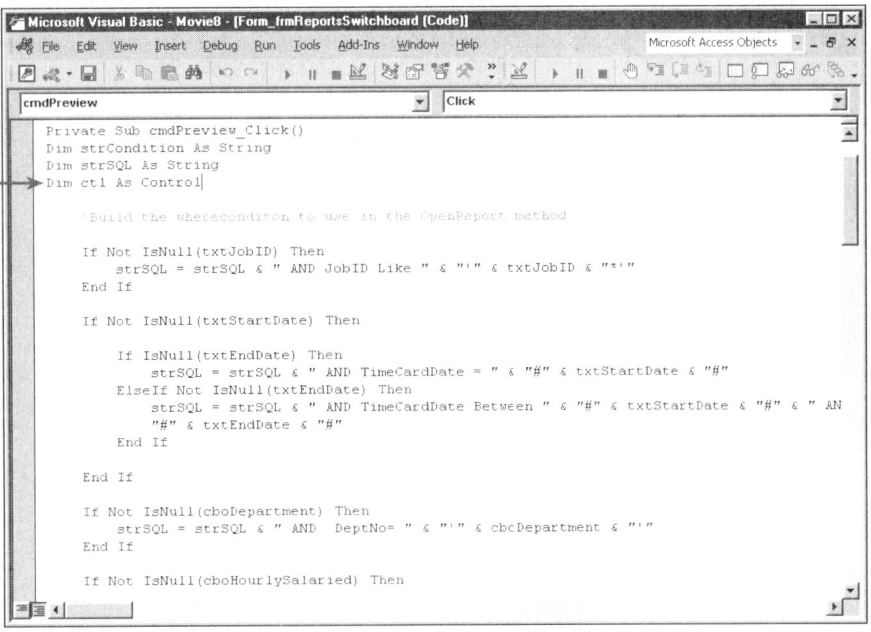

4. Scroll down, position the insertion point at the end of the txtEndDate = Null line, and then press the **Enter** key twice.

5. Type the following comment and statements, indenting and spacing as shown in Figure 8-12.

```
'Enable all of the controls except labels
For Each ctl In Me.Controls
If Not TypeOf ctl Is Label Then
ctl.Enabled = True
End If
Next ctl
```

Figure 8-12 ADDING CODE TO ENABLE ALL THE CONTROLS

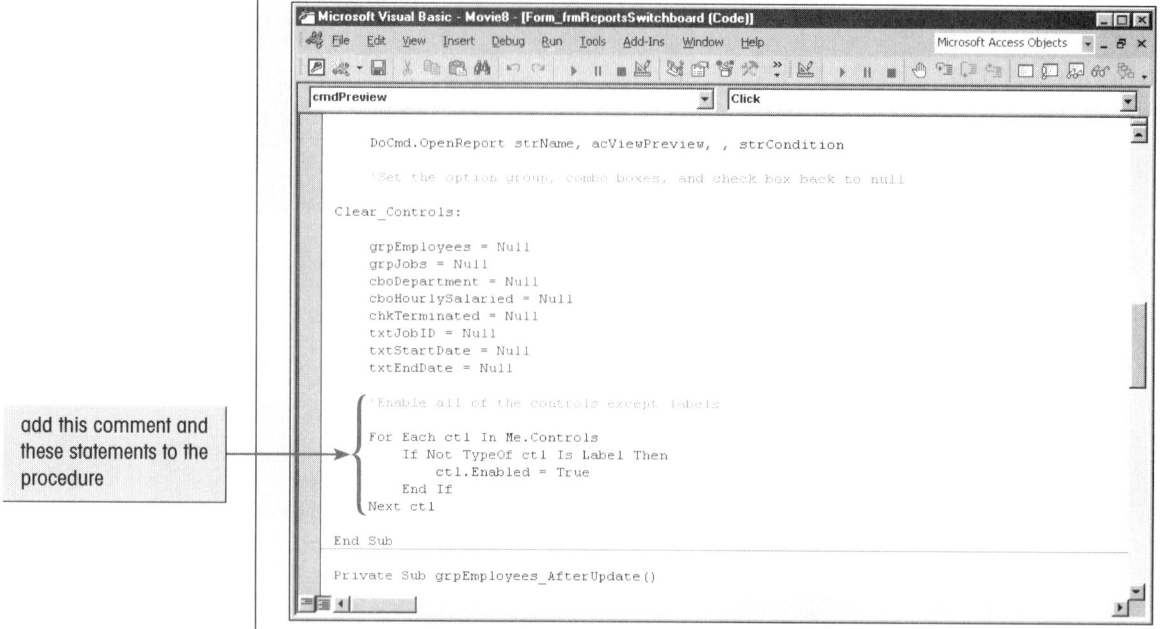

6. Save the changes and then close the Visual Basic window.
7. Switch to Form view, and test the form by clicking the **Job List** option button. The Employee Reports options and the Beginning and Ending Dates text boxes are now dimmed, as shown in Figure 8-13.

Figure 8-13 SETTING THE ENABLED PROPERTY

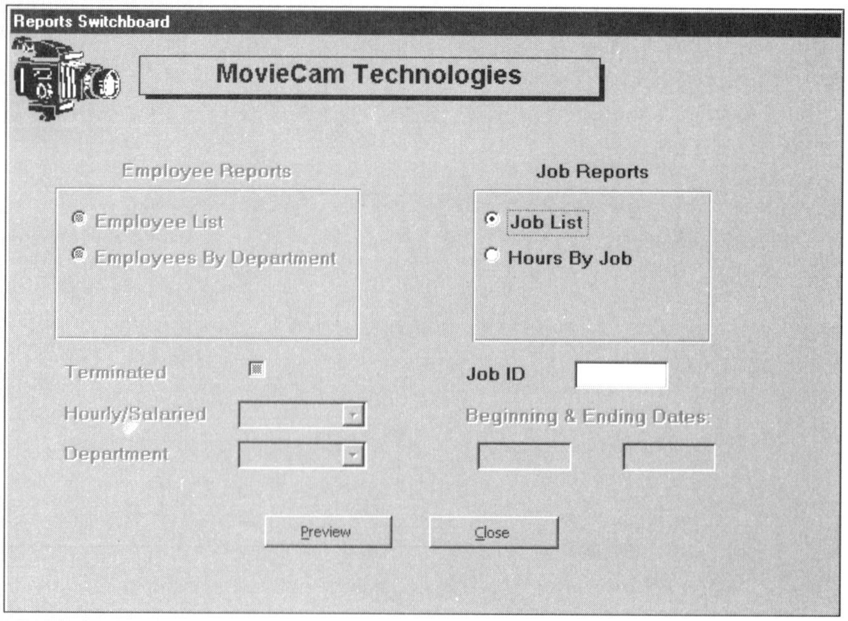

8. Click the **Preview** button and then close the report. The controls are now enabled.
9. Switch to Design view.

You have completed the necessary coding to prevent one type of user error. Next you need to address the problem that occurs when the user does not select a report from one of the option groups. You will review error types and error handling in the following session.

Session 8.1 Quick Check

1. What is a control structure in VBA?
2. The ______________ is used to repeat statements in your procedure until a specified condition is true.
3. The ______________ executes statements a specified number of times.
4. How does the Visible property differ from the Enabled property?
5. Which type of control does not have an Enabled property?
6. The ______________ operator indicates that what follows is an item defined by Access.
7. Which notation—dot or bang—results in a shorter path to an object or property?
8. What is the Me keyword used for?
9. What advantage does CodeContextObject have over the Me keyword?
10. What is the Screen object?

SESSION 8.2

In this session, you will learn about the different types of errors that can occur in Access and VBA. You will write error-trapping code for a VBA run-time error, and learn how to identify an Access run-time error and write code to handle it. You also will learn about the Event and NotInList properties and how they can be used to trap Access errors. You will create a combo box and write code to synchronize records on a form to the record chosen in the combo box. You will learn about ActiveX controls and create a form that incorporates the Calendar control.

Syntax Errors

Syntax errors occur when you violate the VBA syntax rules. For example, a syntax error occurs if you misspell a keyword such as MsgBox, forget the End Select statement in a Select...Case decision structure, or omit necessary punctuation, such as a required comma in a DoCmd.OpenReport statement.

Syntax errors are detected either as you write code in the VBE (Visual Basic Editor), or immediately before the code is run. All syntax errors must be corrected before the procedure can be executed. To be sure that VBA is checking for syntax errors, click Tools on the menu bar in the Visual Basic window, click Options, and make sure that the Auto Syntax Check option on the Editor tab is selected.

Run-Time Errors

Run-time errors occur while the application is running. A run-time error also occurs if the user attempts an operation that the system cannot perform. For example, you might write code that opens a particular report, and then later you change the name of that report. If you do not change the report's name in your coding procedures, a run-time error will occur when the user tries to run the code.

When Access encounters a run-time error during program execution, it selects the line of code that caused the error and prompts you with an error message dialog box. For example, you would receive the error message shown in Figure 8-14 if you renamed the rptEmployeesList report to rptEmployeesLst and then attempted to open the report from the frmReportsSwitchboard form.

Figure 8-14 RUN-TIME ERROR

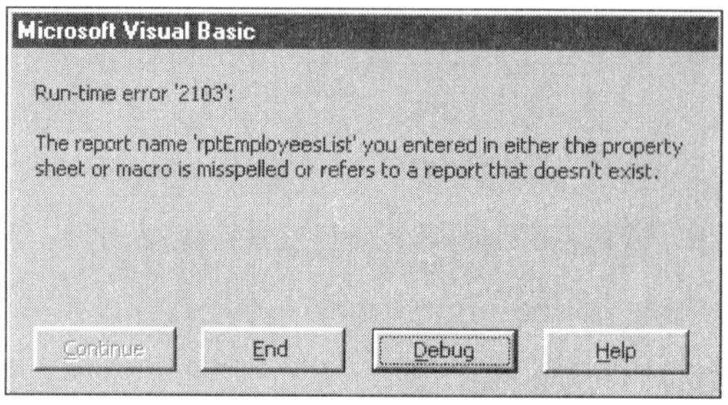

Clicking the Debug button in the error message dialog box opens the Visual Basic Editor so that you can attempt to fix the error. Clicking the End button immediately terminates the program, and clicking the Help button opens related Help topics.

Run-time errors are generally more difficult to fix than syntax errors because there can be many sources of these errors and those sources might not always be obvious. For example, an application might run fine under normal circumstances, but when a user enters a particular type of data, an error results. It is usually difficult to anticipate all possible run-time errors.

Logic Errors

Logic errors occur when your procedures execute without failure, but their results are not what you intended. A logic error can occur when code has been assigned to the wrong event procedure, or when the order of operations in a procedure is incorrect.

Recall in Tutorial 7 when you created procedures for the frmReportsSwitchboard form. You moved the statements that set the controls back to null from the grpEmployees_AfterUpdate() procedure to the cmdPreview_Click() procedure. You moved that code so that the controls on the switchboard were set to null *after* the report opened, rather than after the user chose an option from the option group. If you had not moved those statements, a logic error would have occurred. The controls would have been set back to null, and the report would have opened showing all records instead of the records specified by what you entered in the text boxes. Logic errors can be quite difficult to find, but stepping through code (as discussed in Tutorial 7) is a good way to locate them.

Trapping Run-Time Errors

It's a fact in the programming world that errors do occur. So it's important that you protect your programs and data from the effects of those errors. You can accomplish this by the use of error handling, also known as **error trapping**.

By trapping run-time errors, you make your application more tolerant of them. If a run-time error is generated by a VBA procedure, you handle the error by adding error-handling code to the procedure itself. If the run-time error is generated by the interface, the run-time error triggers the Error event for the active form or report. You can handle this error by creating a VBA procedure for the Error event. The NotInList event property of combo boxes on forms also can be used to create an error handler for a specific type of interface error.

Without error handling in place, the user can be forced to abruptly exit the application, often without knowing why. However, applications that trap run-time errors can handle common user errors without stopping the application. The better you are at anticipating common errors and protecting against them, the less likely that your application will fail.

VBA Errors

To write an error-handling routine to trap the run-time error that occurs when no report is chosen from the option group, you need to learn about the On Error statement, the Err object and its properties, and the Resume statement.

The On Error Statement

You can enable error handling in a procedure by using the On Error statement. When VBA encounters a run-time error, it searches for an On Error statement that indicates there is an error-handling routine included in the procedure. If VBA finds an **On Error statement**, the error is handled, and execution of the procedure resumes either at the statement that caused the error or at a different statement, depending on how the error handler is enabled. If VBA cannot find an On Error statement, execution halts and a run-time error message is received.

The On Error GoTo statement enables an error-handling routine in the procedure and also specifies the routine's location in the procedure. For example, Access would stop execution when an error occurs and go to the statements labeled TestError, if the following statement were used:

```
On Error GoTo TestError
```

Execution would then resume, based on the Resume statement used.

The Resume Statement

The **Resume statement** resumes execution after an error-handling routine is finished. It can have any of the following forms:

- *Resume*: If the error occurred in the same procedure as the error handler, execution resumes with the statement that caused the error. If the error occurred in a called procedure, execution resumes at the statement that last called out of the procedure to the error-handling routine.
- *Resume Next*: If the error occurs in the same procedure as the error handler, execution resumes with the statement that immediately follows the statement that caused the error. If the error occurred in a called procedure, execution resumes with the statement immediately following the statement that last called out of the procedure that contains the error-handling routine, or execution resumes at the On Error Resume Next statement.

- *ResumeLine*: Execution resumes at the line specified in the required line argument. The **line argument** is a line label or line number and must be in the same procedure as the error handler. A **line label** is used to identify a single line of code and can be any combination of characters that starts with a letter and ends with a colon (:). Line labels are not case sensitive and must begin in the first column of the code window. A **line number** is also used to identify a single line of code and can be any combination of digits that is unique within the module where it is used. Line numbers also must begin in the first column of the Code window.

The Err Object

The **Err object** contains information about an error that has just occurred. When a run-time error occurs, the properties of the Err object are filled with information that both uniquely identifies the error and that can be used to handle it. The properties of the Err object are reset to zero or a zero-length string after the Exit Sub or Exit Function statement executes in an error-handling routine. The properties of the Err object are as follows:

- *Err.Number*: The number property is an integer value that specifies the last error that occurred. You can use this property in error-handling code to determine which error has occurred. Each error has a unique number; by default the error's (Err's) number property is set to zero to indicate that no error has occurred.
- *Err.Description*: This property is a string that contains a description of the error. The Description property contains the Access error message. Once an error is trapped, you can replace this message with a custom message that is more user-friendly.
- *Err.Source*: The source property contains the name of the object application that generated the error. For example, if you open Excel from Access and Excel generates the error, Excel sets the Err.Source property to Excel Application.
- *Err.HelpFile*: You can use this property to specify a path and filename to a VBA Help file. The HelpFile property is useful for displaying information about a particular error. That information is more user-friendly and more complete than just the description. By default, the HelpFile property displays more information about a particular error by returning the default Help file that Access uses.
- *Err.HelpContext*: This property is used to specify the Help topic that is identified by the path in the HelpFile argument. The HelpContext property must be used in conjunction with the HelpFile property before a particular Help topic can be shown. By default, the HelpContext property offers more information on a particular error by returning the default Help file that Access uses.
- *Err.LastDLLError*: This property contains the system error code for the success or failure of the last call to a dynamic link library. A **dynamic link library (DLL)** is a file containing a collection of Windows functions designed to perform a specific class of operations. Most DLLs have a .dll extension, but some use the .exe extension. Functions within DLLs are called by applications as needed to perform specific operations.

Using objects and statements, you can build the following error handler to respond to the error that occurs if a report is selected that does not exist in the database:

```
Private Sub grpJobs_AfterUpdate()
  'Set strName equal to report chosen in the option group
On Error GoTo TestError
  Select Case grpJobs
        Case 1
              strName = "rptJobsSummary"
        Case 2
              strName = "rptHoursByJob"
Exit Sub
TestError:
 If Err.Number = 2103 Then
      MsgBox "The report selected does not exist in this
      database"
      Resume Next
      End If
End Sub
```

Error number 2103 is the error that occurs if you attempt to open a report that does not exist in the database. The OnError Goto TestError line tells Access to stop execution and go to the code labeled TestError if an error occurs. The If...Then construct tests the error number, and then returns an appropriate message box. The Resume Next statement causes execution to resume at the Case 2 statement because the report does not exist.

Reserved error numbers range from 0 to 65535. For more information on trappable errors, search for "Trappable Errors" in Microsoft Visual Basic Help, or just search on the word "Error." There are error numbers specific to various components of Access, and sometimes you have to search Help to look up additional information about the error.

Next you will add an error handler to the frmReportsSwitchboard form. The error handler is similar to the one in the preceding example. The error handler that you will add tests for run-time error 2497, which indicates that the action or method requires a Report Name argument.

To add error-handling code to a procedure:

1. If you took a break after the previous session, make sure that Access is running, that the **Movie8** database from the Tutorial.08\Tutorial folder on your local or network drive is open, and that the **frmReportsSwitchboard** form is open in Design view.
2. Click the **Code** button  on the toolbar to open the Visual Basic window.
3. Position the insertion point at the end of the Dim ctl As Control statement, as shown in Figure 8-15, and press the **Enter** key twice.

Figure 8-15 ADDING ERROR-HANDLING CODE TO THE cmdPreview_Click PROCEDURE

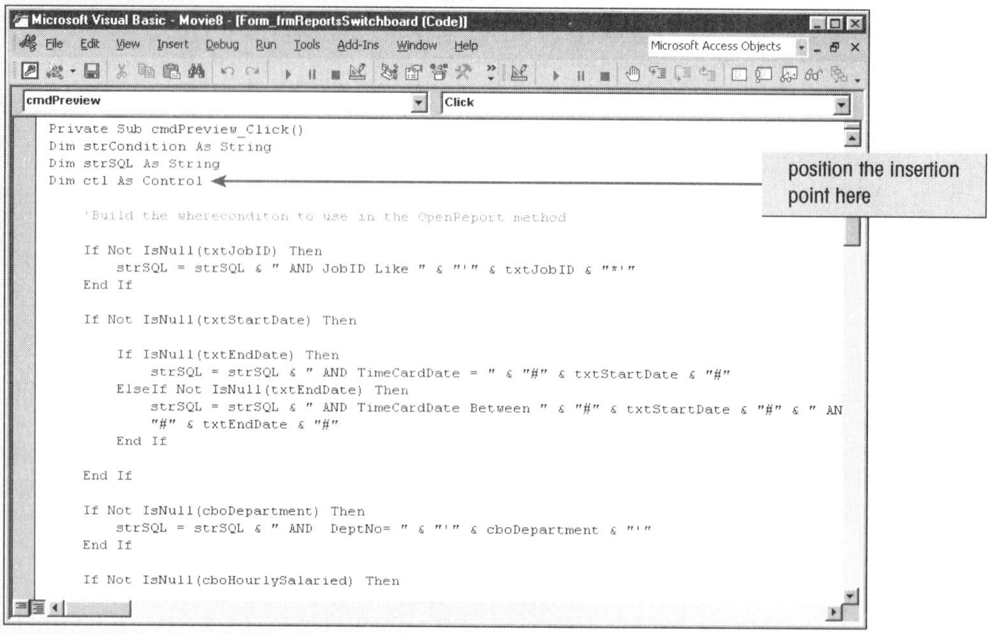

4. Press the **Tab** key to indent, and then type **On Error GoTo PrintError**.
5. Scroll down, position the insertion point at the end of the Next ctl statement, and then press the **Enter** key twice.
6. Type the following comment and code, indenting and spacing as shown in Figure 8-16:

```
PrintError:
If Err.Number = 2497 Then
'No report was selected from the option groups
MsgBox "You must select a report from one of the option
groups"
Resume Next
End If
```

Figure 8-16 **ERROR HANDLER**

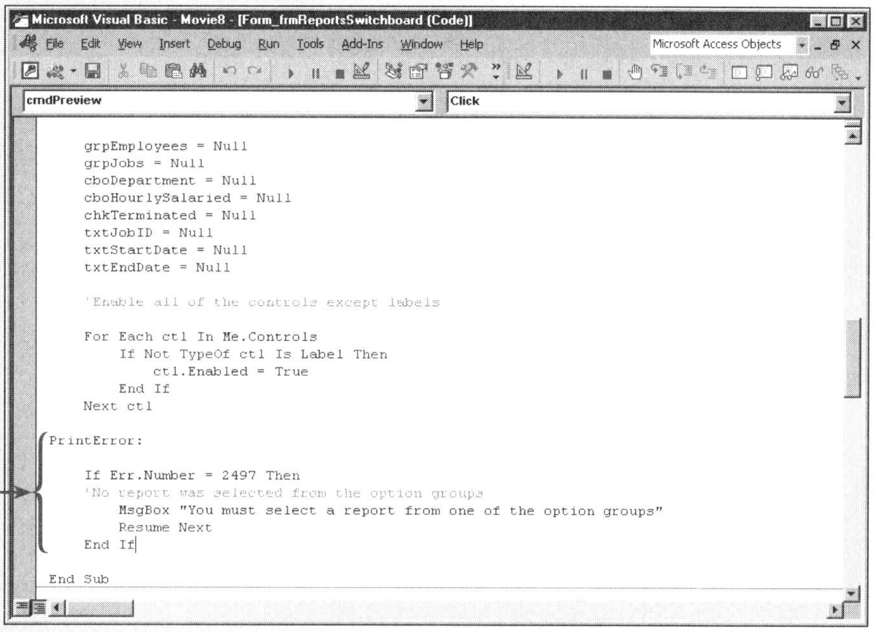

add this comment and these statements to the procedure

7. Click **Debug** on the menu bar, and then click **Compile MovieCam**. If you have any syntax errors, correct them now.
8. Close the Visual Basic window, save the changes, and then close the frmReportsSwitchboard form.
9. Open the **frmReportsSwitchboard** form in Form view, and click the **Preview** button without selecting a report from either option group. You receive your custom error message, as shown in Figure 8-17.

Figure 8-17 **CUSTOM ERROR MESSAGE**

10. Click the **OK** button and then close the form.

Now that you have completed the error handler for the VBA error, you will focus on errors that might occur in the interface.

Access Errors

In the section on error trapping, you learned that Access errors can be handled with the Error event. Remember that Access errors occur in the user interface, as opposed to those that occur in your VBA code.

There is a potential problem with the frmTimeCards form. If the user does not enter a time card number, they receive the Access error message shown in Figure 8-18.

Figure 8-18 ACCESS ERROR MESSAGE

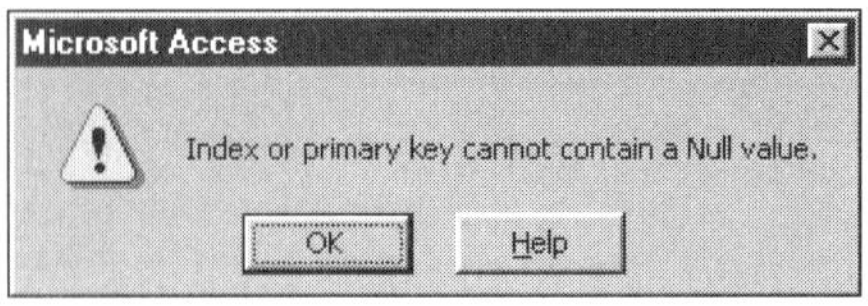

You will use the Error event to trigger error-handling code to deal with it.

Error and Timing Events

Recall that many types of events exist in Access, including the Print events and Data events discussed in earlier tutorials. Error and Timing events are another category of events, and include the following:

- *Error*: This event occurs when an Access run-time error occurs in a form or report. (This does not include run-time errors in VBA.) To run an event procedure when the Error event occurs, set the OnError property to the name of the event procedure.
- *Timer*: This event occurs when a specified time interval passes as specified by the TimeInterval property of the form. To keep data synchronized in a multiuser environment, you use this event to refresh or requery data at specified intervals.

Determining the Error Number

To determine the error number of the Access error shown in Figure 8-18, you will add code to the frmTimeCards form that is triggered by the Error event. The Error event procedure includes several arguments that will help you find out more about the error. The syntax of the Error event procedure is:

```
Private Sub Form_Error(DataErr As Integer, Response As
Integer) OR
Private Sub Report_Error(DataErr As Integer, Response As
Integer)
```

The Error event procedure arguments are:

- *DataErr*: DataErr is the error code returned by the Err object when an error occurs.
- *Response*: Response is the setting that determines whether or not to display an error message. It can be one of the following constants:
  - *acDataErrContinue*: Use this to ignore the error and continue without displaying the default Access error. You can use this setting in conjunction with a custom error message.
  - *acDataErrDisplay*: This is the default setting and specifies that the default Access error message will be shown.

You will use the DataErr argument to determine the code number of the error. You must add code to be triggered by the Error event procedure that in turn instructs Access to display the error number in the Immediate window.

REFERENCE WINDOW RW

Determining the Number of an Access Error

- Use Design view to open the form or report that causes the error.
- Display the property sheet, click the Event tab, click in the On Error text box, and then click the Build button.
- Indent and then type "Debug.Print DataErr" and then press Ctrl + G to open the Immediate window. Minimize the Visual Basic window.
- Execute the action in the form or report that triggers the error, and then maximize the Visual Basic window. The error number is shown in the Immediate window.
- Close the form or report without saving your changes.

After you identify the error number, you can write the code necessary to trap it.

To determine the error number of an Access error:

1. Open the **frmTimeCards** form in Design view, and then click the **Properties** button on the toolbar.
2. Click the **Event** tab if necessary, click in the **On Error** text box, and then click its **Build** button. The Visual Basic window opens.

   TROUBLE? If the Choose Builder dialog box opens, you can click Code Builder in the list box, and then click the OK button to open the Visual Basic window. Or to make sure that the Visual Basic window opens automatically instead of the Choose Builder dialog box when you click the Build button, click the Cancel button in the Choose Builder dialog box to return to Design view, click Tools on the menu bar, click Options, click the Forms/Reports tab, click the Always use event procedures check box to select it, and then click the OK button. Repeat Step 2.

3. Press the **Tab** key, type **Debug.Print DataErr**, and then press **Ctrl + G** to open the Immediate window, as shown in Figure 8-19.

Figure 8-19 DETERMINING THE ERROR NUMBER

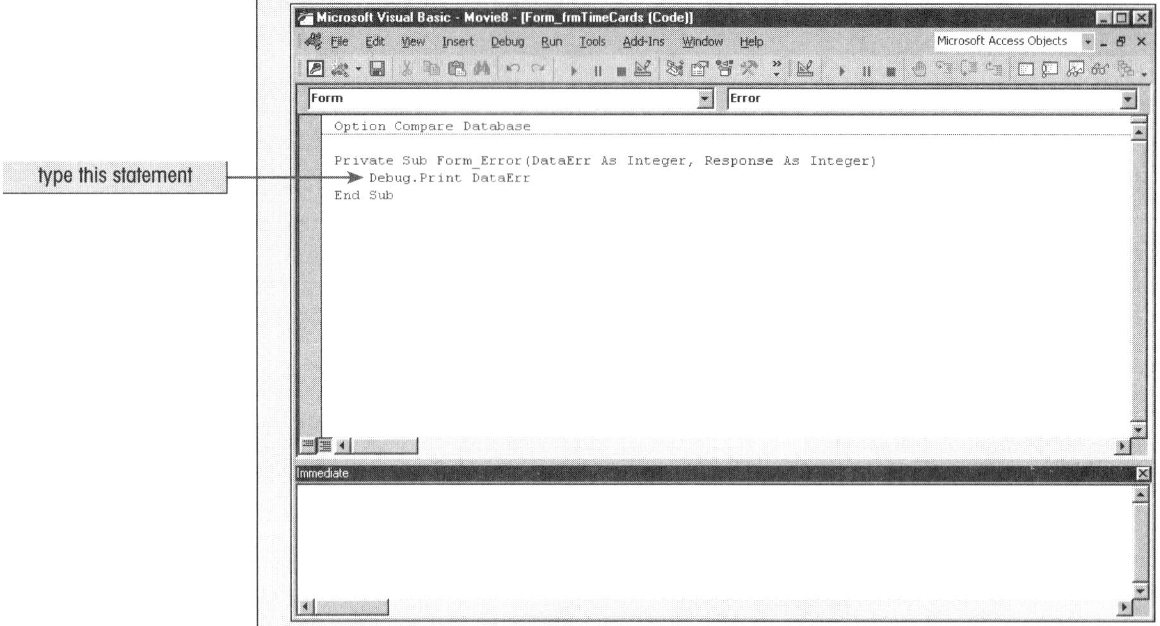

4. Minimize the Visual Basic window, close the property sheet, and then switch to Form view.
5. Click the **New Record** button on the toolbar, press the **Tab** key to go to the Time Card Date field, type **11/9/2004**, and then press the **Tab** key to go to the Employee No field.
6. Type **20** and then press the **Tab** key. The error message "Index or primary key cannot contain a Null value" is displayed (see Figure 8-18).
7. Click the **OK** button, press the **Esc** key to cancel the entry, and then switch to Design view.
8. Redisplay the Visual Basic window by clicking its icon on the taskbar. You see error number 3058 in the Immediate window, as shown in Figure 8-20.

Figure 8-20 **ERROR NUMBER IDENTIFIED IN THE IMMEDIATE WINDOW**

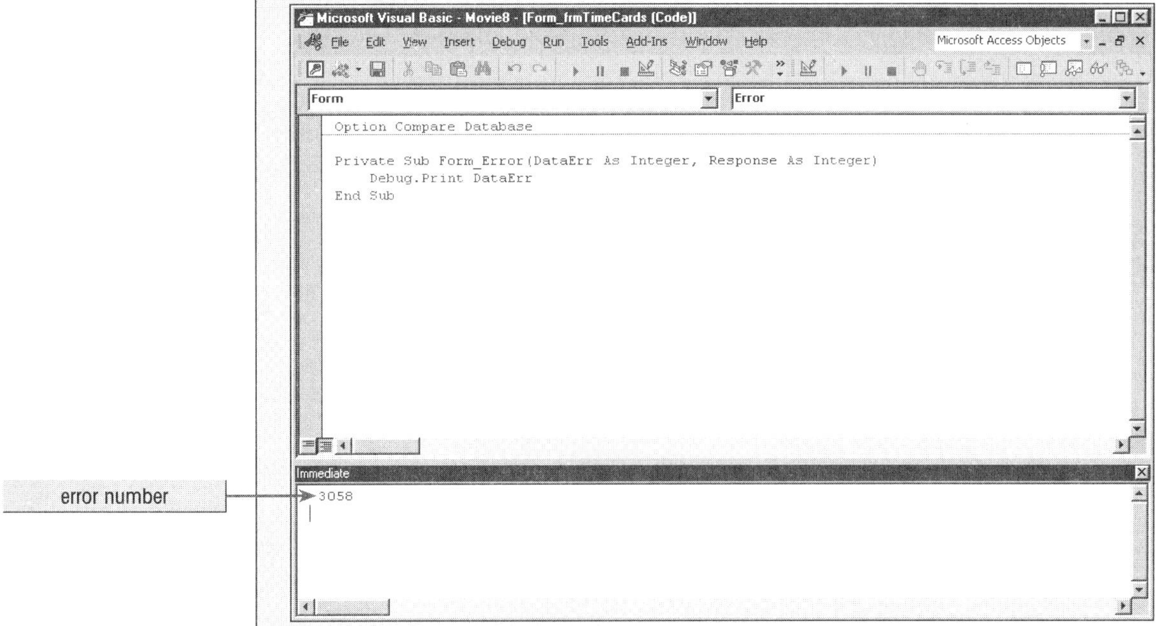

9. Close the Immediate window.

Now you'll delete the statement you used to identify the error and replace it with an error-handling routine. You will use an If...Then...Else construct to test the error number. If the error is 3058, you will display a custom message, position the insertion point in the Time Card No text box, and suppress the default error message. If the error is other than error 3058, you will display the default Access error message.

To write an error handler for error 3058:

1. Delete the **Debug.Print DataErr** statement from the Form_Error(DataErr As Integer, Response As Integer) event procedure.
2. Type the following comment and code, spacing and indenting as shown in Figure 8-21.

```
'Display a custom error message for missing TimeCardNo
If DataErr = 3058 Then
MsgBox "You must type a Time Card No to continue"
Response = acDataErrContinue
DoCmd.GoToControl "TimeCardID"
Else
Response = acDataErrDisplay
End If
```

Figure 8-21 **ERROR-HANDLING CODE FOR MISSING TIME CARD NUMBER**

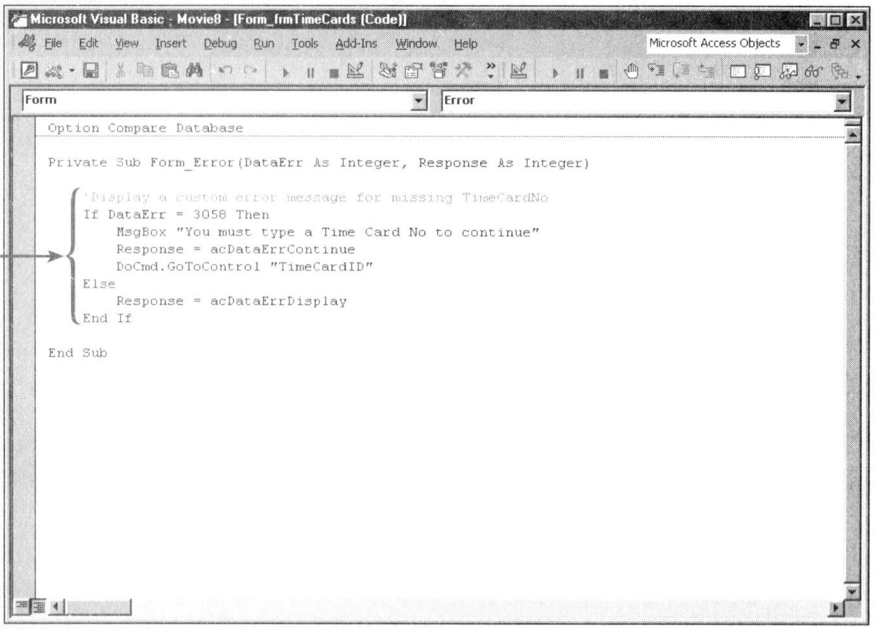

error-trapping procedure

3. Close the Visual Basic window, and then switch to Form view.
4. Click the **New Record** button on the toolbar, press the **Tab** key to go to the Time Card Date field, type **11/9/2004**, and then press the **Tab** key to go to the Employee No field.
5. Type **20** and then press the **Tab** key. You see the custom error message shown in Figure 8-22.

Figure 8-22 **CUSTOM ERROR MESSAGE**

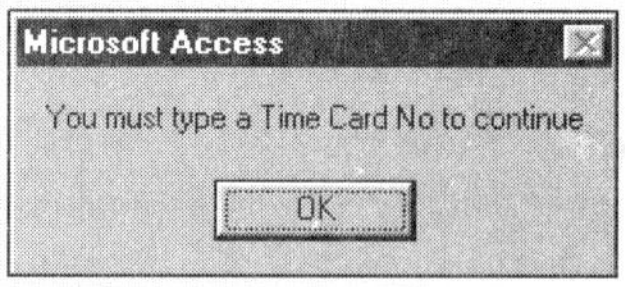

6. Click the **OK** button. The insertion point is automatically positioned in the Time Card No text box.
7. Press the **Esc** key to cancel your changes, and then click the **Save** button on the toolbar.
8. Switch to Design view.

You have completed the code for the error that occurs if a user does not enter a time card number. Now you will work on the other changes that Martin Woodward requested for the frmTimeCards form.

Combo Box Programming

Martin asked you to modify the frmTimeCards form so that a record can be "looked up" by the TimeCardNo field. He wants to be able to type a time card number in a text box or select a time card number from a list and then be able to go directly to that record. You will include a combo box on the frmTimeCards form to accomplish this.

To create the combo box:

1. Make sure that the toolbox is visible and that the **Control Wizards** button is not selected.
2. Click the **Combo Box** button on the toolbox, and then click in the Form Header section above the Time Card Date label to insert the combo box.
3. Click the label control to select it, click the **Properties** button on the toolbar, click the **All** tab, change the Name property to **lblLookup**, the Caption property to **Lookup**, and the Fore Color property to **255** (red), as shown in Figure 8-23.

Figure 8-23 lblLookup PROPERTIES

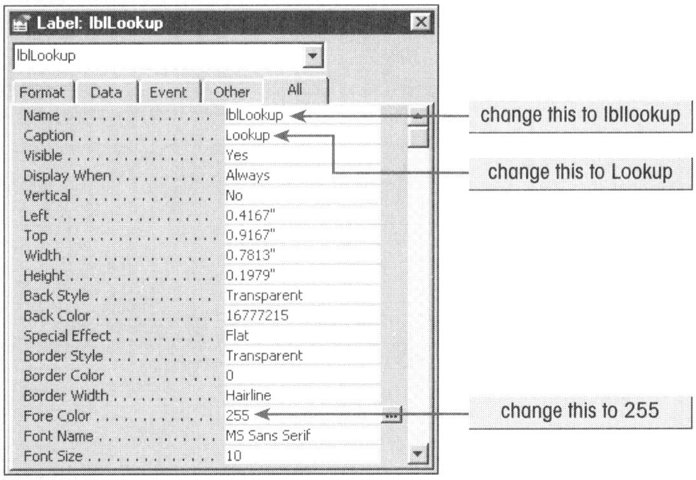

4. Click the combo box control to display its properties, change the Name property to **cboLookup**, click in the **Row Source** text box, and then click its **Build** button. The Query Builder window and the Show Table dialog box appear.
5. Add the **tblEmployees** and **tblTimeCards** tables to the Query Builder window, and close the Show Table dialog box. The Query Builder window should look like that shown in Figure 8-24.

Figure 8-24 QUERY BUILDER WINDOW

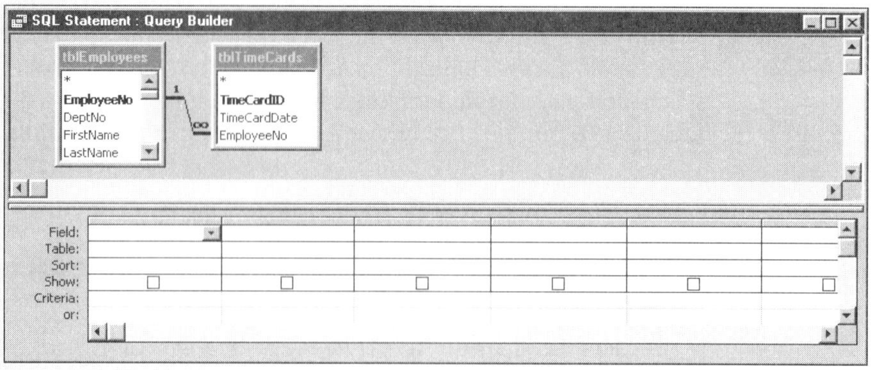

6. Add the **TimeCardID** field from the tblTimeCards table and the **LastName** field in the tblEmployees table to the design grid as shown in Figure 8-25.

Figure 8-25 ADDING FIELDS TO THE QUERY GRID

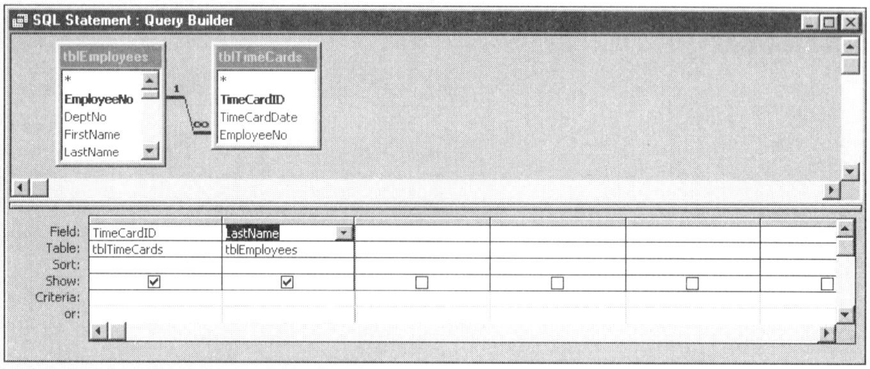

7. Close the Query Builder window, and then save your changes.
8. Change the Column Count property to **2**, the Column Widths property to **0.5";0.5"**, and the Limit To List property to **Yes**, and then close the property sheet.
9. Reposition the label and the combo box so that they do not overlap, and resize the combo box to approximately 2" wide.
10. Switch to Form view and click the list arrow for the **Lookup** combo box. The values for the TimeCardNo and LastName fields should be visible.

    TROUBLE? If either of the fields is not completely visible, return to Design view and widen the combo box.

11. Switch to Design view and click the **Save** button on the toolbar.

Now you will add the Sub procedure to synchronize the record on the form to the one the user chooses from the combo box. The procedure you will write is shown in Figure 8-26.

Figure 8-26 cboLookup_AfterUpdate() PROCEDURE

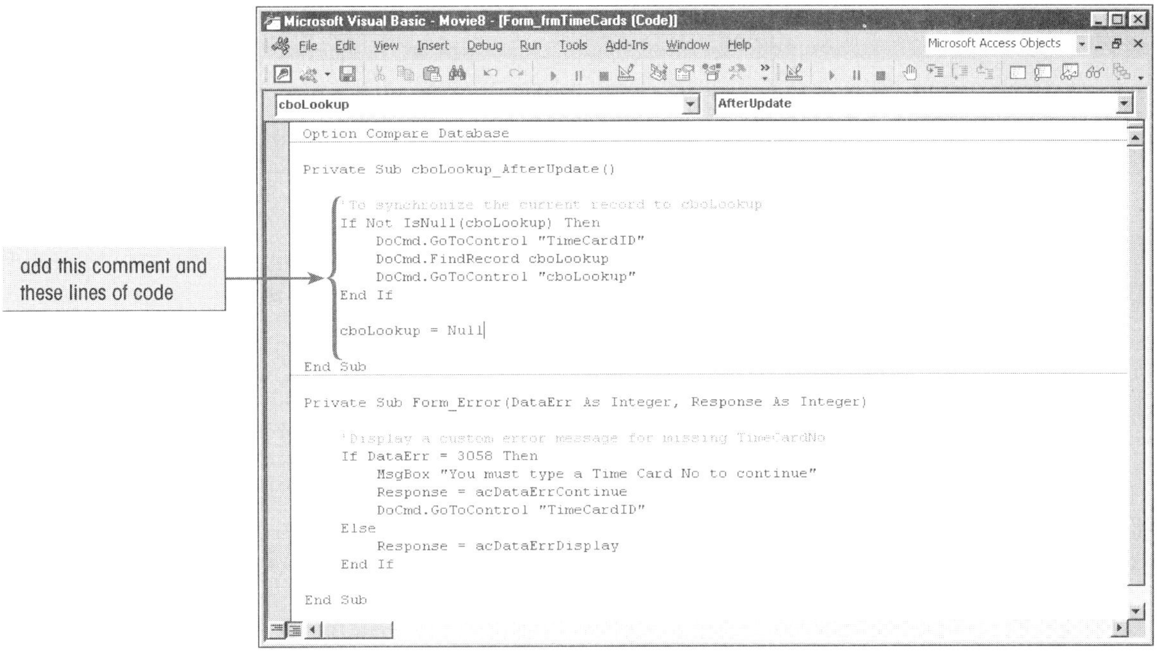

The Sub procedure tests whether there is a value in the combo box. If there is, the Sub procedure moves the focus to the TimeCardID control. Next the FindRecord method looks up the contents of the cboLookup combo box in the TimeCardID field, and finally returns the focus to the combo box with another DoCmd.GoToControl statement.

The code uses two methods of the DoCmd object: DoCmd.GoToControl and DoCmd.FindRecord. These are discussed next.

DoCmd.GoToControl

You can use the GoToControl method to move the focus to a specified field or control in the current record of the open form or table. You can use this method when you want the field or control to have the focus for comparison purposes or to use the FindRecord method. You also can use this method to navigate in a form according to certain conditions. The syntax of this method is:

```
DoCmd.GoToControl(ControlName)
```

Its single argument is ControlName, which is a string expression that is the name of a control or field on the active form or table.

DoCmd.FindRecord

You can use the FindRecord method to find the first instance of data that meets the criteria you specify in the FindRecord arguments. This method also can be used to find records in a form or table. The syntax of this method is:

```
DoCmd.FindRecord(FindWhat, Match, MatchCase, Search,
SearchAsFormatted, OnlyCurrentField, FindFirst)
```

The DoCmd.Find Record arguments are:

- *FindWhat*: This argument is required and is the data for which you are searching. It can be an expression that evaluates to text, a number, or a date.
- *Match*: Use acAnywhere to specify that you are searching for data contained in any part of the field. Use acEntire (the default) to specify that you are searching for data that fills the entire field. Or use acStart to specify that you are searching for data located at the beginning of the field. The Match argument is not required.
- *MatchCase*: Use this argument to specify whether or not the search is case sensitive. Use true (-1) for a case-sensitive search, and false (0) for a search that's not case sensitive. This argument is not required and the default is false.
- *Search*: Use this argument to specify the direction of the search. Use acUp to specify that the search starts at the current record and goes back to the beginning of the records. Use acDown to start at the current record and search down to the end of the records. Or use acSearchAll to search all of the records. This argument is not required and the default is acSearchAll.
- *SearchAsFormatted*: Use true in this argument to search for data as it is formatted, and false to search for data as it is stored in the database. This argument is not required and the default is false.
- *OnlyCurrentField*: Use acAll to specify that the search include all the fields, or use acCurrent to specify that the search is confined to the current field. The current field search is faster and is the default. This argument is not required.
- *FindFirst*: True specifies that the search should start at the first record, and false specifies that the search should start at the record that follows the current record. The default is true and this argument is not required.

Next you will add the code to the form and test it to be sure it works properly.

To add a Sub procedure to the frmTimeCards form:

1. If necessary, click the **cboLookup** combo box to select it, and then click the **Properties** button on the toolbar.
2. Click the **Event** tab, click in the **After Update** text box, and then click its **Build** button. The insertion point is positioned between the stub.
3. Type the following comment and code, indenting and spacing as shown in Figure 8-26:

```
'To synchronize the current record to cboLookup
If Not IsNull(cboLookup) Then
DoCmd.GoToControl "TimeCardID"
DoCmd.FindRecord cboLookup
DoCmd.GoToControl "cboLookup"
End If
cboLookup = Null
```

4. Click **Debug** on the menu bar, click **Compile MovieCam**, close the Visual Basic window, close the property sheet, and then switch to Form view.
5. To test the Lookup combo box, click its **list arrow**, and then click **11**. The record for time card number 11 is shown.

6. Type **125** in the text box portion of the Lookup combo box, and then press the **Enter** key. The record for time card number 125 is shown.
7. Type **500** in the Lookup text box, and then press the **Enter** key. Because there is no such time card number, you receive the error message shown in Figure 8-27.

Figure 8-27 ACCESS ERROR MESSAGE

8. Click the **OK** button to close the error message and return to the form, and then press the **Esc** key until the entry is cancelled (at least twice).

The error message shown in Figure 8-27 is an Access error rather than a VBA run-time error. An Access error occurs when the LimitToList property is set to Yes and a user chooses a value that does not exist. You will use a special event procedure to handle this error.

NotInList Event Procedure

Although the Error event helps you respond to many errors, the NotInList event can be used to trigger code to respond to the specific error shown in Figure 8-27. The NotInList event applies only to controls on a form and does not trigger the Error event. This is important for you to understand because you used code in the Error event procedure in this form, and that code shows the default Access error message if the error is *not* number 3058.

The NotInList event property has the following syntax:

```
Private Sub ControlName_NotInList(NewData As String, Response
As Integer)
```

The arguments are:

- *ControlName*: The name of the control whose NotInList event procedure you want to run.
- *NewData*: A string that Access uses to pass the text the user entered in the text box portion of the combo box to the event procedure.
- *Response*: This setting indicates how the NotInList event was handled. The Response argument can be one of the following constants:
  - *acDataErrDisplay*: This is the default and displays the default message to the user. You can use this constant when you don't want to allow the user to add a new value to the combo box list.
  - *acDataErrContinue*: This constant specifies that the default error message is not shown. You can use this when you want the user to receive a custom message and you want to skip the default error message.
  - *acDataErrAdded*: This constant specifies that the message is not shown to the user. It enables you to add the entry to the combo box list in the NotInList event procedure.

You will use the acDataErrContinue Response argument to provide your own error message and suppress the default message.

To add the NotInList event procedure to the frmTimeCards form:

1. Switch to Design view, click the combo box if necessary to select it, and then click the **Properties** button on the toolbar.
2. On the Event tab, click in the **On Not in List** text box, and then click its **Build** button.
3. Type the following comment and code, indenting and spacing as shown in Figure 8-28.

```
'Display a custom error message and suppress the
default message
MsgBox "The time card number you entered does not exist.
Press Esc and enter the correct number."
Response = acDataErrContinue
```

Figure 8-28 cboLookup_NotInList PROCEDURE

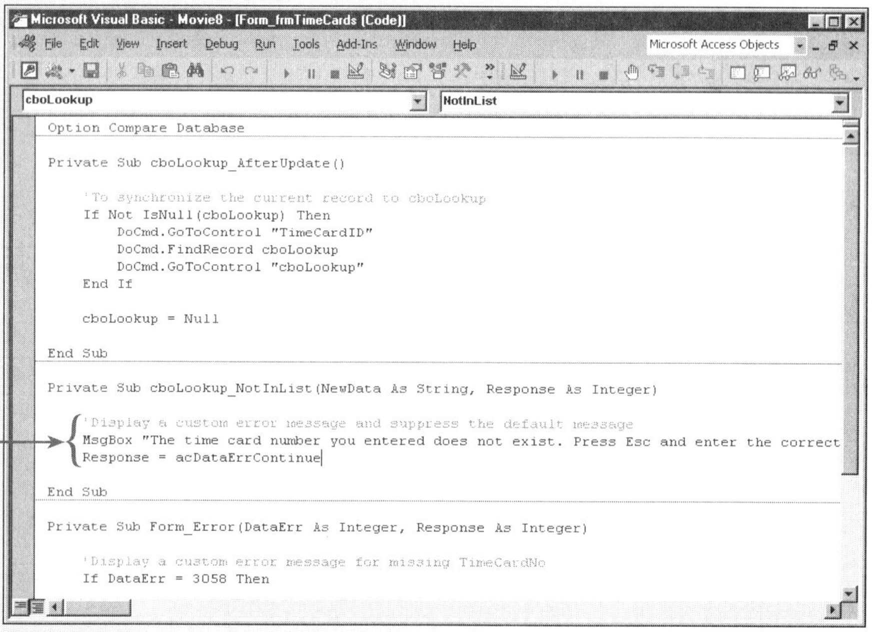

type this procedure

4. Click **Debug** on the menu bar, click **Compile MovieCam**, close the Visual Basic window, close the property sheet, and then switch to Form view.
5. Type **500** in the Lookup text box, and then press the **Enter** key. You will see the custom error message shown in Figure 8-29.

Figure 8-29 CUSTOM ERROR MESSAGE

6. Click the **OK** button, press the **Esc** key twice to cancel the entry, and then close the form and save your changes.

Using this procedure, you are able to display a much more user-friendly and context-specific custom error message rather than just the generic error message provided by Access. This shows that as a developer, you anticipated this error and prepared a helpful response for the user.

The last change that you make to the frmTimeCards form will be to set the Time Card Date text box so that when a user double-clicks it, a calendar menu appears, and the user can click the date. You will use an ActiveX control for this purpose.

ActiveX Controls

In addition to the standard built-in controls in the toolbox, Access supports ActiveX controls. In previous versions of Access these were referred to as OLE (object linking and embedding) controls or custom controls. An **ActiveX control** is similar to a built-in control in that it is an object that you place on a form or report to display data or perform an action. However, unlike a built-in control, the code that supports the ActiveX control is stored in a separate file or files that must be installed for you to be able to use it.

You can install the Calendar ActiveX control when you install Access. There are more than 100 other ActiveX controls available in Microsoft Office 2002, and even more controls are available from third-party vendors.

Other programs, such as Word, Excel, and VBA, support ActiveX technologies. Because each program might support a different set of ActiveX controls, controls that work in some programs might not work in others. If you use a control that hasn't been certified for use in Access, you can receive unpredictable results. If you insert an ActiveX control on an Access form and get the "No Object in this Control" error message, you might have selected a control that is not supported. If you distribute an Access application that uses ActiveX controls, you must make sure that the controls are installed on each computer that runs your application.

ActiveX controls have methods and properties associated with them, just as built-in controls do. You can use these methods and properties to manipulate the control's behavior and appearance. To set the properties for an ActiveX control, display the Access properties dialog box, click in the Custom property text box, and then click the Build button. Custom properties of an ActiveX control also can be manipulated by using VBA the same way you use it to manipulate properties for built-in controls.

Registering an ActiveX Control

The Calendar control is automatically registered with the system when you install the control file. Many ActiveX controls are registered automatically, but some are not. To add a control to a form in Design view, it must be registered.

To determine whether an ActiveX control is registered, open a form in Design view, click Insert on the menu bar, and then click ActiveX Control. If the control you want to use is included in the list, you can add it to a form. If it's not listed, you must register it first. To register an ActiveX control, click Tools on the menu bar, and then click ActiveX Controls. Click the Register button. In the Add ActiveX Control dialog box, navigate to the ActiveX control file, and then click the Open button.

Using the Calendar ActiveX Control

You will use the Access Calendar ActiveX control to build a menu form that can be accessed from any other forms in your application. The calendar form will appear when the user double-clicks a date text box on a form. It will then store the date that the user double-clicks on the calendar control in the text box on the form.

REFERENCE WINDOW RW

Adding an ActiveX Control to a Form

- Use Design view to open the form on which you want to add the control.
- Make sure that the toolbox is visible.
- Click the More Controls button on the toolbox, and then scroll to the ActiveX control you want to add.
- Click the ActiveX control, and then click and drag on the form to draw the control.

Your first step will be to create the calendar form.

To create the frmCalendar form:

1. Create a new unbound form in Design view.
2. If necessary, click **View** on the menu bar, and then click **Form Header/Footer** to eliminate them from the form.
3. Size the form so that it is 2" wide by 1 1/2" tall, as shown in Figure 8-30.

Figure 8-30 SIZING THE frmCalendar FORM

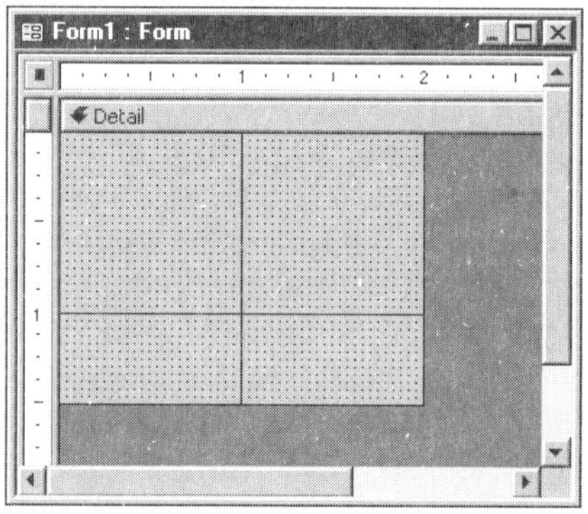

4. Click the **Properties** button on the toolbar to display the form's properties, click the **All** tab, and then change Caption property to **Calendar**, the Navigation Buttons property to **No**, the Pop Up property to **Yes**, the Border Style property to **Dialog**, the Control Box property to **No**, the Min Max Buttons property to **None**, and the Close Button property to **No**. See Figure 8-31. You are setting the Pop Up property to Yes so the form remains on top of any other open forms.

Figure 8-31 CHANGING THE frmCalendar FORM PROPERTIES

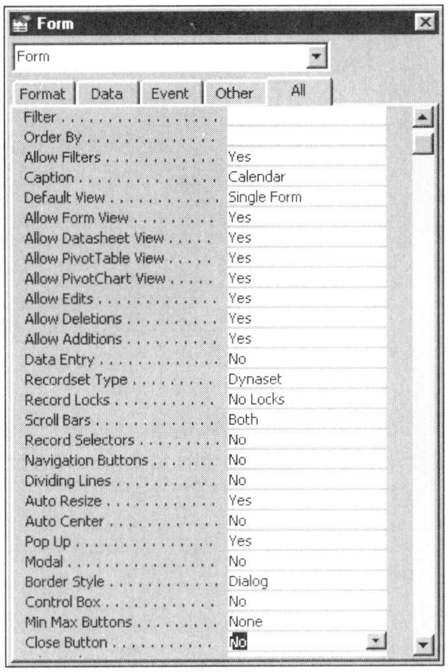

5. Close the property sheet, make sure the toolbox is visible, and then click the **More Controls** button on the toolbox. A menu of ActiveX controls appears.

6. Click **Calendar Control 10.0** in the list, and then click and drag to draw a calendar that fits on the form.

7. Right-click the **calendar control**, point to **Calendar Object**, and then click **Properties**. The Calendar Properties dialog box opens, as shown in Figure 8-32.

Figure 8-32 CALENDAR PROPERTIES DIALOG BOX

the date on your screen will differ

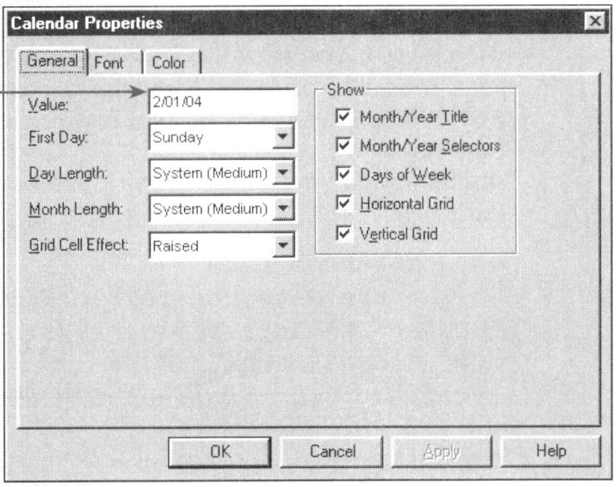

8. Clear the **Month/Year Title** check box so there is more room on the calendar, and then click the **OK** button. The form should look like that shown in Figure 8-33.

Figure 8-33 CALENDAR FORM

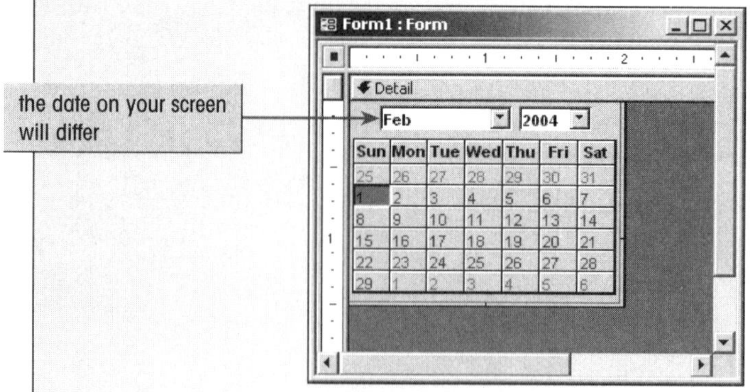

9. Click [icon] on the toolbar to display the property sheet for the calendar control, and then change the Name property to **actlCalendar**. The "actl" prefix is for ActiveX control.

10. Click the **Save** button [icon] on the toolbar, type **frmCalendar**, and then click the **OK** button.

Next you will add a Sub procedure to the DblClick event of the calendar control on the frmCalendar form. The procedure will store the value of the calendar in a dtmDate variable and then close the frmCalendar form. It will then set the active control on the form that opened the frmCalendar form so the control is equal to the value of the dtmDate variable.

To add the Sub procedure to the frmCalendar form:

1. Click the **Code** button [icon] on the toolbar to open the Visual Basic window.

2. Select **actlCalendar** from the Object list, and then select **DblClick** from the Procedure list.

   TROUBLE? If a Private Sub named actlCalendar_Updated(Code As Integer) was created when you selected the actlCalendar option in the Object list, simply delete the Sub procedure. If you need to delete the Sub procedure, make sure you reposition the insertion point in the actlCalendar_DblClick() Sub procedure.

3. Type the following comment and code, spacing and indenting as shown in Figure 8-34.

```
Dim dtmDate As Date
'To set the date control to date selected on the calendar
dtmDate = Me.ActiveControl.Value
DoCmd.Close acForm, Me.Name
Screen.ActiveControl.Value = dtmDate
```

Figure 8-34 **actlCalendar_DblClick() SUB PROCEDURE**

type this Sub procedure

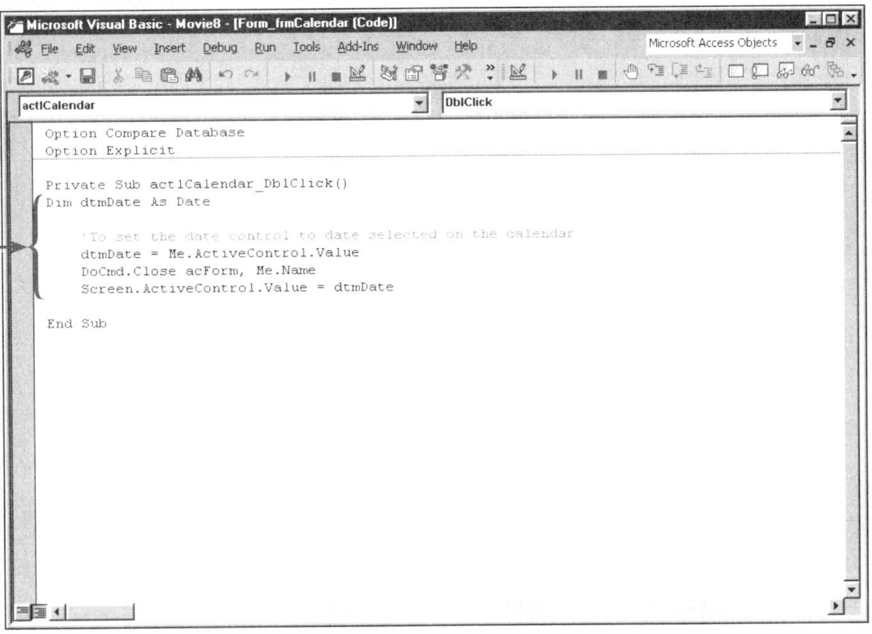

4. Click **Debug** on the menu bar, and then click **Compile MovieCam**.
5. Save the changes and then close the Visual Basic window.
6. Close the property sheet and the form.

Now that the frmCalendar form is created, you can open it from any other form in the database by adding a Sub procedure to that form. You will do this next in the frmTimeCards form. You want the user to be able to double-click the Time Card Date field and have the frmCalendar form open.

To add code to open the frmCalendar form in the frmTimeCards form:

1. Open the **frmTimeCards** form in Design view, and click the **TimeCardDate** text box control.
2. Click the **Properties** button on the toolbar, and then click the **Event** tab.
3. Click in the **On Dbl Click** text box, and then click its **Build** button.
4. Press the **Enter** key to insert a blank line in the TimeCardDate_DblClick(Cancel As Integer) Sub procedure, and then press the **Tab** key to indent.
5. Type **DoCmd.OpenForm "frmCalendar"** and then press the **Enter** key. See Figure 8-35.

Figure 8-35 **TimeCardDate_DblClick SUB PROCEDURE**

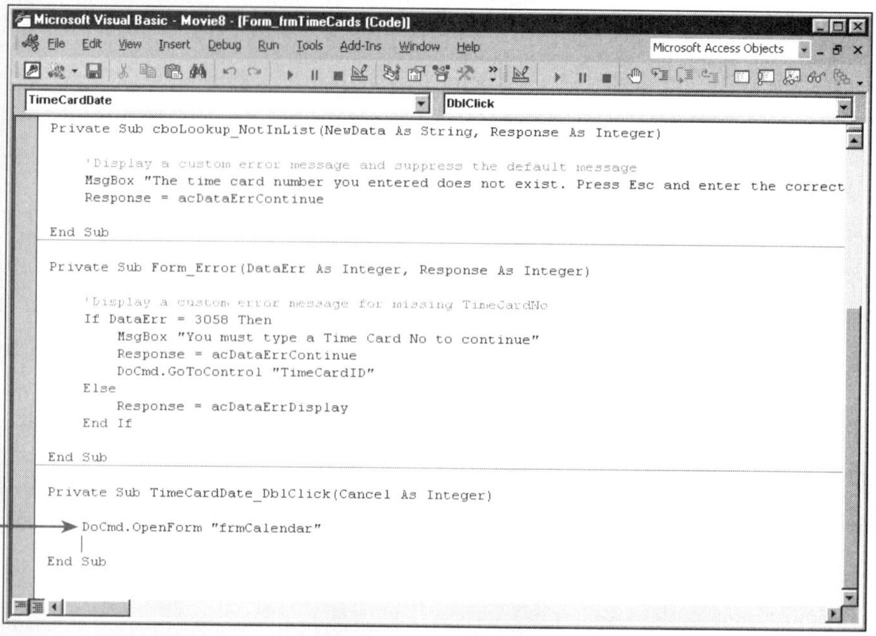

enter this statement

6. Close the Visual Basic window, close the property sheet, and then switch to Form view.
7. Click the **New Record** button on the toolbar, and double-click the **Time Card Date** text box. The frmCalendar form opens.
8. Double-click any date on the calendar to populate the text box. The date appears in the Time Card Date text box, and the frmCalendar form closes.
9. Press the **Esc** key to cancel the entry.
10. Click the **Save** button on the toolbar to save your changes.

Next you will test the functionality of this new date feature.

To test the frmCalendar form:

1. Double-click the **Time Card Date** text box to open the frmCalendar form.
2. If necessary, drag the **frmCalendar** form so you can see the Employee No field, and then click in the **Employee No** text box.
3. Double-click a date on the frmCalendar form. The date is entered into the Employee No text box.
4. Press the **Esc** key to cancel the entry.
5. Close the frmTimeCards form to return to the Database window.

Your test found that the focus can be changed from the frmCalendar form back to the frmTimeCards form before the date is entered in the correct text box. This allows the user to click other parts of the form, and then double-click the date on the calendar. A number of different errors could result from this problem. The user could enter a date into the Time Card No text box or into the Employee No text box. He or she could click on a label and then double-click the date, which would result in run-time error 2448, "You can't assign a value to this object."

Rather than attempt to write code to prevent this situation, you will change the Modal property of the frmCalendar form. This will prevent the user from clicking on any other object and changing the focus until the frmCalendar form is closed.

To change the Modal property for the frmCalendar form:

1. Open the **frmCalendar** form in Design view, and then click the **Properties** button on the toolbar.
2. Click the **Other** tab, change the Modal property to **Yes**, and then close the property sheet.
3. Save your changes and close the form.
4. Open the **frmTimeCards** form in Form view, and click the **New Record** button on the toolbar.
5. Double-click the **Time Card Date** text box to open the frmCalendar form.
6. Try to click on another part of the frmTimeCards form. The focus does not change.
7. Double-click a date on the calendar, and then press the **Esc** key to cancel the change.
8. Close the frmTimeCards form.
9. Close the Movie8 database, and then exit Access.

Martin is satisfied with the functionality you have added to the frmTimeCards form. The combo box provides him with an easy method for finding data, and he likes the visual effect of the calendar feature. You will add code to open the calendar in other data entry forms as well.

Session 8.2 QUICK CHECK

1. Misspelling a key word is an example of a(n) __________ error.
2. What is a run-time error?
3. When VBA encounters a run-time error generated by a procedure, it searches for a(n) __________ statement.
4. What does the Resume statement do?
5. A run-time error that is generated by the interface triggers the __________ event.
6. What is the purpose of the NotInList event?
7. A(n) __________ control is similar to a built-in control, in that it is an object that you place on a form to display data or perform an action.
8. Which ActiveX control included in Microsoft Office is an Access control?

REVIEW ASSIGNMENTS

The Hours8 database is similar to the MovieCam Technologies database you worked on in this tutorial. A form named frmReportsSwitchboard has been created to open reports in the database. You will add some code to this switchboard to deal with errors.

1. Start Access and open the **Hours8** database located in the Tutorial.08\Review folder on your local or network drive.
2. Open the **frmReportsSwitchboard** form in Form view, and then click the Preview button without selecting a report. Run-time error message 2497 appears.
3. Click the End button to close the error message.
4. Switch to Design view, and then click the Code button on the toolbar to open the Visual Basic window.
5. Position the insertion point at the end of the Dim strCondition As String statement, and press the Enter key twice. (*Note*: If all procedures are not visible in the Visual Basic window, click Tools on the menu bar, click Options, click the Default to Full Module View check box on the Editor tab, and then click the OK button.)
6. Type **On Error GoTo ReportError** and then press the Enter key.
7. Scroll down, click at the end of the chkTerminated = Null statement, and press the Enter key twice.
8. Type the following comment and code, indenting and adding blank lines as needed:

```
ReportError:
If Err.Number = 2497 Then
'No report was selected from the option groups
MsgBox "You must select a report from one of the option
groups."
Resume Next
End If
```

9. Compile the code and correct any syntax errors identified.
10. Close the Visual Basic window, and switch to Form view.
11. Click the Preview button. The new error message is shown. Close the error message box.
12. Save your changes and close the form.
13. Close the Hours8 database, and then exit Access.

CASE PROBLEMS

Case 1. Edwards and Company The frmClients data entry form contains a combo box for ConsultantID. The user can enter the ConsultantID number or select an item from the list. Because this combo box is based on the data in the tblConsultants table, an error results if the wrong number is entered. You will determine the error number and write code to deal with it. Complete the following:

1. Start Access and open the **Edward8** database located in the Tutorial.08\Cases folder on your local or network drive.

2. Open the **frmClients** form in Form view, and click the New Record button on the toolbar.
3. Click in the Consultant text box, type **800**, and then press then Enter key.
4. Click the OK button when the Microsoft Access error message box is shown, and then press the Esc key to cancel the entry.
5. Switch to Design view, open the property sheet for the form, click the Event tab, click in the On Error text box, and then click its Build button.
6. Press the Tab key, type **Debug.Print DataErr**, and then press Ctrl + G to open the Immediate window.
7. Minimize the Visual Basic window, close the property sheet, and then switch to Form view.
8. Click the New Record button on the toolbar, type **800** in the Consultant field, and then press the Tab key.
9. Click the OK button to close the error message box, press the Esc key to cancel the entry, and then switch to Design view.
10. Redisplay the Visual Basic window. The error number 3201 is shown in the Immediate window.
11. Close the Immediate window, delete the Debug.Print DataErr statement, and then add the following code, indenting and adding blank lines as needed:

```
'Display a custom error message for incorrect Consultant ID
If DataErr = 3201 Then
   MsgBox "You must type a Consultant ID from the list.
Press Esc to cancel the entry."
   Response = acDataErrContinue
Else
   Response = acDataErrDisplay
End If
```

12. Compile the code and correct any syntax errors identified.
13. Close the Visual Basic window, and switch to Form view.
14. Click the New Record button, type **800** in the Consultant text box, and then press the Enter key. Your error message is shown. Close the error message.
15. Save your changes and close the form.
16. Close the Edward8 database, and then exit Access.

Case 2. San Diego County Information Systems The frmClasses form is used to enter all the classes into the tblClasses table in the ISD8 database. It also contains a field for the class date. You have decided to create an ActiveX calendar control on the form so you can enter a date by double-clicking the date on the calendar control. Complete the following:

1. Start Access and open the **ISD8** database located in the Tutorial.08\Cases folder on your local or network drive.
2. Open the **frmClasses** form in Design view, display the toolbox if necessary, and click the More Controls button.
3. Click Calendar Control 10.0 and then click and drag to draw a calendar to the right of the other controls on the form.
4. Right-click the calendar, point to Calendar Object, and then click Properties.

5. Clear the Month/Year Title check box, and then click the OK button.
6. If necessary, resize the calendar control so that you can read the dates.
7. Click the Properties button on the toolbar to display the properties for the control, and then change the Name property on the All tab to **actlCalendar**. Close the property sheet.
8. Click the Code button on the toolbar, and then add the following Sub procedure, indenting and adding blank lines as needed:

```
Private Sub actlCalendar_DblClick()
Dim dtmDate As Date
'To set the date control to date selected on the calendar
  dtmDate = Me.ActiveControl.Value
  Date.Value = dtmDate
End Sub
```

9. Compile the code and correct any syntax errors identified.
10. Close the Visual Basic window, and switch to Form view.
11. Test the calendar by double-clicking a date.
12. Save your changes and close the form.
13. Close the ISD8 database, and then exit Access.

Case 3. Christenson Homes The frmLots form in the Homes8 database contains a combo box for entering the subdivision. As you test this form, you note that if the user types an item that is not in the list, the following error message is received: "The text you entered isn't an item in the list." You will replace this error message with your own to make the form more user-friendly. Complete the following:

1. Start Access and open the **Homes8** database located in the Tutorial.08\Cases folder on your local or network drive.
2. Open the **frmLots** form in Form view, and click the New Record button on the toolbar.
3. Press the Tab key, type the word **test** in the Subdivision text box, and then press the Enter key. An error message appears.
4. Click the OK button to close the error message box, press the Esc key twice to cancel the entry, and then switch to Design view.
5. Create a Sub procedure that is triggered by the On Not In List event of the SubdivisionID combo box. The code will be similar to the following code used in this tutorial:

```
'Display a custom error message and suppress the default
message
MsgBox "The subdivision you entered does not exist. Press Esc
and enter the correct subdivision."
Response = acDataErrContinue
```

6. Compile the code, correct any syntax errors identified, and then close the Visual Basic window.
7. Switch to Form view and test the form.
8. Save the changes and close the form.
9. Close the Homes8 database, and then exit Access.

Case 4. Sonoma Farms The Sonoma Farms database contains a form named frmVisitors. You would like to add a form to this database that contains the Access ActiveX calendar control that you can access to enter a date in the Date of Visit text box in the frmVisitors form. Complete the following:

1. Start Access and open the **Sonoma8** database located in the Tutorial.08\Cases folder on your local or network drive.
2. Create an unbound form in Design view, and add the Calendar Control 10.0 ActiveX control to the form.
3. Select the form, click the Properties button on the toolbar, and then change the Caption property to **Calendar**, the Navigation Buttons property to No, the Pop Up property to Yes, the Modal property to Yes, the Border Style property to Dialog, the Control Box property to No, the Min Max Buttons property to None, and the Close Button property to No.
4. Right-click the calendar, point to Calendar Object, click Properties, clear the Month/Year Title check box, and then click the OK button.
5. Change the Name property of the control to **actlCalendar**.
6. Using the code in this tutorial as a sample, write the VBA code so that clicking a date on the calendar control enters that date into the Date of Visit text box on the frmVisitors form.
7. Save the form as **frmCalendar**, and close it.
8. Using the code from the frmTimeCards form in this tutorial as a guide, add the code to the frmVisitors form to open the frmCalendar form when the Date of Visit text box is double-clicked.
9. Switch to Form view and test the two forms.
10. Return to the Visual Basic window, print the code, and then close the Visual Basic window.
11. Save your changes and close the frmVisitors form.
12. Close the Sonoma8 database, and then exit Access.

QUICK CHECK ANSWERS

Session 8.1

1. A control structure is a series of VBA statements that work together as a unit.
2. Do...Loop
3. For...Next loop
4. The Visible property can be used to show or hide a control, whereas the Enabled property specifies whether a control can have the focus in Form view.
5. Label controls do not have an Enabled property.
6. dot
7. Bang notation results in shorter pathnames to an object or property.
8. The Me keyword is used to refer to the associated form or report in which the class module is located.
9. CodeContextObject can be used in a standard module, but the Me keyword cannot.
10. The Screen object refers to the particular form, report, or control that currently has the focus.

Session 8.2

1. syntax
2. A run-time error is an error that occurs while the application is running.
3. On Error
4. The Resume statement resumes execution after an error-handling routine is finished.
5. Error
6. The purpose of the NotInList event is to trigger code to respond to the specific error in which the item selected is not in the list.
7. ActiveX
8. The Calendar control is an Access control

OBJECTIVES

In this tutorial you will:

- Compare the ActiveX Data Object (ADO) and Data Access Object (DAO) models
- Study the DAO model collections and objects
- Test DAO object code in the Immediate window
- Use the DAO Recordset object in VBA code
- Identify the different levels of security in Access
- Learn to work with the Workgroup Administrator, and create and join workgroup information files
- Establish user-level security in the MovieCam database
- Create users and assign permissions
- Learn to set and clear user passwords

WORKING WITH OBJECT MODELS AND SECURING THE DATABASE

Working with DAO and Implementing User-Level Security in the MovieCam Technologies Database

CASE

MovieCam Technologies

In Tutorial 8, you added a combo box to the frmTimeCards form. The combo box you added can be used to look up a particular time card number and then show it on the form. Martin Woodward requested that you change the search feature so it shows employee last names, time card numbers, and the date. He wants the data to show records sorted by last name and then by time card number. He likes the pop-up frmCalendar form you created and wants the time card search to operate similarly. You plan to create a pop-up form that contains a list box that looks up time card records in the frmTimeCards form. You have researched coding with Recordset objects in DAO, and you have determined that using Recordset objects is a more efficient way to program the pop-up form feature because recordsets of bound forms, such as frmTimeCards, are DAO recordsets.

Amanda has reevaluated the method that you developed for controlling user access to the database. More users than you anticipated will be using the database, so you need to determine the various levels of rights that users will have to the data and objects. Amanda wants you to implement user-level security on the database, so you also need to create user groups for data entry personnel, for managers that need read-only access, and for administrators, such as yourself or anyone else who might be a future administrator.

SESSION 9.1

In this session, you will study the Data Access Object (DAO) and ActiveX Data Object (ADO) models and compare the two of them. You will learn to manipulate DAO objects in the Immediate window and study the DAO Recordset object, in particular. You will create a form for looking up data. The form you create will contain a list box. You also will learn some of the methods and properties of the Recordset object, and, in turn, use these methods and properties to write the VBA code for looking up data on a form.

Introduction to Object Models

The VBA code that you have written in earlier tutorials fits into a logical framework called the **Access object model**. The Access object model (which was diagrammed in Tutorial 8), contains all the items such as the Forms collection, forms, and Controls collection that you use in an application. You use the object model to interact programmatically with the Access user interface.

Up to this point, changes you have made to the application's data have been handled by Access behind the scenes. For example, if a user changed the data in a form, Access changed the data in the underlying table.

To write VBA code that works directly with the data in your application, you must work with a different object model. To create tables and queries and manipulate records programmatically, you must work with either the DAO library or the ADO library provided with Access.

DAO vs. ADO

The **DAO** (**Data Access Object**) interface has been used to programmatically manipulate data, create tables and queries, and manage security in Access databases since Access 2.0 was released. (Version 1.0 contained DAO 1.0, but it was very restrictive.) The recordsets of bound forms are DAO recordsets, so when you want to work directly with the recordset data underlying a form in Access, you use the properties and methods of DAO to do so.

Many company databases have data created in programs other than Access. For example, many companies use SQL Server, DB2, Sybase, Oracle, or others. These are large client-server databases. In these instances, Access can be used as the front-end, or client, to the data stored in these databases, and is attached to the provider data in the form of back-end tables. In this configuration, the attached tables appear just like Access tables and can be accessed programmatically using DAO in the same way that native Access tables are accessed. The problem with using DAO to manipulate the data in these tables is that it is not particularly efficient. DAO has to communicate with **Open Database Connectivity** (**ODBC**), which is a standard method of sharing data between databases and programs. ODBC drivers use the standard Structured Query Language (SQL) to gain access to external data. Although ODBC can be used to connect to relational databases, it cannot be used to connect to data that is not relational, such as the Microsoft Exchange mail system.

To address this issue and some of the ODBC efficiency problems, Microsoft developed the **OLE DB** technology that provides access to both relational and nonrelational data. The OLE DB interface is essentially a means of providing object linking and embedding technology to a database (data) source. From this standpoint, a data source could be a flat file, a relational database, a directory service in Windows NT or 2000, or some other nonrelational data. This technology has a single programmatic interface called **ADO** (**ActiveX Data Objects**), which is what client applications (such as Visual Basic or VBA) use, regardless of the type of data provider. What this means, for example, is that you use the same syntax with ADO whether you are connecting to tables in SQL Server, tables in Access, or data that is in Microsoft Exchange.

The OLE DB technology provides a means to interface to the data source and presents this to the ADO programmatic interface in a uniform manner so that you can manipulate the underlying data without necessarily having to understand how that data is accessed, updated, or stored. There are separate OLE DB interfaces for SQL Server, Oracle, Access, and other data sources because the objects, syntax, and rules for manipulating the underlying data are different for all of these data sources. This OLE DB interface contains all the correct rules for working with the given data source, so you simply invoke the appropriate OLE DB provider, and this allows ADO to directly call into the data source. As a result, once you have established a connection to the data source with OLE DB, you can use the same set of ADO properties and methods to work with any underlying data source that OLE DB can expose for you. To learn more about OLE DB, search for the key word OLE DB in Microsoft Visual Basic Help.

Microsoft has made it clear that ADO is the interface they will use in the future, and that there will be no further development of DAO, though there is no clear obsolescence date for DAO at the time of this writing.

A **recordset** is simply a set of records, and manipulating recordsets is one of the major uses of ADO and DAO technology. In this tutorial, you will use DAO to manipulate recordsets because recordsets of bound forms are DAO recordsets.

The ADO model is shown in Figure 9-1.

Figure 9-1 ADO MODEL

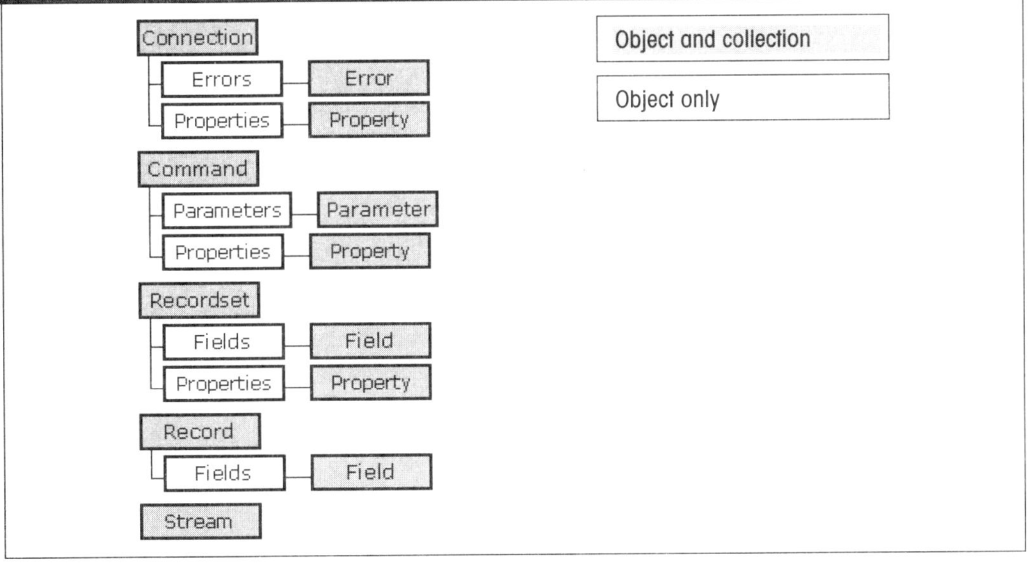

The DAO model is shown in Figure 9-2.

Figure 9-2 DAO MODEL

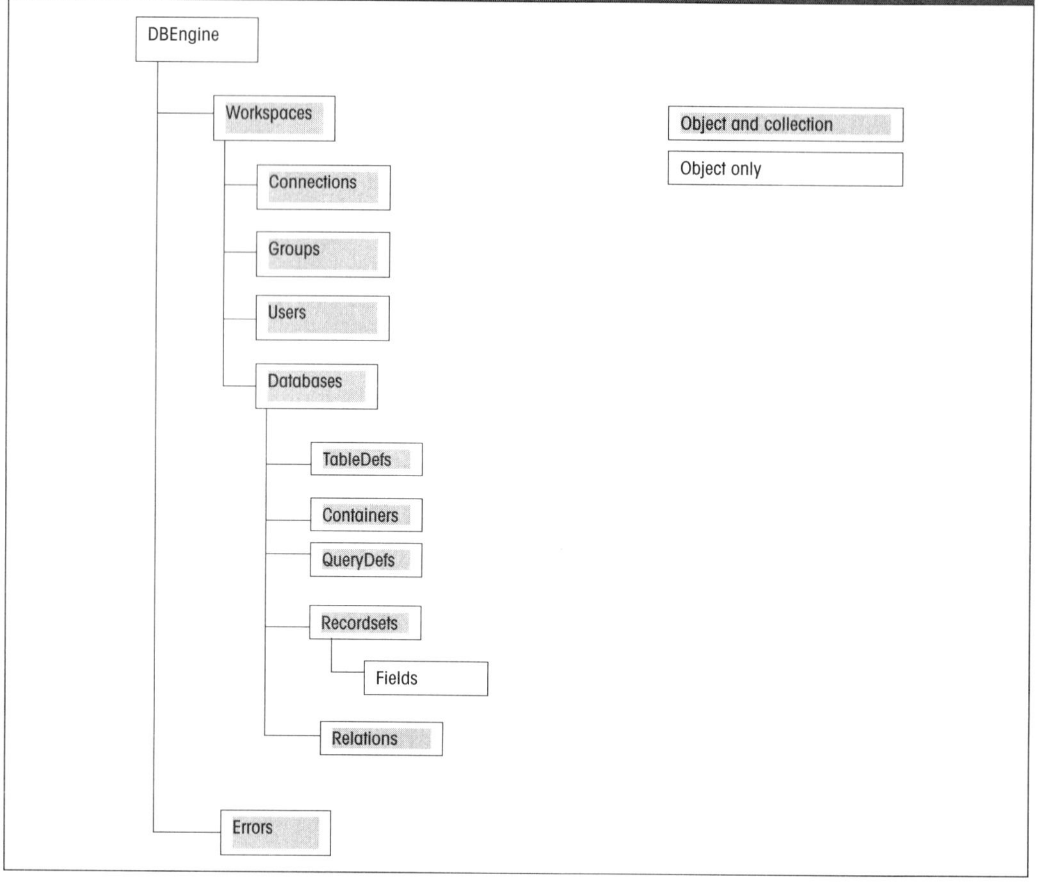

ADO

The ADO hierarchy is simpler than the DAO hierarchy, and starts with the Connection object that represents a connection to a data source. Both the ADO and DAO object models have a Recordset object for working with data in tables and queries, but the rest of each hierarchy is different.

DAO

The DAO hierarchy contains a number of objects, grouped together into collections. The DAO hierarchy is arranged in the same manner as the Access object model with collections of objects, each of which has its own methods and properties. Recall that in the Access object model there is a Forms collection that contains all the open forms, each form has a Controls collection, and so on. Look at Figure 9-2 and you can see that DAO also has collections. It contains an Errors collection, Workspaces collection, Databases collection, and so forth.

The DBEngine Object

In the Access object hierarchy, the Application object representing the Access application is the topmost object; in ADO, the Connection object is the topmost object; and in DAO, the DBEngine object is at the top. The **DBEngine object** represents the DAO interface into the **Microsoft Jet database engine** and ODBCDirect technology. The Microsoft Jet database engine is often referred to as simply the Jet engine and is a database management system that retrieves data from, and stores data in, user and system databases. Such is the fundamental function of any database engine. The Microsoft Jet database engine can be thought of as a data manager component with which other data access systems, such as Microsoft Access or Visual Basic, are built. The ODBCDirect technology can access a remote ODBC data source directly, bypassing the Jet engine. You use the DBEngine object to determine which version of DAO you are using and to access the collection contained in it.

To use the DBEngine object to determine the DAO version:

1. Start Access and open the **Movie9** database located in the Tutorial.09\Tutorial folder on the local or network drive.
2. Press **Ctrl + G** to open the Immediate window in the Visual Basic window.
3. Type **?DBEngine.Version** and then press the **Enter** key. Version 3.6 should be visible in the Immediate window, as shown in Figure 9-3.

Figure 9-3 TESTING THE DBENGINE

The DBEngine object default collection is the Workspaces collection, which is discussed next.

The Workspace Object

The Workspaces collection contains all active Workspace objects of the database engine. A **Workspace object** represents a single session or instance of a user interacting with the database engine. For example, to find out the name of the user currently logged on to the database, you could use the Workspace object. (As you will learn later in this tutorial, you are logged in by default as the Admin user, even in an unsecured database.)

To determine the current user of the database:

1. Type **?DBEngine.Workspaces(0).UserName** in the Immediate window, and then press the **Enter** key. The user name "admin" is returned, as shown in Figure 9-4.

Figure 9-4 TESTING THE WORKSPACES COLLECTION

The Workspace object contains a Users collection and a Groups collection that, in turn, contain details of all users and groups defined in the current system database. The Workspace object also contains a Databases collection, which is discussed next.

The Database Object

Because you normally have only one database open at a time, there will be only one Database object in the Databases collection for the current workspace. Next, you will test the Database object in the Immediate window.

To determine the current database:

1. Type **?DBEngine.Workspaces(0).Databases(0).Name** in the Immediate window, as shown in Figure 9-5.

Figure 9-5 TESTING THE DATABASES COLLECTION

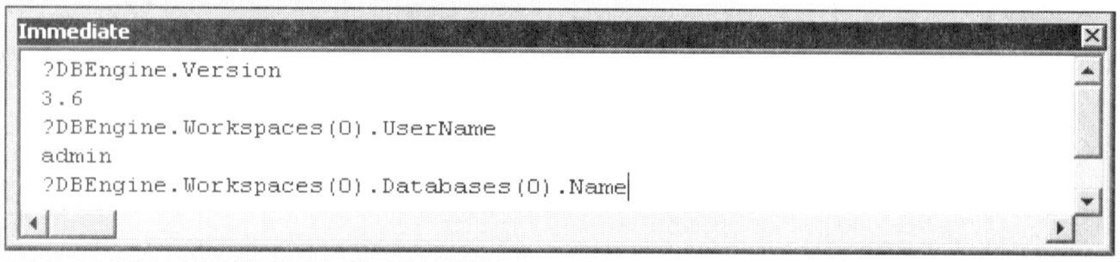

2. Press the **Enter** key. The path and name of the current database are shown. (Recall from Tutorial 8 that you do not need to type the name of the default collection.) The Workspaces collection is the default collection of the DBEngine, and Databases is the default collection of the Workspace object.
3. Type **?DBEngine(0)(0).Name** and then press the **Enter** key. Again, the path and name of the current database is shown. You also can use the CurrentDB shortcut.
4. Type **?CurrentDB.Name()** in the Immediate window, and then press the **Enter** key. The Immediate window should look similar to that shown in Figure 9-6 (you might need to expand the height of your window in order for it to match the figure).

Figure 9-6 DETERMINING THE CURRENT DATABASE

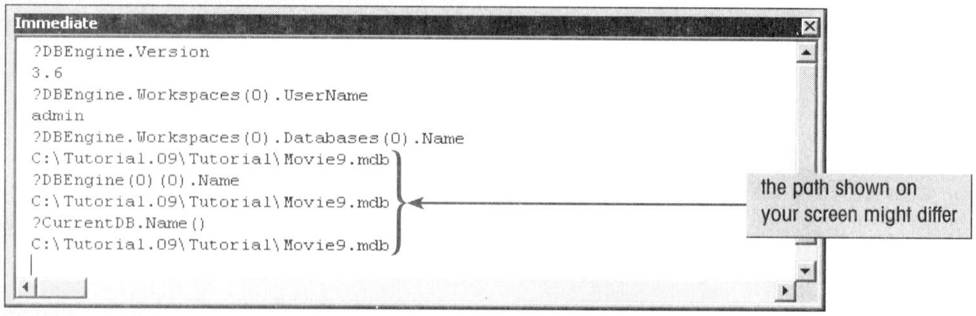

The **Database object** contains five collections: Containers, QueryDefs, Recordsets, Relations, and TableDefs. The Containers collection holds one container object for each collection of documents. The documents contain information about objects in the database and their owners and permissions.

The QueryDefs collection contains one QueryDef object for every saved query that exists within the database. The Relations collection contains one Relation object for every relationship defined between tables in the database. The TableDefs collection contains one TableDef object for every table (including system tables, but excluding linked tables) in the database. Next, you'll use the TableDefs collection to find the number of tables in the database, and the QueryDefs collection to find the number of queries in the database.

To determine the number of tables and queries in the database:

1. Type **?CurrentDB.TableDefs.Count** in the Immediate window, and then press the **Enter** key. The result should be 13, as shown in Figure 9-7.

Figure 9-7 USING THE TABLEDEFS COLLECTION TO COUNT TABLES

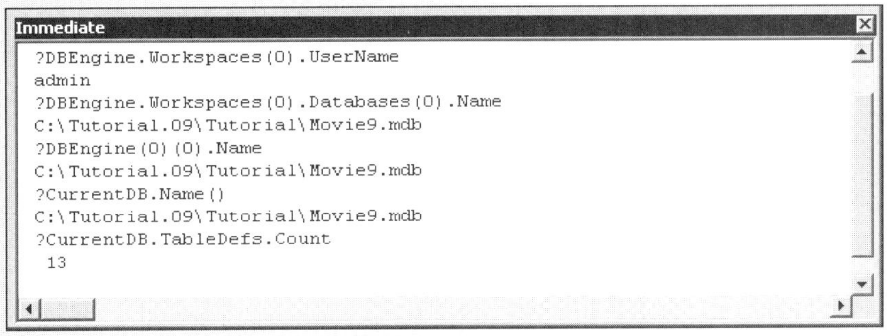

2. Close the Visual Basic window, click **Tables** on the Objects bar of the Database window if necessary, and then count the tables. There should be eight tables.
3. Click **Tools** on the menu bar, and then click **Options**.
4. Click the **View** tab if necessary, click the **System objects** check box to select it, and then click the **OK** button. You should now see five additional system tables listed in the Database window. System tables, such as the MSysObjects table, are database objects that are defined by the user or by the system. You can create a system object by using USys as the first four characters in the object name.
5. Press **Ctrl + G** to open the Immediate window, type **?CurrentDB.QueryDefs.Count**, and then press the **Enter** key. The result is 15, as shown in Figure 9-8.

Figure 9-8 USING THE QUERYDEFS COLLECTION TO COUNT QUERIES

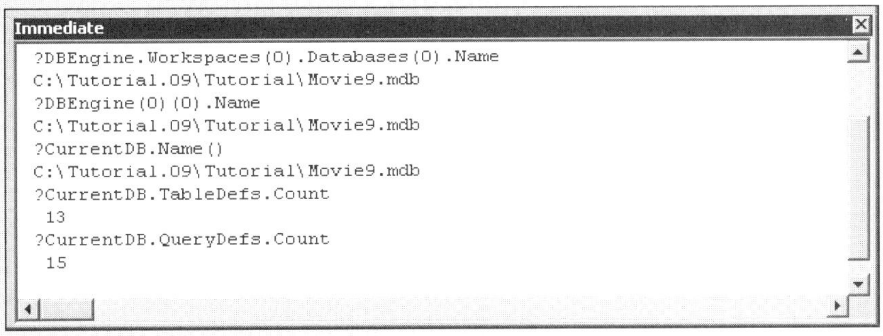

6. Close the Visual Basic window, and then click **Queries** on the Objects bar of the Database window, and count the queries. There are only five. The reason for this is that each time you create a combo box, a list box, a form, or a report that uses an SQL statement as its source, a saved query is created, but is not shown in the Database window.
7. Click **Tools** on the menu bar, click **Options**, clear the **System objects** check box on the View tab, and then click the **OK** button.

The Recordsets Collection

One of the collections used most often in the Database object is the Recordsets collection. The **Recordsets collection** contains one Recordset object for every recordset that is currently open in the database. The Recordset object represents the records in an underlying table or query and can be simply considered a set of records. Following are the types of Recordset objects you can use:

- *Table*: This is the default type of Recordset object and represents a table that you can use to add, change, or delete records from a single table in an Access database. The table can be local or attached.
- *Dynaset*: This type of Recordset object can be the result of a query that contains records that can be updated. This object can be used to add, change, or delete records from the underlying table or tables. It also can contain fields from one or more Access database tables that are either local or attached. A dynaset can be edited and the results of those edits will be reflected in the underlying tables. While a dynaset is open, Access updates the records in the dynaset to reflect changes that other people are making in the underlying tables.
- *Snapshot*: This type of Recordset object cannot be updated and does not reflect changes other users make to the underlying tables. Snapshot is a static representation of the data from one or more Access database tables that are local or attached. One advantage of snapshots is that they are generally faster to create than dynasets.
- *Forward-only*: This type of Recordset object is identical to a snapshot, except that you can only scroll forward through the records; you can read the records one after another, but you cannot go back to previous records. This object also is read-only and does not reflect user changes. This will improve performance when you only need to make a single pass through a recordset.
- *Dynamic*: This type of Recordset object is used for accessing data in remote OBDC databases, as opposed to Access databases. Dynamic is a query result from one or more tables in which you can add, change or delete records. Records that others add, change, or delete also appear in the recordset.

You will test the Recordset object in the Immediate window next.

To test the Recordset object:

1. Press **Ctrl + G** to open the Immediate window.
2. Type **?Currentdb.OpenRecordset("tblTimeCards").RecordCount** and then press the **Enter** key. This opens the recordset underlying the tblTimeCards table and returns a count of the records. The number of records returned is 25, as shown in Figure 9-9.

Figure 9-9 USING THE RECORDSETS COLLECTION TO COUNT RECORDS IN A TABLE

Immediate

```
?DBEngine(0)(0).Name
C:\Tutorial.09\Tutorial\Movie9.mdb
?CurrentDB.Name()
C:\Tutorial.09\Tutorial\Movie9.mdb
?CurrentDB.TableDefs.Count
 13
?CurrentDB.QueryDefs.Count
 15
?Currentdb.OpenRecordset("tblTimeCards").RecordCount
 25
```

3. Close the Visual Basic window, and then open the **tblTimeCards** table in Datasheet view. There are 25 records.
4. Close the table.

You will use a pop-up form containing a list box to look up time cards from the frmTimeCards form, rather than using the combo box you created in Tutorial 8. You think this can make the feature more user-friendly, because a list box shows more columns and rows. The program managers typically search for a time card based on the employee last name, time card number, and date. A list box shows this data more easily. Also, the menu form format keeps the form from being visible while it is not used. You will use DAO Recordset code to program the list box on the menu form. Before you can do that, however, you need to complete the frmFindTimeCards form.

The frmFindTimeCards form properties are similar to the frmCalendar form you created in Tutorial 8. The Pop Up and Modal properties are both set to Yes, the Border Style property is Dialog, and the Navigation Buttons, Control Box, Min Max Buttons, and the Close Button properties are set to No. The form contains neither form header nor footer sections, and is approximately 4" wide by 2" tall. See the form properties in Figure 9-10.

Figure 9-10 frmFindTimeCards PROPERTIES SHEET

Form

Form

Format | Data | Event | Other | All

Order By	
Allow Filters	Yes
Caption	Find Time Card
Default View	Single Form
Allow Form View	Yes
Allow Datasheet View	Yes
Allow PivotTable View	Yes
Allow PivotChart View	Yes
Allow Edits	Yes
Allow Deletions	Yes
Allow Additions	Yes
Data Entry	No
Recordset Type	Dynaset
Record Locks	No Locks
Scroll Bars	Both
Record Selectors	No
Navigation Buttons	No
Dividing Lines	No
Auto Resize	Yes
Auto Center	Yes
Pop Up	Yes
Modal	Yes
Border Style	Dialog
Control Box	No
Min Max Buttons	None
Close Button	No
Whats This Button	No
Width	4"

Next, you will add the list box to the form, and then change some of its properties.

To add the list box to the frmFindTimeCards form:

1. Open the **frmFindTimeCards** form in Design view, make sure that the toolbox is visible, and then click the **Control Wizards** button on the toolbox to turn it on if necessary.
2. Click the **List Box** button on the toolbox, and then click in the upper-left corner of the form to create the list box. The first dialog box of the List Box Wizard appears, as shown in Figure 9-11.

Figure 9-11 LIST BOX WIZARD

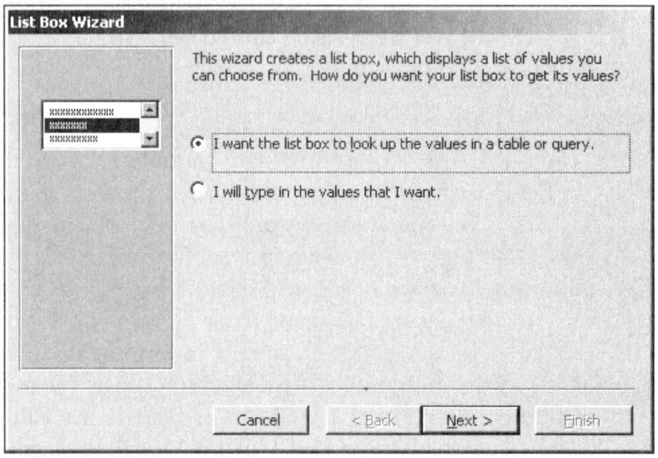

3. Click the **Next** button to accept the default option and to move to the next dialog box.
4. Click **tblTimeCards** in the list of tables, and then click the **Next** button.
5. Add the **TimeCardID** and **TimeCardDate** fields in the list of Available Fields to the Selected Fields list box, as shown in Figure 9-12. You will add the LastName field from the tblEmployees table after you have completed the List Box Wizard.

Figure 9-12 SELECTING FIELDS FOR THE LIST BOX

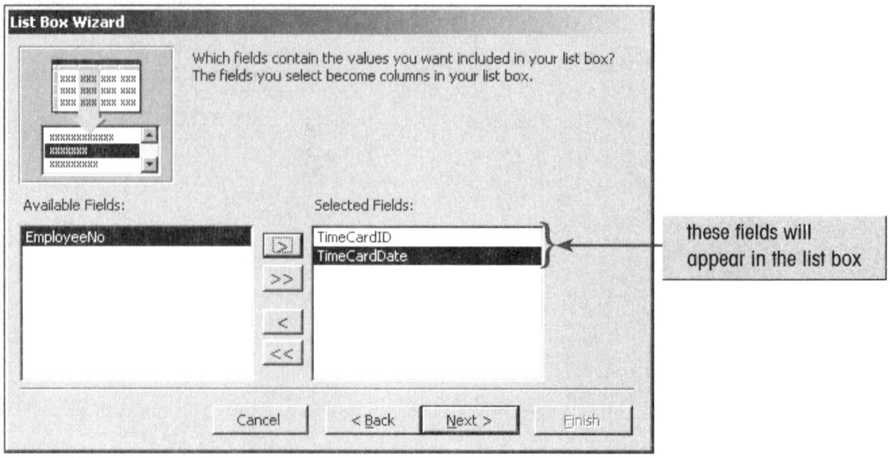

6. Click the **Next** button to move to the next dialog box, clear the **Hide key column (recommended)** check box because you want the TimeCardID field to be visible in the list box, and then click the **Next** button.
7. Make sure that the **TimeCardID** field is selected in the dialog box that asks which value you want to use later to perform an action, and then click the **Next** button. Later on, you will use the TimeCardID field in your code to look up the record on the frmTimeCards form.
8. Type **Select Time Card** as the label for the list box, as shown in Figure 9-13.

Figure 9-13 ENTERING THE LABEL FOR THE LIST BOX

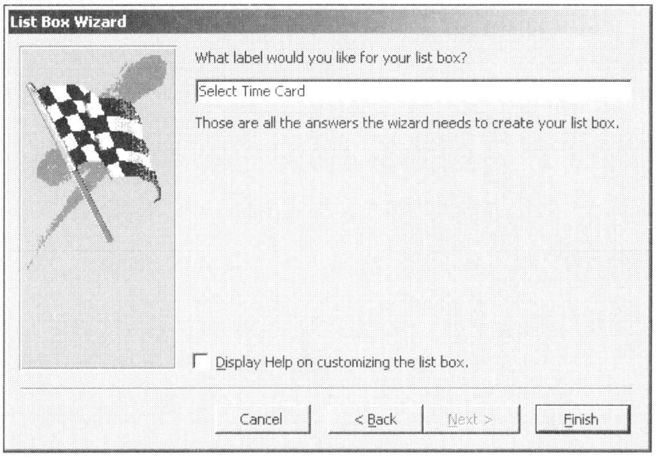

9. Click the **Finish** button.

Next, you need to change the Row Source of the list box so that it also shows the last name of the employee. You will change the list box properties so that the field saved for later use is the second column. Then you will create two command buttons. One will be used to search for the time card after it is chosen from the list box. You will name the button cmdFind. You will change the Enabled property for the cmdFind button to No, so that it is not enabled by default. Later, you will add a Sub procedure to the form class module to set the Enabled property of the button to Yes after a user has chosen a time card from the list box. The other command button you create will be used to close the form.

To change the list box properties:

1. Click the **Properties** button on the toolbar, click the **All** tab if necessary, click in the **Row Source** text box, click its **Build** button, click **Query** on the menu bar, and then click **Show Table**.
2. Click **tblEmployees** in the Show Table dialog box, click the **Add** button, and then click the **Close** button.
3. Drag the **LastName** field from the tblEmployees table field list to the first column of the query grid, click the **Sort** list arrow for the LastName field, click **Ascending**, click the **Sort** list arrow for the TimeCardID field, and then click **Ascending**. See Figure 9-14.

Figure 9-14 MODIFYING THE LIST BOX SQL STATEMENT

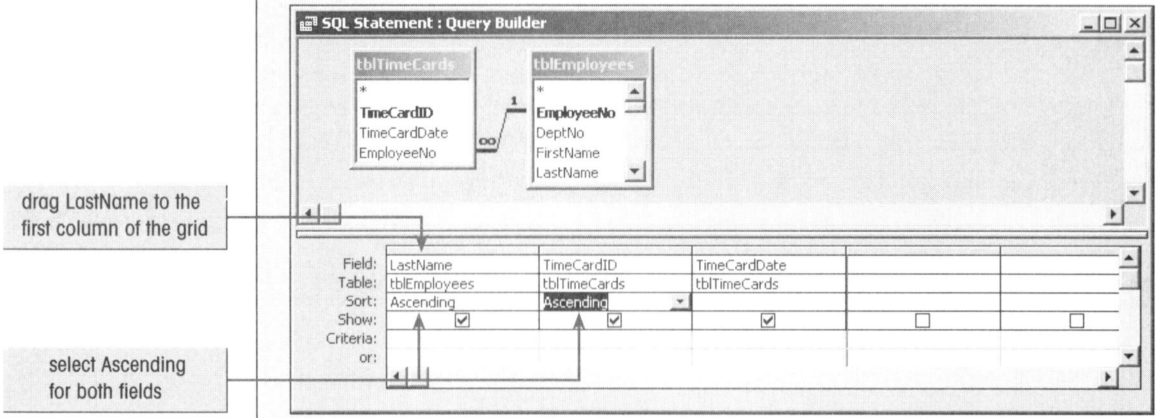

4. Close the Query Builder window and save the changes.
5. Change the list box's Name property to **lstFind** (be sure to type the letter "l" and not the number 1 as the first character), the Column Count property to **3**, the Column Widths property to **1";0.5";0.5",** and the Bound Column property to **2**, and then close the property sheet. These changes allow you to show the LastName field in the first column and to use the TimeCardID field in the second column to look up the record on the frmTimeCards form.
6. Resize the lstFind control and its label as shown in Figure 9-15. The label for the control might be behind the list box, so you will have to use previously learned skills to move the label and list box control to match Figure 9-15.

Figure 9-15 SIZING THE LIST BOX

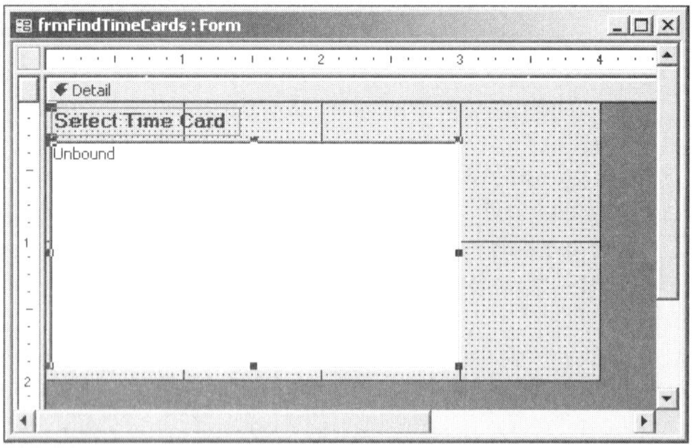

7. Click the **Control Wizards** button  to turn it off, click the **Command Button** button  in the toolbox, click to the right of the list box to create a command button, click **Edit** on the menu bar, and then click **Duplicate**. A second command button is created below the first.
8. Open the property sheet, click the first command button to display its properties, change the Name property of the first command button to **cmdFind**, the Caption to **&Find Record**, and the Enabled property to **No**.

9. Click the second command button to display its properties, change the Name property of the second command button to **cmdCancel** and the Caption to **&Cancel**, and then close the property sheet.

10. Size and align the buttons as shown in Figure 9-16, reducing the form width to 4" if necessary, and then save the changes to the form.

Figure 9-16 ADDING THE COMMAND BUTTONS

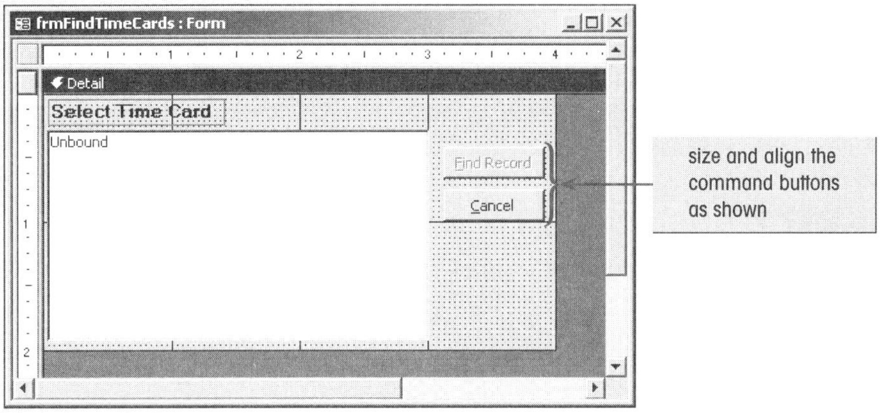

You are ready to begin writing the code for the list box, but first you must make sure that the DAO library is available because the code will use the DAO Recordset object, rather than the ADO Recordset object. You will do that next.

Changing the Object Library Reference

An object library is a collection of prebuilt objects and functions that you can use in VBA code. By default, the ADO library is selected in Access 2002.

REFERENCE WINDOW RW

Changing the Object Library Reference

- Click Tools on the menu bar, point to Macro, and then click Visual Basic Editor, or click the Code button on the Form Design toolbar.
- Click Tools on the menu bar of the Visual Basic window, and then click References.
- Click the Microsoft DAO 3.6 Object Library check box, and then click the OK button.
- Close the Visual Basic window.

Next you will add the DAO library so that you can use its objects in your code.

To add the DAO library:

1. Click the **Code** button on the Form Design toolbar to open the Visual Basic window.

TROUBLE? If the Choose Builder dialog box opens and indicates that you need to select a builder, close the Visual Basic window, click Tools on the menu bar, click Options, click the Forms/Reports tab, click the Always use event procedures check box, and then click the OK button. Repeat Step 1.

TROUBLE? If your Immediate window is still open, close it to provide additional space in your Code window.

2. Click **Tools** on the menu bar, and then click **References**. The References - Movie9 dialog box opens.
3. Click the **Microsoft DAO 3.6 Object Library** check box, as shown in Figure 9-17.

Figure 9-17 SELECTING THE DAO OBJECT LIBRARY

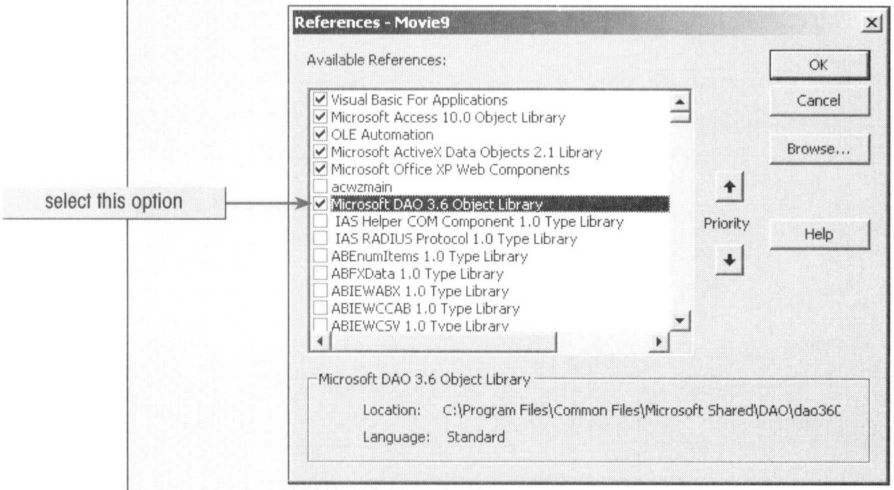

TROUBLE? Your References dialog box might not match Figure 9-17 exactly. Your Microsoft DAO 3.6 Object Library option might appear in alphabetical order with other Microsoft object libraries. If you have difficulty finding this library, ask your instructor or technical support person for assistance.

4. Click the **OK** button and then close the Visual Basic window.

Writing **Code Using the Recordset Object**

The completed VBA Sub procedure that will find the record chosen in the list box on the frmTimeCards form is shown in Figure 9-18.

To understand this code, you need to understand the RecordsetClone property, the FindFirst method of DAO Recordset objects, and the Bookmark property of forms and recordsets. Using these properties and methods, you will see how easy it is to program a professional-looking lookup capability. Recall that the recordset of a bound form, such as frmTimeCards, is a DAO recordset, so you will use DAO to manipulate and move through this recordset.

RecordsetClone Property

Every form has a **RecordsetClone property** that you can use to get a copy of the form's underlying recordset. By creating a copy of the table or query on which the form is based, you can navigate or operate on the form's records independently of the form itself. After you have navigated to or modified the record in the copy, you set the actual recordset of the form equal to the copy. One advantage of using a form's RecordsetClone property is that you then can use the DAO Find methods that cannot be used with forms to navigate through records. You will learn about these methods in the next section.

The Sub procedure will include the following line of code:

```
Dim rst As DAO.Recordset
```

The preceding statement declares an object variable as a DAO Recordset object. The following line of code sets the object variable to the RecordsetClone property of the frmTimeCards form:

```
Set rst = Forms!frmTimeCards.RecordsetClone
```

FindFirst, FindLast, FindNext, and FindPrevious Methods

These methods locate the first, last, next, or previous record in a dynaset or snapshot Recordset object according to the criteria specified. The methods then make that record the current record. These methods are only available in DAO. The syntax for these methods is

```
recordset.{FindFirst | FindLast | FindNext | FindPrevious}
criteria
```

The recordset is an object variable that represents an existing dynaset or snapshot Recordset object. The criteria is a string used to locate the record and is like the WHERE clause in an SQL statement without the word WHERE. (This is similar to the WhereCondition argument in the DoCmd.OpenReport object that you worked with in Tutorial 7.)

If a record that matches the criteria isn't located, the NoMatch property is set to True. If the recordset contains more than one record that satisfies the criteria, the FindFirst method locates the first record, the FindNext method locates the next record, and so on.

The FindFirst method begins searching at the beginning of the recordset and searches to the end. The FindLast method begins searching at the end of the recordset and searches to the beginning. The FindNext method begins searching at the current record and searches to the end of the recordset. The FindPrevious method begins searching at the current record and searches to the beginning of the recordset.

When a new Recordset object is opened, its first record is the current record. If you use one of the Find methods to make another record in the Recordset object current, you must synchronize the current record in the Recordset object with the form's current record. You do this by assigning the value of the recordset's bookmark property to the form's bookmark property.

The statement in the procedure you will write looks like the following:

```
rst.FindFirst "TimeCardID = " & "'" & lstFind & "'"
```

This statement uses the FindFirst method of the Recordset object to find the first record. It searches from the beginning of the recordset to the end.

Bookmark Property

When a bound form is open in Form view, each record is assigned a unique bookmark. The Bookmark property contains a string expression created by Access. You can get or set the form's Bookmark property separately from the DAO Bookmark property of the underlying table or query.

Bookmarks are not saved with the records that they represent and are valid only while the form is open.

In the procedure you will write, you will enter the following statement to set the Bookmark property of the form equal to the Bookmark property of the Recordset object, thus synchronizing the records:

```
Forms!frmTimeCards.Bookmark = rst.Bookmark
```

To write the code for the cmdFind button:

1. Right-click the **Find Record** button on the form, and then click **Build Event** on the shortcut menu.
2. If necessary, select **Code Builder** in the Choose Builder dialog box, and then type the following comment and statements, indenting as shown in Figure 9-18.

```
Dim rst As DAO.Recordset
'Find the record and then close the dialog box
Set rst = Forms!frmTimeCards.RecordsetClone
rst.FindFirst "TimeCardID = " & "'" & lstFind & "'"
Forms!frmTimeCards.Bookmark = rst.Bookmark
DoCmd.Close acForm, "frmFindTimeCards"
Set rst = Nothing
```

Figure 9-18 WRITING THE cmdFind CODE

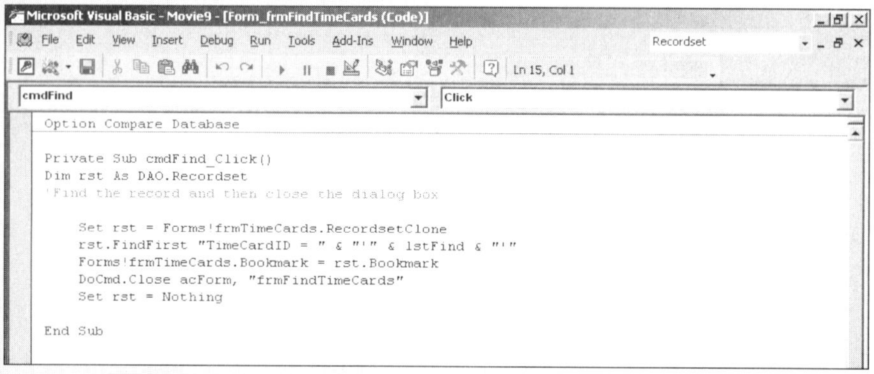

TROUBLE? The control name is lstFind, with the letter "l" as the first character, not the number 1. If you typed the number one (1), change it to the letter "l" and complete the procedure.

3. Click the **Object** list arrow, click **lstFind**, click the **Procedure** list arrow, and then click **AfterUpdate**.

   TROUBLE? If a blank BeforeUpdate Sub procedure was created before you selected AfterUpdate from the Procedure list box, simply delete the BeforeUpdate Sub procedure. Make sure you reposition the insertion point in the lstFind_AfterUpdate Sub procedure before continuing to the next step.

4. Press the **Enter** key, press the **Tab** key, type **cmdFind.Enabled = True**, and then press the **Enter** key. The additional spacing you are adding here makes the code easier to read.
5. Select **cmdCancel** from the **Object** list to create a blank Sub procedure for the click event, press the **Enter** key, press the **Tab** key, type **DoCmd.Close**, and then press the **Enter** key.
6. Click **Debug** on the menu bar, and then click **Compile Movie9**.
7. Click the **Save** button on the toolbar, and then close the Visual Basic window.
8. Minimize the form, open the **frmTimeCards** form in Form view, restore the **frmFindTimeCards** form, and switch to Form view. Both forms are now open in Form view. The frmFindTimeCards form should appear as shown in Figure 9-19.

Figure 9-19 **TESTING THE frmFindTimeCards FORM**

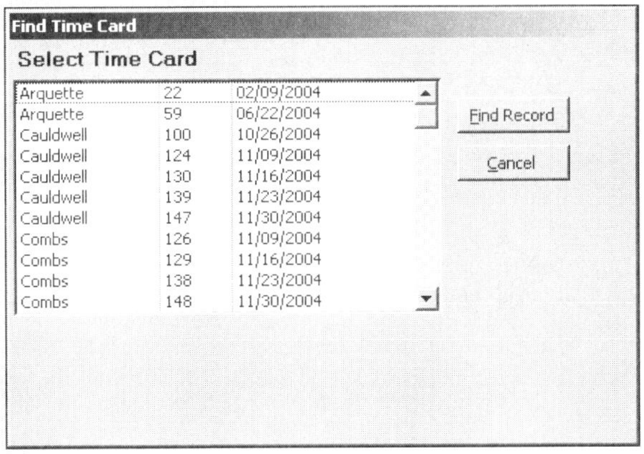

9. Click time card number **139** in the list box, and then click the **Find Record** button. The button is enabled when a selection is made from the list box, the record is shown in the frmTimeCard form, and the frmFindTimeCards form closes.

Next, you will add code to the frmTimeCards form. The code will open the frmFindTimeCards form when the Time Card No text box is double-clicked.

To open the frmFindTimeCards form from the frmTimeCards form:

1. Switch to Design view.
2. Click the **TimeCardID** text box, click the **Properties** button on the toolbar, click the **Event** tab, click in the **On Dbl Click** text box, click its **Build** button, and if necessary, click **Code Builder** in the Choose Builder dialog box.
3. Press the **Enter** key, press the **Tab** key, type **DoCmd.OpenForm "frmFindTimeCards"**, and then press the **Enter** key. The code should appear as shown in Figure 9-20.

Figure 9-20 **ADDING THE CODE TO THE frmFindTimeCards FORM**

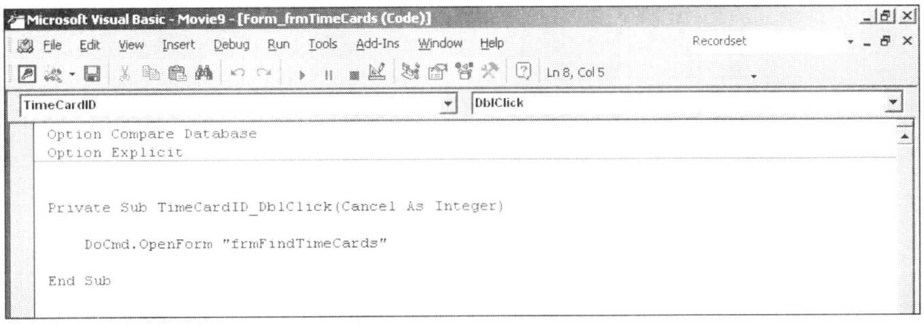

4. Close the Visual Basic window, close the property sheet, and then switch to Form view.
5. To test the code, double-click the **Time Card No** text box. The frmFindTimeCards form automatically opens.

6. Click the **Cancel** button on the frmFindTimeCards form to make sure that it closes.
7. Save the frmTimeCards form, and then close it.

The last thing you will do is add code to the frmFindTimeCards form, so that if a user double-clicks a time card in the list box, the time card will be found as if the user had clicked the Find button.

To complete the frmFindTimeCards form:

1. Open the **frmFindTimeCards** form in Design view.
2. Display the properties for the lstFind list box, click the **Event** tab if necessary, click in the **On Dbl Click** text box, click its **Build** button ..., and if necessary click **Code Builder**. The lstFind_DblClick Sub procedure is inserted.
3. Type the following comment and code, indenting as shown and inserting a blank line before and after the code block:

```
'Find the record that is double-clicked
If Not IsNull(lstFind) Then
      cmdFind_Click
End If
```

4. Compile the code, save your changes, close the Visual Basic window, close the property sheet, and then close the form.
5. Open the **frmTimeCards** form in Form view, double-click the **Time Card No** text box to open the frmFindTimeCards form, and then double-click time card **126**. The record is shown in the frmTimeCards form, and the frmFindTimeCards form is closed.
6. Close the frmTimeCards form.
7. Close the Movie9 database.

The new frmFindTimeCards form meets all of Martin's requirements and he prefers it to the combo box that you created in Tutorial 8. Although the combo box was fairly efficient, the pop-up form provides an additional field of data in a more aesthetically pleasing format. Forms such as frmFindTimeCards are typical features in many Windows-based applications and provide an alternative to the combo box while freeing up additional space on your form, frmTimeCards. You are pleased with the results, and now will turn your attention to assigning security levels to the database.

Session 9.1 QUICK CHECK

1. To write VBA code that works directly with the data in your application, you must work with ADO or ______________.
2. When is it a good idea to use DAO rather than ADO?
3. The ______________ is the database engine that Access uses for all of its native database management.

4. What is the object at the top of the DAO hierarchy? What object is at the top of the ADO hierarchy?
5. What are the types of Recordset objects?
6. How can a user create a system object?
7. Every form has a(n) ____________ property that you can use to get a copy of the form's underlying recordset.
8. The ____________ method of the Recordset object begins searching at the beginning of the recordset and continues to the end.
9. What is an object library?

SESSION 9.2

In this session, you will learn the different security options in Access and will implement user-level security on the MovieCam database. You will learn about the Workgroup Administrator and create a new workgroup information file. You will use the Security Wizard to create groups and users and to set permissions for them in the database. You also will set and clear passwords for users.

Overview of Security

You can apply a number of different security options to an Access database. In Tutorial 6, you changed the Startup properties and disabled the Bypass key to restrict users from opening database objects in Design view. This method is fine for a small application without lots of users, but it is not foolproof. In addition, it does not allow for various permissions for different users or groups of users.

The simplest method for protecting an Access database is to set a password on it. Once a password is set, a dialog box requests that password whenever a user attempts to open the database. Users can open the database only if they enter the correct password in the dialog box. After the database is open, the user has access to all objects in it. But, whenever an employee leaves the company or changes to a position where they no longer need or should have access to the database, you would need to change the database password and communicate the change to the remaining authorized users. This is not very efficient.

The most flexible and extensive method for securing a database is called user-level security. With **user-level security**, a database administrator can grant specific permissions to individual users and/or groups of users for any database object, except data access pages and modules. User-level security prevents users from changing tables, queries, forms, reports, and macros, and also protects sensitive data in the database. It follows a similar model to Windows security, relying on groups and users. The best practices approach is to set up groups and assign permissions to the groups, then you add or remove users from those groups. This makes security maintenance much more efficient and practical.

Workgroup Information File

An Access **workgroup** is a group of users in a multiuser environment who share data. If user-level security is defined, the members of a workgroup are recorded in an Access **workgroup information file** that is read at startup. This file contains the users' names, passwords, and the group to which they belong.

When you install Access, the Setup program automatically creates an Access workgroup information file that is identified by the name and organization information you provide during the installation process. Technically, security is established by default for each Access database you create. The only user in the database is Admin. Admin, by default, has full rights to all objects in the database and has no password. Therefore, each time you open an unsecured database, you open it as Admin with full rights, and no password is required. Each time you create a new database in Access, you create it as Admin, so, by default, Admin is the owner of each database. Owners and administrators have full rights to the database objects.

Amanda wants you to create a new workgroup information file for two critical reasons. The first is that Admin is the default owner and administrator of all databases in Access according to the default workgroup information file. If you do not create a new workgroup information file, users will not be able to use any Access database on the system without knowing the Admin password you created in the default workgroup information file. You must create a new workgroup information file that contains the name and password of a new user who is both owner and administrator.

The second reason is that the default workgroup information file simply contains the name and organization that was provided when the Access software was installed. This information is easy to obtain, and anyone who has it can re-create the default workgroup information file, identify themselves as an administrator account, and gain full rights to the database. To guard against this, you should create a new file that is protected by a workgroup ID.

A **workgroup ID** is a case-sensitive string that contains letters and/or numbers and is four to 20 characters long. Think of the workgroup ID as a password for the workgroup information file. Only someone who knows the workgroup ID can re-create the workgroup information file.

You can create the workgroup information file by running the Workgroup Administrator program that is installed with Access. You run this program by clicking the Tools menu, selecting Security, and then selecting the Workgroup Administrator option. There is also a User-Level Security Wizard that contains a dialog box asking whether you want to use the existing workgroup information file or create a new one.

An important point to remember is that when you join or create another workgroup information file, the default workgroup file, and any others you have created, still exists on your computer or network. If you begin to have difficulty working with a workgroup file, you can always rejoin your default file, so you should never delete the workgroup file that is installed with Access, and you should never alter that default workgroup file. Always create a new one for your purposes rather than edit the System.mdw.

While working with workgroup files, it is possible to assign yourself right out of administrative permissions, so that the next time you open Access and your database, you cannot administer the database. Please follow all the steps in this tutorial very carefully and always make a backup of your database file just prior to implementing security or creating a new workgroup information file. That way, if you make any mistakes, you can always start over by creating a new workgroup file and fall back on a copy of the unsecured database.

Creating a Workgroup Information File

The cleanest approach is to create the workgroup information file as a separate step from running the User-Level Security Wizard. When the wizard is run, the user currently logged into the database becomes the new owner of the database and all of the objects in it. Remember that the owner has full rights. If you create the workgroup information files as a part of running the User-Level Security Wizard, the new owner of the database becomes an unknown user, and you would need to assign an appropriate owner name at a later time or the unknown user name would have full control rights over the database. This would not be a secure situation. It is best to create the new workgroup information file, create a new administrative user named MovieAdmin, log in as MovieAdmin, and then run the wizard. This makes MovieAdmin the new administrator and the new owner of the database, which will save you from having to do some additional work later.

REFERENCE WINDOW RW

Creating a Workgroup Information File

- Click Tools on the menu bar, point to Security, and then click Workgroup Administrator.
- Click the Create button.
- Type a name, an organization, and a workgroup ID, and then click the OK button.
- Click the Browse button, and then navigate to the folder where you want to store the file.
- Type a filename and then click the Open button.
- Click the OK button to accept the change, click the OK button when the new name and path are specified, and then click the OK button again to acknowledge that the file has been created successfully.
- Click the Exit button.

You will create the new workgroup information file next.

To create a new workgroup information file:

1. Click **Tools** on the menu bar, point to **Security**, and then click **Workgroup Administrator** to open the Workgroup Administrator dialog box.

   The Workgroup Administrator dialog box shows the default workgroup information file, System.mdw, preceded by its path on the local or network drive, the name associated with the file, and the company associated with it. You will need to know the location of System.mdw later in order to make it the active file (rejoin it). If an error is made, you might also need to recreate the default workgroup information file later, and you will need all of this information to do that. As an added precaution, you might want to copy the System.mdw file to a floppy disk so that you can simply copy it back to the local or network drive later. See your instructor or technical support person if you need assistance to do this. The current location might possibly be at C:\Documents and Settings\Owner\Application Data\Microsoft\Access\System.mdw. The location of this file depends upon your operating system (Windows 98/2000/XP) and how Access was installed on the computer you are using.

2. Write down the location of System.mdw right now. You will need the exact location to complete the tutorial and the exercises at the end. This is extremely important.
3. Click the **Create** button, type *Your Name* in the Name text box if necessary, and then type **MovieCam Technologies** in the Organization text box.
4. Type **Movie1234** in the Workgroup ID text box, and then click the **OK** button. The Workgroup Information File dialog box opens.
5. Click the **Browse** button and then navigate to the Tutorial.09\Tutorial folder.
6. Click the **Save as type** list arrow, click **Workgroup Files** if necessary, and then type **MovieSecure** as the File Name. See Figure 9-21.

Figure 9-21 NAMING THE WORKGROUP INFORMATION FILE

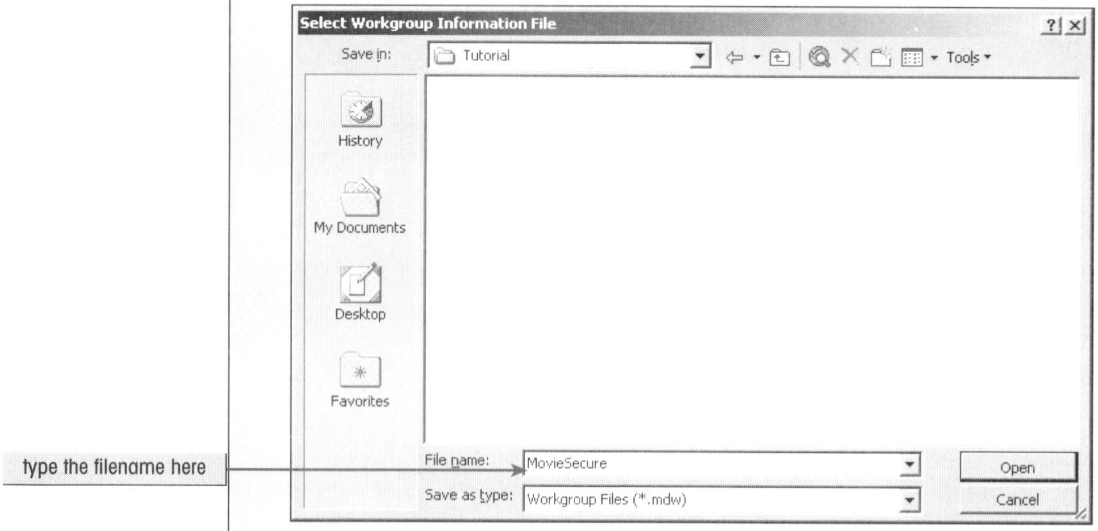

7. Click the **Open** button to complete the operation.
8. Click the **OK** button to accept the change, click the **OK** button when the new name and path are specified, and then click the **OK** button again to acknowledge that the file has been created successfully.
9. Make sure that the new workgroup information file specified is MovieSecure.mdw and that it is located in the Tutorial.09\Tutorial folder.
10. Click the **OK** button to close the Workgroup Administrator.

Rebuilding a Workgroup Information File

If a workgroup information file is damaged or deleted, you can re-create it as long as you have the exact, case-sensitive information that you used when you initially created the file. This information includes the name, company name, and workgroup ID.

Make sure that once you have created the new workgroup information file, you have users rejoin or modify their shortcuts if you've stored the file in a new location or if you have changed the name.

Security Accounts

The workgroup information file you create or use by default contains the following predefined user and group accounts:

- *Admin*: This is the default user account. This account is exactly the same for every copy of Access and for other applications such as VBA and Excel.
- *Admins*: This is the administrator's account group. Users in this group have full rights to all objects in the database. The group must have at least one user at all times. The Admin user is in the Admins group.
- *Users*: This group account contains all user accounts. Access automatically adds user accounts to the Users group when a member of the Admins group creates them. This account is the same for any workgroup information file,

but it contains only user accounts created by members of the Admins group of that workgroup and the Admin user. A user account can be removed from the Users group only if an Admins group member deletes that user.

Creating a New User

Before you make any changes to the users and groups, you decide to make a copy of the database. You will do that next.

To make a copy of the Movie9 database:

1. Open **Windows Explorer**.
2. Navigate to the Tutorial.09\Tutorial folder, right-click the **Movie9** file, and then click **Copy** on the shortcut menu.
3. Right-click an empty area of the window, and then click **Paste** on the shortcut menu.
4. Right-click the **Copy of Movie9** file, click **Rename** on the shortcut menu, type **Movie9TestCopy**, and then press the **Enter** key.
5. Close Windows Explorer, return to the Database window in Access, and then open **Movie9** if it is not already open.

Next, you want to determine the user and group accounts and the database owner. You will then make the changes necessary to establish a new owner and administrator.

To create a new owner and administrator:

1. Click **Tools** on the menu bar, point to **Security**, and then click **User and Group Accounts**. The User and Group Accounts dialog box opens, as shown in Figure 9-22. The Admin user is shown in the Name box, and the Admins and Users groups are shown in the Available Groups list box. The Member Of list box shows that Admin is currently a member of both the Users and Admins group.

Figure 9-22 USER AND GROUP ACCOUNTS DIALOG BOX

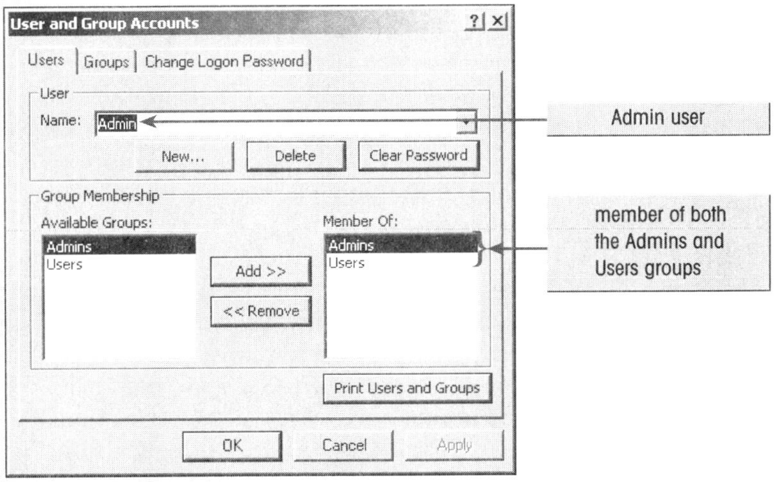

2. Click the **New** button to create a new user, and then type **MovieAdmin** in the Name text box.
3. Press the **Tab** key, type **Movie1234** in the Personal ID text box, and then click the **OK** button. The Personal ID is not the same as a password. It is a case-sensitive, alphanumeric string of four to 20 characters that Access combines with a user account name to identify a user or group in a workgroup.
4. With Admins selected in the Available Groups list box, click the **Add>>** button to make MovieAdmin a member of the Admins group, as shown in Figure 9-23. Recall that there must always be at least one member of the Admins group. You are adding the new user to this group. Next, you will take the Admin user out of the Admins group.

Figure 9-23 MAKING MovieAdmin A MEMBER OF THE ADMINS GROUP

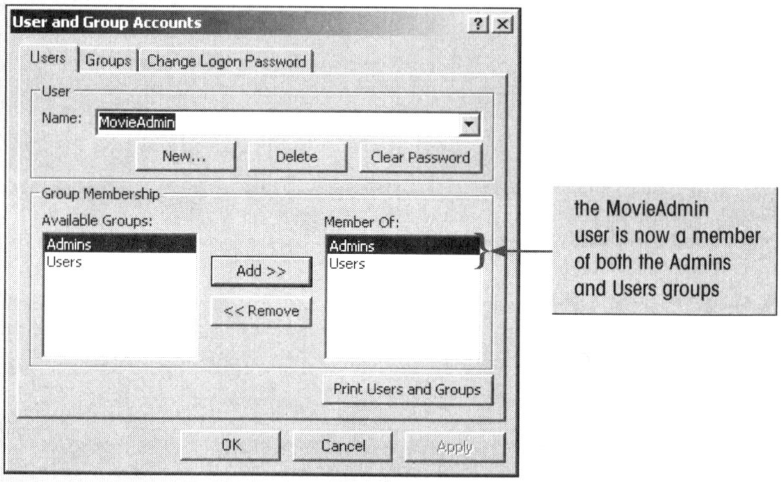

5. Click the **Name** list arrow, and then click **Admin**.
6. Make sure that **Admins** in the Member Of list box is selected, and then click the <<**Remove** button.

If you decide later to give database rights to the Users group, you need to guard against the possibility that someone might create a new workgroup information file with the Admin user in it. You also want to guard against a user joining the default workgroup information file, System.mdw, in which Admin exists but does not require a password. Setting a password now requires a user to use it to log into Movie9 as Admin. In addition, you must set an Admin password for Access to prompt you for a logon name. Because you will want to log on as MovieAdmin before you run the User-Level Security Wizard, you want that prompt to display.

The reason you entered a different Personal ID (PID) from the MovieAdmin user name is to help prevent someone from replicating your security set up. A PID is part of the encryption process. Once a user is created with the PID, there is no way to ever view that PID again, so be sure to write it down and lock it in a safe place. The workgroup information file contains the user and group names, but each database actually stores which users and groups have what type of permissions for each object. Attached to the object permissions for each user name, but hidden from view, is the PID that must be set each time you create a new user.

A workgroup information file can be used for many databases, but each database can only have one workgroup information file. Before using a fully secured database, a user has to join the appropriate workgroup information file, because you should have removed the typical admin rights. By making the PID something different than the user name, as you did above (that is, Movie1234), and safeguarding that information, you are preventing someone else from re-creating the MovieAdmin user the same way you did.

As an example, assume you had created the administrative MovieAdmin user, setting the user name and the PID both to be simply MovieAdmin. If anyone ever found out the administrative logon name (MovieAdmin), they could simply create their own workgroup information file, set up a new MovieAdmin user, using the same name for a PID, and then they would have all the same rights to your secured database as your MovieAdmin user does. But, if you use a different PID (such as Movie1234) for your MovieAdmin user, and someone else created a MovieAdmin user without matching your PID exactly, their version of the MovieAdmin user would not have the same rights as yours does, and your security would not be compromised. Using a PID that is different from the user name is an important step to help prevent someone from replicating your secure workgroup information file just by knowing only user names. Without knowing the PIDs, knowing the user names is worthless for trying to replicate a workgroup file. This is an additional layer of security beyond the workgroup information file's workgroup ID.

Setting a Password

Next, you'll change the logon password for the Admin user. Currently the Admin user is only a member of the Users group.

To add a password for the Admin user:

1. Click the **Change Logon Password** tab in the User and Group Accounts dialog box, as shown in Figure 9-24.

Figure 9-24 CHANGING THE ADMIN PASSWORD

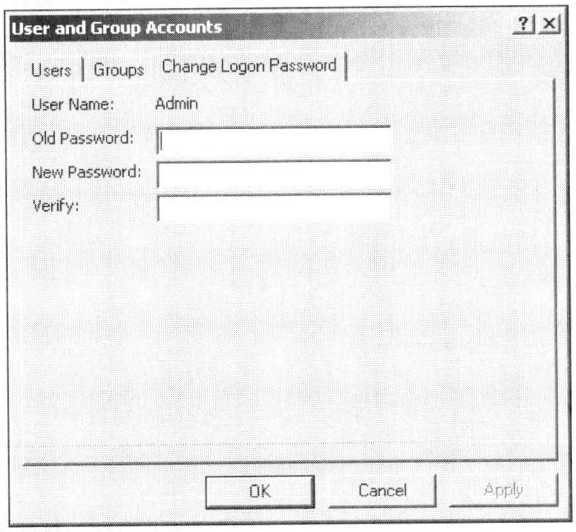

2. Press the **Tab** key to move to the New Password text box.
3. Type **moviecam**, press the **Tab** key, and then type **moviecam** again to confirm.
4. Click the **OK** button. Now you will test the password.

5. Exit Access.
6. Start Access and then open the **Movie9** database. The Logon dialog box opens. Before the database file will open, you need to log on.
7. Click in the **Name** text box, type **Admin**, and then press the **Tab** key.
8. Type **moviecam** as the password, and then click the **OK** button. The Movie9 database opens.
9. Close the Movie9 database, and then exit Access.

The next step in the process is to log on as the new administrator of the MovieAdmin database and assign a password to this account. You also will run the User-Level Security Wizard to secure the database.

User-Level Security Wizard

The User-Level Security Wizard performs the following tasks:

- Gives you the option to create a new workgroup information file
- Secures the objects you select in the database that is open when you run the wizard
- Lets you add new groups with predefined levels of security to the database
- Lets you add new users and passwords to the database
- Assigns ownership of the database and the objects in it to the user who is currently logged in
- Upon completion, prints a User-Level Security Wizard report that contains passwords and user names you create
- Makes a back-up copy of the database using the same name and the .bak extension

Running the User-Level Security Wizard

You will now log back on to the database as MovieAdmin. Although you defined a Personal ID (PID) for this user when you created the MovieAdmin user, a PID is not the same thing as a password. A password is used to access the application; the PID is used as a part of the encryption process. After you create a password for the MovieAdmin user, you will run the User-Level Security Wizard.

To create a password for the MovieAdmin user and run the User-Level Security Wizard:

1. Start Access and then open the **Movie9** database. The Logon dialog box opens.
2. Click in the **Name** text box, type **MovieAdmin**, and then click the **OK** button to open the database.
3. Click **Tools** on the menu bar, point to **Security**, and then click **User and Group Accounts**.
4. Click the **Change Logon Password** tab in the User and Group Accounts dialog box. Note that the current user is now MovieAdmin, as shown in Figure 9-25.

Figure 9-25 MovieAdmin IS THE CURRENT USER

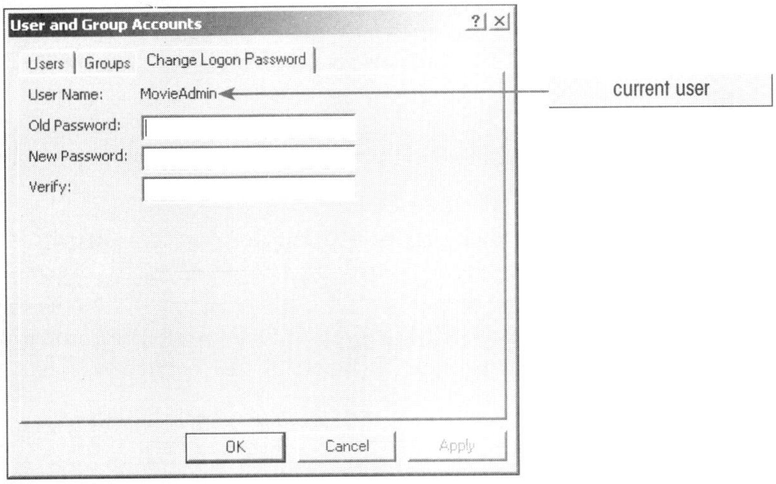

5. Press the **Tab** key, type **moviecam** in the New Password text box, press the **Tab** key, type **moviecam** in the Verify text box, and then click the **OK** button. Note that you are using simple passwords and repeating them. In a personal or business situation, you should create passwords that are at least six characters in length, and use a combination of letters and numbers to make your passwords difficult to determine.
6. Click **Tools** on the menu bar, point to **Security**, and then click **User-Level Security Wizard**. The first dialog box, which is shown in Figure 9-26, gives you the option of creating a new workgroup information file or modifying the existing one.

Figure 9-26 USER-LEVEL SECURITY WIZARD

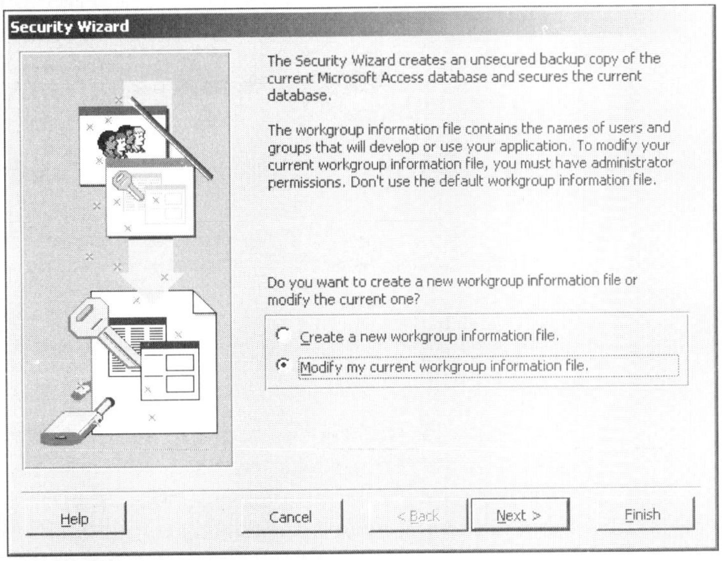

7. Make sure that the **Modify my current workgroup information file** option is selected, and then click the **Next** button. The next dialog box contains a list of objects in the database. All are selected by default to be secured. If you want an object to be unsecured, you would deselect it now.
8. Click the **Next** button.

The next dialog box in the User-Level Security Wizard lets you choose from a list of predefined groups with varying levels of security. Clicking an item in the list displays an explanation of the group permissions for that group. This dialog box creates the group so that you, as database administrator, are then able to add users to the group as you create them. You will add the Full Data Users group for the data entry employees, and the Read-Only Users group for some of the managers. You will add these groups next, and also complete the User-Level Security Wizard.

To complete the User-Level Security Wizard:

1. Click the **Full Data Users** and **Read-Only Users** check boxes, as shown in Figure 9-27, and then click the **Next** button. The next dialog box lets you grant permissions to the Users group. You will not give the Users group any permissions because you have two groups selected.

Figure 9-27 ADDING PREDEFINED GROUPS

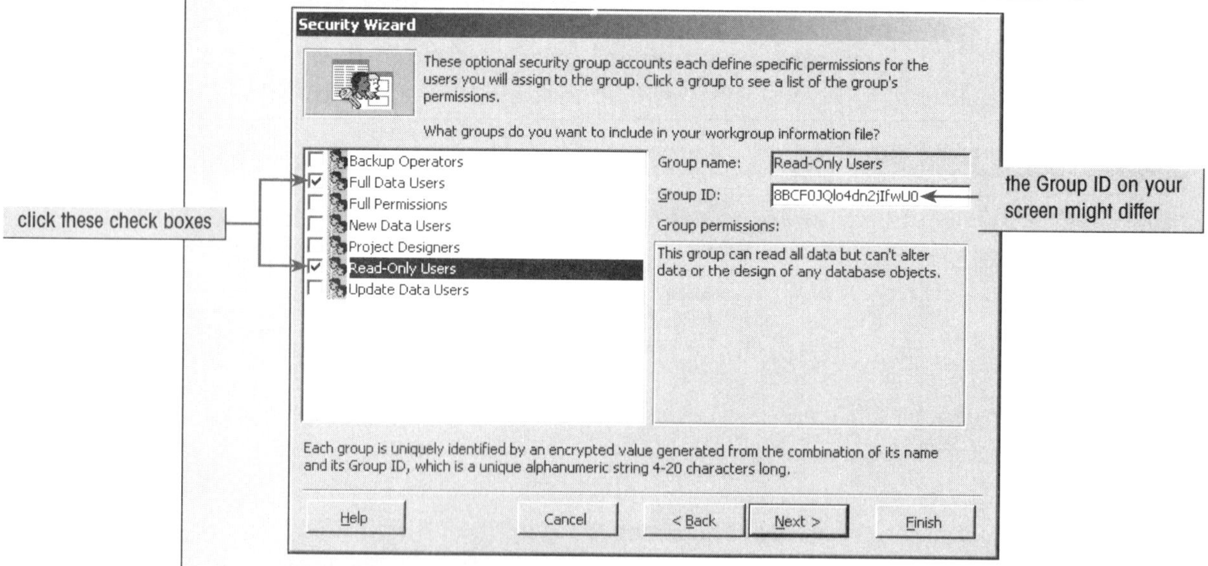

2. Make sure the **No, the Users group should not have any permissions** option is selected, and then click the **Next** button. The next wizard dialog box, which is shown in Figure 9-28, lets you add new users and passwords for these users. A PID is automatically provided. You will add Martin as a new user, but you will not add a password. The users can set their own password the first time they log on to the database.

Figure 9-28 ADDING USERS

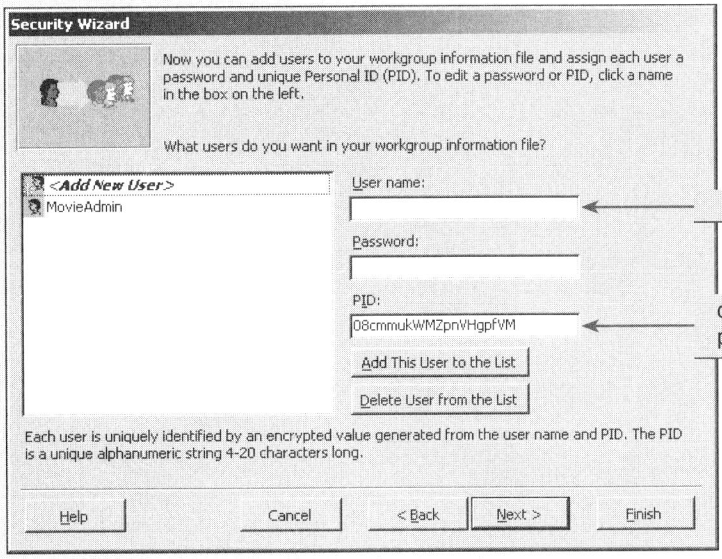

3. Type **mwoodward** in the User name text box , click the **Add This User to the List** button. To include Amanda as a user, type **atyson** in the User name text box, click the **Add This User to the List** button, and then click the **Next** button. The next dialog box, which is shown in Figure 9-29, lets you add database users to specific groups. As you see, MovieAdmin is currently in the Admins group.

Figure 9-29 ADDING USERS TO GROUPS

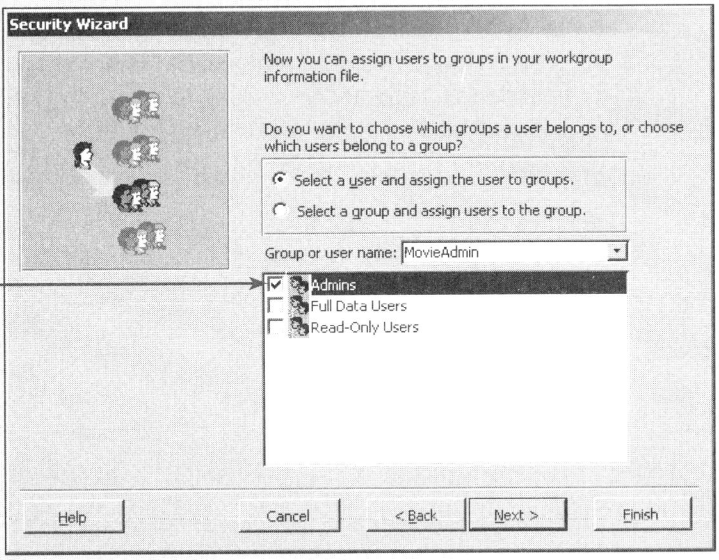

4. Click the **Group or user name** list arrow, click **mwoodward**, check the **Read-Only Users** option, click the **Group or user name** list arrow, click **atyson**, check the **Full Data Users** option, and then click the **Next** button.

5. The final wizard dialog box asks you to choose a name and path for the back-up file the wizard will create. If the wizard is suggesting the name Movie10.bak, change it to Movie9.bak, as shown in Figure 9-30.

Figure 9-30 SAVING THE BACK-UP FILE

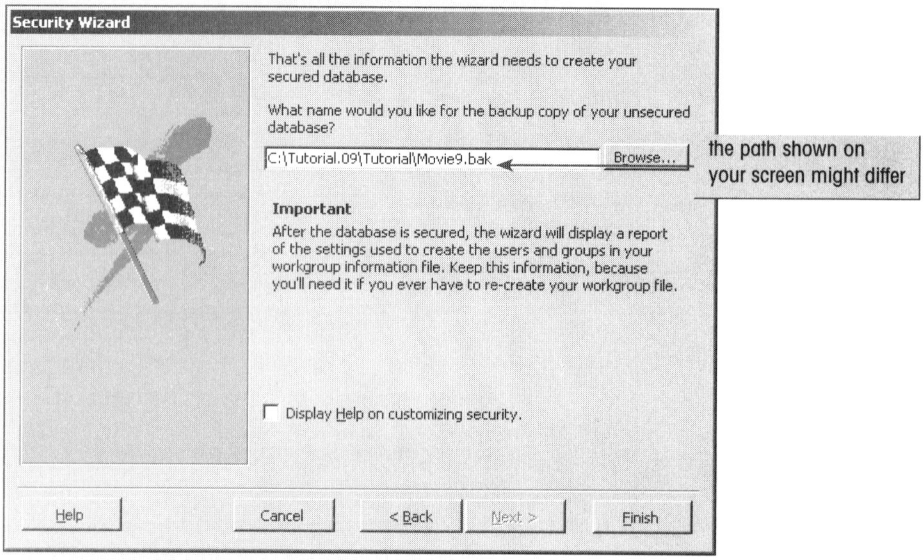

6. After verifying the name and path as being correct for your situation, click the **Finish** button. The One-step Security Wizard Report is shown in Print Preview. This report contains the information you need to re-create the workgroup information file and the list of users of the database. You will export it to Word so that you can print it later.
7. Click the list arrow for the **OfficeLinks** button on the toolbar, and then click **Publish It with Microsoft Word** to export the report to a Word document.
8. Close the Word document, which is assigned the name swz_rptSecure, and then close the report. A dialog box appears and asks if you want to save the report as a Snapshot file. You have saved the report as a Word file, so you will not use the report again in another format.
9. Click the **No** button to return to the Database window.
10. Close the Movie9 database, and then exit Access. You are exiting because you are currently logged on as MovieAdmin. To log on as another user, you must exit Access and then open it again.

Next, you will test the security of the database.

Testing User-Level Security

To test the MovieSecure workgroup information file that is currently in use, you will log on as atyson and test this user's access to various objects in the database. Recall that this user is a member of the Full Data Users group.

To test the security of the Movie9 database:

1. Start Access, open the **Movie9** database, type **atyson** in the Name text box, and then click the **OK** button. Recall that you have not assigned a password to this user.

2. Click **Forms** on the Objects bar in the Database window, click **frmReportsSwitchboard**, and then click the **Open** button. The form opens fine. Now you'll test to be sure that reports can be previewed.
3. Click the **Employee List** option, and then click the **Preview** button. The Employee List report opens in Print Preview.
4. Click the **Close** button to close the report, and then click the **Design view** button to switch to the Design view of the frmReportsSwitchboard form. You receive the error message shown in Figure 9-31.

Figure 9-31 TESTING USER-LEVEL SECURITY ON THE frmReportsSwitchboard FORM

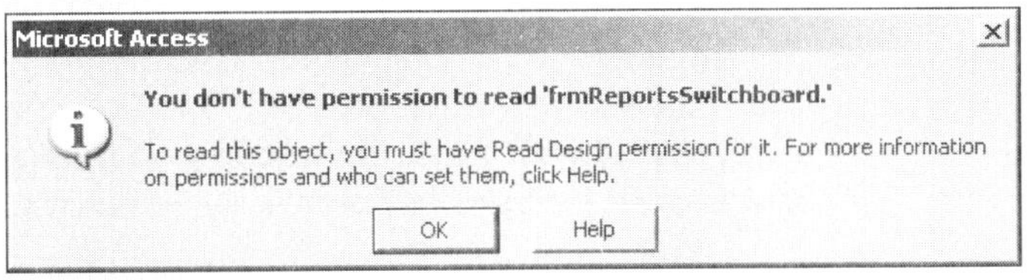

5. Click the **OK** button, and then close the frmReportsSwitchboard form.
6. Click **Tables** on the Objects bar in the Database window, click **tblEmployees**, and then click the **Design** button. You receive the error message shown in Figure 9-32.

Figure 9-32 TESTING USER-LEVEL SECURITY ON THE tblEmployees TABLE

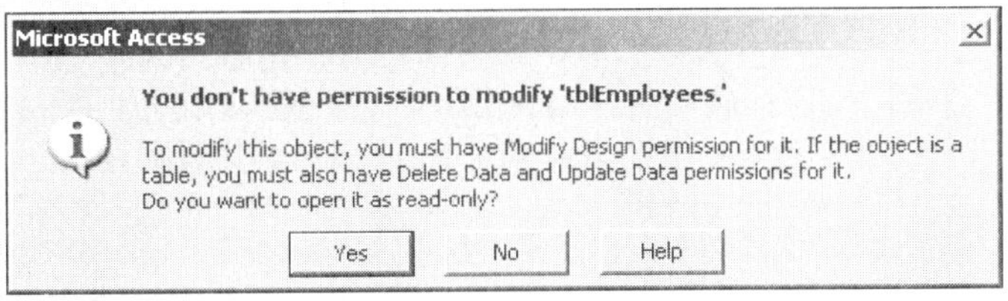

7. Click the **No** button to close the dialog box. You will conduct one more test to determine whether users can make changes to their own permissions.
8. Click **Tools** on the menu bar, point to **Security**, and then click **User and Group Permissions**.
9. Make sure that **atyson** is selected in the User/Group Name list box, that **Table** is selected in the Object Type list box, that **tblEmployees** is selected in the Object Name list box, and then click the **Read Design**, **Modify Design**, and **Administer** check boxes.
10. Click the **OK** button. You receive the error message shown in Figure 9-33.

Figure 9-33 TESTING USER-LEVEL SECURITY ON DATABASE PERMISSIONS

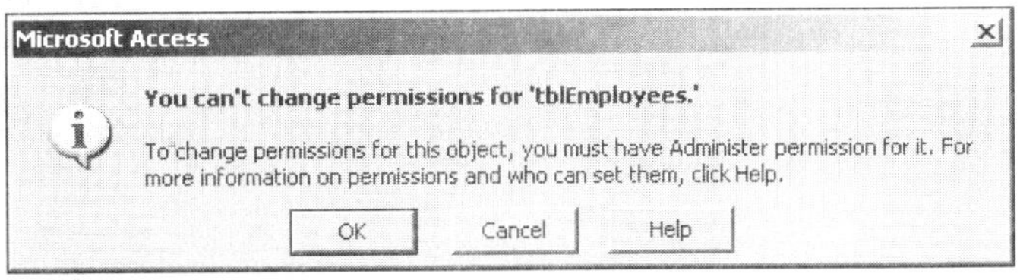

11. Click the **OK** button in the error message, and then click the **Cancel** button in the User and Group Permissions dialog box.

Amanda asks you how this new workgroup information file, MovieSecure, will affect users' access to other databases on which the User-Level Security Wizard has not been run. For example, what would happen if you were to close the secure database, Movie9, and then open the Movie9TestCopy database, which is an unsecured copy? You will test this next.

To test an unsecured database:

1. Close the **Movie9** database, but do not exit Access. This way the current user, atyson, is still logged on.
2. Open the **Movie9TestCopy** database from the Tutorial.09\Tutorial folder on your local or network drive. This is the original file you copied at the beginning of this session.
3. Click **Forms** on the Objects bar of the Database window, click **frmReportsSwitchboard**, and click the **Design** button to open this form in Design view. It opens as it normally would without security implemented.
4. Close the frmReportsSwitchboard form, click **Tables** on the Objects bar of the Database window, and open the **tblEmployees** table in Design view. Again note that the table opens as it normally would. To investigate why these objects open with no error messages, you'll take a look at the security settings.
5. Close the tblEmployees table, click **Tools** on the menu bar, point to **Security**, and then click **User and Group Accounts**. Note that the same users and groups that were defined for the Movie9 database exist in this database as well, as shown in Figure 9-34. This is because you are still using the new MovieSecure workgroup information file. Recall that the users and groups, passwords, and PIDs are all stored in this file. The specific permissions assigned to the objects in the Movie9 database are attached to the user names and PIDs of this workgroup information file. This test copy of the database, backed up before you ran the User-Level Security Wizard, does not have permissions associated with its objects, even though you can still see the users and groups from the workgroup.

Figure 9-34 MovieSecure WORKGROUP INFORMATION FILE ON ORIGINAL DATABASE

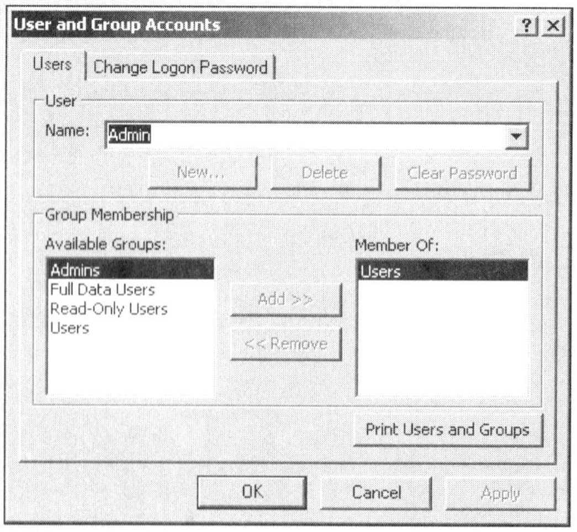

6. Click the **Name** list arrow, and then click **atyson**. Note that atyson is a member of two groups: the Users group and the Full Data Users group. Recall that all new users created by the database administrator are automatically added to the Users group. In the secured Movie9 database, the Users group has no permissions to any of the database objects. Next, you'll see what rights the Users group has in this database.
7. Click the **OK** button to close the User and Group Accounts dialog box, click **Tools** on the menu bar, point to **Security**, and click **User and Group Permissions**.
8. Click the **Groups** option button, click **Users** in the **User/Group Name** list box, and then click the **Object Type** list arrow. If necessary, click **Table**, and then click **tblEmployees** in the Object Name list box. See Figure 9-35. Note the permissions that all Users group members have in an unsecured database. They have permissions to read, write, and change all of the objects. However, in the Movie9 database, members of the Users group have no permissions.

Figure 9-35 PERMISSIONS FOR USERS GROUP MEMBERS IN AN UNSECURED DATABASE

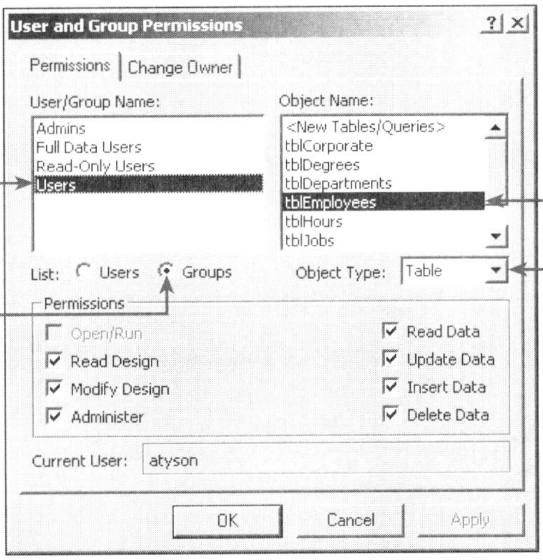

9. Click the **OK** button to close the User and Group Permissions dialog box.
10. Close the Movie9TestCopy database, but leave Access open.

Joining the Default Workgroup

Next, you will rejoin the default workgroup information file, System.mdw, so that it can be used with other Access databases.

To join the default workgroup information file:

1. Click the **Tools** menu, point to **Security**, and then select **Workgroup Administrator** to open the Workgroup Administrator dialog box.
2. Click the **Join** button.

3. Click the **Browse** button, and then navigate to the System.mdw location that you wrote down near the beginning of this session.
4. Click **System.mdw**, click the **Open** button, and then click the **OK** button. The message dialog box opens, as shown in Figure 9-36.

Figure 9-36 JOINING THE DEFAULT WORKGROUP INFORMATION FILE

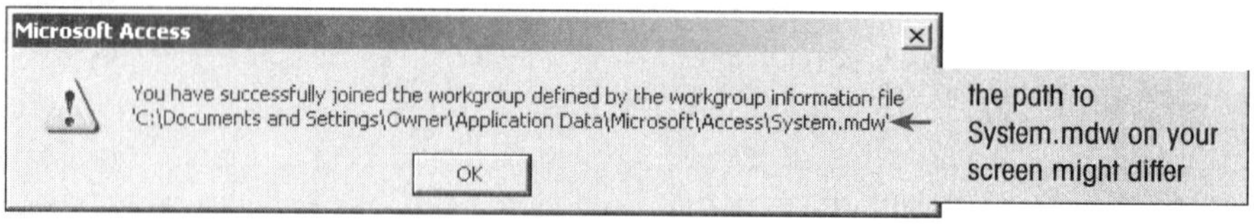

5. Click the **OK** button, and then click the **OK** button in the Workgroup Administrator dialog box.

TROUBLE? The path shown in Figure 9-36 might not match the path to your System.mdw file. If you are having trouble relocating the System.mdw file, use the Find option in Windows Explorer, write down the full path, and then repeat Steps 1 through 5 again.

Next, you'll open an unsecured database to see the effect of using the default System.mdw workgroup information file.

To open an unsecured database while the default workgroup information file is in use:

1. Open the **Movie9TestCopy** database.
2. Click **Tools** on the menu bar, point to **Security**, and then click **User and Group Accounts**. The default user and groups are visible, as shown in Figure 9-37. The only user is Admin and the only groups are Admins and Users. These are the default user and groups specified earlier in this tutorial.

Figure 9-37 DEFAULT USERS AND GROUPS

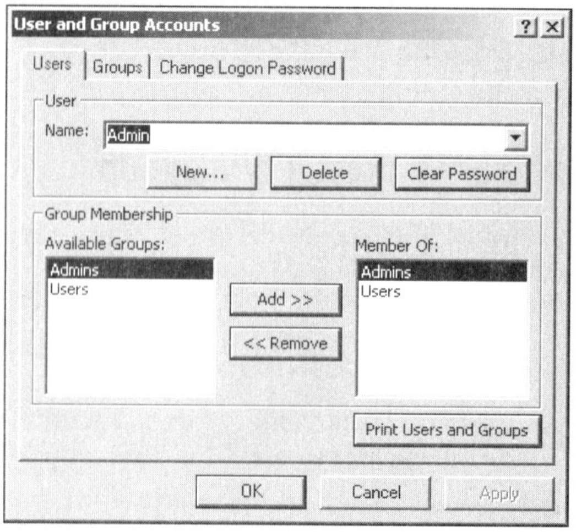

3. Click the **OK** button to close the User and Group Accounts dialog box, and then close the Movie9TestCopy database.
4. Open the secured version of the **Movie9** database. Recall that you have rejoined the default workgroup. You should see the following message as shown in Figure 9-38, if you have followed all previous security steps in this session.

Figure 9-38 PERMISSION TO OPEN DATABASE DENIED

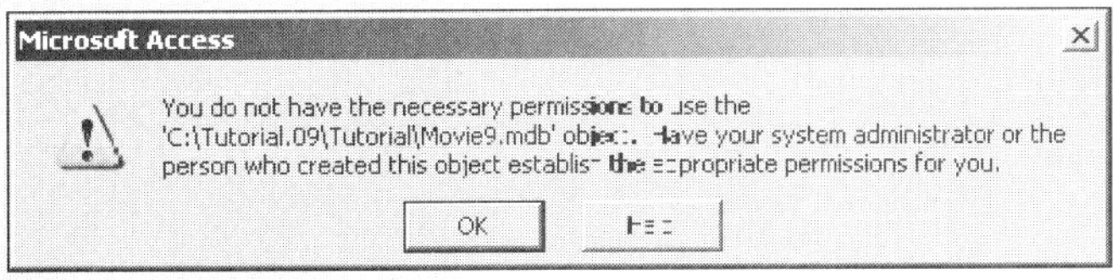

5. Click the **OK** button to close the message box.

Assigning Permissions

You can assign two types of permissions in user-level security: explicit and implicit. **Explicit permissions** are granted directly to a user account and no other account is affected. **Implicit permissions** are granted to a group account. When you add a user to a group, the group's permissions are granted to that user; removing a user from a group takes away those permissions.

A user's security level is based on both the implicit and explicit permissions of that user, and that level is always the less restrictive of the two. This means that you can add a user to a group that has a particular level of permissions, yet still give that user less restrictive permissions than those of a group to which he or she belongs. The simplest way to administer a workgroup of users is to create new groups and assign permissions to the group. You can then add users to the group that has restrictions that are closest to what you want for that user, and, if necessary, add additional permissions to the individual user.

Only a member of the Admins group, or a user who has Administer permission for an object, or the owner of an object, can change permissions.

Owners and Permissions

The user who creates a table, query, form, report, or macro is the **owner** of that object. The same group previously identified as having the ability to change permissions can also change ownership of the database or the objects in it. The simplest way to change ownership of all the objects in the database is to create a new database and import all of the objects, or run the User-Level Security Wizard. The user who is logged on will then have ownership.

Group accounts cannot own databases, but can own database objects. In this case, all the members of the group own the object.

You decide that the Read-Only Users group should have read-only rights to all data except that in the tblEmployees table. Because this table contains salary information, you want only a small group of users to have access to it.

First, you will need to rejoin the secured workgroup you created earlier in this session.

To rejoin the MovieSecure workgroup and open the Movie9 database:

1. Using the Tools menu, open the **Workgroup Administrator** dialog box, and rejoin the **MovieSecure** workgroup that you saved to your Tutorial.09\Tutorial folder on your local or network drive.
2. Open the **Movie9** database and log in as **MovieAdmin** using the password **moviecam** that you created earlier.

REFERENCE WINDOW RW

Changing Permissions

- Click Tools on the menu bar, point to Security, and then click User and Group Permissions.
- Select the Users or Groups option button to select whether you are changing permissions for a user or a group, and then select the user or group from the User/Group Name list box.
- In the Object Name list box, select the object for which you want to change permissions.
- Click the appropriate permissions, and then click OK to close the User and Group Permissions dialog box.

Your first step will be to remove the group's rights to this data. Then you will test the change and assign an individual user the rights to that data.

To change permissions for a group:

1. Click **Tools** on the menu bar, point to **Security**, and then click **User and Group Permissions**.
2. Click the **Groups** option button, and then click **Read-Only Users** in the User/Group Name list box.
3. Click **tblEmployees** in the Object Name list box if necessary, and then clear the **Read Design** check box if necessary, as shown in Figure 9-39. Clearing this check box forces the Read Data check box to be cleared. Access requires that for a user to be able to Read Data, at a minimum, the user must also have permission to Read Design as well.

Figure 9-39 CLEARING THE PERMISSIONS FOR READ-ONLY USERS

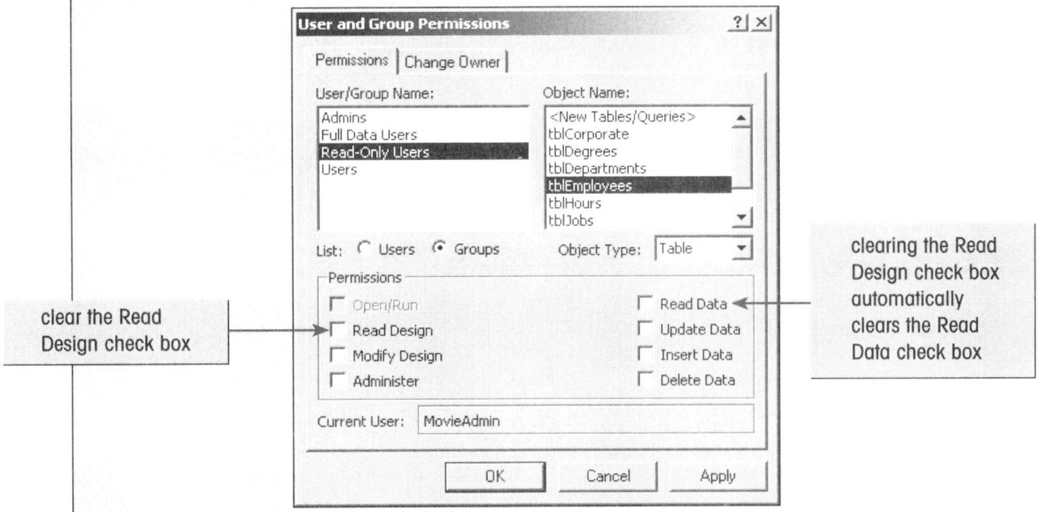

4. Click the **OK** button to close the User and Group Permissions dialog box.
5. Close the Movie9 database, and then exit Access.
6. Start Access and open the **Movie9** database.
7. Type **mwoodward** in the Name text box, and then click the **OK** button. This user is a member of the Read-Only Users group.
8. If necessary, click **Tables** on the Objects bar in the Database window, and then click **tblEmployees**. Now click the **Open** button. This user does not have permission to modify this object.
9. Click the **OK** button to close the message box and return to the Database window.
10. Close the Movie9 database, and then exit Access.

You now know that the change to the Read-Only Users group took effect, so you will add another user to the group—rjenkins. Richard Jenkins is a manager in Human Resources and needs access to the employee data. You will modify his permissions to include the tblEmployees table. You also want to enable his rights to modify data in the tblEmployees table.

To add a new user and change permissions:

1. Open the **Movie9** database, and logon as **MovieAdmin** using the password **moviecam**. You need to log on as an administrator or owner to add users and change permissions.
2. Click **Tools** on the menu bar, point to **Security**, and then click **User and Group Accounts**.
3. Click the **New** button, type **rjenkins** in the Name text box, and then type **rjmovie2468** in the Personal ID text box.
4. Click the **OK** button, click **Read-Only Users** in the Available Groups list box, and then click the **Add>>** button.

5. Click the **OK** button, click **Tools** on the menu bar, point to **Security**, and then click **User and Group Permissions**.
6. Click **rjenkins** in the User/Group Name list box, and then make sure **tblEmployees** is selected in the Object Name list box.
7. Click the **Read Data**, **Update Data**, **Insert Data**, and **Delete Data** check boxes, as shown in Figure 9-40. The Read Design check box is checked automatically when you click the Read Data option.

Figure 9-40 **CHANGING PERMISSIONS FOR rjenkins**

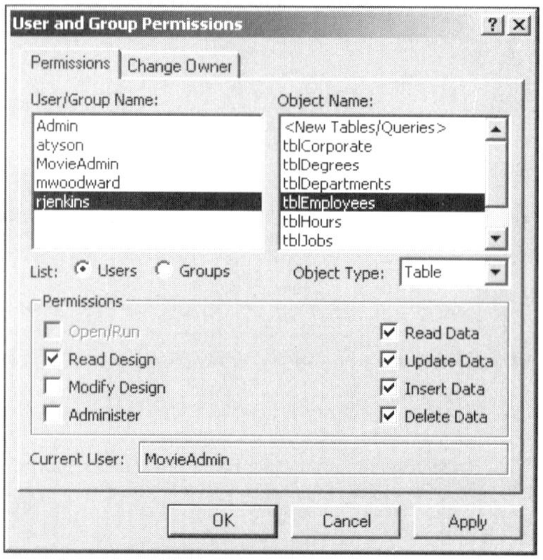

8. Click the **OK** button to accept the changes.
9. Close the Movie9 database, and then exit Access.

Now that you have made the necessary changes to the user account, you need to log on as rjenkins to test them. You will do that next. In addition, you need to determine the method for a user to set up a password when he or she first logs on.

Setting Passwords

Passwords for the user security accounts are created so that no other user can log on using that name. You plan to have users establish their own passwords the first time they log on to the new system. As you have seen, by default, Access assigns a blank password to any new user in the workgroup. For a new user to establish a password, they must start Access, log on with that user name, and then open User and Group Accounts from the Security menu. The password can be entered on the Change Logon Password tab.

REFERENCE WINDOW RW

Clearing a Password

- Open the database and logon as the user for whom you want to create a password.
- Click Tools on the menu bar, point to Security, and then click User and Group Accounts.
- Click the Name list arrow, scroll down, and then click the name of the user for whom you want to clear the password.
- Click the Clear Password button, and then click OK to close the User and Group Accounts dialog box.

A password can be one to 20 characters in length, can include any combination of numbers and special characters, and is case sensitive. Neither you nor your users can recover a password if they forget it. If a user forgets a password, an administrative user must log on and then clear the password for that user.

Next, you will test the changes to the rjenkins permissions, set a password as rjenkins, and then log back on as the administrative user to clear the password.

To set and clear a password:

1. Open the **Movie9** on the desktop, type **rjenkins** in the Name text box, and then click the **OK** button.
2. Click **Tools** on the menu bar, point to **Security**, click **User and Group Accounts**, and then click the **Change Logon Password** tab.
3. Type **test** in the New Password text box, press the **Tab** key, and then type **test** in the Verify text box.
4. Click the **OK** button to accept the change, open the **tblEmployees** table in Datasheet view, tab to the Hourly Rate field for **Thomas Arquette**, and then type **60.00**. Note that the change is accepted.
5. Press the **Esc** key to cancel the change, close the tblEmployees table, close the Movie9 database, and then exit Access.
6. Start Access, open the **Movie9** database, and log on as **MovieAdmin**, using the same password you have previously used for MovieAdmin.
7. Click **Tools** on the menu bar, point to **Security**, and then click **User and Group Accounts**.
8. Click the **Name** list arrow, and then click **rjenkins** from the list, as shown in Figure 9-41.

Figure 9-41 **CLEARING THE PASSWORD FOR rjenkins**

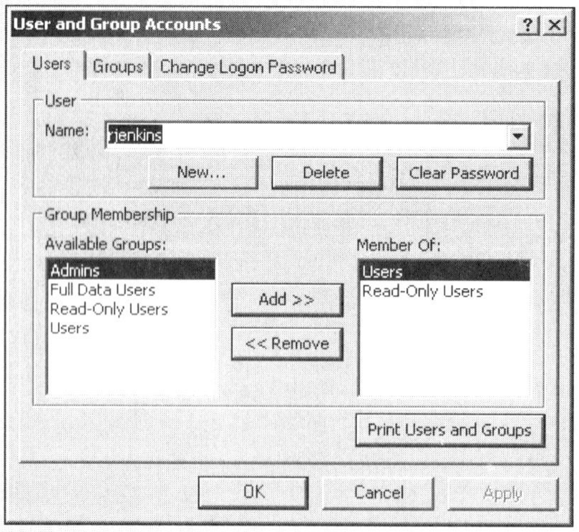

9. Click the **Clear Password** button, and then click the **OK** button to close the User and Group Accounts dialog box.
10. Close the Movie9 database and then exit Access.

Removing **User-Level Security**

There are times when you might need to remove user-level security from a secured database. This is a two-step process. First, log on to the database as a workgroup administrator, and give the Users group permissions on all tables, queries, forms, reports, and macros. Then return ownership of the database and objects to the default Admin user. To do this, exit, log on as Admin, create a blank database, and then import all of the objects from the original database into the blank database. You also should clear any password that you set for the Admin user if the users will not be using the default workgroup information file. Recall that in the default workgroup information file, Admin has no password.

Now that you have set up the groups for the new database, you can add users as necessary. Users will be able to create their own passwords for the system and, as administrators, you can make modifications and changes as necessary to the database objects. You plan to use the menus and switchboards that you developed in earlier tutorials as the user interface to the system, but you will not need to use code to disable the Bypass key now that user-level security is in place.

If you do not do any of the exercises at the end of the tutorial, prior to continuing on with Tutorial 10 you should rejoin your default workgroup by following the steps provided previously for joining the default workgroup.

Session 9.2 QUICK CHECK

1. What is a workgroup?
2. In an unsecured database, the default user is ______________.
3. The default workgroup information file is named ______________.

4. What is the simplest method for setting up database security?
5. The workgroup information file you create or use by default contains what predefined user and group accounts?
6. What is the difference between a PID and a password?
7. The user who creates a table, query, form, report, or macro is the ____________ of that object.
8. Who can change permissions for a user or group?
9. If a user forgets a password, is it possible to recover it?

REVIEW ASSIGNMENTS

The Hours9 database is similar to the MovieCam Technologies database you worked on in this tutorial. You want to implement user-level security on the database. You will create the users and run the User-Level Security Wizard to accomplish this task.

1. Start Access, click the Tools menu, point to Security, and then click Workgroup Administrator to open the Workgroup Administrator dialog box. Make sure that you write down the location of the default workgroup information file, System.mdw, if you have not already done so, in order to rejoin it later. If you are not joined to the default workgroup information file at this time, just be sure you have already written down the path to the default workgroup information file and proceed to the next step.
2. Join the workgroup named **HoursSecure** located in the Tutorial.09\Review folder on your local or network drive.
3. Open the **Hours9** database located in the Tutorial.09\Review folder on your network or local drive.
4. Click Tools on the menu bar, point to Security, and then click User and Group Accounts.
5. Click the New button to create a new user, and then type **HoursAdmin** in the Name text box.
6. Press the Tab button, type **Hours1234** in the Personal ID text box, and then click the OK button.
7. With Admins selected in the Available Groups list box, click the Add>> button to make HoursAdmin a member of the Admins group.
8. Click the Name list arrow, and then click Admin.
9. Make sure that Admins is selected in the Member Of list box, and then click the <<Remove button.
10. Click the Change Logon Password tab, press the Tab key to move to the New Password text box, type **hours**, press the Tab key, type **hours** again to confirm, and then click the OK button.
11. Close the Hours9 database, exit Access, restart Access, reopen the **Hours9** database, type **HoursAdmin** in the Name text box, and then press the Enter key.

12. Click Tools on the menu bar, point to Security, click User-Level Security Wizard, make sure that the Modify my current workgroup information file option is selected, and then click the Next button. All the objects should be checked in the next dialog box. Click the Next button, click the Full Data Users check box, click the Next button, make sure the No, the Users group should not have any permissions option is checked, and then click the Next button.
13. Type **tjames** in the User name text box, click the Add This User to the List button, click the Next button, click the Group or user name list arrow, click tjames, check the Full Data Users option, and then click the Next button.
14. Click the Finish button to accept the default name and location. The One-step Security Wizard Report opens in Print Preview. Close the report. When prompted to create a snapshot file, click No.
15. Change the logon password for HoursAdmin to **hours9adm39**.
16. Close the Hours9 database, and then exit Access.
17. Repeat Step 1 to open the Workgroup Administrator, and then join the default workgroup information file System.mdw again. (*Hint*: It is essential that you perform this step before beginning the Case Problems for this tutorial or beginning Tutorial 10.) Exit Access.

CASE PROBLEMS

Case 1. Edwards and Company User-level security has been established on the Edwards and Company database. The administrative use- and owner of the database is EdwardAdmin. No password has been established. You need to create two new users and add them to the Read-Only Users group. Complete the following:

1. Start Access and then open the Workgroup Administrator dialog box. Note the location of the default workgroup information file, System.mdw, if you have not already done so, in order to rejoin it later. If you are not joined to the default workgroup information file at this time, just be sure you have already written down the path to the default workgroup information file and proceed to the next step.
2. Join the **EdwardSecure** workgroup information file located in the Tutorial.09\Cases folder on your local or network drive.
3. Open the **Edward9** database located in the Tutorial.09\Cases folder on the network or local drive.
4. Type **EdwardAdmin** in the Name text box, and then click the OK button.
5. Click Tools on the menu bar, point to Security, and then click User and Group Accounts.
6. Click the New button to create a new user, and then type **jedwards** in the Name text box.
7. Press the Tab button, type **Edwards1234** in the Personal ID text box, and then click the OK button.
8. Select Read-Only Users in the Available Groups list box, and click the Add>> button to make jedwards a member of the group.
9. Click the New button to create a new user, and then type **medwards** in the Name textbox.

10. Press the Tab button, type **Edwards5678** in the Personal ID text box, and then click the OK button.
11. Select Read-Only Users in the Available Groups list box, and click the Add>> button to make medwards a member of the group.
12. Click the OK button to close the User and Group Accounts dialog box, close the Edward9 database, and then exit Access.
13. Restart Access, open the **Edward9** database, type **jedwards** in the Name text box, and then press the Enter key.
14. Click Tools on the menu bar, point to Security, and then click User and Group Accounts.
15. Click the Change Logon Password tab, type **edwards** in the New Password text box, type **edwards** in the Verify text box, and then click the OK button.
16. Close the **Edward9** database, and then exit Access.
17. Repeat Step 1 to open the Workgroup Administrator, and then join the default workgroup information file System.mdw. (*Hint*: It is essential that you perform this step before beginning Case Problems 2 or 4 or beginning Tutorial 10.) Exit Access.

Case 2. San Diego County Information Systems You are going to implement user-level security on the training database and need to create a workgroup information file to store the new users and passwords. You will create this file next. Complete the following:

1. Start Access and then open the Workgroup Administrator dialog box. Note the location of the default workgroup information file, System.mdw, if you have not already done so, in order to rejoin it later. If you are not joined to the default workgroup information file at this time, just be sure you have already written down the path to the default workgroup information file and proceed to the next step.
2. Click the Create button, type ***Your Name*** in the Name text box, type **San Diego County ISD** in the Organization text box, type **ISD1234** in the Workgroup ID text box, and then click the OK button.
3. Click the Browse button and then navigate to the Tutorial.09\Cases folder on the network or local drive.
4. Change the filename to **ISDSecure**, and then click the Open button.
5. Click the OK button to accept the change, click the OK button when the new name and path are specified, and then click the OK button again to acknowledge that the file has been created successfully.
6. Click the OK button to close the Workgroup Administrator, exit Access, start Access, and then open the **ISD9** database located in the Tutorial.09\Cases folder.
7. Click Tools on the menu bar, point to Security, and then click User and Group Accounts.
8. Click the New button to create a new user, and then type **ISDAdmin** in the Name text box.
9. Press the Tab button, type **ISD1234** in the Personal ID text box, and then click the OK button.
10. With Admins selected in the Available Groups list box, click the Add>> button to make ISDAdmin a member of the Admins group, click the Name list arrow, and then click Admin.
11. Make sure that Admins in the Member Of list box is selected, and then click the <<Remove button. Close the User and Group Accounts dialog box.

12. Open the Database Documenter.
13. Make sure that the Tables tab is selected, click the Select All button, click the Options button, select the Permissions by User and Group option for Include for Table, select the Nothing option for Include for Fields, and select the Names and Fields option for Include for Indexes. Make sure no other options are selected.
14. Click the OK button, and then click the OK button again to preview the report.
15. Print the report, close the ISD9 database, and then exit Access.
16. Repeat Step 1 to open the Workgroup Administrator, and then join the default workgroup information file System.mdw. (*Hint*: It is essential that you complete this step before beginning Case Problem 4 or Tutorial 10.) Exit Access.

Case 3. Christenson Homes The frmLots form in the Homes9 database is used for entering data into the tblLots table and the tblCustomers table. Roberta wants to be able to look up a record by the subdivision and then by the address. On the frmLotSearch form you will create a list box to display the subdivision and lot address. You will open the list box by double-clicking the Address text box on the frmLots form. Complete the following:

1. Start Access and open the **Homes9** database located in the Tutorial.09\Cases folder on the network or local drive. A blank form named frmFindLots has been created in the database.
2. Open the **frmFindLots** form in Design view, and create a list box on the form that looks up the Subdivision name and the Lot address from the tblSubdivisions and tblLot tables, respectively. Name the list box 1stFind.
3. Create a button to find the record on the frmLots form. (*Hint*: This text assumes that you completed all the exercises in the tutorial. If not, you need to add Microsoft DAO 3.6 Object Library as explained in the tutorial.) Type the following code to look up the data, indenting and adding blank lines appropriately as you have learned in previous tutorials:

```
Private Sub cmdFind_Click()
Dim rst As DAO.Recordset
'Find the record and then close the dialog box
Set rst = Forms!frmLots.RecordsetClone
rst.FindFirst "Address = " & "'"& lstFind &"'"
Forms!frmLots.Bookmark = rst.Bookmark
DoCmd.Close acForm, "frmFindLots"
Set rst = Nothing
End Sub
```

4. Create a button to cancel (close) the frmFindLots form. You can use the Command Button Wizard for this.
5. Add the following code to the frmLots form to open the frmFindLots form when the Address text box is double-clicked.

```
Private Sub Address_DblClick(Cancel As Integer)
  DoCmd.OpenForm "frmFindLots"
End Sub
```

Explore

6. Add code to the frmFindLots form that will call the find procedure when you double-click on an address record in the form. (*Hint*: This will be just like you did for the Movie9 database frmFindTimeCards.)
7. Compile the code, fix any errors, close the Visual Basic window, save your changes, switch to Form view, and test the form.
8. Close the Homes9 database, and then exit Access.

Case 4. Sonoma Farms You plan to implement user-level security on the Sonoma Farms database. You need to create a workgroup information file named SonomaSecure. You will run the User-Level Security Wizard to do this. In addition to the Admin group and Users group, you plan to create a Read-Only Users group. You will create a new Admin user name—SonomaAdmin—but will not assign a password. You also will create one new user name—jdowney—and add him to the Read-Only Users group. Complete the following:

1. Start Access and then open the Workgroup Administrator dialog box. Note the location of the default workgroup information file, System.mdw, if you have not already done so, in order to rejoin it later. If you are not joined to the default workgroup information file at this time, just be sure you have already written down the path to the default workgroup information file and proceed to the next step.
2. Create a new workgroup information file named **SonomaSecure**, and save it in the Tutorial.09\Cases folder on the network or local drive. Type ***Your Name***, type **Sonoma Farms** as the name of the organization, and type **Sonoma1234** as the Workgroup ID.
3. Open the **Sonoma9** database from the Tutorial.09\Cases folder.
4. Create a new administrator named **SonomaAdmin** with a PID of **Sonoma1234**, add this user to the Admins group, and then remove Admin from the Admins group.
5. Create a password **Sonoma** for Admin, close the Sonoma9 database, and then exit Access.
6. Restart Access, open the **Sonoma9** database from the Tutorial.09\Cases folder, and log on as **SonomaAdmin**.
7. Run the User-Level Security Wizard, create a Read-Only Users group, make sure that the Users group has no permissions, and create one new user named **jdowney** with no password.
8. Add jdowney to the Read-Only Users group.
9. Print the user-level security report. Do not save a snapshot of the report.
10. Close the Sonoma9 database, and then exit Access.
11. Repeat Step 1 to open the Workgroup Administrator, and then join the default workgroup information file, System.mdw. (*Hint*: It is essential that you to complete this step before beginning Tutorial 10.) Exit Access.

QUICK CHECK ANSWERS

Session 9.1

1. To write VBA code that works directly with the data in your application, you must work with ADO or DAO.
2. Use DAO to write code that makes changes to the structure of tables and queries in a Jet (.mdb) database or to manipulate recordsets behind forms.
3. The Jet engine is the database engine that Access uses for all of its native database management.
4. The object at the top of the DAO hierarchy is the DBEngine object. The Connection object is at the top of the ADO hierarchy.
5. The types of Recordset objects are table, dynaset, snapshot, forward-only, and dynamic.
6. A user can create a system object by using USys as the first four characters in the object name.

7. Every form has a RecordsetClone property that you can use to get a copy of the form's underlying recordset.
8. The Findfirst method of the Recordset object begins searching at the beginning of the recordset and continues to the end.
9. An object library is a collection of prebuilt objects and functions that you can use in VBA code.

Session 9.2

1. An Access workgroup is a group of users in a multiuser environment who share data.
2. In an unsecured database, the default user is Admin.
3. The default workgroup information file is named System.mdw.
4. The simplest method for protecting an Access database is to set a password on it.
5. The workgroup information file you create or use by default contains Users and Admins Group accounts and an Admin user.
6. A password is used to access the application; the PID is used as a part of the encryption process.
7. The user who creates a table, query, form, report, or macro is the owner of that object.
8. The owner of the database or any member of the Admins group can change permissions for a user or group.
9. No. However, their account can be reset so that they can create a new password.

OBJECTIVES

In this tutorial you will:

- Learn how hyperlinks are used in Access
- Create hyperlinks on a form to other database objects
- Create hyperlinks that address e-mail
- Add hyperlinks to a menu bar
- Learn about data access pages and how to use them
- Format controls on a data access page
- Apply a theme to a data access page
- Use grouping levels on a data access page
- Export a query to an HTML document

CONNECTING TO THE WORLD WIDE WEB

Working with Hyperlinks and Data Access Pages in the MovieCam Technologies Database

CASE

MovieCam Technologies

You recently met with Amanda to review your progress on the MovieCam technologies database. Amanda wants you to create the database main switchboard form that users will use to navigate to other switchboards.

Many users have Internet access, and all of them have access to the company intranet. As you may already know, the term "intranet" typically implies all that the term Internet does in relation to Web pages, TCP/IP, and use of Internet-enabled servers, but the intranet exists behind a company firewall and is not accessible to unauthorized users outside of the firewall. To use the company intranet you either have to be physically plugged into the company network on site or authorized to use some secured form of remote access via a modem or perhaps virtual private networking.

Amanda wants you to use the Web features of Access to provide a method for navigating to the Web from within the database. To accomplish this, you decide to add some Web options to the custom menu bar that you already created.

Amanda wants you to integrate the database with the company intranet. This integration would be beneficial to MovieCam employees in several ways. Amanda wants employees who don't have access to the MovieCam database to be able to view their time card records online. She also wants all employees to have the ability to go online and modify certain portions of their employee record, including current mailing address, phone number, and emergency contact information.

Finally, you want to experiment with exporting data to the Web. At times, managers need to see query results so they can complete quarterly or annual reports. It occurs to you that exporting a query to an HTML document might be a simple way to handle infrequent requests for specific data.

After completing Tutorial 9, if you have not rejoined your default workgroup, then do so now by following the steps provided in Tutorial 9 for Joining the Default Workgroup.

SESSION 10.1

In this session, you will study hyperlinks and how they are used in Access. You will insert hyperlinks on a form to objects in the database. You also will insert a hyperlink to an e-mail address. You will complete the MovieCam menu bar by adding Web-related commands to it, including a hyperlink to the Microsoft Home Page.

Introduction

Access contains a number of features designed to let you take advantage of the resources on the World Wide Web (WWW). You can embed hyperlinks on forms, assign hyperlinks to a toolbar or menu command, create data access pages (a new object in Access 2000), and so forth. A **hyperlink** is text or an image that you click to navigate to other parts of a file, to other documents on your computer or network, or to Internet addresses. A **data access page** is an object in the database that lets you display, edit, and manipulate other objects, such as tables, forms, and reports, so that they can be published to the Web using the Internet Explorer Web browser. (Data access pages do not work with all Web browsers.)

You still need to complete the main switchboard form for the MovieCam Technologies database. You want to be able to use the main switchboard to open the frmDataSwitchboard form and the frmReportsSwitchboard form. You also plan to add a button for exiting the database to the main switchboard.

Amanda suggested that you try a main switchboard form that contains hyperlinks to the objects in the database that you want to open, rather than having controls that trigger VBA code. This type of form opens faster than a form containing VBA code.

Using **Hyperlinks on a Form**

You can create a hyperlink on a form to a Web site, another file, an e-mail address, or an object in the database. You create it by inserting a command button, label, or image control, and then setting the control's properties to tell the hyperlink where to jump. The address or the pathname to the file or URL associated with the control is saved with the form and doesn't change, even if you move from one record to another. You also can store hyperlinks in a field in a table and then create a text box on a form that is bound to that field. In this instance, the hyperlink changes with each record as the user navigates through them. If the hyperlink address points to a Web site, the user's Web browser automatically opens when the hyperlink is clicked.

You use the Hyperlink Address and the Hyperlink SubAddress properties to design the hyperlink control. Use the **Hyperlink Address property** to specify the path to a document on the local or network drive or a Web site address. Use the **Hyperlink SubAddress property** to specify a particular location in a document, such as a bookmark in a Word document or a particular object like a form or report in an Access database. Hyperlinks can be used to navigate to:

- *Word or Excel files*: A hyperlink can open any file created in a Microsoft Office application. Specify the path and filename of the document, such as C:\MyDocuments\Report, in the Hyperlink Address property text box.

- *HTML documents*: A hyperlink can navigate to an HTML file on the Web or on a network or local computer. The file is visible in a Web browser regardless of whether it's on a local drive, an intranet, or the Internet.
- *Internet addresses*: A hyperlink can navigate to other areas of the Internet besides the WWW. You can set a hyperlink address to transfer a file from an FTP server or to send electronic mail. To send e-mail, you specify the address in the Hyperlink Address property text box as follows: mailto:krisoxford@msn.com.
- *Access database objects*: A hyperlink can open any object, such as a form or a report, in the same database or in a different database. If the object is in the same Access database as the hyperlink, you leave the Hyperlink Address property blank and specify the name of the form or report (preceded by the word Form or Report) in the Hyperlink SubAddress property text box.

Creating a Main Switchboard

You will create a simple, main switchboard form that looks like the one shown in Figure 10-1. It will contain a button to open the frmDataSwitchboard form and a button to open the frmReportsSwitchboard form. The form also will contain a button to exit the application and a hyperlink to e-mail a help desk address that your network administrator set up for you in case a user needs help with the database or has questions.

Figure 10-1 MovieCam MAIN SWITCHBOARD FORM

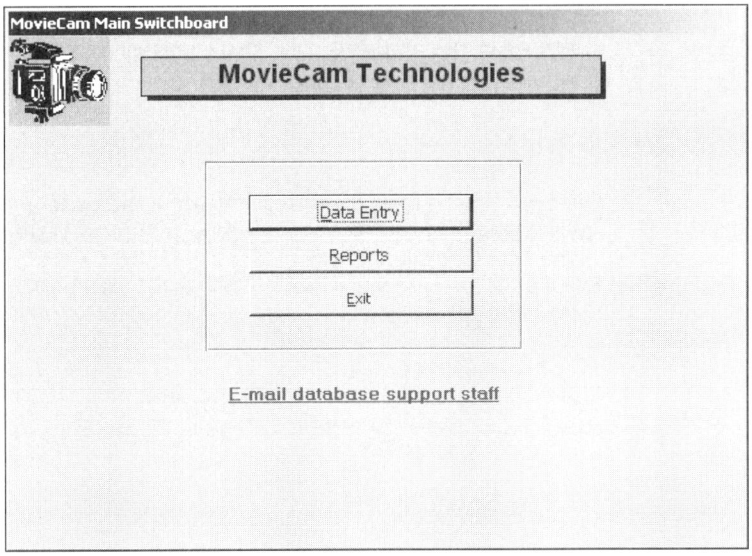

The Data Entry and Reports command buttons will be designed as hyperlinks to the specified switchboard form in the database. Hyperlinks can be formatted to look like standard command buttons and can include a keyboard shortcut just like command buttons that execute VBA code or macros.

REFERENCE WINDOW RW

Creating A Hyperlink to Open a Form

- Create a command button on a form.
- Select the button and then display its property sheet.
- Click the Hyperlink SubAddress text box, and then click its Build button to open the Insert Hyperlink dialog box.
- Click the Object in This Database option in the Link to bar, and then click the expand indicator to the left of Forms.
- Select the form that you want to open, and then click the OK button.

You'll create the Exit button with the Command Button Wizard, and then write a VBA Sub procedure to exit the database. The label at the bottom of the switchboard will be a hyperlink to a special help desk e-mail address that your network administrator set up for you. Clicking it will open Microsoft Outlook Express (or your default e-mail application) and address the e-mail.

To create the frmMainSwitchboard form:

1. Start Access and then open the **Movie10** database located in the Tutorial.10\Tutorial folder on your local or network drive.

   TROUBLE? If you are prompted for a logon, then you have not rejoined the default Access workgroup. Close the Logon dialog box, and then rejoin the default System.mdw workgroup file by following the steps provided in Tutorial 9 for "Joining the Default Workgroup." Once you have done so, close Access and then repeat Step 1.

2. Click **Forms** on the Objects bar in the Database window, right-click **dmfrmMasterSwitchboard**, and then click **Copy** on the shortcut menu.
3. Right-click an empty area of the Database window, click **Paste** on the shortcut menu, type **frmMainSwitchboard** as the new form name in the Paste As dialog box, and then click the **OK** button.
4. Open the new form in Design view, and then maximize the form window. It should look like that shown in Figure 10-2.

Figure 10-2 MAIN SWITCHBOARD FORM IN DESIGN VIEW

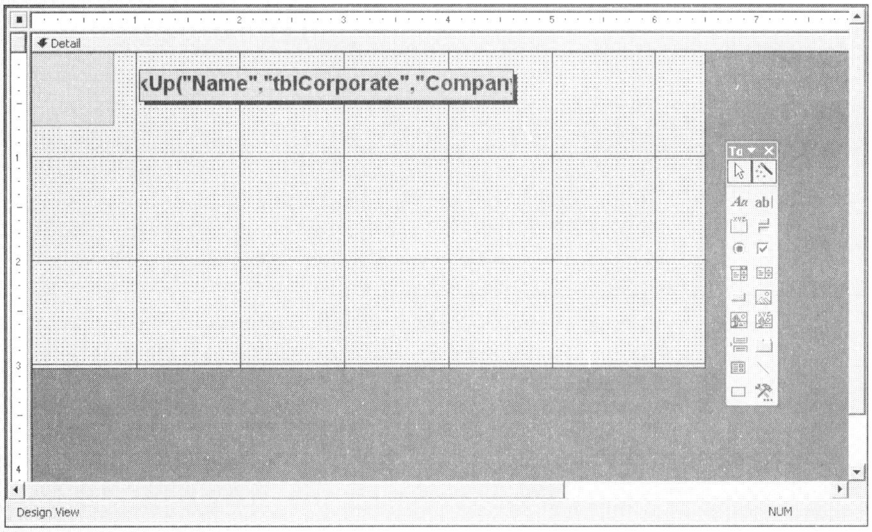

5. Drag the bottom of the Detail section of the form down to the 4" mark, display the toolbox if necessary, make sure the Controls Wizards button is *not* selected, click the Command Button button on the toolbox, and drag to draw a command button, as shown in Figure 10-3.

Figure 10-3 RESIZING THE MAIN SWITCHBOARD FORM

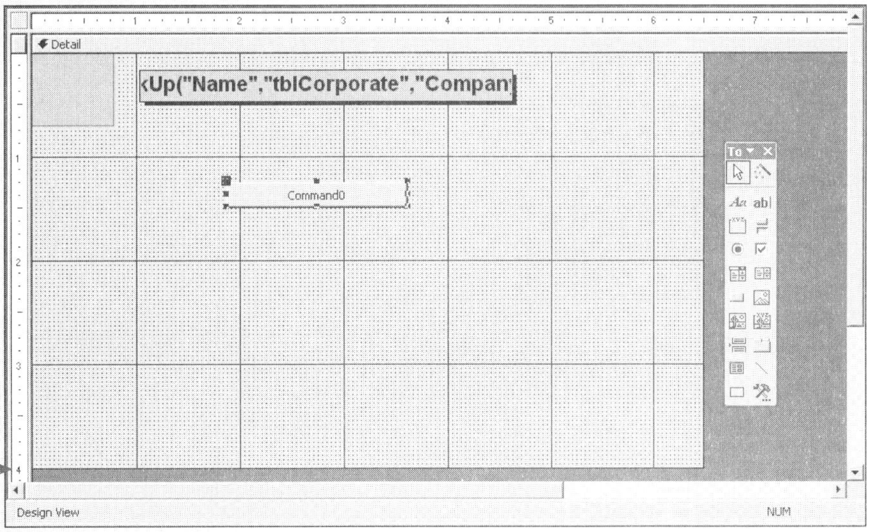

drag bottom of the form to this point

6. Click the **Properties** button on the toolbar, click the **All** tab if necessary, change the Name property to **cmdForms**, the Caption property to **&Data Entry**, click in the **Hyperlink SubAddress** text box, click its **Build** button, and then click the **Object in This Database** option in the Link to bar. The Insert Hyperlink dialog box opens, as shown in Figure 10-4. Your list of recently used hyperlinks might be different than those displayed in Figure 10-4 depending on the sites that you have visited recently.

Figure 10-4 INSERT HYPERLINK DIALOG BOX

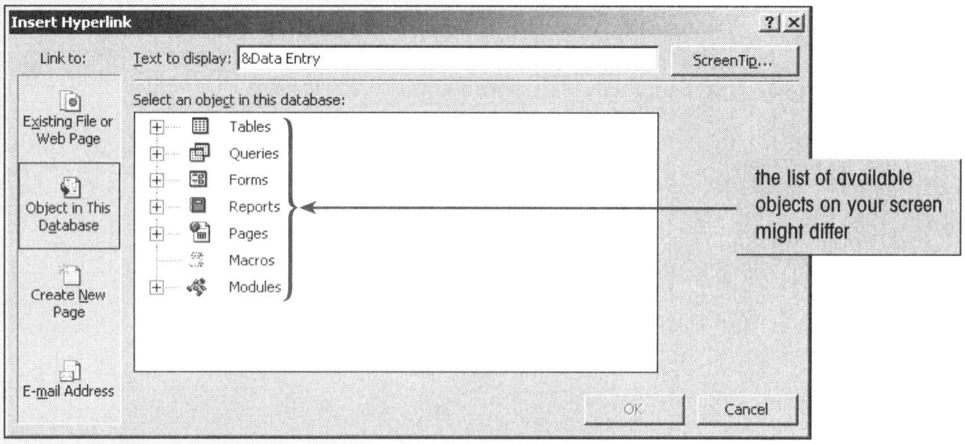

7. Click the **expand indicator** [+] to the left of Forms. All the forms in the current database are shown.
8. Click **frmDataSwitchboard** and then click the **OK** button. The Hyperlink SubAddress text box now contains "Form frmDataSwitchboard."
9. In the property sheet, scroll to and change the Fore Color property to **0** (this changes the text on the button to black), the Font Size property to **10**, and the Font Underline property to **No**. These changes make the hyperlink on the button look like a standard command button.

Next you will add the command button to open the frmReportsSwitchboard form. You will simply duplicate the button you just created, and make the necessary changes to the new button's properties.

To add the command button for the frmReportsSwitchboard form:

1. Make sure that the **Data Entry** button control is selected, click **Edit** on the menu bar, and then click **Duplicate**. A duplicate button is created below the Data Entry button, as shown in Figure 10-5.

Figure 10-5 **DUPLICATING THE COMMAND BUTTON**

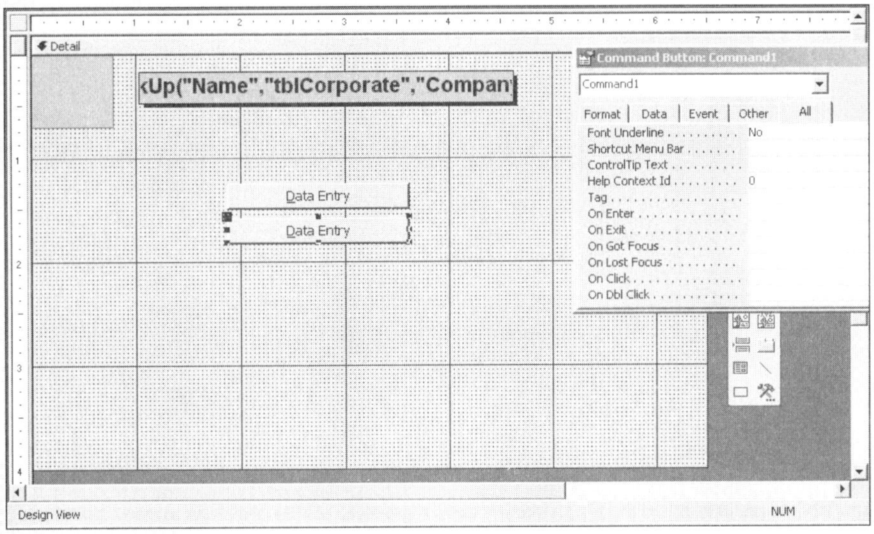

TROUBLE? You might see two menu bars: the mnuMovieCam toolbar you created earlier and the default menu bar. Click View on the menu bar, point to Toolbars, click Customize, click the Toolbars tab, scroll to mnuMovieCam, and click the check box to clear it.

2. Change the Name property of the new button to **cmdReports**, the Caption property to **&Reports**, the Hyperlink SubAddress to **Form frmReportsSwitchboard**, and then close the property sheet.
3. Switch to Form view and click each button to test it, and then use each button's keyboard shortcut key: **Alt + D** for the Data Entry button and **Alt + R** for the Reports button.
4. Switch to Design view, click the **Control Wizards** button on the toolbox to select it, click the **Command Button** button to select it, and then draw a third command button below the first two. The Command Button Wizard opens.
5. Click **Application** in the Categories list box, make sure that **Quit Application** is selected in the Actions list box, click the **Next** button, type **&Exit** in the Text box, click the **Next** button, type **cmdExit** as the name of the button, and then click the **Finish** button.
6. Select all three buttons, right-click the selection, point to **Size** on the shortcut menu, click **To Widest**, right-click the selection again, point to **Size**, click **To Tallest**, right-click the selection, point to **Align**, and then click **Left**.
7. Click **Format** on the menu bar, point to **Vertical Spacing**, click **Make Equal**, click the **Rectangle** button on the toolbox, and click and drag around the buttons as shown in Figure 10-6.

Figure 10-6 **CREATING A RECTANGLE AROUND THE BUTTONS**

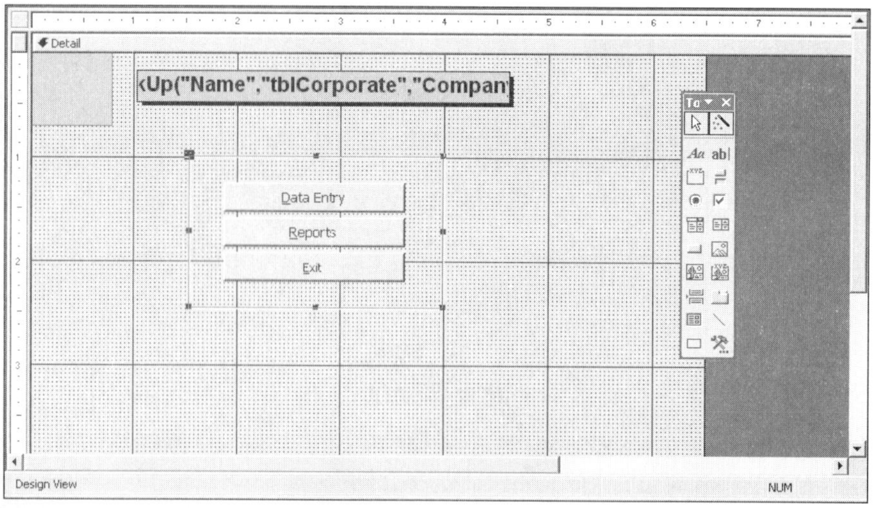

8. Click the **Save** button on the toolbar to save your changes, switch to Form view, and then click the **Exit** button to test it. The Access program closes.

   TROUBLE? If a message box displays asking if you want to exit Access and empty the clipboard, click the Yes button to continue.

The switchboard needs a few finishing touches. You want to add a hyperlink label for sending e-mail to the help desk address, and you want to change the Caption property of the form so that it reads MovieCam Main Switchboard. You'll also add a few ScreenTips to the buttons.

To complete the frmMainSwitchboard form:

1. Start Access, open the **Movie10** database located in the Tutorial.10\Tutorial folder on your local or network drive, open the **frmMainSwitchboard** form in Design view, and then click the **Properties** button on the toolbar. Maximize the form if necessary.
2. Type **MovieCam Main Switchboard** as the Caption property, click the **Data Entry** button to display its properties, change the ControlTip Text property to **Open the data entry forms switchboard**, click the **Reports** button, change the ControlTip Text property to **Open the reports switchboard**, click the **Exit** button, type **Exit Access** in the ControlTip Text property, and then close the property sheet.
3. Change the form width to 5½", and then click the **Save** button on the toolbar. Your form should look like that shown in Figure 10-7.

Figure 10-7 **SIZING THE FORM**

drag to align with the 5½" ruler mark

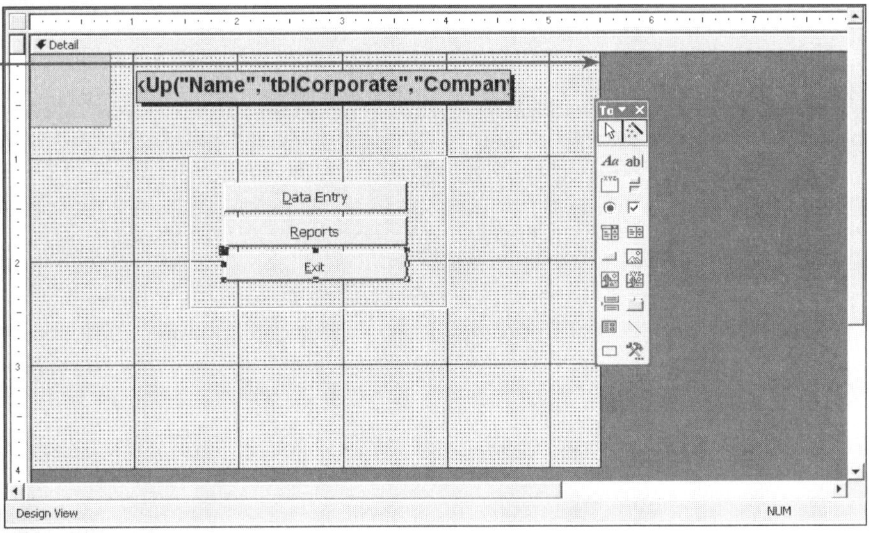

4. Click the **Insert Hyperlink** button on the Form Design toolbar. The Insert Hyperlink dialog box opens.
5. Click the **E-mail Address** option in the Link to bar, type **E-mail database support staff** in the Text to display text box, position the insertion point in the **E-mail address** text box, and then type **helpdesk@moviecam.com** as the e-mail address. Notice that the mailto: portion is added automatically to the beginning of the entry, as shown in Figure 10-8.

Figure 10-8 **CREATING THE E-MAIL HYPERLINK**

mailto: is automatically added at the beginning of the entry

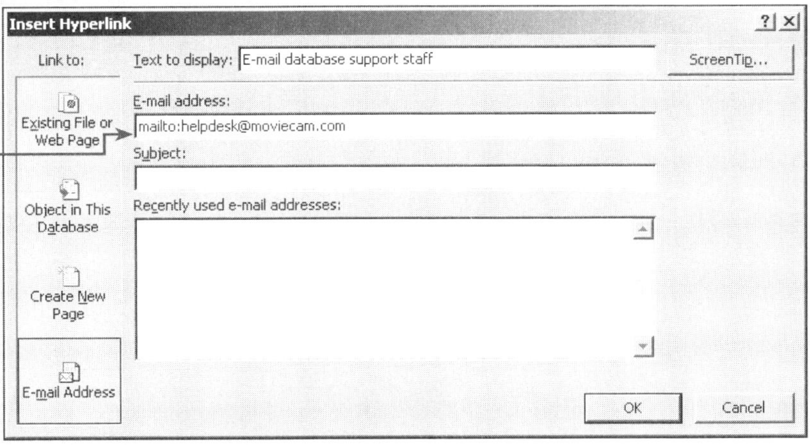

6. Click the **OK** button, and drag the label containing the hyperlink down approximately ¼" below the rectangle that surrounds the command buttons.
7. Click the rectangle that surrounds the command buttons to select it, hold down the **Shift** key, and click the new label containing the hyperlink so that both are selected.

8. Right-click the selection, point to **Size**, click **To Widest**, right-click the selection, point to **Align**, and then click **Left** (or **Right**, depending on how the label is positioned). Your form should look like that shown in Figure 10-9.

Figure 10-9 **SIZING THE LABEL CONTROL**

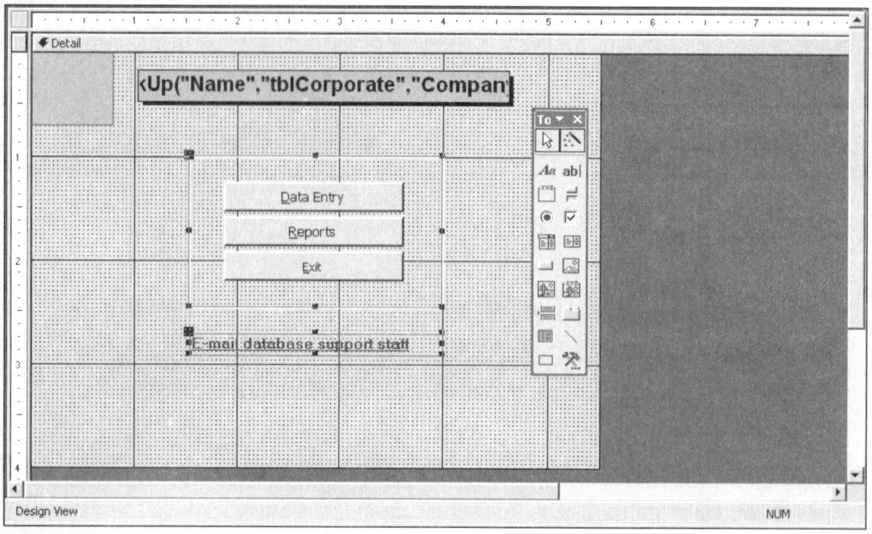

9. Click the **Detail** section of the form to deselect the two controls, click the label containing the hyperlink to select it, click the **Center** button on the toolbar to center the label text inside the box, and then click the **Save** button on the toolbar to save your changes.

Next you will test the hyperlink and the property changes that you made to the switchboard.

To test the frmMainSwitchboard form:

1. Click the **Restore** button so the form is no longer maximized, and then switch to Form view. Your form should look like that shown in Figure 10-10.

Figure 10-10 COMPLETED SWITCHBOARD

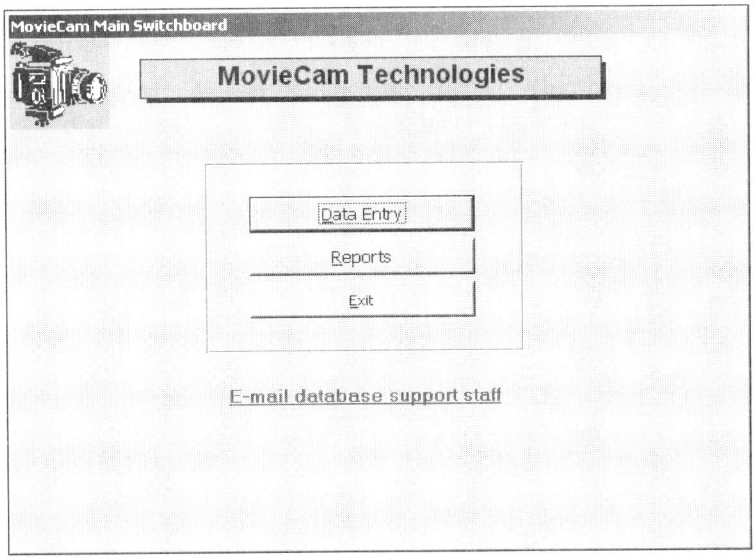

2. Click the hyperlink **E-mail database support staff**. Microsoft Outlook Express opens (if it is installed). and you will see a new e-mail message addressed to helpdesk@moviecam.com, as shown in Figure 10-11.

Figure 10-11 ADDRESSED E-MAIL

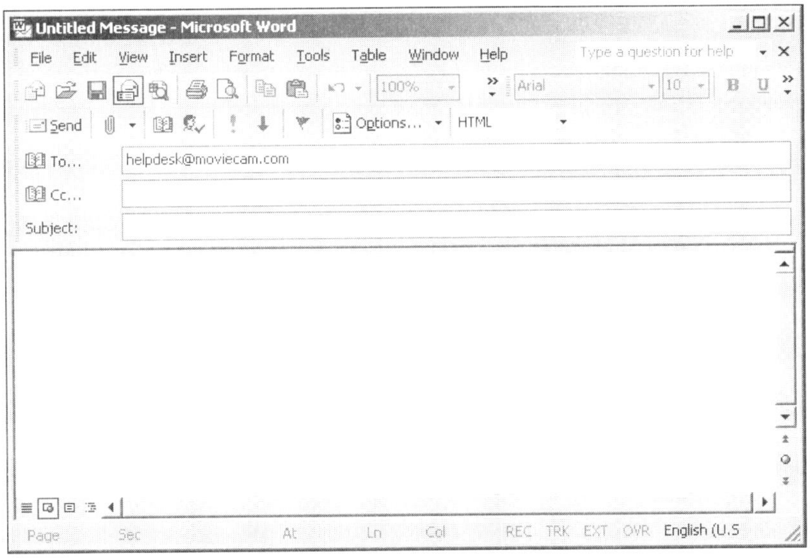

TROUBLE? If Outlook Express is not installed, you might need to skip this step. If another e-mail program is the default e-mail system, a dialog box might display asking if you want to make Outlook Express your default mail client. Your e-mail message might look different than the figure above depending upon what e-mail program you are using. If this happens, click the No button and continue without performing this step or Step 3.

3. Close the New Message window without saving the message to return to the switchboard.
4. Position the pointer over the Data Entry button. The ControlTip is shown.
5. Test each of the two other command buttons to be sure that the ControlTip Text property settings work properly. Press the **Tab** key to move to a button to give it focus, and then pause the pointer over the button to display the ControlTip.
6. To close the form, click **File** on the menu bar, and then click **Close** to return to the Database window.

Amanda is pleased with the frmMainSwitchboard form. It effectively controls the parts of the database to which users have access. When the database is ready for use, you plan to set the Startup properties to open the frmMainSwitchboard form when the database is opened. You also will set other options to hide the Database window, disable the shortcut menus, and set the mnuMovieCam menu bar as the default menu bar. Rather than disable the Bypass key, you will use the Startup settings in conjunction with the secured database and workgroup information file you created in Tutorial 9 to truly secure the system.

Using **Hyperlinks on a Menu Bar**

The mnuMovieCam menu bar that you created in Tutorial 6 now has some additional menu items, Web and Help, as shown in Figure 10-12.

Figure 10-12 mnuMovieCam MENU BAR

The choices on the Help menu include two commands for working with the Access Help system. You want to add Web menu commands to search the Web and to go to the Microsoft Home Page so that users can browse for online training, classes, and other product information.

REFERENCE WINDOW **RW**

Assigning a Hyperlink to a Menu Command

- Right-click the Database toolbar, and then click Customize on the shortcut menu.
- Make sure that the Toolbars tab is selected, and then select the menu bar to which you want to add the hyperlink.
- Click the Commands tab in the Customize dialog box, scroll down in the Categories list box, and then click Web.
- Drag the Hyperlink command from the Commands list box to the menu item to which you want to add the command.
- Right-click the Hyperlink command on the menu, point to Assign Hyperlink, and then click Open.
- Click the Existing File or Web Page option in the Link to bar, type the Web address in the Type the file or Web page name text box, and then click the OK button.

To assign a hyperlink to a toolbar button or menu command, you must add a button or a menu command, and then add the hyperlink to replace the command that is currently assigned to it. You will do this next.

To complete the mnuMovieCam menu bar:

1. Right-click the **Database** toolbar, as shown in Figure 10-13.

Figure 10-13 DATABASE TOOLBAR SHORTCUT MENU

right-click here

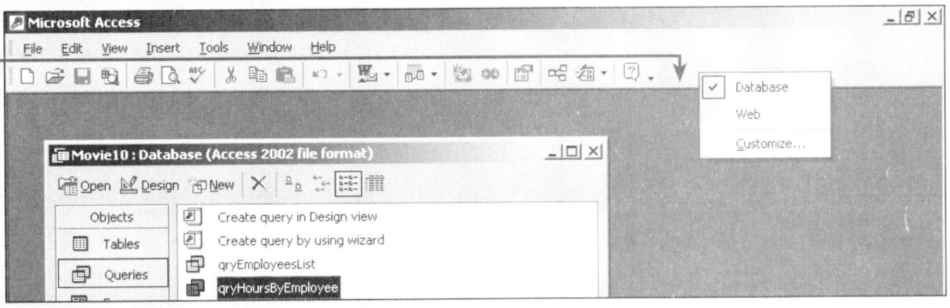

2. Click **Customize** on the shortcut menu to open the Customize dialog box, click the **Toolbars** tab if necessary, scroll down to the bottom of the list, and click the **mnuMovieCam** check box. The toolbar appears.

   TROUBLE? If the mnuMovieCam toolbar is docked, undock it. If necessary, resize the toolbar so that all the menu options appear horizontally aligned in one row (see Figure 10-12), and then proceed to the next step.

3. Click the **Commands** tab in the Customize dialog box, scroll down in the Categories list box, and then click **Web**.
4. Drag the **Search the Web** command from the Commands list box to the Web menu item, and when the Web menu is highlighted, drag the command to the area directly below the Web menu. Release the mouse button. Your screen should appear similar to Figure 10-14.

Figure 10-14 ADDING THE SEARCH THE WEB COMMAND

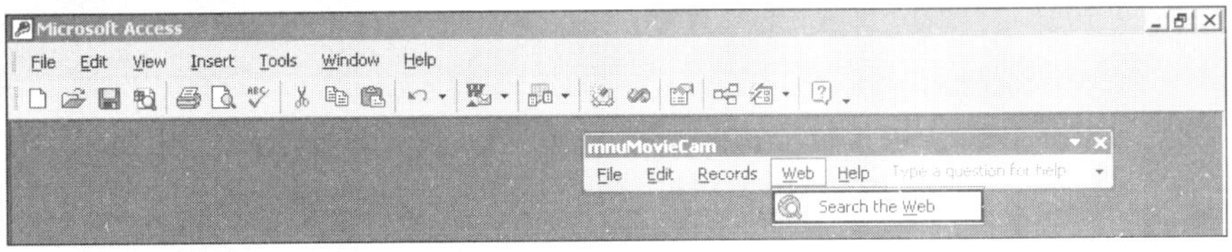

5. Scroll down in the Commands list box, and then drag the **Hyperlink** command below the Search the Web command on the Web menu.
6. Right-click the **Hyperlink** command that you just placed on the Web menu, point to **Assign Hyperlink**, and then click **Open**. The Assign Hyperlink: Open dialog box opens, as shown in Figure 10-15.

Figure 10-15 **ASSIGN HYPERLINK: OPEN DIALOG BOX**

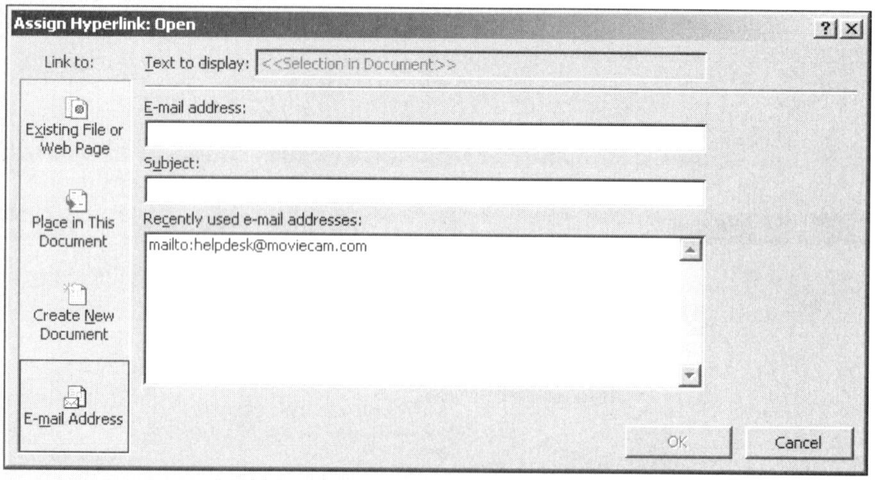

7. Click the **Existing File or Web Page** option in the Link to bar, type **www.microsoft.com** in the Address list box, and then click the **OK** button.
8. Right-click the **Hyperlink** command, click **Name** on the shortcut menu, type **&Microsoft**, click outside the menu, and then close the Customize dialog box. You must be connected to the Internet for the next step to work.
9. If necessary, connect to the Internet, click **Web** on the mnuMovieCam menu bar, and then click **Microsoft**. Internet Explorer launches and the home page for Microsoft is displayed.
10. Close Internet Explorer to return to Access.
11. Right-click the Database toolbar, click **Customize** on the shortcut menu to open the Customize dialog box, click the **Toolbars** tab if necessary, scroll down to the bottom of the list, click the **mnuMovieCam** check box to deselect it, and then close the Customize dialog box. You could also simply click the Close button on the mnuMovieCam toolbar.

The Web commands that you added to the menu bar work well. Amanda is satisfied that the custom menu bar provides the options that users will need from within the database. The main switchboard works well and loads quickly because it has very little VBA code. Now that these items are completed, you are ready to work on the data access pages. In the next session, you will create two data access pages that will be placed on the company intranet.

Session 10.1 QUICK CHECK

1. What is a hyperlink?
2. What is a data access page?
3. What is the advantage of having a main switchboard form that contains hyperlinks to the objects in the database that you want to open, rather than having controls that trigger VBA code?

4. The ______________ property is used to specify the path to a document on the local or network drive or a Web site address.
5. The ______________ property is used to specify a particular location in a document, such as a bookmark or a particular Access database object such as a form or report.
6. How can you assign a hyperlink to a menu bar or toolbar?

SESSION 10.2

In this session, you will create both read-only and updateable data access pages. You will apply a theme to the pages, learn to format controls on a page, and work with grouping levels. You will create a hyperlink to e-mail an employee of MovieCam and create a hyperlink on one page that opens another page. You will open the data access pages in Internet Explorer, navigate between them, and learn to edit data in a page. Finally, you will export a query to an HTML document.

Data Access Pages

Data access pages are Web pages that are separate from your Access database file and allow users with Web access to view and edit data in your tables, in a fashion similar to that of a form or report. A data access page merely provides a dynamic view to the underlying data, but does not store any data itself. You create data access pages in much the same way that you create forms and reports. Data access pages have properties to allow the user to make changes to the data or present the data in a read-only format, just like a form can. Microsoft provides an underlying layer to data access pages that handles bidirectional communication through the browser interface back to the database.

Not all MovieCam employees will have access to or be using the MovieCam database; however, they still need access to some of the database information. You can make this information available via the company's intranet by placing it in data access pages that can then be viewed in the Internet Explorer Web browser.

At Amanda's direction, you will create two data access pages: one read-only page that displays employee, time card, and hours data, and one updateable page that displays employee name, address, telephone number, and emergency contact information. Both pages will be uploaded to the MovieCam intranet.

Creating a Read-Only Data Access Page

The first data access page you create is based on the qryHoursByEmployee query. Figure 10-16 shows the query in Design view.

Figure 10-16 qryHoursByEmployee QUERY IN DESIGN VIEW

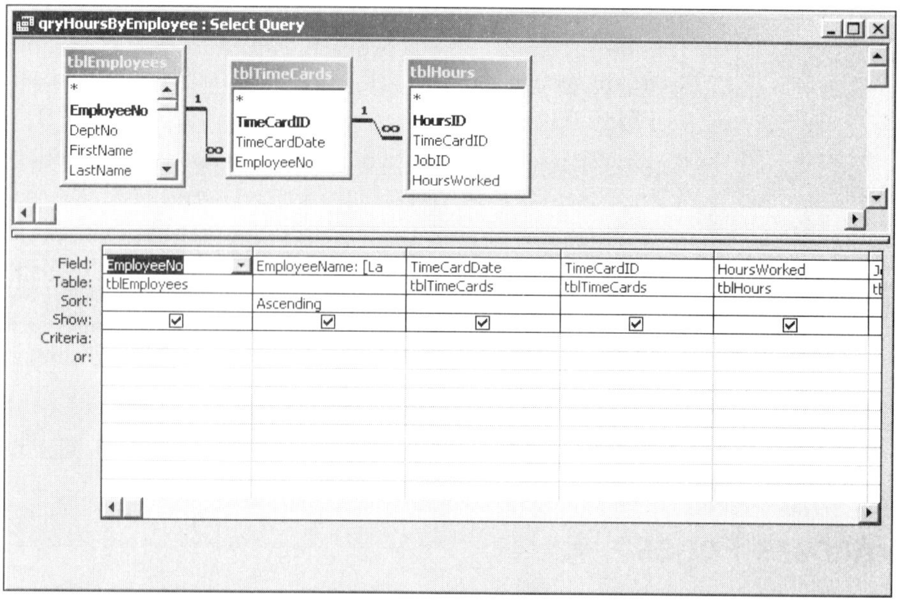

The query contains the EmployeeNo field and the EmployeeName field, and is an expression that concatenates the FirstName and LastName fields from the tblEmployees table, the TimeCardDate and TimeCardID fields from the tblTimeCards table, and the HoursWorked and JobID fields from the tblHours table. Running the query produces the results shown in Figure 10-17.

Figure 10-17 qryHoursByEmployee RESULTS IN DATASHEET VIEW

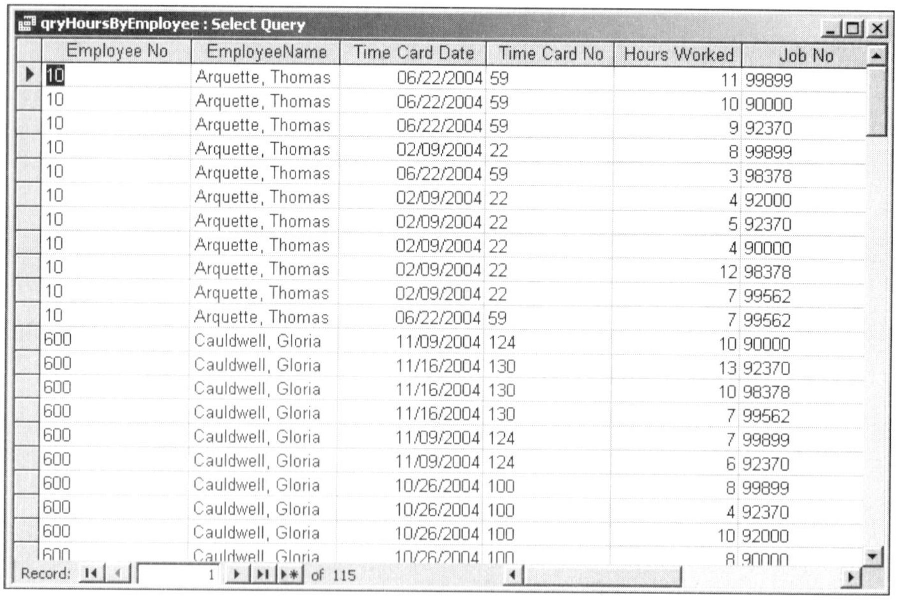
qryHoursByEmployee : Select Query

Employee No	EmployeeName	Time Card Date	Time Card No	Hours Worked	Job No
10	Arquette, Thomas	06/22/2004	59	11	99899
10	Arquette, Thomas	06/22/2004	59	10	90000
10	Arquette, Thomas	06/22/2004	59	9	92370
10	Arquette, Thomas	02/09/2004	22	8	99899
10	Arquette, Thomas	06/22/2004	59	3	98378
10	Arquette, Thomas	02/09/2004	22	4	92000
10	Arquette, Thomas	02/09/2004	22	5	92370
10	Arquette, Thomas	02/09/2004	22	4	90000
10	Arquette, Thomas	02/09/2004	22	12	98378
10	Arquette, Thomas	02/09/2004	22	7	99562
10	Arquette, Thomas	06/22/2004	59	7	99562
600	Cauldwell, Gloria	11/09/2004	124	10	90000
600	Cauldwell, Gloria	11/16/2004	130	13	92370
600	Cauldwell, Gloria	11/16/2004	130	10	98378
600	Cauldwell, Gloria	11/16/2004	130	7	99562
600	Cauldwell, Gloria	11/09/2004	124	7	99899
600	Cauldwell, Gloria	11/09/2004	124	6	92370
600	Cauldwell, Gloria	10/26/2004	100	8	99899
600	Cauldwell, Gloria	10/26/2004	100	4	92370
600	Cauldwell, Gloria	10/26/2004	100	10	92000
600	Cauldwell, Gloria	10/26/2004	100	8	90000

Record: 1 of 115

The data access page you create from the query will contain grouping levels similar to grouping levels you specify in reports. Grouping levels will be discussed in detail later. For now, you should know that pages that contain them cannot be updated; they are read-only. If an employee finds an error in the hours listed for a particular time card, that employee can click a hyperlink that you will insert on the page and e-mail the timekeeper about the error.

REFERENCE WINDOW RW

Creating a Data Access Page Using the Page Wizard

- Click Pages on the Objects bar in the Database window, and then double-click Create data access page using wizard.
- Click the Tables/Queries list arrow, select the table or query on which the page will be based, move the desired fields to the Selected Fields list box, and then click the Next button.
- Select a field to group by if desired, and then click the Next button.
- Type a name for the page, and then click the Finish button.

You will use the Page Wizard to create this page.

To create a data access page:

1. If you took a break after the previous session, make sure that Access is running and that the **Movie10** database from the Tutorial.10\Tutorial folder on your local or network drive is open.
2. Click **Pages** on the Objects bar of the Database window, and then double-click **Create data access page by using wizard**. The Page Wizard opens, as shown in Figure 10-18.

Figure 10-18 PAGE WIZARD OPENING DIALOG BOX

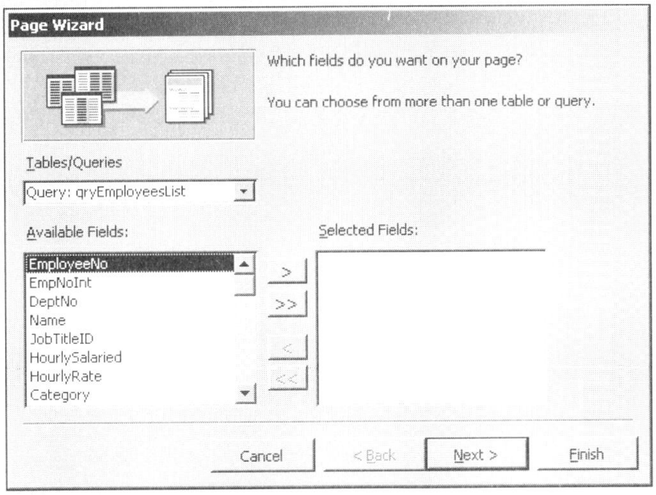

3. Click the **Tables/Queries** list arrow, click **Query: qryHoursByEmployee**, click the >> button to move all the fields in the Available Fields list box to the Selected Fields list box, and then click the **Next** button. The next Page Wizard dialog box, shown in Figure 10-19, asks if you want to add any grouping levels and assumes that you want to use the JobID field to group the items in this page.

Figure 10-19 SECOND PAGE WIZARD DIALOG BOX

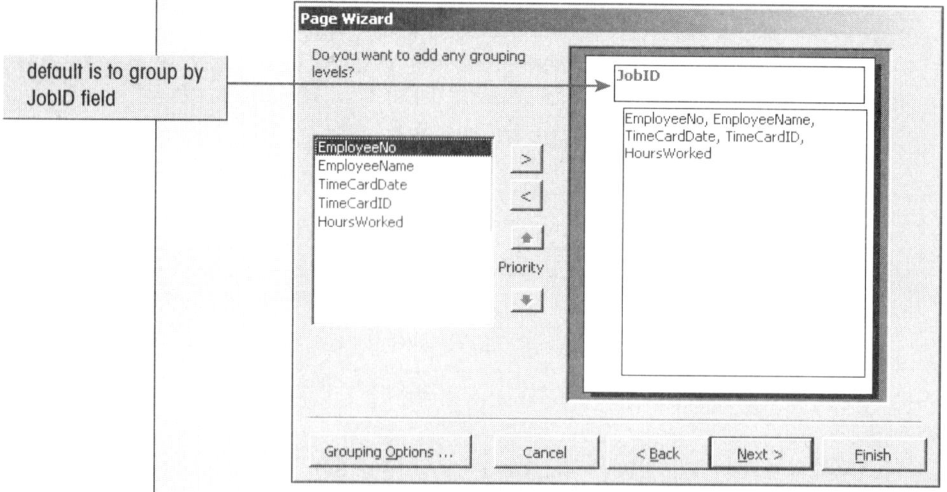

However, you want to group by the EmployeeName field so that all the time cards and hours for a particular employee will be visible on one page. Grouping in data access pages automatically creates an expand control in the page. (This control will be discussed in more detail later in this tutorial.)

4. Click the < button to move JobID back to the list of fields, click **EmployeeName** in the list box on the left, click the > button, and then click the **Next** button. The next screen of the Page Wizard asks for the sort order. You are not sure in what order you want to sort the detail records, so you will leave this blank.
5. Click the **Next** button. The next dialog box prompts you for a title for your page.
6. Type **dapTimeCards** and then click the **Finish** button. The data access page and the field list are visible in Design view, as shown in Figure 10-20.

Figure 10-20 COMPLETED DATA ACCESS PAGE

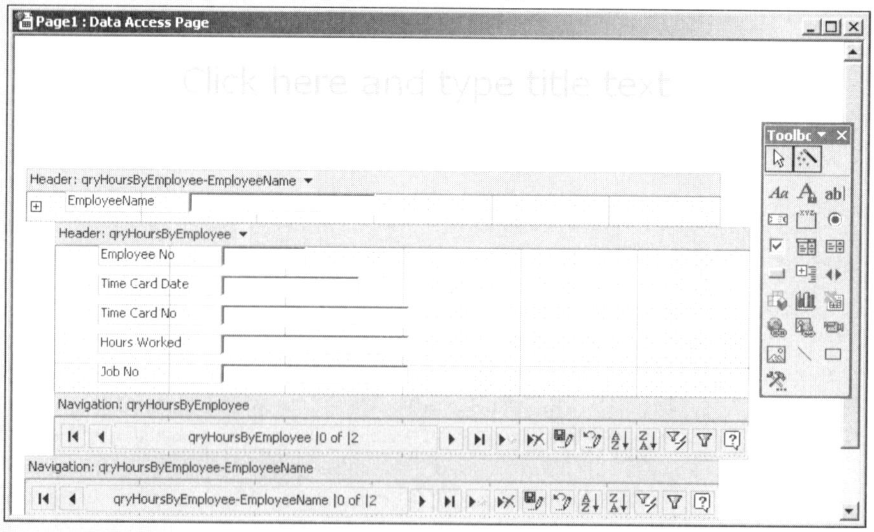

7. Switch to Page view. You see that the data access page needs a lot of work.
8. Switch to Design view.
9. Click **File** on the menu bar, click **Save As**, type **dapTimeCards**, click the **OK** button, navigate to the Tutorial.10\Tutorial folder on your local or network drive, and then click the **Save** button. Recall that the data access page is saved outside the database, so you must tell Access where you want it saved.

   TROUBLE? If you get the message warning you about the connection string, click the OK button to acknowledge and close the message.

Although a data access page looks like an Access form, it is quite different. The controls on the page work differently, the tools for designing pages are not as advanced as those for forms and reports, and you cannot use any of the wizards or expressions that you have used on forms and reports.

Formatting the Data Access Page

Next you will make some changes to the default formatting that the Page Wizard applied to the data access page. You will add a title, change the text inside the labels on the page, and move one of the controls on the data access page to a different section.

To format the data access page:

1. Click the text placeholder at the top of the page that reads *Click here and type title text*, and then type **Time Cards Page**.
2. Click the **EmployeeName** label in the Header: qryHoursByEmployee-EmployeeName section, click the **Properties** button on the toolbar, click the **All** tab if necessary, and then change the InnerText property to **Employee Name**.
3. Click the **EmployeeNo** label in the Header: qryHoursByEmployee section, and then change the InnerText property to **Employee No**.

   TROUBLE? The remaining labels might already include the necessary spaces. If this is the case, skip this step and Step 4.

4. Repeat Step 3 to change the remaining labels as follows: TimeCardDate to **Time Card Date**, TimeCardID to **Time Card No**, HoursWorked to **Hours Worked**, and JobID to **Job No**.
5. Click the **Employee No** text box to select it, and then move it up into the Header: qryHoursByEmployee-EmployeeName section and to the right of the Employee Name control, as shown in Figure 10-21. Note that when you click the text box (and not the label) and then cut, copy, or move it, the label is included in the action. When you click the label and cut, copy, or move it, only the label is affected by your action.

Figure 10-21 MOVING THE EMPLOYEE NO TEXT BOX AND LABEL

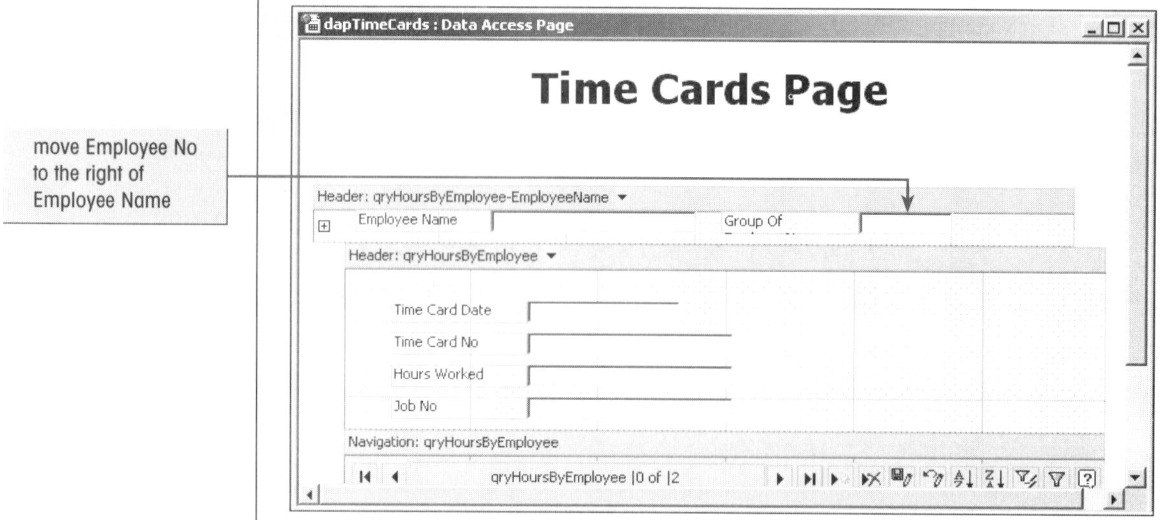

When you moved the Employee No control to the header, Access renamed the inner text of the label to read "GroupOfEmployeeNo." You need to change the InnerText property.

6. If necessary, display the property sheet for the label, change the InnerText property to **Employee No**, and then close the property sheet.

Applying Themes to Data Access Pages

A **theme** is a set of design elements and color schemes for background, font, horizontal lines, bullets, hyperlinks, and controls. Using a theme helps you quickly create professional, attractive data access pages.

REFERENCE WINDOW **RW**

Applying a Theme to a Data Access Page

- Click Pages on the Objects bar in the Database window, and then open the page in Design view.
- Click Format on the menu bar, click Theme, and then select a theme from the Choose a Theme list box.
- Select the Vivid Colors check box if you want to apply this option.
- Click the OK button.

A theme can be applied and then changed at any point in the page development. Themes are installed with Access; additional themes can be downloaded from the Web. In addition to Access themes, you can apply a Microsoft FrontPage theme to data access pages. A number of Web sites offer free themes for FrontPage.

When applying a theme, you can select options to brighten colors, animate graphics, and apply a background to the data access page. Next you will apply a theme to the data access page.

Applying a theme to the data access page:

1. Click **Format** on the menu bar, and then click **Theme**. The Theme dialog box opens, shown in Figure 10-22.

Figure 10-22 THEME DIALOG BOX

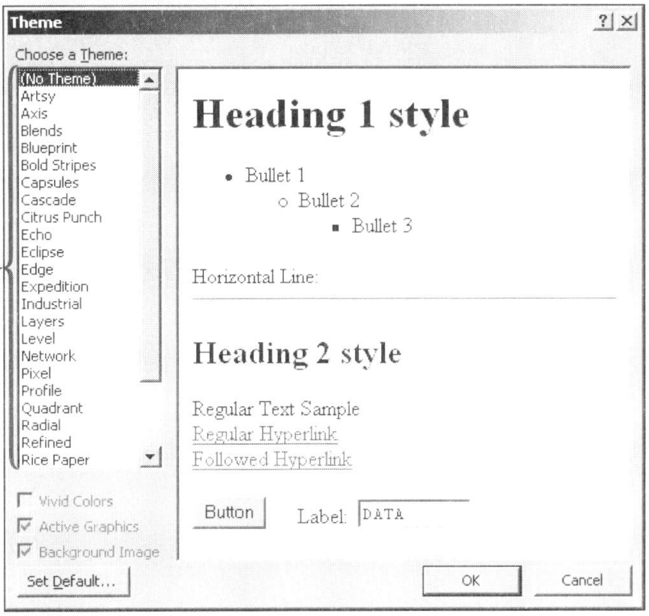

the list of available themes on your screen might differ

2. Click **Expedition** in the Choose a Theme list box, click the **Vivid Colors** check box, and then click the **OK** button.

   TROUBLE? Your Choose a Theme list box might have different themes displayed depending on those installed on the computer you are working on. If Expedition is not included in the list, select another theme.

3. Switch to Page view to see how the form looks with the theme applied. Next you will make some changes to the text boxes, fonts, and labels.

4. Switch to Design view, click the **Employee Name** label, click the **Font Size** list arrow on the toolbar, click **10**, and then click the **Bold** button **B** on the toolbar. Resize the Employee Name label slightly so that both words appear in the label if necessary.

5. Repeat Step 4 to modify the **Employee No** label.

6. Click the Employee Name text box, displays its properties, click the **Format** tab, change the BorderStyle property to **none**, and then change the Font Size to **10pt** if necessary.

7. Repeat Step 6 to modify the **Employee No** text box.

8. Click the **Time Card Date** text box in the Header: qryHoursByEmployee section, change the BorderStyle property to **none**, and then change the BorderStyle property to **none** for the **Time Card No**, **Hours Worked**, and **Job No** text boxes.

9. Switch to Page view, and then click the **expand indicator** + to the left of Employee Name. Your page should now look like that shown in Figure 10-23.

Figure 10-23 **TIME CARDS PAGE**

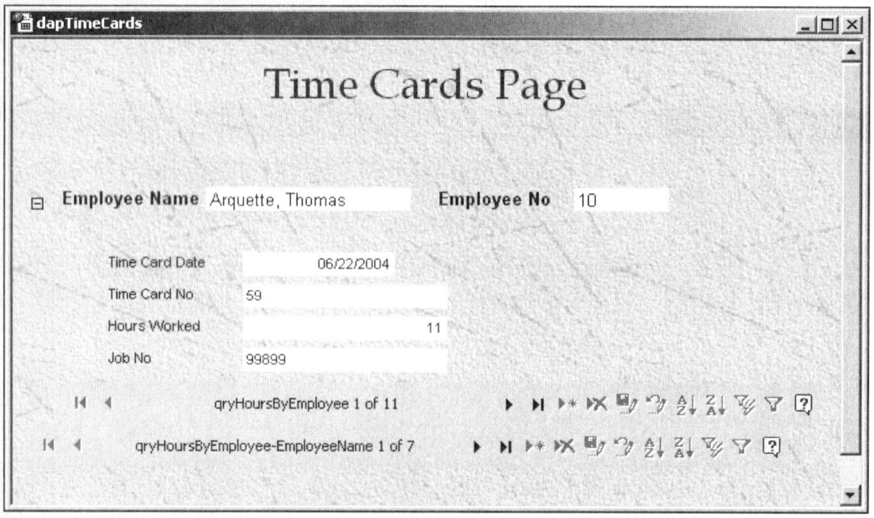

TROUBLE? If your labels wrap to two lines, widen the label in Design view so that the text in each label fits on one line, as shown in Figure 10-23.

Grouping in Data Access Pages

Grouping data in data access pages is much like grouping data in a report. When you specify groups in a page, Access automatically adds an expand control so that users can expand or collapse the records in a group. By working with group-level properties in a page, you can add or delete groups, and define exactly how you want the groups to appear.

Pages have some advantages over printed reports. Pages are interactive so the user can move through the records online and view the data they desire. Plus, pages always contain the most current data because they are connected to the database, whereas a printed report is only as current as the database was at the time the report was printed.

The expand indicator and the record navigation toolbar are added automatically to a data access page for each group specified. They can be removed or modified. Groups can be easily added to, or deleted from, a data access page by selecting a text box, and then choosing Promote or Demote from the shortcut menu. To promote a group means to move it up a level in the grouping hierarchy, and to demote a group means to move it down or further into, a hierarchy.

REFERENCE WINDOW **RW**

Adding a Group to a Data Access Page

- Click Pages on the Objects bar in the Database window, and then open the page in Design view.
- Right-click the field that you want to group the page on, and then click Promote on the shortcut menu.

The page is fine so far, but it is a good idea to group the data in the page so that each time card number and time card date is visible, and so the user can expand a particular time card to view its detail. This way, when there are many time cards in the system, it will be easier to find the specific time card and expand it to see the hours and jobs. Next you will add a new group to the data access page.

To add a group to the data access page:

1. Return to Design view, right-click the **Time Card Date** text box, and then click **Promote** on the shortcut menu. A new group is added to the page.
2. Right-click the **Time Card No** text box, click **Cut** on the shortcut menu, right-click inside the new group header, and then click **Paste** on the shortcut menu.
3. Move the **Time Card No** label and text box to the right of Time Card Date, as shown in Figure 10-24.

Figure 10-24 MOVING THE TIME CARD DATE AND TIME CARD NO TEXT BOXES AND LABELS

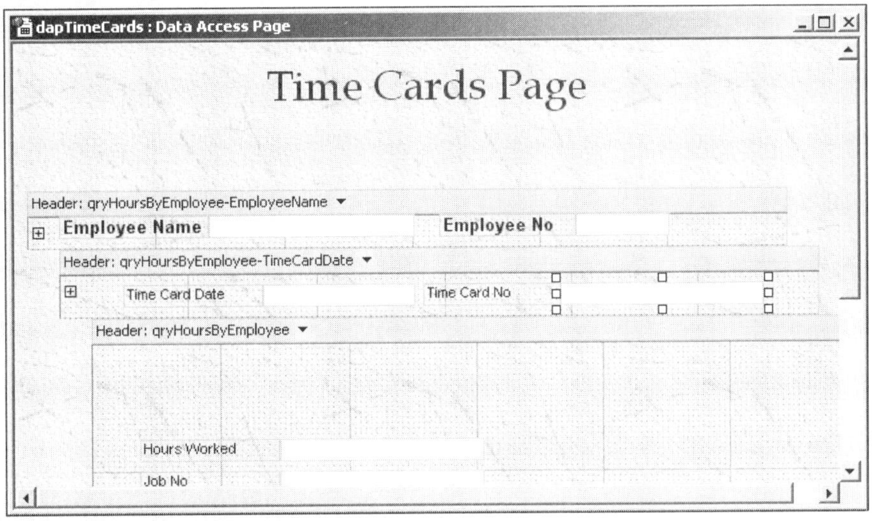

4. Size the Hours Worked text box and the Job No text box so that each is approximately 1" wide.
5. Move the Hours Worked label and text box to the top of the Header: qryHoursByEmployee section, and then move the Job No label and text box to the top of the header section, as shown in Figure 10-25.

Figure 10-25 MOVING THE HOURS WORKED AND JOB NO TEXT BOXES AND LABELS

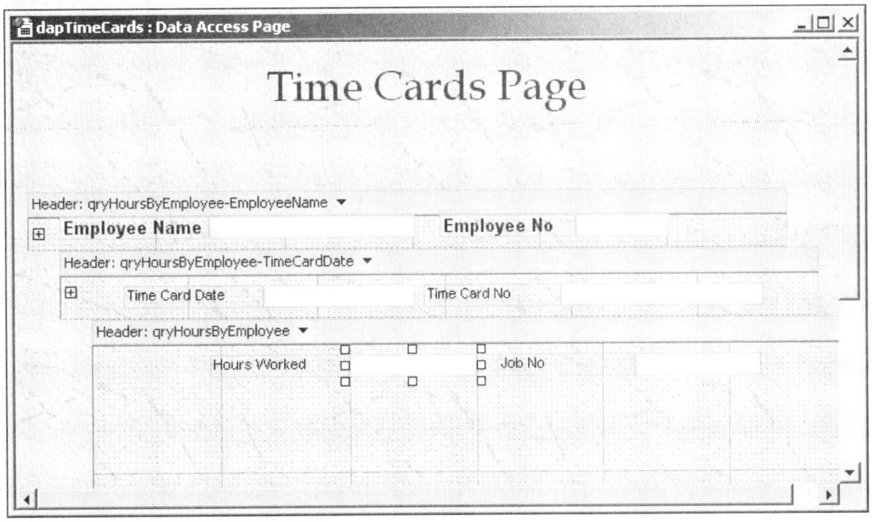

6. Click the **Header: qryHoursByEmployee** section, position the pointer over the handle on the bottom center of the section until the pointer changes to ↕, and then click and drag the section up to the bottom of the controls.
7. Return to Page view, and click the **expand indicator** [+] to the left of Employee Name to show the time cards for that employee.
8. Click [+] to the left of the first Time Card Date to show the hours for that particular time card.
9. Return to Design view.

Changing Group Level Properties

Now you will modify the way the data in the groups is shown on the page. First, you will eliminate the NavigationSection: qryHoursByEmployee section below the Header: qryHoursByEmployee section. Each time card will have only 5 to 10 entries, so the user does not need a toolbar to navigate through these records, as shown in Figure 10-26. You also will eliminate the NavigationSection: qryHoursByEmployee-TimeCardDate section because at this time the number of time cards per employee is not excessive. You can always add this later if it becomes necessary.

Figure 10-26 NAVIGATION TOOLBARS

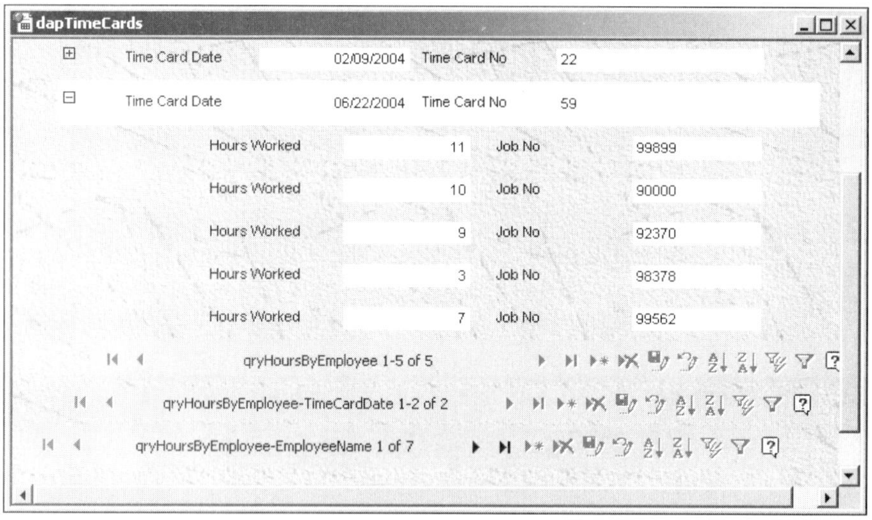

You also will modify the remaining record navigation toolbar in the NavigationSection: qryHoursByEmployee-EmployeeName section to eliminate unused buttons.

Finally, you will change some of group-level properties to determine the number of records shown on each page and to determine which sections you want expanded by default. This will eliminate the need to click the expand indicator. You also will add a caption section to eliminate the repetitive labels in the two innermost sections, qryHoursByEmployee and qryHoursByEmployee-TimeCardDate.

To change the group-level properties:

1. Right-click the **Header: qryHoursByEmployee** section and then click **Group Level Properties** on the shortcut menu. The property sheet opens, as shown in Figure 10-27.

Figure 10-27 **GROUP-LEVEL PROPERTIES**

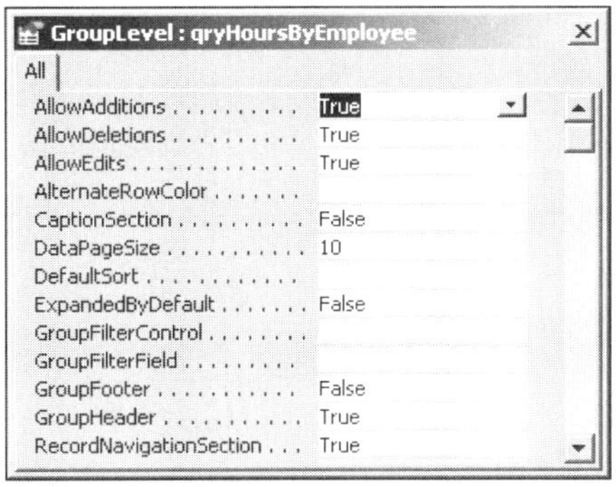

2. Change the CaptionSection property to **True**, the DataPageSize property to **All**, and the RecordNavigationSection property to **False**.
3. Close the property sheet. Your data access page should look like that shown in Figure 10-28. It now contains a new section, Caption: qryHoursByEmployee, which you can use for the labels so they don't repeat for each section entry. The Navigation section is gone.

Figure 10-28 **DATA ACCESS PAGE WITH CAPTION SECTION ADDED**

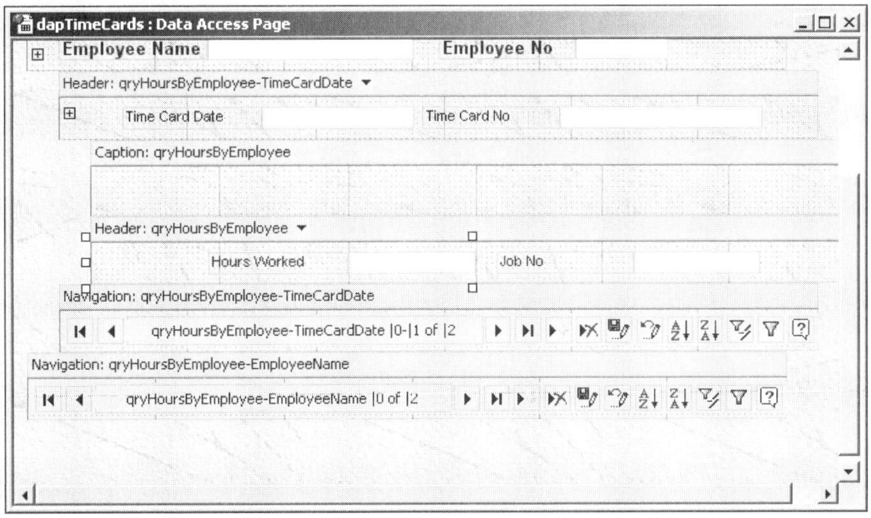

4. Right-click the **Hours Worked** label, click **Cut** on the shortcut menu, right-click the **Caption: qryHoursByEmployee** section, click **Paste** on the shortcut menu, and then move the label so that it is positioned directly above the Hours Worked text box.
5. Repeat Step 4 for the **Job No** label. You might need to size the label smaller for each label in order to position it above its respective text box.

6. Move the pasted labels to the top of the Caption: qryHoursByEmployee section, and then drag the section up beneath them, as shown in Figure 10-29.

Figure 10-29 MOVING THE LABELS IN THE CAPTION SECTION

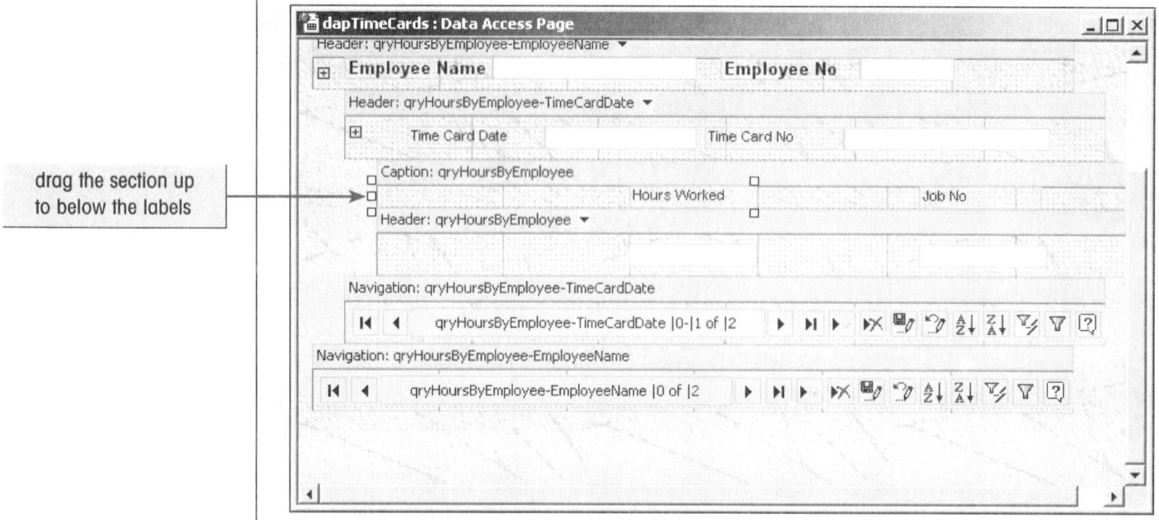

7. Right-click the **qryHoursByEmployee-TimeCardDate** header and choose **Group Level Properties**.

8. Change the CaptionSection property to **True**, the DataPageSize property to **10** (if necessary), the RecordNavigationSection property to **False**, and then close the property sheet.

9. Cut and paste the **Time Card Date** and **Time Card No** labels into the Caption: qryHoursByEmployee-TimeCardDate section, and then repeat Step 6 for this caption section.

10. Switch to Page view and test the page. Click the expand indicators to see the various levels.

Changing Navigation Toolbar Properties

Now that you have completed the changes to the group-level properties, you will modify the remaining record navigation toolbar. It currently contains a label that identifies the qryHoursByEmployee-EmployeeName, and is followed by a string that shows the record number and the total number of records. You want this to read "Employee Name" instead, but you won't change the record number display. You also will eliminate the buttons, including the Delete and Sort Ascending buttons, on the record navigation toolbar that do not work in this type of page.

To change the properties of the navigation toolbar:

1. Switch to Design view, click the navigation toolbar, and then display its property sheet.

TROUBLE? Selecting the area of the navigation section that you want can be difficult. At the bottom of the data access page, try selecting just the area in between the navigation buttons where you see some text displayed (this is actually called the RecordsetLabel), and then open the property sheet for this object.

2. Click the **All** tab, click in the **RecordsetLabel** text box, and then press **Shift + F2** to open the Zoom window.
3. Delete the **qryHoursByEmployee-** string at the beginning of the entry, click between **Employee** and **Name**, and then press the **spacebar**. The Zoom window should now look like that shown in Figure 10-30.

Figure 10-30 CHANGING THE RecordsetLabel PROPERTY

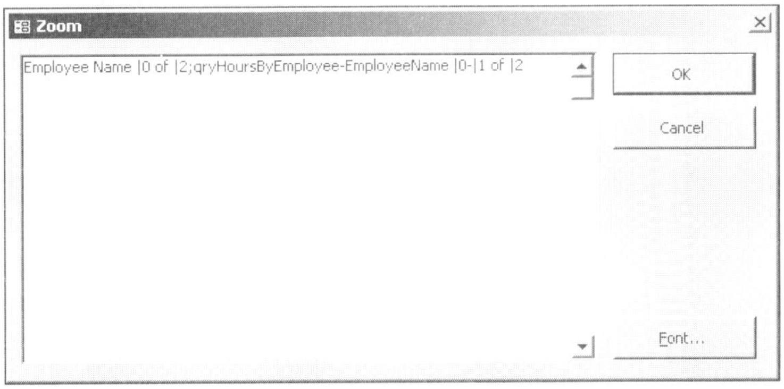

4. Click the **OK** button, and then close the property sheet.
5. Right-click the navigation toolbar, and then point to **Navigation Buttons** on the shortcut menu. A submenu pops out to the side of the shortcut menu. Note there are check marks beside all available button options. To remove buttons, you click on them one at a time in this submenu to remove the check box beside that button name, and the button will be removed from the navigation toolbar. You can also select buttons directly on the navigation toolbar and press the Delete key to remove them.
6. Using whichever method you prefer, remove the following buttons from the navigation toolbar: **New**, **Delete**, **Save**, **Undo**, **Sort Ascending**, **Sort Descending**, **Filter By Selection**, and **Filter Toggle**.
7. Size the record navigation toolbar to approximately 3" wide, and center it, as shown in Figure 10-31.

Figure 10-31 SIZING THE RECORD NAVIGATION TOOLBAR

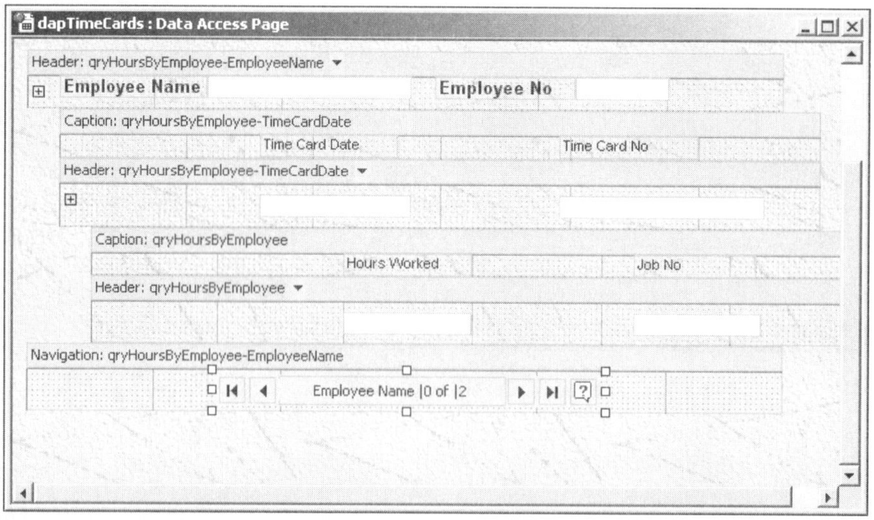

8. Switch to Page view. You want the Employee Name group to expand automatically when a new record is viewed.
9. Switch to Design view and open the group-level property sheet for the Header: qryHoursByEmployee-EmployeeName section.
10. Change the ExpandedByDefault property to **True**. Now the expand indicator will not have to be clicked each time the user navigates to a new employee record. Close the property sheet.
11. Switch to Page view to test your changes.

To complete the dapTimeCards page, you will create a hyperlink to e-mail the timekeeper in case an employee discovers an error in the data.

To add a hyperlink to a data access page:

1. Switch to Design view, make sure that the toolbox is visible, and then click the **Hyperlink** button on the toolbox.
2. Click approximately 1" below the record navigation toolbar. The Insert Hyperlink dialog box opens.
3. Click the **E-mail Address** option in the Link to bar, type **E-mail Timekeeper** in the Text to display text box, and then type **rjenkins@moviecam.com** in the E-mail address text box.
4. Type **Time card error** in the Subject text box as shown in Figure 10-32.

Figure 10-32 **CREATING THE E-MAIL HYPERLINK**

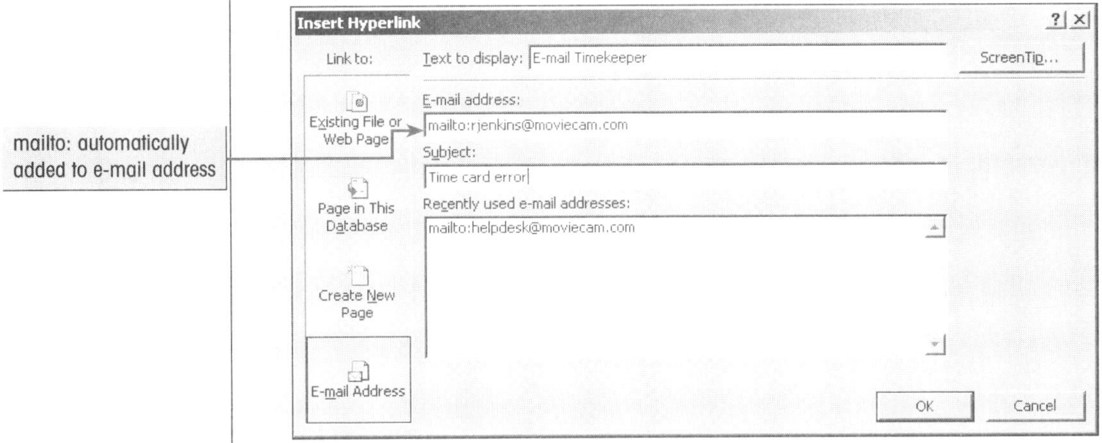

5. Click the **OK** button and then position the pointer on the handle on the right side of the hyperlink text box.
6. Click and drag to make the box the same width as the body of the data access page, as shown in Figure 10-33.

Figure 10-33 **MAKE THE HYPERLINK THE SAME WIDTH AS THE BODY OF THE PAGE**

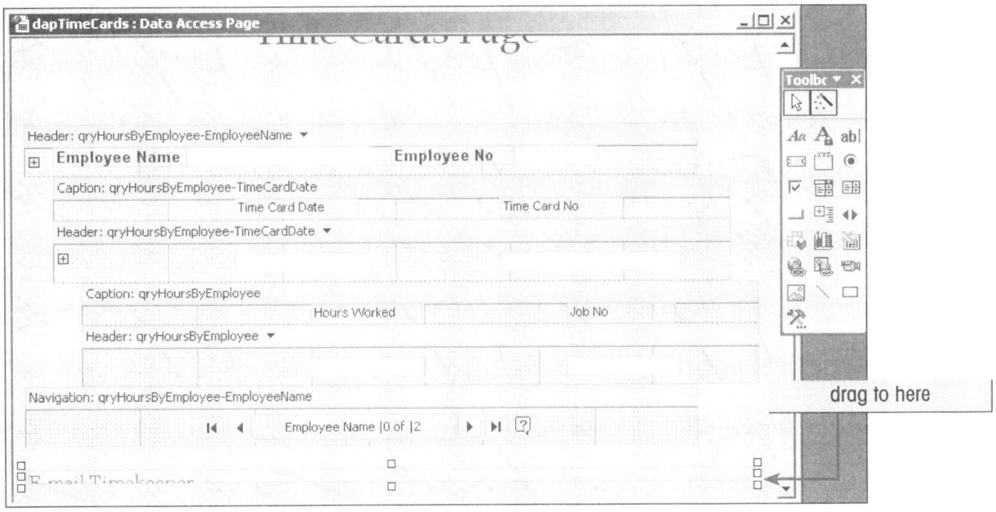

7. Click the **Center** button on the toolbar to center the text inside the box.
8. If necessary, drag the handle on the bottom of the hyperlink text box down so that the text displays completely.
9. Switch to Page view and click the **hyperlink** to test it. Outlook (or your default e-mail application) opens, and an e-mail is addressed automatically.
10. Close Outlook (or your default e-mail application) without saving the message, save your changes to the page, and then close the page.

Creating an Updateable Data Access Page

Amanda sent a memo to all employees to let them know that if they do not want their home address, telephone number, and emergency contact information available on the company intranet, they should send a written request. No one made the request, so you can create a data access page based on the tblEmployees table.

If you want to be able to edit the records in a data access page, you must base the page on a single table, make sure there are no grouping levels, and make sure that only one record at a time is visible. The page that you planned will allow employees to change their address and emergency contact information.

You want to provide users with quick access to their individual record, so you will include a combo box to filter the records by last name. You will apply the same theme to this page as you used on the time cards page, and you also will provide a link on this page to the dapTimeCards page.

To create an updateable data access page:

1. Make sure **Pages** is selected on the Objects bar in the Database window, and then double-click **Create data access page by using wizard**.
2. Click the **Tables/Queries** list arrow, click **Table: tblEmployees**, and then move the following fields from the Available Fields list box to the Selected Fields list box: **EmployeeNo**, **FirstName**, **LastName**, **Address1**, **Address2**, **City**, **State**, **Phone**, **ZipCode**, **EmergencyContact**, and **EmergencyPhone**.
3. Click the **Next** button, and then click the **Next** button again. You do not want to add any grouping levels because employees will be searching for their own information only and do not need a hierarchy that would be provided by grouping.
4. Select **LastName** as the field to sort by, click the **Next** button, type **dapMovieEmployees**, and then click the **Finish** button.
5. Click the *Click here and type title text* placeholder, type **Employees Contact Information Page**, click **Format** on the menu bar, click **Theme**, click **Expedition**, click the **Vivid Colors** check box, and then click the **OK** button.
6. Open the group-level property sheet for the tblEmployees header, change the CaptionSection property to **True**, and then close the property sheet.
7. Make sure the toolbox is visible and that the **Control Wizards** button is selected, click the **Dropdown List** button, and then click in the center of the Caption: tblEmployees section to create a drop-down list. The Combo Box Wizard starts. (The drop-down list looks just like a combo box on a form.)
8. In the Combo Box Wizard dialog box, click the **Next** button to accept the default selection to look up the values in a table or query, make sure the **Tables** option is selected in the next dialog box, click **Table: tblEmployees** in the list box, and then click the **Next** button.
9. Double-click **LastName** in the Available Fields list box, click the **Next** button, click the **Next** button again because the column does not need to be wider, type **Last Name** for the combo box label, and then click the **Finish** button. Your page should look similar to Figure 10-34.

Figure 10-34 ADDING THE COMBO BOX TO THE dapMovieEmployees PAGE

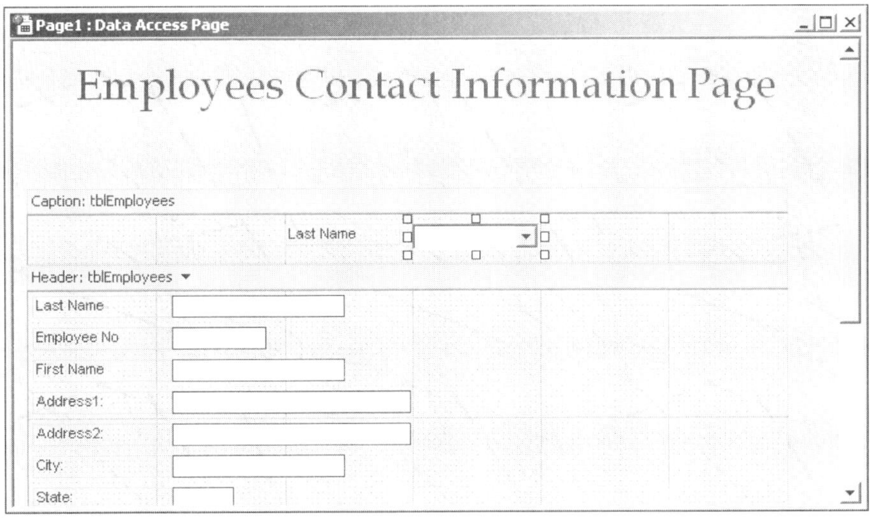

Now you need to set the page to filter the records. If this were a form or report, you would write VBA code to synchronize the combo box record to the record on the page, but data access pages do not require any programming to do this. Because data access pages are designed to run in Internet Explorer, which does not use the same language or event model as Access, you would have to use a scripting language like VBScript or JavaScript rather than VBA if you wanted to do any special programming.

To set the data access page to filter the records:

1. Make sure that the drop-down list text box is selected, and then open its property sheet.
2. Click the **All** tab and then change the Id property to **cboLastName**.
3. Right-click the **tblEmployees** header, and then click **Group Level Properties** on the shortcut menu.
4. Type **cboLastName** in the GroupFilterControl text box, and then type **LastName** in the GroupFilterField text box. The GroupFilterControl property is used to specify the combo box or list box that filters the page. The GroupFilterField property is the name of the field on which this control is filtered.
5. Close the group-level property sheet, switch to Page view, and then test the combo box by clicking the list arrow and selecting a last name from the list. The record in the page will synchronize to the chosen name.
6. Return to Design view, click the **Save** button on the toolbar, type **dapMovieEmployees** in the File name list box if necessary, navigate to the Tutorial.10\Tutorial folder on your local or network drive, and then click the **Save** button. If you get the connection string warning again, click the **OK** button in the message box.

Because the new data access page is linked directly to the tblEmployees table, you need to be sure that records cannot be deleted from the table. Although the Cascade Delete

Related Records option is not in effect between the tblEmployees and tblTimeCards tables, an employee who does not have a record in the tblTimeCards table could be inadvertently deleted. You also don't want the user to navigate to a new record and try to add data, because the purpose of this Web page is to allow employees to update their own information only. You will make these changes to the record navigation toolbar next.

To complete the dapMovieEmployees page:

1. Click the **Last Name** label in the Caption: tblEmployees section, display its property sheet, change the InnerText property to **Last Name Search**, close the property sheet, and then click the **Bold** button on the toolbar. The text wraps in the label, but the label is not large enough for you to see the added text, so you need to resize the label control in order to see all of the text.
2. Drag the left edge of the label to make it large enough so the text fits on one line. The Last Name Search label should already be selected
3. Press and hold the **Shift** key, click the **cboLastName** combo box, right-click the selection, point to **Size** on the shortcut menu, and then click the **Height** button.
4. With both the cboLastName combo box and the Last Name Search labels still selected, right-click the selection again, point to **Align** and then click the **Top** button on the shortcut menu.
5. Move the combo box and label to the left edge of the page as shown in Figure 10-35.

Figure 10-35 MOVING THE COMBO BOX AND LABEL

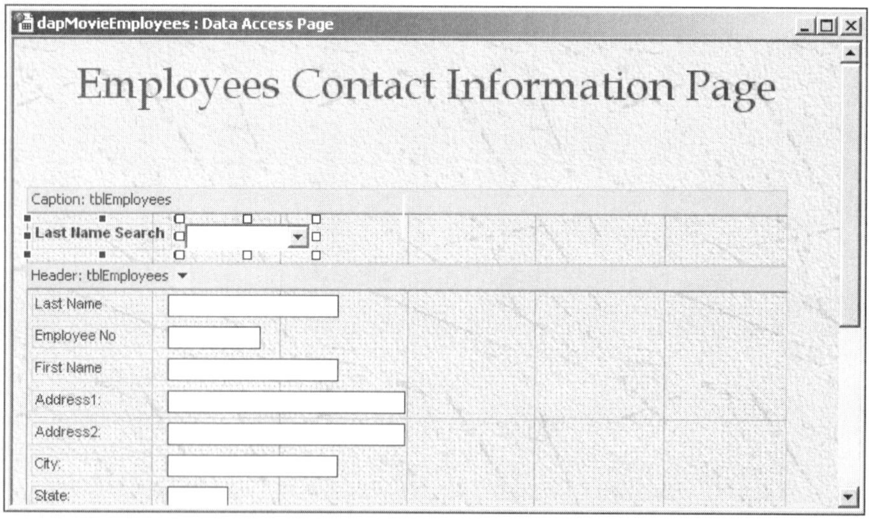

6. Scroll to the bottom of the page if necessary, click only the RecordsetLabel portion of the record navigation toolbar, and then click the **Properties** button on the toolbar, click the **All** tab if necessary, delete **tbl** from the beginning of the InnerText property.
7. Remove the **New** and **Delete** buttons from the navigation toolbar.

8. If the page is maximized, click the **Restore** button so that you can see the title bar of the data access page. Click the title bar to select the page, and then change the Title property to **Employees Contact Information**.
9. Close the property sheet, select the title **Employees Contact Information Page**, and then click the **Align Left** button on the toolbar.
10. Switch to Page view to test the page, click the **Last Name Search** list arrow, and then click **Garcia**. Resize your data access page as necessary so it will appear as shown in Figure 10-36.

Figure 10-36 THE dapMovieEmployees PAGE IN PAGE VIEW

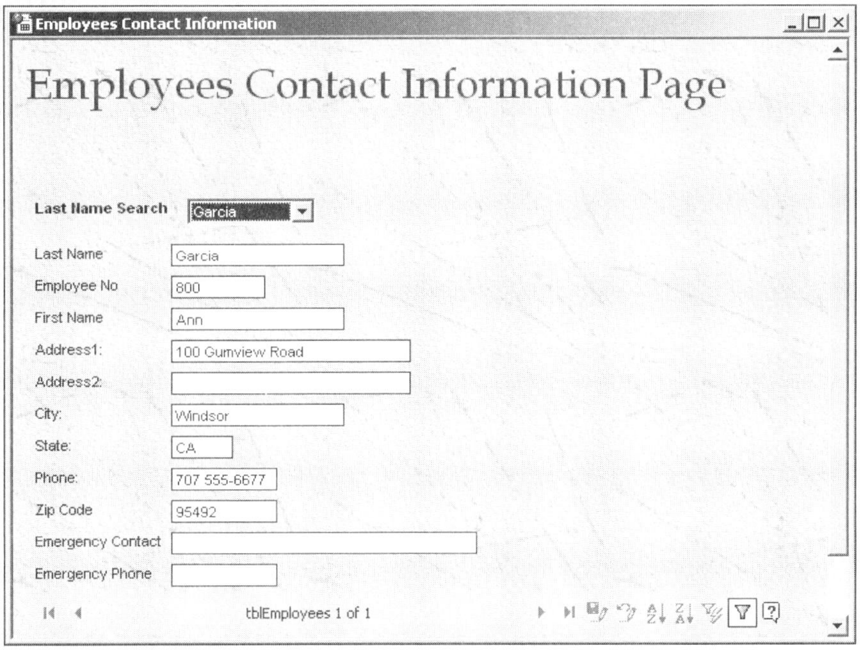

11. Save your changes and close the page.

Testing the Data Access Pages

Now that you have completed the dapEmployees page, it is time to test it. You will open it in Access and then open it in Internet Explorer. The editing features work a bit differently in data access pages than in forms. When you make a change to a record, you need to use the Save Record button on the toolbar to save it. Pressing the Enter key does not move you from text box to text box, so you need to use the mouse to navigate.

You will open the updateable page in Access first.

To edit data in a data access page:

1. Make sure **Pages** is selected on the Objects bar in the Database window, and then double-click **dapMovieEmployees**. If necessary, resize the page so you can see the record navigation toolbar at the bottom of the page.

2. Click the **Last Name Search** list arrow, click **Eichman** from the list, select **722 Blair Place** in the Address1 text box, and then press the **Delete** key.
3. Type **1555 Starr Road** and then press the **Enter** key. The entry seems to disappear.
4. Press the **Backspace** key and the address reappears.
5. Click the **Save** button on the record navigation toolbar to save your change.
6. Click the **City** text box, delete **Santa Rosa**, and then type **Windsor**. Do not press the Enter key.
7. Click the **ZipCode** text box, change the entry to **95492**, and then click on the record navigation toolbar.
8. Close the dapMovieEmployees page.

To complete the next set of steps, you do not need to be connected to the Internet, but you do need a copy of Internet Explorer. You will launch Internet Explorer, and open both data access pages to see how they look.

To test data access pages in Internet Explorer:

1. Start Internet Explorer.

   TROUBLE? Check with your instructor or technical support person to make sure Internet Explorer is installed on your computer or to ask how to start the program if you are not sure.

2. Click **File** on the Internet Explorer menu bar and then click **Open**. You will see the Open dialog box, as shown in Figure 10-37.

Figure 10-37 OPENING A DATA ACCESS PAGE FROM INTERNET EXPLORER

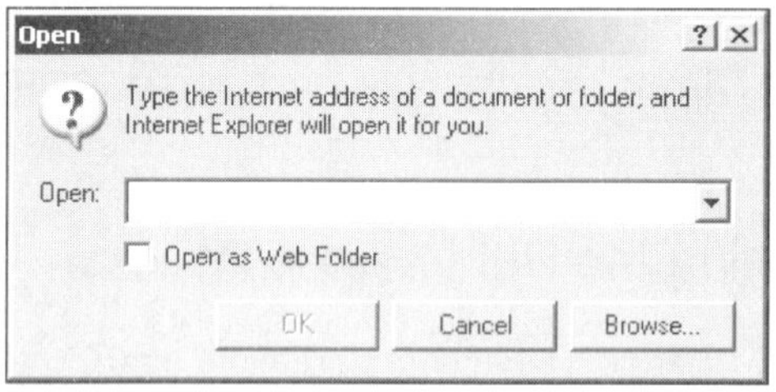

3. Click the **Browse** button and the Microsoft Internet Explorer dialog box opens.
4. Navigate to the Tutorial.10\Tutorial folder containing the data access pages, click **dapTimeCards**, and then click the **Open** button.
5. Click the **OK** button in the Open dialog box.
6. Repeat Steps 2 through 5 to open the **dapMovieEmployees** page.
7. Click the **Last Name Search** list arrow, click **Gerardo**, type **Joyce Gerardo** in the Emergency Contact text box, type **707 555-4999** in the Emergency Phone text box, and then click the **Save** button on the record navigation toolbar.

8. Click the **Back** button on the toolbar to navigate to the dapTimeCards page.
9. Click the **Next** button on the record navigation toolbar until you reach the record for Todd Combs, and then click the **expand indicator** for the 05/25/2004 time card. The page should look like that shown in Figure 10-38.

Figure 10-38 TIME CARDS PAGE IN INTERNET EXPLORER

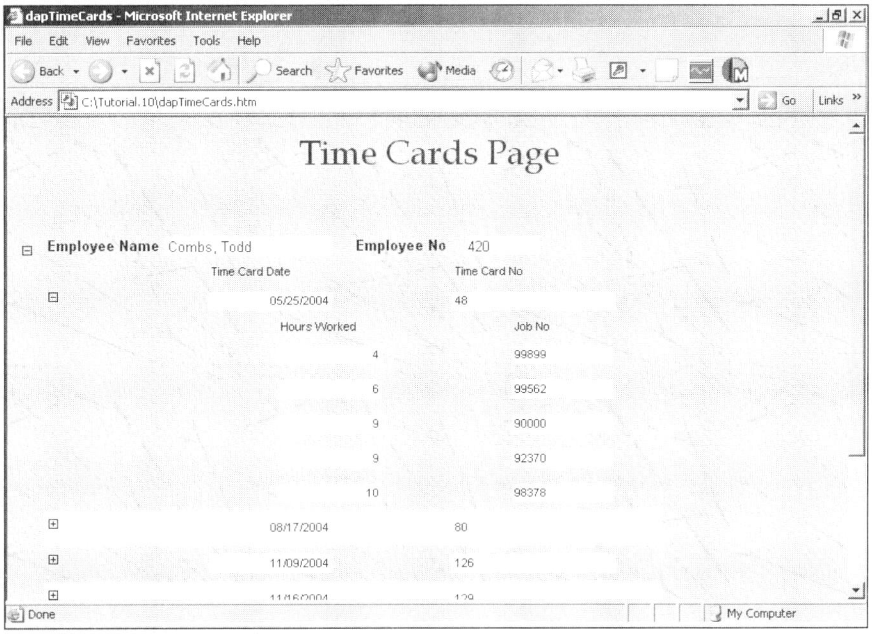

10. Close Internet Explorer.

Adding a Hyperlink to Another Page

You want to provide a link in the dapEmployees page to open the dapTimeCards page. You will do that next.

To add a hyperlink to a data access page:

1. Make sure **Pages** is selected on the Objects bar in the Database window, and then open the **dapMovieEmployees** page in Design view.
2. If necessary, display the toolbox and maximize the window, click the **Insert Hyperlink** button on the toolbox, and then click about 1" below the record navigation toolbar on the page.
3. Click the **Page in This Database** option in the Link to bar, and then click **dapTimeCards** from the Select a page in this database list box.
4. Type **Time Cards Page** in the Text to display text box, click the **OK** button, and then widen the hyperlink text box so that it is the same width as the body of the page, as shown in Figure 10-39.

Figure 10-39 POSITIONING THE HYPERLINK LABEL

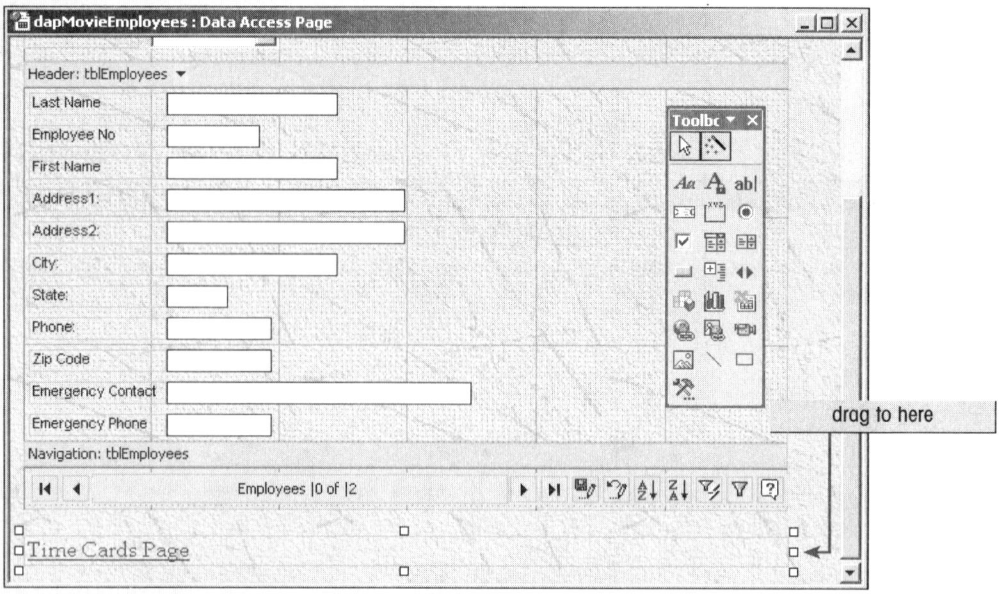

5. Click the **Center** button on the toolbar, if necessary size the hyperlink text box so that all the text is visible, and then save your changes.
6. Switch to Page view, and then click the **hyperlink**. Internet Explorer launches and the dapTimeCards page opens.
7. Close Internet Explorer.
8. Close the dapMovieEmployees page to return to the Database window.

The data access pages work well. You plan to have users test them more before you put the pages on the company intranet server. Because data access pages are stored in files that aren't in your database, Access needs to know where to find these database files on your hard disk anytime you open a page. If you have moved the files to a different location, Access will prompt you to locate the files by navigating to the New folder when you try to open the data access page.

Exporting to the Web

You can export tables, queries, forms, or reports to a Web-ready format by using the Export command on the File menu. To save a table, you can use the HTML Documents format, which is readable with any browser.

REFERENCE WINDOW RW

Exporting an Access Query to an HTML Document

- Click Queries on the Objects bar in the Database window, and then open the query you want to export.
- Click File on the menu bar, and then click Export.
- Click the Save in list arrow, and navigate to the drive and folder in which you want to save the document.
- Click the Save as type list arrow, click HTML Documents, and then click the Export All button.
- Close the query.

The qryJobsTotalDollars query groups all of the jobs and shows totals to date of hours and dollars for each job. The product managers need this information from time to time, but do not need the printed output. One option is to provide the managers with read-only rights to the query. Another option is to export the file to an HTML document on a shared drive of the network where the managers can open the file from their browser. You will export the query now.

To export a query to an HTML document:

1. Click **Queries** in the Objects bar in the Database window, and then double-click the **qryJobsTotalDollars** query to open it.
2. Click **File** on the menu bar, and then click **Export**. The Export Query dialog box opens.
3. Navigate to the Tutorial.10\Tutorial folder on your hard drive or network drive.
4. Click the **Save as type** list arrow, click **HTML Documents**, and then click the **Export All** button.
5. Close the query to return to the Database window.
6. Start Internet Explorer, click **File** on the menu bar, and then click **Open**.
7. Click the **Browse** button to open the Microsoft Internet Explorer dialog box.
8. Navigate to the Tutorial.10\Tutorial folder, click **qryJobsTotalDollars**, and then click the **Open** button.
9. Click the **OK** button in the Open dialog box. The query appears in Internet Explorer.
10. Close Internet Explorer, close the Movie10 database, and then exit Access.

You are satisfied with this solution for providing data to managers. You plan to train managers on how to open exported queries from Internet Explorer. When the managers have a one-time request for summary data, they can e-mail you via the help desk address the network administrator set up for you. You can then write the query, run it, and export the results to an HTML document. With this approach, you won't need to generate a report or change the switchboard or rights in the database to give the managers access to the data.

Session 10.2 QUICK CHECK

1. How is data viewed or edited in a data access page?
2. Data access pages that contain ______________ cannot be updated.
3. A(n) ______________ is a set of design elements and color schemes for background, font, horizontal lines, bullets, hyperlinks, and controls.
4. The ______________ for designing data access pages are not as advanced as those for designing forms and reports.
5. Programming Web pages requires that you use a scripting language like ______________ or ______________.
6. What are the requirements for an updateable data access page?
7. How is editing data different on a data access page than it is in a form?
8. Which Access objects can you export to an HTML document file?

REVIEW ASSIGNMENTS

The Hours10 database is similar to the MovieCam Technologies database you worked with in this tutorial. You want to create a data access page so that employees can update their address, telephone, and contact information via the company intranet.

1. Start Access and open the **Hours10** database located in the Tutorial.10\Review folder on your local or network drive.
2. Create a data access page by using the wizard, select the tblEmployees table, and then move the following fields from the Available Fields list box to the Selected Fields list box: FirstName, LastName, Address1, City, State, Phone, ZipCode, EmergencyContact, and EmergencyPhone.
3. Click the Next button, click the Next button again to skip the step for adding grouping levels, select LastName as the field to sort by, click the Next button, type **dapEmployees** as the label, and then click the Finish button.
4. Click the *Click here and type title text* placeholder, type **Employees Page**, click Format on the menu bar, click Theme, click Industrial, click the OK button. Using the property sheet for group-level properties, change the CaptionSection property to True, and then close the property sheet. (*Hint*: If the Industrial theme is not available, pick another theme.)
5. Make sure the toolbox is visible and that the Control Wizards button is selected. Click the Dropdown List button, and click in the center of the Caption: tblEmployees section to create a drop-down list.
6. Click the Next button to accept the default selection to look up the values in a table or query, click the Tables option button, click tblEmployees in the list box, and then click the Next button.
7. Double-click LastName from the Available Fields list box, click the Next button, click the Next button again because the column does not need to be widened, type **Last Name Lookup** for the label, and then click the Finish button.
8. If necessary, select the drop-down list text box, click the Properties button on the toolbar, and change the Id property on the All tab to **cboLastName**.

9. Display the group-level properties, type **cboLastName** in the Group Filter Control property, type **LastName** in the Group Filter Field property, and then close the property sheet.
10. Move the combo box and label to the left edge of the page
11. Click the record navigation toolbar, delete "tbl" from the beginning of the RecordsetLabel property, and then remove the New and Delete buttons from the navigation toolbar.
12. Click the Save button on the toolbar, type **dapEmployees**, navigate to the Tutorial.10\ Review folder on your local or network drive, and then click the Save button.
13. Switch to Page view and test the page. Close the page.
14. Close the Hours10 database, and then exit Access.

CASE PROBLEMS

Case 1. Edwards and Company Jack Edwards wants you to create a company intranet Web page that consultants can browse for their particular clients. He wants the client name, address, telephone, and contact information displayed so that he does not have to provide each consultant with access to this information in the database itself. The Edwards and Company database contains a query named qryClientByConsultant that contains the fields that you need to complete the page. The data access page will be grouped by the consultant name and will contain all the fields in the query. Complete the following:

1. Start Access and open the **Edward10** database located in the Tutorial.10\Cases folder on your local or network drive.
2. Click Pages on the Objects bar in the Database window, and then double-click Create data access page by using wizard.
3. Click the Tables/Queries list arrow, select Query: qryClientByConsultant if it is not already selected, move all of the fields in the Available Fields list box to the Selected Fields list box, and then proceed to the next step in the wizard.
4. Use the ConsultantName field to group by and sort on the CompanyName.
5. Type **dapClients** as the title for the page, and then click the Finish button.
6. Save the page as **dapClients** in the Tutorial.10\Cases folder. Ignore the connection string warning, if necessary.
7. Click the *Click here and type title text* placeholder at the top of the page, and then type **Clients Page**.
8. Insert a space in the label in the qryClientByConsultant-ConsultantName header so it reads **Consultant Name**.
9. Change the Address1 label to read **Address**.
10. Click Format on the menu bar, click Theme, click Capsules in the Choose a Theme list box, click the Vivid Colors check box, and then click the OK button.
11. Click the navigation toolbar in the qryClientByConsultant section.
12. Click the RecordsetLabel and delete the qryClientByConsultant portions of the string, and use **Client Name** in the RecordsetLabel property. Click the OK button.

13. Remove the following buttons from the navigation toolbar: New, Delete, Save, Undo, Sort Ascending, Sort Descending, Filter By Selection, and Filter Toggle.
14. Size the record navigation toolbar to approximately 3" wide, and center it.
15. Repeat Steps 12 through14 for the navigation toolbar in the qryClientByConsultant-ConsultantName section. Change the RecordsetLabel to display as **Consultant Name**.
16. Switch to Page view, and test the page. Close the page and save your changes.
17. Close the Edward10 database, and then exit Access.

Case 2. San Diego County Information Systems You used the built-in menu bar in the ISD database rather than a custom menu bar and now you want to modify it to include some Web options. You want to add two menu choices: one to navigate to the Microsoft Home Page, and another to navigate to the County home page. Complete the following:

1. Start Access and open the **ISD10** database located in the Tutorial.10\Cases folder on your local or network drive.
2. Right-click the Database toolbar, and then click Customize on the shortcut menu.
3. Click the Commands tab in the Customize dialog box, scroll down in the Categories list box, and then click Web.
4. Drag the Hyperlink command from the Commands list box to the bottom of the Window menu item, and then drag another Hyperlink command to the Window menu below the menu item you just added.
5. Right-click the first Hyperlink command, point to Assign Hyperlink, and then click Open.
6. Click the Existing File or Web Page option in the Link to bar, type **www.microsoft.com** in the Address text box, and then click the OK button.
7. Right-click the Hyperlink command, change the Name property to **&Microsoft**, and then press the Enter key.
8. Right-click the second Hyperlink command, point to Assign Hyperlink, and then click Open.
9. Click the Existing File or Web Page option in the Link to bar, type **www.sandiego-county.org** in the Address text box, and then click the OK button.
10. Right-click the Hyperlink command, change the Name to **&SDCounty**, press the Enter key, and then close the Customize dialog box
11. If necessary, connect to the Internet, click Window on the menu bar, and then click the Microsoft menu item. Your default browser opens the Microsoft Home Page. Close your browser.
12. Close the ISD10 database, and then exit Access.

Case 3. Christenson Homes Roberta asked you to develop a read-only Web page for customers to view the various subdivisions under construction. The Homes10 database contains the query you wrote for this purpose. The query named qryLotsBySubdivision has subdivision and lot information. Complete the following:

1. Start Access and open the **Homes10** database located in the Tutorial.10\Cases folder on your hard drive or network drive.
2. Using the wizard, create a data access page that contains all the fields in the qryLotsBy Subdivision query.
3. Group the data in the page by SubdivisionName, sort by LotID, and save the page as **dapLots** when prompted by the wizard.

4. Type **Lots Web Page** as the title for the page.
5. Modify the labels so that they contain the names of the fields. Use spaces between words in the field names.
6. Format the label and text box in the grouping header so they are 10-point size and bold.
7. Size the Subdivision Name label so that the text fits on one line.
8. Apply the Expedition theme with the Vivid Colors option to the data access page.
9. Delete the Record Navigation section from the qryLotsBySubdivision section.
10. Add a caption section to the qryLotsBySubdivision section, and move the labels into this section.
11. Move the text boxes in the qryLotsBySubdivision section so that they are lined up in a row, rather than a column, and then align their labels over them. Resize the Address text box and label to accommodate more text than the other text boxes. Resize the other text boxes to the same width as their corresponding labels. (*Hint*: Use the property sheet, and once you size and align the labels into the caption section, use the Left and Width properties to align the text box controls beneath their corresponding labels.)
12. Reduce the height of the qryLotsBySubdivision section to approximately 0.333".
13. Click the navigation toolbar in the qryLotsBySubdivision-SubdivisionName section.
14. In the RecordsetLabel, delete the qryLotsBySubdivision- portion of the string, and then insert a space between Subdivision and Name.
15. Remove all of the buttons except the ones used to navigate between records (First, Next, Last, and Previous) and the RecordsetLabel.
16. Open the property sheet for group-level properties for the qryLotsBySubdivison-SubdivisionName header, and then change the ExpandedByDefault property to True.
17. Save the data access page as **dapLots** in the Tutorial.10\Cases folder, and close the property sheet.
18. Switch to Page view and test the page.
19. Close the Homes10 database, and then exit Access.

Case 4. Sonoma Farms The Sonoma Farms database contains the frmCustomers, frmDistributors, and frmVisitors forms. You have decided to use a lightweight switchboard in this database to open each of these forms. You will include hyperlinks on command buttons for each form and also include a button designed with VBA code to exit the database. Complete the following:

1. Start Access and open the **Sonoma10** database located in the Tutorial.10\Cases folder on your local or network drive.
2. Create a new unbound form in the database and save it as **frmMainSwitchboard**.
3. Change the properties of the form to eliminate record selectors, dividing lines, navigation buttons, and the Close, Minimize, and Maximize buttons.
4. Create a label at the top of the form, and type **Sonoma Farms Main Switchboard** as the Caption property.
5. Add three command buttons to the form. Create hyperlinks on the buttons to open each of the three data entry forms in the database: Customers, Distributors, and Visitors.
6. Include a shortcut key for each button, and format the buttons so that they look like standard command buttons rather than hyperlinks.

7. Use the wizard to add a command button to exit the database.
8. Add a hyperlink label at the bottom of the form. Use your e-mail address as the hyperlink, so the user can click it if there are problems or questions.
9. Test the form to be sure that it works properly.
10. Save the form.
11. Close the Sonoma10 database, and then exit Access.

QUICK CHECK ANSWERS

Session 10.1

1. A hyperlink is text or an image that you click to navigate to other parts of a file, to other documents on your computer or network, or to Internet addresses.
2. A data access page is an object in the database that lets you display, edit, and manipulate other objects, such as tables, forms, and reports, so those objects can be published to the Web using the Internet Explorer Web browser.
3. A main switchboard form that contains hyperlinks to the objects in the database that you want to open will open faster than a form containing VBA code.
4. The Hyperlink address property is used to specify the path to a document on the local or network drive or to a Web site address.
5. The Hyperlink subaddress property is used to specify a particular location in a document, such as a bookmark, or a particular Access database object such as a form or report.
6. To assign a hyperlink to a toolbar button or menu command, you must add a button or a menu command, and then add the hyperlink to replace that command.

Session 10.2

1. Data access pages are Web pages that are separate from your Access database file, and allow those who have Web access to use Internet Explorer to view and edit data in your tables.
2. Data access pages that contain grouping levels cannot be updated.
3. A theme is a set of design elements and color schemes for background, font, horizontal lines, bullets, hyperlinks, and controls.
4. The tools for designing data access pages are not as advanced as those used for designing forms and reports.
5. Programming Web pages requires that you use a scripting language like VBScript or JavaScript.
6. An updateable page must be based on a single table, there must be no grouping levels, and only one record is visible at a time.
7. When you make a change to a record, you need to use the Save Record button on the toolbar to save it. Pressing the Enter key does not move you from text box to text box, so you need to navigate using the mouse.
8. You can export tables, queries, forms, or reports to a Web-ready format.

GLOSSARY

A

Access object model
A model that contains all the items you use in an application (such as the forms collection, forms, and controls collection), and is used to interact programmatically with the Access user interface

actions
The individual commands in a macro

ActiveX control
Similar to a built-in control, it is an object you place on a form or report to display data or perform an action; unlike a built-in control, the code that supports ActiveX control is stored in a separate file or files that must be installed for use

ADO
A single programming interface used by client applications, regardless of the type of data provider

***After Del Confirm* event**
A form event that occurs after you confirm record deletions and the records are actually deleted, or occurs after the deletions are canceled

***After Insert* event**
A form event that occurs after a new record is added to the database

***After Update* event**
A form and control event that occurs for new and existing records after a control or record is updated with changed data

allow zero length
A field property, when set to Yes, that allows a zero length string to be entered; applies to Text, Memo, and Hyperlink fields

array
A series of variables of the same data type, arranged contiguously in memory

B

back end
A file that contains tables

bang notation
Uses the bang (!) operator, in place of dot notation when the collection referenced by an object is the default collection

bang operator
An exclamation point (!) used to separate one object from another or from the object collection

***Before Del Confirm* event**
A form event that occurs after one or more records are deleted, but before Access displays a dialog box asking you to confirm or cancel the deletion

***Before Insert* event**
A form event that occurs when you type the first character in a new record, but before the record is added to the database

***Before Update* event**
A form and control event that occurs for new and existing records before a control or record is updated with changed data

bound forms
Forms that are tied to a table or a query, and are used for editing, entering, and reviewing data in that underlying table or query

breakpoint
A selected line of a program where execution automatically stops

C

caption
Field property that displays text other than the field name in Datasheet view

Cascade Delete
Deleting a record in the primary table automatically deletes any related records in a related table

Cascade Update
A change in the primary key of the primary table will automatically be updated in a related table

***Change* event**
A control event that occurs when the context of a text box or the text box portion of a combo box changes

class
The definition for an object, including the object's name, its properties and methods, and any events associated with it

CodeContextObject property
Determines the object in which a macro or VBA code is executing

collection
An object that contains a set of related objects (objects of the same class)

collection index
A range of numbers that begin with a zero, and in turn represent each object in the collection

combo box
A drop-down list of items from which you can select; limits entries in a field

comment
Text included in a procedure; briefly describes what the procedure does

compilation
Process in which Access checks for overall consistency when a program is run and translates the VBA statements into a language that the computer understands

composite key
A primary key that consists of two or more fields

concatenates
Joins items together in a sequence, typically string expressions; for example, combining a first name, a space, and then a last name together into one field or expression is a concatenation of those three items

constant
A meaningful name that takes the place of a number or string

Controls collection
Group of controls of the same type

control structure
A series of VBA statements that work together as a unit

***Current* event**
A form event that occurs when the focus moves to a record, therefore making it the current record; also occurs when you requery a form's source of data

D

DAO
An interface that has been used in programs to manipulate data, create tables and queries, and manage security in Access databases since the release of Access 2.0

data access page
An object in the database that lets you display, edit, and manipulate objects such as tables, forms, and reports so that they can be published to the Web using the Internet Explorer Web browser

data-definition query
A query that uses the data-definition language component of SQL to create objects such as tables and indexes

data dictionary
A list and definition of the individual fields included in each table in a database

data events
Events that occur when data is entered, deleted, or changed in a form or control; they also occur when the focus moves from one record to another

Database Documenter
Allows you to create a data dictionary quickly and easily by generating a document that clearly identifies the database objects and their related properties

database management system
An application used to manage, store, retrieve, and order large amounts of information

Database window
The command center for working with objects

Database window toolbar
Contains buttons for opening, creating, and deleting objects, and for changing views

DatePart function
A function that returns an integer containing the specified part of the given date

DAvg()
A domain aggregate function that returns the mathematical average of the values in the specified field

DBEngine object
Represents the DAO interface into the JET engine and ODBCDirect technology

DCount()
A domain aggregate function that returns the number of records with nonnull values in a specified field

decimal places
Field property that applies to Number and Currency fields and determines the number of decimal places shown to the right of the decimal point

default value
Value, when entered in the Default Value text box, that Access automatically enters into each new record

***Delete* event**
A form event that occurs when a record is deleted, but before the deletion is confirmed and actually performed

delimiter
The characters in a text file that identify the end of one field and the beginning of another field

Detail
Section that represents the main body of the report or form

DFirst()
A domain aggregate function that returns the value in the specified field from the first physical record

***Dirty* event**
A form event that occurs when the contents of a form or the text portion of a combo box change, or when you move from one page to another page in a tab control

DLast()
A domain aggregate function that returns the value in a specified field from the last physical record

DLookup()
A domain aggregate function that returns the value in a specified field

DMax()
A domain aggregate function that returns the maximum value in a specified field

DMin()
A domain aggregate function that returns the minimum value in a specified field

Do...Loop
A type of programming control structure used to repeat statements in a procedure either while a specified condition is true (or false) or until a specified condition is true (or false), depending on how the programmer wants to use the control structure

domain
A set of records

dot notation
Uses the dot (.) operator to indicate that what follows is an item defined by Access

DSum()
A domain aggregate function that returns the sum of the values in a specified field

dynamic link library (DLL)
File containing a collection of Windows functions designed to perform a specific class of operations

E

Err object
Contains information about an error that has just occurred

error and timing events
Events that are used for error-handling and synchronizing data on forms or reports

error trapping
A way of protecting programs and data from the effect of errors

event-driven programming
The use of event properties to run macros or execute VBA code

event procedure
A group of statements that execute when an event occurs and is part of a larger category of procedures called Sub procedures

event property
Associated with each event, it specifies how an object responds when the event occurs

events
Actions that are recognized by an object and for which a response can be defined

explicit declaration
Process in which it is necessary to declare a variable before using it

explicit permissions
Permissions in user-level security that are granted directly to a user account and affect no other account

expression
A combination of symbols and values that produces a result

F

field size
The number of characters a field can contain

field validation rules
Allow you to validate a field compared to a constant

filter events
Events that occur when a filter is applied or created on a form

focus
The ability to receive mouse or user input through mouse or keyboard actions

focus events
Events that occur when a form or control loses or gains the focus

For...Next Loop
A type of programming control structure used to execute statements of code a specified number of times

For Each...Next Loop
A type of programming control structure that executes a group of statements on each member of an array or collection

foreign key
The join field in the secondary table in relationships

form class module
Saved as part of a form, and which contains one or many procedures that apply specifically to that form

form master
A form that contains the controls that are common to all forms in the database

form template
A form on which to base other forms created in the database

format
Predefined standards for entering Number, Date/Time, and other types of fields; does not affect the way data must be entered, only how it will appear after it is entered

format event
Event that occurs when Access determines what data goes in a report section, but happens before the section is formatted for previewing or for printing

front end
A file that contains the queries, forms, reports, macros, and modules

function
A built-in procedure that returns a value and usually requires you to specify one or more pieces of information, called arguments

G

Group Footer
The section that appears at the end of a group of records; it might contain information that can be used to show calculations, such as a total or an average of the records in the group

Group Header
The section that appears at the beginning of a new group of records; it might contain information such as a group name or a picture that applies to the group

Groups bar
Organizes database objects according to subject

H

hyperlink
Text or an image that you click to navigate to other parts of a file, to other documents on your computer or network, or to Internet addresses

I

identifier operators
Operators that are used in expressions, macros, and VBA code to identify objects and their properties

Immediate window
A window that shows information that results from debugging statements in the code or from commands typed directly into the window

implicit declaration
Process in which it is not necessary to declare a variable before using it

implicit permissions
Permissions in user-level security that are granted to a group account

importing
A way to bring data into Access, usually into a new table; a good approach if the data will be used only in Access and not in its original format

index
A separate hidden table that consists of pointers to records or groups of records, and is designed to make sorting and searching more efficient

indexed
Field property that can speed up the process of searching and sorting on a particular field, but also can slow updates

input mask
Composed of a string of characters that act as placeholders for the characters that will be entered into the field; controls how data is actually entered into a field, not how it appears after it is entered

instance
A new object with all the characteristics defined by the class on which it is created

J

junction table
Contains common fields from two tables; is on the many side of a one-to-many relationship with those two tables

K

keyboard events
Events that occur when you type on a keyboard, and when keystrokes that use the Sendkeys macro action or the Sendkeys statement in VBA are sent to a form or a control on a form

L

lifetime
The time during which a variable retains its value

lightweight form
A form that contains hyperlinks to the objects in the database that you want to open, rather than having to use controls designed with VBA code

line continuation character
A character (the underscore _) that is used to continue a line of code to the next line on the screen when the code is too long to fit on a single line

linking
A way to use outside data in Access; it leaves data in its current format and location outside of Access, and is a good alternate method to importing if the data is going to be used both in its original format and in Access

literal
A character in the input mask that you don't have to type, such as dashes in a Social Security number

Locals window
Displays the name, current value, and type of all the variables and objects in the current procedure

logic errors
These occur when your procedures execute without failure, but the results are not what you intended; can occur when code has been assigned to the wrong event procedure or when the order of operations in a procedure is incorrect

M

macro
A command or series of commands, used with forms and reports, that automate database operations

Me keyword
In a VBA class module, it can be used to refer to the associated form or report that contains the class module; always refers to the object that is running the code

menu animation
A term used to describe how the menu opens

method
A procedure that acts on an object

mod operator
An arithmetic operator used to divide two numbers and return only the remainder

module
An object in an Access database that is used to store VBA functions and procedures; a small compact program written in VBA

mouse events
Events that occur in a form or in a control on a form as a result of a mouse action, such as pressing down or clicking the mouse button

N

new value
Field property that can be applied only to fields of AutoNumber data type

NoData event
Event that occurs after Access formats a report for printing when the report has no data, but before the report is printed

***Not In List* event**
A control property that occurs when a value entered in a combo box isn't in the combo box list

O

object library
A collection of prebuilt objects and functions that you can use in VBA code

object variables
Used when you want to declare variables in your procedures to use in place of object names

Objects bar
Contains buttons for viewing each database object

object shortcuts
Provide a quick method for creating an object

On Error statement
A statement that enables error handling in a procedure

one-to-many relationship
Exists when a related table has many records that relate to a single record in the primary table

one-to-one relationship
Exists when one entry in each table corresponds to only one entry in the other table

operators
Used to perform arithmetic calculations, perform comparisons, combine strings, and perform logical operations

orphan record
A record in the related table that does not contain a record in the primary table

owner
In a group, the user who creates a table, query, form, report, or macro

P

page event
Event that occurs after Access formats a page for printing, but before the page is printed

Page Footer
The section that appears at the bottom of every page of a report and may contain information such as date, time, and page numbers

Page Header
The section that prints at the top of every page in a report and may include column headers or the report title

page property
Property that specifies the current page number when a page is being printed

pass-through query
A query that passes an uninterpreted SQL statement to an external database server

precision
Field property that can be applied only to fields of Number data type where the Field Size property has been changed to Decimal; defines the total number of digits used to represent a numeric value

primary key
The field (or fields) that uniquely identifies a record in a table

primary table
Table that contains data about a person or object when there is only one record that can be associated with that person or object

print event
Event that occurs after Access has formatted the data in a report section, but before the section is printed

print events
Events that are found on reports and report sections, and occur when a report is being printed or is being formatted for printing

Private keyword
A keyword that indicates that the procedure can be called only from within the module where it is contained

procedures
In any programming language, a group of statements that perform actions and tasks

property
A named attribute of an object that defines a certain characteristic

Public keyword
A keyword that indicates that the procedure can be called from outside the module where it is contained

R

records
A set of field values

recordset
A set of records; the results (or the records found) of a query; manipulating recordsets is one of the major uses of ADO and DAO technology

redundancy
Duplication of data

referential integrity
Requires that a foreign key value in a related table matches the value of the primary key for some row in the primary table, and prevents the occurrence of orphaned records

related table
In a relationship, it is the table(s) that is not the primary table

relational database management system (RDBMS)
An application that links tables through a common field, and thereby combines data in new objects and minimizes data duplication; also can store a large amount of information

Report Footer
The section that appears once at the end of a report and may be used to show the results of expressions such as totals or averages

Report Header
The section at the beginning of a report that may contain information such as company logo, report title, and company name and address

reports
Used primarily for printing records in an organized, attractive format; might be based on the contents of a table, the results of a saved query, or a SQL statement

required
Field property, when set to Yes, that requires text or a value be entered into the field

Resume statement
A statement that resumes execution after an error-handling routine is finished

retreat print event
Event that occurs when Access must back up past one or more report sections on a page in order to perform multiple formatting passes

run-time errors
These occur while the application is running, or when the user attempts an operation that the system cannot perform

S

scale
Field property that can be applied only to fields of Number data type where the Field Size property has been change to Decimal; also determines the number of decimal places to the right of the decimal point

scope
The visibility and accessibility of one procedure from another procedure

Screen object
The particular form, report, or control that currently has the focus

ScreenTip
A message that appears when the pointer is positioned on a control, form, or button on a toolbar

self-join
The process of joining a table to itself in a query

splash screen
A type of unbound form that opens automatically when a database is opened; it is designed to give the user something to do while the application is loading

step value
Value that lets you increment a For...Next loop by a given amount

Structured Query Language (SQL)
The most common complete database query language that offers the capability to create components of a database as well as to manipulate them

Sub procedure
A series of VBA statements that performs actions but does not return a value

subdatasheet
A datasheet that allows you to view or edit related data in another table

subreport
A report that is inserted in another report

switchboard
An unbound form that is used to navigate to other forms and reports in the database

syntax errors
These occur when you violate the rules of VBA syntax

T

tab-delimited
Text files in which the fields are separated by a tab; each record begins on a new line

table validation rules
Allow you to test the validity of one field compared to another

theme
A set of design elements and color schemes for background, font, horizontal lines, bullets, hyperlinks, and controls

transactional table
Table in which the data entry process is ongoing

trap errors
When a developer anticipates an error that could occur, the default response of Access can be trapped and replaced with custom messages and actions

U

unbound forms
Forms that are not tied to a table or query; used to create an interface that provide users with controlled access to the application

unicode compression
Each character is represented by two bytes instead of by a single byte; represents data in Text, Memo, or Hyperlink fields

union query
A query that creates the union of two or more tables

***Updated* event**
A control property that occurs when an OLE object's data has been modified

user interface
The mechanism by which the user communicates and interacts with the application

user-level security
The most flexible and extensive method for securing a database

V

validation rule
An optional expression (formula) that can be created at the table or field level

validation text
Appears in the warning message box that opens if the validation rule is violated

variable scope
The lifespan of a variable that is determined by its declaration and its location in a module

variables
Named locations in memory that are used to store data of a particular type

VBA expression
A combination of keywords, operators, variables, and constants that yields a string, number, or object

VBA statement
A unit that expresses one kind of action, declaration, or definition in complete syntax

W

window events
Events that occur when you open, resize, or close a form or report

workgroup
A group of users in a multiuser environment who share data

workgroup ID
Case-sensitive string that contains letters or numbers and is 4 to 20 characters long

workgroup information file
A file that, if user-level security is defined, records the members of a workgroup; it contains the user's names, passwords, and the group to which they belong, and is read at startup

Workspace object
Represents a single session or instance of a user interacting with the database engine

INDEX

D

G

H

I

J

K

L

TASK	PAGE #	RECOMMENDED METHOD
Access objects, display hidden	AC 115	Click Tools on the menu bar, click Options, click the View tab, click the Hidden objects check box
Access objects, hide	AC 115	Right-click the object in the Database window, click Properties, click the Hidden check box
Access objects, import	AC 99	*See* Reference Window: Importing Access Objects
ActiveX control, register	AC 380	Click Tools on the menu bar, click ActiveX Controls, click the Register button, navigate to the folder containing the ActiveX control, click it, click Open
ActiveX control, use	AC 382	*See* Reference Window: Adding an ActiveX Control to a Form
Ampersand, display on a control	AC 176	Type &&
Append query, create	AC 97	*See* Reference Window: Creating an Append Query
Breakpoint, use	AC 319	*See* Reference Window: Using Breakpoints to Step Through a Procedure
Can Grow property, apply	AC 195	*See* Reference Window: Applying the Can Grow Property
Chart, create	AC 221	*See* Reference Window: Inserting a Record-Bound Chart in a Report
Choose Builder dialog box, bypass	AC 240	*See* Reference Window: Bypassing the Choose Builder Dialog Box
Code, compile	AC 297	Click Debug on the menu bar in the Visual Basic window, click Compile
Code Builder, use	AC 209	*See* Reference Window: Using the Code Builder
Combo box, create	AC 307	Click the Control Wizards button on the toolbox, click the Combo Box button on the toolbox, click on the form to create the control
Command button, create	AC 174	Click the Command Button button on the toolbox, click on the form or report to create the control
Command button, duplicate	AC 404	Select a command button, click Edit on the menu bar, click Duplicate
Composite primary key, create	AC 57	*See* Reference Window: Specifying a Composite Primary Key
Controls, align	AC 155	Select two or more controls, right-click the selected controls, click Align
Copy, field contents	AC 67	Press Ctrl+' (apostrophe)
Data access page, add group	AC 460	*See* Reference Window: Adding a Group to a Data Access Page
Data access page, create with wizard	AC 455	*See* Reference Window: Creating a Data Access Page Using the Page Wizard
Database Documenter, use	AC 72	*See* Reference Window: Using the Database Documenter
Database Splitter Wizard, use	AC 277	*See* Reference Window: Using the Database Splitter Wizard
Database window, display	AC 267	Press the F11 key
Date, insert automatically	AC 67	Press Ctrl+; (semicolon)
Dates, display a four-digit year	AC 70	*See* Reference Window: Forcing a Four-Digit Year
Default control properties, change	AC 156	Click the control to be changed on the toolbox, open the property sheet

TASK	PAGE #	RECOMMENDED METHOD
Delete query, create	AC 112	*See* Reference Window: Creating a Delete Query
Design view, switch to	AC 12	Click the Design View button
Errors, determine the number	AC 371	*See* Reference Window: Determining the Number of an Access Error
Event procedure, create	AC 295	*See* Reference Window: Adding an Event Procedure
Expression, create in form or report	AC 154	*See* Reference Window: Creating an Expression in a Form
Expression Builder, open	AC 92	Click the Build button on the toolbar
Expression Builder, use	AC 91	*See* Reference Window: Using the Expression Builder
Field expression, create	AC 22	Click in the Field text box, type the expression name, type a colon, type the expression
Field validation rule, create	AC 13	*See* Reference Window: Creating a Field Validation Rule
Fields, drag all to the query design grid	AC 109	Double-click the title bar of the table field list, drag the selected fields to the first column of the design grid
Form, create from a master	AC 151	*See* Reference Window: Creating a Form from a Form Master
Form, select	AC 144	Click the form selector box in the upper-left corner of the form in Design view
Form name, change	AC 33	Right-click the form in the Database window, click Rename
Form properties, change	AC 28	*See* Reference Window: Changing Form Properties
Form section, size	AC 143	Position the pointer at the bottom edge of the section until it changes to the ✢ shape, click and drag
Form template, create	AC 143	*See* Reference Window: Creating a Form Template
Hyperlink, assign to menu command or toolbar button	AC 450	*See* Reference Window: Assigning a Hyperlink to a Menu Command
Immediate window, open	AC 317	Press Ctrl+G
Immediate window, use	AC 317	*See* Reference Window: Testing a Function in the Immediate Window
Import Spreadsheet Wizard, use	AC 103	*See* Reference Window: Using the Import Spreadsheet Wizard
Import Text Wizard, use	AC 87	*See* Reference Window: Using the Import Text Wizard
Index, create	AC 56	Click the field to be indexed, click the list arrow of the Indexed property
Keyboard shortcut, create on a control	AC 176	Type a caption for the control that includes a single ampersand before a character
Label, create on a form or report	AC 147	Click the Label button on the toolbox, click on the form or report to create the control
Linked Table Manager, use	AC 278	*See* Reference Window: Using the Linked Table Manager
Locals window, open	AC 322	From the VBA window, click View on the menu bar, click Locals Window
Macro, convert to VBA	AC 188	*See* Reference Window: Converting a Macro to VBA
Macro Action Arguments pane, move to	AC 170	Press the F6 key

TASK	PAGE #	RECOMMENDED METHOD
Macro Builder, use	AC 175	Display the Properties window, position the insertion point in an Event property, click the Build button, click Macro Builder
Macro window, change settings	AC 173	*See* Reference Window: Changing Default Macro Window Settings
Menu, create	AC 259	*See* Reference Window: Creating a New Menu Bar and Menu Items
Menu, customize	AC 261	*See* Reference Window: Adding Commands to a Menu Item
Menu, display full	AC 252	*See* Reference Window: Displaying the Full Set of Menu Commands
NoData event property, change	AC 203	*See* Reference Window: Changing the NoData Event Property
Object Definition report, export to Word	AC 75	Click the list arrow for the OfficeLinks button, click Publish it with Microsoft Word
Object library, add	AC 405	*See* Reference Window: Changing the Object Library Reference
Option Button Wizard, use	AC 164	Click the Control Wizards button to select it, click the Option Group button on the toolbox
Option Group Wizard, use	AC 163	*See* Reference Window: Using the Option Group Wizard
Page numbers, add to a report	AC 226	*See* Reference Window: Adding Page Numbering to a Report
Password, clear	AC 431	*See* Reference Window: Clearing a Password
Password, set	AC 417	Click Tools on the menu bar, point to Security, click User and Group Accounts, click Change Logon Password tab
Permissions, change	AC 428	*See* Reference Window: Changing Permissions
Picture, add to a form	AC 148	*See* Reference Window: Adding a Picture to a Form
Property sheet, open	AC 144	Click the Properties button
Query, export to Excel	AC 129	Click Tools on the menu bar, point to Office Links, click Analyze It with MS Excel
Query, export to HTML document	AC 475	*See* Reference Window: Exporting an Access Query to an HTML Document
Query, open from the report window	AC 197	*See* Reference Window: Modifying the Query from the Report Window
Query, run	AC 23	Click the Run button
Relationship, create between tables	AC 63	*See* Reference Window: Creating a Relationship Between Tables
Relationships, print report	AC 76	Click File on the menu bar in the Relationships window, click Print Relationships
Report, number items in	AC 212	*See* Reference Window: Using the Running Sum Property to Number Items in a Report
Report, size	AC 35	Position the pointer on the right border of the report so that it looks like ↔, click and drag to the right or left
Report page break, add	AC 34	*See* Reference Window: Applying the Force New Page Property
Report sort order, change	AC 34	Click the Sorting and Grouping button

TASK	PAGE #	RECOMMENDED METHOD
Retangles, add	AC 30	*See* Reference Window: Adding a Retangle to a Form
Self-join query, create	AC 190	*See* Reference Window: Creating a Self-Join Query
Shortcut menu, create	AC 263	*See* Reference Window: Creating a Custom Shortcut Menu
Snapshot, create	AC 199	*See* Reference Window: Sending a Report in Snapshot Format
SQL query, create	AC 119	*See* Reference Window: Creating a Query Using SQL
Startup properties, bypass	AC 269	Open Access, press the Shift key, open the database with Shift key held down
Startup properties, change	AC 267	*See* Reference Window: Setting the Database Startup Properties
Subdatasheet, display related records	AC 69	Click the expand indicator +
Subdatasheet, hide related records	AC 69	Click the collapse indicator −
Subreport Wizard, use	AC 216	Drag the query or table on which the subreport will be based to the main report from the Database window
Table, copy	AC 109	*See* Reference Window: Copying and Pasting a Table Structure
Table, create in Datasheet view	AC 52	Click Tables on the Objects bar, double-click Create table by entering data in the Database window
Table validation rule, create	AC 12	*See* Reference Window: Creating a Table Validation Rule
Text box, create on a form or report	AC 31	Click the Text Box button ab| on the toolbox, click on the form or report to create the control
Theme, apply to data access page	AC 458	*See* Reference Window: Applying a Theme to a Data Access Page
Toolbar, customize	AC 255	*See* Reference Window: Customizing a Toolbar
Toolbar, display more buttons	AC 254	Click the Toolbar Options button
Toolbar, resize	AC 254	Click the move handle and drag the edge of the toolbar
Unique values, find	AC 106	*See* Reference Window: Querying for Unique Values
Update query, create	AC 101	*See* Reference Window: Creating an Update Query
User-Level Security Wizard, use	AC 418	Click Tools on the menu bar, point to Security, click User-Level Security Wizard
Variable declaration, require	AC 300	From the VBA window click Tools on the menu bar, click Options, click the Editor tab, click the Require Variable Declaration check box to select it
Visual Basic window, open	AC 269	Click Modules on the Objects bar, click the New button; or click the Code button
Workgroup information file, create	AC 413	*See* Reference Window: Creating a Workgroup Information File
Zoom window, open	AC 93	Right-click the text box, click Zoom

Access 2002 with VBA File Finder

Location in Tutorial	*Name and Location of Data File*	*Student Creates New File*
Tutorial 1		
Session 1.1	Tutorial.01\Tutorial\Movie1.mdb	
Session 1.2	(Continued from Session 1.1)	Tutorial.01\Tutorial\dapMovieEmployees.htm
Review Assignments	Tutorial.01\Review\Hours1.mdb	Tutorial.01\Review\dapHoursEmployees.htm
Case Problem 1	Tutorial.01\Cases\Edward1.mdb	
Case Problem 2	Tutorial.01\Cases\ISD1.mdb	Tutorial.01\Cases\dapISDStudents.htm
Case Problem 3	Tutorial.01\Cases\Homes1.mdb	Tutorial.01\Cases\HomesLots.htm
Case Problem 4	Tutorial.01\Cases\Sonoma1.mdb	Tutorial.01\Cases\SonomaDistributors.htm
Tutorial 2		
Session 2.1	Tutorial.02\Tutorial\Movie2.mdb	
Session 2.2	(Continued from Session 2.1)	Tutorial.02\Tutorial\doc_rptObjects.doc
Review Assignments	Tutorial.02\Review\Hours2.mdb	
Case Problem 1	Tutorial.02\Cases\Edward2.mdb	
Case Problem 2	Tutorial.02\Cases\ISD2.mdb	
Case Problem 3	Tutorial.02\Cases\Homes2.mdb	Tutorial.02\Cases\Homes2_docRpt.doc
Case Problem 4	Tutorial.02\Cases\Sonoma2.mdb	
Tutorial 3		
Session 3.1	Tutorial.03\Tutorial\Movie3.mdb Tutorial.03\Tutorial\Movie3.txt	
Session 3.2	(Continued from Session 3.1) Tutorial.03\Samples.mdb Tutorial.03\Tutorial\Movie3.xls	
Session 3.3	(Continued from Session 3.2)	Tutorial.03\Tutorial\qryUnionAllTCHours.xls
Review Assignments	Tutorial.03\Review\Hours3.mdb Tutorial.03\Review\Hours3.xls	
Case Problem 1	Tutorial.03\Cases\Edward3.mdb Tutorial.03\Cases\Edward3.txt	
Case Problem 2	Tutorial.03\Cases\ISD3.mdb Tutorial.03\Cases\ISD3.xls Tutorial.03\Samples.mdb	
Case Problem 3	Tutorial.03\Cases\Homes3.mdb Tutorial.03\Cases\Homes3.txt Tutorial.03\Samples.mdb	
Case Problem 4	Tutorial.03\Cases\Sonoma3.mdb Tutorial.03\Cases\Sonoma3.xls Tutorial.03\Samples.mdb	
Tutorial 4		
Session 4.1	Tutorial.04\Tutorial\Movie4.mdb Tutorial.04\Tutorial\Logo.wmf	
Session 4.2	(Continued from Session 4.1)	
Review Assignments	Tutorial.04\Review\Hours4.mdb	
Case Problem 1	Tutorial.04\Cases\Edward4.mdb	
Case Problem 2	Tutorial.04\Cases\ISD4.mdb	
Case Problem 3	Tutorial.04\Cases\Homes4.mdb Tutorial.04\Cases\H4Logo.wmf	
Case Problem 4	Tutorial.04\Cases\Sonoma4.mdb	
Tutorial 5		
Session 5.1	Tutorial.05\Tutorial\Movie5.mdb Tutorial.05\Tutorial\Logo.wmf	
Session 5.2	(Continued from Session 5.1)	
Review Assignments	Tutorial.05\Review\Hours5.mdb	
Case Problem 1	Tutorial.05\Cases\Edward5.mdb	

Access 2002 with VBA File Finder

Location in Tutorial	Name and Location of Data File	Student Creates New File
Case Problem 2	Tutorial.05\Cases\ISD5.mdb	
Case Problem 3	Tutorial.05\Cases\Homes5.mdb Tutorial.04\Tutorial\H5Logo.wmf	
Case Problem 4	Tutorial.05\Cases\Sonoma5.mdb	
Tutorial 6		
Session 6.1	Tutorial.06\Tutorial\Movie6.mdb Tutorial.06\Tutorial\MovieCam icon	
Session 6.2	(Continued from Session 6.1)	
Review Assignments	Tutorial.06\Review\Hours6.mdb	
Case Problem 1	Tutorial.06\Cases\Edward6.mdb	
Case Problem 2	Tutorial.06\Cases\ISD6.mdb	
Case Problem 3	Tutorial.06\Cases\Homes6.mdb	
Case Problem 4	Tutorial.06\Cases\Sonoma6.mdb	
Tutorial 7		
Session 7.1	Tutorial.07\Tutorial\Movie7.mdb	
Session 7.2	(Continued from Session 7.1)	
Review Assignments	Tutorial.07\Review\Hours7.mdb	
Case Problem 1	Tutorial.07\Cases\Edward7.mdb	
Case Problem 2	Tutorial.07\Cases\ISD7.mdb	
Case Problem 3	Tutorial.07\Cases\Homes7.mdb	
Case Problem 4	Tutorial.07\Cases\Sonoma7.mdb	
Tutorial 8		
Session 8.1	Tutorial.08\Tutorial\Movie8.mdb	
Session 8.2	(Continued from Session 8.1)	
Review Assignments	Tutorial.08\Review\Hours8.mdb	
Case Problem 1	Tutorial.08\Cases\Edward8.mdb	
Case Problem 2	Tutorial.08\Cases\ISD8.mdb	
Case Problem 3	Tutorial.08\Cases\Homes8.mdb	
Case Problem 4	Tutorial.08\Cases\Sonoma8.mdb	
Tutorial 9		
Session 9.1	Tutorial.09\Tutorial\Movie9.mdb	
Session 9.2	(Continued from Session 9.1)	Tutorial.09\Tutorial\MovieSecure.mdw Tutorial.09\Tutorial\Movie9TestCopy.mdb Tutorial.09\Tutorial\Movie9.bak Tutorial.09\Tutorial\swz_rptSecure.rtf
Review Assignments	Tutorial.09\Review\Hours9.mdb Tutorial.09\Review\HoursSecure.mdw	Tutorial.09\Review\Hours9.bak
Case Problem 1	Tutorial.09\Cases\Edward9.mdb Tutorial.09\Cases\Edward9.bak Tutorial.09\Cases\EdwardSecure.mdw	
Case Problem 2	Tutorial.09\Cases\ISD9.mdb	Tutorial.09\Cases\ISDSecure.mdw
Case Problem 3	Tutorial.09\Cases\Homes9.mdb	
Case Problem 4	Tutorial.09\Cases\Sonoma9.mdb	Tutorial.09\Cases\SonomaSecure.mdw Tutorial.09\Cases\Sonoma9.bak
Tutorial 10		
Session 10.1	Tutorial.10\Tutorial\Movie10.mdb	
Session 10.2	(Continued from Session 10.1)	Tutorial.10\Tutorial\dapMovieEmployees.htm Tutorial.10\Tutorial\TimeCards.htm Tutorial.10\Tutorial\qryJobsTotalDollars.html
Review Assignments	Tutorial.10\Review\Hours10.mdb	Tutorial.10\Review\dapEmployees.htm
Case Problem 1	Tutorial.10\Cases\Edward10.mdb	Tutorial.10\Cases\dapClients.htm
Case Problem 2	Tutorial.10\Cases\ISD10.mdb	
Case Problem 3	Tutorial.10\Cases\Homes10.mdb	Tutorial.10\Cases\dapLots.htm
Case Problem 4	Tutorial.10\Cases\Sonoma10.mdb	